John T. Cirn, Ph.D., NHA
3463 Donovan Drive
Crete, IL 60417

Phone: (708) 672-7687

*Courses and workshops on
long-term care administration.*

LONG-TERM CARE ADMINISTRATION HANDBOOK

Edited by

Seth B. Goldsmith, ScD, JD
University of Massachusetts
Amherst, Massachusetts

AN ASPEN PUBLICATION®
Aspen Publishers, Inc.
Gaithersburg, Maryland
1993

Library of Congress-in-Publication Data

Long-term care administration handbook / (edited by) Seth B.
Goldsmith.
p. cm.
Includes bibliographical references and index.
ISBN: 0-8342-0374-X
1. Long-term care facilities—Administration. I. Goldsmith, Seth
B. II. Title: Long term care administration handbook.
[DNLM: 1. Long-Term Care—in old age. 2. Long-Term Care—
organization & administration. 3. Nursing Homes—organization &
administration—United States. WT 30 L8474]
RA999.A35L68 1993
362.1'6'068—dc20
DNLM/DLC
for Library of Congress
92-48287
CIP

This publication is designed to provide accurate and authoritative information in regard to the
Subject Matter covered. It is sold with the understanding that the publisher is not engaged in
rendering legal, accounting, or other professional service. If legal advice or other expert
assistance is required, the service of a competent professional person should be sought. *(From
a Declaration of Principles jointly adopted by a Committee of the American Bar Association
and a Committee of Publishers and Associations.)*

Editorial Resources: Lenda Hill
Ruth Bloom
Library of Congress Catalog Card Number: 92-48287
ISBN: 0-8342-0374-X

Printed in the United States of America

1   2   3   4   5

Table of Contents

About the Editor/Contributor

Seth B. Goldsmith, Sc.D., J.D., editor of this book and author of a number of its chapters, is presently Professor of Health Policy and Management at the School of Public Health of the University of Massachusetts at Amherst. Additionally, Dr. Goldsmith is editor of *The Journal of Ambulatory Care Management* and Counsel to the law firm of Bowditch and Dewey in Worcester, Massachusetts. Professor Goldsmith's involvement in long-term care has included teaching both graduate and continuing education courses in long-term care, membership on the New York State Board of Examiners for Nursing Home Administrators, consulting to nursing homes as well as board level appointments to various organizations including membership in the House of Delegates of the American Association of Homes for the Aging, The Association of Massachusetts Homes for the Aging, and the Jewish Nursing Home of Western Massachusetts. In 1990, Dr. Goldsmith's book, *Choosing a Nursing Home,* published by Prentice Hall, was selected as a Book of the Year by *Library Journal.* Additionally, in 1991, the American Association of Homes for the Aging honored Dr. Goldsmith with its Chairman's Citation.

About the Contributors

George A. Balko III, J.D., A.B., is an attorney with Bowditch & Dewey in Worcester, Massachusetts. He is a member of the adjunct faculty, Anna Maria College, and was admitted to the Bar in Massachusetts and the District of Columbia. He is a member of Massachusetts, Worcester County, District of Columbia, and American Bar Associations; and the Association of Trial Lawyers of America. He was recently listed in Marquis' *Who's Who in American Law,* seventh edition, 1992/1993.

Susan S. Bailis, B.S., M.S., is executive vice president and CEO of The A/D/S Group, North Andover, Massachusetts. Ms. Bailis came to long-term care from hospital management at New England Medical Center, Boston, where she aided the institution's entry into the long-term care field and administered a wide variety of operational functions. Ms. Bailis is first vice president of the Massachusetts Federation of Nursing Homes.

Howard L. Braverman, M.H.A., L.N.H.A., is president and CEO of Jewish Nursing Home of Western Massachusetts and its parent holding company, Jewish Geriatric Services, Inc., both in Longmeadow, Massachusetts. He has 18 years experience in senior management positions in the acute and long-term care industries and is active in professional and community organizations.

James N. Broder is an attorney with the Portland, Maine, law firm of Curtis Thaxter Stevens Broder & Micoleau. A former two-term member of the Federal Council on Aging, his national law practice focuses on the representation of nonprofit and proprietary developers and providers of a wide range of residential and long-term care services.

Marian C. Broder, J.D., an attorney, is a consultant to nursing homes on federal and state regulations regarding long-term care. She serves on the adjunct faculty of Western New England College School of Law. She is currently chairperson of the board of the Jewish Nursing Home of Western Massachusetts and has chaired its ethics committee for four years.

Karen L. Cameron is a consultant in the Atlanta office of Jennings, Ryan, Federa & Company. Ms. Cameron has more than 6 years of health care experience, primarily in the areas of strategic and product line planning. Before joining Jennings, Ryan, Federa & Company, she was a health care management consultant with Ernst & Young.

Cathy Sullivan Clark, M.M., is a consultant in the Northampton, Massachusetts office of Jennings, Ryan, Federa & Company. She has served as a management consultant for the last five years. During that time, she has developed a particular expertise in long-term care planning and finance.

Janet Courtney, R.N., M.S.N., is a professor of nursing at Holyoke Community in Holyoke, Massachusetts. In this position, she plans and supervises classroom and clinical learning experiences in care of elderly nursing home residents for nursing students who are preparing for registered nurse practice. She has presented lectures at local and national conferences related to the teaching of geriatric nursing theory and skills as part of an integrated nursing curriculum.

Joan Marie Culley, R.N, M.S., M.P.H., is an associate professor of nursing and coordinator of the Nursing Career Pathway Program at Holyoke Community College in Holyoke, Massachusetts. She is a consultant to hospitals and other health care organizations regarding the teaching of "critical thinking" skills in nursing, and the development of programs for non-traditional learners, and has presented papers on these topics at local and national conferences. She has over twenty-three years of experience in nursing both as a nursing instructor and practicing clinician. Her specialties include medical/surgical nursing, nursing administration, and public health.

Neal E. Cutler, Ph.D., is director of the Boettner Institute of Financial Gerontology at the University of Pennsylvania, and research associate at the university's Population Studies Center. Dr. Cutler recently co-edited *Aging, Money, and Life Satisfaction: Aspects of Financial Gerontology* (Springer, 1992), and co-authored *Can You Afford to Retire?* (Probus, 1992). He writes "Financial Gerontology," a regular column in the *Journal of the American Society of CLU & ChFC*, is a member of the board of directors of the American Society on Aging and chair of its research committee, and is a member of the U.S. Planning Committee for the International Association of Gerontology 1993 World Congress.

David M. Dunkelman, J.D., is president of the Rosa Coplon Jewish Home and Infirmary, a 166-bed long-term care facility located in Buffalo, New York, and president of the proposed Menorah Campus, Inc., located in Amherst, New York. He is an attorney who has a master's degree in long-term care administration. He is also a Ph.D. candidate in organizational analysis and gerontology, and an assistant clinical professor of medicine (geriatrics), School of Medicine, SUNY at Buffalo. Mr. Dunkelman has been the speaker at numerous conferences and author of many articles regarding aging and the health care profession.

Denise Finn-Rizzo, R.N., is the health care coordinator of Applewood at Amherst, a long-term care facility in Amherst, Massachusetts. She received her bachelor's of arts degree with a concentration in nursing from Simmons College.

Herbert H. Friedman, M.S.A.M., M.B.A., is the executive vice president at the Gurwin Jewish Geriatric Center in Commack, New York, and has been the CEO since its founding in 1985. Mr. Friedman has almost 20 years experience in long-term care administration. He is currently a clinical instructor in the Department of Family Medicine, in the School of Medicine at the State University of New York at Stoney Brook and was on the faculty at the Department of Health Services Administration in the Graduate School of Management and Urban Profession at the New School for Social Research and at the Brooklyn College of the City University of New York.

Mary B. Geisz, M.B.A., is an independent management consultant and writer specializing in the research, planning, and analysis of health care services for a variety of provider organizations and industry publications. Her experience includes a focus on the health care needs both of the elderly and of children and adolescents.

Solomon Goldner, M.B.A., M.P.H., is vice president and chief financial officer of Golden State Health Centers, Inc., a multi-facility chain of skilled nursing facilities in Sherman Oaks, California. He was formerly with Coopers and Lybrand and National Medical Enterprises', Hillhaven Division. His degrees in accounting and public health are both from Columbia University.

Anne K. Harrington, Ph.D., is an independent consultant, writer, and gerontologist working in the Boston area. She writes, edits, and produces two publications on aging (one of which she co-founded in 1989) and consults on industry trends, strategic planning, public policy, and communications.

H. Ralph Hawkins, A.I.A., M.P.H., is executive vice president of HKS, Inc., an architectural, planning, and engineering firm specializing in the design of health care facilities. In this position, Mr. Hawkins has worked for more than 17 years in over 35 states designing and planning health care facilities from tertiary medical centers to long-term facilities.

Judith L. Horowitz, M.A., M.B.A., is a vice president in the Atlanta, Georgia, office of Jennings, Ryan, Federa & Company. She has been providing planning and financial consulting to health care organizations for over ten years.

Margo P. Kelly, M.H.A., M.B.A., has 11 years of experience in the health care industry, including hospital administration and financial positions. She has served as a consultant for over 7 years and is currently a vice president in the Jacksonville, Florida, office of Jennings, Ryan, Federa & Company.

Victor L. Klein, B.F.A., is president of the board of directors of Heritage Pointe, a nonprofit senior retirement in Mission Viejo, California. He has worked in the marketing and advertising field for over 40 years. He has held marketing, advertising, training, and sales promotion positions with Grey Advertising, Ford Motor Company, Philco, and Caloric Corporation.

Susanna E. Krentz, M.B.A., is a vice president in the Chicago, Illinois office of Jennings, Ryan, Federa & Company. In over nine years of consulting, she has worked in a variety of engagements regarding long-term care services, including program planning, financial analysis, and feasibility assessment.

Richard S. Lamden, B.B.A., is executive vice president of Handmaker Jewish Services for the Aging, Inc., in Tucson, Arizona, a nonprofit, nonsectarian long-term care organization. He is also the president/CEO of Handmaker Management Enterprises, Inc., a for-profit subsidiary specializing in consultation and management services to long-term care facilities and housing. He is a former officer of the American Association of Homes for the Aging.

Stephen Lawrence, A.O.S., AHCFA, is the director of food service at the Jewish Nursing Home of Western Massachusetts. He has had nearly ten years experience in health care food service administration and is the president-elect of Massachusetts Healthcare Food Service Administrators, Inc.

Steven A. Levenson, M.D., is the medical director of Asbury Methodist Village in Gaithersburg, Maryland. He has been a long-term care physician full time since 1978, and medical director since 1982. He has written over 30 articles, book chapters, and monographs in the areas of geriatrics, medical ethics, medical computing, quality assurance, and medical direction. He is also the editor and principal author of *Medical Direction in Long-Term Care* and *Medical Policies and Procedures for Long-Term Care,* two widely used comprehensive reference sources for the nursing home medical director.

Donna G. Michaels, Ph.D., is president and executive director of Kids Voting Florida, Inc., based in Miami. Her experience includes service as a senior development officer in a university and as a program developer and administrator in state and local level human services organizations. She has also held senior management and marketing positions in the media and communications industry.

Marianne Raimondo, M.S., Ph.D., is a vice president of Applied Management Systems, a consulting firm for health care organizations. Her expertise is in the area of total quality management. She has been involved in quality management in health care for 10 years.

Deborah L. Roland, M.B.A., is principal, information systems consulting for Loeb & Troper, CPAs in New York. Ms. Roland has worked in the health care industry for 19 years, with the last 7 years dedicated to long-term care computerization. She consults with organizations in the planning, selection, and implementation of clinical, financial, and administrative information systems.

Roderic L. Rolett is vice president of Herbert J. Sims & Co., Inc. Mr. Rolett has underwritten in excess of $300 million of tax-exempt bonds to finance the construction, renovation, and expansion of startup and existing continuing care retirement communities and nursing homes. He uses both first mortgage revenue and credit enhanced tax-exempt bonds to finance housing and health care facilities for the elderly. Mr. Rolett is a specialist in using letters of credit to enhance retirement community bond issues. Prior to joining Herbert J. Sims' investment banking department, Mr. Rolett was a vice president of AMBAC, a municipal bond insurance company, and a financial guarantee officer at Aetna Life and Casualty. Mr. Rolett graduated from Phillips Academy Andover and received his bachelor of arts from Pomona College. He earned his master's degree from Harvard University. Mr. Rolett has been with the firm since 1987.

Zev Schostak, D.D., M.A., is director of pastoral services at the Gurwin Jewish Geriatric Center in Commack, Long Island, New York. He is the founder and chair of Gurwin's Ethical Panel and has written extensively on Jewish medical ethics and issues. Rabbi Schostak is a research fellow at the Institute for Medicine in Contemporary Society at the State University of New York at Stony Book, School of Medicine.

Harvey M. Shankman, M.S.S.A., is executive director of the Eliza Bryant Center, a long-term care facility and senior center located in Cleveland, Ohio. Mr. Shankman is a licensed nursing home administrator, a licensed independent social worker, and a member of the Academy of Certified Social Workers. He is an adjunct instructor at the Mandel School of Applied Social Sciences, Case Western Reserve University.

Linda J. Shea, Ph.D., is an associate professor of marketing in the Department of Hotel, Restaurant, and Travel Administration at the University of Massachusetts at Amherst. Her research and teaching emphases are in marketing management, marketing research, and consumer behavior—particularly the elderly consumer. She specializes in marketing applications to the service sector, including health care, education, and hospitality organizations.

Charles D. Schewe, Ph.D., M.B.A., is a full professor at the University of Massachusetts at Amherst and president of University Research Associates, a management and marketing consulting firm offering a broad range of marketing and strategic consultation to health care providers and other organizations. Dr. Schewe has developed a particular expertise in understanding the marketing implications of our 50+ population. He is presently the president of the American Association for Advances in Health Care Research.

Fredlee J. Shore, B.A., has been CFO and owner of Agawam Medical Equipment, Inc., for the past 16 years. In addition to this position, she provides private consulting services to the HME industry on third party reimbursement and is an adjunct professor of parapharmacy at MCP/AHS in Boston, Massachusetts.

Herbert H. Shore, Ed.D., is the executive vice president of North American Association of Jewish Homes and Housing for the Aging in Dallas, Texas. He is also the director of field instruction in the Center for Studies in Aging at the University of North Texas in Denton, Texas.

Ronald L. Skaggs, F.A.I.A., is chairman and CEO of HKS, Inc., an architectural, planning, and engineering firm specializing in the design of health care facilities. During the past 25 years, Mr. Skaggs has been responsible for the planning and design of more than 250 health care projects including many long-term care facilities.

Alan D. Solomont, B.A., B.S., is president, CEO, and founder of The A/D/S Group, North Andover, Massachusetts. His career in long-term care spans almost two decades and began with the direct management of a 130-bed nursing home. Mr. Solomont is past president of the Massachusetts Federation of Nursing Homes and has advised the Commonwealth of Massachusetts on matters relating to long-term care and the elderly.

Peter F. Straley, M.B.A., is a consultant in the Northampton, Massachusetts office of Jennings, Ryan, Federa & Company. He has over 13 years of experience in the health care industry and specialized in strategic and financial planning consulting to health care clients.

Mark E. Toso, M.S.B.A., C.P.A., is president of TriNet Healthcare Consultants, Inc. Mr. Toso has worked in the health care industry for over 18 years. His broad range of experience includes strategic, financial, and organizational analysis for hospitals, nursing homes, and physicians. Before starting TriNet, he was the eastern regional vice president of Amherst Associates Inc. from 1976 to 1985.

Concetta M. Tynan, R.N.N.P., serves as vice president of senior services with Handmaker Jewish Services for the Aging, Inc., a nonprofit, nonsectarian health care facility. She also is the vice president of Handmaker Management Enterprises, Inc., a for-profit subsidiary specializing in consultation and management services to long-term care facilities and housing. Mrs. Tynan has 13 years of expertise in the long-term care field.

James E. Wallace, Jr., J.D., L.L.M., is a senior partner and co-chair of the Labor/Employment Practice Group with Bowditch & Dewey in Worcester, Massachusetts.

Janice Warnke, M.S.W., serves as the director of adult day care services with Handmaker Jewish Services for the Aging, Inc., a nonprofit, nonsectarian long-term care agency in Tucson, Arizona. Ms. Warnke administers three distinct programs that serve disabled, demented, and elderly persons. Ms. Warnke is a licensed nursing home administrator who has held administrative positions in California and Arizona.

Susan Krauss Whitbourne, Ph.D., is a professor of psychology at the University of Massachusetts at Amherst and has extensive experience in gerontological research, teaching, and practice. Her areas of research interest include psychological adaptation to the aging process, personality development in adulthood, and the provision of clinical services to older adults.

Karen-Jo Wills, M.S., is a Ph.D. candidate in clinical psychology at the University of Massachusetts at Amherst. She has experience in direct care to the elderly and in providing psychotherapy to adults of various ages. In addition, she is an active researcher who recently co-authored a major longitudinal investigation of adult personality development.

Charles S. Wolfe, M.A., Ed.S., is a consultant and lecturer in Adventura, Florida. He formerly served as executive director of the Jewish Home of Detroit for 16 years prior to becoming the executive director of the Mt. Sinai Medical Center Foundation.

Preface

A few years ago I wrote a book titled *Choosing a Nursing Home* (Prentice Hall, 1990) that was directed at helping consumers navigate their way through the long-term care labyrinth. As part of my research for the book, I visited nursing homes throughout the country. My travels across America introduced me to a wide range of administrators with backgrounds in social work, nursing, management, hospital administration, and law. From each of these individuals, whether they were responsible for large, small, government, proprietary, or nonprofit homes, or homes that were freestanding or affiliated with hospitals or national chains, I learned of similar frustrations, demands, and rewards. What became abundantly clear from those meetings is that nursing homes of the 1990s are organizations in transition.

No longer are nursing homes merely residences for the frail elderly, but rather they are in the process of becoming an exceedingly interesting amalgam of both social service oriented organizations and technologically sophisticated clinical facilities. All of this is happening at a time when financing for long-term care is precarious; federal, and state legislation is sending mixed public policy messages; and other players in the health and welfare world including hospitals, ambulatory care facilities, and even community centers are struggling with defining their own roles—a definition that sometimes infringes on the territory of long-term care facilities.

This volume is a response to the myriad issues administrators are facing. It is hoped that these chapters, written by some of America's most distinguished experts in long-term care, will serve to clarify problem areas and offer solutions or at least stimulate thinking on critical problems faced by management. From my many colleagues who are practicing nursing home administrators I have often heard it said that these are both the best of times and the worst of times for the profession. It is my hope that this book is a contribution toward the making of better times.

Seth B. Goldsmith
Amherst, Massachusetts

Acknowledgments

A book of this scope and depth is a complex team undertaking. First I want to acknowledge my enormous debt to my fellow chapter authors who responded to my call and delivered their work and revisions in a timely manner. Also, on behalf of my fellow authors, I want to thank all those unnamed persons who generously gave of their time and expertise in many ways, including reviewing manuscripts, suggesting revisions, typing, or simply providing the always needed moral support throughout the process of chapter preparation. Additionally, I would like to thank Mike Brown, Aspen's distinguished publisher, who encouraged and supported me throughout this project; and Ms. Lenda Hill who carefully and thoughtfully squired this complex handbook to its completion. Finally, thanks to my wife Sandra and sons Jonas and Ben for their personal support throughout the years of this undertaking.

Chapter 1

Introduction

For more than two decades I have had the privilege of working with scores of long-term care administrators and visiting nursing homes in 24 states and several foreign countries. As a researcher and educator, I have consistently been impressed with the key role administrators play in long-term care facilities—a role in many ways more significant than the one that health administrators play in other organizations. Indeed, in many instances the long-term care administrator has limited support staff yet is called upon to provide technical expertise and leadership throughout the entire organization. The challenge for administrators in long-term care is extraordinary, and unfortunately little is available to help administrators sort through many of the complicated organization and management issues that must be dealt with.

In this book more than 40 of the leading experts in the field share their analyses of the major issues facing long-term care. The book is divided into four parts. Part I discusses background issues, Part II deals with managing long-term care, Part III examines support systems in long-term care, and Part IV presents the essentials of future-oriented management. Readers should be aware that this is a long and at times demanding book and is not for casual summer reading. It is basically a resource book and should be reviewed as necessary. Furthermore, as with all books of this type, there are limitations. For example, there is little discussion of the physical plant issues that administrators face every day. Also, several functional areas of importance in long-term care, such as physical or occupational therapy, are not covered, and readers will have to consult specialty texts for information in those areas.

Part I begins with a chapter by Dr. Herbert Shore, one of America's most distinguished leaders in long-term care. Dr. Shore provides a history of long-term care that begins with an overview of its Biblical and European roots and then focuses on the American experience. In the next chapter, Dr. Susan Krauss Whitbourne, a psychologist and gerontologist, and Karen-Jo Wills present an important and thoughtful analysis of the psychological issues that arise in institutional care for the aged. This chapter provides a conceptual and theoretical framework for understanding aging, and it also describes how the infantilizing behavior of caregivers can adversely affect residents.

In Chapter 4, Steven Levenson, MD, former medical director of a large geriatric center and a leading authority on long-term care medical departments, analyzes the role of the medical director in the nursing home. In present circumstances, when most nursing homes are admitting older and sicker residents who are in need of more intensive medical care, this chapter is of particular relevance.

Chapter 5, by professors of nursing Joan Culley and Janet Courtney, focuses on the delivery of nursing care. It includes an analysis of the issues that nursing departments face as well as an appendix that contains sample job descriptions for nursing department personnel. Marian Broder, an attorney with extensive experience in long-term care, is the author of the next chapter, which discusses ethical issues that providers of long-term care must confront. This chapter not only provides a conceptual background for understanding these crucial ethical issues but also examines such topics as the Federal Patient Self Determination Act, health care proxies, living wills, advance directives, durable powers of attorney, and transfer rules. Additionally, Broder provides guidance on development of an ethics committee. Chapter 7, by Mary Geisz, a consultant, examines the mental health issues facing the elderly and provides interesting examples of programs that have been developed to address their mental health needs. The final chapter of Part I is by Dr. Neal Cutler, who directs the Boettner Institute of Financial Gerontology at the University of Pennsylvania. The focus of this chapter is on the connections among aging, dependency, and personal care. Some of Dr. Cutler's findings are startling and will give administrators data of the type crucial for successful program planning.

Part II begins with two chapters that I have authored. The first of these examines management in nursing homes. It analyzes the functions of management, the special challenges of management, and expectations for managers and makes some practical suggestions on the subject of entering management. In the next chapter I examine the role and function of boards of directors. In general, this chapter will be of particular interest to administrators of nonprofit nursing homes, but it may also be of value to those involved in for-profit facilities.

In Chapter 11, Jim Wallace, a senior partner in the law firm of Bowditch and Dewey and a specialist in employment law, presents a comprehensive discussion of employment issues. Chapter 12, by Robert Cope, also of Bowditch and Dewey, and me, is designed for managers who are in the process of negotiating their own employment agreements. It contains a summary of a survey we completed as well as alternative strategies for contract negotiations. Cope and I also authored the next chapter, which presents an overview of the legal and political issues involved in a corporate reorganization. Howard Braverman, the president of a major geriatric facility, follows with a case study of what happened in his nursing home when it went through the time-consuming and expensive process of corporate reorganization. Braverman's chapter is an insightful analysis of the power politics often involved in such a change.

The two next chapters focus on marketing. In the first of these, professors Linda Shea and Charles Schewe provide a conceptual overview of the marketing basics that long-term care administrators need to understand in order to develop an effective marketing plan. Following this is a comprehensive case study on the development and marketing of Heritage Pointe in Mission Viejo, California. This chapter is written by Victor Klein, who is president of the Mission Viejo board and was formerly a senior marketing executive with Ford Motor Company and with Philco.

Chapter 17, by Deborah Roland, a leading consultant in the information systems field, examines computer applications that can be used to support the resident care process in nursing homes. In Chapter 18, Marianne Raimondo, also a health care consultant, shares her expertise in Total Quality Management. The following chapter, on financial management, covers the financial organization of long-term care, the elements of health finance, and the budgeting process. This chapter has greatly benefited from the contributions of Sol Goldner, who in addition to his experience as a nursing home administrator was a health care financial management consultant with a major national accounting firm. Chapter 20 is a primer on capital financing in long-term care. In this chapter, prepared by Rod Rolett of the firm of Herbert G. Sims and Company, the four primary methods of nursing home financing are examined. Rolett also includes an outline of the parameters that lenders consider in evaluating capital finance decisions.

The next two chapters are the result of a professional meeting I attended several years ago. At this meeting I heard an interesting presentation by Chuck Wolfe on fund raising for nonprofit nursing homes. I subsequently asked Wolfe to prepare two chapters. In the first of these, he teamed up with Dr. Donna Michaels, and together they prepared an excellent overview of the principles of capital fund raising. In the second article, Wolfe and James Broder, the board president of a Maine nursing home, discuss a fund-raising campaign in Portland that exceeded its own goals. Chapter 23, by consultants Peter Straley and Karen Cameron, uses four case studies to examine the issues surrounding the operation of a financially viable Alzheimer's disease treatment unit. In Chapter 24, consultants Judith Horowitz and Margo Kelly consider the financing issues associated with retirement communities.

Part III focuses on the delivery of services in long-term care. In Chapter 25, Steve Lawrence, the director of food services at a 200-bed skilled nursing facility, provides a comprehensive review of food service management in long-term care. In the next chapter, Harvey Shankman, presently the administrator of a nursing home and previously the director of social services at a large geriatric center, examines the requirements for a nursing home social work department to be effective. Chapter 27 was originally published as a report for the United Hospital Fund of New York. We are pleased to include it as the chapter on activities programs, because it is an outstanding review of what nursing homes in New York City are doing in this important functional area. Chapter 28, by Herb Friedman and Rabbi Zev Schostak, considers the broad range of responsibilities that chaplains presently play or could play in nursing homes. In Chapter 29, Dick Lamden, Concetta Tynan, and Janice Warnke provide a conceptual background for understanding day-care services and a detailed analysis of what is necessary to develop and run a successful adult day-care program in a nursing home.

Two chapters on durable medical equipment (DME) complete this section of the book. In the first of these, Fredlee Shore, a DME consultant and owner of a DME business as well as the former president of the board of a nonprofit nursing home, provides an overview of many of the key issues affecting nursing homes and their potential involvement with DME. The second chapter is by Denise Finn-Rizzo, a nurse who is the health care coordinator for a continuing care retirement community. Her chapter examines DME from the perspective of the buyer.

Part IV looks at the future of long-term care management. In Chapter 32, Mark Toso, a consultant and frequent contributor to the literature, provides a model for strategic planning in long-term care. This model, plus the data presented, should prove useful to many administrators. In the next chapter, architects Ron Skaggs and H. Ralph Hawkins provide a comprehensive analysis of architectural issues of importance to long-term care administrators, including the likely impact on design of the Americans with Disabilities Act of 1990. As an interesting contrast, David Dunkelman, president of a Buffalo geriatric center that has gone through a huge planning and building project, provides in the following chapter an analysis of what it takes from an administrative perspective to develop and implement a new project.

Chapter 35, by Dr. Anne Harrington, is an interesting and timely account of the issues surrounding assisted living, a subject of considerable importance in the long-term care field. Chapter 36, by George Balko, a trial lawyer, provides guidance for avoiding litigation by reviewing what it is that lawyers look for in making a case against nursing homes. Obviously, prevention is less costly than cure, and Balko's observations are worthy of consideration by any risk management program. Chapter 37, by consultants Cathy Clark and Susanna Krentz, although focused on planning long-term care services for a hospital, is also relevant for nursing homes. Last but not least is the final chapter, by nursing home executives and consultants Alan Solomont and Susan Bailis. This chapter examines an important new trend in long-term care, the transfer of administrative responsibilities for a nursing home to a separate management company.

In sum, this book represents the thinking of a broad range of experts, including administrators, consultants, academics, planners, lawyers, architects, and nurses, on a broad range of issues. My hope is that each chapter proves to be valuable to the reader, both conceptually and practically.

Part I

Background Issues

Chapter 2

History of Long-Term Care

Herbert Shore

HISTORICAL SURVEY

The Patriarch Abraham (Gen. 12:6) is credited with originating institutions such as hostels, hospitals, and homes by legends that tell of his tent in the plain of Moreh at the junction of important trade routes. It had openings on four sides and was accessible from every direction. Strangers were welcomed, given food and drink, and made comfortable for the night, and in the morning they were set upon the road headed in the right direction.[1]

"God loves the stranger" (Deut. 10:18) served as inspiration to those who made an effort to accommodate journeyers to Judea. It was the aspiration to holiness that resulted in a whole range of amenities and comforts for those in the community who were deprived. The furnishing of food, clothing, education for children, dowries for maidens, subsidies for orphans, visitors to the sick, support for pregnant women, money for free burials, ransom for captives, aid to the ailing, and shelter for the aged was placed among the highest ideals of mankind (Talmud, B.B. 8b). Maimonides, a physician and Judaic philosopher, supported the position that helping others in need should be a goal not only of the Jewish constituency but of all people alike.

In Ecclesiastes and the Psalms, there are references to the infirmities of the declining years, the failing powers of the aged. Old age was pointed to as a state of inactivity. As a balance, upon the young was placed an obligation to provide for the support and comfort of the old (Ruth 4:5), and without question the Fifth Commandment (Exod. 20:12), asserting that honor should be given to one's father and mother, is in a similar vein.

Accurate information about the origins and early history of institutions for the aged is scanty. Garrison attributes "the credit of ministering to human suffering on an extended scale" to the teachings of Christianity and traces the development of institutions for the sick in the Byzantine Empire following the conversion of Constantine.[2]

Among the specialized hospitals that gradually developed during the fourth century, he mentions *Gerontochia,* for the aged; *Nosocomia,* for the care of the sick alone; *Brephotrophia,* for foundlings; *Orphanotrophia,* for orphans; *Ptochia,* for the helpless poor; and *Xenodochia,* for poor and infirm pilgrims. These functions undoubtedly overlapped in many of the local foundations that grew up in the Middle Ages, especially during the Crusades, under the inspiration of priests and with the support of nobility. In many cases, these foundations were managed and staffed by Catholic orders devoted to the care of the sick.

Medieval and Renaissance hospitals were in actuality only places of refuge for sick strangers and infirm aged individuals without family or friends. There was no organized supervision by physicians. In the poem "The Hye Way to the Spytell Hous" (c. 1536), the author, Robert Copland, inquires from the porter of a London hospital what sort of people obtain help there and receives this reply:

> Forsooth they that be at such myschefe,
> That for they'r lyvying can do no labour
> And have no frendes to do them socour
> As old people seke and impotent. . .

R.M. Clay, in *The Medieval Hospitals of England,* points out that these homes were called indiscriminately "hospital," "Maison Dieu," "almhouse," or "bedehouse."[3] The oldest in England are St. John's in Canterbury, founded by Archbishop Lanfranc in 1084, and St. Cross' in Winchester, founded in 1132 by Henry de Blois, Bishop of Winchester and brother to King Stephen.[4] Both these institutions are still in existence. Ewelme, in Oxfordshire, founded in 1437 by William de la Pole and completed by his wife Alice, a granddaughter of Geoffrey Chaucer, is of particular interest because the mastership of the almshouse is an obligation and also a source of revenue for the Regius Professor of Medicine at Oxford. Sir William Osler's interest in the pensioners and his discovery of priceless old documents in a locked chest are described in Cushing's biography.[5]

W.J. Marx traced the development of charity in medieval Louvain and mentions, among others, the hospice of St. Barbara, which was begun in the last half of the 13th century.[6] Belgium is the chief site of activity of the Béguines, members of lay sisterhoods founded in 1170 by Lambert le Bégue, a priest of Liege. The Béguinage of St. Elizabeth of Ghent, famous for its architecture, has about a thousand sisters, nearly all elderly women, who devote themselves to a life of service without taking monastic vows. The Béguines wear the old Flemish headdress and a dark costume.[7] They support themselves by the manufacture of fine laces and are noted for their kindness to the poor and the sick.

The deterioration and breakdown of the monastic charities all over Europe as well as in England and their gradual supplementation by the action of municipal authorities has been well covered by the Webbs in their classic study of the Old

English Poor Law.[8] The English were stimulated into action by the Spanish scholar Juan Juis Vives (1492–1540), who became friendly with Henry VIII at Bruges and frequently visited England. In his *De subventione pauperum sive de humanis necessitatibus* (1526), he told the authorities of Bruges that they must help the destitute in order to prevent rebellion and because slums are centers of infection and moral contamination. He divided the indigent into three classes: those sheltered in hospitals and almshouses, homeless beggars, and the honest and shamefaced poor living in their own homes. He insisted on an accurate census and recommended medical aid for the sick and segregation of the insane.

The earliest English law for relief of the poor, the statute of Henry VIII (1531), empowered justices to issue licenses to beggars. The parliamentary statue of 1597–1598 authorized the appointment in each parish of overseers of the poor and imposed on them, and on the churchwardens, the duty of providing for all of the destitute, whether able-bodied or impotent, young or old, lame or blind, and gave them the right to raise funds by taxing parish residents. The courts were empowered to jail anyone refusing to work or anyone refusing to pay the poor rate. This poor law, enacted in the reign of Queen Elizabeth, became part of the English common law that was brought to America by the colonists and has formed the basis of our local government activities on behalf of the poor.

With the growth of modern medicine, the hospital became gradually the center for active treatment of the sick, but in France and Germany homes for the aged also took on important functions as centers of medical study and research, often furnishing to distinguished investigators material on which to base valuable contributions to our knowledge, not only of old age and its associated diseases but also knowledge in other areas of medicine. This rich medical tradition is nowhere better exemplified than in Paris, where the Salpétrière (for women) and the Bicêtre (for men) provided refuge for the aged, the chronically ill, and the insane and were even used at various times for the incarceration of criminals. Guillain and Mathieu have written a vivid history of the achievements of the Salpétrière.

> Refuge of thousands of aged, great center of neurology, great center of psychiatry, the Salpétrière has only become adapted to its actual role by stages. It has seen within its walls the men of the 17th, 18th, 19th and 20th centuries according to their successive conceptions, attempt to solve the great problems of public and private charity, of aid to the poor and the aged, of the protection of society against the insane and the defective, of the protection of the defective and insane against society; it has seen...the creation of scientific psychiatry."[9]

Charcot left us an unforgettable picture of this great institution, where he himself worked and taught so brilliantly for many years.[10]

At the Bicêtre, Pinel in 1798 first struck the chains from the insane, as we learn from the often told story of the earliest efforts toward humane care of the mentally affected. Magendie, Cruveilhier, Rostan, Prus, Durand-Fardel, Landré-Beauvais, and Dechambre were only a few of the great French physicians who made important studies of the aged in these Parisian institutions. In the provinces, Emil Demange made excellent clinical and pathological observations during 500 postmortem examinations of the old residents of the St. Julien Hospice at Nancy.[11] Jules Boy-Teissier of Marseille, physician to the Hôpital St. Marguerite, a home for the aged, published in 1895 *Lectures on the Diseases of the Aged,* based on lectures given at the Marseille Medical School.[12] In recent times, Adrien Pic utilized the clinical material of the Hospice of Perron, near Lyon, for his textbook on the diseases of old age.[13]

In the first monograph on the anatomy of the aged by Burkhard Wilhelm Seiler, *Anatomia Corporis Humani Senilis Specimen,* which appeared at Erlangen in 1800, we find the author admonishing physicians connected with homes for the aged to take advantage of the material at their disposal and stressing the necessity for repeated observations before ascribing any manifestation to old age itself.[14] Lorenz Geist based his 1860 monograph *Klinik der Greisenkrankheiten* on his studies of the residents of the Pfrundner Anstalt zum Heiligen Geist in Nürnberg.[15] Carl Mettenheimer (1824–1898) worked at the Frankfurt Home for the Aged for many years.[16] In Austria, the Vienna municipal hospital for the aged was a source of inspiration for Mueller-Deham's *Innere Krankheiten des Greisernalters,*[17] which owes much of its value to some 2,000 autopsies of old people supervised by the distinguished pathologist Jakob Erdheim.

In England, the Royal Hospital in Chelsea, a medical establishment for old soldiers, gave MacLachlan, in 1863, and Lipscomb, in 1932, the motivation to write texts on the medical aspects of old age, and it later stimulated the efforts of Dr. Trevor Howell, who has written so interestingly of its history as well as of its pensioners' maladies.[18]

THE AMERICAN EXPERIENCE

The colonists came to the New World seeking religious and political freedoms and economic opportunity. In addition to their meager possessions, they brought hope, faith, determination, and dreams. They also brought, consciously and unconsciously, the systems of law and the communal structures that had evolved over many centuries in their native lands.

They continued a Calvinistic approach exemplified by Elizabethan poor laws, which attempted to limit and control mendancy by requiring able-bodied individuals to work. They agreed that the lame, sick, blind, orphaned, and elderly could be cared for in communal facilities, which became known as almshouses. (Almshouses were built in Boston in 1622, in Philadelphia in 1713, and in New York in 1736.)

Early in the history of our country, there were no government agencies or programs. Relief was a local responsibility and was dispensed either by the local community or church or by organizations formed to meet the social, cultural, and religious needs of the immigrant groups. Thus there were associations, clubs, and societies to ensure that the poor would be clothed, housed, and fed, the sick visited, the prisoners ransomed, and the deceased buried. These early organizations, some known as the "Ladies Sheltering Aid Society" and similar names, were established so that those without families and in need of help would be cared for.

These "societies" often purchased private houses and converted them into "homes." Whatever was provided for the wards, referred to as inmates, was expected to be appreciated. The facilities, based on the poor farm or asylum model, were created primarily by nonprofit communal groups, but county-run homes were instituted for individuals who were unaffiliated with any such group.

There were several streams of experience. Immigrants who came from Eastern Europe brought with them the communal "collection pot." This "home" served the aged and orphaned, the handicapped and disabled, the mentally deficient and the mentally ill. It was a feared and dreaded fate and was accepted only when there was no other alternative or recourse.

Immigrants from Germany and Scandinavia brought a different model—the Altenheim, a kind of a club-residence for those who had saved and planned for a respectable retirement. These two distinctly different types of facilities coexisted until virtually the end of World War II.

The voluntary, philanthropic, fraternal, ethnic, church-related home was the primary type of facility providing services throughout the 19th century and up to the early 1920s.

The federal government pursued a philosophy of studied avoidance of intrusion into the lives of citizens. It was not until the late 1890s that the Public Health Service was established, not until 1909 that a president used his good offices to call for a White House Conference (on children), and not until 1916 that Congress authorized a study of the problems of housing and the nation's slums.

There were several factors that maintained the status quo. First, the average life expectancy was low, and therefore the need to develop institutions for the elderly was relatively small. Second, every winter fully one-fourth of the population of existing homes (and those on the waiting lists) would die of pneumonia. Pneumonia was popularly called the "old man's friend" because it was most often accompanied by death, resulting in an end to the burdens of old age.

The major economic upheaval of 1929, the Great Depression, proved to be the undoing of the system of welfare on the county and state level. Unemployment and need was so great that the local church and community groups did not have the resources to cope.

Fearful of the "Army of the Aged," the movement begun by Dr. Francis Townsend, which had grown into a significant political force, President Franklin Roosevelt instructed Frances Perkins (the first woman cabinet member and Secretary of Labor) to propose legislation that would deal with the demands for pensions and welfare reform.

In August 1935, the Congress of the United States passed, and the president signed, the Social Security Act. This legislation was designed to accomplish several things and was indirectly responsible for the growth of the nursing home industry.

The Social Security Act provided for a national, unified welfare system through "categorical assistance" programs. In effect, it said that those already aged (over an arbitrary age of 65), those who were blind, and families with dependent children would receive assistance from a federal and state program. The second part of the act established a form of old age and survivors insurance. The idea was that workers, in conjunction with their employers, would contribute to a fund that in their retirement years would provide income security. If a contributing worker died before age 65, his survivors (wife and children to age 18) would be assured a monthly income.

The Social Security Act has been amended a great many times to provide coverage for the "permanently and totally disabled," coverage for certain special refugee groups, and universal coverage.

In the language of the original act were two provisions for the exclusion of beneficiaries. One of these indicated that if an individual had contracted for life care, he or she would be ineligible for old age assistance. The second provision stated that if an individual was in a government or "county" facility, he or she would be ineligible for old age assistance. Consequently, many local (county) homes recognized that if they continued to operate, the residents would not receive Social Security income. If the residents were discharged or transferred, however, they could become eligible, and thus many county homes moved toward closing.

Another result of the Great Depression was that many people were close to losing their homes (due to severe unemployment). Some of these individuals, seeking income to help them make their mortgage payments, were happy to welcome relatives and those being discharged from county homes into their own homes. This gave rise to a new cottage industry consisting of private homes converted into rest homes. In that era of meager regulation, there were no standards of care and no licensing requirements. And finally, once older people had some income and were no longer totally indigent, there was a dramatic shift from thinking of them as inmates to recognizing them as individuals. They became "residents" rather than "wards" or "patients."

THE DEMOGRAPHIC CHANGES

The increased sophistication of medicine, the discovery of new drugs, various technological breakthroughs, changes in rehabilitation, and the shift from acute to chronic care altered forever the demographic landscape and led to the "graying of America."

In the late 1930s and 1940s, the discovery of broad spectrum antibiotics virtually eliminated infectious diseases (the use of sulfa, penicillin, and the myecins reduced the risk of death from surgical interventions).

World War II made drastic changes imperative in the treatment and repair of orthopedic injuries and gave birth to the field of physical medicine and rehabilitation. Previously, older people who had broken a hip were subjected to long periods of traction and often died from other complications. Now age was no longer a factor in treatment. With replacement hardware, antibiotic medication, and transfusable blood, people could recover from or live for long periods with chronic disabilities.

The next major breakthrough was the discovery of the psychotropic drugs. The psychopharmacological revolution made the treatment of depression and aggressive behaviors possible. Individuals who previously could only be cared for in state hospitals could be maintained at home, in the community, or in a nursing home.

The progress of medicine thus altered the demand for services, and the demographic revolution led to the need for a modified health benefits insurance program for the aged.

COLLATERAL DEVELOPMENTS

Licensing of Facilities

In the amendments to the 1950 Social Security Act, Congress mandated that, by 1953, if a facility housed and cared for four or more unrelated individuals receiving Social Security income, the facility would require a license from the state in which it was located. Thus for the first time on a national scale, physical and service standards were established, and nomenclature began to define care facilities.

Introduction of Specially Designed Facilities

The nature of the population in care facilities was changing. Familyless immigrant residents were being replaced by nativeborns. The residents were older (average age on admission increased from around 60 in the 1940s to around 86 in the early 1990s), sicker (they had four or more chronic disabilities and more than half suffered from some form of dementia), and poorer (they had exhausted their funds or divested them prior to institutionalization).

Because of the increased age and enfeeblement of the residents, the federal government, in 1958, convened the first national Conference on Homes for the Aged and Nursing Homes, and the thrust of that effort was to focus on unsafe, unsanitary conditions and to eliminate the possibility of nursing home fires. A steady stream of regulations came forth, calling for fire-resistant structures, sprinkler systems, smoke and heat detectors, and alarm systems. Several federal loan programs made loan guarantees available to replace the fire-hazardous facilities, and a new era of facilities designed for use as nursing homes was ushered in. Some of these new and efficient designs became the foundation for the growth of nursing home chains.

National Organizations

Although there were some sectarian nursing home organizations (Protestant, Catholic, and Jewish), there was no unified national organization representing all nonprofit homes. In 1960, the American Association of Homes for Aging was organized to represent those facilities. There already was an association representing for-profit homes, the American Nursing Home Association, which later changed its name to the American Health Care Association. This group also accepts nonprofits into its membership.

These organizations primarily serve institutions. The American College of Nursing Home Administrators (name changed to the American College of Healthcare Administrators) serves the professionals who manage nursing homes.

The American Association of Homes for Aging became the force for recognition of the "social components of care," which introduced the psychosocial model to long-term care.

With the virtual elimination of infectious diseases and pneumonia, homes began to have large waiting lists, the elderly were increasing in number, as were organizations serving the elderly, and their political clout was felt at the First White House Conference on Aging, authorized by Congress in 1960.[*] At that conference, delegates urged that some form of national health insurance be enacted.

Though originally introduced in the Congress in 1942 by Murray, Wagner, and Dingill, it was not until 1965 that Congress passed the Health Insurance Benefits

---

[*]President Harry Truman called for a National Conference on Aging, which was held in 1950, but the first White House Conference on Aging was officially held in 1960.

for the Aged Act, which established Medicare (an insurance program primarily for physician benefits and hospital and home care payments) and Medicaid (an assistance program for extended care, etc.).

The belief that the government was going to underwrite posthospital extended care was the impetus for an enormous growth in nursing homes and also for the linking of many free-standing facilities to form chains. The emergence of nursing homes as major players in the health delivery system permitted them to create corporate entities and, by going public, to get their stocks traded on the big board. Some of these corporations were bought and sold and traded and were as much economic entities as care-providing entities.

With reimbursement comes regulation, and during President Nixon's administration a major nursing home reform initiative was established that placed new emphasis on the provision of services as well as on the physical plant of nursing homes. Nixon also appointed a special Commissioner for Nursing Homes.

The U.S. Senate Subcommittee on Aging has been interested for many years in the conditions in America's nursing homes. In 1967, Congress passed legislation mandating that every administrator of a nursing home be licensed by 1970, and each state has now established a board of licensure.

The Congress called upon the National Academy of Science's Institute of Medicine to conduct a study to improve the quality of care in the nation's nursing homes. After several years of work and in an effort to identify quality indicators, the report was issued and served as the basis of the Nursing Home Reform Act of 1988, part of the Omnibus Budget Reconciliation Act. The reforms were the most sweeping in ten years and will contribute to the empowering of residents, the creation of restraint-free environments, and the upgrading of nurse aide training.

The modern nursing home is the result of centuries of evolution and refinement. Only a very small portion of the elderly are cared for in institutions (approximately 5 to 6 percent at any given moment), yet those who are in homes tend to be especially frail, fragile, vulnerable, and cognitively impaired.

Free-standing and single-function nursing homes are disappearing. In their place are campuses for serving the elderly in housing and nursing homes and in continuing care retirement communities, which offer a vast array of services.

The modern nursing home offers inpatient, outpatient, and outreach services. In addition to direct services, it can provide education (to its own staff and to college students or others) and can engage in research and demonstration projects.

The nursing home today is the foundation for a comprehensive, community-based continuum of care. With its range of services, it can utilize care management to provide the right service at the right time and at the right cost.

The nursing home is no longer the point of no return. It is the "aging person's destination" and the "thinking person's choice" when the need for long-term care arises.

NOTES

1. J.G. Gold and S.M. Kaufman, Development of Care of Elderly: Tracing the History of Institutional Facilities, *The Gerontologist* 10 (1970):262–274.
2. F.H. Garrison, *An Introduction to the History of Medicine,* 4th ed. (Philadelphia: W.B. Saunders, 1929).
3. R.M. Clay, *The Medieval Hospitals of England* (London: Methuen, 1909).
4. H. Moody, *A History and Description of the Hospital of St. Cross* (Winchester: G. & H. Gilmour, 1844).
5. H. Cushing, *The Life of Sir William Osler* (Oxford: Clarendon Press, 1925).
6. W.J. Marx, The Development of Charity in Medieval Louvain (Thesis, Columbia University, 1936).
7. G. Van Bever, *Les Béguinages* (Brussels: Editions due Cercle d'Art, 1944). See also the *Catholic Encyclopedia* and the *Encyclopedia Britannica*.
8. S. Webb and B. Webb, The Old Poor Law, in *English Poor Law History* (London: Longmans Greedn & Co., 1927).
9. G. Guillain and P. Mathieu, *La Salpétrière* (Paris: Masson & Cie, 1925).
10. J.M.A. Charcot, *Clinical Lectures on the Diseases of Old Age,* trans. by L.H. Hunt (New York: William Wood & Co., 1881).
11. E. Demange, *Étude Clinique et Anatomo-Pathologique Sur la Vieillesse* (Paris: F. Olean, 1886).
12. J. Boy-Teissier, *Leçons sur les Maladies des Vieillards, Faites a l'école de Médecine de Marseille* (Paris: O. Doin, 1895).
13. A. Pic and S. Bonnamour, *Précis des Maladies des Vieillards* (Paris: O. Doin & Fils, 1912).
14. B.W. Seiler, *Anatomia Corporis Humani Senilis Specimen* (Erlangen, Germany: J.J. Palm, 1800).
15. L. Geist, *Klinik der Greisenkrankheiten* (Erlangen, Germany: F. Enke, 1860).
16. C.F.M. Mattenheimer, *Sectiones Longaevorum* (Frankfurt, Germany: Sauerlander, 1863).
17. A. Mueller-Deham, *Innere Krankheiten des Greisemalters* (Vienna: Julius Springer, 1937).
18. D. MacLachlan, *A Practical Treatise on the Diseases and Infirmities of Advanced Life* (London: J. Churchill's Sons, 1863); F.M. Lipscomb, *Diseases of Old Age* (London: Bailliere, Tindall & Cox, 1932); T. Howell, *Old Age: Some Practical Points in Geriatrics* (London: H.K. Lewis & Co., 1944). For further information, see T. Faulkner, *A Historical and Descriptive Account of the Royal Hospital and the Royal Military Asylum at Chelsea* (London: T. Faulkner, 1805); G.R. Gleig, *Chelsea Hospital and Its Traditions* (London: Richard Bentley, 1839).

SUGGESTED READINGS

Abel, N.E. A short history of long term care. *Modern Healthcare,* July 1976, 13–16.

McArthur, R.F. The historical evolution from almshouse to ECF. *Nursing Homes,* April–August 1970.

Rogers, W.W. Historical institutions of long term care. *The Southwestern Journal of Aging* (Southwest Society on Aging) 7, no. 1 (1991).

Tobriner, A. Almshouses in sixteenth-century England: Housing for the poor elderly. *Journal of Religion and Aging* 1, no. 4 (1985):13–41.

U.S. Department of Labor. Bureau of Labor Statistics. *Care of aged persons in the United States.* Pub. No. 489, Oct. 1929.

U.S. Department of Labor. Bureau of Labor Statistics. *Homes for the Aged in the U.S.* Pub. No. 677, 1941.

Zeman, F.D. The institutional care of the aged: Scope and function of the modern home. Unpublished, 1952.

Chapter 3

Psychological Issues in Institutional Care of the Aged

Susan Krauss Whitbourne and Karen-Jo Wills

The psychological concerns of aging individuals have been the focus of four decades of research, beginning with the publication in 1959 of the first *Handbook of Aging and the Individual*.[1] At that time, it was generally believed that aging brought with it a diminution of happiness, level of activity, and self-esteem and an increase in anxiety, susceptibility to stress, and rigidity. However, even in this first edition, Kuhlen[2] pointed out that age alone is not a sufficient basis for predicting adjustment and that personality and life circumstances interact in important ways to influence the individual's level of happiness and adaptability. The theme of personal variability and the influence of situational determinants remained an important concept throughout the subsequent 40 years, serving as the basis for hundreds of investigations into factors affecting adjustment in later life.

PERSON-ENVIRONMENT CONGRUENCE MODELS OF ADAPTATION

Among the variables studied as predictors of adjustment in old age, one of the most important has been the individual's living situation. With the growth of institutions designed to care for the infirm elderly, psychological gerontologists have maintained a commitment to understanding the effect of institutional life on the individual's adjustment, a commitment that began with the early publications in this area by Carp, Coe, Lawton, and Lieberman.[3] Implicit in this research is the understanding that most elderly persons in need of supervised medical care would prefer to live independently in their own homes and fear the institutionalization process,[4] yet health problems and the unavailability of caregivers prevent them from living at home.[5] When institutional care becomes a necessity, the question is to determine how to reduce the negative impact of forced dependence on the psychological health of older people.

Over the past 25 years, the search for ways to minimize the negative effects of institutionalization has led to the development of a model focusing on the concept of congruence, or a matching of the needs of the individual with the characteristics of the institutional environment.[6] According to this model, individuals vary in their needs and perceptions of the environment and are best adapted when they are in a state of congruence (i.e., the environment both meets their needs and is positively perceived). The central assumption is that there are large individual differences in the person-environment congruence equation. Elaborating on the congruence model, the competence model adds the notion that the demands of the environment must be considered in relation to the capacities of the resident.[7] Severely impaired residents are unable to function in environments that are too challenging; conversely, highly competent residents have difficulty adapting to environments that are insufficiently demanding of their abilities. Thus, not only must needs and interests be taken into account when considering the person-environment match, but so must the resources and demands of the person and the environment.

As helpful as the congruence and competence models have proven in stimulating further theory building and research, they have obvious limitations as models for practice when they are implemented in the real world. Institutions, by their very nature, must provide for the "average" person; they are not easily molded to meet the idiosyncratic needs of the varieties of people who live in them. To take a simple example, some individuals prefer rooms that are warm and others prefer rooms that are cool. Yet the heating system of the institution must be set at some average temperature, and by definition this average will fail to satisfy people who prefer or require environments that are warmer or cooler.

Consideration of the emotional climate of the institution leads to more puzzling dilemmas. The emotional needs of institutional residents can be regarded as revolving around the important theme of autonomy-security,[8] a dimension regarded as contributing to personal growth as well as physical and emotional well-being in institutional residents.[9] Apart from their physical needs, some older adults may desire a nurturant environment that fosters dependence; others value their emotional autonomy and wish to preserve it as long as possible. Yet, as with the setting of temperature, the institution adjusts the level of independence to an "average" amount and in the process creates tension between the needs of individuals and the ability of the institution to meet those needs. The natural tendency of caregivers is to err on the side of dependence, as the institution runs more smoothly if staff rather than residents organize daily schedules, decide on activities, plan meals, and structure activities of daily living such as bathing, dressing, and feeding.[10] In the area of toileting, for example, it is more efficient for staff to change a patient than to rely on the patient's schedule of voiding.[11] This tendency to encourage dependence is also fostered by the medical model, in which the resident is regarded as a patient who passively receives treatment.[12] Ironically, although institutions may pride themselves on providing as much support as possible for residents by meeting their daily needs for care, activity, and stimulation, too much support can actually be detrimental, because it will tend to reduce the individual's efforts at self-direction and mastery, leading to greater psychological dependence on the institution.[13]

Even if it were not more efficient to run an institution by having the staff in control, the roles of resident and caregiver almost naturally foster the development of dependence in residents. The resident, whose responsibilities for taking care of home, family, and finances have been removed in the institutionalization process, is placed in a dependent or childlike relationship to the staff, who have taken over the management of the resident's affairs. A self-fulfilling prophecy is set in motion when the caregiver views the resident as too infirm to take independent action, which causes the resident, in turn, to lose self-maintenance skills.

THE INFANTILIZATION PROCESS

Underlying the issue of dependence versus independence is a process that is discussed less frequently in the gerontological literature but seems to play a fundamental role in the lives of the institutionalized elderly. This is the process of infantilization, which involves treating an elderly individual like a child.[14] The infantilization of older adults is reflected in the characterization of later life as a "second childhood."[15] Older adults are seen as unproductive, undisciplined, disruptive, cranky, irrational, silly, and impulsive. Their need for help with the activities of daily living that small children need help with—eating, dressing, and toileting—further supports this characterization of older adults as infantile. Activities that are planned for older adults typically include arts and crafts, birthday parties, and play with toys, all of which are activities that adults make available to children.

Infantilization can also be seen in the way an older person is dressed by caregivers. A woman may have bows, ponytails, or pigtails put in her hair. The clothes she is given to wear are pastel colored, like those used to dress small infants, and on holidays she may be outfitted using colors or pins that are symbolic of the season. Elderly men are often subjected to a similar kind of treatment. For example, a male resident wearing a necktie or a suitcoat might be responded to by flirtatious remarks on the part of female caregivers, who might declare how "handsome" he looks. At the opposite extreme, caregivers may pay little attention to dressing the residents in proper attire, leaving them in pajamas and bathrobes, much as infants are left in their sleepers during the day. Finally, infantilization may take the form of lack of respect for a resident's need for privacy—by dressing or undressing the resident in a public location or without proper safeguards to prevent intrusion.

The language directed at residents is another area in which infantilization manifests itself.[16] Referring to an elderly man as "handsome" is not in and of itself an instance of infantilization; it is when the term is used as synonymous with "cute" that the compliment becomes condescension. Similarly, referring to a resident as "sweetie," "grannie," and "dearie," or using first names only, is patronizing and violates the resident's dignity.[17] Baby talk—speaking with intonations and words that would be used to address a small child—is another manifestation of infantilization.[18] Although it may be argued that such verbalizations can be reassuring and consistent with the role of nurse as caregiver,[19] it is just as likely that the use of baby talk results from a lack of knowledge of alternate methods of communication.[20]

Caregivers may also decorate the environment so that it resembles a kindergarten or preschool rather than a residence for adults. For weeks before the next major holiday, the institution may be decorated with hearts, pumpkins, turkeys, or Santa Clauses (or Hanukkah decorations in a Jewish institution), just like a classroom in an elementary school. At other times, mobiles, stickers, or the artwork of residents may be placed in the hallways and common spaces as a way to add color, contributing further to the school-like appearance of the institution.

It is, perhaps, in the attitudes and general behaviors directed toward residents that infantilization occurs in its most extreme form. These attitudes and behaviors include rewarding residents by patting, touching, or kissing them, which is like cuddling or hugging babies when they are good. Similarly, a caregiver may reinforce childlike fantasies in a resident by giving the resident a doll, for example, and calling it "baby" when the resident starts to treat it as a child. Residents are also given little freedom of choice in the areas of food, dress, and activities, just like children, who typically lack the authority to control the decisions made by parents. If a resident balks or objects to a particular choice, the caregiver is likely to respond in ways similar to those adopted by a parent handling a difficult child. The resident may be publicly scolded or punished by having certain benefits withheld, whereas compliant behavior is rewarded.

WHAT CAUSES INFANTILIZATION?

The most straightforward explanation of infantilization is that it occurs as a function of the elderly adult's being placed in a dependent position with regard to the caregiver. As a result of being placed in this dependent position, the elderly person acquires by association the status of a child, who is also dependent relative to caregivers.[21]

Although both resident and caregiver are likely to make this association between dependence and childlike attributes, it is more probable that the caregiver will act on this association. The resident has an identity as an adult and a sense of continuity of the self over time. The caregiver, who has only seen the resident in the dependent position within the institution, lacks this reference point and sees the resident only as a frail elderly person no longer capable of self-care. In many ways, this situation is comparable to the fundamental attribution error described by social psychologists[22] in which observers discount the importance of situational variables when making judgments about the causes of a person's behavior. The caregiver attributes childlike qualities to the resident despite the obvious fact that the resident's physical frailty or illness has contributed to his or her need for institutional care.

The forming of an association between dependency and childlike status may begin the process of infantilization. Once set in motion, though, infantilization becomes a vicious cycle. The resident, feeling increasingly helpless and dependent, begins to regress behaviorally to the level of a child, and the more helpless the resident feels, the more this regression occurs. Regressive behaviors on the part of the resident trigger complementary behaviors in the staff as their view of the elderly person as a child is borne out. There is a tendency for staff to encourage dependent, compliant behavior and to ignore and even punish more competent, self-reliant behavior.[23] Furthermore, the control that caregivers have over the consequences of residents' behaviors makes residents highly dependent on how caregivers evaluate them. Scolding by caregivers or encouragement to be "good" only aggravates this regressive pattern.[24]

Adding to the regression shown by each resident individually may be interactive behaviors among residents that further confirm the caregiver's view that they are like children. The lack of privacy and space, combined with loss of control over their environment, may lead residents to become competitive and territorial about their claims to occupy certain areas of the institution or to receive certain rewards, such as food and materials. Residents may be drawn into fights and bickering among themselves as they struggle to maintain possession of what they perceive as limited resources to which they have no independent access. Such disputes may be likened by staff to the way that children fight in the playground for desirable toys or access to equipment. Similarly, if a resident complains about having a valued item taken away, this behavior can be used to justify the assertion that residents are like children who cry or become angry when they must give up or share a desired possession.

Not only are residents dependent on caregivers for material rewards, but they are also dependent on them for much of the affection and approval they experience in their lives. Seeing that childlike behaviors are given attention and rewarded may lead residents to enact these behaviors as a route to affection.[25] Furthermore, residents may be willing to put up with the patronizing behaviors of kissing, hugging, and touching for the sole purpose of maintaining human contact, even if it is degrading. In this regard, it is important to point out that caregivers who infantilize in this manner may be doing so out of the best of intentions, because they believe that the elderly residents appreciate this treatment, and, perhaps, because they have no other model of positively relating to residents. Indeed, when interviewed about their feelings toward their work, one sample of nursing assistants described themselves as nurturing, caring, and compassionate individuals who help the infirm elderly.[26]

Finally, infantilization may be furthered by sensory losses, disorientation, and confusion, which make the resident feel more helpless and lead to even greater dependence on caregivers for help in negotiating the environment. Caregivers also take on heightened importance for residents who feel isolated, abandoned, and lonely and cannot bring themselves to interact with other residents. The clearest way to receive attention from caregivers is to comply with the infantilization process by taking on childlike personal qualities.[27]

Professional caregivers are not the only individuals likely to infantilize the elderly. Family members may also become caught up in the process of seeing their elders as children. In part, this attitude is encouraged by popular characterizations of aging families, in which role reversal between adult children and their parents is regarded as almost an inevitable concomitant of the parents' aging process. Adult children may come to anticipate the moment when they will begin to parent their parents, and elderly parents, exposed to similar social attitudes, may unquestioningly follow through with complementary behavioral changes. An unfortunate consequence of the infantilization process when it occurs in the home is that the older adult's grandchildren are likely to take on similar infantilizing attitudes through modeling their own parents. In addition to developing this unfortunate way of behaving toward older adults, young people are more likely to develop negative attitudes toward old age because they associate it with childhood, a period of life they have just left behind. Similarly, adults are more likely to become "gerontophobic," because they are facing the prospect of an old age in which they will be treated like a child.[28]

WHO BECOMES INFANTILIZED?

The infantilization process may be expected to vary according to the individual characteristics of the resident and the standards or norms of the particular institution. The person-environment congruence model predicts that there are individual variations in the way that older adults adapt to the institutional environment. These variations are based on differences in physical status, functional competencies in the physical and cognitive domains, personal needs and motivations, and prior socialization. Two psychological constructs particularly relevant to institutional adaptation are expectancy of personal control[29] and coping strategy.[30]

By expectancy of personal control is meant the individual's sense of whether the outcomes of events in his or her life are determined by factors internal to the individual, such as quality of judgment or appropriateness of decision making, or by external factors, such as fate, chance, luck, or religious or political forces. Although having a sense of internal control over one's life is generally regarded as more adaptive and as enhancing feelings of well-being,[31] there are potential drawbacks, especially when, as in an institution, control is shifted to an external agency (i.e., the institutional staff and administration). In such cases, the individual might maintain adaptability by relinquishing personal control rather than fighting against a system which now, in fact, has control over his or her life.[32] The exception is if the individual is residing in a malleable environment in which autonomy and personal responsibility are fostered.[33]

The coping strategies an individual uses to manage stress are a separate but related dimension influencing quality of adjustment to the institution. Stress, in the context of the institution, may be seen as involved in the initial phases of relocation and as further involved in the day-to-day adaptation to the demands of institutional life, which are different from the demands of living in the community. Rather than being a direct function of events in the environment, stress is regarded as dependent on the individual's perception of a situation as overwhelming. The two types of coping strategies identified within the stress and coping literature are emotion-focused coping and problem-focused coping.[34] In emotion-focused coping, the individual attempts to reduce stress by changing the way the event is perceived so that it is no longer regarded as threatening. Emotion-focused coping strategies include avoidance, escape, and wishful thinking. None of these strategies causes the stressor to disappear, but the individual may feel less stressed and therefore better adapted. In problem-focused coping, the individual attempts to lower stress by changing something in the situation. There are also coping strategies that involve a combination of emotion- and problem-focused coping, such as seeking social support. When people reduce stress through social support, the situation may or may not be changed, but the actions involved in finding others to confide in can lower the perception of stress.

As with locus of control, coping strategies may be seen as more or less adaptive for certain situations. In a situation that cannot be changed, such as bereavement, emotion-focused coping is more adaptive in that the individual can at least eventually come to feel better about the loss. Conversely, problem-focused coping will be more successful if the threat represented by a situation can be reduced by taking some sort of action. In the institutional setting, emotion-focused coping would appear to foster adaptation to the environment. Assuming that the institutional environment is relatively unmalleable, the individual will adapt better by finding ways to feel better rather than by engaging in futile attempts to bring about change.

For the average institutional resident living in the average institutional environment, having an external locus of control and relying on emotion-focused coping would seem to result in the most positive adaptation, at least in terms of the individual's ability to fit into the surroundings.[35] Institutions run more smoothly when residents do not question or challenge the authority of staff, and those residents who manifest a compliant pattern of behavior are likely to be given more positive regard by staff and administrators. Some variation around this normative pattern may be satisfactory, though, particularly in institutions that allow greater autonomy for residents, have active resident governments, or have a resident population that is functioning at high levels of physical and cognitive ability.

In summary, to answer the question of who becomes infantilized, it seems reasonable to predict that this process will develop more rapidly in individuals who live in an environment that fosters compliance and who use modes of adapting to the environment that combine an external locus of control and emotion-focused coping. Less likely to become infantilized are those individuals who have an internal locus of control and rely on problem-focused coping. Whether these individuals continue to resist pressure to become infantilized may depend on the response of the environment to their behaviors and on their ability to resist the pressure to conform.

OUTCOME OF INFANTILIZATION

As the above discussion implies, individuals who have an external locus of control and use emotion-focused coping may be "happier" in the institutional setting because they see no reason to complain about what they are being offered. They may feel comforted by the knowledge that the institution is taking care of them and that the burden of decision making has been lifted from their shoulders. At a deeper level, the infantilization to which they become subject may provide them with feelings of being nurtured, of returning to an earlier state of dependence on parents. If these individuals have been socially isolated before their entry into an institution, the care and concern shown by staff may provide reassurance that they are valued for their personal qualities.

By contrast, individuals who maintain a sense of personal control, try to force change in a rigidly controlling institutional environment, and in the process take offense at being infantilized face a more difficult process of adjustment. It is likely that they will be labelled "troublemakers" and have even more of the autonomy they seek withheld from them. A vicious cycle is set into motion, in which the more these individuals protest, the more they stand to lose and the more likely it is that their resolve will give way to compliance at best or isolation at worst.[36] Unlike their counterparts who entered the institution with a more compliant attitude, these defiant individuals will find great difficulty in accepting institutional control and do so only at a great emotional cost.

Although it is important to identify both the favorable and unfavorable outcomes of infantilization, it is also crucial to identify the potential dangers of infantilization. As was just described, the autonomous individual is likely to become demoralized in an environment that stresses infantilization. The more compliant individual, though perhaps happier, nevertheless loses important adaptational skills. Just because it is more comforting to be infantilized does not mean that the individual is better served when treated like a child. Researchers have consistently demonstrated that the loss of autonomy and control has negative effects on the emotional, physical, and behavioral well-being of nursing home residents.[37] The encouragement of a more adultlike status and set of behaviors would seem to be advantageous for all institutional residents, since it would maximize their functional capacities for as long as possible. Unlike children, these older individuals have developed a set of adult coping skills and behaviors. Divesting them of these through infantilization leaves them as helpless as children at a time in their lives when they should be able to benefit from their wisdom, maturity, and life experiences.

HOW INFANTILIZATION CAN BE AVOIDED

If it is assumed that the outcome of infantilization is more negative than positive, then it would seem that this process should be averted in any way possible. Given the many factors that make it likely to occur in any given institution, administrators and staff must be vigilant in their efforts to eradicate infantilization and maintain an environment in which residents receive more adultlike treatment.

Perhaps the first step in avoiding infantilization is to change the perception by staff that the residents are dependent, and to do this, the residents need to be encouraged to act in more independent, adultlike ways. To facilitate this process, ingrained patterns in which staff take over the daily maintenance functions for residents must be broken by having staff make a conscious decision to encourage residents to do more for themselves without help. To implement this decision, staff can be trained in methods of reinforcing residents to become more independent, such as self-shaving, self-dressing, and self-eating.[38] With residents behaving more independently, staff will be less likely to regard them as childlike and helpless. Even when residents need assistance, they can be encouraged to make their own decisions.[39] To the extent that the institution can foster autonomy by giving residents a voice in the administrative policies, the sense among residents of personal independence can also be enhanced.[40]

A second method of combatting infantilization is to encourage staff to become more empathic to the feelings of residents when they are treated as children. One technique helpful in sensitizing students enrolled in courses on the psychology of aging is to use an infantilization exercise. In this exercise, an activities program is simulated in the classroom, and the students are put in the role of residents and are required to make "decorations" for the "dining room."[41] The decorations consist of simple drawings that the students color using crayons that are passed around. The students are infantilized by the instructor, who behaves toward them in an exaggeratedly patronizing manner, calling them "sweetie" and "dearie," insisting that they "color between the lines," and making a number of intrusive or embarrassing remarks about their personal appearance and demeanor ("Doesn't your hair look pretty today?"). Students resent this treatment, and although they soon gather that the exercise involves role-playing, they nevertheless demonstrate some of the key signs of infantilization, such as regression and compliance. Some students become enraged within the context of the role-playing, however, and refuse to follow the rules set by the instructor. After approximately 15 minutes, the instructor stops the exercise and opens the floor for discussion. Students express their feelings of powerlessness and irritation and recognize that if they were in such a situation in real life, they would feel humiliated and angry. Students who work in institutional settings claim that the experience alters their way of relating to the residents and that they will be on guard against infantilizing them in the future. Such an exercise, if redesigned to be more appropriate for institutional staff, could provide a valuable lesson in the dangers of infantilization.

A third way of focusing the attention of caregivers on the elderly resident as an adult is to emphasize the resident's life history and past accomplishments.[42] The assumption is that the more the resident is presented as an individual rather than as one of many people being cared for, the more likely it is that the resident will receive treatment that respects the resident's rights and adult status. Further, by emphasizing the resident's past achievements, in whatever arena these might be, caregivers can come to appreciate the talents and skills that the individual possesses and will thus be less likely to reduce the individual to the status of a helpless child.

Changes in the physical environment can serve to reduce infantilization by enhancing the resident's ability to negotiate that environment independently. In an environment in which the markings and directions are clear, residents will be able to find their way around without staff assistance. The more the environment encourages orientation, the less confused residents will be, decreasing their reliance on staff for assistance and contributing to the perception by staff that the residents are self-reliant. An environment that is decorated to reflect the personal interests of residents rather than the interests of staff can add to the focus on residents as adults with diverse and mature interests. Caregivers may be less likely to treat residents as children if the environment is not school-like in its appearance. With their personal possessions available in their surroundings, residents can gain greater satisfaction[43] and a sense of connectedness to their preinstitutional existence.

Providing an environment that allows for high levels of personal comfort, as perceived by residents, can also serve to enhance independence. In a more comfortable setting, residents are more likely to initiate activities themselves, to interact with each other socially, and to use their time more productively.[44] When residents are in surroundings they perceive as pleasant, they may feel more supportive of each other and are also more likely to find activities that they find personally involving. Such changes not only build the self-esteem of residents but also lead to their behaving in ways that reinforce the staff's perception that residents are self-directed and mature adults rather than children in need of guidance.

The last suggested intervention involves a more general approach—respecting the dignity of each resident as well as his or her feelings, type-of-care preferences, and expressions of emotion. This intervention may require a two-way process, since residents, as a result of becoming infantilized, sometimes develop ways of relating to caregivers that are insulting, abusive, retaliatory, and depersonalizing. Staff also wish to be treated politely and with respect.[45] Helping residents to recognize their own responsibility to treat staff courteously and considerately may break the destructive cycle that lowers the quality of interactions for both groups of participants.

IMPLICATIONS

This focus on infantilization as a central psychological issue in institutionalization has led to a set of recommendations that have broader implications for the long-term care of older adults. Infantilization is assumed to be a pervasive but relatively unrecognized problem of institutional life, and it is proposed that by reducing its prevalence some of the other difficulties involved in caring for the elderly can be ameliorated as well. If residents could live up to their functional capacity potential, the person-environment congruence model predicts that the institutional environment could be made more challenging. Caregivers would therefore find their workload reduced, if not made less burdensome, as more residents become capable of self-care. For those residents who cannot achieve higher levels of self-care, staff would have more time available to provide support and structure.[46] Unfortunately, changes that promote independence may meet with resistance or with unresponsiveness on the part of caregivers unless caregivers have continuous in-service training.[47]

Improvements in the environment, such as increasing the level of stimulation, can indirectly enhance the morale of residents through the positive effects such stimulation has on caregivers.[48] Interventions designed to increase the quality and quantity of interactions between residents and caregivers can also be of value to residents,[49] since staff nurses can serve as an important source of social support for residents.[50] Heightened contact of a social nature in a context in which residents and staff respond appropriately to one another can further break down the stereotypes that each group has of the other.[51]

By recognizing variations in the ways that people respond to the institutional environment, caregivers can become more attuned to the variations in people's needs for nurturance, on the one hand, and autonomy, on the other. Although attention to the psychological needs of residents cannot eliminate the physical diseases that require institutional care, such efforts can reduce the emotional discomfort of these diseases, both for the elderly residents and the caregivers.

REFERENCES

1. J.E. Birren, *Handbook of Aging and the Individual* (Chicago: University of Chicago Press, 1959.)

2. R.G. Kuhlen, Aging and Life-Adjustment, in *Handbook of Aging and the Individual,* ed. J.E. Birren (Chicago: University of Chicago Press, 1959).

3. F.M. Carp, The Impact of Environment on Old People, *The Gerontologist* 7 (1967):106–108; R.M. Coe, Self-Conceptions and Institutionalization, in *Older People and Their Social World,* ed. A.M. Rose and W.A. Peterson (Philadelphia: Davis, 1965); M.P. Lawton, How the Elderly Live, in *Housing and Environment for the Elderly,* ed. T.O. Byerts (Washington, D.C.: Gerontological Society, 1971); M.A. Lieberman, Institutionalization of the Aged: Effects on Behavior, *Journal of Gerontology* 24 (1969):330–340.

4. P.J. Biedenharn and J.B. Normoyle, Elderly Community Residents' Reactions to the Nursing Home: An Analysis of Nursing Home-related Beliefs, *The Gerontologist* 31 (1991): 107–115.

5. S.J. Newman et al., Overwhelming Odds: Caregiving and the Risk of Institutionalization, *Journal of Gerontology: Social Sciences* 45 (1990):S172–183.

6. E. Kahana, A Congruence Model of Person-Environment Interaction, in *Aging and the Environment: Directions and Perspectives,* ed. M.P. Lawton, P.G. Windley, and T.O. Byers (New York: Garland STPM Press, 1980); M.F. Nehrke et al., Toward a Model of Person-Environment Congruence: Development of the EPPIS, *Experimental Aging Research* 7 (1981):363–379.

7. M.P. Lawton, Activities and Leisure, *Annual Review of Gerontology and Geriatrics* 5 (1985): 127–164.

8. J. Grimley-Evans, Prevention of Age-associated Loss of Autonomy: Epidemiological Approaches, *Journal of Chronic Disease* 37 (1984):353–363; P.A. Parmelee and M.P. Lawton, The Design of Special Environments for the Aged, in *Handbook of the Psychology of Aging,* ed. J.E. Birren and K.W. Schaie, 3d ed. (San Diego: Academic Press, 1990).

9. B.F. Hofland, Autonomy in Long Term Care: Background Issues and a Programmatic Response, *The Gerontologist* 28, suppl. (1988):3–9; S. Lemke and R.H. Moos, Measuring the Social Climate of Congregate Residences for Older People: Sheltered Care Environment Scale, *Psychology and Aging* 2 (1987):20–29.

10. R.A. Kane et al., Everyday Autonomy in Nursing Homes, *Generations* 14, suppl. (1990):67–71; S. Stein et al., Patients and Staff Assess Social Climate of Different Quality Nursing Homes, *Comprehensive Gerontology* 1 (1987):41–46.

11. J.F. Schnelle et al., Reduction of Urinary Incontinence in Nursing Homes: Does It Reduce or Increase Costs? *Journal of the American Geriatrics Society* 36 (1988):34–39.

12. C.W. Lidz and R.M. Arnold, Institutional Constraints on Autonomy, *Generations* 14, suppl. (1990):65–68; J. Wack and J. Rodin, Nursing Homes for the Aged: The Human Consequences of Legislation-shaped Environments, *Journal of Social Issues* 34 (1978):6–21.

13. J. Avorn and E.J. Langer, Induced Disability in Nursing Home Patients, *Journal of the American Geriatrics Society* 30 (1982):397–400; M.P. Lawton, Community Supports for the Aged, *Journal*

of Social Issues 37 (1981):102–115; P.A. Parmelee and M.P. Lawton, The Design of Special Environments for the Aged, in *Handbook of the Psychology of Aging,* ed. J.E. Birren and K.W. Schaie, 3d ed. (San Diego: Academic Press, 1990).

14. I. Milton and J. MacPhail, Dolls and Toy Animals for Hospitalized Elders—Infantilizing or Comforting? *Geriatric Nursing* 6 (1985):204–206; A.R. Tarbox, The Elderly in Nursing Homes: Psychological Aspects of Neglect, *Clinical Gerontologist* 1 (1983):39–52.

15. A. Arluke and J. Levin, Another Stereotype: Old Age as a Second Childhood, *Aging,* August 1984, 7–11.

16. E.H. Dolinsky, Infantilization of the Elderly, *Journal of Gerontological Nursing* 10 (1984):12–19.

17. D.C. Kimmel and H.R. Moody, Ethical Issues in Gerontological Research and Services, in *Handbook of the Psychology of Aging,* ed. J.E. Birren & K.W. Schaie, 3d ed. (San Diego: Academic Press, 1990).

18. L.R. Caporael, The Paralanguage of Caregiving: Baby Talk to the Institutionalized Aged, *Journal of Personality and Social Psychology* 40 (1981):867–884.

19. L.K. Wright, A Reconceptualization of the "Negative Staff Attitudes and Poor Care in Nursing Homes" Assumption, *The Gerontologist* 28 (1988):813–820.

20. M.D. Shulman and E. Mandel, Communication Training of Relatives and Friends of Institutionalized Elderly Persons, *The Gerontologist* 28 (1988):797–799.

21. A.R. Tarbox, The Elderly in Nursing Homes: Psychological Aspects of Neglect, *Clinical Gerontologist* 1 (1983):39–52.

22. L. Ross, The Intuitive Psychologist and His Shortcomings: Distortions in the Attribution Process, in *Advances in Experimental Social Psychology,* vol. 10, ed. L. Berkowitz (New York: Academic Press, 1977); see also S.T. Fiske and S.E. Taylor, *Social Cognition* (Reading, Mass.: Addison-Wesley, 1991).

23. M.M. Baltes et al., Further Observational Data on the Behavioral and Social World of Institutions for the Aged, *Psychology and Aging* 2 (1987):390–403.

24. A.R. Tarbox, The Elderly in Nursing Homes: Psychological Aspects of Neglect, *Clinical Gerontologist* 1 (1983):39–52.

25. L. Herst and P. Moulton, Psychiatry in the Nursing Home, *Psychiatric Clinics of North America* 8 (1985):551–561.

26. T. Heiselman and L.S. Noelker, Enhancing Mutual Respect among Nursing Assistants, Residents, and Residents' Families, *The Gerontologist* 31 (1991):552–555.

27. A.R. Tarbox, The Elderly in Nursing Homes: Psychological Aspects of Neglect, *Clinical Gerontologist* 1 (1983):39–52.

28. A. Arluke and J. Levin, Another Stereotype: Old Age as a Second Childhood, *Aging,* August 1984, 7–11.

29. J.B. Rotter, Generalized Expectancies for Internal versus External Control of Reinforcement, *Psychological Monographs* 80, no. 1, whole no. 609 (1966).

30. R.S. Lazarus and S. Folkman, *Stress, Appraisal, and Coping* (New York: Springer, 1984).

31. J. Rodin, Aging and Health: Effects of the Sense of Control, *Science* 233 (1986):1271–1276.

32. A. Antonovsky, *Health, Stress, and Coping* (San Francisco: Jossey-Bass, 1979); N. Krause, Stress and Coping: Reconceptualizing the Role of Locus of Control Beliefs, *Journal of Gerontology* 41 (1986):617–622.

33. E.J. Langer and J. Rodin, The Effects of Choice and Enhanced Personal Responsibility for the Aged: A Field Experiment in an Institutional Setting, *Journal of Personality and Social Psychol-*

ogy 34 (1976):191–198; J. Rodin and E.J. Langer, Longer Term Effects of Control-Relevant Intervention within the Institutionalized Aged, *Journal of Personality and Social Psychology* 35 (1977):897–903.

34. R.S. Lazarus and S. Folkman, *Stress, Appraisal, and Coping* (New York: Springer, 1984).

35. H.A. Davidson and B.P. O'Connor, Perceived Control and Acceptance of the Decision To Enter a Nursing Home as Predictors of Adjustment, *International Journal of Aging and Human Development* 31 (1990):307–318.

36. A. Arluke and J. Levin, Another Stereotype: Old Age as a Second Childhood, *Aging,* August 1984, 7–11.

37. M.M. Baltes and P.B. Baltes, *Aging and the Psychology of Control* (Hillsdale, N.J.: Lawrence Erlbaum, 1986).

38. D.J. Sperbeck and S.K. Whitbourne, Dependence in the Institutional Setting: A Behavioral Training Program for Geriatric Staff, *The Gerontologist* 21 (1981):268–275.

39. B.J. Collopy, Autonomy in Long Term Care: Some Crucial Distinctions, *The Gerontologist* 28 (1988):10–17.

40. J. Rodin et al., The Construct of Control: Biological and Psychosocial Correlates, *Annual Review of Gerontology and Geriatrics* 5 (1985):3–55.

41. S.K. Whitbourne, The Infantilization Exercise as a Teaching Tool in Courses on the Psychology of Aging, in preparation.

42. M.E. Pietrukowicz and M.S. Johnson, Using Life Histories To Individualize Nursing Home Staff Attitudes toward Residents, *The Gerontologist* 31 (1991):102–106.

43. G.C. Smith and S.K. Whitbourne, Validity of the Sheltered Care Environment Scale, *Psychology and Aging* 5 (1990):228–235.

44. C. Timko and R.H. Moos, Determinants of Interpersonal Support and Self-Direction in Group Residential Facilities, *Journal of Gerontology: Social Sciences* 45 (1990):S184–192.

45. T. Heiselman and L.S. Noelker, Enhancing Mutual Respect among Nursing Assistants, Residents, and Residents' Families, *The Gerontologist* 31 (1991):552–555.

46. S. Lemke and R.H. Moos, Personal and Environmental Determinants of Activity Involvement among Elderly Residents of Congregate Facilities, *Journal of Gerontology: Social Sciences* 44 (1989):S139–148.

47. J.F. Schnelle et al., Management of Patient Continence in Long-Term Care Nursing Facilities, *The Gerontologist* 30 (1990):373–376.

48. E. Kahana et al., Alternative Models of Person Environment Fit: Prediction of Morale in Three Homes for the Aged, *Journal of Gerontology* 35 (1980):584–595.

49. D.J. Sperbeck et al., Determinants of Person-Environment Congruence in Institutionalized Elderly Men and Women, *Experimental Aging Research* 7 (1981):381–392.

50. J.E. Bitzan and J.M. Kruzich, Interpersonal Relationships of Nursing Home Residents, *The Gerontologist* 30 (1990):385–390.

51. F.J. Vaccaro, Application of Social Skills Training in a Group of Institutionalized Aggressive Elderly Subjects, *Psychology and Aging* 5 (1990):369–378.

Chapter 4

Role of the Medical Director in the 1990s

Steven A. Levenson

In 1974, for the first time, the Department of Health, Education, and Welfare (HEW) required every skilled nursing facility to retain a full- or part-time medical director. However, the only guidance offered was the inclusion of a medical director's potential job description. In 1977, the American Medical Association (AMA) issued a booklet of articles about the position of medical director, but since then it has given scant attention to the role of that position in the nursing home.[1] There was little further in-depth discussion of medical direction in the literature until some articles and books began to appear in the mid to late 1980s.[2]

In the 1990s and beyond, the role of the nursing home medical director is certain to expand. The current legal foundation for that role, and the strongest impetus to its further evolution, has come from the extensively revised federal nursing home regulations ("Conditions of Participation for Medicare and Medicaid"). These are known as the OBRA '87 regulations, because the law mandating their revision was part of the 1987 federal Omnibus Budget Reconciliation Act (OBRA).

The OBRA '87 regulations require that there be a medical director in all the nation's nursing facilities (former skilled and intermediate facilities). The only explicit regulatory duties of a medical director are to oversee the medical care and to coordinate the facility's resident care policies. However, other accompanying guidelines also imply that the medical director is obligated to help the facility apply appropriate professional standards and to take action when clinical care is inconsistent with those standards.[3]

This chapter will explore the required and optional responsibilities of the nursing home medical director, including the potential for the medical director to help improve the care of the institutionalized elderly.

THE CHANGING MEDICAL SITUATION IN LONG-TERM CARE

The nursing home has become a primary site for managing advanced old age and the health problems associated with aging. There are currently more people

(1.5 million) in nursing home beds than in acute care hospital beds in the United States.[4] Most nursing home residents are over age 65 (mean age, 80 years or older), predominantly female (approximately two-thirds), physically disabled with respect to basic activities of daily living, and cognitively impaired.[5]

One-fourth of those reaching age 65 will spend some time in a nursing home before they die. Because of shorter lengths of hospital stays under prospective payment reimbursement, nursing homes are receiving sicker patients and providing more medical care than before. More nursing home residents are dying within 30 days of admission, including more terminally ill patients transferred to nursing homes just prior to death.[6]

The nursing home population is very diverse. Facilities and attending physicians must manage a broad spectrum of age groups, illnesses, functional problems, and goals of care. Nursing home residents range from those who enter extremely ill and have a life expectancy of less than six months to those who have a mix of physical and cognitive impairments and will remain for many years.[7]

Thus, nursing homes are changing their functions and relationships, shifting from a predominantly social model providing personal care to a health care model managing illnesses and dysfunctions. Simultaneously, the roles of caregivers within nursing homes are changing, too.

THE PHYSICIAN'S ROLE

More than ever before, nursing home residents need quality medical care. Yet, many facility administrators and nursing directors wonder about the medical director's role in their facilities and how physicians might help them provide and improve care to the elderly population under their custody.

The diversity of the nursing home population requires medical flexibility. The management of a short-stay rehabilitation resident differs significantly from that of a short-stay terminally ill resident or of a long-term ambulatory but cognitively and functionally impaired resident. Many problems of nursing home residents are not medical in nature. If they are medical, they may be only partially treatable by physicians and the tools of modern medicine.

Attending physicians in the nursing home must coordinate their management of diseases, including their orders, with the plans and activities of other staff providing care (e.g., social workers, dietitians, nurses, nurses aides, and physical and occupational therapists). Others impacting care include families, administrators, regulators, ombudsmen, and lawyers. Also, there are greater expectations for the residents' participation in care decisions. The medical director has a responsibility to encourage attending physicians to respect this interdisciplinary approach and to pay attention to the information provided by other staff.

Medical directors can also help improve clinical care by helping attending physicians and other caregivers manage acute and chronic illness more effectively in the nursing home. Nursing home residents have many potentially remediable medical conditions, including malnutrition, dehydration, depression, and infections. Apparently, many such problems could be treated successfully in their earlier stages in the nursing home, thus preventing costly and traumatic hospital admissions.[8]

There are important differences between providing care in acute and long-term care settings. Whereas acute care focuses on treating a medical disease or condition, long-term care focuses on restoring and maintaining functional capabilities, supporting maximal autonomy and quality of life, providing comfort and dignity for those who are dying, managing chronic medical conditions, and preventing and recognizing acute medical and iatrogenic illnesses.[9]

The extent to which the medical problems of a nursing home resident should be treated depends on the available therapies, the prognosis, and the wishes of the resident and family. An effective system to ascertain those wishes must be combined with good communication between and policies and protocols for cooperative management by physicians and other caregivers. Thus, a medical director should possess and promote a broader understanding of the meaning and implications of clinical care in the nursing home, including but not limited to the medical management of acute and chronic illness.

THE MEDICAL DIRECTOR'S REQUIRED AND OPTIONAL ROLES AND FUNCTIONS

In 1988, a group of medical directors met to develop a comprehensive enumeration of roles, functions, and tasks for nursing home medical directors.[10] Exhibit 4-1 lists these major administrative functions.

Only the first three (performing administrative functions, such as coordinating policies and procedures; organizing and ensuring adequate medical coverage; and overseeing care) are required by OBRA '87 regulations. Exhibit 4-2 lists some specific medical director activities relevant to regulatory compliance.

Table 4-1 illustrates the potential depth and breadth of medical director activities. Additional functions represent a broader, more activist physician role that many people believe could help improve the quality of care in nursing homes. It remains to be seen to what extent improvements will occur. The rest of this chapter considers the various tasks associated with these medical director functions.

Exhibit 4-1 Major Medical Director Functions

- Participate in administrative decision making and recommend and approve policies and procedures
- Organize and coordinate physician services and services of other professionals as they relate to patient care
- Participate in the process to ensure the appropriateness and quality of medical and medically related care
- Participate in the development and conduct of education programs
- Help articulate the facility's mission to the community and represent the facility in the community
- Participate in the surveillance and promotion of the health, welfare, and safety of employees
- Acquire, maintain, and apply knowledge of social, regulatory, political, and economic factors that relate to patient care services
- Provide medical leadership for research and development activities in geriatrics and long-term care
- Participate in establishing policies and procedures for ensuring that the rights of individuals are respected

Source: J.J. Pattee and T.M. Altemeier, Results of a Consensus Conference on the Role of the Nursing Home Medical Director, *Annual of Medical Direction* 1, no. 1 (1991):5–11.

MAJOR TASKS AND FUNCTIONS

Administrative Decision Making and Policies and Procedures

Typically, the medical director of a nursing home is the primary or only medically oriented person with administrative responsibilities. These responsibilities concern both the medical staff and the rest of the facility.

Administrative Staff

The medical director should work closely with the facility's departmental and professional leadership (i.e., the administrative staff).

The primary administrative decision makers in the nursing home are the administrator and the director of nursing. The medical director should meet regularly with them, using such meetings to discuss clinical issues and problem prevention and resolution, explain the medical staff's needs to the administrator and the director of nursing, listen to their concerns and needs regarding medical care, review the current status of previous problems, and provide medical input into

Exhibit 4-2 Examples of Medical Director Functions To Comply with OBRA '87 Regulations

---

Admission Rights
- Help create admission policies that clarify the process for approving and accepting prospective residents based on medical and psychosocial needs.

Change in Resident Condition
- Help create policies about notification of physicians of incidents and accidents, changes in resident condition, or death
- Help ensure an effective system for evaluation and triage of significant changes in condition and timely transfer of residents out of the facility for further assessment or treatment in case of serious illness
- Review unexpected deaths and unanticipated discharges as part of quality assurance monitoring

Infection Control
- Work with other facility staff to establish appropriate policies and procedures for prevention and management of infections and the spread of infections
- Help establish policies and procedures for vaccination, isolation, universal precautions, and surveillance
- Establish policies and procedures for physician involvement in the assessment, prevention, and management of infections and infectious outbreaks
- Review all infection reports and analyze pertinent data for trends or potential or actual problems as part of the quality assurance/risk management process
- Participate in relevant infection control committee meetings

Medical Director Oversight of Care
- Ensure that physicians are aware of applicable professional standards
- Communicate and distribute pertinent information about geriatrics and related care standards from the clinical literature
- Help educate attending physicians to understand and apply those standards for care
- Review attending physician performance through quality assurance activities based on those standards
- Create appropriate medical policies and procedures
- Oversee the implementation of other clinical policies and procedures, coordinating the medical and nonmedical aspects
- Evaluate questions and concerns about the care of individual residents and discuss findings with residents, families, staff, and attending physicians, as pertinent
- Observe care on rounds and through record review
- Actively advocate for realistic improvements in the overall quality of care
- Document personal efforts to improve care, especially as part of the quality assurance process
- Ensure timely attending physician visits and follow-up
- Keep records of discussions or correspondence with individual attending physicians regarding care of residents and with physicians who have significant problems complying with regulations and policies

Physician Staffing
- Create a system (bylaws, policies, etc.) that gives attending physicians a clear understanding of their regulatory responsibilities and their facility obligations and privileges
- Help the facility handle situations of significantly noncompliant attending physicians
- Provide the facility, residents, and families with guidelines for selecting or changing attending physicians

Source: S.A. Levenson, *Medical Direction in Long-Term Care,* 2d ed. (Durham, N.C.: Carolina Academic Press, 1993).

Table 4-1 The Medical Director's Roles and Functions

Planning	Organizing	Managing	Leading
		FUNCTIONS	
Help plan facility programs and services	Organize medical services	Participate in administrative decision-making process	Demonstrate appropriate geriatric medical principles through patient care and consultation
Plan for medical staffing and support needs	Establish bylaws and policies and procedures	Create and modify clinical policies and procedures	Advise facility of medical staff need for assistance and support
Plan for research and education activities and programs	Establish quality assurance program	Ensure appropriate and timely quality medical care	Participate in overall quality assurance program and quality improvement process
		Ensure physician compliance with laws, regulations, and policies	Represent the facility to the community
		Investigate and resolve medical staff problems	Participate in an employee health program
		Coordinate medical and other patient care services	Help ensure promotion of residents' rights
		Perform medical quality assurance oversight	Attain and apply knowledge of regulatory, legal, economic, and social factors affecting care
			Participate in research and education activities and programs
		TASKS	
Planning activities	Organizational activities	Physician facilitation and oversight; medically related problem solving	General systems facilitation and problem solving; physician and nonphysician education and training
		SKILLS	
Organizational	Organizational	Clinical	Clinical
Conceptual	Conceptual	Informational	Informational
		Interpersonal	Interpersonal
		Problem solving	Problem solving
		Communication	Communication
			Conceptual
			Decision-making
			Teaching

pertinent decisions. This is an excellent opportunity to emphasize the importance of clinical and administrative coordination in providing good care.

The medical director should also establish effective communication with other professional staff leadership. This may include meeting with them individually or collectively and exchanging information about individual cases or about general issues or problems in the facility.

The medical director may find it helpful to prepare a periodic (e.g., quarterly or annual) report to the administration in order to make known the medical staff's activities and perspectives, summarize medical quality assurance and other activities, and ensure that the administration is aware of the medical staff's concerns and questions.

Admissions

Increasingly, nursing homes take residents with multiple medical, cognitive, behavioral, and functional problems. Therefore, some medical input into the development of general admissions criteria and into the decision process for individual admissions is desirable.

The medical director should advise the facility on appropriate medical criteria for admissions based on knowledge of the facility's goals and mission and the residents' conditions and problems. Also, the medical director should help the facility determine the staffing, services, and programs it needs to care for individual admissions. Related activities might include serving as an advisor to a facility admissions committee and recommending which medical information should be collected in a facility's preadmission assessment process.

Committees

Under the OBRA '87 regulations, the medical director must oversee the resident care policies. The OBRA '87 regulations require only a quality assurance committee. Also common in nursing homes are pharmacy and therapeutics, medical records, and infection control committees.

Committees are an important part of interdisciplinary communication and policy formulation in any nursing home. The medical director must work effectively with committees so that they will support the care.

The medical director and other key staff should decide together on an efficient way to hold these meetings. A combined meeting, in which the same key staff participate in handling several functions consecutively (medical records, infection control, risk management, etc.), can save time and be highly efficient. Many facilities are finding the quality assurance committee to be a valuable focus for solving and preventing problems and for obtaining critical interdisciplinary participation.

Financial Issues

Part of the medical director's role is to help ensure adequate facility resources for patient care. Decisions made by the administrators, owners, and board through the budgeting process determine the priorities for acquiring, distributing, and using these resources.

The medical director should participate in the facility budget process to help ensure that such resources are available. Often the medical director will have little input into anything other than his or her own compensation. In other cases, the medical director will be responsible for certain services, programs, or personnel, such as dues and travel, office supplies, staff physicians, support staff, consultants, or technicians.

Wherever possible, the medical director should be involved in certain steps in the medical budget process. This process begins with the preparation of departmental or medical staff objectives and goals based on current medical activities, a description of accomplishments during the past year, plans for the coming year, and the relationship of these activities and programs to the facility's goals and objectives. Based on these projections and on the medical staff's portion of the facility's revenues and expenses, a medical budget should project revenues and expenses for the coming year and justify any significant changes.

Medical Direction

Every medical director should have a written job description. Writing the description is best done after reviewing medical direction requirements and assessing the facility's desire or need for additional roles and responsibilities.

A physician's time commitment to medical direction will vary with a facility's size, its programs and services, the complexity of the residents' medical problems, and the expectations of the administrator and director of nursing. It also depends on the extent to which the medical director is new to the job or is organizing a new medical staff system, as opposed to improving or refining an existing system. Once a medical director establishes an effective system, ongoing management will take less time.

A medical director's contract should specify responsibilities and approximate time expectations; terms of the relationship (employee, contractor, etc.); compensation and benefits; secretarial support; and any financial support for education, meetings, and acquiring journals and other reference materials. Also, it should ensure that the medical director will receive adequate administrative support and authority to do the job properly.

Given the growing complexity of residents' medical problems, and the expanded responsibilities under OBRA '87, medical directors will probably need at least four to eight administrative hours a week per 100 beds to meet basic requirements effectively. Less than an hour a week is almost certainly insufficient.

Medical Records and Documentation

Though not a requirement, the medical director should help evaluate and improve the quality and consistency of the clinical information available in the nursing home and the quality of the systems for collecting, storing, retrieving, analyzing, and reporting that information. In the future, such systems will be needed not only for patient encounters but for management decisions and regulatory compliance.

Current medical records systems in health care are often inadequate for dealing effectively with complex patient care, especially with high volumes of regulations and standards, and where there is substantial variability in a staff's knowledge, skills, and performance. Poor quality, inaccurate, and inconsistent information should be considered a significant risk factor for the facility and its practitioners, since it contributes to errors of omission and commission. The reliability of sources of clinical information in the nursing home is hampered by the many cognitively impaired residents with a limited ability to give an accurate history and the often limited number of caregivers with adequate assessment skills to gather good quality clinical data.[11]

Partly because of pending requirements to record minimum data set information in a computer-usable format, many facilities are beginning to realize the value of computerizing clinical as well as financial information. The nursing home industry will need to use computers and other technologies creatively to meet growing expectations for quality care for a growing population. The OBRA '87 interpretive guidelines explicitly allow for computerized medical records, provided there are certain safeguards.

Some developments in the computer field that will likely impact significantly on nursing home practice in the next five years include much cheaper and more portable computers, reductions in the cost of linking users in effective networks, growing interest by vendors in nursing home software, and improved voice and handwriting recognition capabilities. Computers and other modern information technologies also offer great possibilities for staff and patient education, staff communication, and collection and use of information for multiple purposes, including clinical care, quality assurance, and regulatory compliance.

Also, "applied intelligence" software is becoming more widely used in many areas of government and industry. This software guides moderately skilled individuals to collect and input data, which are then interpreted by the software according to rules based on the accumulated knowledge, judgment, and experience of experts in the field. This kind of software has the potential to revolutionize the care in nursing homes by allowing modestly trained and skilled individuals to benefit from expertise not immediately available in their facility.

Medical directors should become more knowledgeable about information management and the potential uses for computerized information systems in long-term care. The needs of all caregivers, including the attending physicians, must be taken into account as facilities consider and then reorient toward the creation and future automation of effective clinical information systems that help provide high-quality patient care and meet regulatory and documentation requirements.

Patient Care

The medical director has an important role in helping to establish and achieve overall patient care goals for the facility and to ensure adequate physician participation in the care planning process.

Besides trying to ensure the best possible medical care for facility residents, the medical director should also encourage attending physicians to help the facility satisfy several major regulatory expectations: that treatments and medications are "medically necessary," that negative outcomes are "medically unavoidable," and that residents are able to attain the "highest practicable" levels of function and quality of life.

Policies and Procedures

In any complex system, such as the one delivering care to nursing home residents, policies and procedures are essential guides to performance. Effective policies and procedures are the ground rules that guide a collection of individuals of diverse experience and background toward common standards and expectations and that help ensure a more consistent understanding of essential goals and objectives.

Policies may be defined as officially interpreted general goals, objectives, and expectations. Managers or directors of businesses, departments, facilities, or organizations establish policies for those who work with or for them. Procedures are the specific steps or mechanisms for achieving these goals or objectives.

The medical director is specifically responsible for implementing resident care policies, including policies in such areas as admissions, transfers, and discharges; infection control; physician privileges and practices; emergency care; resident assessment and care planning; accidents and incidents; ancillary services such as laboratory, radiology, and pharmacy; use of medications; use and release of clinical information; utilization review; and overall quality of care.

The medical director should help create and coordinate effective policies and procedures to guide clinical care and related processes. These policies and procedures should incorporate social, medical, and economic information and advances and reflect good care standards. Some will be physician-specific and others will concern general clinical issues requiring physician participation and input. The medical director may share the responsibility for writing and implementing them.

Several references now exist to provide medical directors with comprehensive medical policies that can help them and their attending physicians fulfill their responsibilities under OBRA '87.[12]

For example, when, why, how, and how urgently should nurses notify physicians of changes in a resident's condition? Such changes appear to be a common source of physician-nurse disagreement in many nursing homes nationwide. Nursing home staff need a timely physician response to notification of changes in condition, and physicians desire an effective system to distinguish emergency problems from routine ones. Thus, protocols and policies for notification are important communication and clinical tools.

Regulatory guidelines note that a medical director is expected to help monitor and improve the actual care, not just write and approve policies. Like other managers in the nursing home, the medical director should understand the relationship between quality care and policies and procedures.

Surveys and Inspections

The medical director should help the facility interact with outside regulatory agencies and represent the medical staff at health department and other licensure and certification reviews.

During the actual survey process, surveyors match their evaluation of a facility's care to the OBRA '87 rules and guidelines. Before the licensure survey, the medical director can help improve overall physician compliance with physician-centered regulations such as visit requirements, and he or she should encourage attending physicians to support care by talking to staff and patients and coordinating their orders with staff care plans. The medical director can also recommend to the facility's administration and staff ways of improving general clinical care, communication, information management, and documentation systems.

During and after the survey process, the medical director can help by answering general or case-specific questions on medical care, requesting clarification of citations regarding clinical care, helping to draft corrective actions, and communicating with health department physicians who might understand better the nuances of disputed complex medical issues.

If done fairly and objectively, the survey process is a potentially useful opportunity for getting and giving feedback to confirm and improve care. Based on the results of such surveys, the medical director may want to revise medical or other clinical policies and procedures and help the facility institute or modify quality assurance activities to deal with the issues raised.

Organizing and Coordinating Medical Services

The medical director must ensure adequate and timely medical coverage for the facility's residents. This may be accomplished by

- organizing medical coverage
- helping ensure staffing to meet the facility's needs and goals
- helping ensure the quality, timeliness, and appropriateness of medical care
- credentialing the medical staff
- helping ensure medical staff compliance with facility, federal, state, and local requirements
- ensuring that the medical staff executive committee or its equivalent performs its appropriate functions
- developing and reviewing policies and job descriptions for midlevel practitioners such as physician assistants and nurse practitioners

Typically, nursing facilities have used any of several different physician staffing arrangements. Most still use open staffs of community-based attending physicians. Especially in larger nursing homes (more than 200 beds), some medical directors are turning to closed staffs, sometimes hiring full- or part-time salaried physicians, using nurse practitioners and physician assistants to provide primary care, or using fewer attending physicians, each with more patients.

More medical directors realize the importance of at least some organization of attending physicians. They have found it hard to exercise their responsibility without a system enabling them to assert some authority and fulfill quality assurance oversight functions. Attending physicians must know the regulations, policies, and expectations that determine what constitutes adequate performance.

Bylaws

More medical directors are using bylaws (also referred to as practice agreements) to organize attending physicians and to create a foundation for medical care. Bylaws describe the legal foundations and the structure and functions underlying medical staff activity, establish a broad general framework of expectations for physician performance, create a mechanism for enforcing responsibility, and establish ground rules for the medical staff to carry out its responsibilities to the residents and the facility. They establish the medical staff as a self-governing entity and define its relationship to the governing body, which is ultimately responsible for the care delivered in the facility. Sample nursing home medical bylaws are available from the American Medical Directors Association and elsewhere.[13]

Since the nursing home medical director typically serves the functions of the chief of staff and medical executive committee in an acute hospital, nursing home medical staff bylaws can be simpler than those for a hospital medical staff. These bylaws should at least obligate practitioners to acknowledge that they understand the regulatory and clinical requirements that contemporary nursing homes must meet, are willing to cooperate with the medical director and facility staff to provide good geriatric medical care and help meet those requirements, and are receptive to the medical director's suggestions, based on medical quality assurance activities, about ways to improve care.

Consultative and Emergency Coverage

As much as possible, the medical director should ensure that the facility has access to needed consultants and that such consultants respond in a timely fashion. This objective may be hindered by the limited availability of consultants in many areas of the country. Also, the medical director may need to educate consultants about the special aspects of nursing home residents and long-term care so that they will understand the special problems of prescribing in the facility and in carrying out complicated orders for residents who may not be able to participate in their care.

The medical director should ensure that the facility has access to essential medical coverage, including for emergencies, and that attending physicians and their backups respond in a timely fashion to urgent or emergent problems. Also, the medical director should help ensure that equipment, drugs, and supplies are available in the facility for emergencies. This may include reviewing the emergency cart, the interim medication box, supplies, procedures for resuscitation, and protocols for deciding when to notify attending physicians of new problems or changes in a resident's condition or status.

Outside Affiliations

The medical director should help the facility attain and maintain certain outside affiliations. For example, the medical director might be given the job of initiating, analyzing, and supporting links with hospitals and universities, serving as medical liaison with other facilities, or helping obtain ancillary services (such as lab and x-ray services).

Since most medical directors with nursing home patients are also on the staffs of local hospitals, they have an opportunity to try to improve hospital care of the elderly, which can in turn help the nursing home meet its care responsibilities. Many acute care hospitals and their medical staffs have yet to realize they can play a role in helping nursing homes give better care. Examples of possible improvements include reducing placement of indwelling urinary catheters in nursing home residents who are hospitalized, reducing development or worsening of pressure sores in nursing home residents who are hospitalized, and improving the documentation and discharge instructions regarding ongoing care when hospital patients are transferred to the nursing home. Possible approaches to improving support may include informal discussions and presentations at grand rounds or other medical meetings.

Trainees

Increasingly, the nursing home is an important site for health professional students and trainees to learn about the problems of the elderly and about the practice of geriatric medicine and other health professions.

Students and postgraduate trainees from many different schools who may rotate through teaching nursing homes must be monitored and supervised. The medical staff or medical director will often have some responsibility for these trainees. The medical director is at least indirectly responsible for monitoring trainee activities that might impact on the physical or psychological well-being of the residents. Training programs work best when those being trained and those responsible for them understand each other's needs and problems and make accommodations accordingly. Trainees must appreciate that they are learning within a residence and must not let their presence interfere with the operation of the facility or infringe on the rights of the residents.

The medical director should collaborate with directors of various training programs to ensure that supervision is adequate and appropriate and that the programs are educationally worthwhile. This may necessitate creation of program policies and procedures that describe qualifications, requirements, supervisory responsibilities, other responsibilities, prerogatives and limitations, liability, and conditions for termination of assignment.

Ensuring the Appropriateness and Quality of Medical and Medically Related Care

The OBRA '87 regulations mandate physician participation on a facility quality assurance committee. Most likely, the medical director will serve as the physician member. To function effectively the medical director should have some role in setting up the monitoring systems; deciding how to collect data; reviewing and analyzing the data; identifying high-risk, high-volume, and problem-prone areas; and educating attending physicians based on analysis of the data.

The Joint Commission on Accreditation of Healthcare Organizations has recommended a ten-step process for quality assurance activities.[14] This process includes

1. assigning responsibility
2. defining the scope of care
3. considering the important aspects of care
4. developing key indicators
5. creating evaluation thresholds
6. collecting and organizing data
7. evaluating care
8. taking problem-solving actions
9. assessing the results of those actions
10. communicating relevant information

In some form, these principles apply to all disciplines.

The quality assurance process should focus on education rather than disciplinary action, which should be reserved for the most flagrant and persistent offenders. Education activities may include providing education materials to help staff improve the quality of care, monitoring and evaluating the effectiveness of education programs, providing quality assurance feedback to staff and recommending ideas to improve performance and decrease problems, and ascertaining the national standards for quality care and helping the facility translate these into internal standards.

Medical Staff Quality Assurance

The medical director has a major role in helping establish standards and indicators for quality medical care and physician performance.

The goals of medical quality assurance in the nursing home are to safeguard good care already being provided, recognize opportunities to improve care, and identify and resolve problems. Briefly, a successful medical quality assurance program in a nursing home involves the following steps. The medical director and attending physicians should identify important aspects of care and collaborate in establishing appropriate policies, medical care standards, and quality indicators (criteria for reviewing specific aspects of care). The medical director, perhaps assisted by other medical staff, should then ensure a mechanism for collecting pertinent data, review the data when collected, analyze problems or seek areas for possible quality improvement, provide feedback to attending physicians (both quality assurance information and education), and follow up to see if education and policy making improve care and prevent subsequent problems.

Though responsible for evaluating data and taking follow-up actions, the medical director can rely mostly on data that others already collect or report for other purposes. Medical directors typically evaluate care and identify care problems by reviewing accident and incident reports, pharmacist reports, change of patient condition reports, and infection control reports; by making observations while delivering care and on rounds; by attending quality assurance committee meetings; by helping design special studies and ongoing audits; and by offering consultation and guidance to other caregivers regarding the management of individual residents.

Medical directors may respond to identified problems with care by communicating with individual physicians (orally or in writing), communicating with the medical staff about care problems in general (not pertaining to a specific resident), communicating with nonphysician staff regarding clinical care, participating in facility in-services to correct general care problems, and preparing written reports of actions taken.

Facilitywide Quality Assurance Program

Defining quality care in a nursing home is a complex task, since nursing homes provide both personal and medical care.[15] Demonstrating quality care is also difficult.

As a leader in the nursing home, the medical director should understand and advocate for tactics and systems that help both physicians and nonphysicians work more effectively. According to one perspective, professional and facility leaders must take the lead in seeking continuous quality improvement, promoting a vision of the health care system as capable of continuous improvement, and using modern technical and theoretically grounded tools to improve care processes. It is also important to get physicians to join in the efforts to achieve continuous improvement.

Although the value of the concept of continuous quality improvement in the nursing home remains to be proven fully, it appears that an effective system is critical to providing good care. The medical director should at least encourage and help attending physicians to understand their role in a common effort to improve care instead of seeing themselves primarily as isolated practitioners treating disease in individual patients.

In relation to the facilitywide quality assurance process, the medical director can help

- ensure the relevance of programs and standards to quality patient care
- ensure adequate quality review in areas mandated by laws and regulations
- draft policies and procedures that correct and prevent problems
- establish and monitor factors related to quality of life in the facility
- discuss quality of care issues regularly with other key administrative staff
- establish basic standards and criteria for quality medical care and physician performance

- incorporate new knowledge and quality assurance findings into the patient care–planning process

Risk Management

Risk management may be defined as the preventive arm of a quality assurance program. Risk management activities seek to reduce or eliminate potential problems that may impact negatively on care or on those providing care.

The medical director's role in a facility's risk management program may include reporting pertinent observations (e.g., about safety hazards or potential sources of clinical errors or miscommunications) to the director of nursing and the administrator; becoming involved in the employee health program; and educating physicians to help reduce risks (e.g., by responding quickly to nursing notification of changes in condition, ensuring adequate alternate coverage in case of unavailability, and reducing the use of medications that may increase functional problems such as dizziness and falling).

Utilization Review

The medical director should work with the medical staff to help the facility ensure appropriate, cost-efficient use of beds and services, ensure that patient admissions and placement are consistent with established criteria, and ensure that patients receive the programs and services they need based on the comprehensive assessments and other pertinent findings. The medical director should participate in the utilization review process to monitor delivery of care within economic and social constraints. Although there is no longer a formal utilization review committee requirement for skilled nursing facilities, there may still be state and Medicare requirements.

Developing and Conducting Education Programs

The medical director may play an important role in helping educate the administration and board about care issues in the facility, including appropriate programs, necessary support, realistic expectations, quality of care issues, the medical role in long-term care, and the medical director's responsibilities. The medical director should also update the facility on clinical issues by providing current information gathered from attendance at meetings and conferences and from the medical literature.

An important part of the education process lies in the medical director's individual interactions with staff, administrators, patients, and families. Both formal and informal education should occur regarding clinical, ethical, regulatory, and legislative issues. Patient care rounds are also an excellent opportunity for teaching other staff.

The medical director also represents an important resource for the community. The medical director's role might include

- educating the community about long-term care and the facility
- making speaking appearances
- helping outsiders understand and have more realistic expectations of the facility and of long-term care generally
- educating patients and families about relevant clinical issues
- producing various written materials, such as handbooks, to assist facility staff in dealing with complex ethical and clinical issues

Educating the medical staff might involve

- informing attending physicians about changes in policies, procedures, laws, and regulations
- keeping medical staff informed about medical staff activities
- providing summaries of reports and meeting minutes
- keeping medical staff informed about pertinent policies, procedures, laws, and regulations

Promoting Employee Health, Welfare, and Safety

Employee Health

Employee health is an important but sometimes overlooked part of any facility. There are many areas in which medical input can be of assistance. Overall, the medical director should recommend ideas to decrease legal risks and prevent problems that could adversely impact patient care and the general safety of employees, staff, patients, and visitors. The medical director could play an important role in employee health by

- developing and participating in a pre-employment screening process
- helping to monitor and evaluate employee injuries and illness
- promoting employee wellness programs and ways to prevent job-related injuries and disease
- helping to foster a sense of self-worth and professionalism among employees
- establishing appropriate health maintenance screens and procedures, such as TB testing

- identifying community resources for employees with psychological or social problems
- planning and determining the scope and policies of medical services
- providing overall medical direction for the physical examination program, including initial and ongoing assessments, and determining the scope of the examination
- evaluating the physical capacity of employees to perform their jobs
- discussing and interpreting findings with employees when health problems are found and making appropriate referrals
- evaluating employees' ability to return to work
- helping to establish programs to assist in the employees' return to work after an injury or illness
- reviewing reports from employees' outside personal physicians
- making periodic tours of the physical plant to become familiar with the physical requirements of the various jobs
- helping to ensure employee compliance with infection control requirements
- helping the facility minimize workers' compensation losses
- contributing to a program to monitor, evaluate, and prevent injury and illness
- contributing to the activities of a safety committee
- encouraging proper use of assistive devices by employees
- developing a modified work program for injured employees

Representing the Facility in the Community

Traditionally, nursing homes have a bad reputation among physicians and other professionals. The medical director can help play a role in enhancing the facility's reputation among local professionals, including physician colleagues, by

- participating in pertinent activities of professional organizations, hospitals, and so on
- meeting regularly with other long-term care professionals in the community
- identifying issues and negotiating solutions to problems involving outside institutions and programs
- helping to handle problems with outside organizations or agencies (lab, x-ray, other hospitals, outside physicians, etc.)
- serving as liaison between the facility medical staff and other local medical staffs

- providing grand rounds, conferences, and other information about the facility and long-term care

Programs and Systems

The medical director may also participate in health care planning, including helping the facility develop innovative and cost-effective alternative health care programs and integrating those facility programs with others in the continuum of long-term care. This may involve

- networking with community groups and long-term care organizations
- helping others understand the systems approach to health care
- evaluating and correlating admission patterns relative to community trends and needs

Applying Knowledge of Social, Regulatory, Political, and Economic Factors

The medical director should keep abreast of political, regulatory, legal, and economic developments that could affect care in the facility, such as new mechanisms for long-term care reimbursement and changes in state and federal rules and regulations. Possible applications of such knowledge might include

- suggesting reasonable cost-containment measures (contracts, lab usage, formularies, etc.)
- recommending ways to improve the efficiency and productivity of facility staff
- giving feedback to legislators, policy makers, and local decision makers on existing and proposed rules and regulations

Promoting Research and Development Activities in Geriatrics and Long-Term Care

Most medical directors do not consider research to be a major responsibility. Those involved in research may do the following:

- evaluate and review the feasibility and goals of research projects
- solicit funding for research activities
- learn about basic research methodologies

- ensure proper safeguards for patients involved in research projects, including informed consent protocols
- serve as chairperson of the institutional review committee

Even for a medical director who does not have an interest in formal research, it is worthwhile to try to foster appropriate facility attitudes toward investigation and change by applying a rational problem-solving approach and pertinent research findings from the medical and related literature.

Ensuring That the Rights of Individuals Are Respected

The OBRA '87 regulations heavily emphasize residents' rights. The medical director should be familiar with those rights, ensure that the attending physicians help protect and enhance those rights, and help the facility do likewise. The medical director can assist in the protection of general patient rights by

- helping ensure rights of privacy and confidentiality
- ensuring application of the patient bill of rights
- facilitating choice of physicians
- helping the facility monitor for and handle patient abuse
- becoming knowledgeable about pertinent legal precedents

Ethical Issues

Many elderly people now expect a say in decisions about their care and about the initiation, discontinuation, or withdrawal of treatment. Legal and regulatory guidelines have expanded the rights of recipients of care.

Medical ethics involves clarifying or selecting values and evaluating to what extent treatment options are consistent with specific values and beliefs.

In fact, individualization and selectivity are key values in the care of the elderly. Broad ethical and clinical goals are directed to maximize individual benefit. Not everyone should have to make the same treatment choices, just as not everyone with heart failure should receive the same medications. However, adherence to a consistent process will allow better individualization of outcomes.

Although the physician can best present medical facts (e.g., "These are your options and the likely benefits and risks"), the elderly individual or an appropriate substitute decision maker should evaluate the options and make choices under the guidance of the physician and other caregivers. It helps to remember that making a medical choice is not purely a scientific matter but also has personal, social, and philosophical dimensions.

In geriatric medicine, especially in the nursing home, ethical considerations should be included routinely in the clinical decision-making process. Problems can be reduced or prevented by following appropriate procedures consistently and by presenting information thoughtfully, documenting prudently, and involving residents and families in the decision-making process, as appropriate. All parties should view the use of guidelines as a way to improve geriatric medical practice and to enhance the well-being of residents, not just as a way to avoid being sued.

The medical director's responsibilities may include

- ensuring that patients have a say in their own care through appropriate documents and expression of wishes
- helping establish a program to manage ethical issues
- developing policies and procedures to deal with limited treatment plans
- developing a mechanism for transferring information regarding patient choices through the spectrum of care sites
- participating in an institutional biomedical ethics committee

THE FUTURE OF MEDICAL DIRECTION

The future of long-term care medical direction looks bright. With current regulatory requirements and the rapidly growing elderly population, medical directors will have greater responsibility for organizing medical care and coordinating it with other programs and services, creating and refining policies and procedures, and overseeing medical and general clinical care. Most of all, medical directors can perform a major service to facilities and their residents by helping ensure effective compliance with the expectations for improved quality of life and quality and thoughtfulness of the clinical care, as described in the OBRA '87 regulations and guidelines.

Undoubtedly, the extent of medical director participation and influence in individual facilities will vary widely. The full potential impact of the medical director on clinical care remains uncertain. It will be important to study the effect on outcomes and quality of care of the time that medical directors spend on activities such as quality assurance; employee health, education, and training; and research and development.

Some medical directors feel handicapped by a shortage of attending physicians, the lack of cooperation or interest on the part of some attending physicians, the relative lack of facility support, the quality and skills of nonphysician personnel working in nursing homes, regulations, limited reimbursement, and paper work. However, a substantial minority of medical directors do not appear to face any significant impediments to improving physician or nonphysician care in their facilities.

Currently, a number of nursing facilities have satisfied and effective attending physicians because of effective collaboration between these physicians and their medical director as well as effective collaboration between the medical director and the other facility staff and the administration. Nursing home administrators should encourage and support physicians who are considering serving as medical directors and attending physicians in the nation's nursing homes. In the nursing home of the future, there will be few professionals more valuable than a skilled and committed medical director.

NOTES

1. American Medical Association, *The Medical Director in the Long Term Care Facility* (Chicago: American Medical Association, 1977).

2. S.R. Ingman et al., Medical Direction in Long-Term Care, *Journal of the American Geriatrics Society* 26 (1978):157–166; J.J. Pattee, Update on the Medical Director Concept, *American Family Physician* 28, no. 6 (1983):129–133; W. Reichel, Role of the Medical Director in the Skilled Nursing Facility: Historical Perspectives, in *Clinical Aspects of Aging,* ed. W. Reichel, 2d ed. (Baltimore: Williams and Wilkins, 1983); S.A. Levenson, *Medical Direction in Long-Term Care* (Baltimore: National Health Publishing, 1988).

3. U.S. Department of Health and Human Services, Health Care Financing Administration, Part 483 Requirements for Long Term Care Facilities, *Federal Register* 56, no. 187 (September 26, 1991):48867–48879.

4. AMA Council on Scientific Affairs, American Medical Association White Paper on Elderly Health, *Archives of Internal Medicine* 150 (1977):2459–2472.

5. J.G. Ouslander, Medical Care in the Nursing Home, *JAMA* 262 (1989):2582–2590.

6. AMA Council on Scientific Affairs, White Paper on Elderly Health.

7. Ouslander, Medical Care in the Nursing Home.

8. AMA Council on Scientific Affairs, White Paper on Elderly Health.

9. Ouslander, Medical Care in the Nursing Home.

10. J.J. Pattee and T.M. Altemeier, Results of a Consensus Conference on the Role of the Nursing Home Medical Director, *Annual of Medical Direction* 1, no. 1 (1991):5–11.

11. Ouslander, Medical Care in the Nursing Home.

12. S.A. Levenson, *Medical Policies and Procedures for Long-Term Care* (Baltimore: National Health Publishing, 1990); J.G. Ouslander et al., *Medical Care in the Nursing Home* (New York: McGraw-Hill, 1991).

13. Levenson, *Medical Direction in Long-Term Care;* J.J. Pattee and O.J. Otteson, *Medical Direction in the Nursing Home* (Minneapolis: Northridge Press, 1991).

14. Joint Commission on Accreditation of Healthcare Organizations, *Quality Assurance in Long-Term Care* (Chicago: Joint Commission, 1989).

15. S.A. Levenson, Quality Care in the Nursing Home—Defining and Providing It in a New Era, *Geriatric Medicine Today* 8, no. 8 (1989):29–40.

Chapter 5

Nursing in the Long-Term Care Facility

Joan Marie Culley and Janet Courtney

This chapter is designed to give administrators of long-term care facilities a brief guide and overview of nursing as it can be organized and delivered in the long-term care setting. Nursing provided in this setting and to the elderly population is very different from nursing in the acute care facility, free-standing clinic, outpatient clinic, or the home. This chapter focuses on the development of the department of nursing and the selection of a nursing model to be used as a guide for delivery of care to our elderly population in the long-term care setting.

OVERVIEW

In replacing the term *nursing home* with *long-term care,* the central mission of a long-term care facility may be obscured. This mission is easily articulated by family members or residents of long-term care facilities: It is *nursing care.*

Most people enter long-term care facilities to receive the type of care offered by the facility's nursing department. Reduced ability to perform activities of daily self-care, loss of cognitive skills for self-care and home management, and difficulty moving about in the physical environment are the most common problems that lead an elder and his or her family to seek nursing home residence. The long-term care administrator needs to appreciate the centrality of the nursing care function in the facility and organize the operations of the facility to support that function.

Support for nursing begins with designating the director of nursing as a top management position in the organization. Selection of a director of nursing who is educationally and experientially qualified for the position is the next major step. In a majority of long-term care facilities, the director of nursing has a direct line relationship with the facility administrator and is the second in charge of the administrative aspects of the facility. Because of the importance and scope of responsibilities, the director of nursing should be educationally prepared at the master's level in nursing and should be experienced in the care of the elderly. Experience with the elderly is an extremely important requirement and cannot be overemphasized. (See Appendix 5-A for qualifications and a suggested job description.) A good working relationship between the long-term care facility administrator and the director of nursing is essential for successful institutional management. Indeed, the director of nursing and the administrator frequently share on-call responsibilities.

The responsibilities of the director of nursing in the long-term care setting include

- implementing extensive and complex federal and state regulations
- operationalizing the concept of resident instead of patient
- operationalizing the concept of home
- developing services with the capability of caring for elderly persons, whose presentation of illness is unique and very different from younger persons'
- focusing on residents' potential capabilities rather than limitations

The long-term care setting is unique and demands the use of skilled caregivers who are knowledgeable about and experienced in long-term care. Although many acute care skills may be applied, the long-term care setting requires a nursing leader who clearly understands the differences between acute and long-term care and is able to administer a department responsive to the differences.

The director of nursing should be involved in the development of the philosophy and goals of the facility. The philosophy and goals of the department of nursing complement and enlarge upon those of the long-term care facility. Nursing is viewed by most residents and family members as the major focus of the delivery of care and services. Residents and families judge the quality of the facility by the care delivered at the bedside.

Bureaucracy often seems to engulf long-term care, making it easy to lose sight of the caring and nurturing environment that should determine outcomes and set the course for the services that are delivered to residents. In attempting to meet the many demands of both federal and state regulations, a facility may become obsessed with the tasks to be accomplished rather than with outcomes. Time, energy, personnel, and resources are required to manage the documentation and forms that must be completed.

Residents entering long-term care facilities and their families view the bureaucracy through their own personal set of glasses. They frequently report seeing numerous personnel hustling and bustling around in expensive suits and dresses, carrying paper back and forth between departments, but only two or three actual caregivers on each residential unit. To them, this means a system that is top-heavy with administrative personnel and inadequately funded to provide enough direct care to the residents. They wonder how the money they are spending on long-term care placement translates into direct caregivers and time spent at the bedside.

Speech therapy, occupational therapy, physical therapy, recreational therapy, dietary counseling, social services, psychiatric services, pastoral services, financial counseling, and physician services are all critical services in the inpatient facility. Nursing services differ from these in that nursing is provided on a continuous basis to each and every resident 24 hours a day, 7 days a week, 52 weeks a year, year after year.

Nursing staff are there when Mrs. Yoke is having a nightmare and needs someone to talk with, to ask for some warm milk, to rub her back, and to walk her in the hall until she is calmer. They understand that providing a sedative to Mrs. Yoke causes disorientation and agitation, and thus they have designed a plan for Mrs. Yoke that prevents these upsetting side effects.

Nursing staff are there to plan the celebration for Mr. Brown's 93rd birthday. Mr. Brown is all alone because his friends and relatives have died. They understand that, in order for a resident like Mr. Brown to complete the psychological development tasks of the older adult, related to integrity rather than despair, reflection about the past is essential. They therefore make time to listen to Mr. Brown reminisce about the past. Each night, a nurse finally tucks him safely into bed, remembering to place the urinal within easy reach. Mr. Brown has urinary urgency and needs to have the urinal within easy reach to prevent falls from his attempts to get to the bathroom. The nursing staff know how upset Mr. Brown becomes when he is incontinent and that such "accidents" prevent him from sleeping the rest of the night. A plan has been developed to prevent the incontinent episodes. Now that the urinal is always placed within reach, Mr. Brown only rarely has episodes of incontinence, sleeps well, and has had no further falls at night. In developing such a plan of care, the nursing staff reduced the risk of falls and the number of patient care hours required to change Mr. Brown's bed. Mr. Brown's quality of life has been greatly enhanced by the plan as well.

Nursing staff are there to carefully dry between the surfaces of Mrs. Hernandez's toes so that she will not develop an infection between her toes again. Five months ago Mrs. Hernandez had a foot infection that prevented her from wearing shoes for two weeks. She enjoys walks outside each morning with the nursing assistant but could not take these walks until the infection was cured. When the elderly are restricted in their activities and less mobile, the chance of such complications as thrombophlebitis, pneumonia, and renal problems increases. These complications affect the quality of life for residents, often result in acute care admissions, cost the facility and health care system money, and increase the number of patient care hours needed.

As can be seen from these illustrations, nursing is the focus in the long-term care setting. The ability of the nursing department to perform assessments, establish priorities, develop appropriate plans of care, and deliver and monitor care (making adjustments when necessary) ensures that the long-term care facility will be able to manage resources and productivity effectively, reduce the risk of liability from negligence, and, most important, provide a quality of life for older persons that is respectful of their capabilities.

The director of nursing has the responsibility of organizing the department. The critical elements of this task include (1) the establishment of the philosophy of the department, (2) the development of a nursing care practice model, (3) the selection of personnel, (4) the development of patient care standards, and (5) the development of policies and procedures. Each of these topics is discussed below.

PHILOSOPHY OF THE DEPARTMENT OF NURSING

When defining the philosophy of nursing care that is to be delivered in any institution, it is necessary to delineate the expected outcome of that care. Historically, many long-term care facilities have adhered to a custodial rather than restorative philosophy of care.

With the custodial philosophy, the focus is on providing services to residents, who are viewed as passive recipients of routine assistance with daily living activities. The goal is protection through watchful vigilance. With a restorative philosophy, the focus is on working with the residents, who are viewed as participants capable of reaching their maximum potential. This approach to caregiving is not in conflict with the needs of the terminally ill or cognitively impaired resident. Even terminally ill residents can be regarded as participants capable of determining how their care should be managed. Cognitively impaired residents can be assessed for potential strengths, which can then be used to achieve maximum development of capabilities. Custodial care focuses on weaknesses, not on strengths. It is human nature to focus on problems or disabilities, but an environment becomes nurturing when the focus is switched to the actual and potential capabilities of the individual.

The choice of either the custodial or the restorative approach will be reflected in all services and care provided to the residents. Federal guidelines on reimbursement currently mandate that a restorative philosophy be implemented in long-term care facilities.

For example, although it may seem easier and more efficient to simply diaper Mrs. Ortiz as a way of dealing with her urinary incontinence, it may not be in her best interest. If the restorative goal is to increase her self-esteem and maximize her independence by making her capable of continence, then specific alterations in her environment and care delivery could probably be planned to achieve this goal. Once a thorough assessment of the continence problem is completed, the incontinence might be controllable without diapering by moving furniture in Mrs.

Ortiz's room so that she has a direct path to the bathroom, placing a raised commode seat on the toilet, carefully selecting clothing that Mrs. Ortiz can remove quickly to expedite toileting, and educating and supporting staff in this plan of care.

SELECTION OF THE PRACTICE MODEL

The organizational framework for delivering care to residents operationalizes the restorative philosophy of care. Features of this framework include (1) decentralized authority and responsibility; (2) accountability to the resident and the resident's family; (3) decision making as close to the resident as possible; and (4) staffing the institution with the proper mix and numbers of licensed nurses, certified nursing assistants, and qualified personnel, giving each staff member the appropriate responsibility and authority for completing the required tasks. (See Appendix 5-A for detailed job descriptions for the personnel assigned to the department of nursing.)

Decentralization provides flexibility and promotes greater participation in decision making at the level at which decisions should take place. The role of nursing as the principle provider of care 24 hours a day and as responsible for identifying, treating, and monitoring the physical sequelae of illness places nurses in the position of being managers of care. The nurses, as a result, are accountable for the quality of health supervision and care in the long-term care facility. It should be noted that the role of manager of care may be new to nurses whose clinical experience has been primarily in acute care hospitals, where physicians are usually the managers of care.

In the long-term care setting, it is often nursing that identifies the need for other available health services and intervenes to ensure that the services are provided in a comprehensive, well-organized manner. Nursing is the maestro that orchestrates the harmonic delivery of care.

The restorative philosophy of care requires the proper mix of personnel possessing the expertise to assess resident needs, develop interdisciplinary plans of care, implement care, evaluate the outcomes of care, and make changes in the plans of care when indicated. Long-term care recipients "on the average have four or more chronic illnesses and frequent episodes of acute illnesses."[1] Care must therefore be developed to respond to resident's needs dynamically. This requires a carefully balanced ratio of residents to staff. In other words, it may not be cost-effective in the long run to staff units with mostly unlicensed personnel. Although federal and state authorities provide regulations that guide minimum staffing patterns, it may enhance productivity to place greater numbers of licensed staff at the bedside. Licensed staff have the ability, authority, and responsibility to make decisions and perform assessments quickly, reduce incidents such as falls and skin integrity problems, and enhance the residents' ability to toilet and dress themselves so that they can be more active participants in their own care. When residents' capabilities are utilized and falls and skin integrity problems are prevented, the institution saves time and money.

The environment in a long-term care facility can become much more productive and stimulating if nursing staff are responsive to the residents' feelings of being valued as individuals capable of making decisions, participating in their own care, and reaching their maximum potential. All personnel in the department of nursing must have a clear understanding of the goals and must share in the interdisciplinary approach that is characteristic of a decentralized model. In particular, the director of nursing must demonstrate an attitude toward nursing assistants that is respectful of the important role they play in providing direct care to residents. This includes recognizing their contributions and involving them in interdisciplinary meetings, end-of-shift reporting, and staff development activities. One of the most valuable resources in the long-term care setting is the quality of the direct caregivers—the nursing assistants.

SELECTION OF PATIENT CARE STANDARDS

Standards provide norms for assessing a department of nursing's performance. They serve as a framework for departmental evaluations and as the yardstick by which liability is judged in a court of law. The standards most frequently cited are set by the federal government in regulating long-term care facilities. These are used by survey teams in evaluating long-term care facilities and serve as a reference for analyzing both the organizational structure and direct care services.

In addition to the federal and state written standards, the American Nurses' Association (ANA) has established standards for geriatric nursing practice and organized nursing services in long-term care facilities. Unlike the federal and state standards, the ANA standards do not reflect the minimum level of quality but the optimum level. A long-term care facility must also comply with the standards set by the Joint Commission on Accreditation of Healthcare Organizations (Joint Commission) or it may not be eligible for government funds.

The ANA's Standards for Organized Nursing Services state that the department of nursing must (1) have a philosophy and structure that ensures the delivery of high-quality nursing care, (2) have a qualified administrator who is a member of the corporate administration, (3) have policies and practices that provide for equality and continuity of services, (4) use the nursing process to plan and organize care, (5) provide an environment that ensures the effectiveness of nursing practice, (6) ensure the development of educational programs to support high-quality care, and (7) initiate and utilize research for improvement of care.[2] These standards form the framework used by most nursing executives in the development and organization of their departments.

The departmental and organizational philosophies and goals of a long-term care facility form the basis for identifying what can and should be done. Standards are the articulation of this process. Once the organizational standards are developed and in place, the direct patient care standards are written. The purpose of these standards is to provide the highest level of care possible within the economic and productive capacities of the nursing department. Following are three examples of general resident standards of care:

1. Ninety percent of the time residents will receive pain medication within ten minutes of the request when the request is appropriate and orders are available.
2. One hundred percent of the time residents will receive the correct medication, at the correct time, in the correct dose, and by the correct route.
3. Ninety percent of the time the Minimum Data Set (MDA) will be completed by the interdisciplinary team within one month of admission for a resident.

The formulation of patient care standards can also be plugged into the level of care required for each resident. The standards then show the interventions required for care, identify the desired outcomes of the interventions, and assign cost. This allows the department of nursing to isolate better what is done for residents, how much it costs, and how it can be done more productively and economically.[3] The MDA is now required in long-term care facilities to assess each resident's level of functioning. Once the level of functioning is established, standards identify the interventions required for each area of functioning. A cost can then be assigned to each standard or unit of care.

Role of Quality Assurance and Risk Management

Quality assurance and risk management, although different in focus, work together to identify and solve problems in productivity, quality of care, and cost containment.[4] The object of quality assurance is to use the established standards of care to measure and evaluate the delivery of services at the prescribed productivity levels. Effective, well-stated, measurable standards provide not only a vehicle for the measurement of patient care outcomes but also the foundation for performance appraisals of employees.

The Joint Commission now requires all of its accredited facilities to have a program in place that ensures (1) identification of care and services given, (2) identification of indicators of care and services, (3) establishment of thresholds to measure care and services, (4) collection of data, (5) evaluation of variations of the thresholds, and (6) documentation of actions taken. This new process is called quality improvement. The focus has shifted from the illusive value of ensuring quality to vigilant improvement. Quality cannot be ensured without a concern for improving what is already in place.

Risk management focuses on the identification, prevention, and resolution of potential or actual problems to minimize or prevent damage or loss to the institution or the risk of liability. If proper standards are set and a quality improvement program is in place at the unit level to evaluate the actual outcome of care as compared to the expected outcome, interventions can be instituted quickly to identify potential problems and to prevent liability or loss. Quality assurance and risk management activities are a requirement of accreditation organizations and federal regulating agencies. With an aggressive quality improvement program in place, risk is controlled and liability is reduced.

If a standard of care states that each resident will have a skin integrity assessment completed within 24 hours of admission and an appropriate treatment protocol initiated if indicated, then the responsibility of risk management would be to evaluate (1) whether skin integrity assessments are being completed within 24 hours, (2) whether the appropriate skin protocol is being initiated, (3) whether the treatment plan is being properly implemented, and (4) whether the treatment protocol is resolving skin integrity problems. Note that the focus of quality improvement is ongoing assessment and initiation of changes in the plan when indicated. Retrospective analysis, while still a legitimate activity for certain aspects of the standards, now needs to give way to concurrent and prospective analyses.

SELECTION OF POLICIES, PROCEDURES, AND PROTOCOLS

Policies and procedures provide rules for guiding behavior and consistency in decisions and behavior in an institution. Policies are general directions or rules that create the legal and organizational framework through which the institution and nursing department carry out their goals. They specify the locus of authority and responsibility and the type of behavior needed to achieve a particular purpose. Procedures provide step-by-step instructions that direct individuals in how to proceed in carrying out activities or policies. Without such instructions, chaos might ensue and established standards would probably not be followed.

Imagine, for example, what might happen in a situation where a waste can fire was discovered by a janitor in a resident's room. Chaos might well result if a policy was lacking that clearly identified the evacuation plan, who to report to, who was in charge, the steps to be taken to prevent the spread of the fire, the responsibilities of other staff to protect residents and staff, and a schedule of drills that keep staff updated on their responsibilities and the location, for example, of extinguishers and emergency exits.

Policies and procedures standardize decision making and provide a mechanism for continuity and consistency in the way care and regulations are implemented. Each member dealing with the waste can fire cannot proceed with his or her own method of firefighting. Each must know specifically what his or her duties are and be trained in their performance. Policies are usually developed around such issues as accidents involving residents, staff, or visitors; admissions; autopsies; communicable disease; complaints; consents; deaths; discharge; doctor's orders; protocols for gerontological nurse practitioners; fire regulations; and documentation, to mention just a few.

Policies are developed when (1) there is confusion about the locus of responsibility that might result in neglect or malperformance, (2) residents' and families' rights must be protected, and (3) personnel management and welfare are at risk.[5] A policy manual is developed for the institution and for the nursing department. The manual then becomes a tool for orienting staff, a reference when unexpected problems arise, and a foundation on which to develop procedures and resolve conflicts or differences.[6]

Some nursing departments combine policies and procedures into one manual. Updating and revising this manual (or manuals, if there is both a policy manual and a procedure manual) is an ongoing responsibility. A committee is usually established to undertake this task. Policy and procedure manuals must be located on each nursing unit so that they are accessible to all staff for reference. The procedure manual must be correct, complete, up-to-date, and properly indexed.[7] The manual details such psychomotor skills as how to insert a Foley catheter, care for an intravenous catheter, or care for a deceased resident. Each procedure description comprises (1) a definition of the procedure to be performed, (2) a list of equipment needed to complete the procedure, (3) a statement of the desired outcome, and (4) a step-by-step outline of how the procedure is to be performed.

Procedures should be based on a review of the current literature in nursing and should reflect the most up-to-date findings and developments in the field. The requirements of regulatory agencies should be consulted so that the procedures are in congruence with their standards. Procedures are reviewed and approved by the appropriate nursing committee and medical advisory board. They are then used by all staff in implementing care and provide the standards by which liability and outcomes are assessed.

Procedures can of course be changed. Implementing changes on a trial basis through the use of miniresearch projects is one way to get staff involved in altering behavior and testing the effectiveness of the new techniques.

Protocols are plans of treatment that define specifically what is to be done for residents under specific conditions. Protocols are developed in consultation with the facility's medical director. Approval is gained from the patient care policy committee and each resident's physician. Periodic review of each protocol should be done annually. Gerontological nurse practitioners usually work under protocols approved by the medical advisory board and by the resident physician of record.[8]

Practice Guidelines

One emerging trend is to replace policies, procedures, and protocols with practice guidelines. Policies, by legal definition, are "nonnegotiable" rules. With the development of technology has come increased litigation. Practice guidelines provide negotiable standards that allow for clinical judgment and expertise and truly promote collaborative practice among all health care providers. Practice guidelines are an alternative to care plans and can be used to streamline documentation, provide a basis for outcome-focused quality improvement (assurance), and demonstrate the integration of the nursing and medical plans of care.

The issue of policies versus practice guidelines can be elucidated by describing a common policy in acute and long-term care facilities related to the care of an intravenous (IV) catheter. Most policy manuals require the replacement of an IV catheter every 72 hours, or more frequently if indicated. Suppose, for example, that the registered nurse assessed the condition of an IV located in the right lower forearm of a frail elderly resident, Mrs. Dumas. Aware that the physician expects to discontinue the IV antibiotics tomorrow, the nurse notes that there is no redness, swelling, or obvious need to replace the IV catheter at this point, especially since the IV is scheduled for termination. The nurse is also aware that the staff have had tremendous difficulty locating an appropriate vein in the past and that the procedure of replacing the IV is always painful for Mrs. Dumas. Since the nurse cannot locate any veins that may be used to change the IV, she decides to allow the current IV to stay in place for one more day.

If Mrs. Dumas was to develop thrombophlebitis at the IV site subsequently, causing pain and the potential for more serious complications, Mrs. Dumas and her family could sue the facility for negligence in the management of the IV. The first document to be subpoenaed would be the policy and procedure manual. The nurse indicted in the incident would be questioned about her knowledge of the policy and procedure manual, would be asked if she was able to read, and would most probably be held liable for not following the policies and procedures outlined by the facility. After all, these policies have been approved by medical, administrative, and nursing authorities and been deemed acceptable health care practice. To deviate from the "rules" can be interpreted as negligence.

The corresponding practice guidelines, on the other hand, would describe the competencies of the health care providers responsible for caring for the IV; describe patient, staff, and administrative system outcomes; give indications for implementing the guidelines; define areas of responsibility for assessing, planning, evaluation, documentation, and teaching as well as for implementing actions to be taken if complications arise. The guidelines would provide a more flexible guide for care.

Use of Current Research in Developing Protocols

Following are three examples of the use of current research as the foundation for the development of protocols.

Skin Care

Changes in the skin of the elderly make them especially prone to skin pressure points, tears, and decubitus wounds. This is one of the most important and potentially expensive problems facing the administrator of a long-term care facility. Maintenance of skin integrity is a primary responsibility of nurses. The main focus of care is prevention of skin breakdown. The primary etiologic factor in skin breakdown is pressure combined with shearing force and friction. The daily routines of hygiene, turning, moving, and lifting residents must be carried out with an awareness of the potential of this factor to cause breakdown of the skin. When pressure sores do occur, the nurse is aided by having clear guidelines for assessing and staging the affected skin and implementing measures according to identified clinical criteria. A skin care protocol can provide consistent guidelines that promote continuity in the care of the individual resident. Elements of a skin care protocol include (1) a process for identifying residents who are at risk for developing pressure problems; (2) criteria for assessment and staging of pressure sores; (3) recommended dressing material, a specific treatment procedure, and a schedule for treatment for each stage of the wound; and (4) a time frame for evaluation and further referral.

Urinary Incontinence

Urinary incontinence is one of the major factors leading to the admission of elderly persons to long-term care facilities. The impact of incontinence on the self-esteem and social interaction of elders can be devastating, and the cost of care for incontinence can be substantial.

There are several types of incontinence common in older adults: stress incontinence, urge incontinence, and overflow incontinence. Functional incontinence occurs when advanced cognitive impairment, musculoskeletal disability, or effects of medication render an elder unaware of the need to void or unable to get to the toilet. Until recently, nurses have generally viewed incontinence as a single problem. Research has yielded clearer definitions of the etiologies and defining characteristics of incontinence problems.[9] Treatment modalities include medical

interventions as well as a variety of nursing interventions that can reduce or eliminate incontinence. It is now possible to identify the specific problem and develop
specific protocols and treatment plans that can greatly reduce it. However,
administrators of long-term care facilities must first assign a high priority to
dealing with incontinence and then develop protocols for nurses to implement.

Restraints

Maintaining safety for the long-term care resident has always been a nursing
priority. This is one of the primary focuses of the OBRA '87 regulations. Too
frequently the use of restraints has been a mainstay measure for preventing falls.
The acceptability of this measure has come under attack as the negative physical
and psychological effects of restraint use are better understood. Efforts are now
directed toward developing alternatives to restraint. Cutchins describes a blueprint for care that involves changes in the environment and the operation of the
facility and a reorientation of clinical practice that can give residents maximum
protection in a restraint-free setting.[10]

SELECTION OF PERSONNEL

The scientific basis and specialized practice of nursing care of the elderly has
developed. The long-term care facility is no longer a place where a nurse might
work so as to get a rest from the hospital. No longer is it assumed that nursing
skills necessary for acute care are easily transferrable to long-term care. The
needs of elderly persons residing in long-term care facilities are unique. They and
their families seek out long-term care facilities in the hope that dignity and self-
esteem can be preserved in the face of tremendous losses—the loss of a spouse,
for example, or the ability to walk or to ask for assistance. The nurse who accepts
the care of these elderly persons as a professional responsibility deserves support
and encouragement to pursue professional development in the field of gerontological nursing. The career development paths extend to formal advanced degree
preparation (MSN) and roles as clinical specialists in gerontological nursing (CS)
or gerontological nurse practitioner (MSN or C). For the nurse who does not wish
to enroll in a formal program, recognition for specialized skills can be earned
through the certification process as gerontological nurse (C).

Staffing Regulations

The provision of nursing care in any health care institution is regulated by the
state's board of nursing (or the equivalent government regulatory body). This
agency carries the responsibility for safeguarding the public and promoting high-

quality nursing care. Each state has a nurse practice act that defines the scope of nursing within that jurisdiction. The licensure of nurses is regulated. In the United States, two types of licensure are currently identified, registered nurse (RN) and licensed practical nurse (LPN)/licensed vocational nurse (LVN). Since 1991, training and certification of nursing assistants has been carried out under federal OBRA '87 regulations for long-term care facilities. Specific job descriptions that define the role and scope of practice for RNs, LPN/LVNs, and certified nursing assistants and the expanded scope of practice for nurse practitioners and certified nurse specialists are provided in Appendix 5-A.

The director of nursing is responsible for knowing the regulatory mandates regarding the RN, LPN/LVN, and nursing assistant mix. The use of RNs and LPN/LVNs is constrained by the level of nursing care required by residents in a facility. This determines the staffing patterns in the institution. In general, there is a requirement for the around-the-clock, seven-day-a-week presence of a licensed nurse in the facility and for the availability of supervision by a registered nurse.

In addition to the direct-care nursing staff, the nursing department provides for specialized expertise in the areas of nursing management, direct care, and education. Appendix 5-A includes job descriptions for the types of nursing positions needed in a long-term care facility. The educational preparation for and responsibilities of each position are also described.

Infection Control

An infection control program is required for facilities that receive federal reimbursement as skilled nursing facilities. An effective program begins with an infection control committee composed of members from medicine, nursing, pharmacy, dietary, and housekeeping. The individual who implements the infection control program designed by the committee is usually a nurse. The role of this nurse is to collect data related to infection in the facility, to investigate episodes of infection, to educate the staff, and to develop policies and procedures related to prevention and control of infection. Elderly persons may not present the usual clinical signs and symptoms of infection. Subtle changes in an elder's level of awareness, the loss of appetite, or general complaints of "not feeling good" need to be carefully assessed to rule out the possibility of infection.

High Turnover Rates

Nursing administrators face the complex problem of high long-term care facility turnover rates for both nursing assistants and licensed nurses. Among the reasons for the high rate are "the difficult nature of the work and the residual stigma associated with nursing home work and the deterrents to practice in this setting; noncompetitive salaries compound the problem.[11]

About 8 percent of the RN population work in long-term care facilities, as compared with 67 percent employed in hospitals. Many licensed nurses who are hired by long-term care facilities have little educational preparation in the care of the elderly. They may be unfamiliar, for example, with the manager of care role. In addition, the ethical dilemmas posed by the setting are quite different from those common in acute care hospitals. Therefore, nurses will generally benefit from a strong staff development program that focuses on

1. strengthening the image of long-term care nursing as a specialized field
2. developing the nurses' management skills and leadership qualities
3. getting the nurses to perceive themselves as contributors to the interdisciplinary team caregiving process
4. changing the basis of practice from the medical model to a nursing model that emphasizes the physical, cognitive, and functional capacities of the elderly person
5. building awareness of how reimbursement issues influence long-term care

The nursing assistant's need for ongoing personal and career development must be addressed. Continuing education programs offered in the facility are needed for the renewal of the nurses' aide certification. In addition, programs preparing the nursing assistant for GED certification or offering child care assistance or facility-provided transportation may be added as incentives to promote recruitment and retention of staff.

As financial constraints continue to plague long-term care facilities, it is easy to give a low priority to staff development. Building and maintaining the competence of the nursing staff is an indispensable part of the facility's legal responsibility to the residents it serves.

LINKING LONG-TERM CARE WITH EDUCATION

Nurses who work in long-term care facilities may feel removed from the mainstream of the profession. They may find it difficult to keep current with advances in medicine and nursing. The administrator can assist in this area by promoting opportunities for the facility to link with educational resources in the community. Hospitals, community colleges, and universities would be natural partners in efforts to educate health professionals. There are several excellent models already established.

Currently a Kellogg Foundation–sponsored program, The Community College–Nursing Home Partnership, is in its dissemination phase.[12] Some community college nursing education programs are working with long-term care facilities to include care of the elderly in the clinical education of RNs. In the state of Washington, nurses at the Ida Culver House are collaborating with faculty at the University of Washington (Seattle) School of Nursing to provide a range of services to the elderly, including care in a 74-bed skilled nursing facility.

What these and other models of partnership share is the enrichment gained by each partner as nurses with various types of expertise come together to share knowledge and apply it to meeting the unique needs of elder persons. Advances in technology and knowledge have redefined many of the nursing problems seen in the long-term care facility and require that nurses change some of their traditional practices.

NOTES

1. E. Tagliarani et al., Participatory Clinical Education, *Nursing and Health Care* 12, no. 5 (1991):248.

2. American Nurses' Association, *Standards for Organized Nursing Services,* ANA Pub. No. NS-1 (Kansas City: American Nurses' Association, 1982).

3. B. Rutkowski, *Managing for Productivity in Nursing* (Gaithersburg, Md.: Aspen Publishers, 1987), 228.

4. Ibid., 195.

5. H.S. Rowland and B.L. Rowland, *Nursing Administration Handbook,* 2d ed. (Gaithersburg, Md.: Aspen Publishers, 1985), 101.

6. Ibid., 103.

7. Ibid.

8. Rutkowski, 213–214.

9. P. Turnink, Alteration in Urinary Elimination, *Journal of Gerontological Nursing* 14, no. 4 (1988):25–31.

10. C.H. Cutchins, Blueprint for Restraint-Free Care, *American Journal of Nursing* 91, no. 7 (1991):36–44.

11. C. Eliopoulos, *Caring for the Nursing Home Patient: Clinical and Managerial Challenges for Nurses* (Gaithersburg, Md.: Aspen Publishers, 1989), 241.

12. Tagliarani et al., Participatory Clinical Education; L.S.J. Trippett, Partners in Care, part of a panel presentation entitled "Partnerships in Gerontological Nurse Education and Practice" at the National Conference on Gerontological Nursing Education, Norfolk, Va., February 1, 1992.

Appendix 5-A

Job Descriptions

Nursing Service Director

Common Titles

Director of Nursing, Vice-President for Nursing, Vice-President for Patient Care, Assistant Administrator for Nursing, Chief Nurse.

Education, Training, and Experience

A baccalaureate degree in nursing is a minimum requirement, with a master's degree in nursing administration preferable. Current licensure as an RN by the state board of nursing in the state where the long-term care facility is located is necessary. Five years of administrative experience as a director or as a supervisor of nursing service and experience in care of the elderly are required. Demonstrated stature in the nursing profession and keeping abreast of changes in the profession are a must.[1]

Duties

Has 24-hour accountability for the department of nursing. A leader who interprets nursing both internally and externally and promotes and maintains harmonious relationships among nursing personnel, physicians, other administrators, residents, ancillary personnel, and the public. Is the role model and individual who establishes the professional environment in which efficient, productive, and caring services are delivered. Is able to organize and administer the department of nursing by establishing goals and objectives for the department; establishing the organizational structure of the department; developing, interpreting, and administering administrative policies; preparing and administering the budget for the department; selecting and appointing nursing staff; and directing and delegating the management of professional and ancillary nursing personnel. Also coordinates activities of the various nursing units, plans and directs orientation and in-service training programs, evaluates nursing and implements measures to improve care, and participates in community educational programs.

Assistant Nursing Service Director

Common Titles

Assistant Director for Nursing, Associate Director of Nursing.

Education, Training, and Experience

A baccalaureate degree in nursing is a minimum, with a master's degree in nursing desirable. Current licensure as an RN by the state board of nursing in the state where the long-term care facility is located is necessary. At least one year of management experience and two years of clinical experience in the care of the elderly are required.

Duties

Has 24-hour accountability for the department of nursing. Assists in organizing and administering the department of nursing as delegated by the nursing service director. Implements administrative policies and services by organizing appropriate committees and working directly with supervisors and department personnel. Coordinates and evaluates services to improve direct resident care. Structures an environment in which employees may grow and are rewarded for productive, efficient, and highly competent work. Writes job descriptions for the department and establishes performance evaluation or appraisal policies. Supervises and administers policies so that each individual employed in the department is held accountable for the job responsibilities outlined in his or her job description. Assists in review and evaluation of the department budget and in the implementation of the orientation and in-service programs. Assists in research and quality assurance activities.

Nursing Supervisor

Common Titles

Evening, Night, or Day Supervisor, Specific Unit Supervisor (Level 1 or Skilled Care Unit, Rehabilitation Unit, etc.).

Education, Training, and Experience

A baccalaureate degree in nursing is desirable, as is graduate preparation in gerontology. Current licensure as an RN by the state board of nursing in the state where the long-term care facility is located is necessary. Five years experience as a head nurse, demonstrated supervisory and teaching abilities, and demonstrated excellence in clinical skills in the care of the elderly are necessary.

Duties

Has either 24-hour or 8-hour responsibility for nursing service, depending on the definition and scope of responsibilities. Has the major portion of the responsibility of representing nursing at the unit level. Must be an excellent role model, must be diligent in supervising and providing guidance in direct patient care services, and must demonstrate leadership and excellence in nursing care. Supervises and coordinates activities of department personnel on the evening, night, or day shift so that continuity of care is provided on a 24-hour basis. Maintains direct contact with personnel and residents on the nursing units to ensure quality assurance and adherence to department policies and procedures. Delegates and supervises performance appraisals and any remedial actions to be taken. Works with the nursing service director and assistant director in establishing unit budgets and evaluating needs. Determines staffing needs for each shift. Is the administrative presence in the institution during the evening and night shifts and on the weekends and holidays and must be able to interpret administrative policies, make administrative decisions, and handle emergencies, as appropriate.

Director of Education

Common Titles

Director of Staff Development, In-service Education Coordinator, Director of Education.

Education, Training, and Experience

A baccalaureate degree in nursing is required, along with experience as a head nurse, supervisor or nurse educator. Current licensure as an RN by the state board of nursing in the state where the long-term care facility is located is necessary. Must have a broad and thorough knowledge of nursing skills and be able to evaluate the quality of the nursing care given and the abilities of the staff administering care.

Duties

Plans, organizes, and implements educational programs for nursing staff and often for residents and families as well. May develop, implement, and evaluate nursing assistant certification programs that meet federal and state regulations. Works with nursing administration to evaluate quality assurance and plan remedial actions when necessary. Understands accreditation and federal and state regulations and ensures that the regulations are met. Keeps appropriate training records. Implements orientation and in-service programs and provides ongoing education and training of nursing assistants.

Head Nurse

Common Titles

Head Nurse, Clinical Nurse Manager.

Education, Training, and Experience

A baccalaureate degree in nursing is desirable, as is advanced preparation in the clinical specialty of gerontology. Current licensure as an RN by the state board of nursing in the state where the long-term care facility is located is necessary. Should have five years of experience as a professional nurse in the care of the elderly.

Duties

Usually has 24-hour accountability for nursing services provided on unit. Directly supervises the nursing staff and ensures compliance with policies and procedures on one nursing unit. Directly responsible for the provision of an environment where excellent nursing care may be delivered. Is the vital link between management, the nursing staff, and the residents and families. Is a resource to staff, develops and administers staffing schedules, and writes performance appraisals for staff on the assigned unit. Must be able to evaluate services delivered and to determine and implement appropriate remedial actions and rewards when indicated. This is the individual that most residents and families view as the key individual in the delivery of care on the unit. Therefore, the head nurse must have excellent interpersonal skills.

Staff Nurse

Education, Training, and Experience

Current licensure as an RN by the state board of nursing in the state where the long-term care facility is located is necessary. Education may include a baccalaureate degree in nursing, a diploma in nursing from an accredited hospital school of nursing, or an associate of science degree in nursing. Should demonstrate an interest in care of the elderly.

Duties

Has 8- or 12-hour shift accountability for nursing care provided on a specific unit. The scope of practice of the RN is defined by statutes of the state in which the long-term care facility is located. The long-term care facility may define duties that are narrower than those defined in the state's nurse practice act but may not exceed the duties and responsibilities spelled out in the statutes. Nursing at the RN level is generally defined as the "diagnosis and treatment of human responses to actual or potential health problems."[2] Professional nursing usually means (1) the performance for compensation of acts related to health maintenance, prevention, promotion, and restoration; (2) supervision and teaching of other personnel; (3) administration of medications and treatments prescribed by a licensed physician or dentist; and (4) the application of specialized judgment and skill based on knowledge and application of principles of the biological, physical, and social sciences.[3]

Assists in planning, supervising, and instructing licensed practical nurses, nursing assistants, and students. Develops, implements, and evaluates individual residents' plans of care. Maintains resident records, including the recording of nursing care given. Usually serves as the team leader for the group of personnel rendering care on a specific unit. Is responsible for the minute-to-minute direct service given. Has the responsibility to delegate, supervise, and administer nursing care commensurate with licensing regulations and personnel capabilities.

Most RNs perform activities and treatments such as the following: the administration of medications by mouth, injection, IV, and other prescribed routes and their evaluation; the provision of treatments involving equipment; the initiation, maintenance, and evaluation of IV infusions by peripheral, central line, and subcutaneous access ports; treatment of wounds as prescribed; the taking of temperatures, pulses, respirations, and blood pressures; the performance of physical assessment and implementation of appropriate actions when necessary; the administration and supervision of alternative feeding methods via a gastrostomy or jejunostomy tube; and the performance of other sterile procedures such as urinary catheterization and complex dressing as prescribed.

Licensed Practical Nurse/Licensed Vocational Nurse (LPN/LVN)

Education, Training, and Experience

The LPN/LVN is a high school graduate or has earned a GED and graduated from a recognized one-year practical vocational nursing program. Current licensure as an LPN by the state board of nursing in the state where the long-term care facility is located is necessary.

Duties

Has 8- or 12-hour shift accountability for nursing care provided on specific unit. The scope of practice of the LPN/LVN is defined by the statutes of the state in which the long-term care facility is located. The long-term care facility may define duties that are narrower than those defined in the state's nurse practice act but may not exceed those duties and responsibilities spelled out in the statutes. Works under the supervision of an RN. Is responsible for the minute-to-minute direct services given and for reporting significant changes to the RN. Participates in the assessment and planning of nursing care. Provides direct resident care (as assigned by the RN), which may include bathing; feeding; making beds; helping residents in and out of bed; taking temperatures, pulses, respirations, and blood pressures; collecting specimens; dressing wounds; using sterile procedures such as urinary catheterization; assisting with physical examinations by the physician; transporting patients; recording appropriate information in the resident's chart; and administering and evaluating medications given by oral, injectable, or other prescribed routes. *Note:* Some institutions, in accordance with their state's nurse practice act, train LPNs to start IV infusions, mix specified IV solutions, and discontinue IV infusions. Most LPNs are not allowed to manage the care of central lines or subcutaneous access ports, including the changing of tubing, aspiration of blood specimens, and changing of dressings; administer any drug by IV push; administer blood or blood products; administer chemotherapy; or administer hyperalimentation (TPA).

Nurse's Aide/Nursing Assistant

Common Titles

Certified Nursing Assistant, Nurse's Aide, Orderly.

Education, Training, and Experience

Federal regulations now require certification for all nursing assistants who are employed full time in a long-term care institution for more than four months. Certification is intended to protect the public by obligating nursing assistants to meet minimal classroom theory requirements and demonstrate skill competency.

A certified nursing assistant program requires approval by the state licensing authority. Certification requires (1) combined classroom theory and clinical skill instruction, (2) a supervised clinical experience, and (3) a clinical skills competency exam in which the examinee demonstrates safe practice in at least five of the required skills. Any long-term care facility can develop and administer such a program, but this is expensive and very time-consuming. Most long-term care facilities hire nursing assistants who have already completed an approved certification program sponsored by either private or state-supported sources. A list of approved certification programs may be obtained from the state regulating agency. Some certification programs do not include the clinical exam component. The clinical skills competency exam may be administered by any long-term care facility that has been approved by the state regulating agency. Most long-term care facilities apply for this approval and are then able to hire individuals who have completed the educational component of the certification process but still need to pass the clinical skills exam.

Note: Many nursing students are looking for part-time work and make excellent employees. Nursing students who have completed 75 hours of clinical instruction meet the educational requirement of the certification process, but they must still pass a clinical skills competency exam. Consult with the state regulating agency for specific requirements. Note that nursing students who are only part-time employees do not technically need to be certified.

Duties

Certified nursing assistants provide most of the care in a long-term care facility. This is one important difference between long-term care facilities and skilled nursing and acute care facilities, where most, if not all, of the care is delivered by licensed RNs and LPNs. It is therefore essential that the nursing assistants are chosen, trained, educated, and supervised with extreme care. Also, because of the minimal education and training received in a certification program, it is vital that ongoing training and education be conducted by the long-term care facility. The quality of care delivered is dependent upon the nursing assistants' insights regarding residents' needs and their ability to grow professionally and increase their skills. Most nursing assistants, if asked, will indicate their desire for ongoing training and supervision. Nursing assistants perform tasks delegated and supervised by either an LPN or RN. Such tasks usually include bathing and feeding residents; assisting with toileting; making beds; ambulating; helping residents in and out of bed; taking temperatures, pulses, respirations, and blood pressures; and collecting certain specimens.

Ward Clerk

Education, Training, and Experience

The following are required: high school diploma or GED; ward secretary certification if available; training in English, typing, spelling, and arithmetic. Ward clerks usually receive on-the-job training.

Duties

General clerical duties, including maintaining records on the unit; completing lab and other requisition forms; recording temperature, pulse, and respiration on residents' charts; keeping files of old records on the unit; maintaining inventory of supplies; ordering and replenishing supplies as needed; keeping records of residents transferred or discharged; answering the phone on the unit; and typing various records, schedules, care plans, or communications with physicians. It is often the ward secretary with whom the residents and families have first contact. The ward secretary must have excellent interpersonal skills and be able to answer the phone and greet people in a way that suggests the high quality of care provided in the institution.

SPECIALIZED ROLES AND TITLES

Clinical Nurse Specialist in Gerontological Nursing

Title

Registered Nurse, Certified Specialist in Gerontology (R.N., C.S.).

Education, Training, and Experience

Certified clinical nurse specialists have a master's or higher degree; have clinical preparation in a specialty such as gerontology, medical-surgical nursing, or adult psychiatric health; and have passed a certification examination developed by the appropriate professional society. The title RN certified specialist is reserved for individuals who hold credentials beyond degree preparation. Certification requires not only master's degree but certification and the demonstration of continued clinical competence and expertise. Clinical nurse specialists in gerontology are recognized as experts in the field. Current licensure as an RN by the state board of nursing in the state where the long-term care facility is located is necessary. Current evidence of certification should be kept on file.

Duties

The purpose of employing clinical nurse specialists is to place expert clinicians at the bedside. Clinical nurse specialists are usually put in staff rather than line positions. They do not have direct authority over other personnel and are typically responsible to the director of nursing. Clinical nurse specialists function as expert clinicians, administrators, teachers, researchers, and consultants. Clinical nurse specialists in gerontology have advanced knowledge and clinical skills in the care of the elderly, with a focus on the physical, psychological, and sociocultural dimensions of such care. Most long-term care facilities hire one certified clinical nurse specialist in gerontology to provide consultation.

Gerontological Nurse Practitioner

Title

Registered Nurse, Certified Gerontological Nurse Practitioner (R.N., C.).

Education, Training, and Experience

Gerontological nurse practitioners earn their specialized license and certification through (1) master's degree preparation or (2) a certification program that involves at least nine months (one academic year) of full-time study. Certification requires not only appropriate educational preparation but the passing of a certification examination and the demonstration of continued clinical competence and expertise. Gerontological nurse practitioners are able to practice in most states and are allowed an expanded scope of practice defined by state statutes. They have special nursing licenses that enable them to practice in this expanded role. Their licenses are renewed upon evidence of their meeting special requirements.

Duties

Gerontological nurse practitioners assume expanded roles in providing care to older adults. They possess in-depth knowledge of physical assessment and can manage stable, chronic, and minor acute illnesses or conditions. These practitioners collaborate with other health professionals to provide care. Their functions may include assessment of patient status, nursing diagnosis, goal setting, development of nursing care plans, implementation of care plans, and evaluation of progress.[4] They usually are put in staff rather than line positions. They do not have direct authority over other personnel and are typically responsible to the director of nursing. Protocols that gerontological nurse practitioners follow must be approved by the medical advisory board and the individual physician of record.

Most long-term care facilities hire one gerontological nurse practitioner to provide consultation. Long-term care facilities can be reimbursed under Medicare for services provided by gerontological nurse practitioners.

Gerontological Nurse

Title

Registered Nurse, Certified in Gerontology (R.N., C.).

Education, Training, and Experience

A nurse, in order to get this generalist certification, must have (1) an active RN license and (2) a minimum of 4,000 hours of practice as a licensed registered nurse in gerontological nursing practice (1,600 of the 4,000 hours must have occurred within the past two years). Certification requires not only appropriate clinical preparation but the passing of a certification examination and the demonstration of continued clinical competence and expertise.[5]

Duties

The purpose of the gerontological nurse certification is to recognize the skill and commitment of RNs who choose to work with the elderly as their primary focus. Gerontological nurses are able to identify and use the strengths of the elderly and to assist the elderly in maximizing their independence. These specialists encourage the elderly to be actively involved in the development of their plans of care. All RNs in the long-term facility who meet the educational and clinical requirements should be encouraged to seek this certification and be compensated for its achievement. Award of the certification indicates attainment of advanced and specialized knowledge and skill beyond what is required for safe practice.[6]

NOTES

1. H.S. Rowland and B.L. Rowland, *Nursing Administration Handbook,* 2d ed. (Gaithersburg, Md.: Aspen Publishers, 1985), 82.

2. ANA Board Approves a Definition of Nursing Practice, *American Journal of Nursing* 55 (1955):1474.

3. Ibid.

4. American Nurses' Association, Inc., Center for Credentialing Services, *1990 Certification Catalogue* (Kansas City: American Nurses' Association, 1990).

5. Ibid.

6. A.M. Rhodes and R.D. Miller, *Nursing and the Law,* 4th ed. (Gaithersburg, Md.: Aspen Publishers, 1984), 31.

Chapter 6

Ethical Decision Making in Long-Term Care

Marian Broder

INTRODUCTION

Ethical issues have always been an integral part of health care delivery. Historically, discussion about these issues occurred primarily in hospitals. However, recently ethical issues are being examined in the long-term care setting.[1]

Nursing homes, having to cope with instituting ethical decision making, are attempting to redefine ethical principles to fit the long-term care environment. They are concerned with establishing policies, guidelines, procedures, and educational programs to guide residents, families, and staff in making ethical determinations. With the availability of technology and more skilled staff, higher levels of care are now being provided in nursing homes. Important decisions on how long technological support should continue and when appropriate circumstances exist for termination of care are being made with increasing frequency.

DIFFERENCES BETWEEN HOSPITALS AND LONG-TERM CARE FACILITIES

Consideration of ethical issues in hospitals is different than in long-term care institutions. In hospitals the patient is admitted, treated, and discharged. The length of stay is short. Medical treatment focuses on acute illness and recovery and, in many instances, uses technology. "Do not resuscitate" orders are for brief periods or for the duration of the hospitalization. Physicians dominate the decision-making process. Autonomy issues are dealt with according to a traditional model. If the patient has decision-making capacity, the patient makes the medical decisions. If the patient lacks the necessary capacity, a surrogate makes decisions on behalf of the patient using either the substituted judgment or the best interest standard.

The situation is totally different in long-term care facilities. In a nursing home, the stay is generally prolonged. The term *resident* instead of *patient* and the term *placement* instead of *admission* correctly suggest that a long-term care facility is primarily a home rather than a health care institution. The care is more often based on medical treatment or rehabilitative or palliative care rather than equipment and procedures. Treatment issues and decisions are made over a longer period of time rather than in response to an acute illness. The care team is interdisciplinary. The nursing staff is primarily responsible for providing care, and physicians play a smaller role than in the hospital. Physicians join with nursing staff; social workers; physical, occupational, and recreational therapists; and others in developing care plans. Because many residents have varying degrees of diminished mental capacity, decisions involving autonomy and other issues must respect individual variations and not be based on simple categorizations of residents as having or not having capacity. Finally, because of the length of the residents' stays, orders and directives for care must be periodically reviewed and kept current.

ADVANTAGES OF THE NURSING HOME ENVIRONMENT FOR ETHICAL DECISION MAKING

The nursing home has a responsibility to provide opportunities for ethical decision making. Education and communication must take place between the resident, the family, and the staff. Planning can be done in advance; the resident's values can be documented prior to a crisis. Conflicts can be anticipated and attempts made to avoid them. The interdisciplinary team of daily caregivers can be involved in decision making. As the resident's values or medical condition change, decisions can be reviewed, updated, and documented. Rather than merely mirror the hospital situation, the nursing home can proactively assist its residents and staff.

BASIC PRINCIPLES OF BIOMEDICAL ETHICS

Among the most basic principles of biomedical ethics are the principles of autonomy and beneficence.[2]

The term *autonomy* is derived from the Greek *autos* (self) and *nomos* (rule) and means self-rule . The principle of autonomy is that each individual should be in control of his or her own person, both body and mind. In the health care environment, the principle entails that each individual has a right to be free from nonconsensual interference with his or her body. Justice Cardoza, in 1914, stated that "every human being of adult years and sound mind has a right to determine what shall be done with his own body."[3] The doctrine of informed consent grew out of this. A competent individual has the right to accept or refuse medical treatment.

The principle of beneficence is that what is best for each person's welfare should be accomplished. It incorporates two obligations: the first is to do that which is for the good of the individual; the second is to do no harm to the individual (nonmaleficence). In some instances the two obligations must be balanced against one another, that is, the amount of good to be done balanced against the amount of harm. For instance, a resident with advanced terminal cancer may be offered chemotherapy, but the adverse side effects of the drug might increase the pain and suffering. Or in the case of a resident undergoing cardiopulmonary arrest, resuscitation may be offered. Although the procedure is frequently successful when administered to healthy individuals whose attack is witnessed by someone else, the procedure, when performed on nursing home residents, often results in fractured ribs, punctured lungs, and increased pain and suffering and has little chance of success.[4]

The principles of autonomy and beneficence come into conflict when an individual wishes to refuse a treatment that others believe would be beneficial. Generally the principle of autonomy has been accepted as primary in medical ethics and the principle of beneficence as secondary. However, in the nursing home setting, where state and federal regulatory policies to provide care must be complied with, the principle of beneficence may override the principle of autonomy.

Residents who are admitted to nursing homes with their full capacities can consent to admission and to medical treatment. However, residents who are suffering from substantial physical and mental difficulties are not able to exercise autonomy.

Autonomy in a nursing home environment must be defined and measured differently than autonomy in an independent living situation. In the latter, autonomy is characterized as freedom, self-choice, privacy, and control of decision making. Placement occurs when the individual, because of age, illness, dependent behavior, or dementia, requires personal and medical support. The nursing home, to meet both state regulatory standards and provide care in a cost-effective manner, has routines and schedules for eating, bathing, dressing, medications, activities, and bedtime that deprive the resident of choices they would have had in independent living. Privacy in both living space and public space is limited. Some autonomy is sacrificed for the benefits of the care offered.

A report based on the Hastings Center Project on Responsible Caring: New Directions in Nursing Home Ethics urges that the concept of autonomy be rethought in the nursing home setting.[5] "Because of the limitations most residents face...and the social functioning of nursing homes,...autonomy and dependency cannot be seen as opposites. Instead, they must be seen as intertwined facets of one's life and one's state of being." Furthermore, the difficult problem of "justifiable limitations on individual freedom of choice and the institutional management of behavior" must be reconsidered.[6]

Some elderly residents prefer to delegate the primary responsibility for making their medical decisions to others (e.g., their physicians, family members, or friends). Although health care institutions and physicians should do all that is possible to encourage residents to make their own decisions, they should also recognize that autonomy includes the freedom of the individual to waive decision-making rights. However, before accepting and acting on the waiver of these rights, the physician should be certain that the person's preferences have been expressed unambiguously, that they are documented in the medical record, and that guidance has been given to the surrogate decision maker by the resident.[7]

MAXIMIZING AUTONOMY

An ethical goal of a long-term facility should be to maximize the autonomy of all residents within the facility. Historically, elderly patients have been treated in a paternalistic manner by physicians, staff, and family. Misconceptions exist about the degree of dementia in the elderly. Residents must be viewed individually and given the greatest possible opportunity to make their own decisions.

Initially the decision has to be made about whether the resident is competent or has decision-making capacity. Competency is a legal concept, and only through a formal legal proceeding can the determination be made that a person cannot make legally effective decisions regarding his or her own affairs. If the person is judged incompetent, a guardian is appointed by the court to make personal, financial, and medical decisions on the person's behalf.

Medical decision-making capacity is not strictly a legal issue. It must be determined by the physician in relation to the specific medical decision that must be made. Individuals with capacity are able to make their own decisions about medical care whereas those without capacity must have decisions made by a surrogate. The Massachusetts Health Care Proxy Law defines "capacity to make health care decisions as the ability to understand and appreciate the nature and consequences of health care decisions, including the benefits and risks of and alternatives to any proposed health care and to reach an informed decision."[8]

Residents should be given an opportunity to demonstrate their highest level of functioning. To protect the rights of the residents, facilities should develop guidelines to assist the medical staff in assessing a resident's capacity to give informed consent. Many different types of tests of capacity exist, and physicians should be able to provide the staff with examples of available tests.[9] Four standards that have been suggested are (1) the ability to communicate choices, (2) the ability to understand information about treatment decisions, (3) the ability to appreciate the situation and grasp the relevant consequences, and (4) the ability to manipulate the information provided in order to compare the benefits and risks of the various treatment options.[10]

Decisional incapacity is not always clear-cut. A medical determination should be made about the underlying cause of the loss of capacity. Capacity can fluctuate or waver. Incapacity can be a temporary condition resulting from a reversible physiological abnormality such as an illness, a physical or emotional trauma, overmedication, or another treatable condition. Efforts should be made to change the underlying situation. It is critical to identify and evaluate depression when determining competency to make medical decisions.[11]

To enhance the resident's autonomy, the assessment of capacity should provide specificity about particular decision-making responsibilities and not be global. Simple mental status tests can be used for an initial screening of mental function but do not provide details. Health care team members who observe the resident daily often can provide the necessary details better than a psychiatric or neuro-logic evaluation. For instance, a resident who cannot manage financial decisions may be able to decide about a roommate or surgery. Residents should be able to make the decisions that they are capable of making (e.g., residents who can no longer dress themselves should be encouraged to select the clothes that they wish to wear). Recognition should be given to life time patterns[12] (e.g., the resident who never ate breakfast should not be forced to eat in order to comply with state regulations). Expanded autonomy within the community improves the institutional environment and enhances the quality of the resident's life.[13]

The principle of autonomy must be balanced against the principle of benefi-cence when health care staff believe that the resident is making an incorrect treatment choice. The risks and benefits must be weighed. The resident's values history, personal goals, motivation, immediate care goals, and long-term goals must all be built into the equation.

AUTONOMY IN MEDICAL DECISION MAKING

The Patient Self-Determination Act

Long-term care facilities can foster autonomy in medical decision making for their residents through policies and guidelines, an environment that fosters full disclosure, and a commitment to gaining truly informed consent regarding medical treatment. Residents must be informed of diagnosis, treatments, risks and benefits of treatments, prognosis with and without treatment, and alternatives. Paternalistic patterns of behavior by physicians and families, who tend to shelter the elderly from information in the belief that they do not want to or are unable to make decisions, must be changed.

The Patient Self-Determination Act requires facilities participating in Medicare and Medicaid to provide at time of admission written information about the rights of a patient under state law to make health care decisions.[14] Providers are required to provide state-specific information and documents. Included is the right to accept or refuse treatment and the right to execute advance directives. Facilities must inform residents of their policy on implementing advance directives. Documentation of whether or not an individual has executed an advance directive is to be placed in the medical record. The law does not require execution of an advance directive, nor can the provision of care be conditioned on whether or not an individual has executed an advance directive.

The Use of Agents and Directives

Autonomy for the resident can be furthered by encouraging the competent resident to appoint an agent to make future medical decisions for the resident when the resident can no longer do so and by encouraging the resident to express and document his or her values and opinions on treatment issues to that person. The resident is able to choose a person whom the resident trusts and who he or she believes will express his or her preferences.

The appropriate timing for this undertaking is difficult to determine. Each facility must establish a policy or set guidelines that reflect state regulations. Some facilities ask for this information at the time of placement. State regulations for nursing homes may require advance directive data to complete the medical record. Facilities subject to such regulations sometimes find it convenient to have new residents and their families complete the paper work at the time of admission. Family members, who are not always available, may be gathered together for this process.

Some argue, however, that admission is not a good time to complete advance directive documents. The process is stressful to a new resident and his or her family, and the resident should be given the opportunity to adjust to the facility prior to making advance directive decisions.

Many documents and planning tools are available: health care proxies, durable powers of attorney, advance or medical directives, living wills, and values statements. These documents vary according to state, and any documents completed by residents must conform to state law. Through a combination of one or more of these documents, the resident will be able to designate a surrogate and provide the information necessary to make the surrogate's decision reflective of the resident's viewpoint.

Health Care Proxy

A health care proxy is a legal document that allows a resident ("the principal") to appoint a person (the "proxy" or "agent") to make health care decisions for the resident if the resident no longer has the capacity to make or communicate those decisions. The proxy has the same access to medical information and the same authority to make decisions that the resident would have had if she or he could make decisions.

Durable Power of Attorney

A power of attorney is a legal document that allows a competent person to appoint an agent to act on his or her behalf for purposes that are described and limited in the document. Traditionally, the power of attorney has been used for financial and real estate purposes. A problem with the document was that its authority expired upon the "incapacity" of the principal and it could not be used for managing the affairs of elderly individuals who lost their capacity. To solve this problem, a durable power of attorney was developed. The authority of this document is not affected by the incapacity of the principal.

Durable powers of attorney for health care list specific powers to make health care decisions regarding, for example, the admission, discharge, or transfer of an individual to or from a health care facility; the selection of health care professionals to treat the individual; access to medical records; and consent to the provision of medical treatment, including the withholding or withdrawal of medical care.

Responsible Party

Responsible parties are required to cosign admissions agreements with the residents in many nursing homes. Generally they agree to fulfill certain obligations related to financial matters. The designation of someone as a responsible party does not give that person any power to make medical decisions; thus, a health care proxy or durable power of attorney must also be completed.

Advance Directive

An advance directive is a written statement that is prepared in advance of any serious illness and indicates how the person completing it wants medical decisions to be made if he or she no longer has the capacity to make or communicate the decisions. Included are instructions about medical treatments that the person wants or does not want and circumstances in which these instructions are to apply.

Advance directives take a number of different forms. Where state laws exist, the directives need to comply with the regulations or the form adopted in the state. Sometimes the health care proxy or durable power of attorney for health care document includes instructions about medical treatments that the person wants or wishes to avoid. Instructions may be included in a private letter using the person's own language or in a printed form. Forms are titled "Advance Directive" or "Medical Directive" or "Living Will" and include choices about specific treatments in specific situations.[15] For example, the form may list a treatment such as cardiopulmonary resuscitation or mechanical breathing and then list various situations in which a person may wish to have or not to have the treatment.[16]

Living Will

A living will is a type of advance directive or medical directive. It is a document in which a competent person provides directions regarding medical treatment in the event that the person can no longer communicate or make medical decisions. It is called a *will* because it expresses a person's will regarding medical treatment. It is called a *living* will because it takes effect before a person dies. Over 40 states have passed living will statutes. These statutes specify the types of decisions that a person can make and provide immunity to physicians and health care professionals for following the directives. Many living wills are limited to medical decisions regarding the withholding or withdrawal of medical treatment when an individual is terminally ill, is in an irreversible coma, or has "an incurable or irreversible mental or physical condition with no hope of recovery."[17]

Values History

A values history is a questionnaire that can assist a surrogate decision maker in predicting the preferences of the principal. Rather than asking a person about specific types of medical treatment, the questionnaire focuses on the "premises and processes" a person uses. It contains questions about "preferences in specific medical circumstances, general values, medical values, relationships with family, friends, and health care providers, religious views, financial preferences and other issues."[18] A values history can be used to motivate conversation between the resident and the surrogate. Through such conversations, the surrogate's ability to exercise accurate substituted judgment will be strengthened.

Periodic reviews of the directives and values history are necessary. Unlike hospitals, where the medical orders are of short duration, nursing homes may have residents with medical orders that are in effect for longer periods of time. It is necessary to have residents periodically review the documents to be certain that they still reflect their views. Some nursing homes look at these documents during regular review of residents' care plans. In addition, they request that, when there is a significant change in the resident's condition, the resident or his or her family review and update them.

Some ethicists and physicians advocate the use of the health care proxy or durable power of attorney for health care decisions. The advantage of these documents is that the physician can discuss the medical treatment with a person who has the legal authority to make a health care decision. Unlike a living will or medical directive, which specifies consent to or rejection of specific medical treatments and may be limited to certain medical conditions (such as terminal illness), a health care proxy or durable power of attorney gives the agent the flexibility to make all types of medical decisions in all circumstances. To safeguard this flexibility, it is advised that specific limitations not be written into the health care proxy or durable power of attorney document.[19] Principals are encouraged to inform their agents either orally or in a private letter of their preferences.

Selection of the Surrogate Decision Makers

Generally, when a nursing home resident no longer has the capacity to make health care decisions, an agent or a surrogate makes the decision on behalf of the resident. Deciding who is to be the surrogate decision maker is critical for ensuring the autonomy of the resident, whose own desires and preferences are intended to be reflected in the surrogate's decisions.

A clear-cut choice is made when the surrogate is appointed by a court through a guardianship proceeding or is designated by the resident through advance planning in the form of a health care proxy or a durable power of attorney. In some states, when there is no specific surrogate, statutes, regulations, or judicial precedents provide guidance. Without such guidance, it is customary for the decisions to be made by family members. This policy is based upon the belief that the family knows best what the resident would have wanted and has the resident's best interests in mind.

Although the process is time consuming and difficult, a nursing home, in order to protect the residents and itself, must develop policies and guidelines for informal substitute decision making. Copies of these policies and guidelines should be provided to residents and families at the time of admission. Consideration should be given to requiring a consensus among family members for any substitute decision. When there is disagreement among family members or the decision appears to contradict the implied preferences of the resident or contradict the position of the physician or staff, then the facility, for its own sake as well as for the sake of the resident, should encourage the family to initiate a formal legal intervention or should initiate a legal intervention itself to resolve the disagreement.[20]

Surrogate Decision Making

The surrogate, in making a decision, employs the substituted judgment standard, which requires the surrogate to try to determine what decision the principal would make if confronted with the situation at that time. In making the decision, the surrogate should have the same medical information that the principal would have had available, such as descriptions of diagnosis, prognosis, treatment, and risks and benefits. In addition, the surrogate must search for information that indicates how the principal would have decided. The surrogate may consider the resident's past preferences (expressed in writing or orally) and religious beliefs, the impact on the family, the extent of suffering, present and future incompetency, and other relevant factors. If the surrogate lacks such information, then the surrogate can make the decision based on the best interests standard, which requires the surrogate to choose what he or she believes would be in the best interests of the patient.

WITHHOLDING OR WITHDRAWING MEDICAL TREATMENT

One of the most critical ethical decisions in nursing home care is whether to administer or to withhold treatment that is within the scope of usual medical care. Withholding treatment is considered only when an individual is suffering, beyond hope of recovery, unable to respond to therapy, or living a life that the individual would not want to live. Withholding a necessary treatment might allow death to occur naturally and with dignity. Deciding whether to withhold treatment might involve subsidiary decisions regarding transfer to the hospital, surgery, cardiopulmonary resuscitation, the use of antibiotics, and nutrition and hydration. These decisions are made more difficult when the resident lacks the capacity to make them and had expressed no preferences prior to incapacity.

The objectives of the care for the resident must be set by the resident, the physician, and the family prior to making any decision regarding the withholding or withdrawal of medical treatment. Is the objective to restore the resident to a previous state? Is it to provide rehabilitation? Is it to prolong life? Is it to provide comfort? Is it to provide relief of pain and suffering?

Care planning requires adequate data. In the nursing home environment, there is generally adequate time for the compilation of the necessary information. Included should be an assessment of the resident's physical and emotional status; the prognosis with and without treatment; the risks and burdens of treatment; the resident's level of intellectual functioning; an assessment of the resident's quality of life; the previously expressed wishes of the resident and family; and the recommendations of caregivers, the family, and the physician. Ordinarily there should be consensus among the resident's family, the physician, and other health care workers. Data and decisions should be documented in the resident's medical record.[21]

Following is a suggested list of 11 questions that might provide a framework for making a morally and legally sound decision:[22]

1. Does the resident have a severe, progressive, imminently fatal disease?
2. Is the resident in an irreversible coma or a chronic vegetative state?
3. What steps have been taken to substantiate the diagnosis?
4. Is the therapy beneficial or is it burdensome or futile?
5. Does the patient want the therapy under consideration continued or stopped?
6. If the patient cannot communicate, what evidence is there of his or her wishes?
7. What does the family want?
8. Is the family united in their wishes for the resident?
9. Are all concerned parties communicating?
10. Has any concerned party been omitted from the decision-making process?
11. What is the law in the state regarding withholding or withdrawing therapy?

Facilities should have policies or guidelines on the process available as well as required information before making withdrawal or withholding decisions.

"DO NOT TRANSFER" AND "DO NOT HOSPITALIZE" DECISIONS

Decisions about where to undertake treatment occur frequently in nursing homes. Determining whether to issue a "do not transfer" or "do not hospitalize" order is among the most important ethical decisions made in long-term care. Hospitalization is required for evaluation and treatment, including surgery. Hospitalization decisions should be made in accordance with the treatment objectives for the individual. The benefits of hospital treatment must be measured against the risks of hospitalization. Frequently nursing home residents transferred to hospitals suffer confusion, falls, adverse drug reactions, bed sores, and infections.

Decisions not to hospitalize should not be absolute. In some instances, hospitalization may be required to alleviate pain and maintain comfort. For example, surgery may be necessary for broken bones or a laparotomy for a mechanical intestinal obstruction. Pneumonia or respiratory distress may require oxygen or parenteral antibiotics.

ALLEVIATION OF SUFFERING

The alleviation of suffering and pain and the provision of care and comfort should be part of every nursing home's medical treatment program. No resident should suffer from physical pain. Analgesic or psychoactive drugs used appropriately can provide comfort. Care plans that include skin care, turning, bowel and bladder management, and oral and eye hygiene can provide comfort to both residents and their families.

DEVELOPING AN INSTITUTIONAL FRAMEWORK FOR
ETHICAL DECISION MAKING

Institutional policies and guidelines for ethical decision making have been devised by committees or departments, depending on the organization of the facility. Administrative, medical, and nursing staff adopt policies in response to government regulations. The Omnibus Budget Reconciliation Act of 1987 set the standards for patient rights. In some states, the Department of Public Health requires policies about cardiopulmonary resuscitation. Treatment, care, and competence decisions are made by the physician in consultation with the family and the resident. Issues of patient autonomy and self-determination are concerns of interdisciplinary committees developing individual care plans. Social workers deal with the issues of identifying surrogates for residents who are unable to speak for themselves.

Although nursing homes already have mechanisms for considering ethical issues, a centralized ethics committee can foster an institutional environment that is especially sensitive to such issues. The ethics committee can also bring medical, legal, social, and religious issues into consideration as well, and it can develop policies (mandatory) and guidelines (advisory) to handle ethical issues; educate residents, staff, family members, and the community about ethical issues and ethical analysis; perform case reviews; and provide consultation to residents, staff, and families.

Prior to developing guidelines and policies on specific issues, the ethics committee must define the value system or orientation of the institution. This is particularly true in a nonprofit religious institution, where religious views may establish the parameters for decision-making guidelines. When policies reflect these views, residents should be informed of them prior to admission.

Among the topics that the ethics committees consider are those related to end-of-life decisions (e.g., "do not resuscitate" and "do not transfer" orders and decisions to withhold or withdraw medical treatment or technology). When many residents have some form of cognitive impairment, the topics of competency, autonomy, valid informed consent, decision-making capacity, surrogates, and the role of the family in decision making become prominent. Legal and legislative changes as well as policies for advance directives, living wills, and durable powers of attorney for health care are also addressed. In addition, the ethics committees will probably be involved in case consultation regarding these very issues.

THE ETHICS COMMITTEE

There are guides published on how to start an ethics committee.[23] Defining the mission and purpose of the ethics committee will help determine its size and composition. Membership on a typical committee includes nurses, social workers, an administrator, a physician, an attorney, a clergy, and a resident or resident representative. Ombudsmen, family members, community members, and representatives from the board of trustees can also be included. If education is an important role of the committee, participation of the education director is essential. All participants must be aware of resident privacy and the duty of confidentiality in the discussion of cases.[24]

Educational Role

The educational role of the ethics committee is an important one. Through educational programs, the ethics committees can help to create an environment that supports ethical decision making by residents, family members, the clinical team, and the physician.

Initially, ethics committee members themselves need to be educated and oriented. Committee members must be given a common background understanding of the field of biomedical ethics and health care decision making. The concepts of autonomy, beneficence, and nonmaleficence must be defined and discussed. At each meeting, a case study or an article related to ethical issues can be reviewed. New members should be briefed on past committee decisions.

Educational programs should be planned for staff and families as well as residents. Movies, videos, discussion of articles, speakers, brochures, and visual displays can be used for educational purposes, as can ethics conferences or ethics rounds.[25]

Case Review Function

An ethics committee does both retrospective and concurrent case reviews. Retrospective case reviews assist the committee to identify clinical situations that require policies, guidelines, or educational programs. They assist committee members in evaluating their own ability to provide guidance on a particular issue and to interact with other nursing home committees.

In concurrent or advisory case review, the committee acts in a consultative capacity, providing assistance to residents, families, and staff. The committee must act skillfully and cautiously in order not to intrude on the physician-resident relationship or assume direct responsibility for resident care decisions. The advisory function should be assumed by the ethics committee only after it has completed its education and has developed policies and guidelines.

Each institution should have its own process for determining how cases are to be brought before its ethics committee and how the committee is to transmit its opinion to the parties. The process should identify who can contact the committee and how the contact should be made. Information gathering may be done by the whole committee or selected members. The committee generally meets in private and communicates its recommendations, either orally or in writing, to the person or persons referring the case and to the physician. Typically the recommendations of the committee are advisory and not binding.

CONCLUSION

There are many ethical issues that need to be resolved in the long-term care setting. As the resident population becomes more acutely ill and more cognitively impaired, residents, families, and staff will need to confront these issues. Facilities should develop and implement policies and guidelines. There should be an initial focus on methods to increase the autonomy of each resident. Equally important are policies related to termination of medical treatment, resident competence, resident autonomy, and choosing surrogates. Staff particularly need educational programs and case review to assist them in understanding and carrying out clinical decisions based on bioethical principles.

NOTES

1. P. Boyle and B. Jennings, eds., *Responsible Caring: Ethics Resources for Nursing Homes* (Briarcliff Manor, N.Y.: The Hastings Center, 1991); R.A. Kane and A. Caplan, eds., *Everyday Ethics: Resolving Dilemmas in Nursing Home Life* (New York: Springer, 1990); M. Waymack and G. Taler, *Medical Ethics and the Elderly* (Chicago: Pluribus Press, 1988).

2. T. Beauchamp and J. Childress, *Principles of Biomedical Ethics* (New York: Oxford University Press, 1989).

3. Schloendorf v. Society of New York Hospital, 211 N.Y. 125, 105 N.E. 92 (1914).

4. D.J. Murphy, Do-Not-Resuscitate Orders: Time for Reappraisal in Long-Term-Care Institutions, *JAMA* 260:2098–2101.

5. B. Collopy et al., New Directions in Nursing Home Ethics, *Hastings Center Report* 21, suppl. (March-April 1991).1–16.

6. Ibid., 3.

7. M. Knapp, Medical Empowerment of the Elderly, *Hastings Center Report* 19 (July-August 1989):5–7.

8. *Massachusetts General Laws,* Chapter 201D.

9. J. Janofsky et al., The Hopkins Competency Assessment Test: A Brief Method for Evaluating Patients' Capacity To Give Informed Consent, *Hospital and Community Psychiatry* 43 (February 1992):132–136.

10. P. Appelman and T. Grisso, Assessing Patients' Capacities To Consent to Treatment, *New England Journal of Medicine* 319 (1988):1635–1638.

11. E. Howe et al., Medical Determination (and Preservation) of Decision-Making Capacity, *Law, Medicine, and Health Care* 19 (Spring-Summer 1991):27–33.

12. B. Collopy, Autonomy in Long Term Care: Some Crucial Distinctions, *The Gerontologist* 28, suppl. (June 1988):10–17.

13. B. Collopy et al., *New Directions.*

14. The Patient Self-Determination Act, passed as Sections 4206 and 4751 of the Omnibus Budget Reconciliation Act of 1990.

15. L. Emanuel et al., Advance Directives for Medical Care: A Case for Greater Use, *New England Journal of Medicine* 324 (1991):889-895; L. Emanuel and E. Emanuel, The Medical Directive: A New Comprehensive Advance Care Document, *JAMA* 261 (1989):3288–3293.

16. Ibid.

17. Living Will Declaration, Society for the Right to Die, 250 West 57th Street, New York, NY 10107.

18. P. Lambert et al., The Values History: An Innovation in Surrogate Decision-making, *Law, Medicine, and Health Care* 18 (Fall 1990):202–212.

19. G. Annas, The Health Care Proxy and the Living Will, *New England Journal of Medicine* 324 (1991):1210–1213.

20. M. Knapp, Family Decisionmaking for Nursing Home Residents: Legal Mechanisms and Ethical Underpinnings, *Theoretical Medicine* 8 (1987):259–273.

21. R. Besdine, Decisions To Withhold Treatment from Nursing Home Residents, *Journal of the American Geriatric Society* 31 (1983):62–66; J. Lynn, Ethical Issues in Caring for Elderly Residents of Nursing Homes, *Primary Care* 13 (June 1986):295–306.

22. R. Carlton, Defining the Limits of Treatment: When May It Be Withheld or Withdrawn? *Journal of Critical Illness* 6 (February 1991):138–147.

23. J.W. Ross, *Handbook for Hospital Ethics Committees* (Chicago: American Hospital Publishing, 1986); R.E. Cranford and A.E. Doudera, eds., *Institutional Ethics Committees and Health Care Decision Making* (Ann Arbor, Mich.: Health Administration Press, 1984).

24. B. Brown et al., The Prevalence and Design of Ethics Committees in Nursing Homes, *Journal of the American Geriatrics Society* 35 (1987):1028–1033.

25. L. Libow et al., Ethics Rounds at the Nursing Home: An Alternative to an Ethics Committee, *Journal of American Geriatrics Society* 40 (1992):95–97.

Chapter 7

Mental Health Care
and the Elderly

Mary B. Geisz

The elderly individual living in the community may face a complex set of challenges that affect his or her ability to live a satisfying and independent life. These
challenges may include physical infirmities, lack of emotional and social support
as a result of the deaths of spouse and peers or the relocation of adult children,
and limited financial resources. Any of these factors may cause mental distress in
the elderly individual. In addition, he or she may continue to grapple with previous untreated mental illness or may fall victim to a range of mental or emotional
disorders as a result of disease, neurological deterioration, or medication reaction. In all of these cases, the elderly individual could benefit from appropriate
intervention and treatment; in most of these cases, the elderly individual receives
little or no help.

The diagnosis and treatment of mental illness in the elderly have been given
only minimal attention by medical and mental health professionals and those
responsible for the funding of health care for the aged; yet, the level of functioning and the quality of life of many older persons would be significantly improved
if their mental health needs were addressed. The issue is a complicated one, with
many overlapping elements preventing the development of one comprehensive
response. However, inroads are being made through a variety of programs that
target specific problems and seek to meet defined goals. The expansion of these
services and the continued development of others have the potential over time to
improve the mental health status of the elderly community and enhance the ability of older persons to live fulfilling, independent lives.

PREVALENCE VERSUS TREATMENT

Mental health problems afflict a significant proportion of the elderly (over age
65) population, estimated to be between 15 and 25 percent.[1] The disorders preva-

Source: Reprinted from *The Journal of Ambulatory Care Management,* Vol. 13, No. 2, pp. 43–51,
Aspen Publishers, Inc., © 1990.

lent among the elderly include dementia, that is, Alzheimer's disease, and other types of cognitive impairment. It has been estimated that between 3.5 million and 5.5 million Americans suffer from dementias ranging from mild to severe, with 25 percent of those over the age of 85 affected by severe dementia.[2] Although major depression is not found to be as prevalent among the elderly as in the younger population, less severe depressive illness is found in over 10 percent of the elderly population and is considered to be a risk factor in elderly mortality.[3]

Other causes of negative mental status among older persons include adjustment problems with life changes (e.g., the death of a spouse or relocation to a child's household), negative reactions to medication or the effects of multiple drug inter-action, psychological symptoms associated with somatic disease, and the aging of mentally retarded persons or those with longstanding mental disease.

Although many older persons are in need of mental health services, only a small percentage of the elderly actually receive the treatment they need. Despite constituting close to 12 percent of the population, the elderly account for only 6 percent of the client load at community mental health centers and about 2 percent of the client load of private therapists.[4] They also comprise only about 5 percent of the admissions to psychiatric emergency departments.[5]

The need for treatment is clear. That treatment is not occurring with the expected frequency is the result of a number of factors that serve to prevent the elderly individual from obtaining relief from his or her suffering and leading a more rewarding life.

OBSTACLES TO TREATMENT

The factors that influence the provision of mental health care to the elderly fall into four broad areas: those related to (1) the perceptions of the elderly individual, (2) the practices and perspectives of health care providers, (3) the accessibility of services to the elderly, and (4) the availability of financial resources to pay for the services.

Individual Perceptions

An older person who experiences confusion, depression, loss of appetite, insomnia, or other similar symptoms is most likely to attribute them to a somatic disease or to the effects of aging. As a consequence, these symptoms will generally be presented to the primary care physician, if mentioned at all, and may not be adequately addressed.[6]

Even if the presence of an emotional disorder is identified by a health care provider, a family member, or the individual, the older person may reject the idea of treatment due to a perceived stigma regarding the issue of mental health care.[7]

The elderly are less comfortable than younger persons with admitting that they may have an emotional or mental problem and less willing to be treated by a mental health professional, seeing such an interaction as an indication that they are "crazy."

The elderly individual may be aided in his or her self-deception by family members or physicians who are concerned about the threat of institutionalization or who believe the situation to be part of the aging process.[8] As a result, the older person may not receive the treatment that could improve daily functioning, assist his or her ability to manage a physical disease, and enhance independent living and overall quality of life.

Provider Perspectives

Many older persons are very attached to their primary care physician, an often long-standing relationship, and it is these physicians who are in the best position to identify an emotional or psychiatric problem. Unfortunately, they often do not recognize the problem or, if they do, may not refer the patient to the appropriate professional for treatment. Waxman and Carner, in a study of elderly patients and their treatment by primary care physicians, found that 22 percent "showed mild to moderate psychiatric impairment [yet only 9.3 percent of these] had visited a psychologist or psychiatrist in the previous year."[9]

Many medical conditions may produce symptoms that can be confused with psychiatric problems. Some medications, either alone or interactively, may cause symptoms indicative of mental disorders. In addition, many physicians pay less attention to the emotional concerns of their elderly patients than to their physical problems.[10] As a result, the primary care physician may not provide an adequate response to the mental health needs of the older patient.

Even when a mental or emotional problem of an older person has been identified, the individual may still not receive appropriate treatment due to the pessimism of the referring physician or of the mental health professional regarding the effectiveness of mental health treatment for the elderly client. Clinicians spend more time with and have more interest in younger patients because they have greater expectations of progress with these patients.[11] German and colleagues found, however, that "the likelihood of attention to the emotional problems for older patients"[12] increased if providers were made aware of these issues through use of a screening test.

Accessibility of Treatment

Certain factors may limit the access of mental health services. Lack of transportation to the treatment site may prevent an elderly individual from getting the care he or she needs. The setting of the treatment facility may be threatening to the elderly client due to difficulties negotiating the physical layout, insensitive treatment by staff, or discomfort with other clients.

Homebound individuals are at a particular disadvantage in receiving treatment because only a limited number of programs exist that provide service right in the home. It is these individuals, however, who may be most at risk for institutionalization if their needs are not addressed.

Availability of Financial Resources

Lack of adequate financial resources is a major constraint on the ability of the elderly to receive mental health services in two ways.[13] The number and size of programs developed are limited due to an absence of funding, and the ability of an individual to receive treatment is greatly reduced when little or no reimbursement is available.

Outpatient mental health services for elderly patients are reimbursed through the following sources: Medicare, Medicaid, commercial insurance and managed care plans, government contracts and foundation grants, and self-pay. The Omnibus Budget Reconciliation Act of 1989 expanded Medicare coverage of outpatient mental health services. Although a 50 percent coinsurance requirement remains, there is now no annual dollar cap on Medicare payments. In addition, clinical psychologists may bill Medicare directly for providing diagnostic or therapeutic services in any setting, and clinical social workers may bill Medicare directly in settings other than hospitals and skilled nursing facilities. Outpatient mental health benefits account for less than 0.1 percent of total Medicare expenditures.[14]

Medicaid generally covers outpatient mental health treatment in the same way as other outpatient care, without restriction on diagnosis. Coverage of hospital-based outpatient services is mandated by federal regulation. Services rendered in a clinic setting are covered at the option of the individual states, and virtually all states cover clinic services. Payment amounts may be quite low, which limits access to certain providers and programs. Medicaid is also the payer of last resort; all other sources of payment must be exhausted first.

A portion of the elderly have commercial insurance or managed care plans retained from their working days, which may provide a reasonable level of benefits. Those individuals who elected to terminate health insurance upon retirement thinking that Medicare would cover their needs have been disappointed to find that the comprehensive coverage provided by their employer is not duplicated by Medicare. Some long-term care insurance policies provide home health benefits, which may or may not cover mental health treatment, depending on the policy.

Some funding of mental health programs for the elderly is provided by government contracts and foundation grants. However, this type of support is vulnerable to federal and state budget cuts and changes in the focus and size of foundation budgets.

A final source of reimbursement is the direct payment for services by the elderly client or by the client's family. Private agencies, in particular, dealing with middle-class clients, have found that a revenue source can exist in the family concerned about the safety and well-being of an elderly spouse or parent. The availability of private payment is obviously limited to those individuals with some financial means or an involved family, but this group exists and can be an important source of revenue in certain areas.

ELEMENTS OF SUCCESSFUL TREATMENT PROGRAMS

Although, as discussed above, a variety of factors may prevent elderly individuals from receiving needed mental health treatment, successful programs exist that have been designed to provide service in a manner that responds to the needs of the elderly population. These programs incorporate a number of common elements.

Treatment Approach

Successful treatment of the mental problems of the elderly client is built around a team approach that is able to identify and address both the physical and the mental status of the client. More than with younger clients, the older individual in need of mental health services may also be affected by physical diseases and conditions that mimic or exacerbate mental symptoms and that may influence the success of treatment. Therefore, the client's physical health must always be considered in the development and implementation of treatment plans.

The evaluation of the client's medications is critical to appropriate treatment. The potential side effects and interactive effects of the often multiple drugs taken by the elderly individual must be considered so that a true assessment of his or her mental condition can be made and steps taken to minimize or, preferably, eliminate the medication-induced symptoms.

In addition to a broad focus on the older client's health status, it is important to address the other aspects of the individual's life that may affect mental health status and the ability to be receptive to treatment. Such factors may include housing issues, social support systems, and the need for transportation.

Program Format

Although each program has its own mission and objectives, programs able to fulfill their mission and meet their objectives tend to have some common elements. The programmatic approach is extremely supportive of the client, furthering his or her sense of personal control over treatment progress. It is flexible, with latitude to address multiple needs and try a variety of methods in order to assist the client. It is also structured, providing a confidence-building framework in which treatment can take place.

Programs attentive to the full needs of the client include the client's caregivers and other concerned family members in the design of treatment programs. These individuals are important in several ways: They can provide information to the clinician that will enhance treatment; they can assist in making the client available for treatment; and they may actually participate in the treatment where indicated.

Program Accessibility

Perhaps the most critical element of a successful program to serve the mental health needs of the elderly is access to the program. In many cases, real access requires that service be provided in the home. Many older persons are homebound as a result of physical infirmities. Others are reluctant to leave their home due to lack of adequate transportation or concern about personal safety. Services that are available in the home have the best chance of reaching those elderly individuals most in need of treatment. Other locations for treatment programs that will allow elderly access include senior centers and senior housing facilities.

Although the senior population in general has a difficult time receiving needed treatment for mental disorders, elderly linguistic minorities are particularly limited in their access to treatment. A multilingual program can serve a population that is otherwise very limited in its treatment options. Such programs are very rare, however, due to the scarcity of bilingual clinicians.

Access to most elderly mental health services occurs through a variety of referral sources. These include hospital discharge planners and social workers, physicians, home health agencies, visiting nurses, other agencies dealing with the elderly, senior centers, managers of elderly housing facilities, family members, friends, and neighbors. Ongoing cultivation of referral sources will increase the accessibility of treatment to those who can benefit from it.

A SAMPLE OF MENTAL HEALTH PROGRAMS FOR THE ELDERLY

Across the country, public agencies and private firms are attempting to meet the challenge of providing mental health services to the elderly in need. The following examples from Massachusetts, California, and Texas are representative of the kinds of programs being offered throughout the country that strive to address the mental health needs of the elderly population.

The Visiting Nurse Association of the Greater Milford–Northbridge Area, Inc.

The Visiting Nurse Association (VNA) in the greater Milford–Northbridge area of central Massachusetts developed its Psychiatric and Mental Health Program in 1982 in order to provide services to the chronically mentally ill. Patients discharged from the state mental hospital and other psychiatric facilities often did not keep their referral appointments at community clinics, a situation that frequently led to a return to the hospital. In response, the VNA, under contract with the state, developed this program to serve those who are unable or unwilling to access mainstream services.

Although the state contract covers clients 19 years of age and older, 60 percent of the individuals served are 60 years old or more. All services are provided in the client's home, and other assistance, such as traditional home health nursing care or occupational therapy, is available where indicated. In addition to the state funding, available third parties are billed.

Over time, the VNA found, after assessment, that many individuals presenting with psychiatric symptoms actually suffered from neurologic disorders. As a result, state funding was obtained for a separate Alzheimer's program.

Training has been provided to other visiting nurse associations interested in establishing similar programs, programs that are not within the traditional scope of services offered by these organizations.

An advantage of the VNA program is its image as an organization of helping persons rather than as a mental health program. Consequently, the staff have found acceptance by elderly clients and families reluctant to admit to a mental problem. The program is very busy and constantly has a waiting list.

Mental Health Care at Home, Inc.

Mental Health Care at Home is a private company that provides psychiatric nursing care in the home or another residence, such as a nursing home, life-care community, or halfway house. Headquartered in Dedham, Massachusetts, the firm serves clients in eastern Massachusetts, southern New Hampshire, and Rhode Island. Approximately 40 percent of its clients are elderly.

The firm deals with a range of client problems, from affective disorders (e.g., depression and anxiety related to medical conditions or life changes) to chronic mental illness.

Mental Health Care at Home receives no government funds. A move by the state of Massachusetts to serve Medicaid patients through managed care plans may provide an opportunity for state funds as the state seeks to provide services in less restricted settings.

Approximately 20 percent of the total caseload is private pay, with the percentage somewhat higher among elderly clients. Visits are also reimbursed by commercial insurance and managed care plans providing coverage for retired clients. In some cases, adult children of elderly clients will cover their parents' bills, particularly for a package program.

Mental Health Care at Home strives to prevent or minimize costly hospitalizations through its program of home services of varying intensity. As a result, the firm is able to demonstrate cost savings to third-party payers. In addition, its home services assist in the long-term improvement of mental health status, improvement that does not generally result from hospitalization. Although hospitalization provides an initial safe haven for the client, a setback often occurs.

The company has marketed its services through contact with social workers and discharge planners at hospitals in its service area, meetings with visiting nurse associations, and community presentations at elder centers and elderly housing complexes.

In addition to direct therapy, the company's clinicians (psychiatric clinical nurse specialists) provide precertification, counsel families unclear about where to turn for help with older relatives, and collaborate with clients' personal physicians and psychiatrists.

Geri-Day Program

Boston Community Services, a community mental health center, offers the Geri-Day Program, an adult day health program that serves the long-term mentally ill elderly. Its daily program is designed to allow elderly individuals who might otherwise be hospitalized or admitted to a nursing home to continue to live in the community through participation in a structured, supportive set of activities on a regular basis. The program also provides respite care for families caring for an elderly relative at home.

The focus of the program is on the long-term mentally ill, and 75 percent of the clients fall into this category. The remaining quarter exhibit short-term problems due to issues related to life changes. The participants range from highly functional individuals living independently at home to others from rest homes or group houses. The major problems seen include organic brain syndrome, affective disorders such as anxiety and depression, and schizophrenia.

Referrals to the program are made by physicians, hospitals, clergy, and word of mouth. Approximately 90 percent of the clients are covered by Medicaid; the remainder of funding is provided by the state through the mental health clinic and by private payment. The Geri-Day Program is the only adult day health program in Massachusetts that specifically serves elders with mental health needs.

Senior Health and Peer Counseling Center

The Senior Health and Peer Counseling Center, located in Santa Monica, California, provides a range of physical and mental health services to the surrounding elderly population. In particular, its peer counseling program links older persons in need of emotional counseling and support with volunteer counselors of the same age group.

Peer counselors are recruited through newspaper advertisement and word of mouth. They undergo a free intensive training program and must commit to seeing at least three clients per week and to participating in a two-hour weekly supervisory session with a professional staff member. The peer counselors work primarily on a one-on-one basis with individuals. They may also meet with couples or even, if especially experienced and confident, lead client support groups, such as a group for widows and widowers. Clients are typically seen once each week; the length of treatment varies widely depending upon client need. Cases beyond the scope of the peer counselor are referred to the professional staff, which includes a geropsychiatrist, a geropsychologist, and a licensed social worker.

The peer counseling program receives some funding from the city of Santa Monica, the Los Angeles County Area Agency on Aging, and the Los Angeles County Department of Mental Health, but it is primarily funded through private donations. Third parties are not billed.

The program has been replicated both nationally and internationally as a result of training and consultation provided to groups across the country and around the world. The similar age and experience of the peer counselors and their clients contribute to the development of positive therapeutic relationships. The program has been effective in providing counseling to older persons otherwise reluctant to meet with a mental health professional.

Gerontology Assessment and Planning Program

The Gerontology Assessment and Planning Program (GAP Program) at Texas College of Osteopathic Medicine in Fort Worth, Texas, uses a three-hour intensive workup to analyze client problems and needs and to identify treatment options for frail elderly persons suffering some type of mental impairment, primarily dementias (Alzheimer's disease and others) and depression.

The workup includes a medical history; a physical examination; and an assessment of the client's mental, social, financial, functional, and nutritional status. A six-month follow-up is offered for those who enter community rather than college treatment programs.

The GAP Program staff (geriatrician, master's level gerontologist, and gerontological nurse practitioner) employ a team approach in working with the client's caregiver to help understand the problem and how the client can be helped. The team particularly focuses on the use of community resources to assist the client and family and provides recommendations to the primary physician if the client requests.

The GAP Program receives financial support from the college and also bills available third parties. Referrals to the program have come primarily through word of mouth and from physicians in the college's department of internal medicine. The program is the only geriatric clinic in a county with a total population of over one million people, of which 14 percent are elderly. As a result, a six- to eight-week waiting list exists. The practices of the college's geriatricians continue to expand as many program participants seek the geriatricians' services to carry out the treatment plan developed through the assessment.

The assessment provides clients, families, and other caregivers and health care providers with a plan to address the individual's mental and emotional concerns, along with an introduction to the resources available to assist in the process.

MEETING THE CHALLENGE: FUTURE EXPECTATIONS

The importance of good mental health for the elderly is obvious. Not only does it allow a higher level of independence and daily functioning, but it is also a factor in the progress of somatic disease through its influence on the patient's ability to follow treatment regimens. Good mental health is an important contributor to quality of life.

In spite of the importance of mental health, many persons do not receive the treatment they need. One key to change is the education of physicians, mental health professionals, caregivers, and the elderly themselves about the mental disorders that affect older people, their causes, and the potential for successful treatment. Everyone who cares for and about the elderly must be aware that the mental and emotional disorders of this age group can be treated and that the distress that the problems engender can be alleviated or, in some cases, eliminated altogether.

Even education will not change the current situation if funding is not available to allow the development of programs targeted at the elderly. The current climate of budget deficits on a federal level as well as in many states and localities limits the potential for government funding. In addition, when funds are allocated for social programs, the elderly increasingly are having to compete with other pressing needs (e.g., children's services, the homeless, education, and drug addiction). The elderly are viewed as less and less competitive as these other needs are considered.

In considering the funding of services, it is important for lawmakers, insurers, and granting agencies to recognize that intervention and treatment of a mental or emotional disorder on a timely basis in the outpatient setting is extremely cost-effective in preventing or minimizing hospitalization or other costly treatment. The allocation of dollars now will reduce the dollars needed later.

The programs that are developed must meet several key criteria if they are truly to meet the mental health needs of the elderly community. They must take a holistic approach to their clients because the elderly are particularly prone to psychiatric responses to physical and social causes. The provider must go to the client—in the home, the elder center, the nursing home—because the elderly person may be physically or emotionally incapable of coming to the provider. Finally, the programs must offer a highly supportive therapeutic environment in which a range of treatment approaches and additional assistance services (such as home health care, housekeeping, transportation, and so forth) can be accessed as needed.

Education, funding of cost-effective programs, and program development that is designed to provide service to the elderly in their own setting in a manner that considers the whole person are the critical factors in meeting the mental health needs of the elderly, thereby increasing their overall functioning and ability to live independently, and enhancing their quality of life.

NOTES

1. A.S. Fleming et al., *Report on a Survey of Community Mental Health Centers,* vol. 1 (Washington, D.C.: Action Committee To Implement the Mental Health Recommendations of the 1981 White House Conference on Aging, 1986).

2. U.S. Congress, Office of Technology Assessment, *Losing a Million Minds: Confronting the Tragedy of Alzheimer's Disease and Other Dementias,* pub. no. OTA-BA-323 (Washington, D.C.: U.S. Government Printing Office, 1987).

3. D. Blazer, Current Concepts: Depression in the Elderly, *New England Journal of Medicine* 320 (1989):164–166.

4. E.R. Roybal, Mental Health and Aging: The Need for an Expanded Federal Response, *American Psychologist* 43 (1988):189–194.

5. H.M. Waxman and E.A. Carner, Physicians' Recognition, Diagnosis, and Treatment of Mental Disorders in Elderly Medical Patients, *The Gerontologist* 24 (1984):593–597.

6. P.S. German et al., Detection and Management of Mental Health Problems of Older Patients by Primary Care Providers, *JAMA* 257 (1987):489–493; Roybal, Mental Health and Aging.

7. R.M. Glass, Psychiatric Megatrends and the Elderly, *JAMA* 257 (1987):527–528.

8. Waxman and Carner, Physician's Recognition, Diagnosis, and Treatment of Mental Disorders.

9. Ibid., 596.

10. Ibid.

11. German et al., Detection and Management of Mental Health Problems.

12. Ibid., 493.

13. T.G. McGuire, Outpatient Benefits for Mental Health Services in Medicare, *American Psychologist* 44 (1989):818–824.

14. Ibid.

Chapter 8

Population Aging and Dependency: Caregiving in the 21st Century

Neal E. Cutler

DEPENDENCE, FUNCTIONAL LIMITATION, AND PERSONAL CARE

This chapter focuses on the connections among aging, dependency, and personal care. It is increasingly recognized that an aging society does not necessarily mean a dependent society. The good news, after all, is that 95 percent of older people do not live in nursing homes, and 75 percent do not have functional disabilities. Realistically, however, an aging society does mean that we have a responsibility to identify the kinds of dependency that are likely to increase and plan private and public responses accordingly.

Questions of aging, functional limitations, dependency, and long-term care are typically considered in the context of institutional care (e.g., nursing home care). Yet it is becoming widely acknowledged that most older men and women can and do continue to live in the community and in their own homes. They do so even if they arc ill, cven if they have some level of functional disability.

A variety of interventions, including enhanced medical procedures, sophisticated pharmaceuticals, innovative prosthetics, and community-based nutrition and social support services, each contribute to the increased capacity of older individuals to continue to live in families, homes, and neighborhoods. Such interventions provide many older women and men with the means to avoid the institutionalization that in an earlier era might have been the only plausible solution to a condition of dependence and functional limitation.

The challenge for social policy, both public and private, is to identify those kinds of decrements in ability and functionality that need not be responded to by the "nursing home solution." As it turns out, there is a range of problems that only

Revision of the Opening Address to the Seventh National Conference on Aging and Independence in the 21st Century, Sponsored by the Forum for Health Care Planning, Washington, D.C., December 1990.

require the assistance of another person in the household environment. In particular, when an individual experiences difficulties with certain activities of daily living (ADLs), such as eating or taking a bath, then the logical solution is to provide personal assistance rather than take the more drastic step of assigning the individual to a nursing home.

A substantial amount of gerontology and health research has focused on this kind of situation. Research and practice now have more or less standardized methods for conceptualizing and measuring older people's limitations in ADLs.[1]

The importance of a standard measure of ADLs is illustrated by such developments as the substantial investment of public funds in large-scale population surveys of health and aging that include the ADL measures, the increasing use of ADLs as a trigger in private health and long-term care insurance benefits, the focus upon ADL measures in recent state-federal disputes over the allocation of Older Americans Act social services, and the inclusion of ADL measures in the 1990 census. The standard measure of ADLs identifies an individual's limitations in five areas of everyday life: bathing, dressing, moving from bed to chair, going to the toilet, and eating.

The connection between limitations in the performance of ADLs and institutionalization is fairly straightforward: If the assistance of another person is not available, an older person with limitations will have to be institutionalized. As Chappell has aptly noted in this regard, "One of the greatest indicators of long-term institutional care of elderly people is not medical need but, rather, the lack of social support when need arises. Older people with few or limited family relationships are prime candidates for institutionalization when they become sick."[2]

For economic reasons as well as humanitarian reasons, it seems clearly senseless to relegate an older woman or man to a nursing home when regular personal assistance in getting dressed or bathing is all that is needed. Unfortunately, this view is not universally shared. In defense of narrow nursing home insurance policies, for example, some insurance analysts have recently suggested that home care is not less expensive than nursing home residential care. Of course, the analytically appropriate question here is the conditional question: Under what conditions is home care less expensive than nursing home care? In its absolute form, "Is home care more expensive, yes or no?" the question has neither policy nor analytic value. Unless research reveals that nursing home care is always less expensive, then personal care in the home must be a component of policy debates and gerontological analyses.

THE DEMAND FOR AND SUPPLY OF PERSONAL CARE

If we accept the view that for some older persons personal care in the home is a feasible and desirable alternative to nursing home residence, then two key questions arise. First, given the strong correlation between advanced age and patterns of functional limitation, how much home care (i.e., ADL-related personal care) will society require over the next few years? Second, where is this care likely to come from?

Table 8-1 documents the strong correlation between advanced age and functional limitation. For each of the five activities of daily living, the older the man or woman, the higher the rate of need for personal care. On the other hand, whereas each of the ADLs is strongly age-related, the magnitudes vary, as portrayed graphically in Figure 8-1. Eating has the lowest overall rate and the weakest relationship with aging. More older persons require help with taking a bath, and bathing shows the strongest relationship to age.

The age patterns in Table 8-1 and Figure 8-1 include a composite ADL measure: An older individual is considered in need of personal care if he or she needs

Table 8-1 ADL Rates per 1,000 Persons

	Male	Female	Total
Bathing			
65–74	33.4	36.7	35.2
75–84	68.2	88.8	80.9
85+	194.9	227.9	217.2
Dressing			
65–74	32.5	26.8	29.3
75–84	56.6	47.3	50.8
85+	126.5	135.7	132.3
Moving			
65–74	17.4	17.9	17.7
75–84	28.8	41.8	36.7
85+	66.7	99.1	89.6
Toileting			
65–74	13.6	11.4	12.4
75–84	22.7	33.4	29.3
85+	56.4	95.3	82.6
Eating			
65–74	8.5	4.7	6.3
75–84	17.6	13.9	15.3
85+	23.9	29.0	27.4
1+ ADLs			
65–74	48.1	46.7	47.4
75–84	89.5	98.6	95.2
85+	218.8	247.7	238.8

Sample *N*(65+) = 11,497.

Source: Supplement on Aging, 1984 Health Interview Survey.

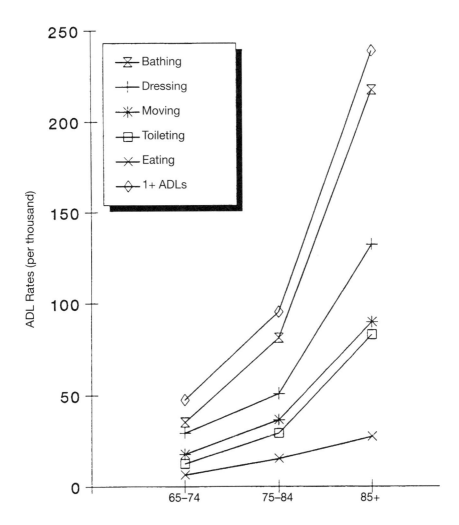

Figure 8-1 Age Patterns in ADLs

assistance with any one or more of the five standard activities of daily living. This "1+" measure naturally shows the highest rate of needed assistance. The rates of ADL limitations are from the *Supplement on Aging* of the 1984 Health Interview Survey, which included a nationally representative sample of 11,500 respondents age 65 and over.

The demand and supply analysis begins with an initial working assumption about the validity of the 1984 rates, an assumption we later modify. The initial assumption is that these 1984 rates are characteristic of the older population in the short run, that is, over the next 10–20 years. What happens in the longer run, as the health habits of today's middle-aged persons translate into future old-age health and functional ability, remains to be seen. For this first part of the analysis, however, we use the 1984 ADL rates, specified by age and gender (the 1+ measure in Table 8-1), to estimate the overall amount of functional limitation in the older population. In turn, these estimates measure the aggregate societal demand for personal care over the next 20 years.

The 1984 age-gender ADL rates were multiplied by the parallel age-gender census projections for 1980 to 2010, and the results were aggregated in Table 8-2. Overall, there were 2.0 million persons (age 65+) with one or more (1+) ADL limitations in 1980. This is estimated to increase to 3.6 million persons in need of personal assistance by 2010, an increase of 80 percent. Within this overall increase is an even more dramatic increase among older-old men and women: In the 85+ age group, there is an estimated 173 percent increase in the need for personal care (again calculated by applying the 1984 rates to the 1980–2010 census data).

Who are the providers of personal care? Systematic case study research as well as anecdotal observations suggest that most personal care is provided by the daughters and daughters-in-law of the older care receivers. From a policy perspective, however, the relevant question is this: How can we estimate the *national supply* of potential or likely caregivers?

To answer this question, it would be useful to have nationally representative surveys of the kind of complex parent-child patterns that are reflective of caregiving relationships. In the absence of such surveys, we use the "demographic supply" of middle-aged women (age 55–64) as the surrogate measure of the number of daughter and daughter-in-law caregivers. The actual (1980) and projected numbers of this caregiver group are given in the bottom row of Table 8-2. In the same period (1980–2010) that the overall national need for personal care rises by

Table 8-2 Projected Need for Personal Care: Population Estimates of Persons with One or More ADL Limitations

	1980	1990	2000	2010	Percentage of Change 1980–2010
65–74	737,139	869,412	863,487	996,042	35.1
75–84	735,990	945,052	1,142,015	1,159,308	57.5
85+	535,386	779,486	1,106,664	1,462,926	173.2
Total	2,008,515	2,593,949	3,112,166	3,618,276	80.1
Potential caregivers (women age 55–64)	11,551,000	11,260,000	12,601,000	18,257,000	58.1

80 percent and the need among the older-old rises by 173 percent, the number of middle-aged women increases by 58 percent.

THE CAREGIVER RATIO

The trend data in Table 8-2 identify the demand and supply components of the caregiver relationship: the number of older persons with one or more ADL limitations and the supply of potential caregivers (middle-aged women). This relationship can be summarized by a caregiver ratio, which indicates the number of caregivers per one care receiver. In Figure 8-2, two versions of the ratio are compared. The versions differ in their definitions of the care receiver population. The top line, based on the ADL measure of demand for personal care, suggests that across the 1980–2020 period the range will be about five or six potential caregivers per each care receiver.

The lower line in Figure 8-2 is based on a definition of the care receiver population as all older-old (85+) men and women. The caregiver ratio drops noticeably, since the same number of middle-aged women caregivers is allocated to a substantially larger number of care receivers. In the first decade of the 21st century, the caregiver ratio declines to about three potential caregivers per older-old person.

Since we know that not all older-old persons will need personal care, why is this latter definition of care receiver included for comparison? First, although the age 85+ version of the caregiver ratio is an unrealistic portrayal of the need for personal care, it helps to define a worst-case limit, identifying in numerical terms what could happen if (or when) increasing numbers of older persons do in fact become dependent on personal care. Second, both the ADL and the age 85+ version show an improvement during the first decade of the 21st century, reflecting the importance of the supply factor (the baby boomers will be reaching their mid-fifties).

ALTERNATIVE VIEWS OF THE FUTURE

The analysis so far is based on the assumption that the national ADL rates identified in the 1984 Health Interview Survey will remain descriptive of the older population over the next two to three decades. Yet despite improvements in old age mortality, research also suggests that morbidity and therefore dependency within the older population is increasing. As new medical discoveries and procedures help to keep people alive for a longer period, at least some of these men and women are kept alive in a less healthy, more dependent state. Just as the eradication of tuberculosis increased the supply of older persons vulnerable to cancer and heart attacks, successful treatment of these latter diseases increases the num-

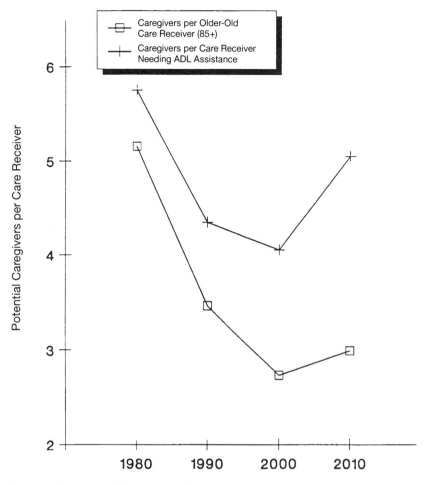

Figure 8-2 Comparison of Two Versions of the Caregiver Ratio for the Period 1980–2010

ber of older persons who are likely to suffer from Alzheimer's disease or in other ways become more functionally limited. As a recent symposium on aging and health care recently concluded,

Agreement appears to exist among the authors published here that an increasing proportion of the future disease burden will be taken up by nonfatal, chronic, often disabling conditions, such as cataracts and osteoarthritis. Furthermore, those saved from usually fatal conditions such as cardiovascular disease and cancer may suffer substantial levels of disability.[3]

In the long term, we may achieve the goal of the squaring of the longevity curve—keeping each person healthy and without any functional limitation until he or she succumbs to total system failure upon reaching the century mark. But in the short term, increased longevity may well be accompanied by increased societal levels of illness and dependency.

Variations in Demand

How might increased longevity affect the need for and availability of personal care? The probability of increased longevity certainly suggests the need for personal care and assistance will be greater than the ADL rates documented for 1984. To examine alternative futures, we simulated two additional sets of caregiver ratios using increased ADL rates (again starting with the 1+ ADL rates in Table 8-1). The two sets of simulated rates assumed ADL rates 25 percent higher than the 1984 rates and 50 percent higher. We returned to the 1984 age-gender rates, increased them by 25 and 50 percent, multiplied the new rates by the appropriate age-gender population projections, and then reaggregated these separate rates to estimate the population numbers.

The results are shown in Table 8-3. Using the 25 percent rate increase, we calculated that the total number of older persons (age 65+) with one or more ADL limitations would increase from 2.0 million in 1980 to 4.5 million in 2010, or 125 percent. If the 1984 ADL rates were to increase by 50 percent, the need for personal care would increase by 170 percent overall, and by more than 300 percent among persons 85 and older.

Table 8-3 Revised ADL Population Projections Using Higher ADL Rates (Compared to 1984)

| | 1980 | 1990 | 2000 | 2010 | Percentage Change | | |
					1980–1990	1980–2000	1980–2010
Projections with 25% Higher ADL Rates							
65–74	737,139	1,086,765	1,079,359	1,245,053	47.4	46.4	68.9
75–84	735,990	1,181,315	1,427,519	1,449,135	60.5	94.0	96.9
85+	535,386	974,357	1,383,330	1,828,657	82.0	158.4	241.6
Total	2,008,515	3,242,437	3,890,207	4,522,845	61.4	93.7	125.2
Projections with 50% Higher ADL Rates							
65–74	737,139	1,304,118	1,295,230	1,494,063	76.9	75.7	102.7
75–84	735,990	1,417,578	1,713,023	1,738,963	92.6	132.8	136.3
85+	535,386	1,169,228	1,659,995	2,194,388	118.4	210.1	309.9
Total	2,008,515	3,890,924	4,668,249	5,427,414	93.7	132.4	170.2

Variations in Supply

In addition to variations on the demand side of the caregiver ratio, it is also important to consider variations on the supply side. Even though we used the total number of middle-aged women to estimate the total potential supply of caregivers, it is obvious that not all middle-aged women are daughters or daughters-in-law of dependent older persons.

Furthermore, even among those potential caregivers who have living parents, many may be unable or unwilling to provide such care. Many middle-aged "empty nest" wives have returned to the paid labor force, others live too far from their parents, and still others may simply not wish to engage in caregiving activity. For these and other reasons, we included a 50 percent reduction in the number of middle-aged female potential caregivers as part of the analysis of this alternative future.

Figure 8-3 shows the two extreme versions of the caregiver ratio based on these combinations of caregiving demand and supply. The top line uses the basic 1984 ADL rates to define the demand for personal care and 100 percent of the middle-aged women to define the supply of caregivers. The more pessimistic scenario, the lower line, is arrived at by using 50 percent higher ADL rates and 50 percent fewer caregivers. As expected the caregiver ratios in the latter scenario are noticeably worse; that is, there are many fewer caregivers for each care receiver. The caregiver ratio declines substantially through the year 2000 and then increases when the baby boomers enter middle age in the early years of the 21st century.

IMPLICATIONS AND ACTIONS

Caregiver ratios and their simulated variations do not, of course, describe relationships among real family units. Recent studies of real parent-child family relationships identify the factors that are likely to promote or inhibit the rendering of personal care. Walker and her colleagues, for example, quantified the importance of a range of demographic and situational factors (e.g., daughter's income and marital status and daughter's and mother's health) for the success of the caregiving relationship.[4]

Because this was an in-depth analysis of 141 mother-daughter pairs in Oregon, the more general estimate of the parameters of supply and demand—even using such crude definitions of caregiving likelihood as the age of the daughter—remains a necessary part of the overall picture. These simulations, in other words, assess in demographic terms what the pattern of caregivers and care receivers might look like under varying conditions. Like such statistical portraits, however,

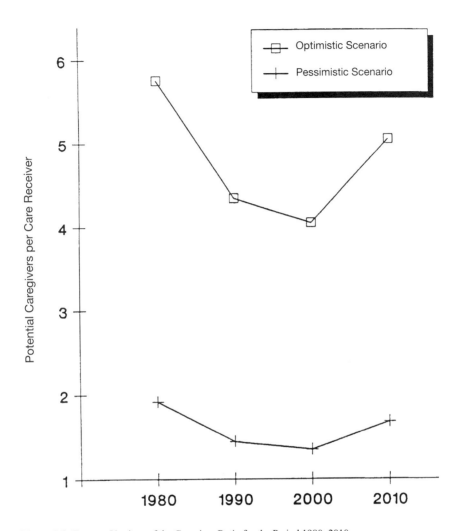

Figure 8-3 Extreme Versions of the Caregiver Ratio for the Period 1980–2010

the analysis utilizes a heuristic model of real relationships as a basis for considering the implications of various trends and dynamics in the social environment.

Whether the need for personal care in the older population will really rise by 50 percent in the 21st century, or whether only half of all daughters will actually provide such care, it is quite likely that the magnitude of the societal need for care will increase—a little in the shorter run and a lot when baby boomers move from caregiving middle age to care receiving older age.

We return to the caregiver ratios a final time to explore the following question: Which of the two components of the relationship, supply or demand, is more likely to strongly affect trends more over the next 20 years? To explore this question, we calculated two sets of caregiver demand and supply ratios. In the first set we held the supply factor constant at 100 percent of the demographic supply of middle-aged women and calculated the caregiver ratio using three demand levels: the basic ADL rates, 25 percent higher rates (ADL+25 percent), and 50 percent higher rates (ADL+50 percent).

In the second set, we held the supply factor constant but at a lower level, using the assumption that only half of all middle-aged women will be caregivers (CG–50 percent). We then calculated the ratios using this lower supply level and the same three levels of demand (basic ADL rates, ADL+25 percent, ADL+50 percent).

The patterns in Figure 8-4 suggest rather clearly that it is the supply of caregivers rather than changing levels of ADL-based demand that is the stronger factor in determining the society's capacity to provide personal care. All three of the caregiver ratio trend lines using the larger supply factor produce "better" or higher ratios of caregivers to care receivers. Alternatively stated, when the lower supply factor (CG–50 percent) is used, the caregiver ratios are always lower for the 1980–2010 period.

CONCLUSION

The analysis suggests that social and policy efforts should be directed at increasing the supply of personal caregivers. In part, this is a manpower issue. If, for whatever reasons, family members are unavailable to supply personal care, then "society" will be called upon to respond to the demand. And while motivation, recruitment, and training are essential for meeting the manpower challenge—as home care agency and nursing home administrators will testify—so is money. We cannot hope to attract and retain motivated and caring people to take care of our parents and grandparents if we pay them only minimum wage or less.

Meeting the need for home care is both a public and a private sector responsibility. Public policies should endorse home care and personal care health benefits alongside the supportive social services now available. Medicare should emphasize well-compensated personal care as a matter of general long-term health care policy. Similarly, private insurance should include generous home care and personal care provisions and benefits. Indeed, the more innovative long-term care insurance policies in this newly developing insurance market are those that offer home care as an alternative benefit.

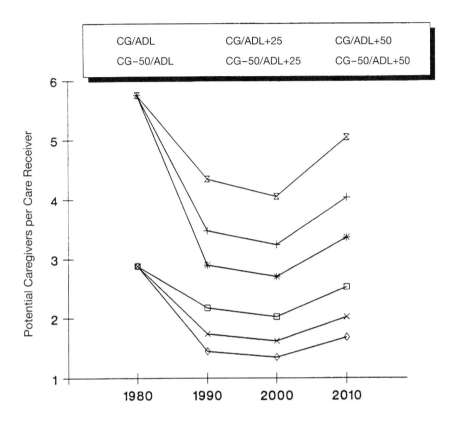

Figure 8-4 The Impact of Caregiver Supply and Demand

In both sectors, public and private, the compensation and benefit structure should be sufficient to attract, compensate, and retain quality caregivers. These final years of the 20th century are crucial for establishing goals, defining solutions, and making notable progress in the enhancement of personal caregiving and the minimization of dependence and institutionalization for older men and women. For as is well known (and redocumented here), demographics will produce an even more difficult situation in the 21st century than the one we face now.

NOTES

1. S.T. Katz et al., Progress in the Development of the Index of ADL, *The Gerontologist* 10 (1970):20–30; H.M. McNeil et al., Disability, *Functional Limitation, and Health Insurance Coverage: 1984/1986* (Washington, D.C.: U.S. Government Printing Office, 1986).

2. N.L. Chappell, Aging and Social Care, in *Handbook of Aging and the Social Sciences,* ed. R.H. Binstock and L.K. George, 3d ed. (San Francisco: Academic Press, 1990), 438–454.

3. M.N. Haan et al., Living Longer and Doing Worse? Present and Future Trends in the Health of the Elderly, (Introduction) *Journal of Aging and Health* 3 (May 1991):133–137.

4. A.J. Walker et al., The Benefits and Costs of Caregiving and Care Receiving for Daughters and Mothers, *Journal of Gerontology: Social Sciences* 47 (1992):S130–139.

Part II

Managing the Enterprise

Chapter 9

Management
of Nursing Homes

Seth B. Goldsmith

The management of nursing homes presents a unique challenge in the field of health care administration. This uniqueness results from the particular circumstance that nursing homes are both social and clinical institutions in which residents, and to a lesser extent families, are totally immersed as full-time members of an organic community. For the residents, the nursing home is the place where they live, work, play, grow older, and, in time, die. For the nursing home manager, the job is a 24-hour-a-day commitment that encompasses all the facets of running a labor-intensive and expensive medical institution plus those of managing a housing complex and a social services program. This chapter explores the role and function of management in nursing homes by first defining management and then developing a challenge for management. Next, there is an examination of the functions of management, followed by an analysis of the special challenges of management in nursing homes. Then the chapter looks at what is expected of managers and concludes with an analysis of ideas that prospective nursing home managers might consider in deciding whether to enter the critical field of long-term care management.

DEFINING MANAGEMENT

Virtually every textbook dealing with management at some point offers the reader a definition of the subject. For example, in 1947, Cornell answered the question, What is management? by noting, "The work of management is to plan, direct and control the organization and to weave together its various parts so that all factors will function properly and all persons cooperate—that is, work together efficiently—for a common purpose."[1]

In perhaps one of the grandest understatements, Drucker, in his best-selling book *Management*, suggests that "management is tasks, discipline, people and practice."[2] Management must be viewed as both an art and a science. On one hand, it deals with sharply defined areas, such as productivity and efficiency, that are exemplified best in current times by the operations research–management science approach to problem solving. On the other hand, it also deals with more diffuse areas, such as leadership and motivation.

THE MANAGERIAL CHALLENGE

For a manager, this sets up the following challenge: How does a manager construct or reconstruct an organization so that it maximizes efficiency and effectiveness for its various external constituencies and simultaneously minimizes stress, disaffection, and unhappiness for its internal constituencies? It should be recognized that this statement of the problem or challenge is value laden, as are most definitions of management and concepts of the manager's role. The emphasis in this statement is on satisfying external constituencies, performing efficiently in economic and financial terms, being effective, and, finally, respecting the human dignity of workers. If, for example, workers are considered drones, peasants, or simply inputs for a resource system, the challenge might be restated to eliminate concern for disaffected workers. Indeed, the manager's concept of the meaning of work can dramatically shift his or her perspective.

A management approach based on a value system—and all approaches are based on a value system to some degree—must examine that system if it is to be responsive and continue to function as a mechanism of achieving organizational goals.

THE FUNCTIONS OF MANAGEMENT

The specific activities of management vary from one organization to another, as well as from time to time in the same organization. The sum total of management in an organization tends to be relatively stable, however; the same managerial functions are carried out in all organizations, although circumstances, organizational needs, and personalities dictate which of these functions predominates at any given time. The most often cited management functions are planning, organizing, staffing, directing, controlling, coordinating, and representing.

Planning

Planning involves those activities associated with setting objectives, making policy, and creating strategies for attaining the objectives within the organizational policy framework. It is considerably more difficult to identify objectives, particularly in the health field, than it appears at first glance. Organizational objective setting is a process that requires global vision, diplomatic skill, and considerable good fortune. Planning normally results in an output—a written plan. Such a document can cover time frames that vary from rather short periods, such as six months or a year, to periods as long as five or ten years. An effective plan results in a positive outcome for the organization; a bad plan has the potential to destroy an organization.

Because of their size and organizational depth, most free-standing nursing homes, as opposed to those belonging to a for-profit or nonprofit chain, do not have a full-time planner. Rather the responsibility for planning is in the hands of the owner, board planning committees, and, quite clearly, management. The actual development of a plan or plans may be a group activity involving the aforementioned people and groups and, with increasing frequency, consultants. The role of a consultant in the planning function is to introduce into the planning process a level and range of expertise not available in the organization. However, the value of the consultant's work is significantly related to the quality of input the consultant receives from the nursing home's management. Indeed, it is an illusion to think that top management can delegate the responsibility or authority for planning to a planner or consultant.

In the best of situations, a plan functions as an organizational control device. With a plan, management can continually identify expectations (goals) for people, programs, or projects and measure the progress and the rate of progress being made toward these goals. In some cases, a manager will prefer to utilize the lack of a plan as a control device for the organization; the only plan is what is in the manager's head. In this way, the manager maintains total control and great flexibility but reigns over a situation that may often be close to disaster.

Organization

Organization is a second function commonly associated with management. This is the function of determining what activities will be carried on by the nursing home, how these activities should be grouped, and who shall have the authority and responsibility for carrying out these activities. The organization chart is the graphic representation of the decisions made regarding this function.

In nursing homes, legal and fiscal constraints, including Medicaid and Medicare reimbursement formulas, may dictate the most cost-effective organizational structure. For example, during a two-year period, I observed a staff member shifted to three different units as the result of an administrative search to find a way to get a state Medicaid program to pay her salary. Tradition and a sensitivity to professionalism will often dictate a particular configuration, as evidenced by the fact that nursing directors rarely report to anyone other than the chief executive or chief operating officer. Similarly, it would be a rare nursing home where a director of food services reported to the head of nursing.

Although organizing and reorganizing seems to be in the blood of managers, it should be recognized that reorganizations are often not the solution to deep-seated organizational problems. Indeed, shifting mediocre staff members to new organizational boxes usually provides the illusion but not the substance of positive change. To have the substance of change, nursing homes, which are like most other health care organizations in being basically labor-intensive, must not merely change the organizational structure but also focus on getting the right people the first time. And that is the task of the staffing function.

Staffing

Staffing is perhaps the most obvious and most critical of management functions. Basically, it involves getting the right people for the jobs and developing them. To be most effective in this managerial area, the executive and his or her staff must be adept at using personnel management tools such as job descriptions and specifications, be fine judges of character, and be master detectives capable of ferreting out what is between the lines of a letter of recommendation.

For any organization, the cost of each new hire is extremely high. This cost involves all expenses related to recruiting, training, and turnover. Fortunately, a nursing home will sometimes find superb people who easily fit into the organization and develop with the job. Occasionally, however, much time, money, and energy will be expended on someone who must be terminated, with all the attendant costs and ill will.

The unfortunate reality is that for many people nursing home jobs are viewed as second choice positions in the health field. The challenge that management must accept is to convince potential recruits of the importance and indeed excitement of a position in long-term care, plus the possibility of a fulfilling career.

However, if employees are to avoid dead-end jobs and management is to make good on its promises, management must take a number of important steps. First, it must be philosophically committed to the professional development of each employee. Second, it must provide financial support for a broad range of development activities, such as taking academic courses, attending in-service training, and going to professional meetings. Finally, management must be prepared to support an employee's advancing career, which may mean giving hiring preference to internal candidates, developing clearly defined career ladders, and encouraging excellent but underemployed staff to leave the organization and develop their careers in a different organization.

In sum, staffing is a process that begins with the identification of an organization's staff needs and continues through staff development. The job of management is to avoid mistakes and develop potential. Mistakes can most often be avoided if managers pay as much attention to process and requirements as they pay to "feel" or "intuition." Too often people are hired because of a good interview that has not been confirmed by a review of credentials, recommendations, or second interviews. Once the "right" decision has been made, the new employee, if he or she is to be most valuable to the organization, must be supported in the development of his or her potential.

Direction

Direction is the function most often associated with management. Indeed, in many instances the title of the most senior administrator is Executive Director.

Direction is also the function most associated with the image of managers as individuals who sit in their offices, no doubt quite removed from any part of the operation, and bark out orders to a compliant group of employees. Except in rare cases, this is a fantasy. Managers may like to view themselves as the captain of a ship, but their word is no longer the law. Rather, they must use their position to guide, persuade, or coach subordinates. Even in highly bureaucratic organizations, such as universities or hospitals, management is by consensus, and the effective manager must shepherd subordinates toward agreement.

In practice, directing an organization is not giving orders or commanding staff, it is closer to pointing out a direction or goal and leading employees toward the goal by coaching, training, encouraging, and occasionally commanding and threatening.

Controlling

Controlling is based on the measurement of performance against predetermined standards. Two elements must come together if the manager's control is going to be effective: There must be standards, and there must be information systems to indicate the progress that is being made toward meeting those standards.

Standards can range from performance indicators to budget indicators. For example, assume a manager has set standards for the marketing representatives, such as 25 confirmed and signed contracts with deposits by a given day. The goal is clear and both the manager and marketing representatives are able to measure progress toward the goal. A more ambiguous target, "Do the best you can," results in confused expectations as well as the possibility of unfair managerial practices.

Setting the standards against which an employee's or unit's performance will be measured is difficult in long-term care because of the complexity and diffuseness of mission of most long-term care organizations. If, for example, the goal is to enhance the quality of care given to residents, how does one measure success? Is it merely the amount of care given? A decrease in complaints? An increase in resident or family satisfaction? A decrease in bedsores, falls, or medication problems? Unfortunately, the waters are a bit murky when it comes to quality of care and quality of life issues.

On the other hand, managers can exercise a considerable amount of control through the budgetary process. In this process, usually after a complicated and protracted negotiation, a unit can project its revenues and expenses and be given the funds to meet its goals. When this occurs, management's job is to track progress toward the goal and follow up on deviations from the budget plan. Finally, management is responsible for decision making to solve or mitigate mid-budget problems.

Coordinating

Coordinating is one of the least important functions. Traditionally, a coordinator has plenty of responsibility and little authority—analogous to the carpenter who is given wood and nails but no hammer. It appears that the most successful coordinators are those with real or apparent authority, a total commitment to the program, or extraordinary skills as a persuader. To put it differently, important managerial problems are often too deep-rooted to be solved through coordination. They must be "managed" in an affirmative manner.

Representing

The seventh traditional function is representing—being the spokesperson for the unit, organization, or industry. A department head represents the department and its case on the division level, and the director represents the organization to the government, a foundation, or even the board.

Representation is a critical managerial function. Those at the top of each component usually represent the component to those at the next higher level. Representation is a time- and energy-consuming function that requires a political sensitivity to the needs of a constituency (or unit) and a similar sensitivity to the needs of those to whom the constituency is being represented. Presentation, debate, analysis, and articulation skills are critical, since they can help to influence the opinions of those who are listening to the presentation.

SPECIAL CHALLENGES OF NURSING HOME MANAGEMENT

Nursing home management has its own special set of challenges that are related to the mission of nursing homes, their relatively small size, and the particular situation of nursing home residents.

The first of these challenges is a function of the complex mission of long-term care organizations—providing quality of care services and quality of life services to the elderly. The two goals are difficult to quantify and are often elusive. For management, whether dealing with a board of a nonprofit facility or the owners of a proprietary home, this apparent diffuseness of mission consistently presents problems. For example, how does one argue for more resources such as an additional staff person in the activities department when the person is not required under state law and you can only hypothesize that an increased staffing level will enhance the quality of the residents' experience.

Equally problematic for managers is the issue of the "bottom line" and its relationship to mission. Virtually every decision is likely to have an impact on the profitability of the home, and the balancing act between money and mission is a delicate one. Consider again the decision whether to hire an additional activities staff person. The cost of hiring, perhaps $20,000, can represent a significant part of a proprietary home's annual profit or require considerable fund-raising activity for the nonprofit home.

A second issue that differentiates nursing home management from other areas of health care administration is the size of nursing homes, which tend to be small and intimate and have a small but quite consistent set of clients. The manager of a typical 100-bed home might have to work with 85 employees organized into three shifts. Additionally, the residents are likely to have an average length of stay of two and a half to three years. This means that residents (and their families) inevitably become knowledgeable about the home and often quite demanding about what happens in it. The administrator also becomes an intimate friend and counselor to residents and families, a role absent from a hospital, where a patient's total stay is usually five or six days.

A third challenge relates to the government oversight of nursing homes. For a host of reasons, some legitimate, others questionable, nursing homes are simply not trusted by society. The result of this is myriad regulations and inspections. For the manager, this means a constant flow of outsiders evaluating the home and causing disruption and periodic ruffled feathers. The manager is responsible for representing the home—dealing with deficiencies, correcting what needs to be corrected, and sometimes challenging the findings and conclusions of the outside experts. The manager must also show constant vigilance in trying to detect changes on the horizon that could affect the organization, such as reimbursement formulas or eligibility criteria for admission. Vigilance allows the manager to plan and organize political activity to help the home and its residents.

A final crucial challenge is dealing with a staff that must work on a daily basis with people who are getting older and sicker and dying. Additionally, the staff members themselves are aging and perhaps becoming less physically able to deal with the constant demands of assisting residents with their activities of daily living.

Thus, in a sense, the nursing home manager functions as the mayor of a small community who is called upon to perform an extraordinarily broad range of functions. As often happens in small and intimate organizations, management operates in the proverbial fishbowl. Indeed, in most nursing homes, there are few secrets and little that escapes the scrutiny and evaluation of staff and residents. Additionally, because of the visibility and accessibility of managers, they are not insulated from the impact of their decisions.

To effectively deal with these challenges, management must act in a manner that is consistent and equitable. To not act in such a way is to court disaster by demoralizing the staff and residents. Yet, although the balancing act in management is difficult, the rewards are high. Nursing home management is perhaps the one type of health care management that presents opportunities for a single administrator to have a dramatic impact on an organization. Indeed, in many nursing homes the administrator wields a significant amount of power, often substantially more than a hospital's administrator might wield. This power, which may be related to the lack of a medical staff or the relatively small size of the management team, means that nursing home managers have the opportunity to truly manage their organizations.

EXPECTATIONS FROM MANAGERS

What should be expected from a manager? In answering this question, two dimensions must be considered: behavior and values.

Both fiction and reality present a picture of managers as "organization men." Their loyalty is to the organization, and the most important professional person in their lives is their boss. The image is of a tight hierarchical structure and operations that respond to that structure. Regardless of the theoretical "flatness" of an organization, there is always someone on the top who has the authority and responsibility to represent the organization and negotiate in its interest—at least that person's conception of its interest.

A clear example of this is the attempted takeover of McGraw-Hill by American Express. This takeover was viewed as an anathema by McGraw-Hill's chairperson, Harold McGraw, Jr. Because of his personal view, he waged a relentless and successful campaign against the invasion. He stated in a letter to the chief executive officer of American Express that American Express lacked "integrity, corporate morality and sensitivity to professional responsibility." He went on to criticize the management and behavior of American Express. All of this was done with the express approval of stockholders, many of whom clearly stood to gain by such a merger.[3]

A different perspective on management is presented by Michael Blumenthal. During his tenure as Secretary of the Treasury, he prepared an article for *Fortune* titled "Candid Reflections of a Businessman in Washington."[4] In it, he contrasted his experiences as a senior government official in charge of an agency employing 120,000 people with his experiences as chairperson and chief executive officer of the Bendix Corporation. Control, he suggests, is related to the ability to "hire and fire," and he identified his problem in government thus: "Out of 120,000 people in the Treasury, I was able to select twenty-five, maybe. The other 119,975 are outside of my control."[5]

It was noted earlier that top management is involved in setting goals and organizing activities that allow the goals to be attained. The contrast between the private sector and the public sector is highlighted in Blumenthal's article by his comment that the senior executives in industry can control who is and who is not involved in policy development and implementation, but that in the government, because of the plethora of official and nonofficial interest groups, many of whom have influence and power, the policy process is considerably more complex.

A final point is that management in industry does most of its business in private. Government executives and, to a lesser extent, managers of nonprofit community organizations, however, must function under the spotlight of the press. How then do performance expectations for health care managers differ from those for industrial managers? In a magazine article about the recipient of the Young Hospital Administrator of the Year Award, it was pointed out that the award winner had "superior administrative capability," which was demonstrated variously, including by the hospital's quality of care, physical and programmatic growth, financial health, and positive professional image. As if that were not enough, the article continued with a description of the administrator's activities as a local and national leader and ended with a statement regarding his "positive spirit." An analysis of this article suggests that, to be successful, at least in the eyes of one professional organization, managers must be joiners and innovators, accept their organization's goals as their own, and invest their spiritual and physical energy in building the organization.

Among the essentials of management are technical skills and the ability to recruit and retain able subordinates. Technical skills are often underemphasized, but they contribute substantially to a manager's credibility and value to an organization. For example, can the manager accurately forecast the utilization of services based on a high-quality assessment of needs, likely demands, and competition? Can the manager develop an appropriate strategic plan or budget for the organization? This is not to suggest that the manager must write the budget personally, but he or she must plan, organize, and review the budget before it is placed in the hands of the board or the owners. Mistakes, conceptual or mechanical, are earmarks of a careless or technically unskilled manager, particularly at the beginning of a career. Indeed, if there is one shortcoming of new managers, it may be an over-reliance on the importance of their image as managers and an under-reliance on the technical tasks that constitute the essence of their job.

Since few managers, even workaholics, have the time and ability to do everything themselves, they must rely on subordinates for their own success. A manager's ability to find people who will be supportive and complement his or her own skills is crucial. Some managers view high-quality subordinates as threats and respond by hiring sycophants. Others view subordinate managers as tools to carry out unpleasant jobs and hire "hatchet men." A third group view subordinates as key colleagues, and they attempt to surround themselves with the best people available. One problem with the "best and brightest" is that they tend to move on if new challenges are not forthcoming. However, for the manager who is comfortable with talented subordinates and invests in their growth and development, the rewards are significant.

ENTERING MANAGEMENT

In his book *Management*, Drucker identifies six common mistakes in designing managerial jobs.[6] These mistakes are (1) designing "the job so small that a good man cannot grow"; (2) designing jobs that are not really jobs; (3) designing jobs that do not combine work with managing; (4) designing jobs that require continuous meetings and continuous cooperation and coordination; (5) giving out titles rather than jobs; and (6) creating "widow-maker" jobs, that is, jobs that are simply impossible to do. Drucker's advice is particularly useful for a chief executive officer who must establish or reorganize an organization. However, it is also useful for a manager who must decide whether to accept a new position. So with apologies to Drucker and acknowledgment of him as the source, following is a list of six ideas to consider when entering or shifting positions on the managerial ladder.

Take a job in which you can grow. In the field of nursing home administration, growth is both a function of the job and the organization. In selecting a position, consider the growth potential. What will you learn on this job? What challenges and opportunities are associated with this job? How, in three to five years, will you be better off as a result of having had this job?

Do not be a gofer for another person. Nonjobs are particularly common in the health industry and are well described by Drucker as positions whose title includes "assistant to." A manager's performance should be observable by the total organization, and his or her position should not depend on the good will of the manager next in line. In small health care organizations, particularly at the entry level, this kind of dependency is difficult to avoid. Some managers attempt to avoid it by continually defining and redefining their positions in writing (via a series of memos). If there is good will and if those higher in the organization feel secure, there are few problems with this method. If the junior manager is simply another tool in the senior manager's bag, all the memos in the organization are insignificant compared with the opinion of the "boss." To the extent possible, then, the job should represent a commitment from the organization, not from the manager next highest in the chain of command.

Take a job in which you work and manage. No one can suggest that management is not hard work, but quite clearly there is a tendency for young managers to ensconce themselves in pleasant offices, deal only with those who seek them out, respond only to those higher in the hierarchy, and "play the manager role." Periodically, however, managers should get their hands dirty. For the physician manager, this might mean seeing patients occasionally. For the nonphysician manager, it might mean handling special projects or observing certain operations. Managers must continue to develop their own competencies and periodically test them. Such development and testing can have positive effects in terms of self-esteem and respect from colleagues and subordinates. An analogy with academia might clarify this concept further: A dean should not only administer the school but should also work by teaching and doing research. In one nursing home I visited, the executive director spent at least several hours per week helping out on the resident units and directly delivering care—clearly she was both working and managing.

Avoid a position with a great deal of nonproductive time. Most people are measured by their output or the outcomes of what they do, not the processes used to attain the outcomes. Although processes are critical for reaching goals, it is easy to forget that a process is not, in fact, an outcome. For example, meetings can become more important than the decisions reached and the implementation of the decisions. All positions include some nonproductive time, but new managers must look for positions in which it is either minimized or can be controlled. Many new managers look back over their first few years on the jobs and realize they have spent most of their time in meetings and have done few things that have had much effect. Organizations want the bases touched but also want runs scored.

Get your objectives straight. Knowing what you really want is extremely difficult, because there is a strong current impelling managers toward accepting the objectives of the organization as their own. Soul-searching is often tiring and time consuming, but it is necessary if managers are to understand what they really want from their position. Is it power, prestige, security, glamour, intellectual stimulation, money, or a combination of these and other objectives? A manager who has come to grips with his or her personal objectives is in a much stronger position to make career choices. Not only that, but the manager will be less likely to suffer from unnecessary and possibly debilitating anxiety.

When in doubt, maximize your potential for success by taking proven jobs. Managers should not risk their future on a widow-maker job, a job that others have tried and failed at. The payoff for being a hero is high, but when other qualified people could not handle the job, new managers must be careful not to slip on their own egos. A proven path is a more sensible choice and less fraught with uncertainties and danger. Here, again, objectives come into play, since some people find a well-constructed ladder less appealing than a greased flagpole.

CONCLUSION

Managers of nursing homes play an absolutely crucial role in the lives of hundreds of employees and residents. The tone they set for the organization reverberates throughout the facility. They have the power to create a cold, stressful, indeed unhealthy environment. They also have the power, fortunately, to construct a warm, caring, and productive organization—the type of place where most of us would choose to work or, if necessary, live.

NOTES

1. W.B. Cornell, *Organization and Management in Industry and Business* (New York: Ronald Press, 1947), 46.
2. P. Drucker, *Management* (New York: Harper & Row, 1973), xiii.
3. *Fortune*, In the News, (February 12, 1979), 16.
4. *Fortune*, Candid Reflections of a Businessman in Washington, (January 29, 1979), 36–49.
5. Ibid.
6. Drucker, *Management*, 405–410.

Chapter 10

The Role and Function of Governing Boards

Seth B. Goldsmith

Governing boards are a fact of life for managers of nonprofit nursing homes. State statutes set a host of requirements for these boards, ranging from the number of members on the board to voting requirements. These same statutes then invest the board with the legal responsibility and authority for the operation of the enterprise, and in some instances they even limit the liability of the board for its decisions if a prudent decision process has been followed. The board in turn normally delegates a significant amount of its power to a full-time managerial staff headed by a paid chief executive officer.

BOARD FUNCTIONS

In discussing board functions, Heen identifies eight areas of board activity:

(a) policy decisions with respect to products, services, prices, wages, labor relations; (b) selection, supervision and removal of officers and possibly other management personnel; (c) fixing of executive compensations, pension/retirement, etc., plans; (d) determination of dividends, financing and capital changes; (e) delegation of authority for administrative and possibly other action; (f) possible adoption, amendment and repeal of by-laws; (g) possible participation, along with shareholders, in approving various extraordinary corporate matters; and (h) supervision and vigilance for the welfare of the whole enterprise.[1]

Although a few of these functions are not applicable to nonprofit homes, most of them are central to the responsibilities of health care organization board members.

The problem of board effectiveness and involvement is common to all organizations. For example, when the famous bankruptcies of W.T. Grant, Lockheed,

Eastern Airlines, and hundreds of banks and savings and loan associations occurred, who claimed to be uninformed? The board! Does it seem possible that board members of major industrial concerns, the elite of America's business establishment, could be so unaware?

Drucker, in his book *Management*, titles a chapter "Needed: An Effective Board." He argues that boards, because of their very nature, the ambiguity of their mission, and the divergence of interest of their members, are programmed for failure.[2] It is a common experience in health care to find executives whose performance is excellent in business but who cannot function effectively on the board of a nonprofit organization. This can be partly understood by considering the composition of boards—health care or industrial. Data from a Heidrick and Struggles study of directors indicate that most board members are well into middle age (the average age being 57), that most are selected for their personal or professional stature, that functional area of expertise is a second but significantly less important reason for selection, and that availability is a considerably less important reason in selection.[3]

This is a pattern seen almost universally in the health care field. A review of a typical board's membership (with the exclusion of community-based programs such as neighborhood health centers) is like reading the who's who of the local area. Boards generally are not representative of any group other than the upper middle class of the community. The justification for this skewed representation is that such a group is likely to bring greater financial and intellectual resources to a board. Addressing the issue of board composition in an amusing article, Chandler suggests (somewhat backhandedly) that a balanced board must be the goal and that various criteria must be used, "from the subjective—candor, enthusiasm, manner of presentation (articulation and appearance), willingness to serve community, cooperativeness; to the more objective—age, occupation, standing in the community, place of residence, etc."[4]

Indeed, my own work with nursing home boards throughout the country supports these observations: Few board members are under 35 years old; most boards are male-dominated; board juntas, cliques that are on a board for life, are common; and virtually no boards have community representatives (i.e., elected and voting resident or family representatives).

BOARD-MANAGEMENT RELATIONS

For the nursing home administrator, the fundamental question is, How can a manager have an effective relationship with a board? At one extreme, the manager must cope with a necessary evil; at the other, the manager is able to utilize the resources that a board can offer. Many managers view their relationship with their board as adversarial. This was well articulated by J. Peter Grace, the chief executive of the multi-billion-dollar W.R. Grace conglomerate, when he said,

> Do you mean to tell me that if I work 100 hours a week for 4.3 weeks a month on average so that I'm working 430 hours a month, some guy is going to come in and in three or four hours outsmart me? I mean that's crazy! No matter how smart you are, if I work 100 times harder than you on a given subject, you have no way of catching me.[5]

As a reflection of his perspective, Grace's board room does not have the traditional conference table but rather is arranged more like a college classroom. In dealing with his board, Grace keeps them fully informed. For example, for one monthly meeting he provided board members with a report over 400 pages long.

Is this typical? Based on the Heidrick and Struggles study, it seems most companies provide their directors only with minutes of the previous meeting, some financial data, and an agenda for the next meeting. In most cases, no summaries of board committee meetings subsequent to the last board meeting, no marketing data, and no data to support agenda items are provided. It can be concluded that only those board members who are involved with committees, which is usually the group making critical decisions, or those who are extremely well informed about agenda items, can offer much of worth at a given meeting. Going back to the Grace example, it must be recognized that without an independent staff or a major investment of their own time, board members would find it impossible to digest or evaluate critically the 400 pages sent to them. Management, then, through its control of information given to the board, has the potential to have a major impact on the effectiveness and value of the board.

The issue of the relationship between management and the board is a recurring theme in the literature. For example, in a 1980 review article on governance, Umbdenstock noted that,

> for hospital trustees, administrators and physicians, many of the same issues in hospital governance remained in the forefront throughout the 70s. What are the board's proper roles and responsibilities? What are the proper relationships with management and the medical staff? What about the board's need to represent the community? Who ultimately directs the institution and how do trustees ensure the quality of care provided in the hospital?[6]

Several years earlier, the U.S. Chamber of Commerce, in its 1974 publication *A Primer for Hospital Trustees,* cautioned the trustees about their balance of involvement.[7] The advice given was to set policy but stay out of implementation. The administrative perspective and concerns are perhaps best identified in a 1973 document from the American College of Hospital Administrators titled *Principles of Appointment and Tenure of Executive Officers.* In it, the authors noted that "some board members in some hospitals cross over into line management, consciously or unconsciously."[8] When that occurs, directors become potential adversaries. As a preventive medicine measure then, the behavior suggested by Grace is almost a necessity for survival.

In 1974, the Macy Foundation produced its landmark study on the governance of voluntary teaching hospitals in New York City. Nelson, the former president of Johns Hopkins Hospital, found the major teaching hospitals in New York City facing many serious problems, some of which related to the board and most of which still plague the nursing home industry:[9]

- There is confusion of authority among governance, management, and medical staffs resulting from the duality of mission of the teaching hospital, which faces toward the medical school in the performance of its teaching and learning functions and toward the community and its doctors' patients in the performance of its service functions.
- Boards of trustees are predominantly white, male, and business-oriented, and there is only token representation of other interests.
- Board leadership is concentrated in small, entrenched groups complacent about the quality of their leadership.
- Except for leadership groups, board members are poorly informed about hospital goals and problems and uninformed about outside forces impinging on hospitals.
- Trustees are frustrated by the lack of information and involvement but nervous about getting involved in financial and medical problems.
- Chief executives lack the authority and backing required for effective negotiation with outside forces and effective control of medical affairs.
- Administrative staffs are generally strong at the top level but lack depth of expertise in finance, law, medical staff orientation, and other specialties.
- Communities are mistrustful of institutional goals and critical of institutional services.
- There is a lack of any standards of performance for hospital trustees or methods of evaluating quality and effectiveness of governance.

The picture of boards painted by Nelson and the others is gloomy indeed, and unfortunately, two decades later, little has changed. Who or what is responsible for this state of affairs? Among the causes might be that board members are sometimes picked on the basis of bad reasons—a person who has the prestige but lacks the time might be selected over someone with the time but limited prestige.

Potential wealthy contributors may be considered more important than those with expertise and interest.

Of course, some managers may want a weak board (and an uninformed board is weak). This is perhaps understandable, yet a strong board can offer dramatic leadership. Individually and collectively, board members can represent and promote the organization's interest; can serve as a sounding board or as a review and comment mechanism for innovation; and, with proper development, can serve as the major organizational evaluation mechanism.

KNOWLEDGE AND UNDERSTANDING OF DIRECTORS

Several years ago, while conducting an executive education program, I met with a group of 26 senior health administrators and asked them what they thought was most important for directors to know or understand about the health system and the role of the manager. Responses to the question varied widely. Some managers wanted their boards to be focused on national affairs, looking at the broad legislative and policy issues and planning alternative health systems; others were more interested in having directors focused on the role their own organization might play in a community or in developing quality services. To put it in conceptual terms, some managers view the board as an external reporting and sounding panel, whereas others see it as part of the internal drive mechanism of the organization.

When this same group of managers considered what they wanted the directors to know and understand about the manager's job, there was considerably less variance. Virtually all wanted their directors to know more about management and fiscal problems and issues. Additionally, a number of managers felt it was important that board members understand the importance of delegating authority and responsibility—a particularly troubling option considering that many board members do not appear to delegate authority in their own organizations.

THE BOARD IMPERATIVE

During a recent visit to a large midwestern geriatric center, I met with the newly elected board president and the center's chief executive officer. Both were successful and competitive men in their midforties, and each was trying to dominate the other as well as the organization. Several months after the meeting, the CEO was unemployed and the organization was in chaos (and fortunately later rescued by a very competent new CEO).

Could the firing have been avoided? Could the period of chaos and its long-term effects have been prevented? Perhaps none of this would have happened if the board's role was less ambiguous. It is absolutely imperative that a board be properly structured, operate within clear guidelines, be focused on the organization's mission, and periodically step back and examine its own performance.

Proper structuring requires a clear delineation of the authority and responsibility of the board and its managers, plus an implementing mechanism. In practical terms, this means the board must meet regularly, have a committee structure that functions, have clear lines of communication with the administration, and have a structure that supports its policy orientation and precludes any drift in the direction of micromanaging the institution.

The board must operate within clearly understood guidelines. For example, it must have its own internal rules about attendance, participation, and conflicts of interest. Individuals should be appointed or elected to the board because of their capacity to serve the organization, not because of a desire to be served. Nothing is more detrimental to the continued health of an organization than having board members who serve for the wrong reasons, such as enhancing their status in the community or, worse yet, using the power of the board to garner business from the organization. Guidelines should also deal with the role board members should have in dealing with staff and programs. Board members must limit the sharing of their expertise to the board room. Administrators need to be assured that their management team will not be undermined by board members who do end runs around administration by cultivating staff for "inside information."

Of paramount importance to any board's future is its ability to keep focused on its mission, which includes constantly re-examining that mission. For this reason, the mission must be clearly articulated and written down, and important decisions should be consistent with the mission statement. Management is responsible for ensuring that decisions reflect the organization's mission and for preparing the ground work for a re-examination of the mission through periodic mission-focused retreats.

CONCLUSION

A board can be a valuable asset of a long-term care facility, but only if it is properly selected and nurtured. Membership selection is crucial. Here, myth must be distinguished from reality. For every story about a board person who gave a building, there are a hundred other stories about someone who "we thought would give a building but died and gave nothing." Organizations should approach the selection of directors with considerable seriousness and select only those people who will enhance the value of the organization because of their expertise, availability, and, yes, in some cases, prestige. One way to approach the possible selection of a candidate is to ask this question: If time and effort are invested in this person, will there be a return on that investment? A negative answer suggests that the search process should be continued.

Once an appropriate new board member has been selected, the administrator must invest time and energy in educating the new member. First, the administrator should learn as much as possible about the new member, including his or her experience, profession, or business. This first phase should include an assessment of the new member's strengths, weaknesses, and interests. Doing this diagnostic workup demonstrates an interest in the board member's personal and professional development while simultaneously permitting an evaluation of how and where the new director might best fit into the organization. Second, the board member must be educated about the major issues and problems facing the long-term care industry and how those issues and problems are affecting the nursing home. Third, the board member needs to be routinely informed about the big picture (i.e., developments in long-term care) and the smaller picture (i.e., the nursing home). Finally, the board member must be asked to work for the good of the nursing home through service on committees, representation functions, or other appropriately useful activities. Most board members do not want to feel like proverbial bumps on a log.

In sum, a board that is tuned into and committed to the mission of the organization can make an invaluable contribution to the success of the manager and the organization as a whole.

NOTES

1. H.G. Heen, *Handbook of the Law of Corporations* (St. Paul, MN: West Pub. Co., 1970), 415.

2. P. Drucker, *Management* (New York: Harper & Row, 1973), 627–636.

3. Heidrick and Struggles, *The Changing Board* (1975), 5.

4. R.L. Chandler, Filling Empty Board Seats, *Hospital and Health Services Administration* 25, no. 1 (Winter 1980):85.

5. Peter Grace's Love-Hate Relationship with His Board, *Forbes* (May 15, 1976), 76.

6. R.J. Umbdenstock, Governance: A Decade of Steady Growth, *Trustees* 33 (1980):17.

7. U.S. Chamber of Commerce, *A Primer for Hospital Trustees* (Washington, D.C.: U.S. Government Printing Office, 1974), 25.

8. American College of Hospital Administrators, *Principles of Appointment and Tenure of Executive Officers* (Chicago: ACHA, 1973), 4.

9. The Macy Foundation, *The Governance of Voluntary Teaching Hospitals in New York City* (New York: Macy Foundation, 1974), 8–9.

Chapter 11

Termination without Litigation: Practical Advice for Separating Employees

James E. Wallace, Jr.

In this era of exploding wrongful discharge and employment discrimination litigation, employers view even the most justifiable termination with hesitation and reluctance. Faced with the inevitable disruption caused by litigation and the potential exposure to awards of compensatory and punitive damages and attorneys fees, employers may allow unsatisfactory performance or unacceptable behavior to persist longer than is desirable or wise before taking the step of terminating employment. Some caution is prudent, of course, and it is certainly necessary to review the circumstances of a proposed termination before executing the decision. However, if an employer has been careful throughout the employment relationship, from hiring to termination, termination without litigation is still possible.

In most states, employment is "at will," meaning either the employer or the employee can terminate the relationship at any time and without notice, for any reason or for practically no reason at all. The right to terminate employment at will is not absolute, however, because that right may have been given up or modified by express or implied contract, and termination of employment in violation of specific laws, such as antidiscrimination statutes, is unlawful.

This chapter outlines the factors and considerations that should be reviewed prior to terminating an employee's employment, the goal being to reduce the risk of claims of breach of contract, discrimination, wrongful discharge, and related causes of action. (This chapter assumes that the employer is a nongovernmental employer with a nonunion work force. Issues particular to public employers or unionized work forces are beyond its scope.)

James E. Wallace, Jr., a partner in the Worcester and Framingham, Massachusetts, law firm of Bowditch & Dewey, is cochair of the firm's Labor and Employment Practice Group and represents management in discrimination and wrongful termination litigation. The writer acknowledges the contributions of Bowditch & Dewey attorneys David M. Felper and Karla J. de Steuben to this chapter.

THE NATURE OF THE EMPLOYMENT RELATIONSHIP

To properly assess whether problems may arise from ending the employment relationship, one must go back to the beginning of that relationship. The consequences of termination may flow from the very formation of the employment relationship.

Whenever termination is being considered, the following checklist should be reviewed.

I. Is there a written contract of employment (or an offer letter)?

    A. Does it specify a term of employment or require cause or notice for termination?

    B. Does it specify grounds for termination?

    C. Is the termination in accordance with the contract?

    D. Is there cause for termination? Does there need to be?

    E. Is termination pay specified?

II. If there is no written contract, is there an enforceable substitute for a written contract?

    A. Oral representations. In most states, a verbal promise of employment for more than one year is not enforceable.[*] But a verbal promise of employment for less than one year may be enforceable under the statute of frauds; likewise, an oral promise of lifetime or permanent employment may be enforceable since the employment could be performed within one year if the employee should die.

        1. Reliance or promissory estoppel. Oral representations of secure or long-term employment, if made to induce acceptance of employment, upon which the employee relies to his or her detriment (e.g., in accepting the offer of employment, the employee relocates or leaves secure employment), may be enforceable even though such promises would otherwise violate the statute of frauds. Thus wild promises or unauthorized offers (e.g., long-term or lifetime employment) must not be permitted. Employers should limit the number of people who are

---

[*] The Massachusetts Statute of Frauds, M.G.L. c.259 §1, is typical: "No action shall be brought. . .upon an agreement that is not to be performed within one year from the making thereof. . .unless the promise, contract or agreement upon which such action is brought, or some memorandum or note thereof, is in writing and signed by the party to be charged therewith or by some person thereunto by him lawfully authorized."

authorized to make offers of employment and ensure that all employees involved in the hiring process are trained.

2. Misrepresentations. Intentionally false statements on which the employee relies to his or her detriment may also be enforced.

B. Written representations.

1. A writing, such as a memorandum, may be sufficient to satisfy the statute of frauds and make what was thought to be an unenforceable verbal promise of long-term employment enforceable.

2. Personnel policy manuals or employee handbooks.

a) In some states handbooks or manuals may be considered implied contracts of employment that limit an employer's right to terminate at will. A court will consider the following factors as evidence that the manual should not be regarded as a contract:

(1) The employer reserves the right to amend or modify the handbook unilaterally.

(2) The handbook states that it is intended only as "guidance" or information.

(3) The handbook contains "at-will" and "no contract" disclaimers (see Appendix 11-A).

(4) The terms of the handbook were not negotiated prior to hiring.

(5) The handbook was distributed to the employee only after commencement of employment.

(6) The handbook was not signed.

(7) The handbook has in fact been amended unilaterally by the employer from time to time.

b) If these factors are not present and the manual is considered a contract, the employer's right to terminate may be limited if the handbook or manual:

(1) Contains representations to terminate only for cause and/or specifies the grounds for termination.

(2) Implies that termination after passing an initial probationary period can only be for cause by emphasizing that employment can be terminated for any reason during the probationary period (or promises "You'll always have a job here as long as you do your job").

(3) Requires notice for termination.

(4) Provides a discipline, grievance, or appeal procedure.

(5) Provides the opportunity to improve poor performance.

In such circumstances, termination of employment without following the policies or procedures spelled out in the handbook might be grounds for a claim of breach of contract by the employee.

3. Past practice may create "expectations" of treatment and an attendant need for justification of departures from that past practice.

PREPARING FOR TERMINATION

Obviously, since the employee was considered qualified enough to be hired, the reason for terminating employment arises during the employment relationship. Termination is usually the result of one of the following circumstances: misconduct, unsatisfactory performance, lack of work and need for a reduction in force, and reorganization or new management. It is rare that an employee is terminated for no reason at all. Whatever the reason, the following guidelines should be kept in mind:

1. Use written performance appraisals or evaluations on at least an annual basis. Be candid and honest in an evaluation, and review it thoroughly with the employee. Provide the employee the opportunity to comment on it, and have him or her acknowledge receipt of it.
2. Establish and apply uniform, progressive disciplinary standards. (But leave flexibility that allows you discretion to deviate when you decide it is appropriate.)
3. If business conditions allow it, afford the employee a reasonable opportunity to correct any deficiency cited in an evaluation before taking adverse action. Be as fair as you can.
4. Ensure that the rules and policies to which you hold employees accountable are reasonably related to legitimate business considerations and needs.
5. Ensure that all such policies are communicated and understood by employees. Reserve the right to amend, abolish, or add to such policies without notice and to deviate from them when you believe it is necessary or desirable.
6. Enforce rules and policies uniformly and consistently, and fully document in writing (with supporting evidence where possible) all violations. Make sure you know and follow your own rules.
7. Establish internal procedures to ensure that all adverse personnel actions, particularly terminations, are fully and fairly investigated. Use internal prob-

lem-solving procedures to give employees "due process." Advise the employee of the nature of the offense and, where appropriate, afford him or her the opportunity to be heard.

8. Use an exit interview to attempt to correct any misconceptions the employee may have about the termination and to uncover and defuse a potentially litigious situation. (You may even elicit an "admission" of misconduct or agreement with the decision.) Be candid about the reason for the termination but do not engage in a debate about the decision.

9. Conduct disciplinary or termination interviews in the presence of another management witness, who should take notes of what is said and done. You should both date and sign the notes. Be courteous and respect your employee as a human being; you'll gain nothing (and may lose much) by being rude or arrogant.

10. A member of senior management should be responsible for reviewing in advance all potential discharge cases to ensure that an offense was actually committed, that it was thoroughly investigated and documented, that all company rules and policies have been followed, that possible claims of discrimination and/or wrongful discharge have been identified and eliminated (see below), that the penalty (termination) is proportional to the offense, and that the penalty is consistent with past practice. (The same review should be done in cases of lesser offenses and discipline and regardless of the reason for termination.)

11. If there are any questions about the appropriateness of any disciplinary or termination decision, get competent legal advice. Your lawyer would rather take part in the decision-making process than read about the decision for the first time in a complaint.

12. Keep the reasons for an employee's discipline or discharge as confidential as possible and only discuss it with those individuals at work who have an absolute need to know of it. Do not make an example of the employee or use him or her to teach a lesson to the other employees. Claims of defamation and invasion of privacy are the inevitable result.

DISCRIMINATION AND WRONGFUL DISCHARGE

Every termination should be scrutinized to answer the following questions:

1. Is there a basis for a claim of discrimination (age, sex, race, color, national origin, sexual orientation, marital status, pregnancy, religion, or handicap), failure to accommodate (religion or disability), or retaliation (e.g., sexual harassment)?[*]

- Is this employee being treated differently from other employees in similar circumstances? If so, why?
- Is there a legitimate, nondiscriminatory reason for termination?
  — Misconduct
  — Poor performance
  — Failure to meet standards
  — Reorganization
  — Reduction in force

Most cases of discrimination are not proved by direct evidence (e.g., a memorandum that states, "Let's terminate all employees over age 65"), because in most cases such direct evidence does not exist. A case of discriminatory termination is usually made out in the following way: The plaintiff (employee) presents evidence that he or she was in a protected category (e.g., black, female, over 40), that he or she was performing at a level that met the defendant's (employer's) legitimate expectations, that he or she was terminated, and that after the termination the defendant sought a replacement or replaced the plaintiff with a person not in the protected category. A plaintiff who presents such evidence makes what is called a prima facie case, and the defendant then must rebut the presumption of discrimination that is created by the prima facie case. The defendant does this by presenting evidence of legitimate nondiscriminatory reasons for the plaintiff's termination. The plaintiff then has the burden of proving that the explanation given by the defendant is pretextual, that is, is not true or is not believable (in other words, is a cover-up for a discriminatory motive). Failure to follow company policy or past practice, inconsistent or contradictory application of policy, and inconsistent or contradictory explanations of the reason for termination (e.g., a sudden finding of unsatisfactory performance when all prior written evaluations indicate excellence) may all be considered evidence of pretext. If the plaintiff convinces the judge or jury that the defendant's explanation is pretextual, the plaintiff wins.

---

*The most frequently invoked federal statutes are Title VII of the Civil Rights Act of 1964 (concerns discrimination on the basis of race, color, sex, religion, national origin, and pregnancy as well as harassment; applies to employers with 15 or more employees); Civil Rights Act of 1966 (42 U.S.C. §1981) (race, national origin; all employers); Age Discrimination in Employment Act of 1967 (age; 20 employees); Americans with Disabilities Act of 1990 (ADA), effective July 26, 1992, as to employers of 25 or more employees and July 26, 1994, as to employers of 15 or more employees; Civil Rights Act of 1991 (effective November 21, 1991, amending Title VII and ADA and adding new 42 U.S.C. §1981A). In addition, most states have antidiscrimination laws that parallel the federal laws.

2. Is there a basis for a claim of breach of the implied covenant of good faith and fair dealing?

   - Is the termination in *bad faith*—without good cause and intended to benefit the company financially at the employee's expense by depriving the employee of compensation earned for past services (e.g., commissions) or by preventing the imminent accrual of benefits (e.g., pension vesting)?
   - Is the termination *unfair*—without good cause and also not in bad faith or with ill motive but with the result that the employee would lose reasonably ascertainable future compensation based on past services?

   If the answer to either question is yes, the decision to terminate should be reconsidered or some monetary compensation should be considered.

3. Is there a basis for a claim that the reason for the discharge is contrary to public policy?

   - Is the employee being terminated for refusing to do something that public policy prohibits (e.g., refusing to commit perjury)?
   - Is the employee being terminated for doing something that public policy favors (e.g., filing a workers' compensation claim, taking time off to serve on a jury, reporting company violations of law [whistleblowing])?

   If the answer to either of these questions is yes, you are headed for trouble.

REDUCTIONS IN FORCE

Reductions in force (RIF) have their own distinctive characteristics and almost always run the risk of provoking claims of age discrimination. In age discrimination litigation, judges and juries must often decide whether the reduction in force was genuine or only a pretext to discriminate against older employees. The answer to that question usually means the difference between winning or losing the case.

Below is a checklist of factors that indicate whether an RIF is genuine or a pretext. If the factors listed in group 2 are present, the RIF may be in the danger zone.

1. Evidence indicating genuineness of an RIF

   - Written analysis of economic conditions necessitating reduction and a written plan to reduce costs by job elimination

- Objective evidence of adverse business conditions
- Exhaustion of alternatives to RIF
  — Attrition
  — Hiring freeze
  — Voluntary early retirement or incentive exit programs
- Objective, written criteria for determining which jobs or functions are to be eliminated
- Written instructions on how to implement the reduction
  — Criteria for selection of specific employees (seniority, qualifications or skills, performance, or evaluations)
  — Review by committee or higher levels of management
  — Documentation of reasons
- Plan showing consideration of impact on protected groups (e.g., statistical profile before and after reduction)

2. Evidence indicating pretext

- Replacement of plaintiff by or delegation of responsibilities to a younger employee of equal or lesser qualifications
- Failure to follow the RIF plan or guidelines
- Failure to follow seniority policies or practices
- Unclear seniority practices or RIF guidelines
- Hiring or job advertising soon after RIF
- Using high salaries as the main reason for selection
- Layoff of employees whose pension vesting is imminent
- Flawed performance evaluation used as the reason for selection
  — Unexplained or undocumented evaluation
  — Inconsistent application of standards or criteria
  — Subjective evaluation
  — Abruptly negative evaluation without prior warning
  — Uncorroborated or contradicted evaluation
- Undue encouragement of older employees to elect early retirement by reference to poor future business prospects, past poor performance, or tenuous future with the company
- Unjustified favorable treatment of younger employees
- Use of code words suggesting age ("youth movement," "deadwood," "young blood," "vigorous and aggressive")

SEXUAL HARASSMENT

Sexual harassment is a violation of Title VII of the Civil Rights Act of 1964 as well as the employment discrimination laws of various states. Sexual harassment occurs when an employee is asked or forced to submit to unwelcome sexual advances, requests for sexual favors, or other verbal or physical conduct of a sexual nature in exchange for some job benefit or to prevent some job benefit from being taken away. This is often referred to as "quid pro quo" sexual harassment. Sexual harassment also occurs when conduct of a sexual nature has the purpose or effect of "unreasonably interfering with an individual's work performance or creating an intimidating, hostile, or offensive working environment." This is often referred to as "hostile environment" sexual harassment.

Most lower courts have held employers strictly liable for quid pro quo sexual harassment engaged in by supervisory personnel regardless of whether the employer knew or should have known of the supervisor's conduct. In hostile environment sexual harassment cases, however, the employee has to show that the employer knew or should have known of the harassment and failed to take proper remedial action.

Sexual harassment may arise in the termination context in a number of ways. The victim, having complained about the harassment and having received no satisfaction from the company, may voluntarily leave employment and claim that she (or he) was constructively terminated because the working conditions were intolerable and she was forced to quit. The victim may be terminated in retaliation either because she resisted the sexual advances or complained about them. Finally, the alleged harasser may be terminated because the company believes the harassment occurred.

To decrease the risk of liability from sexual harassment claims, employers should adopt a specific written policy regarding sexual harassment that states such conduct will not be tolerated and that includes a description of the procedure for reporting and investigating any instances of sexual harassment. Once the policy is adopted, the employer should make sure that employees are aware of its contents by publishing it in handbooks, posting it on bulletin boards, circulating it periodically, and holding training sessions.

The following are the minimum steps for an effective investigation of the sexual harassment complaint:

1. Investigate promptly.
2. Treat complaints seriously and confidentially and discuss only with employees who have a need to know, making sure they understand the need for confidentiality. Stick to the facts and do not leap to conclusions.
3. Interview the complaining party. If the complainant wishes to remain anonymous, advise the complainant that you may not be able to investigate as thor-

oughly as desirable. Assure the complainant of freedom from retaliatory treatment.

4. Confront the alleged harasser, describe the information you have received, and obtain an explanation from that person. Warn against retaliatory treatment of the complainant even if the complaint is ill-founded.

5. Do not simply accept the alleged harasser's denial or explanation. Interview other employees who were or might have been in a position to observe the alleged conduct or aftermath (e.g., the victim crying or distressed), but do not disclose information to them unnecessarily.

6. If the harassment is admitted or substantiated, or if the complainant presents a believable story that the alleged harasser simply denies, take appropriate disciplinary action against the alleged harasser, including written warning, suspension, transfer, or termination if warranted. Respect the privacy rights of the alleged harasser, too.

7. If separation of the two parties is warranted, try not to put the burden of moving on the victim; do not "reward" the alleged harasser.

8. Report to the complainant what action is being taken.

9. Do not fail to investigate even if the complainant declines a formal investigation or withdraws the complaint.

10. Apply the investigation procedure and disciplinary policy consistently from case to case.

11. Document the steps of the investigation.

RELEASES OR WAIVERS

One way to reduce the prospect of litigation resulting from the termination of employment is to have the employee sign a release or waiver of claims. Employees who have signed releases or waivers are less likely to try to avoid the legal effect of that release by bringing litigation. However, in order to be valid and enforceable, a release must comply with the requirements of federal or state law. In particular, to be valid under the Federal Age Discrimination in Employment Act (ADEA), as amended by the Older Workers Benefit Protection Act of 1990, a release must have the following components:

1. The release must be part of an agreement between the employee and the employer that is written in understandable language.

2. The release must specifically refer to rights or claims arising under the ADEA.

3. The release may not waive rights or claims that may arise after the date the release is executed.

4. The release must be in exchange for consideration in addition to anything of value to which the employee is already entitled.

5. The employee must be advised in writing to consult with an attorney before executing the release.

6. The employee must be given at least 21 days to consider the agreement or, if the release is requested in connection with an exit incentive or other employment termination program offered to a group of employees, the employee must be given at least 45 days to consider the release.

7. The release must provide in writing that the employee has 7 days following the execution of the release to revoke the release, and the release may not become effective or enforceable until that 7-day period has expired.

8. If the release is requested in connection with an exit incentive or other group employment termination program, the employer must, at the beginning of the 45-day period mentioned above, inform the individual in writing as to (a) the group of employees covered by such a program and the eligibility factors and any time limits applicable, and (b) the job titles and ages of all employees eligible or selected for the program and the ages of the employees in the same job classification or organizational unit who are not eligible or selected for the program.

If you are not an employer covered by the ADEA (i.e., you have fewer than 20 employees), it is still advisable to structure the release so it complies with the first five requirements listed above. That will ensure its enforceability under most state laws as well.

CONCLUSION

No termination should be carried out without thorough analysis and preparation, and legal advice should be sought if any of the problem areas described above are encountered.

Such analysis and preparation can reduce the risk of claims of defamation, injury to reputation, invasion of privacy, intentional and negligent infliction of emotional distress, intentional interference with advantageous or contractual relations, and negligence (e.g., negligent supervision or evaluation) in addition to claims of breach of contract, discrimination, and wrongful discharge.

Consistency, common sense, caution, courtesy, and care, along with familiarity with the applicable laws, can enable you to achieve a most desirable result: termination without litigation.

Suggested Disclaimer Language

Employment Application

I understand that nothing contained in this employment application or in the granting of an interview is intended to create an employment contract between the Company and myself for either employment or for the providing of any benefit. No promises regarding employment have been made to me, and I understand that no such promise or guarantee is binding upon the Company unless made in writing. I understand that no employer, manager, or other agent of the Company, other than the President of the Company, has any authority to enter into any agreement for employment for any specified period of time, or to make any agreement contrary to the foregoing. Any amendment to the foregoing must be in writing and signed by the President.

I certify that the information contained in this application is correct to the best of my knowledge and understand that concealment or falsification of this information is grounds for dismissal or nonhire. I authorize the references listed above to give you any and all information concerning my previous employment and any pertinent information they may have, personal or otherwise, and I release all parties from all liability for any damage that may result from furnishing same to you. I understand that my employment and compensation can be terminated, with or without cause, and with or without notice, at any time, at the option of either the Company or myself.

Employee Manual or Handbook

The contents of this manual are presented as a matter of information only and as guidance as to the Company's policies and are not to be understood or construed as a promise or contract between the Company and its employees. I understand that my employment and compensation can be terminated, with or without cause, and with or without notice, at any time, at the option of either the Company or myself.

The Company reserves its rights to modify, change, disregard, suspend, add to, or cancel at any time, without written or verbal notice, all or any part of the manual's contents at will, as circumstances may suggest.

Employee Acknowledgment

I have received a copy of the Employee Manual. I understand that any provisions of this Manual may be amended, revised, or cancelled by the Company at any time without notice. I also understand and agree that nothing in this Manual in any way creates an express or implied contract of employment between the Company and me. I also understand that my employment and compensation can be terminated, with or without cause, and with or without notice, at any time, at the option of either the Company or myself.

Chapter 12

Negotiating Managerial Contracts

Seth B. Goldsmith and Robert DeN. Cope

INTRODUCTION

In the 1986 American Hospital Association publication *Evaluation of the Hospital Board and the Chief Executive Officer,* there is a chapter entitled "Contracts for the CEO" that begins as follows: "Until recent years, contracts for the CEO have been a rather rare item."[1]

Although hospital CEOs without a contract may be a rarity, the same cannot be said about nursing home CEOs. This chapter discusses a range of practical contract issues. It begins with a report of the results of a survey that queried administrators about their contracts and the negotiating process, then it describes the central elements that should appear in a contract. It concludes with a description of three alternative approaches to negotiating employment contracts: the power approach, the agent approach, and the principled bargaining approach.

CONTRACT SURVEY

The survey results presented here are based on an exploratory study of the administrator-board contract and negotiation process. Data were collected on 15 employment relationships (involving 13 administrators) from across the country. The questions asked concerned three broad areas: contract formalities, contract terms, and the contracting process.

In terms of contract formalities, of the 15 relationships, only 2 involved formally written contracts, both of which were four pages in length. As regards the remaining 13 relationships, 7 administrators had a piece of paper, usually a short memo or short letter (less than a page) acknowledging the appointment and stating the basic terms of the agreement. In 6 cases there were no written memorials of an agreement.

155

When an employment contract or memo existed, it usually covered the administrator's salary and fringe benefits and occasionally the length of the contract period. Rarely were termination benefits or performance and evaluation standards discussed.

The process of contract negotiation most often involved the administrator initiating the process by contacting several key members of the board. Next some secretive and murky activities occurred at the board level followed by the board effectively telling the administrator what the package would be for the relevant contract period.

The vast majority of respondents had negative feelings about the process, and comments included "I feel like I have to take a token zetz (slap)," "It's like squeezing blood out of a stone," and "We need to do something to take the edge off the negotiations."

Subsequent to collecting and presenting the data at a professional meeting of nursing home administrators, additional observations were offered that suggest some interesting dimensions to this problem of contracts. For example, one distinguished administrator who was five years away from retirement voiced concern about spending 30 years in one job without a contract and being vulnerable to termination by a new board president. A younger administrator, newly hired at a top salary, dismissed these concerns, stating that contracts were merely an impediment to doing a good job.

In summary, the exploratory study indicates that the process is quite variable, many administrators are less than happy with their status (which they perceive to be essentially that of an "employee at will"), but the power relationship precludes them from doing much about their uncomfortable situation.

Under the ideal situation, an administrator would have a formal contract that provides clarity to the employment relationship. The next section describes and discusses the elements of such a contract.

THE ELEMENTS OF AN EXECUTIVE CONTRACT

The executive contract is normally the written memorial of the oral agreement that has been reached between an organization's board of directors (or their appointed representatives) and the CEO. In the best situation, the contract accurately reflects the oral agreement and also becomes an effective mechanism for clarifying ambiguities that arise during the negotiations. Certain elements are of prime importance in CEO contracts. A review of these follows.

The first section of the contract should specify the parties to the agreement. Although this point may appear self-evident, specifying the parties is both a necessity from a legal perspective and a useful reminder that the agreement is between the CEO and the organization, not the CEO and some individual who is sitting as president of the board for a one- or two-year term.

Next there should be a statement of the term of the contract. For example, is this a one-year or multiple-year contract? It is useful to include in the contract the dates of contract renewal and any automatic renewal features.

The next section should be as clear a delineation as possible of the CEO's authority and responsibility. It is also appropriate to note the organizational goals and the role the CEO is to play in meeting the goals. Additionally, this section of the contract should specify who reports to the CEO and to whom the CEO reports. Although some of this information may be contained in a job description or job specification, it is still suggested that this information be restated within the contract.

An exclusivity and best efforts clause should follow in the next section. Such clauses emphasize the bilateral nature of the contract and remind the CEO that he or she is undertaking a full-time commitment to the job. If the agreement is otherwise (e.g., the CEO will be allowed a percentage of his or her time for outside consulting), then this should be stated in the contract, along with any restrictions that may apply.

One section of the contract should be devoted to compensation. The compensation package should be delineated as clearly and thoroughly as possible.

The description of fringe benefits is best not included in the compensation section. If the benefits are exactly those of other employees, then that too should be acknowledged in the contract. More likely, the CEO has a different type of benefit package, and for the sake of mutual understanding that should be specified. Typically, a CEO's benefits include an automobile, health care, vacations, coverage of the costs of professional memberships and attending professional meetings, and contributions to a pension plan.

Life insurance coverage may be a separate item. It is probably unwise for a nursing home to agree to provide a specified amount of coverage for a CEO because of the vagaries of obtaining insurance coverage. The better solution, perhaps from all perspectives, is for the nursing home to agree to contribute up to a specified amount of money per year to be used for life insurance coverage.

The next item that a CEO should have in the contract is an indemnification clause that provides indemnification for any lawsuits that arise from his or her activities as CEO of the nursing home. Such a clause should also contain indemnification for other related expenses, such as attorneys fees.

The CEO must expect that the contract will not be lopsided in his or her favor but will contain quid pro quos. Among the quid pro quos will likely be sections on confidentiality and noncompetition. Here the employer is basically attempting to gain assurance that the confidential information the CEO learns by virtue of his or her position will not go beyond the organization. The CEO should also expect a noncompetition clause. Obviously moving from the CEO position in one home to that of another home in the same competitive market can be damaging to the first home. The protection a home can seek is via a noncompetition clause, although such clauses, if not written with care, may not be enforceable.

The delineation of performance standards and a description of the system of evaluation are also worth incorporating into an employment contract. As indicated by the survey, such items are rarely incorporated into the contracts of nursing home executives. However, by including a section that clearly establishes performance standards as well as the mechanism for periodic evaluation, the board and the CEO are on notice as to what is expected and when it is expected. The inclusion of such a section will go a long way toward mitigating conflicts between the board and CEO.

An increasingly important issue for inclusion in a contract is termination benefits. The contract should specify the different benefits for the different types of termination, including termination for cause, for the convenience of the employer, or by natural circumstances. The items that need to be considered include continuation of salary for a specified time, health insurance coverage, relocation expenses, payments to spouse and family in case of death, outplacement services, and use of the organization's premises for conducting a job search.

Finally, it is suggested that the contract include a clause that deals with the process of resolving disputes. There are a number of options, including mediation and arbitration, but the delineation of the process is useful.

ALTERNATIVE APPROACHES TO THE BARGAINING PROCESS

There are three basic approaches to bargaining. The most prevalent in board–CEO bargaining situations is the *power approach.* This approach is based on perceptions of the negotiators and the power that is engendered by those perceptions. If the board feels that the organization cannot do without the CEO, then the CEO is in the superior position and can make all but the most outrageous demands. It should be noted that the objective validity of the board's perception has no impact on the power relationship. Conversely, the board will be in the superior position if it is prepared to let the administrator resign and the administrator is not prepared to go into the job marketplace.

Because power bargaining is a function of a group or an individual's power at a moment in time, the power relationship has a tendency to shift over time—and also to leave a residue of ill will.

The *agent approach* is favored by the rich and famous but is also applicable to executives, especially at the CEO level. Under this approach, the CEO appoints someone to act as his or her representative in negotiating the contract. Executive recruiters frequently perform this function during the initial placement of an executive but rarely become involved in later contract negotiations. When this does occur, the tension of face-to-face negotiation is diffused, the board can say things to the agent that might be offensive if said directly to the CEO, and the CEO can say things to the agent that are best not said to the board.

The third approach is the *principled bargaining approach,* which is best explicated by Roger Fisher and William Ury in their book *Getting to Yes.*[2] This approach searches for objective criteria, that is, principles for bargaining. For example, the survey discussed at the beginning of the chapter discovered that one administrator had his salary determined by the average salary of the 15 highest paid administrators in his state, and annual increases were also based on the average increases for the 15 highest paid administrators. Other principled positions include setting salary increases as a function of a combination of the annual inflation rate and some incentive, such as the financial position of the organization.

Finally, regardless of the formula selected, the idea is the same: Tie compensation to criteria that are clear, readily understandable, and fair. If principled bargaining is the accepted method, then negotiations take place over the criteria rather than the specific compensation. Principled bargaining is probably a less emotionally loaded and more equitable approach to contract negotiations than power bargaining and has the benefit of putting less stress on the administrator–board relationship.

CONCLUSION

A great deal is at stake in contract negotiations, and it is important to find constructive alternatives to the traditional and often destructive power bargaining approach. Additionally, because so much is at stake, boards and CEOs are well advised to put their agreements into writing. Carefully written contracts provide all parties with a level of clarity and security that all too often is missing in the long-term care industry. Finally, such clarity and security leads to a level of organizational continuity that benefits not only the boards and CEOs but also the residents whose lives and well-being are in their hands.

NOTES

1. R.P. Moses, *Evaluation of the Hospital Board and the Chief Executive Officer* (Chicago: American Hospital Publishing, 1986), 82.
2. R. Fisher and W. Ury, *Getting to Yes: Negotiating Agreement without Giving In* (Boston: Houghton Mifflin, 1981).

Chapter 13

Corporate Reorganization for Nonprofit Nursing Homes

Robert DeN. Cope and Seth B. Goldsmith

A significant percentage of nonprofit nursing homes is presently operating with antiquated legal and organizational structures. By continuing to operate without a structure that is responsive to the likely problems of the 1990s and the first part of the 21st century, nursing homes are placing themselves and their assets at risk. One mechanism by which nursing homes may maximize their ability to deal with a range of emerging problems is corporate reorganization. The final product of this process is the establishment of several corporate entities (i.e., for-profit and nonprofit corporations) that accomplish the various goals of the typical nursing home. This chapter examines the reasons for undergoing a corporate reorganization, the basic steps involved in implementing a reorganization, and some legal aspects of corporate reorganization.

THE OBJECTIVES OF CORPORATE REORGANIZATION

About 15 years ago voluntary hospitals in the United States, in response to the pressures placed upon them by Medicare and Medicaid, started to reorganize. Most often the reorganization involved the transformation of a single charitable [501(c)(3)] hospital entity into at least four separate organizations, which typically included a 501(c)(3) parent acting as a holding company, an operating hospital subsidiary that was also a 501(c)(3) corporation, a 501(c)(3) private foundation, and a for-profit subsidiary. The pressures that were faced by hospitals in those days were not dissimilar to the pressures faced by voluntary nursing homes today.

To begin with, there is the pressure to maximize reimbursement from Medicaid, Medicare, private insurers, and private payers. Maximizing reimbursements requires a provider to include as many allowable costs as possible in its reimbursement formula and simultaneously to be certain that as many income offsets as possible are not in the formula. For example, hospitals learned that gift shop income would offset expense, thus lowering reimbursement. The solution was, at least theoretically, to move the gift shop into a separate corporation. Additionally,

160

in order to avoid the problem of consolidated income and expense statements, it became necessary to move the gift shop into an uncontrolled corporation.

Some may argue that maximizing reimbursement is not a reason for corporate reorganization in voluntary nursing homes because Medicare does not represent a sizable portion of income for most voluntary nursing homes. Further, it may be argued, under many Medicaid systems reimbursement is not likely to be affected by corporate reorganization. There are two responses to the Medicaid assertion. First, some reimbursement systems are indeed responsive to the allocation shifts that will result from corporate reorganization. For example, in some systems profits from a snack bar would be an offset to expenses. But if the snack bar was a separate corporation, no offset would occur and the reimbursement would thus be increased. Second, we suggest that the Medicaid programs are in the process of federalization. In practice, this means that within the next decade the differences presently seen in reimbursement systems will be dramatically narrowed, if not eliminated. Finally, we can expect a nursing home reimbursement system to emerge that closely resembles the Medicare diagnosis-related group system or some other case mix system, such as New York's RUGGS.

A second financial reason for reorganization is to protect assets, in particular, endowment and building funds. Many voluntary nursing homes have sizable funds of this nature that are presently segregated from operating funds only by accounting devices. As states continue to be plagued by fiscal difficulties, they will look to those funds for first-dollar offsets to their own spending for nursing home care. Separation of endowment funds from operations by the establishment of a new subsidiary corporation to provide the nursing home care is one step in the process of protecting assets. Seeking new charitable gifts through an affiliated foundation represents a major step in protecting them from the hands of a financially starved state administration.

Another aspect of asset protection involves isolating assets as a potential way of minimizing their exposure to liability claims. Although nursing homes have not suffered from the same malpractice and other liability problems as hospitals, many interested observers anticipate that one of the consequences of caring for older and sicker residents will be an escalation of claims against homes. In case of a judgment against a home, endowment funds held in a separate corporation may be much better protected than those that are simply in a separate account of the single nursing home corporation.

Revenue diversification is a third and popular reason for considering a corporate reorganization. Often a health care organization develops a particular expertise that has significant independent market value. A charitable provider may find it difficult for a variety of reasons, primarily tax and operational considerations, to take advantage of the resulting opportunities. An affiliate organized as a for-profit subsidiary would potentially be more responsive to these market opportunities. Additionally, the for-profit subsidiary may also avoid numerous government regulations that are intended only for the provider of health care. Avoiding the regulatory scheme allows an organization to be competitive without having to reveal its strategies to rival organizations.

An increasingly important goal of corporate reorganization is to protect the parent organization's 501(c)(3) status. A significant federal interest in this subject is perhaps best indicated by the 1988 article of James J. McGovern, Director of the Internal Revenue Service's Division of Employee Benefits and Exempt Organizations, who stated:

> In 1950, Congress attempted to create rules that would prevent exempt organizations and their subsidiaries from competing unfairly with taxable businesses. Nineteen years later, in 1969, Congress recognized that the problem had not been solved by its 1950 legislation and created additional rules to restrict exempt organizations' use of taxable subsidiaries. Now, once again nineteen years later, Congress may find it necessary to enact yet more legislation attempting to prevent exempt organizations from using taxable subsidiaries to compete unfairly with other taxable businesses. Certainly Congress' concerns in this area are nearly identical to the concerns that Congress expressed in this area prior to enacting legislation in both 1950 and 1969.[1]

A final yet rarely mentioned reason for corporate reorganization is development of additional and focused community support by opening new opportunities for personal service. For example, establishing a foundation may provide opportunities for groups of interested members of the community to become active in fund raising without being involved in the nursing home's operational problems. Conversely, there are always individuals more interested in operational issues than in fund raising.

Assuming that a decision is made to proceed with a corporate reorganization, the next problem is to determine what steps will probably be required to implement the process.

THE PROCESS OF CORPORATE REORGANIZATION

The goal of the corporation reorganization process is to separate purposes and activities through the establishment of new corporations and the shifting of responsibility and authority between them. The steps required to implement the initial decision are, unsurprisingly, tedious, expensive, and crucial. Furthermore, they do not happen overnight. The next sections of this chapter provide an outline of the most important aspects of the reorganization process.

The starting point of a corporate reorganization must be a mission statement— or the answer to the famous question, "What business are we in?" From a corporate perspective, this is the corporate purpose question. From a governance perspective, the important thing is that the answer establishes the basis for all future evaluation of progress and performance. To answer this question, with clarity, is a major and critical step—and critical in the right direction. In the case of Presbyterian-St. Luke's Hospital in Denver, the answer to the question caused the board to sell the hospital system and establish a health care foundation for the mountain region. There are few shortcuts to answering this question. Committees must meet and hash out the answer, and in the process consider the various alternatives, including exiting from the nursing home business.

Assuming that a clear mission statement has been formulated, the next step is the development of a strategic plan. Such a plan must analyze the likely demand for long-term care services. Demand should be examined through population and demographic analyses and research on the market and competition. The strategic planning process should also include forecasts of likely regulatory impediments to change, an evaluation of developments in financing care, an examination of options for revenue enhancement, and an evaluation of the organization's strengths, weaknesses, and future opportunities.

Finally, the board and management of the home will be ready to make a decision about their corporate alternatives. In most cases the home will want to retain the parent organization as a nonprofit entity with several nonprofit subsidiaries and perhaps one for-profit subsidiary. To effect these changes requires a considerable amount of legal activity. The next section describes some of the major legal issues that need to be dealt with before the corporate reorganization is completed.

LEGAL ASPECTS OF CORPORATE REORGANIZATION

Once a decision is made to implement a corporate reorganization, myriad legal activities must take place before the project is completed. Although the scope of this chapter does not permit a thorough examination of all of these activities and issues, following is a review of the two major areas where advice of legal counsel will be required: traditional legal issues associated with the development of corporations and special regulatory issues associated with health care organizations. Legal advice is critical to the success of the governance effort.

Traditional Legal Issues Associated with the Development of Corporations

The end product of a corporate reorganization is the establishment of a system of interrelated for-profit and nonprofit corporations. What is crucial is for the system to be totally integrated and each component corporation to be organized to play its correct part so that the final outcome for the system is better or greater than it would have been had the initial single corporate entity been maintained.

The first and crucial step in the project should be a careful review and analysis of the status of all existing corporate documentation, in particular, the nursing home's corporate charter and bylaws and the evidence of its 501(c)(3) status (e.g., its application to the IRS and the determination letter that resulted). It is absolutely imperative that the organization be certain that it has the power under present documentation to develop the desired corporate structures. If the stated purposes of the corporation or its bylaws preclude the development of subsidiaries or for-profit corporations, or alternatively dictate how such activities should be developed, then it will be necessary to choose between following the prescribed course and amending the existing documents. The IRS review is also crucial because the organization will not want to do anything that might threaten its 501(c)(3) status.

Establishing corporations in every state requires the completion of a number of discreet tasks, such as selecting a corporate name, developing articles of incorporation and bylaws, developing corporate purposes, selecting corporators and directors, developing the "best" governance structure, clarifying which employees will be shifted into which new corporation, deciding on the transfer of assets, capitalization, and so forth. Additionally, if it is desired that any of the new organizations have 501(c)(3) status, it will be necessary to apply to the IRS to establish entitlement to a tax exemption.

Each and every one of these activities is time consuming and those who have gone through the process realize how emotionally loaded each of these decisions can become. For example, in an ongoing reorganization that we are involved with, the CEO and CFO agonized for days over the name of the corporation's for-profit subsidiary. When the word came back from the secretary of state that the name was available and reserved for them, it was almost as if a birth had taken place.

Unfortunately for health care organizations, the process of corporate reorganization may not end with the decision of a governing board, the selection of a model for reorganization, the preparation of the documentation by a lawyer, and the filing of the documents with the state. For most health care organizations, there may also be regulatory problems with such reorganizations.

Special Regulatory Problems

As suggested earlier the tax-exempt status of the parent organization and subsidiary 501(c)(3) corporations should be of paramount concern in a reorganization. The establishment of a for-profit subsidiary is not the signal for private inurement to begin. In light of the IRS's increased scrutiny of charitable corporations, it is particularly important for nonprofit corporations to be careful about the relationships between their various subsidiary corporations and the employees involved with these entities.

A second major issue faced by health care organizations is dealing with the state health bureaucracy. There is no easy way to describe the myriad problems that may be posed by such a reorganization other than to say that each state seems to have its own regulatory hurdles. Some hurdles may be obvious, such as certificate-of-need requirements, but others are less obvious, such as building codes that apply to newly established corporations but not already existing ones. All relevant regulations must be examined and all regulatory issues must be resolved.

Reimbursement is another area of concern. In the best situation, a financial model should be developed that forecasts the implications for the total system of the reorganization. Once a model is developed, it may prove useful to discuss the planned changes with the reimbursement authority to ensure that the new system will not in any way be financially detrimental or introduce unintended consequences.

CONCLUSION

In this chapter we have highlighted some of the important issues involved in corporate reorganization. The process requires a considerable investment of time and energy by a host of people, including management, the board, lawyers, accountants, and sometimes consultants. In our judgment the time has arrived for voluntary nursing homes to position themselves for the future by implementing a corporate reorganization.

NOTE

1. J.J. McGovern, *Tax Notes,* 1988.

Chapter 14

Corporate Reorganization of Nursing Homes: The Administrative Perspective

Howard L. Braverman

These past few years have seen major developments in the long-term care industry. For example, many long-term care facilities have changed from being homes for the aged to being "junior hospitals"—skilled care facilities serving older and sicker clients. Many factors have contributed to this change, factors that have also led organizations to review and reassess their present situation and their outlook for the future.

The aging of America has become a recognized phenomenon. The elderly population is now the fastest growing segment of our society. Since the turn of this century, the total population in this country has tripled, but the elderly population has grown fivefold. By the year 2000, the age 65 and over group will account for almost 20 percent of the population.

One of the factors contributing to this elderly population growth is a substantial increase in life expectancy. People are living longer today than they have at any time in history. The average life span in 1900 was only 47 years; it has dramatically increased to 74 plus today. By the end of the first quarter of the 21st century, the average life span will be approaching 100 years.

Our society has made great strides in improving the quality of life as well as prolonging life. New and better antibiotics have been created, causes of disease have been discovered, and technology has been developed for earlier and better diagnosis. Given that all these advances have occurred in such a short time, it seems impossible not to believe that the future will bring even greater advances in the preservation of life.

Another key factor in the increase in life expectancy has been a societal change in life styles. We have become so much more health conscious. People have stopped smoking and they exercise and watch their weight. They are taking better care of themselves and their bodies.

The aging of our population, coupled with the increase in life expectancy, has had a major effect on the operation of nursing homes. The resident population has changed dramatically, in some ways mimicking what has occurred in the larger community. At the time of the advent of Medicare and Medicaid, the average age of nursing home residents was 67 years. Today the average age is 86 years.

The older resident population is also a more infirm population. Many more residents require one or more skilled nursing services as well as multiple assistance with activities of daily living. This shift in acuity levels is partially the result of the hospital reimbursement system.

In the mid-1980s, Medicare introduced a new prospective payment system for hospitals. This system was based on diagnosis-related groups. In essence, a hospital is paid a set rate according to the patient's particular diagnosis. If the hospital can provide all the care necessary within that rate, it can make a profit. If the care costs more, it loses money. The incentive for the hospital, therefore, is to discharge patients as quickly as possible—usually to a nursing home. As a consequence, nursing facilities are providing levels of care and service that were unheard of 10–15 years ago.

Provision of these levels of service has of course proven costly. To meet the residents' needs, there have been increases in professional licensed and nonlicensed nursing personnel as well as ancillary staff, such as occupational, physical, and speech therapy staff. In addition, there have been increases in the quantities and scope of medical supplies and equipment needed and used. The result has been an ever-rising cost of care.

For most nursing facilities, the primary payer is state government. In Massachusetts, Medicaid accounts for the payment of almost 75 percent of all resident days. Obviously, nursing home reimbursement contributes substantially to the cost of government and so is subject to the economic conditions of the times.

During the last few years, the nursing home industry has been under a great deal of fiscal pressure. The increased costs of doing business have strained the reimbursement system while state tax dollars have dropped as a result of the current recession. The end result has been decreasing reimbursement rates. For Massachusetts nursing facilities, this drop has come via the restructuring of the reimbursement system—from a retrospective to a prospective system that utilizes a case mix methodology based on a management minute questionnaire. For the Jewish Nursing Home of Western Massachusetts, for example, the average weighted per diem in 1991 equaled our 1989 final rate as determined by audit by the rate setting commission.

Another factor threatening the long-term viability of the Jewish Nursing Home is competition. Over the last few years, a number of new nursing homes opened within ten miles of the facility. Also, a number of continuing care retirement communities have been recently built and others have expanded. Because of Medicaid reimbursement regulations, there has also been a restructuring of a number of nursing homes in the area to achieve "non-profit" status, although they continue to operate in a proprietary manner. Hospitals, home care agencies, and other community agencies are expanding their services to meet the needs of the elderly.

PROPOSAL OF REORGANIZATION FOR THE SPRINGFIELD JEWISH HOME FOR THE AGED, INC.

Faced with these changes in its operating environment, the Jewish Nursing Home needed to respond. A corporate reorganization was proposed as the strategy for ensuring the long-term survival of the Home.

The Jewish Nursing Home of Western Massachusetts is a 200-bed skilled nursing facility. It was founded in 1912 as the Daughters of Zion Home by the Rechamo Silverman Organization, a women's service organization. In 1938 it incorporated as the Springfield Jewish Home for the Aged, Inc. when it relocated to larger quarters in Springfield. The corporation was established as a 501(c)(3) not-for-profit corporation under Massachusetts law. Its purpose was stated as follows:

> To establish and maintain a charitable, benevolent, and religious home for aged Hebrews. To cultivate and promote charity, benevolence, morality and social culture among the inmates of the Home for their mutual benefit. To provide medical care and attendance for the inmates. To collect funds and receive subscriptions, donations and bequests with which to maintain the Home, or to promote any of its purposes. To purchase, hold, sell and convey real and personal property suitable to its purposes, and have all other powers and privileges that like charitable institutions enjoy according to law.

The Jewish Nursing Home has traditionally provided a higher level of care and service than other nursing homes. The decision to offer more intensive care was made by the board of directors in response to the expectations of the community. Thus the Home exceeds the minimum standards established by regulation. For example, it employs a full-time physician medical director who also serves as the primary care physician for many of the residents. Nurse staffing levels are maintained in excess of those required of skilled nursing facilities. The result is that the Home operates at a yearly deficit.

In the 1980s, the Home began to expand its service base. Having moved from Springfield to a new state-of-the-art facility in Longmeadow in 1972, the Home, serving as the sponsoring corporation, created a new housing corporation in 1981, Genesis House, Inc. Genesis House pursued, and received, a Section 202/ Section 8 grant from the Department of Housing and Urban Development to construct 48 units of subsidized housing for the well independent elderly. These units were opened in 1984.

That same year, the Jewish Nursing Home's adult day health care program moved into a new facility attached to the existing nursing home. This program had been started eight years earlier under a grant from the Commonwealth of Massachusetts, the first operational program in the state.

The early 1980s also saw the Home enter into an agreement with the Jewish Community Center and Greater Springfield Senior Services to be a provider of kosher meals to a congregant feeding program at the center. The Home provides 115 meals per day to the site, with approximately 50 percent being delivered to the homebound elderly. The program operates five days a week.

By the mid-1980s, the Home had become a geriatric center serving the institutional and noninstitutional needs of the elderly community.

The Home had proved itself to be very efficient and effective at delivering service. As a result, for eight decades the Home had been the focal point for community fund raising. Capital gifts were commonplace. Yearly fund-raising programs enabled the Home to meet its operating deficits and allowed for the growth of the Home's "building fund," a fund within the financial structure of the Springfield Jewish Home for the Aged, Inc.

Though the old way of operating worked well, in this new era of regulation and reduced reimbursement, and with perceived threats to the assets of the corporation, including its building fund, management proposed reorganizing the corporation.

Corporate reorganization is not foreign to the health care industry. In the mid-1970s, hospitals around the country responded to the financial pressures placed upon them by Medicare and Medicaid by reorganizing. The single non-profit 501(c)(3) hospital became a multiple corporate entity, generally a 501(c)(3) parent holding company, a 501(c)(3) operating hospital subsidiary, a 501(c)(3) foundation, and sometimes a for-profit subsidiary. The pressures faced by hospitals then are very similar to the pressures faced by non-profit nursing homes today.

First and foremost is the pressure to maximize reimbursements from all payers, including Medicare and Medicaid. The goal is to see that as many of a facility's costs as possible are in the reimbursement formula and that incomes that offset costs, and hence, lower reimbursement are not. For example, income from the sale of food is a direct offset against the costs of the operation of the department.

In order to meet funding shortfalls, facilities are faced with the pressure of generating greater revenues. Reorganization provides a vehicle for diversification. It enables revenues to be generated by new business ventures—revenues not subject, in many cases, to regulatory oversight or control. It also allows for the protection of an organization's non-profit status by limiting unrelated business income.

Another of the pressures is the need to protect the corporation's endowment or building funds from consideration in the reimbursement formula. As the states struggle with chronic fiscal problems, concern arises that the states might mandate the use of these funds for facility operations, thus reducing their payments.

The corporation gains another advantage by segregating the endowment assets; it minimizes their exposure to liability claims. Though not much of a factor in the past, suits against nursing homes are becoming a greater concern as residents are more informed and their care more complex. A judgment against a nursing home could affect these funds if they are not protected.

On a number of occasions, the issue of reorganization was presented to the board as "food for thought." In many discussions regarding problems or issues, the need for reorganization came to the surface. For instance, Department of Public Health regulations in Massachusetts prohibit nursing homes from having their own in-house pharmacy. Each time the vendor contract was up for discussion, the question whether to start our own would always arise. The usual response was, "We can't. However, if we were to reorganize, perhaps we could start one by leasing nursing home space to a new for-profit corporation that would run a pharmacy." No action was taken on this, as there were always other priorities.

In the spring of 1989, Massachusetts nursing homes were faced with a major challenge. What was once the "Massachusetts Miracle" had come to an end. A recession hit the Commonwealth. Anticipated revenues were down sharply, and the cost of government was rising. State-funded programs were running out of money. In April, the Medicaid program did not have sufficient funds to pay for nursing home services. As a result, facilities were confronted with catastrophic cash flow problems. Some facilities had to petition the Department of Welfare for payment, while others were forced to the marketplace for credit lines and loans. It was at this point that the board of directors formally approved a corporate reorganization.

As with many institutions, it takes a crisis to spur a board to action. The impetus for changing our organizational structure was the perceived threat to our building fund monies. The discussions of the executive committee of the board focused on the possibility that these funds were in jeopardy. The fact that the Department of Public Welfare was taking the position that facilities with reserve funds could utilize those funds as one means of meeting their cash flow deficits supported the committee's fears. It was felt that in the long term the department would take the position that building fund or endowment fund income, and for that matter the funds themselves, should be used as an offset against costs and would hence reduce Medicaid reimbursement rates. The primary goal of our reorganization, therefore, was to separate the building fund monies from the operating accounts of the Home.

Aside from this fundamental goal, the reorganization was also intended to help the organization meet other objectives. One was diversification. The separation of corporations would allow for the creation of new related business ventures that would assist the organization in meeting community needs and generating increased revenues without jeopardizing reimbursements.

The reorganization would also allow the organization to generate additional community support through the new multiple boards. New individuals could be brought onto the operational and fund-raising boards, thereby creating broader community interest and commitment. It would also provide future leadership vital to the success of the corporations.

The first action taken was to engage a law firm. In the course of the initial discussions of the executive board, one of the members of the committee, a past president of the Home, noted that his law firm had recently put together the purchase of a number of area nursing homes for a client and that these facilities were being established as non-profit corporations. As a "service" to the Home, his firm could do the tax work for the Home (i.e., creating the new corporations and filing the IRS tax-exempt applications) at a reduced cost. The remainder of the work (licensure of the nursing home, dealing with Medicaid and Medicare issues, etc.) could then be done by our Boston counsel.

The Home has used a Boston law firm that specializes in health care and rate-setting matters. One of the principals of the firm spent a number of years as an assistant attorney general representing state agencies in health law-related regulatory matters prior to opening the practice and had been retained by the Home in a number of matters it addressed before the Rate Setting Commission. The firm, which has done legal work for the state nursing home associations, also had been legal counsel for a number of hospital reorganizations.

The local law firm assumed the responsibility for restructuring the corporation, taking the role as lead counsel. This was agreed upon by both firms.

To oversee the work of the reorganization, the president of the board of directors appointed a task force, the Board Organization Task Force. This task force consisted of members of the board as well as a number of community volunteers. The task force members were selected carefully so that all factions of the organization were represented.

The first issue to be addressed was the method of restructuring. Two options were presented by the health care attorneys. The first was a "push-up" method, which would allow the existing corporation to remain as the operating entity and would create a new parent entity. The second was a "push-down" method, which would make the existing corporation the parent entity and would create a new subsidiary operating entity.

The recommendation of legal counsel, which was adopted by the board, was to use the push-down method. Using this method, the existing health care corporation divests itself of ownership and operational control of the nursing home and all its activities by "pushing them down" to a new organization. The corporation's existing articles of organization are restated and the bylaws amended to reflect the fact that the corporation will act to support and benefit the nursing home, and any reference to the corporation's ownership or operation of the nursing home or performance of any other health care activities is deleted. This reorganization method allows the building fund or other endowment funds to be maintained by the parent, the original entity. It also provides a holding company with resources available to invest in new ventures or to undertake new projects.

A push-down method is more complex and hence more costly than a push-up method. The primary difference is that, after pushing down activities, the new regulated corporation will have to be licensed, new provider numbers will have to be obtained, and other regulatory approvals will have to be sought and won.

As the push-down method met the primary goal of the board's reorganization decision, the board readily adopted the recommendation of counsel. It was at this time that responsibilities were assigned for the completion of the reorganization.

The health care legal counsel provided a comprehensive checklist of activities that needed to be done to complete the reorganization. This checklist proved to be an excellent tool for the lawyers and also for management. It provided guidance as to those details that needed to be addressed. It outlined necessary actions, structural issues regarding the parent and the subsidiary corporations, necessary approvals, steps to be taken with regard to employees, tax issues to be considered, and operational actions. It also focused on financial and public relations matters.

With tools in hand, work on the reorganization commenced. The first consideration was the structure of the corporations themselves. The existing entity had been a 501(c)(3) non-profit corporation under the Internal Revenue Service Code. It qualified as a 509(a)(2) non-private foundation by the IRS. This designation means that the corporation met one of the IRS tests that would exempt it from the definition of private foundation normally afforded 501(c)(3) corporations.

Section 509(a)(1) excludes from the definition of private foundation, among other entities, publicly supported organizations (i.e., organizations that normally receive at least one-third of their total support in each taxable year from government units, public contributions, or a combination of these sources). Medicare and Medicaid payments constitute gross receipts from the exercise or performance of exempt activities and therefore are not included in the term *support* for purposes of this test.

Section 509(a)(2) sets forth another exemption from the definition of private foundation. To qualify, an organization must meet two support tests: (1) the one-third support test (i.e., the organization normally receives more than one-third of its support in each tax year from any combination of gifts, grants, contributions, and gross receipts from admission or performance of services), and (2) the not more than one-third support test (i.e., the organization normally receives no more than one-third of its support in each year from the sum of gross investment income and the excess of unrelated business taxable income over the tax imposed on such income). Income from activities directly related to the organization's exempt function is included in this section, and thus Medicare and Medicaid income are included.

A third test is set forth in Section 509(a)(3). This section excludes from the definition of private foundation organizations that support publicly supported organizations. To qualify, the organization must be organized and at all times thereafter operate exclusively for the benefit of, to perform the functions of, or to carry out the purposes of one or more publicly supported organizations; the organization must be operated, supervised, or controlled by or in connection with one or more publicly supported organizations; and the organization must not be controlled directly or indirectly by disqualified persons other than foundation managers.

Much discussion ensued regarding under which IRS section should the new corporation apply and what should be the status of the reorganized entity. It was generally recommended by Boston counsel that there be as much separation of corporations as possible. The objective was to establish a corporate structure that would make it especially difficult to "pierce the corporate veil." It was decided, therefore, to establish the parent entity, Jewish Geriatric Services, Inc., as a Section 509(a)(1) non-private foundation and to qualify the new nursing home, Jewish Nursing Home of Western Mass., Inc., under Section 509(a)(2).

The rationale was that as a 509(a)(1) non-private foundation we would be able to establish a more distant relationship between the parent entity and the operating entity. We would qualify as a publicly supported organization, since it was likely a good portion of our support would come from gifts, grants, investment income, and contributions from the public.

With the establishment of the IRS designations, the paper work phase of the reorganization could begin. Applications for incorporation, IRS exemption, and licensure, as well as bylaws and articles of organization, needed to be developed and completed. Local legal counsel was given the responsibility of preparing the application for tax-exempt status under Section 501(c)(3) of the Internal Revenue Code, Form 1023, and its accompanying documents. The Board Organization Task Force was charged with the responsibility of structuring the two corporations and developing their bylaws.

Development of the bylaws was a long and, at times, a controversial process. Board politics was a major factor in the deliberations and the development of the final documents.

At the time the task force was created, the Home's board structure consisted of a board with a membership of approximately 80 individuals that met three times a year. An executive committee, consisting of the officers of the corporation as defined by the bylaws, and the past presidents of the Home (of which seven were active participants), met monthly. The bylaws provided that past presidents would be life members of the board with voting rights, but there were no specific provisions regarding their serving and voting on the executive committee. This group had given many years of service to the Home and remained active and voted on all matters. Because of this, they exerted much influence on the decisions of the board. Two past presidents were members of the task force.

At one of the early meetings of the task force, an orientation was given to the members as to the present structure of the organization and its board. During that session, the subject of the role of the past presidents in the new corporations surfaced. It was the one issue that consistently influenced the decision-making process, and it eventually led to compromising on specific items. The history of the Home had to be taken into account.

To assist the task force in developing the bylaws, local counsel provided a draft of "generic bylaws." These were augmented by the facility's current bylaws as well as copies of bylaws from other homes and other health care organizations that had undergone reorganization in recent years. These documents proved helpful not only in drafting the new bylaws but in educating the members of the task force as to what had been happening in the health care industry. Why reinvent the wheel when there were excellent models to study and guide the group?

There were a number of critical issues in both sets of bylaws that needed to be addressed. The first was membership. In the old structure there was a non-dues-paying group of corporators (an effective way of garnishing community support). The group's sole responsibility was to elect the board of directors. It was decided, therefore, to continue to have a community group for Jewish Geriatric Services. However, this membership group would be dues paying and would thus serve as a new fund-raising source. Its function would also be the election of directors of the corporation. As for the nursing home subsidiary, the sole member of that corporation would be the parent corporation.

The size and organization of the boards themselves were then considered. As mentioned earlier, the board of the original Home was large and cumbersome. There was a feeling on the part of some individuals that their roles as directors were meaningless. They had no responsibilities, yet they were legally and morally accountable for the operation of the Home and the care rendered. As they expressed it, they were tired of just attending "rubber chicken dinners" and doing nothing. The consensus of the members of the task force was that the boards of directors should be smaller and that each board should be empowered to act for its own corporation. It was agreed that each corporation would be governed by an elected board of 18 members. There were also provisions for appropriate ex-officio members.

In establishing this reorganization, it was felt by the task force that there should be a means of coordinating the activities of the corporations. To this end, it decided to have the chairperson and treasurer of each corporation sit as ex-officio members of the other corporation's board along with the senior paid executive of the corporations. It was also considered appropriate to have the medical director of the Home sit as an ex-officio member on the nursing home board and to have the president of the auxiliary sit on the parent board.

Compromise was also necessary on the issue of participation of past presidents on the board of the nursing home. According to one of the past presidents serving on the task force, their long and active participation made them experts and therefore valuable to the Home. Although they did have a great deal of experience to offer, other task force members felt that having all of them on the board would tend to close the board to new individuals with new ideas. As a compromise, it was agreed to have the three most recent past presidents of the Home on the board.

The terms of all board members were fixed in the reorganization. All terms would be for three years, and the maximum of service would be six years. Under the old bylaws, terms were fixed but unlimited. By establishing limited terms, the task force met one of its objectives—creating a structure that would allow for the infusion of new blood into the organization.

One of the past criticisms of the Home by some of its board members was that the structure "locked out" new members and did not allow them into the power structure. Many on the executive committee were sensitive to this criticism and realized it was not in the long-term best interest of the Home to keep out new members. The Home needed closer and stronger ties to the community. The reorganization became a vehicle for opening up access to the power structure.

The task force then focused on the officers of the corporation. The consensus was that the officer corps should also be streamlined. In the current structure there were six vice-president, two secretarial, and two treasurer positions. The individuals filling these positions had titles and no responsibility. Therefore, officer positions in the new corporations were limited.

Members of the task force also recognized that in today's world operating a long-term care facility was more complex than previously. Issues once in the purview of the board needed to be delegated to professional management. They conceived the role of the board to be to set policy, not micromanage operations. Therefore, the officer structure, it was agreed, should be based on the "corporate" model. The board leadership would consist of a chairperson, vice-chairperson, treasurer, and clerk, along with the paid professional who would be president of the corporation. Previously the paid professional served as the executive vice-president of the corporation and administrator of the Home. All officers, except the president, would be included in the total of 18 board members and subject to the relevant terms of service.

The task force recommended that the current paid professional assume the duties of president of both corporations, serving as chief executive officer of the Home and chief operating officer of the parent. Making the president only chief operating officer of the parent was one of the compromises. Although members were willing to give the president the power to operate the Home, there was concern that the president would have too much control if given the position of chief executive of the parent entity. The president did have full voting privileges on both boards.

Terms for officers were also set but were different for the two corporations. The parent corporation's terms were fixed at two years, and an officer could serve no more than two consecutive terms. For the operating entity, terms were one year, with a maximum of two consecutive one-year terms. The rationale for shorter terms for the nursing home officers was to allow for greater community participation and leadership development.

Another area of debate was the makeup of the nominating committee. Under the current bylaws, the nominating committee consisted of all the past presidents of the Home. There was strong sentiment on the part of one of the past president members of the task force that the old structure would benefit the Home. He felt that the past presidents "best understood the needs of the Home." Others on the task force were concerned that keeping the old structure would be detrimental and would not open the Home to others. The past presidents were older and did not know the "future" leaders of the community. After considerable debate, a compromise was reached.

Under the new bylaws, the nominating committee was to become a committee of the parent entity, but with representation from both corporations. It became a committee of the parent because the parent was the sole member of the nursing home and hence elected the Home's directors and officers as well as its own officers. Serving on the committee are two persons appointed by the chairperson of the corporation from among those of its directors who are not current officers and were not past chairpersons of the corporation or its predecessor organizations or the subsidiary, two persons appointed by the chairperson of the subsidiary from among those of its directors who are not current officers and were not past chairpersons, and the three most recent past chairpersons of the parent. The president serves as a non-voting ex-officio member.

The last item addressed in the bylaws was the oversight controls that the parent would exercise over the subsidiary. In deliberations it was determined that there would be limits on capital expenditures by the operating entity. It was arbitrarily set at $5,000 per transaction or in excess of $25,000 on an annual basis. Expenditures in excess required approval by the parent.

The remainder of the committees for each corporation were established to meet the operational needs and purposes of the corporation. There was strong agreement among task force members to limit the number of committees to avoid a bureaucracy and allow maximum participation of directors.

It took approximately eighteen months for the task force to complete the bylaw development process. A final document was agreed upon by the participants and presented to the executive committee for endorsement. At that meeting one of the past presidents on the task force strongly expressed his view that all past presidents should have life tenure on the parent corporation board. The general view of the task force was that these individuals should not be treated like past presidents but should be asked by the nominating committee to serve as directors of the parent for appropriate terms, guaranteeing them at least six more years of service to the organization. At the meeting, the member advocating life tenure motioned to amend the drafted bylaws. A discussion ensued in which all members of the committee had the opportunity to voice their feelings and concerns about the matter. In the end, and in an attempt to get the bylaws finalized and the reorganization completed, the executive committee voted in a split vote to make all past presidents of the corporation and its predecessor corporation voting members of the board of the parent entity for life.

Concurrent with the development of the bylaws was the development of the IRS application for tax-exempt status for the new nursing home corporation. This document could not be submitted without an approved set of bylaws and articles of organization. Thus the delay in completing the bylaws delayed the application submittal. Staff support was provided to the local counsel for completion of Form 1023. Descriptive information as to the scope of services provided by the Home was developed, as were pro forma financial statements for both corporations. Much of this information was also used for the supportive documents for the articles of organization. The key in developing these documents was to make sure the language substantiated a tax-exempt purpose for both corporations.

With the formal approval of the boards of directors of the two corporations of their bylaws and articles of organization (restated for the existing corporation) and the completion of the final application documents, legal counsel filed the necessary documents with the Secretary of State for incorporation of the corporations. This was followed by the submission of the application for tax-exempt status to the IRS.

It was the intention of the board, legal counsels, and auditors to effectuate the reorganization on January 1. This date was chosen because it coincided with the fiscal year of the original corporation and the rate-setting year for Medicaid. Our timing was precarious, as the filing with the Secretary of State was done only a month earlier. Formal incorporation was granted three weeks before the end of the year. This caused a number of problems.

Advice from local counsel was, "Don't do anything until we file and receive the okay from the secretary of state." This did not seem to management to be the best advice. Much needed to be done to finalize the reorganization and guarantee the smooth operation of the Home.

One requirement was to ensure the Home's licensure and recertification for participation in the Medicaid program. This phase of the reorganization was to be handled by the Boston health care counsel.

To begin this process, it was first necessary to submit a Notice of Intent application to acquire the "old" nursing home. The purpose was to allow the State to determine whether the new corporation was deemed suitable and responsible for ownership and licensure of the facility. The Department of Public Health makes this determination by investigating the background of the individuals on the board of directors and assessing the financial capacity of the facility to operate in accordance with state and federal regulations. The determination could only be accomplished after the election of the directors, which was held at a meeting on December 19. We were fortunate to have all the necessary forms signed by the directors and ready for submission at this time and were able to receive notification of suitability dated December 31. The determination of suitability and responsibility was effective for a time period not to exceed 45 calendar days. Health care legal counsel was of great assistance in expediting this process.

Legal counsel and the Department of Public Health together reviewed the nature of the reorganization. The discussions were fruitful and resulted in an opinion from the department that the reorganization did not necessitate a determination-of-need process. If this had not been the case, the reorganization would have been delayed for a substantial period of time, at some cost to the organization.

The next step was to complete the formal application for licensure, which included state license and ownership disclosure forms and other federal applications, such as Medicare and Medicaid applications (HCFA-671) for the continued certification in the Medicare and Medicaid programs and the ownership disclosure statement (HCFA-1513). Management quickly completed the necessary forms for submission. The application required a copy of the articles of organization and a copy of the signed purchase and sale agreement or other legal document showing the applicant had a legal right to the business. Long-term care facility licensure regulations required that the completed license application be filed within 48 hours after the transfer of ownership. A copy of the license application had to accompany the Medicaid application.

The Home faced a major obstacle in the transfer of the real property. The mortgage on the building was held by a consortium of banks. After the incorporation, local counsel approached the lead bank regarding the transfer. A meeting was held with the bank and its legal counsel to review the rationale for the reorganization. Not all of the other five participating financial institutions understood the rationale behind our actions, and repeated attempts were made to meet with them to discuss the matter. Health care counsel drafted for their benefit a comprehensive explanation. To complicate matters, one of the lenders had been taken over by the Resolution Trust Corporation. An effort was made to close the property transfer before the end of the year, but the lack of understanding and the uncertainty on the part of the banks delayed the reorganization into the new year. Local counsel worked effectively with the lenders, educating them about the reorganization and assuring them of the parent corporation's guarantee of the note. After a couple of postponements, the appropriate documents were signed and the transfer of property was completed. This occurred approximately six weeks after the beginning of the fiscal year. With the consent of all parties, documents reflected the January 1 date of transfer.

The Boston counsel played a significant role at this juncture. The lawyers' contacts within the Department of Public Health proved valuable. They were able to negotiate with the department to recognize the actual transfer and the creation of the new nursing home entity as having occurred on the first of the year. Thus we were able to effectuate the reorganization on the date we intended, but with additional costs for legal services.

The delay in filing also caused another major problem regarding the operation of the new corporate structure. On the first of the year we did not have a tax-exempt ID number for the new nursing home corporation. This could not be obtained until receipt of the confirmation of our tax-exempt status from the Internal Revenue Service. Thus the new entity was faced with the potential financial burden of paying sales tax for all purchases.

One of management's responsibilities was the notification of all contractors, vendors, regulatory and accreditation agencies, professional organizations, and others of the reorganization. With the assistance of the Boston counsel, letters were drafted for each category for mailing. Because of the large number of individuals and organizations needing to be notified, temporary clerical assistance was obtained. In the course of this work, management had the opportunity to clean up and reorganize the relevant files.

Management also began an education program for all staff, residents, volunteers, and families. The administrator, as part of his regular meetings with staff, explained the reorganization, emphasizing that it would have a limited effect on employees. They were reassured that they would not lose wages, benefits, or seniority as a result of their transfer to the new nursing home corporation. They were told that the only thing asked of them would be completion of new W-4 and I-9 forms.

The administrator met with the residents' council to explain the reorganization and, through correspondence, informed families and legally responsible parties. Presentations were also made to the board of the Home's auxiliary and a number of community groups.

With the close of the recent fiscal year, the Home's auditors began the final audit of the original nursing home corporation. They needed to complete final cost reports for Medicare and Medicaid as well as final financial statements.

From an administrator's perspective, there were a number of lessons learned in completing our reorganization. Certain mistakes cost the organization in both time and money.

LESSONS LEARNED IN REORGANIZATION

Lesson 1. Use only one law firm. Using two firms is somewhat counterproductive. At times there was a lack of coordination. Management was occasionally caught in the middle between opposing viewpoints. In our situation, the local lawyers were serving as lead counsel and thus we felt we needed to do it their way. However, since they were not familiar with the complexities of regulatory agencies, it may have been more advantageous to have reversed the roles.

Contact with other organizations that have undergone reorganization also indicates that having only one law firm can be beneficial. The process will probably flow more smoothly and be better coordinated, and administrators will consequently feel less burdened.

Lesson 2. Use a law firm with previous experience in health care corporate reorganization. This is a must. Your lawyers should be very familiar with the industry. They need to know the details of federal and state regulatory requirements. It proved helpful to have lawyers who knew whom to contact in both the Department of Public Health and the Department of Public Welfare. It would be wise to interview a number of firms, accept proposals, and make a well-researched and educated decision.

Lesson 3. Plan ahead. The problems we encountered in the transfer of property could have been avoided with a little planning. Advance contact with all the parties could have paved the way for a quicker resolution of the problem. Educating all the lenders and having them as partners in the process would have ensured the timely transfer of all real property.

Lesson 4. Try to keep the politics out of the process. This may prove difficult, but it will facilitate the process. Politics should be avoided in choosing legal counsel, in developing bylaws, and in completing the reorganization. Reorganization is a major step in the life of an organization, and as many unnecessary obstacles should be skirted as possible.

Lesson 5. Have concrete goals for the reorganization. Fortunately, we did. We knew exactly why we were doing it and what we wanted to accomplish. This facilitated discussion and decision making. We had a focus.

Corporate reorganization may not be right for all organizations. It requires a considerable investment of time and energy by the management, the staff, the board, lawyers, and accountants. It is also costly. A reorganization can easily cost approximately thirty to fifty thousand dollars. Therefore, it must fit into the organization's strategic plan. In our case, it has provided us with a direction for the future and has ensured the long-term viability of the nursing home.

Chapter 15

Marketing for the Long-Term Care Organization

Linda J. Shea and Charles D. Schewe

INTRODUCTION

Health care administrators are recognizing the benefits that flow from applying basic marketing principles to health care organizations. As they struggle for long-term survival in this increasingly competitive industry, they are carefully analyzing competitive strengths, weaknesses, and growth opportunities, and they are conducting marketing research and positioning their organizations by zeroing in on target market segments. They are carefully designing promotion strategies to raise awareness and interest in their product-service mix and crafting pricing and other decisions to entice purchase. These, then, are some key activities of strategic marketing planning that administrators of the 1990s are finding essential for maintaining a healthy organization.

As the population continues to age over the next decade, the need for long-term care will increase enormously. Although only about 4 percent of the U.S. population live in institutions at any one time, nearly 25 percent will eventually spend some time in an extended care facility.[1]

The pattern of illness and disease for those over age 65 has altered since the turn of this century. Acute conditions have become less prevalent whereas chronic conditions are more frequent. The leading chronic conditions facing the elderly are arthritis, hypertensive disease, hearing impairments, and heart condition. Also, more hospital visits are for chronic conditions. Heart disease and circulatory difficulties, digestive and respiratory system problems, and cancer are the leading causes of hospitalization among those above age 65. Further, chronic illness is even more pronounced among women, who generally outlive men. Additional pertinent long-term health care facts about our 65-plus market include the following:

- Between 15 and 20 percent of the elderly have serious symptoms of mental illness.
- A full 27 percent of state mental hospital residents are 65 or above.

- Whereas only 15 percent of people aged 65–69 report having difficulty performing one or more personal care activities, this rises to 49 percent for those 85 and above.
- Those 65 and over are hospitalized about twice as frequently as the younger population and stay 50 percent longer.
- The lifetime risk of institutionalization in a nursing home for those at age 65 is estimated at 52 percent for women and 30 percent for men.[2]

As our health care market continues its maturing, the importance of long-term care provision will only heighten. As competitors vie for a share of this growth market, those organizations best meeting the needs and preferences of long-term care consumers by soundly designing and effectively executing marketing plans will be the industry survivors.

This chapter focuses on the key components of a marketing plan. A marketing plan is directed by the overall organization strategy, which is the outcome of the strategic planning process. And that process begins by looking internally and externally to determine the strengths and weaknesses of the health care organization and the opportunities and threats lurking in the environment. The next section provides a description of the marketing concept. This is followed by explanations of (1) the uncontrollable environmental constraints that shape the organization's strategy and marketing activities, (2) the strategic planning process, (3) marketing research, (4) segmentation, and (5) positioning. Finally, the elements of the marketing mix, that unique, company-specific blend of activities that serve the market, are reviewed. These elements (product, price, distribution, and promotion) provide the foundation for guiding long-term health care managers as they make decisions about which services to offer, how to make them available when and where patients need them, and how services should be priced and communicated to current and potential patients.

Effective strategic marketing demands creativity and innovation. Although long-term health care has lagged behind in embracing marketing philosophy and action, many other health care providers have understood the rewards of implementing the practice of marketing. This chapter provides success stories from many corners of health care provision in order to breathe life into the conceptual material and, perhaps more importantly, provide a wealth of ideas for adaptation and adoption by long-term care organizations.

THE MARKETING CONCEPT: FOCUSING ON THE CONSUMER

The marketing concept is a philosophy. It guides the activities of the organization. The marketing concept means identifying consumer needs and wants and developing products and services to satisfy those needs. It realizes that consumers are the lifeblood of the organization; they are its reason for existence. Although the focus is on the consumer, two other elements are required for adoption of the marketing concept. First, the consumer orientation must be accepted and practiced by all members of the organization, not just the marketing department. Second, this marketing orientation must be accomplished while maintaining a profit or achieving nonprofit organizational goals.

The customers of a health care facility are the patients, and patient satisfaction is the primary focus of a marketing strategy. Several needs have been identified. Among those are cures from illness, information and education for self-help therapy and preventive medicine, a place to stay while getting well, and a place to wait while loved ones are helped.[3] Additional concerns for long-term care patients in particular might include comfort, reduction of fears and apprehension, preservation of personal independence, and provision of companionship and care. These additional concerns are examples of psychological *wants*. Often, psychological wants rather than physical needs make the biggest difference in the evaluation of health care facilities because patients cannot perceptually assess the quality of their health care. Recognizing this, one hospital created this motto: "People don't care how much you know until they know how much you care." Northwestern Memorial Hospital in Chicago designed "niceness training" seminars for doctors, nurses, orderlies, and staff. These marketing-oriented sessions encourage such psychological therapy as smiles and even fresh flowers served with dinner.

Identifying needs and wants is at the heart of the marketing plan. The marketing plan involves developing desirable products and services, pricing them according to patient ability and willingness to pay, designing effective promotional programs to gain attention and encourage usage, and making the services available at the right time and place. A review of the marketing environments will guide decision making in the development of a marketing plan.

ENVIRONMENTAL OPPORTUNITIES AND CONSTRAINTS

Truly understanding consumer needs and wants goes beyond knowing those articulated by current and potential health service users. It also requires knowledge about the uncontrollable environments that affect consumers' needs as well as the ongoing operation of health care facilities. Uncontrollable variables include political and legal issues, sociocultural trends, demographic changes, economic conditions, and the competitive environment. The intensity and direction of trends in these external forces must be monitored continuously and carefully and be reflected in the long-term health care provider's marketing plan.

Within the political and legal environment, changes in the Medicare and Medicaid programs, lobbying efforts by the American Association of Retired Persons, and the enactment of legislation regarding euthanasia are examples of events that could have an impact on a marketing program. The consequences of such events will guide changes in treatment and service offerings, pricing strategy, and other marketing decision areas.

Tracking sociocultural trends also provides direction for the marketing plan. One such trend is the increased social value placed on health maintenance and illness prevention over illness cures such as surgery. This emerging want indicates a greater need for such products as health education, self-help treatments, and preventive measures in the long-term care segment. In response, some hospitals offer educational seminars on stress management, clinics to stop smoking, and workshops on managing diabetes. St. Mary-Corwin Regional Center in Pueblo, Colorado, opened the Pueblo Senior Care Center to encourage independent living for the elderly. The program provides seminars on finding transportation, writing wills, handling insurance claims, taking prescription drugs, and getting help for psychosocial needs. The opportunities created by this sociocultural trend seem almost endless.

Demographic changes will continue to have the greatest impact on the marketing of long-term care. Currently, more than 50 million Americans are over age 55. Projections show that by the end of the year 2010, one-fourth of the U.S. population will be at least 55 years old, and one out of seven will be aged 65 or above. Further, by the year 2000, over half of the elderly population will be older than 75 years of age. The increase in the number of Americans above age 65 was ranked number one on a list of the top ten trends in long-term care for the 1990s.[4] To accommodate this trend, a shift is necessary from an acute illness to chronic illness orientation and toward increased ambulatory care for the diagnosis and treatment of elderly patients. Services to promote independent living for the elderly are also needed. Community Medical Center in Toms River, New Jersey, offers several programs for the elderly, including grandparenting classes, book discussion groups, and adult medical day care.

One major economic fact of the 1990s is the lack of federal funding to finance comprehensive long-term care proposals. Further, any recession is accompanied by increased payment difficulties facing older patients. To counteract these payment problems, Central DuPage Hospital in Winfield, Illinois, created the Patient Accounts Volunteer Experience (PAVE) program. PAVE allows patients to pay off delinquent bills by volunteering their services. Typical services include transporting patients in wheelchairs, providing room service, delivering flowers, and performing clerical work. About 600 volunteers contribute 90,000 hours a year.

In addition to national economic trends, hospitals and other care facilities must examine medical trends to predict the economics of future health care. For instance, cancer is expected to affect three out of four families and will account for over 20 percent of health care expenditures in the 1990s. This suggests the need to develop specialized cancer treatment facilities.

The competitive environment often has the most direct and dramatic impact on specific marketing decisions. Analyzing the competition in the long-term care industry will reveal which needs are currently being sufficiently met and which are not. The results will direct the type of health care specialties and services offered, the specific segments served, the location, and the communication and pricing structure.

Although environmental influences are uncontrollable and often viewed as constraints on the marketing activities of an organization, they should instead be regarded as "open windows" of strategic opportunity. During economic recessions, for example, some hospitals have attracted new clients by offering price incentives to cost-conscious patients. Waiving the deductible or offering reduced prices for checking in on weekends for elective surgery are examples. Looking for strategic opportunities is the first step toward developing an overall organizational strategy and ultimately a sound marketing plan.

CREATING THE STRATEGIC MARKETING PLAN

The importance of strategic market planning cannot be overstated. A recent study of 66 hospitals in both the for-profit and nonprofit sectors showed that the 51 with strategic plans had an average total profit margin of 3.16 percent, compared with –1.07 percent for the 15 without strategic plans. Within the for-profit segment, the difference is even more pronounced. For-profit hospitals with strategic plans earned 4.89 percent margins, compared with –6.4 percent for those without plans—and this was regardless of how the plans were implemented.[5]

Strategic planning addresses three questions: Where are we? Where do we want to go? How are we going to get there? The strategic planning process occurs at multiple levels in the organization. The marketing plan represents the implementation of the organizational strategy. The strategy follows the guidelines established as a result of the overall strategic planning process. Thus, the marketing objectives and strategies must be consistent with the objectives and strategies of the organization as a whole.

The first question addressed in the strategic plan suggests a situation analysis. Particular strengths and weaknesses of the health care organization must be identified, and matched with the opportunities and threats recognized in analyzing the environmental factors. Each long-term health care organization must have distinct competencies setting it apart from competitors. In-house data on occupancy rates, the number and type of scheduled surgeries or illnesses, and the composition of patients served may be used to help pinpoint possible strengths and weaknesses. For example, analysis of discharge forms led one Chicago hospital to begin advertising in Spanish to better serve its predominant customer base.

Another method for identifying strengths and weaknesses is through market share analysis. There are standard measures of market share, such as the number of patients served out of the total number or the share of the long-term care dollar, but an institution can look at market share from multiple perspectives. For instance, share can be calculated for several markets: share by geographic area, by type of illness, by pharmaceutical sales, by department, or by demographic group.[6] Analyzing market share with such scrutiny offers an enriched understanding of a long-term institution's strengths, weaknesses, and opportunities for improvement.

The situation analysis lays the foundation for strategic planning. It helps identify the businesses in which the organization competes and the businesses in which it should compete. Next comes establishing objectives. The objectives are based on the fit between the external opportunities and internal strengths or competencies. Objectives provide direction and control. Neither the strategic plan nor the marketing plan can be fully developed or evaluated without them.

Marketing objectives for long-term health care operations must be consistent with overall organizational objectives. Marketing-related objectives might be established with regard to market share, growth, room or bed occupancy, new product or service development, awareness among specific market segments, or image improvement, to name but a few areas. For example, a nursing home might pursue the goal of lowering its resident base, adding an Alzheimer's disease treatment service, or increasing recognition of its name by 3 percentage points among 46- to 60-year-olds, who are often involved in making nursing home decisions for their parents. Specific and measurable objectives guide the long-term care provider's strategic plan and marketing program.

The strategic plan is developed to answer the question of how to reach the objectives or how to compete more effectively. The plan may call for such strategies as market penetration, product and service development, market development, and diversification. For instance, product development focuses on new services offered to the health care provider's present clientele; market development concentrates on attracting previously untapped patient segments.

The marketing plan is the heart of strategy implementation. It specifies actions for carrying out marketing objectives. A marketing plan identifies target markets and the appropriate marketing mix. The remainder of the chapter is devoted to development of the marketing plan. Information gathering provides a solid foundation for marketing planning.

MARKETING RESEARCH FOR HEALTH CARE SERVICES

Marketing research provides information to allow effective marketing decisions. Common methods of information gathering include informal methods, such as experience surveys, secondary research (e.g., scanning published information), and focus groups, and more formal ones, such as observation and survey research.

In an experience survey, experts in the industry are interviewed. Discussions with effective administrators of long-term health care facilities or those with expertise in a related field provide useful insights about common marketing problems. For example, interviews with leading diabetes researchers could offer valuable information and advice to a health care provider exploring the possibility of adding a diabetes treatment program.

Secondary research uses information previously gathered inside and outside the organization. Periodic in-house reports are helpful for pinpointing trends, indicating gaps in the market or in the marketing program, or monitoring changes in the competitive environment requiring a response. For example, one long-term care provider found internal records showed a lack of patients from a nearby suburb. This resulted in a focused advertising campaign to this geographic segment to increase utilization. Reference books, journals, and government documents available in libraries also provide useful data for long-term health care organizations. The *U.S Census of Population* or the local City and County Data Book, for instance, can be used to estimate the size of any geographic or demographic market area for long-term patients. The *Journal of Health Care Marketing, Modern Healthcare's Eldercare Business,* and *Healthcare Marketing Abstracts* are among the publications reporting research in the health care field.

A focus group consisting of a small number of patients, potential patients, or sponsors meeting in a relaxed, informal atmosphere can be used to discuss topics related to extended care. A session may address the issue of fear about nursing homes or perceptions of area facilities. Although focus groups are exploratory in nature, they are easy to arrange, relatively inexpensive, and generally provide abundant information.

The most useful formal research tool for long-term care is the survey. Surveys can be conducted using personal interviews, over the telephone, or through the mail. The most common type in the health care industry is the patient satisfaction survey. Satisfaction levels of current patients can be monitored by asking them to rate the facility along a number of dimensions. Ratings for physicians and staff, administrative procedures, physical surroundings, and additional services reveal the likes and dislikes of patients. The Hanover Healthcare nursing home chain recently added a stock of toys for visiting children in response to suggestions in one of its quarterly surveys of residents and their families. In addition to patient satisfaction surveys, questionnaires can be used to evaluate promotional strategies, determine the best location for a new facility, or estimate the demand for a particular service.

Marketing research is an integral part of planning and is applicable to all phases of marketing strategy development. For effective target market development, attention must be given to the way consumers select health care services and the influences bearing on their decisions.

THE CONSUMER DECISION PROCESS

Who makes the decisions about long-term care—the decision to obtain treatment, the selection of the physician, and the choice of the health care facility? Is the decision maker different from the recipient of these services? What criteria are used in the decision process? Who and what influences these decisions? Answers to these questions are critical.

A general model of the consumer decision process includes five sequential steps:

1. problem recognition
2. information search
3. evaluation of alternatives
4. choice
5. postdecision evaluation

Problem recognition for long-term care most often occurs when an individual is no longer able to care for him- or herself or when the family and friends are no longer able to provide adequate care. It may occur when a disease such as Alzheimer's is initially diagnosed or when the disease reaches a certain point in its progression. Determining the common situations that lead to recognition of the need for long-term care is essential, since they are indicators of when information will be needed and can suggest ways of communicating with potential patients and other key decision makers.

Consumers (potential patients or their sponsors) seek information about extended care from personal sources such as friends, relatives, doctors, and even pharmacists. They can also obtain useful information during on-site visits with a long-term care facility's admissions personnel. Other marketer-dominated sources of information include listings in the yellow pages, brochures, newspaper and magazine advertisements, and television and radio commercials. Finally, some public information sources are available. Two frequently used sources are listings and descriptions of nursing facilities in local senior centers and newspaper articles profiling long-term health care organizations. Providing information to neutral and personal sources will enhance marketplace awareness and improve a health care organization's probability of being considered for selection. To reach elderly consumers in a small suburb of New Orleans, East Jefferson Hospital launched a program to circumvent referring doctors. Its Elder Advantage Program, a membership club, provides elderly consumers with a number of benefits, including physical exams, counseling services to help with health care-related paperwork, and interest-free financing for hospital charges above the insurance coverage amount. The members, over 13,000 of them, pay only $25 for a lifetime membership.

An information search typically results in defining a set of options to consider. The evaluation stage ultimately results in a choice. During this phase, consumers evaluate the options by comparing them against a particular set of criteria. The importance of the criteria varies according to the type of medical care sought.[7] In one study, nursing home resident sponsors indicated that cleanliness, safety, personnel skill, and services available to residents were the primary factors in their selection of a nursing home.[8] Financial aspects and costs, general appearance, and proximity to the sponsor's home were identified as the least important. Interestingly, though, the sponsors reported living within ten miles of the care facility, with the majority located within a five-mile radius. Each institution must determine the key criteria used by its target segments and properly manage the market's perception of how it meets those criteria. This may involve improving the facility, adding new services, or simply communicating better about what already exists.

Once the criteria are weighed and unwanted alternatives are eliminated, a decision is made. The decision to consider long-term care and the search for information is often carried out by the sponsor; however, the final choice decision still primarily rests with the elderly person. Failure by the long-term care provider to resolve the concerns of both parties may result in rejection.

The decision stage is followed by a postdecision evaluation. In this phase, the new resident of the long-term care facility measures perceived quality of service against expectations. If the quality exceeds expectations, the resident is satisfied; if quality fails to meet expectations, dissatisfaction results. This suggests the futility of making promises that cannot be lived up to. Follow-ups with residents and sponsors are useful for monitoring expectation and satisfaction levels. Understanding consumer perceptions is also critical in establishing or changing a positioning strategy.

POSITIONING THE LONG-TERM CARE ORGANIZATION

The "position" of a long-term care organization is determined by how customers perceive the organization and how they differentiate it from other providers. Consumers rely on their image of health care organizations to evaluate health care options. It is important for the organization, then, to create a clear, distinct, unambiguous position that is consistent with the preferences of target consumers. Several positioning approaches are appropriate for the health care business: positioning by attribute, by user group, by usage occasion or type of care, and by dissociation. The following are some examples of these positioning strategies.

Positioning by Attribute or Benefit

The most direct method of positioning is to focus on one or two key attributes or benefits considered most important by potential residents or their sponsors. Communicating an image with slogans such as "Our home is your home" or "Give us the white glove test" keys in on the attributes of a homelike atmosphere and cleanliness that consumers look for in a nursing home.

Positioning by User Group

The American Hospital Association reported that women visit doctors 25 percent more often than men do and account for 63 percent of all surgery. Furthermore, of the 20 most common surgical procedures, 11 of them are performed on women only. In response, Women's Health Centers of America has created a "one-stop body shop" where women can receive total basic care. Each of the dozens of clinics across the country provide everything from mammograms and treatment for osteoporosis to advice on weight control and psychological counseling.

Positioning by Usage Occasion or Type of Care

Doctors' Hospital of Detroit is becoming known as "the place to go for emergency care." An advertisement shown on cable television promised that patients seeking emergency treatment would be seen within 20 minutes or receive free care. Baylor University Medical Center opened the Tom Landry Sports Medicine and Research Center focusing on rehabilitation, research, and fitness.

Positioning by Dissociation

People generally perceive nursing homes as undesirable, "last resort" options. Placement is often accompanied by other traumatic role changes such as widowhood, loss of independence, and loss of control over seemingly trivial matters. It is important, therefore, to develop a position for such an institution that defies those negative images. Emphasizing living with dignity, enjoying some comforts of home, and easing the financial burden all serve to dissociate an extended care facility from its undesirable perception.

Product positions are strengthened through promotion, pricing, and distribution strategies. The particular position an organization chooses to establish is dependent on the consumer segment it targets.

IDENTIFYING HEALTH SERVICES SEGMENTS

Consumers have varying needs; satisfying all potential consumer needs and wants with a single marketing program is virtually impossible. The case for long-term care is no exception. A marketing plan designed to please everyone rarely satisfies anyone. Instead, consumers can be divided into more homogenous sub-groups, along such dimensions as ability to pay, type of illness, or religious preference and a marketing plan developed to meet and satisfy the needs of one or some of these groups. The more well defined the target segments, the more precise and effective will be the marketing plan to reach those consumers.

Potential users of long-term care can be grouped by similarities in demographic characteristics, by physical condition or health need, by psychographic characteristics, or by benefits sought, to name a few. Generally, the most effective and most recommended method for identifying health care market segments is by benefits sought, or "benefit segmentation."[9] Benefit segmentation applied in the health care industry classifies individuals according to their needs and preferences for medical care. In this procedure, consumers provide importance ratings for a list of health care provision characteristics and are then grouped according to which characteristics they rate similarly. One study produced four distinct segments. The first was coined the "take care of me" segment. This group is most concerned about physical comfort during a hospital stay. The "cure me" segment consists of those who count on privacy and a quiet environment. The third was the "pamper me" segment that wants to be cared for, but doesn't want to be bothered by anything else. It also strives for psychological comfort. A fourth group is concerned with medical and administrative proficiency.[10]

Once possible segments are described, specific product, place, price, and promotion decisions can be directed toward meeting their desires. From the previously described segments, for instance, the pamper me group would be most appreciative of decorative bedding, fresh flowers in the room, and a body massage. The fourth segment described, however, is concerned about physician credentials and would prefer convenient parking and itemized billing statements. Advertising one of these sets of services would create a position for the care provider and attract a specific market segment.

THE LONG-TERM CARE "PRODUCT"

While health care is viewed as a service industry, many traditional product concepts in marketing can provide insights useful for effective marketing. Of particular relevance to the long-term health care market are the concept of the total product, branding issues, and product extensions.

The term "total" product refers to a bundle of tangible and intangible attributes providing satisfaction of consumer wants and needs during the entire stay "experience." A long-term health care product is the perception of the tangible (for example, the physical facilities and equipment, the perceived skills of individual doctors and nurses, the food, and opportunity for social interaction) and intangible features (such as the reputation of the provider and the perceived attitudes of personnel). Among the factors rated as extremely important in the selection of a health care provider are (aside from the formal qualifications of a doctor), how well the doctor listens, the willingness to discuss stress issues, and the willingness to discuss treatment alternatives.[11] Furthermore, since most health care consumers believe they lack the competence necessary to evaluate a physician's performance, they rely instead on personality, quality of interaction, and "art-of-care" to judge the quality of treatment.[12]

Any "brand" or name associated with a long-term care center serves to establish or strengthen an organization's position and improve name recognition. Some facilities have adopted brand names denoting specific types of surgery. Dallas-based Republic Health Corporation's hospitals, for instance, use "You're Becoming" (cosmetic surgery), "Gift of Sight" (cataract surgery), and "Step Lively" (podiatric surgery).

Research has shown that the words used to describe the long-term care institution convey meaning to potential residents and their sponsors. In a study where sponsors rated nine different institution titles in terms of desirability and how accurately they describe the function of the nursing home, none of them ranked high on both variables.[13] The name ranked highest in desirability was "extended health care facility." However, it was ranked only fifth in accuracy. The name ranked highest in accuracy was "extended care for the elderly." It was, however, ranked as one of the least desirable titles. "Nursing home" was ranked seventh of the nine in desirability, but second in accuracy. There clearly is considerable potential for improvement in long-term care institution titles.

Creating product line extensions, or expanded services, is another strategy used by health care organizations to distinguish themselves from competitors. For example, United Hospital in St. Paul and the Metropolitan Medical Center in Minneapolis market Nutritious Cuisine, a line of frozen dinners for the elderly. Mt. Sinai Medical Center sells soup under its own name. This, it believes, creates the image of a "warm and soothing" place. The center, located on 5th Avenue in New York, also employs a concierge to greet patients and assist in any special arrangements (such as preparing a conference room for a business meeting) during the patient's stay.

CREATIVE PRICING

Innovative pricing strategies are an effective tool for increasing health care demand and ultimately market share. Health care administrators tend to rely too heavily on cost-oriented pricing. Demand-oriented pricing offers more flexibility and opportunities to attract new customers. This approach recognizes that the value of a product or service is determined by patients' willingness and ability to pay. Although costs are rarely mentioned as the most important consideration in long-term care selection, price incentives can make the difference when choosing among options perceived as otherwise similar.

Several discount and allowance options are available to attract both private-pay and public-assisted patients. Some hospitals are waiving the Medicare deductible for inpatient care of senior citizens. Others are providing interest-free financing for charges not covered by Medicare or other insurance.

Off-peak pricing offsets costly overhead during slow occupancy periods. Sunset Hospital in Las Vegas offers a unique program to increase off-peak use of its services. If patients check in on Friday or Saturday, they are automatically entered in that week's prize drawing for a round-trip "recuperative cruise" to the destination of their choice. In another incentive program, Sunrise Center offered $5^1/_4$ percent rebates on charges for patients checking in on Friday or Saturday. Long-term care occupancy may not fluctuate weekly, but facilities do experience occupancy lulls that could benefit from an off-peak pricing strategy.

Bundling services into packages and offering them at varying prices may be perceived as an attractive alternative to consumers of long-term care. They often feel they are getting a better value by selecting the services and extras important to them and not having to pay for those that are either inappropriate or unwanted. Furthermore, certain packages can be offered to appeal to different clienteles, such as "no frills" and "deluxe" versions of similar services.[14]

Other appropriate pricing strategies include offering cash discounts to private-pay patients who pay in advance or quantity discounts to those who stay for a certain length of time. Finally, for elderly individuals or their families reluctant to make a long-term commitment, the first month's stay could be offered free as a trial period.

APPLYING DISTRIBUTION CONCEPTS TO LONG-TERM CARE

The distribution component of the marketing mix comprises the physical environment (atmospherics) and the distribution or location of services.

Atmospherics

The physical environment plays an important role in the health care selection process. Just as consumers use the retail store atmosphere to judge the quality of its products, research has shown that patients use the quality of the physical surroundings to judge the quality of treatment.[15] To this end, "designer" decorated delivery rooms have been created for the upwardly mobile maternity patient. Pacific Presbyterian Medical Center in San Francisco offers rooms with Jacuzzi baths and a view of the Golden Gate Bridge. The Women's Hospital of Texas provides a limousine service and hors d'oeuvres for its maternity patients. St. Mary's Hospital in West Palm Beach supplies video equipment for taping birthing events. Patients claim some of these fashionable clinics look and feel more like a Ritz Carlton Hotel than a hospital.

In the case of nursing homes specifically, residents want the look and feel of a real domicile; they wish for some similarities to their former homes. A homelike appearance might include increased emphasis on residential as opposed to institutional furniture, wallpapered walls, a pleasant view from the window, and a place to display personal mementos.[16]

A sense of independence and control can also be maintained through thoughtful physical design. For instance, rooms can be designed to facilitate mobility and enhance independence for residents in wheelchairs by lowering closet rods and keeping other items easily accessible.[17]

Residents who are able to exercise some control by making choices on their own will experience greater satisfaction than those feeling completely dependent. Providing space for sitting, allowing room temperature control, accommodating eating preferences (including dining times), and respecting privacy will give residents a sense of autonomy.

Distribution of Services

The location of an institution is an important factor in long-term care. Given the knowledge that sponsors place elders in extended care facilities located near their homes, competition is kept primarily at the local level.

Other location options include bringing the care to the elders or establishing branch facilities for special services. The "Doc in a Box" concept was developed with this in mind. A "Doc in a Box" is a neighborhood center set up by a hospital for cash customers who need quick advice on cuts, colds, and other minor problems that are not viewed as serious enough for an emergency room visit.

Some institutions provide extended care service in elders' homes through the use of visiting nurses until it becomes necessary to transfer them to a permanent facility. The trend toward bringing the "place" to the patient is further evidenced by Meals on Wheels, mobile units for diagnostic testing, and even the return of physician house calls.

COMMUNICATING WITH TARGET MARKETS

The final element of the marketing mix is promotion. The purpose of the promotional strategy is to inform, persuade, and remind consumers of the benefits offered by the organization. The major components of promotion are advertising, publicity, personal selling, and sales promotion. Advertising refers to any paid form of nonpersonal communication from the identified marketer to the customer. Not long ago, advertising in the health industry was perceived as unethical; now it is generally accepted as a legitimate competitive activity. Advertising in the health care industry increased tenfold between 1983 and 1986 (expenditures went from $50 million to $500 million), and it continues to soar. More recent estimates put expenditures as high as $1 billion a year. Television and magazine advertising are useful for reaching large numbers of potential consumers over a wide geographic area, whereas radio and newspaper advertising generally have greater local penetration. Each of these media is heavily used in the health care industry.

The University of Chicago Hospital discovered through marketing research that its staff was not perceived as warm and approachable. Its solution: The hospital's ad agency produced a series of 20-second testimonials from several staff physicians for a television ad campaign. Faith Family Hospital in St. Louis ran profiles of its doctors in newspaper ads. Instead of using staff physicians, the Women's HealthCare and Wellness Center in Oak Park, Illinois, signed up Dorothy Hamill, Ann Jillian, and Rita Moreno as spokespersons to promote its opening.

Publicity, usually in the form of press releases, is the most common type of promotion in the health care industry. Publicity is not paid for by the organization; however, the press releases are not always published and the information is not always positive. One recommended strategy for developing media relations is to write an information column in the local newspaper. Administrators or staff could offer advice on such topics as identifying chronic illnesses or financial preparations for extended care. Information columns increase visibility, are less expensive than advertising, are more likely to be published than a press release, demonstrate social responsibility, and create a positive image.

Exercising another publicity option, the Franciscan Health System of New Jersey created House Calls, a cable television program. Viewers in 1.5 million homes are informed about health matters and the hospital's services. St. Agnes Hospital in Baltimore found another way of building community goodwill and promoting its services. It operates an in-house print shop for use by community organizations who publish newsletters. The service is offered without cost, and the hospital uses the excess space in the newsletters to promote its programs.

Personal selling involves face-to-face communication with the target customer. St. Elizabeth Medical Center in Dayton, Ohio, employs an unusual personal selling technique. It uses the "tupperware party" approach, complete with games, prizes, and refreshments, to inform potential patients of its services. Doctors and nurses conduct the parties in people's homes, providing answers to medical questions in a relaxed, informal atmosphere. This technique seems most appropriate for long-term care; potential residents and sponsors have much to learn.

Personal selling in the extended care facility occurs primarily during the on-site interview. In a study of first impressions in the nursing home interview, sponsors of prospective residents expressed clear preferences for a rather formal look of dress (sport coats rather than suits or sweaters) for facility personnel. The interview should be viewed as a selling opportunity; however, the soft-sell approach is likely to be most successful in this situation.

Sales promotion makes use of a wide array of tools, such as displays, coupons, event sponsorship, price specials, samples, and contests. Long-term care sales promotion opportunities are plentiful. Open houses for the community, special educational events for residents and their families, and sponsorship of local events are all appropriate and useful means of communicating with current and potential residents. Masonic Home and Hospital in Wallingford, Connecticut, caters to its residents' families (a primary referral group) through various programs that bring the residents and family members together. Its Masonic Railroad Club, for example, uses an elaborate model railroad displayed in one of the old wards to appeal to both residents and their grandchildren. The Greenhouse Club offers gardening activities and operates solely on donated plants and flowers. Residents, their families, and members of the community may join to learn more about gardening or just enjoy the attractive displays.

Each of these promotion methods has the potential to create community awareness of a long-term care facility, to communicate benefits and services offered, and to strengthen the facility's position.

CONCLUSION

Creating a marketing plan involves identifying potential consumers and developing a marketing action program. The effectiveness of the marketing plan depends largely on the extent and accuracy of the planning phase. Analyzing the organization's strengths and weaknesses, identifying marketing opportunities, and understanding the uncontrollable environmental factors provide the basis for a sound marketing program. A thorough knowledge of consumers' needs and wants will provide essential assistance in targeting market segments, designing a positioning strategy, developing health service offerings, specifying pricing and distribution strategies, and communicating to consumers the quality of care they can expect.

This chapter presented the basics for establishing a long-term care marketing program. Much more can be done, however, to fine-tune marketing decisions. The long-term care marketer must set up internal controls to monitor the environment, must institute market surveys to gauge resident satisfaction, and must continually evaluate and modify its product, price, place, and promotion strategies. Marketing must be viewed as a process and a philosophy; it is not just something to do but "a way to be."

NOTES

1. R.C. Atchley, *Aging: Continuity and Change* (Belmont, Calif.: Wadsworth Publishing, 1987).

2. For these facts and more, see U.S. Senate Committee on Aging, *Aging in America: Trends and Projections,* 1987–88 ed. (Washington, D.C.: U.S. Government Printing Office, 1988), 96–124.

3. J.A. Miller, Marketing Basics for Hospital Managers, *Hospital Forum* (July-August 1980):7–12.

4. R.C. Coile, Long-Term Care: Top Ten Trends for the 1990s, *Hospital Strategy Report* 3, no. 9 (July 1991):1–5.

5. J. Greene, Hospitals Can Boost Profits by Going According to Plan, *Modern Healthcare* 21, no. 31 (1992):36.

6. S. Majaro, Market Share: Deception or Diagnosis, *Marketing* (March 1977):43–47.

7. J. Boscarino and S.R. Steiber, Hospital Shopping and Consumer Choice, *Journal of Health Care Marketing* 2, no. 2 (1982):15–23.

8. M. Rogers et al., First Impressions: Preferences of Sponsors of Nursing Home Patients in the Search and Interviewing Processes, *Journal of Health Care Marketing* 8, no. 3 (1988):33–41.

9. D.W. Finn and C.W. Lamb, Jr., Hospital Benefit Segmentation, *Journal of Health Care Marketing* 6, no. 4 (1986):26–33.

10. Ibid.

11. D.W. Stewart et al., Information Search and Decision Making in the Selection of Family Health Care, *Journal of Health Care Marketing* 9, no. 2 (1989):29–39.

12. A. Cartwright, *Patients and Their Doctors* (New York: Atherton Press, 1967).

13. M. Rogers et al., First Impressions.

14. J.A. Miller, Marketing Basics for Hospital Managers.

15. P. Kotler and R.N. Clarke, *Marketing for Health Care Organizations* (Englewood Cliffs, N.J.: Prentice-Hall, 1987).

16. W.J. Brown, Tips on How To Plan for the Resident-Oriented Environment, *Provider* (1988):25–28.

17. J. Baker and C.W. Lamb, Jr., The Roles of Physical Environments in Health Care Marketing, paper presented at the Advances in Health Care Research Conference, Jackson Hole, Wyoming, March 1991.

Chapter 16

Marketing a New Project: The Heritage Pointe Experience

Victor L. Klein

Marketing a new project can seem like a formidable undertaking. However, the marketing assignment can be broken down into a series of relatively simple tasks, and acting on these simpler tasks will provide an overall positive approach to the whole marketing activity.

In order to make effective use of this chapter, it may be necessary to do some interpretation and application of market facts and the problems that are particular to the individual market. The general guidelines and suggestions contained in these pages are the result of the author's experience helping to develop a successful marketing program for a new 179-unit nonprofit retirement facility in Mission Viejo, California, together with his 40 years of marketing experience in a variety of fields. The facility, Heritage Pointe, offers independent and assisted living and has continued to meet its projected development goals.

GATHERING THE INFORMATION

A new project is much like a blank sheet of paper, and successfully marketing the project requires knowing as much as possible about the project, the community, and the people the project will serve.

The first step is to determine the size of the market. The library and the county or city government offices will be able to provide a lot of information about the demographics of the market. One objective is to learn what appeals to and what turns off the particular community. It is also important to try and evaluate perceptions held by the community about the project and about long-term care in general. It is always helpful to inspect and survey other similar facilities in the service area. Not only is this kind of research a good source of information about community needs, but it represents a start in the profiling of the competition.

Depending on available resources, it may be worthwhile to commission a professional demographic study to ascertain the need for the project and create prospect profiles. Such a study can also be helpful in determining the perceptions of the area prospects regarding the kind of services the project plans to offer and in projecting the rate of fill-up.

THE TONE OF THE PROJECT

Once all available information has been gathered, the next step is to begin to develop the tone or image of the project. Tone is established and amplified in written and spoken communications about the project and through the project's name, logo, stationery, color scheme, signage, and so forth.

It is often helpful to establish a philosophy statement that describes the types and levels of care to be provided and the market that is targeted. Once this statement is established, those assigned the task of designing logos, choosing furnishings, and so forth, can develop a graphic and verbal identity for the project that is consistent with the overall philosophy. Establishing tone and quality level early in the project's development can assist management and staff in making "close call" decisions on a variety of issues that will affect the success of the project. Naturally budgets are an important consideration, but a clearly defined philosophy can provide solid direction in many instances. It helps to define the corporate culture of the project.

THE MARKETING PLAN

A marketing plan (or marketing schedule) puts on paper the many components of the marketing function. Depending on the level of sophistication and the needs of the project, the marketing plan can be as simple as calendarizing the things to be done or as complex as writing a detailed narrative longer than this chapter. Perhaps the key benefit of a marketing plan is the very exercise of putting it all down on paper, making sure that all areas are covered, and creating a road map that allows timely sales, advertising, and marketing decisions.

Exhibit 16-1 is a six-month marketing schedule initially created for Heritage Pointe as a tool for planning the marketing function. Although many changes were made during implementation, the basic plan provided Heritage Pointe with a pathway to success. Exhibit 16-2 is a sample six-month marketing schedule, and Exhibit 16-3 is a quarterly marketing schedule form.

The easiest way to proceed in creating a marketing plan is to lay out a calendar ending on the intended date of the opening of the facility. Then, depending on the length of time before the opening, a general plan can be drawn up. The schedule for the next 90 days should be as detailed and as specific as possible. Included in

Exhibit 16-1 Six-Month Marketing Schedule Created for Heritage Pointe

MARKETING SCHEDULE FOR: Heritage Pointe

Prepared by: Barbara Kleger
Date: December 8, 1989

Part 1
Monthly

Month	Direct Mailing		Ads (theme)	Publicity	Collateral Materials	Special Events	Staffing		Expectations (net leases) Mo./Cumm.
	External (mass mailing list)	Internal (project lead list)					People	Programs	
1 DEC		• 200+ cover letter for priority applicant & brochure • 350+ project lead list & brochure & postcard • 550 Mazel Tov	• Theme #2 Fancy bldg. on sale (flag now accepting priority applications)		• See attached schedule		• MW & JC	• Telephone survey (move offices)	
2 1990 JAN	• 4000 self-mailer Jewish surname 65+ (same concept as theme #2)	• Review/preview newsletter (print 1000+) (special charter program) Intro M.W. & J.C.	→	• Publicity & networking to be coord. thru "PR agent" • Announ. staff • HP Info Cntr open		• Networking reception	Add • Recept. (1 Sec'y) • Mktg Asst Move-in Coord.	• Start reservation of applic. (mt w/ P.A.) (start cold call on 65+)	
3 FEB		• 600 invitation to private reception • 600 letter—ending Charter Program	• Theme #3 "Why is this Passover different than all other Pass-overs—this year at Heritage Pointe"		• Residency Agreement	• Private reception for applic. prospects?		→	
4 MARCH	• 20,000 purchase/ borrow new mailing list self-mailer same as theme #3	• Invitation letter to Passover brunch at Heritage Pointe		• Ongoing P.R. include events, staff i.e., Passover brunch • Exec. Dir.		• Passover brunch		• Extend Charter	
5 APRIL						• (move-in)		• Begin 1st year prog. (details to be determined)	First residents to move in April
6 MAY						• Grand opening			

P.A. = priority applicants.

Courtesy of Senior Living Associates, Media, Pennsylvania.

Exhibit 16-2 Sample Marketing Schedule

MARKETING SCHEDULE FOR: Sugarland Retirement Community Date: _____ 19____ Part 1 Monthly

Month	Direct Mailing — External (mass mailing list)	Direct Mailing — Internal (project lead list)	Advertising (theme)	Publicity	Collateral Materials	Specials	Staffing — People	Staffing — Programs	Expectations (net leases) Mo./Cumm.
1 JAN	• 10,000 self-mailers "introducing"	• Invite private seminar • "Telegram" invite	• Introducing new concept in rental retirement living	• Groundbreaking announcement • Info. Ctr. open • Mgr. named	• See attached start-up schedule	• Private seminar	1 Mgr. (Sr. Counselor) 1 Retirmt. Counselor 1 Sect./Asst.	• Accept Charter appls. (refundable fee)	
2 FEB		• Newsletter #1 (rental retirement/who involvd)	• Seminar • Thank you	• Seminar • Advisory Board • Staff		• Publicized seminar		• Start processing appls.	(35 appls.)
3 MARCH		• Open house postcard	• Open House (Info. Ctr.)	• Open house	• Welcome pamphlet	• Open house (prior to Easter)		• Select apt. • Sign leases	+5
4 APRIL	• 10,000 self-mailers An alternative to trad. ret. liv. (model open hs)	• Newsletter #2 "progress"	• An alternative to traditional retirement living	• Architect/designer					+8 = 13
5 MAY		• Invitation to model apartment open house	• (Flag Ad for Open House)	• Staff • History	• Visitor's welcome	• Model apt. open house (prior to Memorial Day)	• Move-In Coord.	• Announce ending Charter Program	+7 = 20
6 JUNE		• Letter—Charter Ending	• Our rental program can change your retirement future	• Topping out		• Biweekly on-site luncheons			+8 = 28

Exhibit 16-3 Sample Quarterly Marketing Schedule Form

MARKETING SCHEDULE FOR: _____

Prepared by: Barbara Kleger
Date: _____

Part 2
Quarterly

Quarter	Direct Mailing		Ads (theme)	Publicity	Special Events	Networking /Outreach	Collateral Materials	Telemarketing	Staffing		Expectations (net leases) Mo./Cumm.
	External (mass mailing list)	Internal (project lead list)							People	Programs	
1											
2											
3											
4											

Courtesy of Senior Living Associates, Media, Pennsylvania.

the plan should be advertising, direct mail, telemarketing, sales planning, sales training, special events, follow-up activities, and anticipated results.

A marketing plan is a living document and is constantly changing, being updated, and revised. It is essential to review the marketing plan regularly and make needed adjustments. Reviewing is an excellent way of making sure no opportunity to present the project has been overlooked. It also helps in assessing whether staff are performing as planned. Following is a discussion of some of the components of a marketing plan.

Advertising

Once the overall marketing plan has been devised, the next step is advertising. The first task is to establish a budget. This will determine what types of advertising are affordable. Then come decisions about what to say and where to say it. It is always a good idea to collect ads run by other facilities in the area, carefully analyze what they say, and note where they are run. It is also worthwhile to ask contacts in other areas to collect ads. A file of advertisements run by similar facilities in other markets is a wonderful resource.

It is advisable not to put too much in a single ad. The more that goes into each ad, the more diluted the message. A single ad cannot be expected to tell the entire story of the project. Advertising is designed for one purpose only, and that is to get people to express interest and to seek additional information. The ads should have a call to action—a phone number or a coupon to allow tracking of responses. The ads should be keyed by publication so the results can be compared by publication. It has often been said that over half of advertising is wasted, but there is no telling which half. Using coupons, tabulating responses, and keeping careful records help reduce advertising waste.

When Heritage Pointe began advertising, we used a simple, straightforward announcement approach (see Figure 16-1). We stated what we were offering and included a coupon. We coded each ad so we would have some idea of the effectiveness of the publication and the ad. The main purpose of the advertisement was to generate interest and leads for our sales force to follow up. Since we could not be specific about when people could move in and were not completely sure of the services we would provide, we devised a priority deposit system. Anyone who made a $100 deposit received a priority number, starting with 100. Priority numbers were used for several reasons. First, we wanted to demonstrate to our bankers that there was a need and demand for a nonprofit project like Heritage Pointe. Second, we wanted to establish a fair order to contact prospects as soon as we finalized the details and timing of our services. The system was very successful. We generated over 400 priority deposits in approximately 90 days.

Figure 16-1 Heritage Pointe Announcement Advertisement. *Source:* Courtesy of Heritage Pointe, Mission Viejo, California.

The second ad was designed to answer a community perception that developed early in our fund-raising campaign. That perception was that Heritage Pointe was only for the wealthy. People questioned us about the purchase of such an expensive facility. We developed an ad (Figure 16-2) that used a headline alluding to the perception, and the ad's copy was directed at addressing the community's concerns. This is a good example of how advertising can be used effectively to combat a negative perception. Such perceptions, however, are easily formed and sometimes difficult to dislodge, requiring constant positive reinforcement.

Direct Mail

If the target market, the type of message, and the tone of the facility have been determined, direct mail can be a practical medium of publicity. The most difficult task in a direct mail program is developing or acquiring a good list. Considering the cost of printing and postage, direct mail can be wasteful if not approached properly.

Why Did Heritage Pointe Buy Such A Fancy Building?

Because It Was On Sale.

Heritage Pointe, the first Jewish retirement community in Orange County, represents a unique opportunity for the Jewish Community. For less than the cost of a worn-out, older building, we purchased one of the finest—and the newest—senior housing facilities in California.

Does this mean that Heritage Pointe is only for the rich? Of course not.

Heritage Pointe is for all Jews. As a not-for-profit organization, our fees are as low as possible, and financial assistance will be extended to 30% of the residents.

And as our capital campaign continues to be successful, Heritage Pointe will be able to offer financial assistance to an ever-increasing number of residents.

So what is it like to live at Heritage Pointe? For many seniors, it's the best of all possible worlds. You'll enjoy the privacy of your own spacious apartment, while having dozens of conveniences and recreational facilities right on site.

And only Heritage Pointe gives you the opportunity to enjoy delicious kosher meals in a gracious community dining room, and attend religious services.

Occupancy is planned for Spring, 1990, and so far, the response has been tremendous. After all, when a facility like Heritage Pointe goes on sale, it's too good an opportunity to miss.

Call (714) 364-9685 for more information. Or return the coupon to Heritage Pointe, 27356 Bellogente, Mission Viejo, CA 92691.

Heritage Pointe

Retirement living in the Jewish tradition.

- ☐ Tell me more about Heritage Pointe.
- ☐ Please contact me to make an appointment.

Name _____

Address _____

City _____

State _____ Zip _____

Telephone ( ) _____

SH

Figure 16-2 Heritage Pointe's Second Advertisement. *Source:* Courtesy of Heritage Pointe, Mission Viejo, California.

Naturally the list should contain all prospects—all inquirers and likely customers. Names can be purchased from direct mail organizations, broken down by age, income, and Zip code location. Depending on the size of the list and the mailing budget, the direct mail piece can be as simple as a letter from the facility's president giving the community an update or as elaborate as a colorful brochure plus a cover letter.

It is always wise to include a special offer (e.g., a special introductory charter rate offer) and a call to act now. Perhaps a small gift might be sent if the prospect calls or writes for more information, or special rates might apply if the prospect acts by a certain date. Direct mail is always more effective if done in a series, with an appropriate time interval between mailings. If the list is exceptionally large, it is acceptable to mail a portion of the mailing on one date and follow a week later with the balance.

It is likely that, after a mailing, the phones will *not* "ring off the hook." A response of .5 percent is considered good by professional direct mail companies. The goal is to achieve quality, not necessarily quantity. There is also an additional communications benefit to be derived from good informative direct mail. Such mail can inform the community of the progress of the project. It is usually a good idea to include community leaders, local politicians, the board, and management on the mailing list as a way of keeping them informed.

Direct mail is also useful in targeting a special group for information about the facility. Physicians, health care professionals, and discharge planners in the area could be invited by letter to a special series of tours of the facility. This is a way of developing a relationship with key groups that could be helpful in recommending patients or residents at the proper time.

If direct mail is used, records of responses and the quality or interest of the respondents will be of great assistance in discovering what works in the market and what does not.

Telemarketing

It is important not to overlook the potential of telemarketing, which is marketing by using the telephone. Telemarketing, properly done, is especially effective in dealing with an elderly market, because it can generally reach elders more easily and allows the message to be geared to the respondents' needs. The keys to effective telemarketing are message, delivery, and follow-up.

A staff member who has a good telephone personality and is warm and friendly should place a call to each prospect in a group previously picked out by marketing and sales. The call is a follow-up to find out if there has been a change in the prospect's health or situation. It also allows an update on the progress of the project. Every time there is a significant addition of services, a major change in the project, or the establishment of new dates or timetables, the prospects should be informed. This shows that the organization cares.

It is advisable to dry run the message that the telemarketers will deliver. The calls are both to inform prospects and to gather information useful to the marketing staff. The telemarketers must accurately mark a prospect card indicating change of health or status and when to call again. The follow-up is so important. It lets prospects know that the organization is interested in them, which will pay off when they are ready to make a decision. Telemarketing is not mysterious, but it takes time and a continuing commitment, plus a system to track its effectiveness.

Special Events

A carefully planned series of special events can accomplish much in developing prospects as well as introducing the project to the community. The events do not have to be major productions involving lots of people. They are intended merely to provide a reason for potential customers to come and see what the organization has to offer. As in other forms of communication, decisions regarding the timing, the audience, and the anticipated costs and results must be made.

Special events should be planned regularly and need only include light refreshments. Invitations can be in the form of a letter. It is a good idea to include the local media on the invitation list. Depending on the type of event, the media might well cover it, which would result in some excellent publicity for the project. Inviting the media to special events can also build relationships with reporters. Finally, an invitation might spark interest in a feature story about the project.

Here is a partial list of types of special events worth considering:

- national holiday celebration (e.g., a party held on Presidents' Day)
- appearances by a local dignitary (e.g., a local county commissioner or the city mayor)
- musical events (e.g., a concert or a recital by a local singer or musician)
- religious holiday celebration (e.g., a Christmas or Easter party or a Passover Seder)
- opening of a portion of the facility
- installation ceremony for a major piece of equipment
- groundbreaking or dedication (these events tend to be quite elaborate and require a great deal of careful planning)
- appointment ceremony for key staff
- project "firsts" (e.g., taste the first dessert prepared in the kitchen)

Special events are opportunities to let the imagination run wild. Yet they still require basic planning and execution. And it is also important to track and record how many people were invited, how many attended, what was spent, and what were the results.

Public Relations

Probably the most misunderstood component of any marketing plan is public relations, which is defined by different organizations in various ways. For our purposes, public relations is nonpaid print commentary about the organization, not paid advertising. In promoting a new project, the goal is to ensure that the project is seen in a positive way and that the press knows about it and writes about it in a manner that is in keeping with the organization's objectives. Professional public relations people and agencies are readily available in most markets. Depending on the marketing budget and the perceived public relations needs, it may be desirable to hire a public relations person or use an agency on a retainer basis (so much per month based on the agency's experience, the daily rate, and the type of program needed).

Good public relations is much more than writing and releasing stories, although stories are a very important component. Public relations begins with cultivating a relationship with the various media people that report on similar kinds of projects for newspapers and radio and TV stations. The objective is to get them to think of the organization first when they want information on long-term health care. A good rapport can be established by getting them the information they seek and by being honest and straightforward. After all, they have a job to do and they desire cooperation. They value direct responses to their inquiries and the timely returning of their calls. Information not immediately available should be tracked down and provided later. It is imperative to follow through on promises made to the media. Once an honest rapport is established, the media will be inclined to run newsworthy items supplied to them.

It is extremely helpful to plan public relations opportunities. A list can be made of all the things that are going to happen in connection with the organization in the next 90 days that the community might want to know about. This becomes the public relations release list. This list can be the source of a steady flow of stories about the project. It is a smart idea to reproduce good stories from publications and use the copies as handouts and mailers. Third parties are generally more believable than interested parties. All activities should be covered and releases should go out on even the most insignificant developments. It is important to have a reliable source for follow-up questions and to respect reporters' deadlines. Reporters should be given promised information on time or be told it is not available.

Reporters are pressed for time and cover a lot of stories and subjects. They will only be attracted by stories that are news in their eyes and the eyes of readers, not yours.

A staff member should be assigned to monitor and clip local papers to discover what the media are saying and how they are saying it. A scrapbook of stories about the project will be a useful archive and can become a valuable marketing tool.

SALES AND MARKETING PERSONNEL

After the basics of the marketing plan are in place, or at least have been addressed, careful thought and consideration should be given to the sales staff. All marketing and advertising efforts are aimed at generating leads and getting a sales representative "voice to voice, face to face" with a prospect. How the representative handles this opportunity will make the difference between a move-in and a disappointed prospect. Planning the sales function and selecting, training, and monitoring the sales personnel will lay the foundation for success.

PLANNING THE SALES FUNCTION

The available budget, the hours of business, and the size of the project help determine the number of sales representatives needed. At Heritage Pointe we had decided to be open 9–5 Monday through Friday and all day Sunday. Sunday is a key day because of typical family involvement in making an important decision such as the move to a facility like Heritage Pointe. As a nonprofit Jewish organization, we were closed for business on Saturday. We determined that two full-time sales representatives were needed. These were hired after advertising, screening, and intensive interviews. We looked for warm, sincere people who were interested in seniors and had experience in marketing to the senior market. A classified ad was developed and run in the local papers. (See Exhibit 16–4 for a sample advertisement.)

At the time Heritage Pointe was looking for sales representatives, the responses were good, interviews were established, and we selected two women and hired them. They were the team that successfully launched the project. We compensated the sales representatives with a salary and a commission structure that enabled us to direct their activity, depending on what was needed. In the early stages, we were interested in priority deposits, which were $100 each. The sales representatives were compensated $25 per deposit received. When we moved into the next phase, the priority deposit bonus was dropped. We paid a bonus on signed agreements of lease. We also instituted a graduated move-in bonus scale.

Exhibit 16-4 Classified Advertisement for Sales Manager

SALES MANAGER. Exciting position for self-starter to do personal interviews, tours, telemarketing and rental contracts for area's most prestigious retirement apt. complex. Maturity, self-confidence, and the poise to interact w/sophisticated, well-educated clientele a must. EOE (equal opportunity employer). Resume to:

The combination of salary and estimated bonus roughly equaled the going rate in the area for top-quality sales representatives.

During the priority deposit period, we took possession of the facility and were inundated with people in the community who wanted to tour the facility. We made use of our core of volunteers. We wrote a guided tour package complete with the most commonly asked questions about Heritage Pointe. We held a training session and had volunteers take potential customers on a tour. When the tour guides found a hot prospect, they turned him or her over to a sales representative. This made excellent use of the representatives' time and enabled us to conduct a lot of tours and raise awareness of the project in the community. The volunteers were scheduled from ten o'clock to noon and from two to four o'clock Sunday and Thursday. There were two to a shift, and the program was extremely successful. After several months, the requests for tours diminished and we eliminated the tour guides and used the sales representatives for this function. However, we always had a trained core of tour guides ready for special events to supplement our marketing efforts. Naturally, we publicly acknowledged and thanked our volunteers and made them feel as important as we could. If volunteers are available, they can be used effectively in a variety of areas.

Sales Training

Management plays a key role in the area of sales training. First, it is imperative that management knows what sales representatives are telling prospects. Second, management has the vital responsibility of keeping the sales representatives up to date on changes or modifications. Much of this can be accomplished with a formal sales training program. After the sales representatives have been hired, they should be provided with all printed materials, management communications, advertisements, position papers, and so forth—anything and everything that will help them develop their presentation to prospects. After they have digested the material, a "skull session" with management and sales staff should be held. The sales staff should be asked questions about the project, and their answers should be carefully analyzed for both substance and form. This skull session is of utmost importance because the sales staff are the primary contact with the community, and whatever they say is what prospects will believe and retain.

If possible, it is helpful to use tape and video recording devices to check the sales representatives' information and their presentation.

Regular update sessions with the sales representatives should be scheduled, and they must be on appropriate information distribution lists so they will get the accurate information they need in a timely manner. They must also be on the distribution list for press releases. Press releases give sales representatives a steady stream of "official facts" that are very useful in their sales presentations.

Another tactic is to arrange for an elderly person to visit the project and note the information given. This tactic could become part of a formal motivational program. In the automobile industry, such visitors are called mystery shoppers. Sales representatives who make a good presentation to a mystery shopper might receive a prize or a cash bonus. The variations are endless.

The most important principles for creating an effective sales training program are as follows:

- Make sure sales staff have up-to-date information.
- Make sure that you review what they are saying and how they are answering questions.
- Monitor and check the sales staff.

The Sales System

This is not the right place to recommend a sales system, but it is appropriate to impress upon the reader how important a system is. The system can be informal or it can be quite sophisticated. The basics of a successful sales system are spelled out below. They can be modified, supplemented, or expanded to fit the needs of almost any project or organization.

Registration Card or Book. Registration cards are used to get the names and addresses of visitors and inquirers and other basic information. Everyone in the organization that has contact with the public should use registration cards. They are an excellent source of leads, prospects, and sales.

Prospect Card. After a sales representative makes follow-up contact with someone listed on a registration card or in the registration book, the updated information goes onto a prospect card. In addition to name, address, and phone number, the card should contain plenty of room for comments on the prospect's apparent physical condition and present living situation and the date for follow-up. Prospect cards are the sales representative's most important tool, and they are helpful to management in reviewing the status and history of particular prospects.

Activity Report. The purpose of the activity report is to monitor the total activity of a sales representative and to enable management to direct the representative into areas that need additional attention. The report, which is completed weekly, should contain a record of the following:

- number of calls made (including new and follow-up calls)
- number of facility visits arranged
- number of off-site presentations
- number of on-site presentations
- number of tours given
- number of sales closed (leases, sales written)
- number of move-ins completed
- sales representative comments and suggestions

The sales system will help track what the sales representatives are doing and accomplishing and is a fundamental tool for managing the sales staff.

CONCLUSION

Marketing a new project is similar to marketing any product or service. It is necessary to set the tone, detail the benefits, establish the systems, check and monitor the results, and then check again. Paying attention to the basics is the key to success.

Chapter 17

Clinical Computerization in Long-Term Care Facilities

Deborah L. Roland

INTRODUCTION

The purpose of this chapter is to describe the criteria for computer applications to support and document the resident care process in nursing homes. It aims to inform administrators, nursing directors, and clinical staff of the issues involved in the evaluation and selection of clinical information systems for use in long-term care facilities.

The focus is not technical but managerial. Consequently, the chapter is intended to assist those responsible for managing the resident care process, although it may be useful for computer systems designers and vendors as well.

BACKGROUND

Several factors contribute to the current interest in automated, clinically oriented information systems:

- the pervasiveness of computers in health care organizations, primarily in the administrative and accounting areas
- personal use of computers, if only for word processing, spreadsheets, and small databases
- the volume of resident data that must be collected, documented, processed, communicated, and reported
- the emphasis on resident assessment and care planning, the eventual automation of the Minimum Data Set (MDS), and the potential use for case mix reimbursement

The Omnibus Budget Reconciliation Act of 1987 (OBRA '87) provides much of the impetus for clinical automation in long-term facilities today. This legislation mandates a "comprehensive assessment as the basis for developing a plan of care to assist the resident to attain or maintain the highest practicable physical, mental and psychosocial functioning possible."[1] Nursing facilities are required to conduct a "comprehensive, accurate, standardized, and reproducible assessment"[2] of each resident's functional capacity using a Resident Assessment Instrument (RAI) specified by the state.

Increasingly, clinicians, researchers, government officials, and consumers have raised concerns about the quality of care in some nursing homes. Investigations by federal and state agencies conducted in the 1970s showed that compliance with quality of care regulations varied widely among facilities. In 1984, the courts ruled that the Department of Health and Human Services was responsible for ensuring quality of care for residents. Soon after, Congress funded a study by the Health Care Financing Administration (HCFA) and the Institute of Medicine (IOM) of the National Academy of Sciences to analyze existing regulations and provide recommendations that would help facilities provide satisfactory care.

The HCFA/IOM recommendations to standardize resident assessment were incorporated into OBRA '87. One of the major reforms called for in OBRA '87 was the development of a uniform system to assess each resident's ability to perform daily life functions and to identify significant impairments in each resident's functional capacity. A collaborative effort by HCFA, the Research Triangle Institute (North Carolina), The Hebrew Rehabilitation Center for the Aged (Boston), Brown University (Rhode Island), and the University of Michigan resulted in the development and refinement of the RAI system.

The Resident Assessment Instrument consists of three components:

1. Minimum Data Set (MDS), which consists of a minimum core of assessment items, with definitions and coding categories needed to comprehensively assess a long-term care facility resident
2. Resident Assessment Protocols (RAPs), which provide the problem-identification link between assessment and care planning (RAPS include definitions of "triggered" conditions as well as structured frameworks for organizing assessment information)
3. Utilization Guidelines, which are specified in the state operations manual and explain the use of the MDS and RAPs

Although OBRA '87 mandated the RAI, it allowed states to specify an alternate assessment instrument. For those states participating in the Multistate Nursing Home Case Mix and Quality Demonstration (NHCMQ), a slightly different version of the MDS, MDS+, is used as the resident data collection tool. The MDS+ will be used for both payment classification and quality monitoring. The plus sign after the MDS distinguishes the two forms, which differ in the order of sections and number of items, with the MDS+ having more items.[3] In addition, many states have implemented variations of the MDS to meet reimbursement requirements or address other quality of care issues. The variations in or modifications of the MDS move the industry further away from the original concept of a standardized assessment.

With respect to automation, system developers may label their software as MDS-compliant, but that, by itself, does not guarantee compatibility with the MDS+ or a state-specific MDS instrument. The MDS in one state may not be the MDS in another. Both the forms and the interpretation of compliance requirements differ from state to state. With some states requiring facilities to computerize the MDS, the electronic submission specifications are state-specific as well.

In general, the market for RAI software is embryonic and somewhat fragmented. Many states have implemented variations of the RAI, causing a regionalization of vendors and multiple versions of the systems to meet state-specific requirements.[4]

BARRIERS TO CLINICAL COMPUTER SYSTEMS

To date, many products have not met the needs of the clinical staff, especially the practicing nurses. There are many new, untested systems and companies, and just as many problems as successes. In addition to the problem of truly standardizing the assessment instrument, there are several barriers to overcome before clinical computer systems are widely accepted in long-term care.

One primary barrier to overcome is the lack of computer systems experience within nursing and other clinical departments. Since most nursing schools do not provide computer courses as part of the curriculum, the responsibility of training nursing and clinical staff on computers falls on the facility. Second, the process to select and implement these systems is time consuming. This is especially a problem if the facility is short-staffed. A third barrier is cost. Although computer hardware cost is declining while power is growing, cost remains an obstacle. Connecting every nursing unit or clinical department is expensive. Hardware and software typically are responsible for less than half the total cost. The major costs are people costs—these systems can take months of effort to implement and require ongoing training. The optimistic predictions by vendors of cost and time savings are difficult to achieve. A fourth barrier, user resistance, is decreasing as computer use becomes more widespread at home, in schools, and in the workplace. Users generally are less resistant if they have participated in the entire planning, selection, and implementation process. A major reason for user resistance is often change itself; clinical systems, often by design, attempt to standardize aspects of the resident care management process. There is a fine line between dictating practice and ensuring that the facility's philosophy and standards of care are incorporated into the system. Systems that provide little reward for the effort or add to the workload instead of decreasing it can also lead to user resistance. Sabotage and a failed implementation are often the result.

Despite these barriers, however, facilities are rushing to automate. Pressure is mounting in the entire health care industry to move toward a computerized patient record (CPR). The IOM published a report in 1991 entitled *The Computer-based Patient Record: An Essential Technology for Health Care*. It "advocates the prompt development and implementation of computer-based patient records.... CPRs and CPR systems have a unique potential to improve the care of both individual patients and populations and, concurrently, to reduce waste through continuous quality improvement."[5]

WHY AUTOMATE?

The reasons to automate the resident care process are just as diverse as the systems in the marketplace. Typically, there are four basic objectives, each of which is at a different level in terms of comprehensiveness:

1. *Meet regulatory requirements for electronic submission of assessment data.* The nursing home's objective in this case is to computerize only what must be computerized. OBRA '87 contemplated electronic submission of MDS data, but there is now some question as to whether HCFA will require national submission. However, some states plan to use the MDS+ as the data collection instrument for case mix reimbursement and are already requiring electronic submission.

2. *Link MDS/MDS+ and comprehensive care planning.* This objective builds on the previous one in that the data are collected for electronic submission and linked to resident care planning. An important distinction is that the assessment tool for this objective is the federal- or state-mandated minimum assessment instrument.

3. *Incorporate a facility-defined assessment with comprehensive care planning.* This objective differs from the previous objectives in that the assessment tool is facility- and often discipline-specific. The assessment instrument and resident database are developed using the facility's existing assessment tools and incorporate the federal or state MDS/MDS+ items. At this level, the MDS/MDS+ is the output, not the input. Facilities with this objective recognize that the MDS/MDS+ is "minimum" and prefer to automate the complete assessment of every discipline.

4. *Integrate facility-defined assessment, comprehensive care planning, orders, scheduling, results, and progress notes.* At this level, the objective is a comprehensive resident care system and possibly even an electronic chart.

ELEMENTS OF A RESIDENT CARE MANAGEMENT SYSTEM

The major purpose of implementing an automated resident care information system is to support the resident care process. This process entails activities involving nursing and all clinical staff and includes communication and documentation as well as the ongoing and iterative process of assessment (data collection), diagnosis, establishing desired outcomes, planning interventions, providing care, and evaluating progress.

In 1973, the American Nurses' Association (ANA) established standards of care for nursing practice that are applicable across settings, including long-term care, and all clinical specialties, including the interdisciplinary team. Each of these standards involves the management and interpretation of resident data; thus, there are implications for an automated resident care information system. The standards can serve as a foundation but require some changes in terminology and focus to conform with the intent of OBRA '87. These changes include the following:

- Substitute "resident" for "patient/client."
- Include "quality of life" and "functional status" along with "health status."
- Change "diagnosis" to resident "needs and problems."
- Replace "nursing" with "interdisciplinary team."
- Replace "nursing care plan" with "comprehensive care plan."

The standards, as modified, are as follows:[6]

Standard I. The collection of data about the status of the resident is systematic and continuous. The data are accessible, communicated, and recorded.

Standard II. Resident needs and problems are derived from an assessment of health status, functional status, and quality of life data.

Standard III. The comprehensive care plan includes goals derived from the needs and problems of the resident.

Standard IV. The comprehensive care plan includes the priorities and the prescribed interdisciplinary approaches or measures to achieve the goals derived from the resident needs and problems

Standard V. Interdisciplinary actions provide for resident participation and health and functional status promotion, maintenance, and restoration.

Standard VI. Interdisciplinary actions assist the resident to maximize his or her health capacities, functional status, and quality of life.

Standard VII. The resident's progress or lack of progress toward goal achievement is determined by the resident and the interdisciplinary team.

Standard VIII. The resident's progress or lack of progress toward goal achievement directs reassessment, reordering of priorities, new goal setting, and revision of the comprehensive care plan.

Resident care management systems currently on the market can generally be grouped into the following four categories:

Level 1: MDS/MDS+ Data Collection and Electronic Submission Capabilities. These systems are designed for those facilities that want a system that meets the minimum government regulations for submission. Most of these systems simply collect the data in the state-mandated format for transmission via diskette or over a modem. Some states even provide free software to nursing facilities. The software provides little or nothing in terms of reports, as its main purpose is to collect the raw data for submission to the state.

Level 2: Linkage of MDS/MDS+ Assessment with Comprehensive Care Plans. These systems use the federal MDS/MDS+ or an alternate state assessment instrument and link to a care-planning module. In these systems, the data entry screens follow the items on the federal- or state-mandated assessment form; some allow further information or comments tagged to the MDS item. When the assessment data are entered, the system prints the assessment form, identifies the RAPs that were triggered, and suggests areas for inclusion in the care plan. These systems are designed to meet the requirements for electronic submission and to provide the facility with the capability to automate both the MDS assessment and the care-planning processes.

Level 3: Incorporation of User-Specific Assessments into Comprehensive Care Planning. These systems are designed for increased flexibility in the assessment software module. This dictates a greater responsibility for system setup and ongoing operation by the user. These systems typically require the user to define every assessment item, the valid responses to the question, the order or placement of the questions in the screen flow, and the report formats. The facility, with vendor assistance, needs to ensure that all elements of the MDS/MDS+ or state alternate instrument are incorporated into the assessment module design and that electronic submission requirements are met. These systems have the potential to reduce duplication, as a single assessment entered by every discipline "feeds" the MDS and the comprehensive care plan.

Level 4: Comprehensive Resident Care Information System. These systems automate the entire resident care process, including assessment, care planning, orders, results, schedules, and progress notes. These systems are both communication and documentation systems and are intended to replace much of the paper chart and reduce the time spent relaying resident information between staff. Although some progress has been made toward a computerized resident record, level 4 systems are more of a goal than a reality today.

A system that facilitates the resident care management process should at the very least accommodate the necessary data elements:

- resident demographics
- assessment data
- problems (etiology, risk factors, evidenced by)
- goals or outcomes, with dates for achievement
- discipline-specific interventions
- discipline-specific orders
- progress notes
- resident schedules[7]

The system should be integrated or interfaced with other elements of the resident record. At a minimum, the census information entered at admission, transfer, and discharge should be available to the resident care management system. Other resident data, including medical orders, medications, and lab results, are often automated, but in an entirely different computer. The clinical staff should be able to retrieve this information without looking at another printout or going to another computer terminal or computer system.

The system should eliminate redundant data entry. Demographic data and assessment responses should be carried over to the resident care management system and the care plan. This saves time and minimizes errors. For example, assessment data could also be used to gauge staffing needs, with the MDS as the foundation of an acuity-based staffing system.[8] Even though minimizing duplicative data entry is important, the system should facilitate the assessment, problem identification, and validation process, not *replace* it. For example, problems could be flagged for insertion in the care plan; however, no problems, goals, or interventions should be transferred automatically to the care plan without the clinician's explicit approval.

The system should provide for electronic data transfer to other systems. OBRA '87 planned for electronic transfer of the MDS data by October 1992, but HCFA postponed this schedule. However, some states, especially those planning to use the data for case mix reimbursement or quality assurance studies and survey purposes, are requiring electronic transmission. These states often provide software to the facilities. However, these systems have minimal functionality, and many facilities desire a more comprehensive system that has the capability for electronic transmission in the state-specified format.

The system should be designed to facilitate information retrieval and manipulation for clinical decision making, quality assurance monitoring, and research. Several existing systems were designed only as documentation systems and are capable of printing the assessment form and the care plan only in the format in which it was collected; some are little more than word-processing systems. For uses such as quality assurance, education, staffing, and research, it is necessary to aggregate data for several residents and from the same resident over a period of time. Database systems are more useful for resident care management. For example, retrieval of assessment data should permit identification of all residents with a particular problem, or retrieval of care planning data should permit identification of those for whom a specific intervention was successful. The system should provide the capability for flexible retrieval for the variety of uses that the clinicians may have. Additionally, users of the system should be capable of generating reports and queries without the assistance of a programmer. Most facilities cannot afford a programmer on staff, nor can they afford to wait for the information.

The system should be flexible enough to permit customization of the facility's conceptual framework and vocabulary. Although each facility's approach to the resident care process may be somewhat different, a functional nursing diagnostic category, as opposed to a body system or medical diagnosis approach, is preferred.[9] The development of a facility's standardized nomenclature for problems, goals, and interventions is a prerequisite for any computerized assessment and care planning system. Even though most systems supply a problem-goal-approach "library," review of this database is necessary in order to customize it to the facility's philosophy, standards, policies, procedures, and resources. The federal survey process varies from state to state and surveyor to surveyor, and the level of detail in the care plan reflects both facility-specific and regulatory influences. Examples of key design concepts utilized by systems include these:

- *Cross-reference.* An item in the assessment module is linked to a care-planning problem or problems. For example, a response of "incontinent" to the MDS item on "bowel incontinence self-control" would be linked to the care plan library for (a) skin breakdown potential/actual, (b) bowel/bladder incontinence, and (c) therapeutic diet. Alternatively the RAP trigger, not the actual MDS item, is linked to a care-planning problem.

- *Problem-Goal-Approach Linkage.* In some systems, several goals are linked to the problem independently from the approaches. Other systems use a hierarchy where several approaches are connected to a goal and then several goals (and their associated approaches) are connected to the problem.

- *Problem Definition.* Some systems define problems very narrowly, which results in a large number of problems in the database. Other systems define problems very broadly. Limitations in the problem definition or descriptor field exist because of screen size, report format sizes, and database restrictions and design. For example, one system allows 15 lines of 21 characters for the problem definition, another allows an unlimited number of lines of 30 characters for the problem.

Automated resident care management systems should be more efficient in terms of data entry and retrieval than existing manual methods. While this requirement is a worthwhile objective, it is difficult to achieve. Some facilities that have automated the assessment process have the clinical staff record the MDS on the paper form and then have someone enter the data into the computer. This method increases, not saves, time. Even when the clinicians enter the assessment items directly, poor typing skills can act as a barrier to full and efficient use of the systems. In addition, when only the MDS is automated, the clinical staff continue to complete an additional discipline-specific assessment, which is additional work. Systems need to replace the entire assessment process to achieve efficiencies. Also, alternatives to keyboard entry, such as optical scanners, light pens, touch screens, and mouse and pen devices, should be applied in these settings.

Systems should provide the proper balance of structured data entry and free-form text. Free-form narrative text takes a long time to type, and information retrieval is more costly, less reliable, and may be impossible. To achieve speed of data entry and facilitate retrieval, data should be pre-defined and coded. For example, if there were five approaches that were typically utilized for a specific problem and expected outcome, they should be recorded as menu choices. However, to facilitate customization for a specific resident, it may be desirable to slightly modify one of the five approaches or to add a completely new approach specific to that resident. The challenge is to find a system that prompts the clinical decision maker with valid and appropriate choices without taking away the user's ability to prepare a plan of care unique to the resident.

Data security and integrity take on increased importance in resident care management systems. Systems should be designed to preserve the safety and integrity of the clinical record if the automated record is to be the legal record. The clinical staff needs assurance that the record will be secure and confidential. "Access should be restricted to only those with a need to know and requiring positive identification before access is granted."[10]

Systems need safeguards to protect against unauthorized alterations and deletions. The ability to purge a record from a system should be restricted to select individuals. Alterations should be restricted to those responsible for the data. For example, if the social services department is given responsibility for entering selected items or questions on the MDS, other disciplines should not be permitted to change that data.

The software should also permit updates of the data without destroying the old data. For example, regulations specify that two years of MDS assessments should be maintained in the record; automated systems should be expected to meet or exceed this standard and to display and report assessment responses over time. Similarly, it may be desirable to maintain on-line or archive resident care plans over time. Of course, there are costs associated with maintaining this volume of data; storage requirements could be substantial. Nonetheless, the system must be capable of maintaining more than the current care plan or assessment.

LEARNING FROM THE HOSPITAL AUTOMATION
EXPERIENCE

Computers are everywhere. Today, it is unusual to find a health care facility without at least one personal computer. Traditionally, long-term care facilities have automated the financial applications first, and only recently have they considered computerizing the clinical areas.

This is similar to the path that acute care hospitals have taken—to first computerize the financial areas, then automate the administrative functions in patient care areas such as patient tracking, order processing, and work flow as an extension of cost control. As these management systems are extended to affect work closer to the point of patient care delivery, they are becoming the forerunners of the hospital clinical systems of the future. Ultimately, these systems will allow an all-digital medical record, an electronic chart, displacing the paper version of the patient chart.[11]

However, the use of information technology in hospitals has not been a total success.[12] It is important not to repeat the mistakes in rushing to automate in nursing homes. In *Health Care Computer Systems for the 1990's: Critical Executive Decisions,* Bernie Minard summarizes the issues:

Without a strong management structure to plan and define comprehensive and useful information systems (in acute care hospitals), the systems that evolved were weak and fragmented. Major forces driving changes in use of information technology came from outside institutions, in the form of requirements that were defined by government regulations, reimbursement specifications, external auditors' recommendations, physicians' occasional interests, and vendors' marketing efforts.

Reacting to these forces, hospitals installed diverse islands of automation. Large computers (usually called *mainframe computers)* and small computers (usually called *minicomputers*) became fixtures throughout hospitals. The equipment (*hardware*) and computer programs (*software*) came from many vendors; consequently, operating and usage procedures differed widely among the installed systems.

These differences were due partly to unique departmental requirements, but some may have resulted from selections calculated to facilitate escape from centralized management influence and control within the hospital.

The resulting collection of information systems was often disparate, disappointing, confusing, and almost impossible to manage. Billing systems frequently used separate and different technology from that of the very registration systems that collected raw billing data. Outpatient registration and billing systems were sometimes incompatible with those used in the very similar inpatient registration processes. The institution's financial accounting system and financial reporting system often used separate and different technology from that of its patient billing systems. Computer systems supporting clinical processes and laboratories were almost always distinct and physically removed from those supporting administrative functions. And, although the industry had high hopes for merging administrative and clinical data from several information systems into a computerized medical record that was to be a cost-effective substitute for voluminous paper processing, that promise was not realized.[13]

Several lessons can be learned from the information systems planning mistakes made by hospitals. As in hospitals, clinical information systems are a recent development in long-term care. However, the need for management involvement in planning, selecting, and implementing these systems is not new. A systematic analysis of objectives, gathering information on how to meet them, formulating strategies, and monitoring progress are just as important, if not more important, when selecting a resident care management system.

CENTRALIZED VERSUS DISTRIBUTED APPROACHES

Systems should be designed to provide accessibility, and equipment should be conveniently located. Several different approaches can be utilized for data entry. Some facilities have elected to use a centralized approach for entry of both the assessment and care-planning data. Employing this approach, the individuals responsible for the data entry gather the completed assessment responses from each discipline, enter the data, generate the assessment and care plan reports, and distribute them. Equipment is located in a single location, which could be a clinical department office (e.g., nursing, medical records, etc.), the care-planning team conference room, or data processing. This can be an efficient and cost-effective approach if the only objective is automating the MDS/MDS+ (Level 1) or the MDS/MDS+ and the comprehensive care plans (Level 2).

However, when user-defined assessments (Level 3) or a comprehensive resident management care system (Level 4) is the objective, it becomes more important for the clinicians to enter their own data. With a distributed approach, the equipment is located on the nursing unit and in the other clinical areas (e.g., physical therapy, social services, dietary, etc.). Some facilities choose a portable computer or a hand-held input device. The goal of using a distributed approach is to replace the process of completing a paper form and entering the data in the computer; the staff in each discipline would enter their responses directly into the computer. This hands-on data entry by clinical staff is used more frequently by larger facilities where the assessment and care-planning process is the basis of a more comprehensive resident care system or by smaller facilities where assistance from data entry clerks is not available.

Before deciding if a centralized or distributed approach is best for a facility, it is important to determine what functions the clinical system will encompass and what "level" is desired. For example, for a large facility, a single, centralized location may not be adequate for entering assessments, selecting and editing care plans, scheduling MDS and care plan reviews, entering orders, coordinating team conferences, and printing and distributing all the reports. Alternatively, the ultimate goal may be a distributed approach, but initially it is considered acceptable to enter the data at a central location, in batch. Once all components of the system are operational, the data entry would be distributed to the clinical staff. It is important to outline these objectives before evaluating systems, as several systems are single-user.

CLINICAL AND FINANCIAL SYSTEMS: INTEGRATED OR STAND-ALONE?

All things being equal, a single, integrated clinical and financial system is preferred. Acute care hospitals learned this lesson the hard way when they had to adjust to diagnosis-related groups (DRGs). One database of resident information should be maintained and shared among the various financial, administrative, and clinical modules. At the time the resident is admitted, discharged, on hospital leave, transferred, and so forth, the information would be available to all components of the system. In reality, however, the census component of many nursing home financial systems is not updated on a real-time basis; admission, discharge, and transfers are often not entered until just prior to the billing process. Monthly or weekly entry of census data is inadequate for a clinical system; the resident data must be entered immediately after the census transaction occurs.

In addition, the demographic data kept in many financial systems are very basic and do not include much of the resident-related information desired by the clinical disciplines.

As mentioned previously, nursing homes traditionally implemented financial systems first. As a result of the initial implementation of financial systems, the controller is most often the manager responsible for information systems. When the issue of clinical systems is brought up, this individual may feel uncomfortable selecting and implementing a system that deals with resident care. The information system needs of the accounting department are more concrete, stable, and well defined. Clinical systems are more conceptual, are subject to interpretation by different clinical disciplines, are based on facility-specific philosophies of resident care, and are constantly changing. As a result, some fiscal managers are reluctant to become involved in the selection and implementation of clinical systems.

Due to these factors, many facilities elect to implement a stand-alone clinical system instead of resolving the operational and managerial issues. Duplicative data entry may be a small price to pay for a stand-alone system that may better meet the clinical information needs, especially if the volume of census transactions is small. And if the facility selects a level 1 or level 2 objective instead of wanting a comprehensive resident care information system that affects all departments and all disciplines, then a stand-alone system can be the right choice.

However, in the event that the assessment instrument (MDS+) is ultimately used for Medicare and or Medicaid reimbursement, a single, integrated system will take on increased importance. Although interfacing stand-alone clinical and financial systems is technically feasible, in reality this approach has met with little success. The problems typically arise with the timing of the transfer of data (batch versus on-line, real-time), the comparability of the data between the systems (size, type, and definition of data elements), and the cooperation of the vendors (who are competitors).

VENDOR EVALUATION AND SELECTION

There are more than 60 vendors offering long-term care clinical software. The design, scope, and cost of these systems vary widely and correspond to the differing needs or objectives of the nursing home industry. Still in the early stage of the product life cycle, these systems are evolving and will continue to evolve for some time. It is important to determine which of the four objectives previously described is the objective of the facility and to eliminate the vendors that do not match. The issue of centralized versus distributed data entry and the requirements of integrating or interfacing the clinical system with other systems in the facility must be considered, as must the question of whether a single-user or multi-user system will be necessary. Evaluating these factors early in the selection process will narrow the number of possible vendors to a manageable size.

Several factors should be considered when selecting a resident care management system vendor. Most of the questions that should be asked are the same questions that would be asked of any software vendor. However, some of the items take on increased significance when evaluating clinical systems vendors. These items are discussed below.

Vendor Characteristics

The size of the company, its years in business, and its financial viability are important. Experience with MDS, MDS+, and state-specific instruments is critical. What is the composition of the staff? Do the staff members have long-term care experience? What clinical disciplines are represented on the staff? Are there any physicians, nurses, or pharmacists or just accountants and computer techies? How familiar are staff members with OBRA '87 and other long-term care clinical issues? Is the vendor office conveniently located and can it provide state-specific customer references?

Software Functionality

In addition to the issues of the level or system scope, software capabilities, and data security, an evaluation should be made of the user interface. The software should be easy to learn and use from the clinician's perspective. The automated process of assessment and care planning through recording outcomes should seem intuitive. If the software provides a library of care plans, its depth and breadth should be evaluated. Is it comprehensive? Does it link to the assessment and incorporate the philosophy and terminology of the RAPs and Directives? Can it be customized to reflect the facility's mix of residents, standards of care, and resources? Will the system save time over previous manual methods? Does it have the potential to improve the resident care management process? Will it facilitate truly individualized care plans or make it too easy to produce "canned" care plans? One vendor advertises that its software eliminates human intervention in choosing from possible problems, goals, and approaches. It is important to search for a system that supplements, not substitutes for, the clinician.

Does the system provide prompts or on-line help when the user needs assistance? Can the user modify the database or define reports easily?

Is the software designed to permit multiple users to enter data or access a resident profile simultaneously? Is the system modular? Is the configuration designed to provide accessibility for the clinical staff?

Is the system operational, and exactly which components or modules are in use? If the system is in development, what is the schedule for release, testing, and production? Will the facility be the first user, a "beta site"?

System Support and Maintenance

This factor is related to vendor characteristics, but the focus is on the vendor's capability for service and support. What training is provided? Is it face to face, on-site, or through a videocassette? What are the credentials of the trainers? Does the vendor have a toll-free number for telephone support? What are the hours of operation and do they coincide with when the system will be used at the facility?

What is the policy for upgrades and enhancements? Some states are changing the form periodically as they prepare for the different uses of data for survey and reimbursement. Does the vendor have the financial wherewithal to make major modifications in response to regulatory mandates? Does it have adequate pro-gramming staff to make the changes to ensure timely implementation?

If the state agency reviews, certifies, or licenses vendors, software, or print-outs, has the vendor obtained the necessary approvals? How open is the vendor to enhancements suggested by individual users or user groups? Is there a cost for these changes?

What kind of service and support track record does the vendor have? Are the references comparable in size and complexity to the facility?

Equipment

The software choice will often dictate the hardware. Is it compatible with exist-ing systems and hardware? Is it capable of interfacing with other systems and producing data files that conform to industry-standard file formats? Is a modem required for on-line vendor support or for transmission to the state? Can the sys-tem accommodate the state-required media for submission—8", 5.25", or 3.5" diskettes or 9-track tapes?

Does the vendor write software for IBM personal computers (PCs) and com-patibles? Does it operate under the DOS family of operating systems as single user? Or does it use operating systems that were designed for multi-user, multi-tasking, such as OS/2, UNIX, Xenix, and Novell? These systems can potentially handle multiple tasks and multiple users simultaneously if the software was writ-ten to take advantage of these capabilities. This functionality has been present in mainframe and minicomputer systems for years, but it is a more recent develop-ment in PC-based systems. Just because a system is "network-compatible" does not mean the software makes comprehensive use of networking technology. If networking and multi-user capability are important, consider both minicomputer and PC-based software and request a demonstration of these features.

Are the storage requirements adequate given the data retention requirements? Does the system print data on preprinted, pin-fed forms requiring a dot-matrix printer? Does it print the full form with shading and special fonts, requiring a laser printer? How fast or slow is form printing on a line or dot-matrix printer compared to a laser printer?

Cost

Lastly, it is important to analyze the onetime and ongoing costs for hardware, software, and support. Current systems differ markedly in terms of design concepts and costs, with software prices ranging from "free" to over $100,000. Several years from now they will become more alike, with common features and functions; they will also be priced more alike.

CONCLUSION

The need to manage the resident care process more effectively and efficiently has never been greater. With the nationwide mandate for standardized resident assessment based on a uniform minimum data set, it is not too soon to consider automation, especially since it has the potential to improve the completeness and accuracy of assessments and link the assessments to comprehensive care plans. Indeed, in the states requiring electronic submission for case mix reimbursement, computerization is not optional but required. The challenge is to determine which components of the resident care management process should be automated, to select a system that addresses the relevant needs, and to implement a system that is accepted by both clinicians and administrators.

NOTES

1. J.N. Morris et al., *Resident Assessment Instrument Training Manual and Resource Guide* (Natick, Mass.: Elliot Press, 1991), 1–11.

2. Ibid., 2–3.

3. J.N. Morris et al., *Multistate Nursing Home Case Mix and Quality Demonstration Project Training Manual* (Natick, Mass.: Elliot Press, 1991), 2–6.

4. American Health Care Association (ACHA) and Arthur Andersen, *Computerizing the Resident Assessment Instrument,* Special Report, September 1991, 3A.

5. M.J. Ball, Computer-based Patient Records: The Push Gains Momentum, *Healthcare Informatics* 9 (January 1992):36.

6. R.D. Zielstroff et al., adapted from *Computer Design Criteria for Systems That Support the Nursing Process* (Kansas City: American Nurses' Association, 1988), 3.

7. D.L. Roland and E. Girado, MDS: Foundation for an Automated Clinical Information System, paper delivered at the 30th Annual Meeting of the American Association of Homes for the Aging, San Francisco, November 1991.

8. A. Hegland, Resident Assessment Pinpoints Staffing Needs, *Contemporary Long Term Care* 15 (January 1992):52.

9. L.H. Carpinito, *Handbook of Nursing Diagnosis* (Philadelphia: J.B. Lippincott, 1985), ix.

10. M.J. Ball and M. Collen, *Aspects of the Computer-based Patient Record* (New York: Springer-Verlag, in press).

11. B. Minard, *Health Care Computer Systems for the 1990's: Critical Executive Decisions* (Ann Arbor, Mich.: Health Administration Press, 1991), 5–6.

12. J.A. Worthley and P.S. DiSalvio, *Managing Computers in Health Care* (Ann Arbor, Mich.: Health Administration Press, 1989), 4–10.

13. B. Minard, *Healthcare Computer Systems for the 1990's,* 7.

Chapter 18

Total Quality Management

Marianne Raimondo

Quality has become one of the most prevalent business topics of the decade. Quality of products, quality of service, quality in management. The health care industry has not been immune to this quality revolution. Increasing attention is being paid to the problem of appraising and improving the quality of health care and health services. The complexities of defining quality, finding valid measurements of quality, and ensuring quality in health care organizations continue to be debated by providers, payers, regulators, policy makers, and researchers in the industry, not to mention patients.

In the search of how to best ensure quality in health care organizations, the latest entry is total quality management (TQM). Since the late 1980s, hospitals, health centers, managed care organizations, and physician clinics have begun to implement TQM. Very recently, long-term care organizations have also begun to recognize that TQM holds potential for them as well. TQM has grown naturally out of the steady progression in quality assurance from implicit peer review to medical audits to systematic quality assurance. It is the next step in the evolution of quality assurance and provides solutions to many of the weaknesses that characterize traditional quality assurance methods. Many contend that TQM will result in major advances in the quality and effectiveness of health care.[1]

TQM represents a much broader approach to quality than traditional quality assurance, which can be viewed mainly as a method of evaluation. Quality assurance is a function, lodged in the quality assurance or nursing department, and its basic purpose is to monitor the quality of products or services produced and delivered by an organization in order to identify poor quality outcomes and the persons responsible for the problems or errors. It has been referred to as a "search for bad apples."[2]

TQM is a much more encompassing management approach to organization-wide quality improvement. Also referred to as continuous quality improvement, TQM is a management philosophy and practice that establishes quality as an organization's highest priority—as a fundamental determinant of an organization's viability and growth. It is based on the premise that a focus on quality will ultimately manage costs in an organization and offer improved value. As an organization attempts to provide quality products and services, it will focus on "doing the right things right the first time," thereby reducing duplicative effort, rework, and waste and consequently improving efficiency and productivity and reducing costs. An organization that differentiates itself on the basis of quality will enhance its reputation, which will lead to increased market share and organizational growth.

TQM has been formally defined as an approach to management that focuses on giving top value to customers by building excellence into every aspect of the organization and by creating an environment that encourages everyone to contribute to the organization. It also encourages the development of skills that enable people to scientifically study and constantly improve every process by which work is accomplished.[3]

Simply put, TQM puts quality as the top priority in an organization—quality that is defined by the customers, that is achieved, not by inspection, but by the improvement of work processes, and that requires the total cooperation of everyone in the organization.

Not to be viewed as a short-term program or project, TQM is a long-range strategy or process intended to mold organizational culture so that it is driven by a relentless search for quality, and to implement management practices and systems that ensure the delivery of quality products and services. TQM is often referred to as a way of running a business, a structured, systematic process for creating organizationwide planning and for implementing continuous improvements in quality.

THE ESSENTIALS OF TOTAL QUALITY MANAGEMENT

Customer Focus

At the core of the total quality management principle is a focus on the customer. According to TQM, quality begins with delighting customers. In fact, TQM defines quality as meeting or exceeding the needs and expectations of customers. Customers can be internal or external to an organization. External customers of a nursing facility comprise those who receive and use the products and services of the facility, including residents, families, physicians, payers, hospitals, and the community. Regulatory agencies such as HCFA and the state department of health and accreditation bodies such as the Joint Commission on Accreditation of Healthcare Organizations (Joint Commission) are also customers. Individuals within organizations, however, receive from other individuals products and services that are necessary for performing their job. That is, within an organization there exists a chain or network of internal customer–supplier relationships. Employees are customers when they receive a product or service from fellow employees and are suppliers when they provide a product or service to someone else who relies on that product or service.

Examples of internal customer–supplier relationships in long-term care facilities include the interaction between housekeeping and nursing, dietary and nursing, pharmacy and nursing, and admissions and billing. The expectations, requirements, and needs of the final or ultimate external customer, the resident or resident's family, can only be met when the requirements and needs of all internal customers are met.

To gain knowledge of customer needs, requirements, expectations, and satisfaction, TQM long-term care facilities use proactive methods such as focus groups, surveys, and interviews, recognizing that annual or quarterly resident satisfaction surveys are often biased and insufficient to gain insights about customers.

These insights are then translated into the provision of quality services through the improvement of the systems and processes by which work is accomplished. Unlike traditional quality assurance, which is essentially an evaluation or monitoring process to detect errors, adverse outcomes, or problems, TQM is directed toward building quality into work processes and systems. Monitoring outcomes such as patient falls, medication errors, complications, and infections may identify isolated problems but often fails to identify the causes of those problems. Furthermore, quality problems are most often due, not to human errors, but to system or process failures. Quality by inspection is costly and is provided too late—the quality problem has already occurred, resulting in waste, rework, duplicative efforts, and perhaps dissatisfied customers.

Contrary to this approach of monitoring final outcomes, TQM is based on the premise that quality is improved by understanding how processes work. Sorting through failures does little to guarantee that a process will do the right things, the right way, the first time, and every time. Systems that focus on identifying bad outputs and that fail to associate output failures with variations in the process do not improve quality as effectively as systems that prevent quality failures before they happen. In TQM, quality is built in during the process, not inspected at the end. Examples of work processes in a long-term care organization include admissions, administering medications, feeding patients, billing, and purchasing.

Quality Improvement Tools

Process improvement is accomplished though systematic problem solving and decision making based on data and factual information rather than anecdotes, innuendo, or guesswork. According to W. Edward Deming (whose theories contributed most to TQM as we know it today), the first step in quality control is to judge and act on the basis of fact supported by quality improvement tools, including flow charts, histograms, Pareto charts, check sheets, control charts, run charts, and scatter diagrams. These tools, briefly described below, facilitate the problem-solving process, enabling data to be collected and analyzed so that process operations can be understood and the root causes of problems can be identified and eliminated. The quality improvement tools described are also useful in identifying and measuring variations in systems and processes. Uncontrolled variations in processes prevent managers and staff working in the processes from ensuring desirable outcomes. Once sources of variation in a process are identified, they can be removed, increasing the consistency and predictability of output.

Flow Chart. A flow chart (Figure 18-1) is a pictorial representation showing all of the steps of a process. Flow charts provide excellent documentation of a process or project and can be useful for examining how various steps in a process are related to each other.

Pareto Chart. A Pareto chart (Figure 18-2) is a special kind of vertical bar graph that helps in determining which problems to solve in what order. It is based on the Pareto principle, which suggests that most effects come from relatively few causes.

Histogram. A histogram (Figure 18-3) displays the distribution of measurement data. It reveals the amount of variation that any process has within it.

Cause and Effect (Fishbone) Diagram. A cause and effect diagram (Figure 18-4) is a special type of chart that is used to organize all the causes of a problem. It helps to identify the root causes of a problem and how the causes relate to each other.

Control Chart. A control chart (Figure 18-5) shows how much variability in a process is due to random variation and how much is due to unique events or individual actions in order to determine whether a process is in statistical control.

Run Chart. A run chart (Figure 18-6) is used to monitor a process to see whether or not the long-range average is changing.

Employee Involvement

Statistical thinking is certainly a key component of a total system. TQM is based on the principle that the quality of services cannot be realized unless processes are understood and controlled. Another fundamental principle is that quality cannot be improved without involving employees in the improvement process.

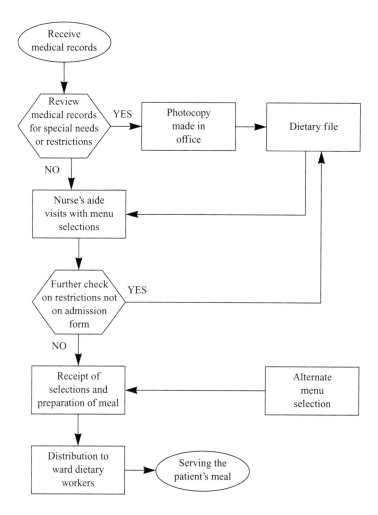

Figure 18-1 Flow Chart for the Process of Serving Meals

The underlying idea is that most employees in an organization want to do a good job and do seek to participate in and contribute to efforts to improve quality in their organization. Deming proposes that management should accept that employees want to do their best and are not willfully lazy or incompetent. It then becomes management's responsibility to provide employees with the necessary training and education as well as clear descriptions of expectations, systems that work, and assistance removing whatever obstacles prevent them from doing a good job.

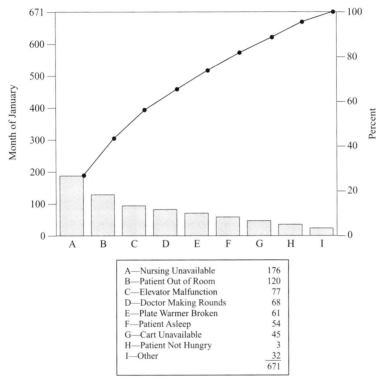

A—Nursing Unavailable   176
B—Patient Out of Room   120
C—Elevator Malfunction   77
D—Doctor Making Rounds   68
E—Plate Warmer Broken   61
F—Patient Asleep   54
G—Cart Unavailable   45
H—Patient Not Hungry   3
I—Other   32
                               671

Figure 18-2 Pareto Chart of Reasons for Patient Receiving Cold Food. *Source:* Reprinted from *Total Quality Management Concepts and Methods,* p. 30, with permission of Applied Management Systems, Inc., © 1992.

It is management's job not simply to delegate responsibility of fixing problems to employees but to help employees do their jobs better and to involve them in decisions that affect their work. Believing that employees want to contribute to organizational improvements, TQM embraces an approach to management that empowers employees by involving them in problem solving and decision making and providing opportunities for them to contribute to the achievement of quality goals. Specifically, TQM requires teamwork in an organization, since employees offer different experiences, talents, skills, and knowledge that must be tapped for maximum gain. If an organization is to be truly excellent in every function, activity, work process, and provided service, everyone in the organization must work together to improve processes.

Teamwork means two things: first, a spirit of loyalty and collegiality throughout the organization, and second, extensive use of team and participative processes in the conduct of business. Teamwork of both kinds results from a

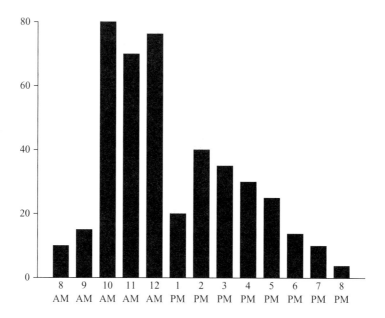

Figure 18-3 Distribution by Time of Discharge

common understanding of the organization's vision and values, a dedication to pleasing customers, an understanding of the organization's systems and processes, and a shared commitment to the ongoing improvement of those systems and processes. All employees in a quality organization understand where their work fits into the larger systems and processes and know how their work relates to the final products or ultimate users or customers. Optimizing individual or departmental quality does not necessarily result in organizational excellence. TQM requires emphasizing cooperation and collaboration across functions and departments that are working in concert for organizational goals.

Quality improvement teams represent one way employees are involved in quality improvement efforts. Quality improvement teams are composed of employees from all organizational levels who are responsible for performing the work in a particular process. Teams follow a systematic problem-solving approach, using the quality improvement tools previously described.

Finally, from the perspective of TQM, quality is the result of a never-ending cycle of continuous improvement. Unlike quality assurance, which establishes standards as the tool for quality, TQM treats standards as minimum requirements. Quality leaders are dissatisfied with the status quo; their goal is not getting by but getting better.

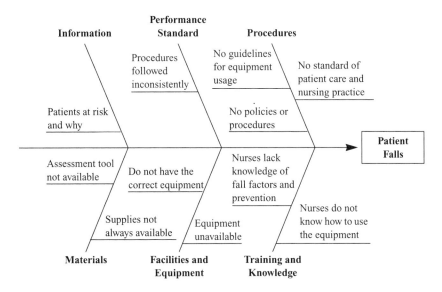

Figure 18-4 Cause and Effect Diagram for Patient Falls. *Source:* Reprinted from *Journal for Healthcare Quality,* Volume 14, Issue 5, with permission of the National Association for Healthcare Quality, 5700 Old Orchard Road, First Floor, Skokie, IL 60077-1057. Copyright © 1992. National Association for Healthcare Quality.

HISTORY

The concepts and principles of TQM are mainly credited to W. Edward Deming, an American statistician who developed, taught, and wrote about management practices and statistical techniques required to design, produce, deliver, and market quality products and services. Deming's ideas and methods were employed by American manufacturers during the 1940s for wartime production, but after the war his teachings on quality were ignored as American companies focused on quantity, production, and short-term profits. Deming's teachings, however, were heeded by the Japanese, who became familiar with his work while he was in Japan assisting the U.S. Secretary of War conduct a population census after World War II. Deming spent over 30 years in Japan, lecturing, consulting, and writing about his statistical techniques and his method of management. Many attribute the rebirth of Japanese industry and Japan's rise as a worldwide economic force to Deming. Joseph M. Juran, an engineer who followed Deming to Japan, is also credited with some of TQM's concepts. He is noted for his ideas on planning for quality.

Total quality management was introduced to the health care industry in the middle to late 1980s. The impetus came from several fronts. The Hospital Corpo-

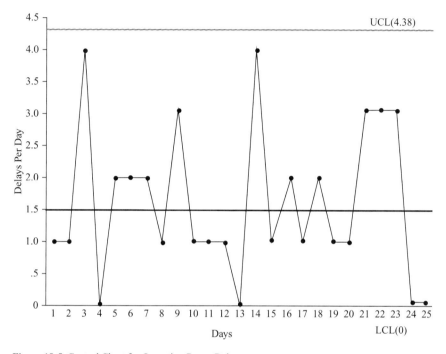

Figure 18-5 Control Chart for Operating Room Delays

ration of America (HCA), a for-profit company that owned and managed over 390 hospitals throughout the United States and abroad, made a corporate-level decision to implement an adapted version of the Deming method of TQM entitled Hospitalwide Quality Improvement Process (HQIP). By 1990, HCA had 75 of their hospitals voluntarily involved in this program.

In 1987, Dr. Donald Berwick, Vice President for Quality of Care Measurement at the Harvard Community Health Plan, initiated with Dr. Blandan Godfrey, then an executive with AT&T Bell Laboratories, the National Demonstration Project (NDP) on Industrial Quality Control in Health Care Quality. Twenty-one health care organizations, including Beth Israel in Boston; the University of Michigan Medical Center, Ann Arbor; Ferry Hospital in Atlanta; and Strong Memorial in Rochester, New York, were trained by professionals from 21 manufacturers, including Xerox, AT&T, and Ford Motor Company, to apply TQM methods to health care processes. The project, funded by the Hartford Foundation, was intended to assess whether quality management theory and techniques could be successfully applied to health care. Given the success of the initial project, the NDP was refunded and expanded. It included more health care organizations, provided training seminars and conferences on TQM,

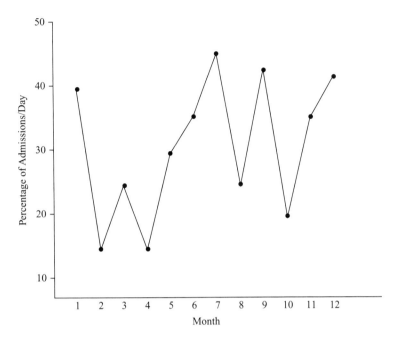

Figure 18-6 Run Chart for Emergency Room Admissions

and sponsored networking opportunities for organizations involved in TQM to share information and experiences.

Hospitals throughout the country have since announced their commitment to TQM implementation. The initial group included the Alliant Health System, Louisville, Kentucky; the University of Michigan Medical Center, Ann Arbor; Henry Ford Health System, Detroit; and Rush Presbyterian St. Luke's, Chicago. In the fall of 1991, the NDP became the Institute for Health Care Improvement (IHI). Headed by Dr. Berwick, the institute was formed to offer educational programs on TQM for hospitals and other health care entities.

Long-term care facilities are beginning to adopt TQM as well. Examples include the Sherrill House, Boston; the Evanswood Center for Older Adults, Kingston, Massachusetts; Villa Clement Manor, Greenfield, Wisconsin; and the Jewish Home for the Aged of Worcester County, Worcester, Massachusetts.

The Joint Commission has also begun to embrace TQM. Changes in the *1992 Accreditation Manual for Hospitals* reflect the beginning of a transition from quality assurance to quality improvement. The chapter called "Quality Assurance" has been changed to "Quality Assessment and Improvement," and new standards are intended to promote (1) more interdepartmental and interdisciplinary quality improvement activities, (2) a focus on processes and systems and not just individual performance, (3) increased efforts to improve the performance of the entire organization rather than focusing only on outliers, and (4) increased communication and collaboration. The manual also contains new leadership standards that require the leadership of hospitals to set priorities for organizationwide quality improvement activities, provide training and education in quality improvement for staff, foster communication and collaboration within the organization, and become personally involved in quality improvement. Some speculate the Joint Commission will eventually change its standards for nursing facilities to reflect TQM.

IMPLEMENTATION

The implementation of a total quality process begins with management's intense commitment to quality and its belief that TQM is the means to achieve not only improved quality but increased market share, improved customer satisfaction, improved productivity, and reduced costs. Although there is no roadmap or instruction manual for becoming a total quality organization, there are some key components of the TQM implementation process, which are described below.

Assessing Readiness

The total quality process can only be initiated after an organization's senior management group is educated in TQM concepts and methods. This can be accomplished through attending conferences, seminars, and courses and making site visits to long-term care and other organizations already using TQM. This awareness-building effort is critical to getting off to the right start. Once senior managers are knowledgeable about TQM and what the approach will involve, they can begin to explore its applicability to their organization.

Before implementing a total quality process, administrators in a long-term care facility should assess whether TQM is compatible with the values, goals, and management practices in their organization. The long-term success of TQM will require intense commitment and dedication of management to the values of quality, customer focus, teamwork, employee involvement, and continuous improvement. Managers should answer several key questions:

- Why implement TQM in the organization?
- What are the potential benefits?
- What obstacles might be encountered in the implementation process?

Administrators should only decide to implement TQM if it makes sense for them based on their leadership style and the organization's goals. Further, the CEO must remain personally involved in the implementation process to ensure a long-term strategic commitment to change and must be willing from the start to maintain that involvement and leadership.

Managers should also articulate a vision of their organization. This vision answers these questions:

- What kind of organization do we want to be?
- How will we look as a total quality organization?

For example, the Evanswood Center for Older Adults developed the following vision statement as part of its ongoing efforts to create a quality culture.

The Evanswood Vision

We pledge uncompromising dedication to excellence in helping older adults grow in spirit, live with a sense of fulfillment, experience dignity, and meet the challenges of their changing lives. We aspire to be consistent in our quality of care, distinctive in our approach, outstanding in performance, and to provide leadership in the field of service to older adults. We welcome others who will join us in pursuit of our vision.

Laying the Foundation

The implementation process begins with senior managers laying the foundation for the total quality process. During this initial phase of implementation, administrators revisit their organizational mission to assess its compatibility with total quality values. The mission statement should answer these questions: Why do we exist as an organization? What is our purpose? What business are we in? The statement should clearly articulate the key customers of the organization, the services provided, and the expected outcomes of such services.

In addition to establishing the organizational mission and vision, an organization implementing TQM should also identify and articulate the values and norms that guide and hold meaning for the employees. The values emphasized by TQM include quality, the primacy of the customers (especially the residents), internal teamwork, employee involvement, and continuous improvement. Finally, the organization may also establish a broad definition of how it defines quality.

Simply drafting mission, vision, quality, and value statements and posting them up throughout the organization is not sufficient to create a total quality organization. They must be communicated constantly to establish and maintain quality-mindedness among all employees.

This initial phase of the quality improvement process is often initiated at a one- to two-day retreat for the organization's senior managers and steering council. The objectives of this session are to explore the benefits of TQM for the organization, to begin to identify potential barriers and obstacles to the process, and to begin to lay out the strategic plans and goals.

Quality Planning

Once the foundation is laid for creating a total quality organization, a plan is developed that outlines the strategy for the implementation process and the expected outcomes of the process. The quality plan is not a static document but is revised throughout the implementation process.

The quality plan lays out the steps of the implementation process, including training managers and employees, forming quality improvement teams, recognizing and rewarding teams for quality improvement, building employee awareness of quality concepts and organizational values and goals, establishing strategies to empower employees, and introducing mechanisms to communicate the quality initiatives continuously. The plan should also include outcome objectives that define how the total quality process should improve quality. These objectives are usually measured in terms of patient satisfaction, employee satisfaction, clinical outcomes, productivity and efficiency, and market share. TQM implementation therefore requires ongoing evaluation to assess whether the process is progressing as planned and objectives are being met. The information gained as a result of this assessment guides the ongoing implementation of TQM.

Gaining Knowledge of Customers

The customer is clearly the focus of the total quality process; the quality improvement process is driven by customer needs, expectations, and requirements. This means that a TQM organization must remain close to its customers, whether they be residents, residents' families, payers, or community agencies. Knowledge of customers can be gained through surveys, focus groups, or interviews. Long-term care organizations implementing TQM need to identify their key customers and then organize efforts to determine customer needs, expectations, and requirements. Task forces are often convened to help in these efforts.

Senior managers should also encourage middle managers to undertake activities to understand internal customers better. Satisfying internal customers is the way to delight external customers. Departments that rely on each other for supplies, products, information, and other services should initiate strategies to learn more about each other's work processes, needs, and requirements. When customer–supplier relationships are strengthened, system improvements can be pursued to increase the quality of the organization's services and products.

Customer satisfaction (of internal and external customers) must be measured on an ongoing basis. Meetings, focus groups, and interviews with residents, employees, hospitals, physicians, and other customers are more effective ways to learn of customer satisfaction than annual, often abbreviated, close-ended surveys.

Making Process Improvements

Knowledge about customers is translated into quality products and services through systems design and process improvement. The emphasis in TQM is prevention, not inspection.

Process improvements are pursued not only by managers of those processes but also through the involvement of employees who perform the work. Quality improvement teams are composed of five to ten employees from all levels in an organization (e.g., nurses, housekeepers, clerks, supervisors, social workers, technicians, etc.) who have knowledge of how work processes operate. Teams are led by team leaders, who are individuals who have ownership of and responsibility for the processes being improved. Team leaders are often supervisors or managers, but they need not be. They are responsible for guiding and directing team efforts, and they are members of the teams and participate fully in the work of the teams. Teams are also guided by facilitators. Unlike team leaders, facilitators are not members of teams; they are outside consultants who remain neutral and objective in providing technical assistance to teams, helping them stay on track and reach consensus.

Quality improvement teams utilize a systematic approach to problem solving to enable them to understand how processes operate, identify and quantify problems in current processes, identify the root causes of the problems, and implement improvements in the performance of the processes.

Much of a quality improvement team's activities involve data collection and analysis supported by the quality improvement tools described previously. These tools enable teams to base decisions on data rather than anecdote, innuendo, or guesswork. The motto adopted by many organizations engaged in quality improvement is: In God We Trust; All Others Bring Your Data.

Use of all quality improvement tools and techniques is not required for every improvement process. Combined they represent a toolbox of available instruments that can be utilized as needed.

Team leaders and facilitators receive extensive training to help them develop the interpersonal and analytical skills required for effective teamwork. Training courses for team leaders and facilitators cover problem solving, how to conduct effective meetings, the use of quality improvement tools, data collection and analysis, team building, and group dynamics.

Quality improvement is a long-term process; teams often meet routinely (usually weekly) for six months or more to improve processes or design new systems. In addition to actual team meetings, team members often work in data gathering, flow charting, and other activities between meetings.

In addition to the actual improvement of work processes, there are many positive outcomes from teamwork in organizations. Teamwork builds respect and understanding among team members from different departments, which leads to greater cooperation and collaboration. As team members gain greater understanding of each other's work and their needs as internal customers and suppliers, they are more likely to work together to improve quality.

Involving employees in resolving problems and improving the processes that affect their everyday work also fosters increased pride of workmanship and an increased sense of ownership. Teamwork also provides an opportunity for employees to learn new tools, develop new skills, and gain new knowledge that will enable them to continue pursuing improvements in their work.

Communication

Communication is critical to the quality improvement process. What should be communicated? First, the basics: The organization's mission, vision, plans, and objectives should be communicated, not in a brochure that is provided at employee orientation or formally recited at an annual staff get-together, but constantly during staff meetings and management meetings and in daily conversations. Communication of the big picture builds teamwork in an organization; employees feel that their work is not menial or trivial but makes an important contribution to the organization.

Second, the values of the organization: Quality, customer focus, continuous improvement, and teamwork must be communicated. This begins during the hiring process, is emphasized in employee orientation, and is continuously re-emphasized daily by all managers.

Third, achievements and progress of the quality improvement process must be communicated, including an announcement of the teams formed, the progress of the teams' work, and team successes. It is crucial that feedback from customer surveys, interviews, or focus groups be communicated, whether it be positive or suggest opportunities for improvement.

Celebrating quality initiatives, besides communicating progress and success, recognizes and rewards employee efforts. Many TQM organizations hold events for teams such as luncheons with the board, recognition dinners, or "team days," which are special days set aside to allow quality improvement teams to present their work at a poster session open to all employees or through formal presentations open to the entire organization. Existing communication mechanisms such as newsletters, bulletin boards, and staff meetings should also be utilized to incorporate quality improvement initiatives and successes.

Quality Deployment

Quality improvement teams, being mostly cross-functional in nature, provide a mechanism to horizontally integrate quality values and initiatives in an organization. However, to infiltrate an entire organization with quality thinking and action also requires vertical alignment. That is, TQM thinking, methods, and practices must be filtered from the top to all departments in a long-term care facility (see Figure 18-7).

Eventually, all managers (i.e., department heads and supervisors) must be educated in TQM concepts and methods and encouraged to pursue quality improvement in their functional areas. This requires that all managers clearly articulate their mission and vision for their departments, establish means to better meet customer requirements and improve customer satisfaction, develop the problem-solving skills of their employees, and build teamwork not only intradepartmentally but interdepartmentally. Most important, it requires that all managers promote the philosophy of continuous quality improvement and be role models for quality improvement practices by constantly seeking ways to get close to customers, pursuing improvement rather than being content with the status quo, being impatient with guesswork, and fostering teamwork.

Systems Integration

If TQM is meant to be a way of life in an organization, then it must mean more than scattered customer surveys or a few isolated teams in the entire organization. It must be integrated into existing organizational rituals, events, activities, and systems, such as planning, budgeting, marketing, information systems, quality assurance, and human resource systems. Systems integration is necessary to ensure constancy of purpose in an organization, consistency in values, and compatibility of organizational objectives. For example, if an organization's priority truly is quality, then performance appraisal systems may need to be revised to recognize an employee's contributions to quality. If an organization truly values

The total quality management model has three major focuses:

1. Vertical alignment through leadership and planning
2. Horizontal integration through teams and customer-driven improvement of processes
3. Daily control through systems, statistical methods, and employee involvement

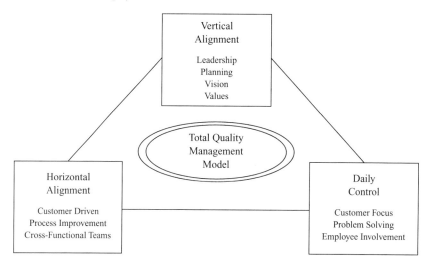

Figure 18-7 Organizationwide Integration of Quality Improvement

teamwork, then performance appraisals should recognize and reward team efforts rather than individual accomplishments, which may have been realized at the expense of collaborative relationships. Likewise, if managers are serious about quality, then management objectives, discussions, strategies, and plans should focus on ways to improve quality rather than contain cost or increase productivity. Managers committed to the concepts of TQM recognize that if processes are improved, duplicative effort, waste, and rework are reduced, thereby decreasing operating costs. Again, if an organization improves the quality of its products and services, it will improve its reputation for quality, thereby increasing market share.

Assessment and Evaluation

The implementation of TQM requires evaluation or assessment to ensure that expected outcomes are attained and that the process that guides those outcomes is continuously improved. A successful total quality process is measured in terms of improved patient satisfaction, improved employee satisfaction, reduced costs, improved productivity, increased market share, and improved performance.

An infrastructure for total quality management must be developed. It should include a leadership body or group, an implementation coordinator, and teams of employees to pursue quality improvements. The leadership body, typically referred to as the quality steering council or committee, energizes the efforts by developing the TQM implementation plan, establishing expectations and objectives for the total quality process, providing resources for training and education, supporting and assisting quality improvement teams, establishing priorities for process improvement, and integrating TQM with other management systems. The steering council is typically composed of senior managers or a combination of senior managers and middle managers. Some steering councils also include a board member. Steering council meetings are scheduled on a weekly or biweekly basis and are held in addition to routinely scheduled management meetings.

The TQM coordinator is responsible for facilitating teams; providing some of the training for the organization; providing assistance and guidance to teams; maintaining a library of information resources and training materials; communicating quality efforts organizationwide; organizing events to recognize and celebrate QI efforts; arranging for seminars, workshops, courses, and other educational opportunities; and working with managers in Human Resources, Finance, Information Systems, and QA to integrate such management systems with TQM. Often the TQM coordinator facilitates the steering council and has direct responsibility for developing the TQM implementation plan. The background of the TQM coordinator can vary. In long-term care organizations, the coordinator could be an administrator, department director, nurse manager, quality assurance professional, staff development coordinator, or human resources manager. The TQM coordinator should report directly to the administrator.

THE ROLE OF MANAGEMENT IN TQM

For some managers, TQM may represent a transformation of their management practices. Rather than a directive, controlling style of management, TQM requires a more participative approach, including open communication with employees and the involvement of employees in decision making. It requires that managers be leaders, exemplars, and teachers of quality. To translate these objectives into action managers must

- be advocates for quality
- see themselves as suppliers to a variety of customers

- seek ways to determine customers' needs, expectations, and requirements and initiate improvements to meet those needs
- seek to improve systems instead of seeking someone to blame
- listen to employees at every level to learn of employees' concerns, problems, or ideas
- help remove obstacles preventing employees from providing quality services and products
- understand how to manage processes and that unless variation is removed from processes, optimal outcomes may be unrealistic for employees to achieve
- become impatient with guesswork and require that data be collected to ascertain the facts
- continuously communicate organizational plans, strategies, problems, goals, issues, concerns, and successes
- provide resources for education and training for employees to improve job skills, understand TQM concepts, and develop the skills necessary for pursuing quality improvement
- find out what stands in the way of teamwork in their organization
- find out what would make employees feel more a part of their organization
- continuously seek ways to integrate quality thinking into existing management systems, such as planning, marketing, quality assurance, and management information systems
- commit to providing jobs for employees instead of creating the fear of job loss
- promote ways to bring employees closer to their customers
- commit to continuous improvement instead of being content with the status quo
- support the work of quality improvement teams by becoming knowledgeable about their activities, providing assistance as needed, and working with them to implement improvements
- seek ways to find out what customers need or expect and initiate improvements to meet those needs or expectations

BARRIERS TO TQM IMPLEMENTATION

There are many barriers to implementing a total quality process. The first barrier is thinking that total quality is a program to be overlaid on traditional management practices rather than a way of life in an organization. TQM should not be equated with a guest relations program or quality circles. It is a comprehensive approach to managing an organization. Managers should not be seduced into thinking they are implementing TQM because they have launched quality improvement projects or teams. Quality improvement teams do achieve laudable results and are excellent vehicles for education, but in and of themselves they do not represent a transformation. TQM is not intended to be a haphazard, fragmented effort but rather an organizationwide, systematic effort. It requires planning, training, direct management involvement, intense commitment, and long-term vision. Managers who form quality improvement teams but fail to change their leadership style to involve employees in decision making, fail to remove obstacles facing employees, continue to focus first on budgets and the bottom line rather than quality, and continue to base performance appraisals solely on tasks performed or objectives met rather than on collaborative teamwork are not implementing TQM. Likewise, managers who, under the guise of improving quality, attempt to use TQM as a cost-cutting tool will probably not be able to rally the support and cooperation of employees, who will tend to view TQM as just another management trick to cut staff, cut budgets, and make them work harder.

Another barrier to implementing TQM in long-term care organizations, a barrier that may not be as significant in hospitals, is the relatively low educational level of employees. Although this problem does not preclude a successful quality improvement process, it needs to be recognized and addressed. Managers in long-term care organizations must be willing to invest in training and education for their staff. Trainers hired should also be sensitive to the fact that the learning process may be gradual and should be experienced in presenting material so that it is understandable and relevant to staff-level employees. Members of quality improvement teams who experience difficulty in data gathering and analysis will need to be assisted and coached by trainers, team leaders, facilitators, and their managers.

Viewing TQM as a quick fix, short-term project is also a way to sabotage quality improvement efforts. TQM is a strategy for long-term improvement; it requires patience. Although some improvements in process performance and employee morale will be experienced within the first year of implementation, increased customer satisfaction, cost reductions, and improved productivity will take longer.

A very real threat to TQM is pseudo-participation. Pseudo-participation occurs when managers form quality improvement teams, communicate to the teams that they are empowered to make changes and improvements, then ignore or reject the teams' recommendations or fail to help the teams implement their improvements. Telling teams they can meet to identify problems but then failing to involve them in the decision to implement improvements is a signal to employees that TQM means business as usual—decision making by management alone. Employees will soon view TQM as a facade and become discouraged and skeptical of management's motives.

Finally, the biggest mistake organizations make in trying to implement TQM is failing to provide education and training for managers and employees. Training and education should be viewed as an investment in human resources. For the total quality improvement process to be effective, employees need to be trained to focus on their customers, work as members of teams, and develop problem-solving skills.

CONCLUSION

Because TQM has only recently begun to be implemented in health care, there has been no formal evaluation of its effectiveness. Early reports of its application have provided some anecdotal evidence of cost reductions, improved customer satisfaction, improved process performance, and improved clinical outcomes, especially in the hospital area.

It is still too early to determine whether TQM is a fad or an approach to management that has significant potential for improving quality in health care. Yet the challenges administrators face in running long-term care facilities in an environment characterized by fragmented and shrinking reimbursement systems, older and sicker patients, higher costs, and intense regulation suggest that TQM is at least worth looking into.

NOTES

1. D.M. Berwick et al., *Curing Health Care: New Strategies for Quality Improvement* (San Francisco: Jossey-Bass, 1990).

2. D.M. Berwick, Sounding Board: Continuous Improvement as an Ideal in Health Care, *New England Journal of Medicine* 320 (1989):53–56.

3. B.L. Joiner, *Total Quality Leadership vs. MBO* (Madison, Wis.: Joiner Associates, 1985), 1–10.

Chapter 19

Financial Management of Long-Term Care Organizations

Seth B. Goldsmith and Solomon Goldner

A central premise of this book is that long-term care facilities are increasingly complex organizations functioning in an extremely demanding and often hostile regulatory environment. The complexity of organization results from the demands being placed on homes to provide a broad array of services to residents needing basic custodial care up to what could be classified as subacute hospital care. Regulatory demands range from those that have a broad application, such as the Americans with Disabilities Act, to those that are more targeted at nursing home reform, such as certain sections of the Omnibus Budget Reconciliation Act of 1987. Unfortunately the problem with many of these well-meaning legislative initiatives is that they cost the long-term care facility money that is simply not fully reimbursed. To deal with this situation requires a strong and informed management that can read and understand financial statements, deal with reimbursement issues, and work with the financial team on developing creative and effective mechanisms to collect all revenues due the institution, generate new sources of revenue, and control expenses without compromising the quality of care provided to the residents.

To meet these challenges, managers in long-term care institutions need a basic understanding of three major topics: (1) the financial organization of long-term care institutions and programs; (2) the elements of health finance, including the revenue cycle; and (3) the budgeting process.

THE FINANCIAL ORGANIZATION OF LONG-TERM CARE INSTITUTIONS

Managers of long-term care organizations are most often in the situation of having major financial decisions made by a top level of owners, corporate officers or, in the case of nonprofit homes, a governing board. This top level of decision making is usually not involved in the day-to-day financial management of the organization but rather exerts its control by allocating funds through annual capital and operating budgets, approving new jobs, and establishing approval levels for spending, such as requiring owner, corporate, or board approval for any expenditure in excess of $2,000. To a large extent, the size of the home may dictate the expectations owners or trustees have of management as well as the resources management has available for financial management. For example, in a 50-bed home it is unlikely that a manager will be able to afford much more support than a bookkeeper, with the result that owners or trustees may themselves try to direct the fiscal management of the home or alternatively may expect that the manager is in fact primarily a finance person. Additionally, the nature of services provided in a home, as well as a state's Medicaid reimbursement system, may dictate either a higher or lower level of financial involvement by the licensed administrator than the owners or trustees expect.

Quite often when there is a board of directors at the top, it will delegate responsibility for the finance function to a subordinate committee. This committee may have limited direct authority or may be just a fact-finding group for the entire board. There is, of course, no simple formula for how all this should work. The key point is that in many organizations the board of directors or owners are ultimately responsible and do indeed exercise that responsibility. This responsibility includes a critical role in ensuring that the home's assets are properly utilized and that all major decisions are financially sound. Although the board and the owners are most often involved in the kind of financial policy making that establishes the parameters of decision making for management, they must also continually oversee the fiscal health of the organization. This is simply not a responsibility that can be delegated to management.

It should be noted that these overseers of the organization's financial health are under no obligation to select only "financial wizards" to serve on the finance committee or to be their guiding light on financial matters. In some instances, a board's finance committee is composed of lawyers or businesspeople who have no particular expertise in finance, much less long-term care finance, and have learned what they need to know by years of experience. For example, in one nursing home, the long-time board treasurer was a stockbroker who had no knowledge of the intricacies of long-term care finance. On one hand, such a situation may be helpful, in that the staff must make its case understandable to those who have only a general knowledge of finance. On the other hand, the board is almost entirely dependent on the staff for its information and is in a sense a captive of its own employees.

Within the long-term care organization or program, the focus of financial activities is the comptroller or vice-president for finance. The nomenclature is so unstandardized that the same position may have scores of different titles. Most comptrollers are trained in accounting. Sometimes they are certified public accountants, and occasionally they have special training in finance. The comptroller is the chief financial officer of the organization and plays a major part in developing and policing the systems that gather, analyze, and interpret financial and related operational data. In some organizations, the comptroller and his or her staff play a key role in all managerial decisions, since they most often have the clearest understanding of the financial implications of any decision.

The major problem with such an accounting and finance staff (and, some might say, their major value) is that they often lack experience in and a perspective on long-term care operations. For example, most of the training programs in accounting and finance focus on the for-profit sector of the economy. Working in long-term care, particularly for the government or nonprofit sector, requires an understanding of slightly different accounting systems, new nomenclature, and different objectives—some of which present problems to a person trained on Exxon financial statements. To compensate for these differences, many organizations send promising individuals to special training programs and encourage them to enroll in the various health-related professional societies. Such educational and professional involvement serves two major purposes: It acquaints these people with the nature of long-term care organizations and their concerns, and it assists them in utilizing their professional skills to maximum effectiveness in the organization. It is also essential that financial officers attend professional meetings, such as the annual meetings of the American Health Care Association or the American Association of Homes for the Aging.

The administrator, whether called president or executive director, is the person who is most accountable for the financial management of the organization. Usually, administrators are not formally trained in finance or accounting but have a general management education background, which typically includes some minimal coursework in accounting and finance. The result of this situation is that administrators utilize the input of their finance staff in making crucial institutional decisions that involve weighing the broad range of quantifiable costs against unquantifiable benefits. So, for example, one administrator pushed ahead on a money-losing day-care program because she felt it was important to the relationship between her nursing home and the community. From a purely financial perspective, it might have been a bad decision; from a political perspective, it was certainly a reasonable choice.

Others in long-term care organizations are also important to the financial management of the organization. Among these are business office staff, who are involved in the credit and collection systems of the organization; data processing staff, who are involved in the systems that set up and record transactions; purchasing staff, whose decisions affect the cash flow and hence the financial health of the organization; and the personnel department, which through its policies affects turnover, vacation substitutions, and a range of other activities that can be translated into dollars and cents. Also, of increasing importance are the medical staff, who should play a role in educating staff, owners, and board members on the implications of new technology for the institution and its residents.

Essentially then, any long-term care organization operates with a series of cash registers that, if properly utilized, take in or ensure the receipt of revenues and disburse money in an organized and objective-related way. For example, the nurse on the resident care floor of a nursing home must ensure that the proper form is filled out when physical therapy is ordered; otherwise, the business office will not bill the resident, Medicare, or Medicaid for the service. If a service is not billed, then the organization has expended resources, such as the nurses' and therapist's time, the machinery and supplies to perform the test, and all the overhead systems necessary to support the physical therapy, without even the opportunity to be reimbursed. Thus, everyone in an organization is part of the revenue-generating function.

ELEMENTS OF LONG-TERM CARE FINANCE

Taxes

Most long-term care organizations are incorporated as for-profit organizations and are taxed as any other organization is taxed. Approximately 25 percent of nursing homes are incorporated as nonprofit organizations and are typically exempt from a range of federal, state, and local taxes. These exemptions do not preclude nonprofit nursing homes from making a profit or force them to operate at the break-even point or at a loss; rather, it requires that any profit made by such organizations must not directly benefit any single person or group of stockholders. In general, the tax laws differentiate between related and unrelated income. Income from activities that are related to the operation and objectives of the organization, such as a profit-making cafeteria run for the convenience of the staff and residents, is tax-exempt. Clearly unrelated income would be taxable. For example, if a nonprofit organization owned a spaghetti factory, the profits from the spaghetti factory would have to be taxed before they could be transferred to the nonprofit organization. Farfetched example? Not really, since the Mueller Spaghetti Company was for many years owned by New York University's law school. Perhaps of greater importance is the increasing vigilance by the Internal Revenue Service regarding the activities of tax-exempt organizations and the increasing pressure by local taxing authorities to collect real estate taxes from nonprofit organizations.

Philanthropy

Occasionally, a wealthy benefactor wills a nursing home or university millions of dollars. While that type of philanthropy is becoming rare, philanthropy on a smaller scale has continued to play a role in financing institutions. However, as a percentage of total revenue, philanthropic giving has declined. Philanthropy is important to an organization for spiritual as well as financial reasons. Spiritually, it tells the organization that it has friends and supporters, and in today's often hostile climate of management and regulation, such statements of support are comforting. From a financial perspective, philanthropy provides funds. Many of the philanthropic gifts that long-term care organizations receive, however, are specially targeted funds, that is, given for a single purpose, such as funds for a building or a program endowment. When money is put into an endowment, the use of the principal is restricted and the interest is available for the purposes of the endowment. Typical problems regarding philanthropic gifts include the source of the money, the restrictions placed on the money, and the cost of getting the money. When money is given, it appears to be less often transferred to the recipient in an unrestricted fashion than it was in the past. The problem with conditions on the money is that operational costs are rarely endowed; thus, for example, money may be provided for a new wing at a nursing home but not for maintenance, heat, or cleaning, and it is the cost of these items that is sometimes too high for an organization to bear. Finally, it should be noted that it takes considerable time and money to raise funds for any organization. Long-term care organizations must compete for limited charitable dollars with a range of other health care programs, particularly hospitals, as well as a broad range of important social programs.

Revenues and Reimbursement

Revenues of long-term care organizations can be broken down into two categories: operating and nonoperating. The operating revenues are generated by the clients or residents who request the services that the organization is in business to offer. The nonoperating income is generated independently of the residents in the organization, although it is directly related to the organization's existence and mission. Operating income from residents may be financed by one of a variety of sources, including the government (through Medicare and Medicaid), private insurers, and the residents themselves. Each of these different payers operates with a different set of reimbursement rules for services, and this translates into different billing and often different collection services. To further complicate matters, each state has different rules affecting nursing home rates. For example, Massachusetts allows nursing homes to charge private-pay residents whatever the home wishes, whereas Minnesota sets the private rate in concert with the Medicaid rate. The income itself is generated by the resident who uses the nursing or professional services. In nursing homes, because of differing agreements with the various payers, residents who have similar limitations, diagnoses, and treatment regimens and are being treated by the same physicians in similar accommodations may in fact generate different revenues for the nursing home. This is analogous to the airline business: Despite the fact that all the passengers on a plane are flying between the same two cities, they are not all paying the same fare. Some are paying first class fare, others are paying full economy fare, others are paying excursion fares (and staying over Saturday night), others are traveling on half-fare coupons, and so forth.

Managing Medicaid and Medicare reimbursement is perhaps the core of financial management for most institutions. State variability in Medicaid methodology and reimbursement is significant. For example, several years ago I visited three comparable nonprofit homes in Dallas, Texas; Kansas City, Missouri; and Fairfield, Connecticut. The Dallas home was reimbursed under a flat rate system at $34.60 per day, the Missouri home received $51.60 per day, and the Connecticut home received $93.84 per day. Yet the Texas home was able to operate with the least restrictions regarding numbers of private-pay residents, whereas the Connecticut home had to respect a tough access law that required it to admit residents on a first-come basis. Finally, if there is an immutable law in Medicaid reimbursement, it is probably that nothing is certain. For example, in 1991 Connecticut relaxed its tough access law in order to allow homes to build their private-pay census and thus cross-subsidize the Medicaid recipients.

Medicare is a program that some homes have been reluctant to develop for a variety of reasons, including a fear of not making money on this program, which is one of the last of the cost-reimbursement programs. This fear may be exaggerated for several reasons. For example, Medicare "cost" includes overhead expenses from every department, including administrative salaries. Thus, every dollar of overhead that is legitimately shifted to a Medicare cost center removes a dollar of overhead from the flat-rate residents, who are usually private-pay residents and in some states Medicaid recipients. In addition, Medicare Part B services, such as physical, occupational, and speech therapy, are often overlooked as sources of revenue. Many nursing homes, while providing space and equipment for these services (as well as the clients), literally give way to outside vendors, who direct bill for the services and leave the nursing home with no fiscal benefit but some real expenses.

Obviously in the world of reimbursement there are numerous tricks of the trade, most of which are based on careful and thoughtful cost accounting, proper recordkeeping, and capturing of all charges. Attention to these details may mean the difference between fiscal viability and insolvency.

Nonoperating revenue comes from grants for projects or development, philanthropy, and other activities, such as parking lots, cafeterias, and gift shops. This income is important, particularly when operating revenues are tight, since funds generated from these sources can often provide the seed money for future development and thus help the organization maintain a competitive edge in its area.

This competitive edge is equally dependent on the effective management of the revenue cycle.

The Revenue Cycle

Effective management of the revenue and accounts receivable cycle is key to the survival of a long-term facility. No matter how good the service is, if the facility does not bill for the service and collect accounts receivable, it cannot stay in business for long. It sounds too simple, but in many organizations there is a significant loss due to unbilled charges through preventable omissions and errors, resulting in the ultimate noncollectibility of accounts. Long-term collection results will depend on effective systems and controls—every step of the way.

Intake and Admissions

A key element of the entire process is the presence of proper intake and admitting procedures. This starts with the building of an accurate and complete database from the time an inquiry for service is received by facility personnel. The persons taking inquiries should be well trained in the financial aspects of the admission process as well as the marketing aspects. They must be capable of developing a preliminary assessment of a prospective resident's condition, needs, and financial resources while simultaneously marketing the facility to the prospective resident. The data gathered is evaluated and a determination is made as to the appropriateness of the admission.

Verification of the prospective resident's third-party coverage should be an integral part of the admissions process. Additionally, because of the debilitated health status of most applicants, a visit to the hospital to meet with and evaluate the prospective resident may help avoid inappropriate placements. The need for and extent of these measures will depend on the relationship with the referral source. Ideally, the nursing home will build relationships of trust with referral sources over time, and they will be able to work with each other effectively to meet the needs of all parties involved.

If the applicant is admitted to the nursing home, the next step in the admission process is a review and execution of the admission agreement. Such agreements have become complex legal documents in their own right, with new requirements added every day. It is imperative that the new resident and his or her representative understand the obligations they are undertaking as well as their rights as health care consumers. If the resident is deemed incompetent, a duly authorized representative who can legally act on behalf of the resident must be identified and assume the role of "responsible party."

When discussing payment, it is important that the resident or responsible party know what is included in the facility's base rate and what is extra and that it is a possibility that, after proper notice, rates and payment arrangements will change. Likewise, care must be taken that they understand what third-party coverage might be available, as well as the limitations of any such coverage. In some states, such as California, Medicaid requires that a "liability" be met by the resident before Medicaid coverage commences, a concept very much akin to a deductible in private insurance policies. Similarly, Medicare has certain deductibles and coinsurance that must be met by the resident or responsible party. If the resident is private pay, it is recommended that the facility collect a deposit equivalent to several months' charges at the time of admission, and the ground rules as to when payment is expected on an ongoing basis should be discussed. Generally, private-pay residents should pay in advance for the month upcoming.

One dilemma often facing the facility is how to deal with residents who have applied for Medicaid but have not yet been approved. These residents are commonly referred to as Medicaid pending and present a risk to the facility inasmuch as it remains questionable whether it will be paid for its services. Where applicable, a deposit covering at least the first 30 days of care should be requested and a thorough evaluation of the resident's Medicaid application performed. Here, too, the extent to which the family cooperates in the process and the known experience and accuracy of the referral source are factors that can minimize the facility's exposure.

Medicare admissions are among the most complex, since a number of additional steps must be performed. In addition to verifying the resident's Medicare coverage, a determination must be made as to whether the resident's condition meets Medicare's strict eligibility criteria from a level-of-care standpoint. This determination is based on a combination of the resident's diagnosis and the nature and extent of "skilled care" required. For this reason it is important to have the input of a qualified nurse who is well versed in the Medicare program. If it is determined that Medicare coverage is not applicable, the facility is required to issue to the resident or responsible party a "Medicare denial letter." The resident may challenge the facility's determination and request that an independent review be performed by the facility's Medicare intermediary. This can be done by requiring the facility to submit a "demand billing" to the intermediary and await its decision. The facility cannot request payment for services until a decision is made by the intermediary, which could have a negative impact on cash flow. However, in most cases effective communication between the facility and the resident or responsible party will obviate many of these problems.

Medicare admissions also require screening other coverage such as HMO membership, since Medicare regulations mandate payment to be sought first from any other existing coverage. This screening is required under the regulations commonly known as the "Medicare secondary payer" rules. In fact, with the accelerating growth of HMO senior plans, in which Medicare participants sign over their benefits to the HMO in return for full medical coverage by the HMO, the facility should routinely check out other coverage for all admissions. Besides the fact that Medicare will generally not pay for the stay of residents enrolled in an HMO, most HMOs require the facility to have a contract with their plan before authorizing services or to contact them, at least, for prior authorization.

Clearly, the best protection for avoiding problems in collection down the road is to have good policies and procedures up front during the admission process as well as well trained staff performing the intake and admission functions. It is the job of the staff to be sure that these policies are well explained to the resident, the family members, or the responsible party. A possible approach that provides additional protection to the facility against costly mistakes in this area is to have all admissions signed off by a committee consisting of the administrator, director of nursing, and business office manager.

Billing for Services

Once again, having proper systems and procedures throughout the billing cycle is of paramount importance. Controls must exist that ensure that charges are generated and posted for all services and supplies that are considered chargeable. A complete "chargemaster," that is, a facility-specific comprehensive price list identifying these items and reflecting appropriate mark-ups over cost, is essential, as is the frequent monitoring of the nursing staff. In this regard, a central supply person who has the full backing and support of management is key to the program's success. Equally important is having proper documentation in the residents' records, such as physician orders and nursing notes detailing usage. One of the most effective ways of achieving control in this area is by utilizing a bar code system, such as the one described later in this chapter.

The three major categories of revenue that we are concerned with are the following:

1. *Basic care.* This is also referred to as room and board. The key here is maintaining an accurate census at all times. It must be balanced daily and reflect all admissions, discharges, and transfers virtually immediately. This type of up-to-the-minute accuracy is essential for the efficient operation of the intake and placement activities as well as for controlling billing.

2. *Ancillary review.* This type of revenue includes physical, speech, and occupational therapy, laboratory and x-ray services, pharmaceuticals, and billable supplies. It represents an increasingly significant source of revenues, since patients are being transferred to nursing homes with higher acuity than ever before. A major portion of this revenue is covered by Medicare Part B, which has the advantage that it is not subject to a specific cap, as is the "routine cost" associated with room and board under Part A.

3. *Personal items.* Revenue can be generated through such items as personal laundry, television rental, beauty shop, and so on. Policies vary from facility to facility as to how these items are charged for, if at all. Given the cost of these items, they should not be overlooked as a potential source of revenue.

The key to maximizing revenue is to avoid lost charges that disappear through cracks in the system, often through staff indifference and lack of controls. A tight, fully integrated order entry and charging system is essential, as discussed earlier. Another significant control step with regard to ancillary charges is to tie the processing of the vendor invoices for contracted services or supplies to the billing cycle. Evidence that a charge has been posted to the revenue system should accompany the invoice sent to accounts payable for processing.

The information generated from the census and the charging systems is then posted to the resident's account, along with any cash receipts and adjustments, and the facility is ready to bill. The concepts are the same whether the facility uses a computer for billing or a manual system. The key here from a cash flow perspective is to condense the cycle as much as possible so as to get the bills out as quickly as possible. In addition, the following suggestions are offered as ways to speed up cash flow:

- Prebill private residents for the next month's room and board charges, mailing statements between the 20th and 25th of the month. Cut off charges for ancillary services and personal items on the 20th of the month, billing the charges from the 21st through the end of the month on the following month's statement.
- Consider "split-billing" Medicaid accounts, sending out two semimonthly invoices instead of one monthly invoice (in those states that allow this). This will have the effect of evening out cash flow over the month.
- Process ancillary charges soon after month's end so that Medicare bills can be mailed early in the month. Securing cooperation from outside vendors in furnishing their invoices soon after month's end is a very important step.

Follow-up and Control

The administrator should, as an integral part of his or her job, monitor the billing process on an ongoing basis, being alert to identify possible bottlenecks or snags in the system. It is ultimately the administrator's responsibility to ensure that a bona fide source of payment exists for every resident who is admitted to the facility and that the systems for billing and collecting for services are in place and functioning properly. The administrator can be aided in this task by receiving at a minimum the following key reports:

- *Monthly revenue and billing report.* This report would indicate revenue by resident type (e.g., Medicare, Medicaid, private, etc.) and category (e.g., room and board, ancillary, personal items) *actually billed.* By comparing these data to the census and other indicators, the administrator would be able to identify and research any variances.
- *Monthly unbilled report.* Complementing the first report is a detailed listing of those accounts *not billed,* along with an explanation as to why each could not be billed, such as "awaiting Medicaid approval." It is critical that the administrator periodically follow up on these unbilled accounts and use this report as a control document.

In addition, the administrator should receive a monthly aging of accounts receivable report, review it, and initiate appropriate follow-up billing and collection activity. Left unattended by the administrator, follow-up activities tend to take a back seat to current, ongoing activities in the business office. The result is that unresolved accounts get older and become progressively more difficult to collect. The simple fact is that the earlier a problem with an account is detected, the greater the likelihood collection will be successful. Therefore, the facility should have a comprehensive collection policy that outlines the various actions to be taken at different times (e.g., a telephone call on fifth of month if no payment is received, followed by letter on the tenth, etc.). Letters and calls should become progressively stronger, with the ultimate action being eviction or the filing of a lawsuit. The point is that the facility should pursue real collection efforts and should not be inhibited in asking for money it is entitled to for services rendered and for which the client has undertaken to pay.

Expenses

The other side of the financial equation is expenses. In most long-term care organizations, the major expense is labor. Depending on the organization, anywhere between 55 and 60 percent of the budget is devoted to salaries and wages, with an additional 10–15 percent going toward taxes and fringe benefits. One 210-bed nonprofit facility in Connecticut offering a range of community services issued an annual report in 1991 that broke down its expenses as follows: wages, salaries, 55.1 percent; employee benefits, 15.9 percent; interest expenses, 4.4 percent; fuel utility and depreciation expenses, 9.3 percent; and supplies and expenses, 15.3 percent.

Cost

The trick for most long-term care organizations, in particular nursing homes, is to maximize their revenue or reimbursements for the services they offer. As previously noted, residents, like airline passengers, each pay a different amount for the same service. While Medicare is a federal system using a cost-based methodology, Medicaid, a joint federal-state program, is the major source of income and headaches. States take differing approaches to Medicaid, ranging from cost caps to paying on the basis of intensity of care provided. Regardless of the system utilized, it is imperative that the nursing home examine the methodology so that it can capture all potential costs. To do this, the home must first have in place a cost-accounting system that can accurately identify costs, and then these costs must be converted into billable charges, which must be followed by timely collection.

Further, it should be recognized that within the commonly accepted principles of accounting and finance, there is considerable discretion for cost allocation to maximize reimbursement. In some instances, institutions have reorganized to take advantage of the reimbursement formulas. Caution should be used, however, because reimbursement strategy is one of the most complex and technical areas long-term care organizations have to deal with. For that reason, expenditures for specialized consultants are often worthwhile.

Cost Containment, Avoidance, and Reduction

Much of the regulatory activity that has occurred over the past few years in the health field has been intended to prevent further escalation in the costs of health care. In general, several strategies can be followed by organizations wishing to contain, avoid, and reduce costs. These strategies include paper work improvements, productivity improvements, scheduling, and training. Typical problems faced by many long-term care organizations include cash shortages, overstaffing, poor utilization of present staff, low productivity, and equipment breakdown. With regard to cash shortages, an organization can establish a budgeting system that contains mechanisms for more accurate forecasting. In order to ensure appropriate cash flow billing and collection, systems must be developed and maintained. The key word is *systems*. It is always amazing to find out how poorly many long-term care organizations handle billing. Even a day's delay in sending out bills or asking for reimbursement is costly to an organization. In one horrendous example, a nursing home failed to collect from a private-pay resident who eventually was $40,000 in arrears.

Rare is the organization that does not have too many staff in certain departments and poorly utilized staff in others. Both under- and overutilization are costly and can be alleviated by better planning and coordination of personnel actions. It cannot be emphasized too strongly that, in a labor-intensive industry such as long-term care, all steps must be taken to ensure the most efficient and effective utilization of staff. This, unfortunately, is not often done.

The related problem of low productivity could be a function of numerous factors. For example, low productivity may result from recruiting inappropriate staff (i.e., people with poor skills or the wrong kind of skills). Productivity problems are often the result of poorly developed expectations for workers, a problem that can be solved by analysis of the jobs in question and related activities. Sometimes low productivity is related neither to production standards nor to the caliber of staff but rather to the basic systems for getting the job completed. The potential for this kind of problem occurs in any process that requires input or material from any other component of the organization before it can proceed. On the Ford assembly line, each of the various functions must be carefully articulated with the previous ones, and materials must be readily available. Without the wheel assembly, the tires cannot be put on, and so forth. Even within nursing homes there is a considerable amount of integration required: The work flow on a nursing unit can bog down because of a breakdown in the laundry, or the business office can be slowed down because information has not arrived from the ancillary service areas or other revenue-generating parts of the facility. All of these breakdowns are expensive simply because they result in unproductive staff time that must be paid for.

Management of Working Capital

Because most nursing homes are dependent on receiving funds from Medicaid, they are increasingly being held hostage to the fiscal machinations of state governments. Whether it is the use of IOUs (as in California) or delayed payments (as in Massachusetts), the problem presented to nursing homes is to pay bills and meet payrolls. To avoid having to borrow money, a home must carefully manage its working capital. Working capital can be thought of as those assets of the organization that are essentially current, such as cash, accounts receivable, and inventory, as opposed to its fixed assets, which might include land and buildings. The basic idea of working capital management is to utilize the current assets to keep the organization in the strongest financial position. Regarding the management of working capital, there are three especially important areas of concern: inventory, accounts receivable, and accounts payable.

Inventory

The basic concern in inventory control is to balance the cost of not having enough with the cost of having too much. Inventory costs money to purchase, and this money is essentially out of circulation until the inventory is used and then converted back to cash. In addition, inventory costs money to store. A final problem is that some items have a limited shelf life; if not used during their shelf life, they must be destroyed. A typical question facing a long-term care manager is how many disposable underpads to buy: a day's supply at a time, a week's supply, a month's supply? It is not so very different from the question the consumer faces when the supermarket has a special on tuna fish. How many cans should the consumer buy? If the consumer uses the entire grocery budget for tuna, then no money is left over for other needs. The consumer also deals with limitations of storage space and shelf life. So it is with the disposable underpads. All the money in central supply cannot be allocated to this item, even if it is bargain priced and the cost is going up in the future, since central supply needs other items that are equally important.

An additional factor in the inventory equation may be the likely availability of the product from suppliers. The reason most people do not maintain large inventories of groceries is that large inventories are readily available in neighborhood stores. An interesting example in the acute care field occurred several years ago when a hospital in Brooklyn, New York, took this approach with its oxygen systems. Since oxygen tank supplies were readily available, why should the hospital install a more expensive (capitalwise) central system that required a large storage tank? Rather, the administration reasoned, it would be better to buy tanks in small amounts and bring in new supplies a few times weekly. This worked well until a strike occurred and the oxygen tanks could not be found. Finally, an imminent disaster was averted when oxygen was located some 50 miles away in New Jersey. When things settled down, the hospital began work on its new central oxygen system, having changed its attitude toward the cost-benefit ratios.

One emerging method for maintaining inventories is the bar code scanning systems typically seen in grocery stores. One of the many systems that presently exist was explained by Michael Barrett of the Minneapolis-based Red Line Corporation, who noted that Red Line's ORBITS system uses bar codes and portable scanners to "track the use of products and services to specific residents and bill it to the appropriate financial class." He went on to note that, when inventory is dispensed, the system automatically records usage and produces reports identifying reorder points based on predetermined levels. As with other automated systems, ORBITS has the capacity to generate budgeting and Medicare reports, case-mix data, and specific usage patterns by individual resident, groups of residents, or units.

Accounts Receivable

Accounts receivable constitute an integral component of cash management, since they are the monies owed the organization for services rendered. Most long-term care organizations operate on a noncash basis; residents or third parties are billed for services, and these bills take some period of time to collect. On the other hand, the organization has obligations to pay the staff who have rendered the services that generate the bills. A nurse is not told that she will be paid as soon as Medicaid pays Mrs. Smith's bill. Rather, the nurse and the rest of the staff are paid periodically, even though a good deal of receivables do not come in on such a regular basis.

The key in accounts receivable is to set up an efficient billing and collection system so that bills are sent expeditiously and contain all the proper information (this is particularly important when dealing with the third-party reimbursers) and that follow-up takes place. As noted earlier, receivables can deteriorate to such a point that it becomes progressively more difficult to collect on them, particularly from private-pay residents. There are no easy solutions to accounts receivable problems, but the importance of organized systems must be emphasized. Organizations should carefully evaluate what have in the past been unacceptable alternatives, such as the use of credit cards or the development of time payment schemes for residents. Finally, it must be recognized that a dollar collected today is worth more than a dollar collected in two months and that investment in a good system therefore can have clear financial benefits.

Accounts Payable

To some extent, accounts payable are the other side of the equation. They are monies the organization is paying out for services and supplies that it has acquired or is planning to acquire. The major account payable for most long-term organizations is the payroll. From an organization's financial perspective, it is best to pay over the longest stretch possible. For example, a monthly payment of staff means 12 processings a year, which saves the organization considerably more cash on hand each month than under a weekly system, where 52 processings a year are required (and higher costs are involved). In business, suppliers often offer incentives for rapid payment, such as 1 percent off the bill if it is paid within ten days. In one nursing home, the working capital was so poorly managed that the home was months and months behind in its payments (some argued that this was actually good management). In some instances, suppliers had cut off deliveries to the home until old bills were cleared up, and thereafter they would supply the home only if cash was paid for the supplies. Again, the key is having an organized system for paying obligations, but this system must be integrated into the total working capital system, which is designed to ensure that money owed the organization is received as rapidly as possible and that funds are properly expended in purchasing inventory.

THE BUDGETARY PROCESS

A budget is essentially a statement of expected expenses and expected revenues over a certain period of time. Most organizations have some sort of budget and a budgetary process. Some organizations, such as nursing homes, must meet federal and sometimes state requirements for budgets of varying lengths. Indeed, some states (e.g., Connecticut) use the budget as a key regulatory device. Also, virtually every government-run or government-financed program is required at the least to prepare a budget at its outset. In theory, then, a budget is a financial timetable, a plan for the organization that has been translated into dollars and cents. Such an approach means that a budget can serve as a guide, a target, and a yardstick for measuring results. A different way of viewing the budget is as a political document that often involves a complicated bargaining process within the organization. Thus, forecasting (or in some cases educated guessing) becomes a key element in the entire budgeting process. Because of the political nature of budgeting and the control that management has when it makes decisions affecting department budgetary levels, the budget and the process can become very significant management tools.

For practical purposes, there are three types of budgets many organizations use: cash, capital, and expense. The cash budget is concerned with cash receipts and disbursements; it is developed to ensure that the business of the organization proceeds at a smooth pace. The capital budget is concerned with capital acquisitions, such as buildings, land, or equipment. Finally, the major budget is the expense budget, which is essentially a statement of the planned operation for a subsequent period of time. The budgetary document, at least superficially, does not vary much from organization to organization, but the process to get to that document does vary substantially. In the end, though, a financial document is prepared. Some documents are program-based, whereas others itemize each expense individually (line item budgets), but with minor effort each type can be translated into the other.

Traditional Budgetary Process

The typical budgetary process has four stages: (1) dissemination of instructions, (2) preparation of initial budget, (3) review and adjustment, and (4) appeal. Dissemination of instructions is exactly that. The instructions to be followed in the preparation of next year's budget are sent to those people who have been designated as responsible for their section of the budget. This is in reality the beginning of management's political statement about the budget and its seriousness about the budget. The first question is, Who prepares the instructions? Is budget preparation by fiat from the management or finance department, or is the instruction rule-making process itself open to question and negotiation? The instructions must also contain some parameters and forecasts, which again provides an opportunity for management to use its control. For example, in the instructions, it might say, "Because of our tight fiscal situation, do not budget any new positions in your department or plan expense for consumable supplies at a level of 2.25 percent higher than last year."

Effectively, management has sent a stark message to the department through the process itself. Another way management makes an important statement about the budget is by its choice of staff to prepare the budget. In one large organization, the department secretaries were responsible for budget preparation, while in another it was the department heads. Different message?

Having read through and digested the mechanics of the instruction, someone within the department is now ready to prepare the initial budget. Within a given department, the budgetary process may reflect the entire organization's approach or the management style of that department's manager. For example, the department may have an open process in which members of the department discuss their plans for the coming year and the money needed to translate those plans into action, or the manager may decide what should happen next year and plan accordingly. Sometimes there is no room in the budget for more than incremental financial plans for the future.

Review and adjustment occurs at the next higher management level (perhaps the second level of management). Here requests are pruned and coordinated. Since the final budget must be adopted at the highest management level (in many organizations, the board or corporate level), it is in everyone's interest to make sure that the document, when finally presented, is as defensible as possible. A strong defense of requests is possible when the forecasts are good and the requests are reasonable. In the review stage, it is important to see that each department has interpreted the forecasting data properly and is using assumptions similar to those of other departments. The review stage also provides an opportunity to ensure that there is no duplication.

The budget is then returned to the originating department. Depending on management's approach, a final appeal to top management is possible. If the department secretary has prepared the budget, there will be few appeals, since the secretary is not likely to be in a power position. Also, by asking the secretary to prepare the budget, management has said that it really considers the process just an academic exercise. On the other hand, if the process is serious and has consumed much energy of "powerful" department-level personnel, an appeal process to override decisions of the coordinating-level managers may be necessary. Here, the case for an increase or change is again made and the budget may be adjusted. It should be remembered that the budget may be reviewed by the board's finance committee before it goes to the full board.

At every one of these stages of review and negotiation, questions are asked. If clarifications are not forthcoming, the budget may not be adopted. Negotiation is the key to this type of process. In many senses, top management and lower-level management are negotiating. The two groups are, to a degree, adversaries, and if each is operating at a high level of competence, the organization stands to benefit from the competition. For example, different groups may have different forecasts based on different interpretations of trends; it behooves the organization to analyze these interpretations before making a decision on the budget. In a closed and managerially dominant system, the opportunity for interaction and negotiation is limited, which is probably not in the best interests of the organization.

Even the timetable of the budgetary process is a statement of how serious and open management is about the process. Too short a timetable gives management total control of the process and the input data for decisions, whereas a reasonable timetable gives the individual departments the opportunity to analyze their own experiences and plans.

The final budget should be an important and weighty document that presents management with a tool to evaluate department heads regarding their ability to meet expectations. Additionally, since the budget sets up the targets, variances from the budget act as flags alerting management of the need to investigate financial problems in a timely manner. Without timely intervention, financial problems simply get out of hand.

CONCLUSION

In sum, money is the fuel of long-term care organizations. A wisely managed institution will use its economic resources well and plan for the future. A poorly run institution not only endangers its own fiscal viability but compromises the health of its residents.

Chapter 20

Capital Financing in Long-Term Care

Roderic L. Rolett

INTRODUCTION

The financial markets offer four primary ways of financing nursing homes: bank loans, tax-exempt and taxable bond issues, Federal Housing Administration insured mortgages, and loans from real estate investment trusts. Each of these ways is a form of debt financing. Equity financing is also available but only on a limited basis, and it is much more difficult to obtain. The focus of this chapter is construction and permanent financing for nursing homes. Seed money and other forms of preconstruction financing are available, but they are generally obtained through informal sources (e.g., partnerships) and are difficult to obtain through the institutional capital markets.

Debt-financing techniques for for-profit and nonprofit nursing homes are dissimilar. Under current federal rules, only nonprofit nursing homes may use tax-exempt bonds. Both for-profit and nonprofit nursing homes may use each of the other methods of debt financing. The first section describes the key variables that must be evaluated when considering alternative financing methods. The second section describes how to present a project (a construction, acquisition, expansion, renovation, or refinancing project) to prospective lenders and the basic steps required to obtain financing under each of the primary methods. The last section compares and contrasts the key differences between the alternative methods as an aid in determining which method may best meet a particular project's needs. Finally, a glossary is provided in Appendix 20-A.

The key parameters to evaluate when considering alternative financing options for your nursing home project include these:

1. *Equity requirements.* Equity represents costs (both construction and non-construction) of the project that are paid by the borrower with its own funds. Lenders' equity requirements vary. The minimum percentage of project costs that each lender requires the borrower to pay with equity depends upon the lender's credit criteria.

2. *Maturity and amortization features.* Maturity represents the term of the loan or the number of years over which the borrower is permitted to repay the loan. Amortization represents the schedule of principal payments the borrower is required to make to the lender. Each lender has its own maturity and amortization requirements, and these requirements reflect the constraints imposed by the lender's own source of funds.

3. *Debt service coverage ratio requirements.* Each lender imposes minimum requirements for the ratio of historic and forecast funds available for debt service to debt service payments due on the lender's loan.

4. *Working capital requirements.* Each lender has its own requirements for borrower liquidity. A key measure of liquidity is the borrower's historic and forecast working capital (i.e., current assets minus current liabilities).

5. *Management experience requirements.* Lenders often use subjective criteria to evaluate management experience. In your first meeting with each lender, ask detailed questions about the lender's expectations for management experience so that you may determine if your team meets the minimum criteria.

6. *Variable and fixed interest rate levels.* Lenders offer a variety of fixed and variable interest rates. Generally, variable rates are lower on a current basis than fixed rates, because lenders know that as market interest rates move up, their variable rate loan will also move up, so they are hedged against increasing rates. Fixed interest rates offer borrowers the advantage of locking in their interest expense.

7. *Collateral and security requirements (e.g., mortgage and lien on revenues).* Lenders require various levels of collateral for their loans, ranging from only a general obligation (promise to repay the loan) to a first mortgage on the financed assets and other property and a lien on the project revenues and the revenues and investments of the borrower's other projects.

8. *Lender familiarity with your state's reimbursement system.* Third-party reimbursement (e.g., Medicaid and Medicare) represents a large part of most borrowers' revenues. Therefore, you want to determine how familiar and comfortable each lender is with this source of revenues as a key component of the project funds available to pay debt service.

9. *Contractor and architect requirements.* For new construction, renovation, and expansion projects, each lender imposes its own requirements for contractor bonds, experience, liquidated damages, form of construction contract, and architect experience. When evaluating alternative lenders, be sure to obtain information about these requirements.

10. *Market analysis or appraisal.* Each lender performs or asks the borrower to engage a professional to perform a demand analysis to demonstrate need for the nursing beds to be built, refinanced, or renovated. Banks may require an appraisal of project value rather than a demand analysis. Make

sure you understand the form of analysis and the level of demand each lender seeks for the loans it makes.

PREPARING TO FINANCE A PROJECT

In order to properly prepare to apply for a construction or refinancing loan, you want to first analyze your project's financial feasibility and pull together the basic information that any lender will need to review. The primary tool used to analyze financial feasibility is a five- to ten-year financial forecast, which may be prepared on a personal computer spreadsheet program. The forecast should include a balance sheet, income statement, and cash flow statement, all prepared according to generally accepted accounting principles. The key to preparing a useful forecast is to select assumptions that are realistic (not optimistic) and to test the project's viability under various less favorable assumptions (sensitivity analysis). If you are forecasting results for an existing facility, explain any future assumptions that differ from the facility's historic performance. Provide an attachment to the forecast that lists the key occupancy, financial, contractual allowance, payor mix, and expense and revenue assumptions incorporated in your forecast. Other important information includes a summary of competitor facilities and their occupancy levels and payor mix (if available) and competitor-proposed expansion projects, résumés of key management and development team members, a detailed list of proposed project costs, and a project timeline. For refinancing, expansion, or renovation of an existing facility, you should provide three years of historical occupancy and payor mix data and audited financial statements.

ALTERNATIVE FINANCE METHODS

Bank Loans

The key step to obtaining a bank loan is familiarizing yourself with the bank's credit criteria. In your initial meeting with a bank loan officer, it is important to determine the bank's loan-to-cost and loan-to-value requirements, parameters for amortization and maturity, and collateral requirements. The loan-to-value and loan-to-cost requirements will determine how much equity versus debt the bank will let you use in financing your project. The value of the project is determined by a certified appraisal prepared by an appraiser selected by the bank.

The bank's amortization parameters will determine how rapidly your project will pay back the bank's principal. Generally, the longer the amortization period, the lower the annual debt service requirement of the loan. A lower debt service requirement will assist in making the project more financially feasible. Of course, if the project can afford to rapidly repay the bank loan, you may want to select a shorter amortization, but remember to allow room in your financial forecast sensitivity analysis for worse than expected performance and less than planned cash available for debt service. The bank's maturity requirement, in conjunction with its loan amortization parameter, will determine your project's refinancing risk. If the bank loan amortization period extends beyond the bank loan maturity, you will need to refinance the remaining principal at the maturity of the loan. Refinancing could present problems if your project is not meeting its financial forecast, if lenders are generally reticent to lend to nursing homes at that time, or if interest rates have significantly increased.

The bank's collateral requirements will determine whether a mortgage on your project's property, together with a lien on its revenues, is deemed by the bank to be sufficient security for its loan. In some cases banks request additional collateral in the form of mortgages on other properties or cash and investments that may be held by the bank until its loan is retired.

Tax-Exempt Bonds

Tax-exempt bonds are issued by a municipality, a state, or a government authority. The government entity then loans the proceeds to a nonprofit nursing home corporation (under current tax law, for-profit nursing homes may not use this form of financing). The nursing home pledges to repay the loan from the government entity, and the nursing home's monthly debt service payments are made directly to a trustee, who then distributes the interest and principal payments to the investors who bought the tax-exempt bonds. Typically, an investment bank purchases (underwrites) the bonds from the government entity at a negotiated interest rate and then resells the bonds to institutional or individual retail investors.

Bond issues typically contain 30-year maturities and are structured with level debt service payments (very similar to single family home mortgage loans). Most bonds are secured by a first mortgage and lien on the project revenues. Because the bond interest payments are tax exempt for the investor, the interest rates are lower than the taxable interest rates set on bank loans and taxable bonds.

Borrowing money through tax-exempt bonds requires you to assemble a finance team that assists in structuring and selling the bonds on your behalf. Before the underwriter may offer the bonds, you, the underwriter, and a bond, borrower, and underwriter counsel must draft a loan agreement, mortgage and trust indenture. The trust indenture directs the trustee to collect the borrower's monthly payments and pay the bondholders on a semiannual basis. The loan agreement describes the restrictions and flexibility permitted the borrower in the areas of additional debt, mergers, asset transfers, and financial ratio requirements. You will also select a feasibility consultant (unless your bonds are credit enhanced) who will forecast, in a format approved by the American Institute of Certified Public Accountants, your project's ability to pay the interest and principal of the bond issue.

Once these documents are complete, the underwriter drafts an offering statement and markets the bonds to prospective investors. After confirming investor interest, the underwriter agrees to purchase the bonds at a specified interest rate. At the closing for the bond issue, the underwriter wires funds equal to the bond principal amount, less his or her fee, to the trustee. The trustee then disburses funds to the borrower for the preapproved purposes outlined in the trust indenture (e.g., refinancing or construction or soft costs).

Real Estate Investment Trusts

A number of real estate investment trusts (REITs) specialize in financing long-term care projects such as nursing homes. Generally, these trusts obtain their capital by selling stock or debt to the public. The funds obtained from the sale of securities to the public are lent to the nursing home borrower. Most trusts prefer to lend for refinancing, expansion, and renovation rather than startup construction. Because the trusts obtain a significant part of their capital from short- and medium-term (1- to 10-year) debt offerings, they prefer to make loans with medium-term maturities (5 to 10 years). It is possible to obtain longer term amortizations (up to 25 or 30 years), but refinancing will be necessary if the amortization extends beyond the term of the loan.

The key feature that distinguishes REIT loans from other sources of financing is the participation terms. The trusts generally require the borrower to pay them a portion of the project's positive cash flow in addition to the upfront points and ongoing interest payments.

Federal Housing Administration Insured Loans

Under Section 232 of the National Housing Act of 1959, the federal government is able to insure the payment of principal and interest on qualifying loans. This insurance program is often referred to as FHA (Federal Housing Administration) insurance. The FHA oversees the granting of FHA insurance commitments for nursing homes through U.S. Department of Housing and Urban Development (HUD) regional offices throughout the country. FHA insurance is available to both for-profit and nonprofit nursing homes. The FHA will insure payments of interest and principal for a 40-year fixed interest rate amortization and maturity. For this reason, the insured loans are typically purchased by lenders in the public debt markets (tax-exempt bonds and the Government National Mortgage Association) rather than commercial or savings banks.

HUD has approved a number of mortgage banks around the country as mortgagees for the Section 232 program. The mortgagees assist the borrower in preparing the FHA application, placing the insured loan, and servicing the insured loan. Application for an FHA insured loan is a three-step process comprising (1) a site analysis and market appraisal, (2) a conditional commitment, and (3) a firm commitment. In this three-step process, the FHA professionals evaluate the demand for the nursing beds; the suitability of the proposed site; the operating assumptions contained in the financial forecast; the project costs; the design, permit, and approval requirements; the ability of the borrower (or a professional management firm) to manage the project; and the ability of the architect and contractor to properly design and build the project.

The FHA program requires that the borrower contribute at least 10 percent equity toward the cost of the project and provide certain letters of credit during construction and initial fill-up for working capital. The FHA insurance fees include 1.3 percent of the loan at closing, the annual servicing fee, and an annual insurance premium equal to 0.5 percent of the principal balance outstanding. Generally, the borrower must count on working with the mortgage bank approximately eight months on the application process before receiving a firm commitment for insurance.

ADVANTAGES AND DISADVANTAGES OF ALTERNATIVE METHODS

Bank Loans

Banks are an obvious source to consider for nursing home construction and permanent financing. The advantages of bank loans include the relatively simple application and credit review process, fast responses (approvals and disapprovals), straightforward documentation, and relatively simple debt structures. The disadvantages include banks' reliance on appraisals, their unfamiliarity with state reimbursement systems, short amortization and maturities, and confusion over whether to treat the loan as a real estate loan or a loan to a health care corporation.

Bond Issues

The primary advantage of bonds is that they provide access to a segment of the capital market different from the commercial bank market. When banks are suffering from capital shortages, regulatory pressures to reduce loan volume, or lack of capacity for new health care loans, bond investors will still typically want to buy bonds and finance nursing homes. Also, the approval and evaluation process is quite different from that employed by banks, since underwriters examine feasibility studies and not real estate-based appraisals to determine the adequacy of the loan security and project credit. The primary disadvantage of a bond issue is the number of entities involved in structuring the various documents and the time required to prepare and review these documents with each of the parties. However, an experienced underwriter is able to coordinate each of the parties and document preparation in an orderly fashion.

Real Estate Investment Trusts

Several REITs specialize in nursing home loans and, as a result, are quite familiar with the industry trends and understand how to analyze loan requests. This specialization makes the trusts a ready source of cash for projects that meet their credit criteria. On the other hand, the trusts tend to lend to only the healthiest projects, because they generally require each project to share a portion of its cash flow with the lender (i.e., a participating loan). Nonprofit nursing homes do not usually use this form of finance, since tax-exempt bonds almost always provide a less expensive source of financing than a participating loan.

Federal Housing Administration Insured Loans

The low fixed interest rate and 40-year amortization available through the FHA's program make it very attractive. However, the FHA requirements are quite detailed, and the process may be lengthy and time consuming compared to the other methods of finance. Borrowers who use FHA-insured loans are required to comply with the federal Davis-Bacon wage act, which may increase the costs of the building construction. For-profit borrowers that are unable to meet a bank's lending standards and do not like the participating loan requirements of a trust may find this program quite attractive. Experienced nonprofits with substantial resources may obtain terms almost as attractive as the FHA loan terms through a tax-exempt bond issue.

Appendix 20-A

Glossary

Amortization. The term over which the principal of the loan is repaid.

Maturity. The date on which all the remaining principal of the loan is due.

Interest rate. The annual rate of interest paid to the lender on the outstanding principal balance of the loan.

Credit criteria. The objective and subjective standards that a lender uses to analyze each loan request and to determine if the borrower qualifies for a loan.

Credit enhanced bonds. Bonds that contain a promise from a third party, like a bank or insurance company, to pay principal and interest if the borrower defaults on its loan payments.

Debt service payments. The periodic (usually monthly) payment of principal and interest to the lender.

Debt service coverage ratio. The ratio of funds available for debt service (usually net income plus noncash expenses less noncash revenues) to debt service.

Equity. The owner's contribution of its own funds toward costs of the project financed with the loan.

Chapter 21

Principles of a Successful Capital Campaign

Donna G. Michaels and Charles S. Wolfe

PHILANTHROPY: OUR ROOTS, OUR STRENGTH

Peter F. Drucker, management guru wrote,

> America needs a new social priority to triple the productivity of the non-profits and to double the share of gross personal income—now just below 3% they collect as donations.
>
> Federal, state and local governments will have to retrench sharply, no matter who is in office. Moreover government has proven incompetent at solving social problems. Virtually every success we have scored has been achieved by the non-profits.[1]

Drucker sees the nonprofits as constituting the social sector of society, which could become as significant as the public sector (government) or the private sector (business).

Drucker's formula for success in the social sector is as follows: "The average non-profit must manage itself as well as the best managed do. . . we need a change in the attitude of government and government bureaucracies. . . and finally non-profits have to learn how to raise money."[2]

Nonprofit nursing homes serving older people have played and continue to play an exceptionally important role in our society. As the public sector continues to withdraw support from these homes, the gap between what is minimally required and what is responsibly desirable will continue to grow.

Philanthropy has often been the means of providing the physical plant, equipment, special services, and desirable levels of staff and of fulfilling our social contract with the elderly of our communities. Today perhaps more than anytime in our past, the need for increased philanthropy is clear.

Although appropriate fund raising is a complex and carefully developed activity that must be based on individual circumstances, we will attempt in this chapter to provide a framework for understudying how the fund-raising process flows. We believe this chapter should be viewed as a springboard to further inquiry and as an aid in assessing any particular environment's potential for sustaining a capital campaign.

The United States has a history of encouraging its citizens to concern themselves with social problems and to underwrite constructive change privately. This unique facet of American society is described in de Tocqueville's familiar quote:

> These Americans are the most peculiar people in the world. You'll not believe it when I tell you how they behave. A citizen may conceive of some need which is not being met. What does he do? He goes across the street and discusses it with his neighbor. A committee comes into existence, and then the committee begins functioning on behalf of that need, and you won't believe this, but it's true: All of this is done without reference to any bureaucrat. All of this is done by private citizens on their own initiative.[3]

The word *philanthropy* derives from the Greek words *phil,* meaning love, and *anthropos,* meaning man. The term *philanthropie* first appeared in the English language in 1628, but philanthropy can trace its earliest roots back thousands of years to the Greeks, Romans, Hebrews, Egyptians, and ancient Chinese. Philanthropy has funded wars, erected temples, built universities, established monuments, transformed the image of tyrants into benevolent statesmen, preserved the arts, and changed the course of world history.

Although the first U.S. charitable foundations appeared after the Civil War, they are considered a phenomenon of the 20th century. By 1915, only 27 foundations had been set up, including those of Andrew Carnegie (1911) and Rockefeller (1913). By 1985, over 32,000 foundations had been formed. The Foundation Center estimates over 95 percent have been established since World War II.[4]

A FRAMEWORK FOR DEVELOPMENT

Development, in its broadest sense, includes the destiny of an institution and can be realized only by an effort on the part of the institution to analyze its philosophy and activities, to crystallize its objectives, and then to project them into the future.

A development program has three major objectives:

1. building acceptance for the organization

2. providing the kind and quality of membership that the institution wants and can best serve
3. obtaining financial support for current operation, special projects, and capital growth

A comprehensive program for financial support will include:

- the annual fund
- ongoing efforts to fund specific projects
- a planned giving program
- major capital funds

Such a program is best managed by a development department responsible for a range of functions. These functions include marketing research, development of marketing strategies, and development of a long-range plan. The department also prepares brochures and newsletters to inform constituents. It has a primary responsibility for developing and directing the several separate giving programs, such as annual giving, deferred giving, and capital giving, as well as requests for foundation funding and government funding. Additionally, the department provides leadership for a speakers bureau, handles gift acknowledgments, and maintains accurate and effective gift-reporting systems.

Ideally, the development department should be managed by a senior development officer, whose responsibilities include the direction and overall supervision of the staff and volunteers who are part of the development effort. The senior development officer has the main responsibility for designing the development program and recommending appropriate goals to the CEO and the board of directors, including specifying the programs and activities necessary to meet funding priorities. The senior development officer also serves in special situations as the spokesperson for the organization and bears the responsibility for organizing support services and materials for development volunteers. The senior development officer plays the role of chief of staff in identifying and cultivating major gift prospects. In this role, the senior development officer will be involved in motivating and training the CEO, the board, and the staff to become an effective fundraising team.

MANAGING A CAPITAL CAMPAIGN

A capital campaign is basically an intensive and concentrated program to raise an agreed-upon amount of money for specific needs. Such a campaign is usually launched and carried out in a limited time period. This means that the institution's leadership (staff and volunteers) will need to devote significant amounts of time and energy to this endeavor. The involvement of a large number of people working together will be required. There should be a clearly defined financial goal. The target amount is essential if the institution's organizational goals are to be accomplished. Setting a financial goal suggests that the institution has engaged in long-range planning. From this planning, specific organizational plans have emerged to address well-defined needs.

The campaign should set datelines. There is some urgency to raise money within those datelines so that the organizational goals can be accomplished. Capital gifts are usually received for specific projects over and above the annual giving budget. Often, the projects are construction-related, such as a new building or an addition to or renovation of an existing building. However, capital gifts may also be used to build an endowment or for specific endowed projects, such as endowed chairs or endowed scholarship programs.

Launching a fund-raising campaign requires a major institutional commitment. Time, energy, financial resources, and willingness to take risks are all necessary in the planning and implementation of the campaign. The commitment to fund raising does not develop all at once. This type of commitment evolves over time, especially if fostered by success. Achieving success requires the implementation of a systematic program to create the conditions under which people will want to contribute. Ultimately, the board and administration control the creation of the conditions necessary for success. According to Crawford,[5] the requirements are

- public awareness of how donations will impact the institution's ability to fulfill its mission
- the direct involvement of persons of affluence and influence (people give when they are involved)
- public awareness that the institution seeks and receives financial support (people give if they are asked and if they know that others are giving too)
- acknowledgment that the institution appreciates the support (people continue to give when they feel appreciated)

The Benefits of a Capital Campaign

A well-conceived capital campaign will raise the dollars immediately needed for the project in question and will increase interest in and good will toward the institution. There are multiple positive campaign outcomes that the CEO and the board of directors need to consider, such as rearticulating the mission of the organization and reviewing and possibly realigning priorities. A capital campaign helps the organization to develop a new leadership base, enhance the loyalty of its constituency, and create a better understanding among its friends and potential supporters. It also helps to provide a more in-depth information base about constituents and potential donors for future fund-raising efforts.

Requirements for Success

For capital campaigns to be successful, several criteria must be met. The sponsoring organization needs an identifiable and relevant constituency that has the potential to meet the fund-raising objective and is also prepared to give the project a reasonably high priority. In addition, the constituency must understand the need and accept the plan. The organization must be prepared to follow sound standards based on time-tested fund-raising principles. There must be a visible plan and a timetable that is experientially based. The plan must be undergirded by an organization built on informed, influential, and effective leadership and a sufficient corps of volunteer solicitors. The campaign must have adequate staff to support the technical work and the volunteers. Above all, the senior leadership group must be unified and possess a sense of common purpose.

BASIC PRINCIPLES OF CAPITAL CAMPAIGNING

Implementation of important fund-raising principles is essential for success. Capital campaign fund raising is unique in several important ways:

1. It is usually done for purposes of an urgent nature.
2. It seeks much larger amounts than normal giving to annual causes.
3. It schedules payments of installments over a period of time.
4. It invests its returns in permanent property or programs.
5. It takes place only when absolutely necessary.
6. It requires planned effort and often involves giving of securities or property.

THE BIG GIFT

The generalization that 80 percent of the funds in a successful capital program come from 20 percent of the donors is a useful guide for most programs. No matter how sophisticated and experienced the organization leadership may be in fund-raising matters, the importance of major gifts cannot be stressed enough. Energy and attention must be focused on obtaining the top 15 to 20 gifts that will be needed in order to establish the pace and pattern of support essential to accomplish the objective of the campaign.

What Leads a Donor To Make a Major Gift?

Dunlop suggests that the specific experiences of each major gift giver are bound to be different.[6] Nonetheless, there are some stages of the process of deciding to give that are common to all. Understanding these common steps can provide insight into how to help others go through the same steps, which will increase the likelihood of their making a major gift. Dunlop outlines the five steps as follows:

1. *Awareness* is critical and can be brought about by a wide range of stimuli: the printed word, comments by a friend, a speech, a broadcast, a public event, or a private experience.

2. *Knowledge* and understanding do not always follow awareness. Knowledge of an institution or a project can only be developed from the information that is made available and that the prospect chooses to assimilate.

3. *Caring* for an institution or a project does not necessarily follow knowledge. Some of the factors that make a person care about a project are personality, values, experience, interests, proximity, relevance, timing, and friendships.

4. *Involvement* develops from caring. Some gifts are made by people who simply care and are not involved. Substantial giving usually results from caring that has turned into involvement. Without involvement, even caring people give only token gifts. Involvement is the key to shifting a person's perspective of an institution or a project from the third person to the first person. When that shift occurs, the process of giving is a matter, not of giving resources away, but of giving to a purpose the giver has become invested in.

5. *Commitment* occurs when the elements of relationship between a person and an institution create in that person a feeling of being a part of a community. The prospective giver will seek out means to express his or her commitment most effectively. The term *commitment* is often used as synonymous with *gift* or *pledge*.

THE PRECAMPAIGN PHASE

In his seminal work, Seymour states that precampaign procedures are paramount.[7] What one does ahead of time usually decides a success or failure. If the services of a professional could be had for only one period, before or during the campaign, the preference would clearly be before the campaign. A capital fund-raising campaign usually involves the conduct of a feasibility or planning study to find out how much can be raised, who will contribute, who will help raise the money, and who will provide campaign leadership. This process begins with a needs assessment aimed at achieving agreement between the administration and trustees concerning essential programs and projects. The needs are concisely described in a prospectus or case statement, which is then shared with those who will be interviewed as part of the needs assessment. Interviews with people who can make or implement the largest gifts to a campaign are critical elements of feasibility studies. Of equal importance are interviews with those who might offer effective leadership. About 50 interviews are usually sufficient to get an overview of the situation. The number will depend on the size of the institution and the number of different constituencies that support it. For smaller institutions, as few as 25 interviews may suffice, but for larger institutions, 100 may be needed. After a list of candidates for interviewing has been developed (the list should be about one-third longer than the number of interviews planned), a letter from the chairperson of the board and the CEO should be sent to the candidates. The letter should explain the nature of the proposed interview and be mailed along with the prospectus.

The Feasibility Study

A feasibility study is essential to the development of a campaign plan because it provides necessary information. Properly carried out, such a study can test the general attitudes of donors and community leaders toward the goals of the campaign. It can reveal unseen problems that may affect the conduct of the campaign. The study will probe reactions, determine the potential level of support, and measure the relative willingness and enthusiasm of the organization's constituencies regarding support and participation in the campaign. It will help to discover appropriate promotional themes and to build early support. The organization should not underestimate the potential of the study for identifying the key leaders and organizations that will be necessary to ensure success.

For public relations purposes and to bring more people into the planning process or to cultivate them as donors in advance of the campaign, it is helpful to add several consultation or focus groups to the individual interviews. Focus group meetings require the attendance of an institution's CEO. They are intended to bring together potential campaign leaders and donors for a presentation of plans and future needs. The guests are invited to question the various proposals and to offer comments and suggestions. When the interviews are completed and the focus groups have met, the feasibility study report is compiled. It should contain suggestions and recommendations regarding every facet of the proposed campaign, including points of emphasis to be made in the promotional case statement and the campaign goal. The report may contain anonymous interviewee quotes. These are often the most carefully read portions of the report.

A feasibility study may require as much as two or three months from start to finish. Ample time is required to arrange and conduct interviews. Depending on the size of the study, it can cost from several thousand dollars to many tens of thousands. The majority of studies range between ten and twenty-five thousand dollars. The investment is usually justified, since the feasibility study is the foundation on which the capital campaign is built. One direct result of the study is the central campaign case statement.

The Case Statement

According to Seymour, the case statement is the definitive document of the campaign.[8] It tells all that needs to be told, including answering all the important questions and explaining the proposed plan for raising the money. With the development of a solid case statement, half of the fund-raising communications task is already completed. The case statement becomes the database. From the case statement, all other materials will flow.

Researching and planning for the case statement should involve directors, key executives, and volunteers who are large gift donors. The case statement should be clear, concise, and compelling; is usually 10–20 typewritten, double-spaced pages; and should be aimed at convincing prospective donors why they should invest their resources in the institution or project. The basic ingredients of a good case statement are as follows:

1. A statement of the need to be addressed by the project. Clear documentation is essential.
2. A clear description of the project the institution has designed to respond to the need. Be specific. For example, describe the

   - program objectives
   - operating procedures
   - expected results (or options)
   - professional staffing
   - timetable
   - costs
   - evaluation and reporting methods

3. Evidence that the institution is capable of carrying out the program. Include the institution's

- history
- achievements and recognition
- professional capabilities
- capacity to serve

4. Dollar requirements for the project and where the institution intends to seek support. List gifts and contributions to date and names of major donors.
5. The project's operating timetable and cash flow requirements and the time-table for fund raising.
6. An explanation of how success in this effort will benefit the project's clientele, society at large, and the donors.
7. A request for a specific gift. Be sure to indicate how a gift can be made.

Selecting a Model for the Campaign

Three kinds of campaigns dominate the philanthropic marketplace: (1) traditional or building fund campaigns, (2) campaigns to build endowment, and (3) combined campaigns that merge capital, endowment, and annual fund objectives.

The selection of the appropriate campaign model will be influenced by a number of factors. The key factors include the experience and abilities of the campaign leadership, the potential for cultivating major prospects, the range and scope of the campaign effort, and the experience and abilities of the development staff. The selection will also depend on the level of sophistication and maturity of the development program and the organization's commitment to strategic planning. It is important to understand that there is no one correct campaign model. What is crucial to remember is that the goal must be reasonable, credible, attainable, and challenging. In the development of the goal, the key actors must be aware of the organization's fund-raising history and the quality of the data in the feasibility study. In addition, the abilities of the campaign leadership and the potential size of the top ten gifts are crucial factors. Finally, the experience of similar institutions in such campaigns and the nature of local experience are important to consider. The development team that ignores these factors risks failure.

The campaign plan delineates organizational requirements, timetables, deadlines, job descriptions, prospect review procedures, the publicity plan, the record-keeping system, and campaign policies. The plan must fix the responsibilities of the staff, leadership, volunteers, and board. And of course it must be approved by the campaign steering committee.

THE ROLE OF LEADERSHIP IN A CAPITAL CAMPAIGN

Nothing is more fundamental to a successful campaign than committed leadership from the top volunteers. The leadership must be the first ones to give, and they must give at a level appropriate to their means, or beyond. They must be among the largest donors. They bear witness that the campaign is personally important, and their donation commits them to the success of the project. It is these leaders who must be depended upon to raise campaign funds from others. Potential donors often prefer to be asked by their peers for support. They do not like to be hit for money by fund-raising professionals and may suspect such professionals of being self-serving, less than candid, or the recipients of unacknowledged benefits. The volunteer leader who has already shown commitment by giving is able to motivate prospects to positive action.

In a good campaign, the fund-raising professional focuses on planning, acts as a resource, and deals with the nuts and bolts. It is the enthusiastic volunteer armed with the plan who goes out and wins the hearts and minds of the donors.

The integration of fund-raising responsibility and values into the thinking of the board of directors is essential for creating the proper climate for the development program's efforts. It is the board's responsibility to establish the fund-raising goal and to be prepared to commit an appropriate portion of the organization's resources, including board member time, to the achievement of the goal. Every board meeting should have time devoted to the progress of the fund-raising effort. The board and key staff should understand that they are expected to participate in training programs that hone their fund-raising skills and enhance their effectiveness in the recruitment of campaign volunteers. The organization and the board should be prepared to show appreciation to the volunteers and to organize appropriate events to honor them.

THE CAMPAIGN CHAIR: THE KEY TO SUCCESS

The campaign chair is the key leader of the campaign. No individual is too important for this post. The best that the community has to offer is just barely good enough. The chair must be a person who can command respect without demanding it, who has the determination to overcome all obstacles. Problems will arise in every campaign. To someone with the right abilities, they are but a signal to go to work. There is an axiom in fund raising: People give and work for people, not for causes. There are many good causes that lack support until a person of influence and ability assumes command. Such a person should have power and influence and be willing to use it. It is also axiomatic that it is impossible to do a first-team job with second and third teams. In fund raising, this means that the chair must have access to the top business structure of the community and must be a person of proven capabilities, dedicated to seeing that the job gets done on schedule.

Duties of the Campaign Chair

1. To serve as chair of the campaign cabinet and hold regular meetings.
2. To follow the campaign plan and schedule and the procedures outlined.
3. To recruit the division chair.
4. To exercise influence on behalf of the campaign, be willing to make a pacesetting personal investment, and be willing to secure dramatic pacesetting investments.
5. To be accessible to the campaign director and other key leaders of the campaign for consultation.
6. To inspire the division chair and ensure that he or she is meeting his or her assigned campaign responsibilities on schedule.
7. To attend meetings and special functions when necessary for the success of the campaign.

CULTIVATING DONORS

Prospect Identification

This is what Benjamin Franklin had to say about getting people committed to a cause:

> My practice, is to go first to those who may be counted upon to be favorable, who know the cause and believe in it, and ask them to give as generously as possible. When they have done so, I go next to those who may be presumed to have a favorable opinion and to be disposed to listening, and secure their adherence. Lastly, I go to those who know little of the matter or have no known predilection for it and influence them by presentation of the names of those who have already given.[9]

Evaluation and prospect review is the process of identifying potential sources of large gifts and determining what would be a reasonable request. Evaluation should answer the question, "How much can this prospect give if interested and seen by the right person?" It is a painstaking process and must involve key volunteer leaders who are knowledgeable about potential donors. The evaluation must be in relation to the required standards for giving—the top gift, the top ten, and top hundred according to the plan. Amounts must be both realistic and challenging. The acceptance of the evaluation by the key campaign leaders and the advance gift prospects will add credibility to the campaign plan.

Helping Donors Make the Right Gift

The key to obtaining the best gift possible is matching the gift opportunity that most interests the donor with the donor's assets and the most suitable gift method. The assets can include cash, securities (marketable or closely held), life insurance, real estate (a residence or vacation property), and tangible personal property (art, antiques, yachts, etc.). Additionally, the general methods of giving include an outright gift; a bequest; a trust providing income to the organization for a period of years, after which it reverts to the family of the donor or the beneficiaries; and a trust providing income to the donor and beneficiaries until the donor's death, after which the assets are transferred to the organization.

Acknowledging Donors

The responsibility for acknowledging gifts in an accurate and timely fashion is a development office responsibility that cannot be underestimated or overlooked. The senior development officer must ensure that appropriate systems are in place for this to be done. Dedications, memorials, and appropriate signs and symbols are just some of the ways to recognize major gifts and principal donors. Additionally, it is essential to ensure compliance with federal, state, and local rules applicable to exempt organizations.

CAMPAIGN COSTS

You cannot raise money without spending money. Within reasonable limits, the return is likely to be commensurate with the investment. In all campaigns, the cost will vary with scope, time, and size of goal. Annual campaigns run for less than 10 or 15 percent of return have all the cost respectability anyone has a right to expect—and in some communities perhaps a touch of uniqueness. Capital campaigns might go as high as that when the goals are low, but the ambitious ones often keep their costs well below 5 percent.

With good management and planning, the expenses will be minimal. Every campaign should have a budget. The following is a guide to preparing a sound campaign budget:

1. salaries and fees

   - professional staff, clerical staff, consultants
   - federal deductions and fringe benefits
   - fees for professional firms, auditors, etc.

2. organization expenses

   - luncheons, dinners, and meetings
   - local and long-distance travel

3. promotion and publicity

   - printed materials
   - artwork
   - models and visualizations
   - direct mail
   - stills and motion pictures
   - special presentations
   - radio and TV

4. general operating expenses

   - rent
   - furniture and fixtures
   - business machines
   - office supplies
   - telephone
   - postage
   - freight and express
   - messenger service
   - electricity and water
   - service and repairs
   - insurance
   - bank charges and interest

5. contingencies

FUND-RAISING CONSULTANTS

A good consultant can provide the expertise and management of detail and technical requirements that are so necessary to a successful campaign. The consultant can maintain momentum during slow periods by keeping on schedule and maintaining the enthusiasm. The consultant's experience and professional objectivity can facilitate problem solving. The professional consultant can bring a critical perspective to both failures and successes. The consultant can also generate excitement and creativity by understanding what is unique and by suggesting remedies. Comradeship is essential in a campaign, and the consultant can help spread the spirit of comradeship among the staff and lay leadership. Most important, hiring a consultant means there is someone who assumes accountability for the problems that can occur.

The following list enumerates the tasks that a campaign consultant will typically be assigned:

1. performing a feasibility or planning study and making recommendations
2. developing and drafting the case statement
3. creating a detailed campaign plan and a timetable
4. setting realistic financial goals based on study results
5. helping with the hiring of appropriate staff
6. helping with the recruiting of the volunteer leadership
7. assisting with office systems, such as the computerization of donor records
8. drafting a fund-raising letter and special proposals for foundation and major gift prospects
9. helping to set up the public relations and communications programs
10. training volunteers
11. providing volunteer support or engaging in donor solicitation
12. performing prospect research
13. determining the campaign budget and maintaining cost controls
14. assisting with postcampaign planning

A fund-raising consultant can do many things and help the organization with many others, but he or she cannot do it all. Particularly, a consultant cannot raise money. The campaign leadership and volunteers have to do that. Of course, a consultant can help. But a consultant cannot replace the keys to good capital fund raising, such as a good case for support, strong and committed leadership, a potential donor base, and sufficient volunteers. A consultant will not relieve the organization staff and board of their campaign responsibilities. In fact, their responsibilities and workload will most likely increase.

Selecting the Right Consultant

The first thing to consider is who should research and short-list the potential consultants and who should sit on the selection committee. The committee should probably include the CEO, the development officer, and representatives of the organization board, the staff, and the volunteers.

After creating a list of consultants who appear to match the institution's needs and who have successful track records, those responsible should interview the candidates and prepare a short list of no more than three. They should then invite the chosen candidates to make formal presentations to the selection committee. The committee members should ask themselves the following questions:

- How well were the candidates prepared for their presentation?
- Did they answer all questions?
- What is their professional reputation?
- Have they had success with other campaigns?
- Do they have good references?
- Do they offer a campaign approach designed to meet the unique needs of the institution?
- Do they have experience in fund raising?
- What is their record on cost per dollar raised?
- Is their style compatible with the institution?

General guidelines can be the starting points for making the final decision, but they are no substitute for in-depth analysis. A good fund-raising consultant will have integrity, experience, commitment, and adaptability in addition to the characteristics required by the particular situation of the institution.

The Contracts

After making the decision on which consultant to hire, the organization will want to state the terms of the business arrangement in a written contract. Although a consultant can be brought in at any time during a capital campaign, many consultants prefer to enter as early as possible (i.e., as soon as the organization begins to consider a campaign seriously). By entering early, a consultant can help develop the strategic fund-raising plan, can convince volunteers that fund raising is crucial to an institution's long-range finances, and can act as the catalyst in making the decision to proceed.

SOLICITOR TRAINING

A good development department places substantial emphasis on the effective training of solicitors. The following model of an ideal solicitor should form the basis of the solicitor training program.

John D. Rockefeller, Jr., said, "Never think you need to apologize for asking someone to give to a worthy objective, any more than as though you were giving him an opportunity to participate in a high-grade investment. The duty of giving is a much his as the duty of asking is yours."[10] Solid commitments from prospects are not obtained by browbeating. They will give if the solicitor

- believes in the mission of the organization
- understands the needs for building projects and endowment programs
- understands something of the background, interests, and capabilities of the prospect
- brings personality to the solicitation
- is not afraid to ask
- knows how to ask open-ended questions, listen, overcome objections, and adapt
- proves by example that the project is worthy of the prospects' support

HOW MUCH TO ASK FOR

Staff and committee evaluation will result in a general range of gift amounts for consideration. It is advisable to aim high enough to challenge and flatter the prospect. If the figure is too high, the prospect will reduce the request. However, very few prospects give more than the amount requested. Setting a solid, high figure in advance of the meeting is crucial to the success of sequential fund raising. Keep in mind the possibility of asking for a pledge for installment payments over a five- or ten-year period as well as the possibility that the prospect's company, family, or private foundation may wish to join together in a gift.

One of the objectives of aiming high and asking the prospect to make the largest possible commitment is that it raises his or her sights. Along with an amount, it is worthwhile to consider how the money will be used. There will be tangible results from receipt of the gift, and a special dedication of a space, floor, or building could be proposed. There are also many special endowment opportunities that provide the satisfaction of having given a perpetual gift.

Like many of the decisions that need to be made before a visit to the prospect, determining the right combination of opportunity and amount is based on the knowledge obtained about the prospect, especially his or her interests and financial situation.

SOLICITATION

A fund-raiser once said, "You don't get a good pickle by squirting brine on a cucumber, you have to let it soak awhile." A good gift will result after proper attention is given to the donor. A two-visit system has proven to have positive results. The first call is more for probing and cultivation. The fact that a solicitor is serious enough to persist will impress the people who are being called and will also begin to raise their sights. It is generally ineffective to mail a sample pledge card. The key to success is face-to-face solicitation.

The First Visit

There is no need to be concerned about closing a gift on the first visit. The first visit is just that—a first visit. A thoughtful gift is usually made on the second visit, after careful consideration of an earlier presentation. Accordingly, it is appropriate to just talk about the facility, its recent achievements, and its future needs. Ultimately, convincing the prospect of the worth and promise of the facility should be the only goal.

The solicitor should try to learn what interest the prospect may already have in the facility. One way to do this is by mentioning a gift opportunity at the appropriate financial level. Mention could be made of the possibility of a combination gift or a gift named to honor the donor, the donor's family, an individual, a corporation, a foundation, or another organization. It is important to use polite locutions like "We hope you will consider giving x dollars" or "We would like to suggest naming y project" rather than "We have you down for x dollars" or "Will you give x dollars?" The prospect should be informed that the suggested gift is proportionate with what others are being asked to consider and that a five- to ten-year pledge period is also an option.

Assessing the Prospect's Reaction

There is no need to worry about closing a gift on the first visit. An excuse may not mean no; it could just mean "not yet." A lower amount suggested by the donor may ultimately be acceptable, but it should not necessarily be either accepted or rejected out of hand. It is essential to listen without judging.

The Follow-up Visit Appointment

One way to make an appointment for a follow-up visit is to say, "I can appreciate that you will want to think this over before making a commitment. Why don't we meet next week at this same time?" Coming back also provides the opportunity to determine the right response to unanswered questions. If, for example, the prospect wants more information about a specific issue, an opportunity to return has been created.

The Pledge Card

Whatever happens, it is essential to keep control of the pledge card and not leave it with the prospect. Too often, leaving the unsigned card results in a much lower gift than anticipated or eventual loss of the prospect completely. It is common practice to leave behind the gift opportunity material or questions and answers and any specifically prepared proposal. The prospect should also be encouraged to discuss the matter with family, business associates, and financial advisors.

The Follow-up Visit

The follow-up visit should be used to review just how important the proposed gift is and to discuss the details of the gift. It is preferable to secure the pledge verbally and then use the card to record the pledge and the details of how it will be handled. The solicitor should review it with the donor and state that a confirming letter will be sent from the development office. To avoid misunderstandings, the solicitor needs to listen carefully and then restate to the prospect what has been heard. If there is any uncertainty about the donor's position, the solicitor can offer to return with a written proposal for the donor to consider and sign. It is often better to turn down a gift or postpone acceptance if a commitment is made that is considerably below expectations. Even if the gift is turned down, the prospect now has a greater understanding of the organization, and an opportunity for a future relationship has been established. Soliciting major gifts is not a science but an art. Usually, if there is one variable that determines success or failure, it is the degree of enthusiasm the solicitor conveys to the prospect. A solicitor must feel excited about the campaign and show it.

CONCLUSION

Philanthropy, despite its centuries' old history, is still an evolving and dynamic field. It is growing and changing to keep pace with the changes in human needs and the priorities of communities. This chapter has presented the basic principles and guidelines for capital campaigns that every professional development officer should know. However, it is important to keep in mind that, in this changing world, creativity, imagination, and the willingness to modify and innovate are the cornerstones of successful philanthropic campaigning.

NOTES

1. P.F. Drucker, *Wall Street Journal,* December 19, 1991, A 14.

2. Ibid.

3. A. de Tocqueville, *Democracy in America,* trans. H. Reeve, ed. R.D. Heffner (New York: New American Library, 1956).

4. E.F. Andrews, *Philanthropy in the United States* (New York: The Foundation Center, 1978).

5. J. Crawford, Perspectives on Consulting: Part I, *Journal of the National Association for Hospital Development,* (Spring 1988):27–29.

6. D. Dunlop, *Concepts for Educational Fundraising,* Presentation. (Miami: University of Miami, 1984).

7. H.J. Seymour, *Designs for Fund Raising,* 2d ed. (Ambler, Pa.: Fund Raising Institute, 1984).

8. Ibid.

9. B. Franklin, *Familiar Quotations,* ed. John Bartlett (Boston: Little, Brown, 1980), 12.

10. J.D. Rockefeller, Ten Principles (Address on Behalf of United Service Organizations, New York, July 8, 1941), 8.

Chapter 22

The Cedars: Promises Kept

Charles S. Wolfe and James N. Broder

At one time the authors of this chapter were in a fund-raising consultant–client relationship. Broder hired Wolfe to do a job and Wolfe did the job. Out of that relationship came the story shared below and a continuing collaboration assisting nonprofit nursing homes and housing providers in their fund development and physical development efforts.

HISTORY

Broder: I moved to Portland, Maine, in 1983. Two of the first people I met were Tanya and Greg Shapiro. Tanya was a volunteer and cultural affairs coordinator at Portland's Jewish Home for the Aged, and Greg was its vice-president and the chair of its long-range planning committee. I am an attorney who has focused most of my practice representing nonprofit sponsors of facilities for the aged in their development efforts—sort of a developer for hire. Greg was somewhat frustrated by a seemingly endless planning process that was going nowhere because the board and community had not yet been aroused to the need for change. Even to me, a newcomer, the need was quite evident.

The original Jewish Home for the Aged was built in 1927–1928 and opened in 1929. It is a two-story wood frame structure that had long outlived its usefulness. There were additions in 1951, 1962, and 1973. The facility housed 88 residents (approximately half of whom were Jewish) and had a reputation for providing quality care. However, this care was provided in a hopelessly outmoded physical plant. The need for radical change seemed obvious. The facility was a potential firetrap.

I dove into the task with all the zeal of a novice, really unaware of the history and self-imposed limitations extant in the community. In short, the community had never seriously asked itself if it could do better and had never had the self-assurance to try.

Call it confidence, call it brashness, call it ignorance, or just call it the knowledge gained from having faced this type of situation many times before in my law practice, but it was clear to me how I would be spending my volunteer time for the next few years.

THE PLANNING PROCESS

With the broad-based support of the home's executive committee, the president, Barry Zimmerman, an excellent lawyer who is a native Portlander, Shapiro, and I reached an agreement. We would each serve as president of the home for a three-year term, thereby ensuring continuity of leadership and commitment to the development effort for almost a decade. That decision was a good one, as it created an ensured base from which all of the members of the team could push forward with some safety and with the conviction that we could and would stay the course.

We first examined whether we could rehabilitate the existing structure. We hired a nationally acclaimed architect who had done a good bit of work in Portland. I led a selection process culminating in interviews with the committee. Several local architects and this fellow "from away" were interviewed. The process itself was quite interesting, because it was the first time a broad cross-section of the board saw the difference specialization could make. It was as if they realized that you did not ask a small town general practitioner to do brain surgery. This was a breakthrough of enormous ongoing significance, because we realized we did not need to limit our horizons to what Portland might have to offer with respect to professionals.

The analysis of the rehabilitation option took at least a year and included design efforts and budget analysis. During this period, there was a growing involvement of more and more board members in the process. Ultimately, the rehabilitation concept was abandoned because of cost constraints and the difficulty of completing so substantial a rehabilitation in an occupied nursing home. As an aside, I have since represented several nursing homes that have actually done major rehabilitation projects while occupied, and the reality is much worse than we had feared.

SITE SELECTION

The next step involved finding a new site, and for that purpose we retained a new staff member, Dick Beach, a man with drive and bulldog determination and with a strong background in development of facilities for the aged. The location ultimately selected after a long and interactive process was a wooded site of more than six acres within the city of Portland and some two miles from the existing site. Having obtained an option to acquire the site, we went about simultaneously obtaining local approvals, preliminary design and cost estimates, and an evaluation of financing options. Our conclusion was that, while a substantial debt service load would be reimbursable through the fixed cost component of the Medicaid reimbursement formula, in order to meet our own internal standards significantly more would need to be spent to move the project from the government's definition of adequate (or necessary) to our own definition of desirable.

GO FOR THE BEST

The strategic decision to not settle for the minimum was another milestone in the process, because it demanded that we go to the community to raise significant capital funds to support a vision that was clearly in excess of what the government would consider adequate and would therefore reimburse. In a community that had never asked very much of itself, in a community that thought of the home as a public utility that was the government's problem, this was a significant issue. We had to convince the community that our goals were a legitimate expression of its own aspirations and that we were not crazy liberal newcomers who wanted to change everything around.

Once we realized we needed to raise money (our initial estimates were in the range of one and a half to two million dollars), we opened a dialogue with the Jewish Federation, the fund-raising arm of the community. Their response—as it turned out, unfortunately for them and fortunately for us—was "No way!" So we knew early on that we would need to do the fund raising ourselves.

CONSULTANT SELECTION

One of our strengths was that our leadership knew what it did not know. Despite the fact that we had all been community fund-raisers before, we really did not feel comfortable with a capital campaign without outside help, so it fell to me to find a fund-raising consultant. We formed another committee and began the search. We found that there were a number of very successful fund-raisers out there who knew that process very well, but as we went through the interview process, we found that none of them had any real sense of our mission or our message. It was clear to us that fund-raising success was a byproduct, albeit an important byproduct, of a community buy-in process, an acceptance of our vision and a self-generated demand for its accomplishment. For that purpose we needed a gerontologist–fund-raiser. Through the nursing home network we identified Charles "Chuck" Wolfe as the man for the job. A former nursing home executive director and lecturer on gerontology, then working in fund raising for a large health care facility in Florida, he combined, we felt, the ability to tell our story with the ability to organize our efforts. While we knew very little about fund-raising methods, the fit seemed right and we engaged Chuck.

READY, AIM, FIRE

Wolfe: Jamie is only partially correct. First, they didn't hire Chuck Wolfe, they hired a team led by Wolfe. I had served for 16 years as executive director of the Jewish Home of Detroit prior to becoming the executive director of Mt. Sinai Medical Center Foundation. I was joined in my engagement by Dr. Steven Marcus and Melissa Tonkin of the Mt. Sinai Foundation. Second, they hired us initially to do a feasibility study, not to be fund-raising consultants.

The purpose of the study was to determine the home's image within the community and the potential for raising the two million dollars Jamie had indicated was needed to help finance a state-of-the-art nursing care facility (Phase I) and an adult congregate living facility (Phase II). These people clearly had a vision, and they asked me to determine if that vision could be realized.

We conducted 46 interviews with a cross-section of community leaders, the home's board and leadership, and potential fund-raising prospects. I also looked around a bit myself and got a good sense of the construction and financing climate, the staff capability at the home, and the regulatory climate in state government.

We found that the people closest to the home, including current and former families, viewed the care as excellent. Those in the next ring of proximity were unclear in their assessment, although most believed the service was basically positive. A final more peripheral group had little real knowledge of the home's quality and service. It was generally felt that the home had not been sending out a consistent message on its mission or on the quality of its service.

The need for a new facility was fairly clear, as there was virtual unanimity that the existing facility was antiquated, inefficient, and nonrehabilitatable. Residents were basically delighted with the campus concept. There was understanding of the costs being projected and a high level of comfort that the fund drive would ensure the construction costs would be covered, with the balance used as an endowment.

My experience told me that as few as 10 percent of the donors would probably contribute as much as 90 percent of the dollars. As a result, the assessment of the major-gift potential to support this campaign was critical. It was clear to me that not only was the potential adequate for the stated goal, but, because of the home's extended constituency, an even larger goal could be funded. A note of caution was required, however, as the track record of giving within the basic constituency was poor. Given this fact, the role of leadership emerged as the central pillar to success. I felt the campaign would stand or fall based on the involvement of the home's board of directors. My philosophy of campaigns is that giving goes from the inside out and from the top down. Many felt the board members would have to greatly intensify their participation in and support of the home. Adding new blood to the board would add stature to the home's image and importance.

CAMPAIGN PROCESS

After completing our study, we told the committee that we thought the campaign was feasible but that an improved image was required. This involved a two-phase approach. In the first phase, the leadership and executive staff would be required to articulate clearly the home's mission, goals for quality and service, and objectives for implementation. The second phase would consist of a well-planned community awareness program.

Delineating the mission and goals of the home in a form that could be communicated to major-gift prospects and to the community at large was essential. The fund-raising goal of $2,000,000 was realistic, and an additional $500,000 to $750,000 was possible if at least one major gift could be garnered at an early stage of the campaign.

We also felt that, in order to be successful, high standards of giving must be established by key leaders and prospects, with the standard in the six figure range for these groups. We recommended that a campaign cabinet and steering committee be created immediately. We wanted the general chairperson to be a respected and well-known community member and a leader of the home. It is a general principle of fund raising that an honorary chairperson of the campaign should be chosen from among the largest contributors.

TOP DOWN, INSIDE OUT

As I have said, fund raising should be sequential: from the major-gift prospects to the lesser-gift prospects, and also inside out, from the top board leadership to the home's best outside prospects and finally to the broader community.

Motivating donations depends on presenting a clear case for support that convinces prospects of the need for the new facilities and thus creates the willingness to give. The case should describe existing financial conditions, the current physical condition of the facility, how the new building will be financed, and opportunities for dedications and tributes. It was clear that making the case for support could be approached obliquely as part of our public awareness campaign as well as directly through campaign parlor meetings and materials.

All of the elements for a successful campaign existed. Creating the right perceptions for giving is a matter of education and cultivation, proper campaign management and leadership, and a highly structured solicitation process. Our team felt that recruiting leadership and setting a high enough standard for giving would be this campaign's greatest challenges.

Broder: I felt, on the other hand, that getting our message out clearly and having the community buy into our vision of the future and believe in themselves enough to actually do it was going to be the challenge.

LEADERSHIP

Wolfe: During the feasibility phase, president-elect Greg Shapiro was frequently mentioned as an ideal candidate for the prime position of campaign chairperson. He was deeply involved in the home, as was his family. He had a variety of significant roles in the general Portland community and was a successful and highly respected businessman. It was also clear to me that community expectations of his giving potential (mid five figures) and, I might add, his own view of what a lead gift meant were at odds with my own belief of what it would take to jump-start this campaign.

I did one solicitation in this campaign, and that was of the campaign chairperson. His deep level of involvement in and commitment to the project resulted not only in his accepting the campaign's leading role but in his reporting, at the public announcement of the campaign, his family's gift, which was fully five times larger than anyone had anticipated.

Broder: The event at which this lead gift was announced was an elegant half-day-long symposium on the problems of growing old, masterfully led by Chuck. The audience, a group of community and business leaders, could not help but be touched by Chuck's eloquence and by the recognition that the problems affected their parents and eventually would affect them. When the chairperson's gift was announced at the end of the symposium, there were audible gasps.

Wolfe: This gift became the springboard for the dramatic increase in the standard of giving for the campaign. People literally said, "If he is giving at that level, I need to re-examine my own level of giving," and they did.

With Jamie, a nationally prominent attorney, coordinating the actual development process, and with the president-elect becoming the campaign chairperson, the environment was ripe for putting in place an outstanding campaign cabinet of home and community leaders. This team met every Tuesday morning at 7:30 AM for almost a year.

It was clear to the entire community and even its most casual observer that the Cedars project had become the most important broad-based communal effort of the current generation.

Broder: Early in the campaign development, Greg asked a longtime friend who was CEO of a prominent local bank to serve as an honorary co-chair of the campaign. This person was viewed throughout the community as a leader and as someone who would be an objective evaluator of the communal worth of the project.

His role was pivotal both in generating the involvement of the corporate community in fund raising and in raising the level of giving. Educational lunches with business leaders of the community were arranged by him, and attendance was always excellent.

The major message of the corporate program was the extent to which the home provided broad-based services and was a facility in which the entire community could take pride. The message rang true. The result was that the corporate gifts constituted over 10 percent of the entire campaign commitment. Needless to say, the positive relations that developed during this period have substantial implications for the future of the home, both financially and in terms of potential clients.

STAFF FUNCTIONS

Wolfe: Our method of consultation makes use of on-site staff to perform day-to-day support functions for the fund-raising initiative. For the Cedars, the project manager, Dick Beach, was at the helm, and the major staff force was the assistant director for development, Tanya Shapiro. Serendipitously, Tanya had a long-term relationship with the home as a professional and a volunteer and was also the spouse of the campaign chair, Greg Shapiro.

The staff's familiarity with the home, the community, the leadership, and the campaign's strategy proved to be invaluable. Although retained for only 32 hours a week, Tanya devoted an average of 40 to 60 hours a week for months on the project. She took a key role in motivating the leadership, following up on solicitations in process, coordinating the public relations consultants, ensuring good communication, setting up special events, and coordinating signage as well as numerous other jobs.

Broder: I want to add that the home's entire staff was involved throughout this entire process and performed in the most exemplary fashion. In fact, they conducted their own highly successful fund-raising campaign for the new facility.

COMMUNITY AWARENESS

Wolfe: Of prime importance was our public relations and community awareness initiative. Great pains were taken to prepare materials that were crisp, clear, and concise. Brochures, newsletters, fact sheets, descriptions of gift opportunities, and other printed materials used the new corporate logo and the theme phrase of the entire campaign: "The Cedars, Promises to Keep."

In addition, a video was created that beautifully captured the unique history and special qualities of the home. The need for a new facility was graphically illustrated. Through small group presentations and office and organizational meetings, the Cedars message was communicated to the widest possible audience. Special activities for raising awareness about aging included lectures, films, and tours of the home project.

Once again, these activities have multiple positive short- and long-term impact, and thus they have continued to be used. They will, no doubt, be an integral part of the home's future marketing and education strategy.

REFLECTIONS ON THE PROCESS

Broder: At this writing, the commitments to the campaign have exceeded $4,500,000, representing approximately 450 gifts. The intensive solicitation period was concluded in nine months. The building was built on time and within budget and has received two national awards for design excellence.

The new 99-bed home is opened, occupancy is at the maximum, and the reaction to both the services and physical plant by residents, family members, staff, and visitors is universally wonderful.

Wolfe: An ongoing fund-raising apparatus has been put in place to continue the cultivation and solicitation process for the future. The staff from the home who worked throughout this program did an incredibly fine job, the leadership was every fund-raiser's "dream team," and the combination made for a most gratifying professional experience.

Broder: When I walk through the new facility, I naturally feel a strong sense of pride and accomplishment. But I also recognize that, in many ways, I was only a cook who was given all the ingredients and equipment to do the job. I knew the recipe, but the community provided everything else. As a community, Portland learned that it needed to make a promise and then, through innovation, cooperation, dedication, and commitment, to keep it. It did.

Chapter 23

Operating a Financially Viable Alzheimer's Disease Treatment Unit

Peter F. Straley and Karen L. Cameron

Alzheimer's disease has become a subject of increasing national attention. In particular the disease's effects on the individual and the family; clinical research advances into its causes, effects, and diagnosis; and the growing recognition that it is far more prevalent than previously suspected have become prominent topics in the national media.[1] The number of Alzheimer's Association chapters, which provide education and support for victims and their families, has grown to over 200 in less than 10 years. A recent report to Congress noted the following statistics:[2]

- Alzheimer's disease is estimated to affect as many as 4 million Americans today.
- The disease has a prevalence of 10 percent among those over 65 years of age.
- Over 47 percent of the population aged 85 years and older are estimated to have Alzheimer's disease, whereas the prevalence is only 3 percent in the 65- to 74-year age cohort.
- Alzheimer's disease is the fourth leading killer of adults, resulting in over 100,000 deaths annually.
- The costs of providing care to these patients are estimated at $80 million annually.
- By the year 2040, 14 million people are expected to have Alzheimer's disease unless significant developments result in a dramatic change in our ability to diagnose and treat the disease.

In response to increased demand for specialized treatment services, many hospitals and nursing homes have developed Alzheimer's disease treatment units, some dedicated solely to patients diagnosed with Alzheimer's disease, others

Source: Reprinted from *Topics in Health Care Financing,* Vol. 17, No. 4, pp. 32–41, Aspen Publishers, Inc., © 1991.

offering special services to Alzheimer's disease patients. Despite the national attention and the increased prevalence of dedicated treatment units, little is known about the underlying causes of Alzheimer's disease. It can be diagnosed only through elimination of a variety of other medical conditions or through autopsy; it has no known cure; and professionals differ on what constitutes the preferred care of patients with various stages of the disease. Partially because of this uncertainty, no effective financing mechanisms are in place to finance care for patients with Alzheimer's disease. This chapter examines the unique care and treatment needs of the Alzheimer's disease victim, some ways in which providers are responding to these needs, and the financial implications of operating a dedicated Alzheimer's disease treatment unit.

TREATMENT NEEDS

Alzheimer's disease is the most prevalent of more than 70 different conditions that can cause dementia. Victims of Alzheimer's disease and related dementias suffer from increasing impairment of intellectual abilities, which ultimately robs them of their ability to function independently and inevitably results in their death due to complicating factors.[3] As Alzheimer's disease progresses, victims show various behavioral traits, such as the tendency to wander and increased confusion and levels of frustration, which have significant implications for caregivers. As the disease progresses, victims lose their ability to sustain the activities of daily living and require increasing levels of supervised and assisted care.

Most practitioners stress the need to treat the psychosocial needs rather than focusing only on the medical needs of the individual with Alzheimer's disease. In the early stages of the disease, victims are physically well, but their behavior is problematic. The traditional approach to such behavior is to apply physical restraints, but most Alzheimer's disease treatment units practice only passive restraints (through facility design) and nonconfrontational tactics. These, in turn, require specially trained staff and, usually, a greater number of staff to lead the activities of the day. In the later stages of the disease, victims frequently require high levels of hands-on nursing care as they begin to lose physical as well as mental functioning.

FINANCING CARE

Treatment for Alzheimer's disease patients is provided primarily outside of an acute care setting. Most researchers believe that the preponderance of care is provided in the home by families rather than through any organized or coordinated system of care. Institutional care is provided largely in a nursing home environment, spanning the continuum from custodial care facilities to skilled nursing facilities. Some adult day-care centers also accept Alzheimer's disease victims.

Although this disease affects primarily elderly persons (or at least manifests itself in such a way that additional care is required for elderly victims), there are no specific provisions within the Medicare payment regulations related to Alzheimer's disease. Alzheimer's disease patients covered by state Medicaid programs receive no special coverage related to the disease—victims receive the standard benefits, and eligible providers receive the mandated payment rates.

Private health care insurance, either traditional indemnity coverage or one of the newer long-term care insurance mechanisms, typically provides no specific benefits for Alzheimer's disease patients. In fact, many policies specifically exclude benefits for Alzheimer's disease patients.[4] Given the increasing prevalence of Alzheimer's disease, policies with such exclusions may impose a significant limitation of benefits on a large number of policyholders. A recent model regulation for long-term care insurance prepared by the National Association of Insurance Commissioners specifically recognizes Alzheimer's disease and indicates that it cannot be excluded from benefits coverage.[5]

In its 1988 to 1989 report, the Advisory Panel on Alzheimer's Disease recommended that "both public and private long-term care insurance programs must be unambiguous in their coverage of the care required by the Alzheimer Disease and related dementia patients."[6] Furthermore, the panel recommended, "a Federal long-term care insurance plan is needed to replace Medicaid as the principal mechanism available for supporting our Nation's long-term care needs."[7] In the meantime, while funding sources are debated and researchers investigate the disease's causes and treatments, providers must care for Alzheimer's disease victims within the financial and clinical constraints that exist today. The specific case examples that follow demonstrate some of the models for care of Alzheimer's disease patients in operation today.

THE ALZHEIMER S DISEASE TREATMENT UNIT: CHARACTERISTICS AND CASE EXAMPLES

The exhibits provide profiles of four different Alzheimer's disease treatment units, each of which provides care to residents in a unique setting but all of which share several common characteristics.

Some common characteristics of these and many other specialized programs are as follows:

- High levels of programmed activities for the residents, engaging them in structured exercises and tasks in an attempt to maximize the residents' use of existing capabilities and to keep them motivated to their highest level.

- Facility design considerations geared to providing passive controls for the residents, such as fenced-in outdoor areas for wandering, locked units so residents cannot leave unattended (although this is less of an issue for victims in the early stages of the disease), and simple layouts and decorative schemes to minimize confusion of the residents.
- A philosophy of care designed to meet the specific needs of the residents and avoid confrontation and stressful situations.
- A belief that the psychosocial care needs of the Alzheimer's disease patient are unique and better met through a dedicated treatment unit.
- A commitment to educate specialized staff members, undertaken primarily internally, to serve the unique needs of the Alzheimer's disease victim.
- Careful entrance screening programs to ensure that residents are suited for the particular facility in question.
- Marketing of the programs through community awareness and cooperation with area agencies and providers rather than through extensive reliance on advertising and other traditional forms of direct promotion.
- A significant percentage of residents brought from out of state, primarily because many families prefer to admit their relatives to a facility near the family's community rather than the resident's original community.

Each of the case examples is described more fully below and in the accompanying exhibits.

Case 1: The Arbors

The Arbors in Shelburne, Vermont, is a privately owned 64-bed facility built exclusively for the care of Alzheimer's disease and memory impairment victims (Exhibit 23-1). The facility, which was built in 1988, is a Victorian-style structure with three central corridors and rooms off the side. Each unit has a small activity area, and there is a common activity area and dining area. Residents furnish their rooms with their own furniture and pictures; all rooms are decorated differently, allowing for easy identification. A fenced-in outside area allows for directional wandering, with paths leading back to the facility.

One unique attribute of this facility is the use of a secure care-monitoring system, which uses an electronic ankle bracelet to track residents. The main purpose of this system is to maintain a restraint-free environment and to minimize the use of medications. The system is used so that patients can be located when they wander. Additionally, the Arbors has a respite program to meet individual family needs. The program allows residents to be taken in for several hours or days at a time.

Exhibit 23-1 The Arbors, Shelburne, Vermont

Configuration: 64 beds in a specially designed Victorian building—32 private, 16 semiprivate

Rates: Private room—$120 per day; semiprivate room—$105 per day

Staffing patterns: For each 32-bed unit, average 4 hours per day per patient

Day shift: 1 licensed nurse, 1 care coordinator, 6 care assistants (nurse assistants)

Evening shift: 1 licensed nurse, 1 care coordinator, 5 care assistants

Night shift: 1 licensed nurse, 1 care assistant

Activities programming: 10 hours per day, 7 days per week

Points of note: Primarily private-pay patients

Marketing approach: Linkages with local agencies and hospitals, word of mouth

Clothes are disbursed as needed from a central clothing room rather than allowing residents to "layer" clothing, as they often do. Residents do not leave the center for basic medical care, as the Arbors contracts with a dental hygienist, a physician, and a podiatrist, all of whom make house calls. Numerous facility designs, such as programmed light switches for all common areas, make the environment less challenging for residents.

Activities are programmed for ten hours per day, seven days per week, and include therapeutic recreational activities, music and art therapy, and other activities designed to engage the residents, many of whom are not self-directed and need structure to involve them. There are also monthly family and staff support groups. Per diem rates are set to be market competitive at $120 for a private room and $105 for a semiprivate room. Historically, at these rates the unit breaks even at approximately 85 percent occupancy. However, an increase in salary costs, fuel prices, or other related expenses can increase the break-even occupancy percentage.

The owners of the Arbors also own two other long-term care facilities in the state that are not specifically dedicated to Alzheimer's disease patients. In comparison to these other facilities, the actual costs of building the facility ($72 per gross square foot) were no higher than for a typical nursing home, but the design is different. The difference in cost of operating the facility relates directly to the higher overall staffing levels of caregivers (four care hours per resident per day) and the higher levels of activities (ten hours per day) offered to the residents.

Exhibit 23-2 The Arcadia Units of Manor Care North, York, Pennsylvania

Configuration: 54 beds in two units of the nursing home

Arcadia 1: 6 private, 12 semiprivate rooms

Arcadia 2: 12 semiprivate rooms

Rates: *Arcadia 1:* Private room—$106 per day; semiprivate room—$96 per day

    Arcadia 2: Semiprivate room—$90 per day

Staffing patterns: Arcadia unit director averages 40 hours per week; each nursing unit averages 3 hours per day per patient

Day shift: 1 licensed nurse, 3 nursing assistants

Evening shift: 1 licensed nurse; 3 nursing assistants

Night shift: 1 licensed nurse; 2 nursing assistants

Activities programming:

Arcadia 1: 10 hours per day, 7 days per week

Arcadia 2: (which treats more advanced stages of Alzheimer's disease): 5–5.5 hours per day

Therapy: Physical, occupational, and speech therapy provided as needed

Points of note: Primarily private-pay patients, will accept medical assistance patients as well; resident assessment allows for placement in the proper unit and provides continuous feedback to the families of the residents; facilities design has been used at 40 other Manor Care Arcadia units.

Marketing approach: Outreach through community education support group and involvement with the local chapter of the Alzheimer's Association.

Case 2: The Arcadia Units of Manor Care North

The two Arcadia units of Manor Care North in York, Pennsylvania, have been in operation since 1989 (the first unit was opened in 1987). The units consist of two separate wings of a 151-bed nursing and rehabilitation center (Exhibit 23-2). Arcadia 1 is a 30-bed unit and Arcadia 2 is a 24-bed unit. Each has a central activities and dining area and a single hallway with a nurse's station. They share an outside fenced-in courtyard with circular paths that promote safe walking and gardening activities.

Both units are designed to offer a low-stimulus environment, with neutral colors and parabolic screens on lights to reduce shadows. As with the Arbors, the philosophy encourages education of the caregivers and is nonrestraint oriented and resident centered. The primarily internal training is geared toward educating the caregivers on appropriate behavioral interventions and encouraging the residents to remain as functionally capable as possible.

Overall care staffing, coordinated by the Arcadia unit director, is three hours per resident per day. The Arcadia 1 unit is primarily for residents who are in the early stages of Alzheimer's disease and remain physically quite functional. Staff members and therapists provide ten hours per day of programmed activities for these residents. Programs are designed to meet the individual cognitive, functional, and psychosocial needs of the residents. The Arcadia 2 unit is for residents who are in the more advanced stages of the disease and are consequently less functionally capable. Residents in Arcadia 2 have five hours of activities per day. In this unit, there is a greater need to attend to the physical needs of the residents, and more hands-on nursing is required. Staff of both units also provide counseling to families of the residents.

The per diem rates of $106 for a private room in the Arcadia 1 unit and $96 and $90 for a semiprivate room in the Arcadia 1 and Arcadia 2 units, respectively, reflect the increased staffing levels of the units and the increased activities planned for the residents. Recent changes in regulations from the 1987 Omnibus Budget Reconciliation Act require that all nursing assistants become certified, which will increase training costs in the future. (Many states already required this, but Pennsylvania did not.) Manor Care North accepts medical assistance patients but notes that in the region average per diem reimbursement rates for intermediate care (Arcadia 2's classification) range from $50 to $60, well below the costs of operating the unit.

Case 3: The Broadway Wing of the Church Home

The Church Home in Baltimore, Maryland, is a 114-unit domiciliary care subsidiary of the Church Hospital and Home. The Broadway Wing consists of 22 private rooms on the first floor of the Church Hospital that were renovated in 1987 to develop a dedicated Alzheimer's disease treatment unit (Exhibit 23-3). The development of this unit was stimulated by the observed unique needs of patients in the Church Home who had Alzheimer's disease, the state's estimate that there would be 20,000 residents in Maryland with Alzheimer's disease, and the delicensing of acute care beds in the hospital.

The unit, though located within the hospital itself, is designed to look like a home. There is a single carpeted corridor with a common dining area, an activity area, and a nurse's station, where all potentially harmful medicines and objects are well enclosed. Residents furnish their own rooms, all of which are private. The unit is L-shaped and opens onto a central, enclosed courtyard where residents can wander, with paths leading back to the facility. The unit was renovated

Exhibit 23-3 The Broadway Wing of the Church Home, Baltimore, Maryland

Configuration: 22 private rooms in a renovated first floor wing of Church Hospital

Rates: Private room—$126 per day

Staffing patterns: Average 4.5 hours per day per patient

Day shift: 1 head nurse, 1 registered nurse, 4 nurse assistants

Evening shift: 1 licensed nurse; 3 nurse assistants

Night shift: 1 licensed nurse; 1 nurse assistant

Activities programming: 12 hours per day, 7 days per week

Points of note: Private-pay patients only; residents may be subsidized through interest from an endowment fund; residents are screened for financial capability and, once accepted, may stay for life, with the all-inclusive fee covering all their health care and other expenses

Marketing approach: Primarily word of mouth, as well as linkages with other subsidiaries of the Church Home and Hospital

to be self-contained, with locking doors linked with the hospital's fire alarm system, and entry to "support areas," such as trash and laundry areas, from the outside so that such activities would not disrupt the residents.

An unusual characteristic of the Broadway Wing is that it has the highest care staffing levels of the four units studied, at 4.5 hours per resident per day. The nurse's assistants who staff this unit have special training in leading group activities. This allows them to simultaneously staff the unit for care purposes and engage the residents in activities. This continuity of care and activity, the directors believe, provides a unique opportunity for the tailoring of the daily experience to each resident's needs. Through linkages with local community colleges, the Broadway Wing is able to attract activities therapists with master's degrees to work with residents on a regular basis.

Another unique characteristic of this program is that it is priced and offered in a fashion similar to a life-care unit. Patients, once admitted, are guaranteed care for life, including medical care at Church Hospital. All residents of Church Home are private payers. Rates are set by a simple calculation of the total costs and a 3 percent add-on. This results in an average per diem rate of $126 for the Broadway Wing versus $87 per diem for the rest of the facility. The difference in rate is attributable to the high-care staffing levels and does not reflect any significant differences in facility costs.

Included within this flat rate is payment for the Blue Cross/Blue Shield Medigap policy, coverage of all health care expenses (except dentistry and prostheses), and all health care supplies and medications. In addition to the medical and psychosocial screening, patients undergo a financial evaluation as well to ensure that they will be able to afford the program for their average life expectancy (the average patient age is 82 years). Currently, residents of the Church Home are eligible to receive subsidies, which are funded by the interest on the home's endowment (just under 25 percent of the residents receive some form of subsidy). The Broadway Wing has not yet established its own endowment fund.

Case 4: Budd Terrace, Wesley Woods Center

Budd Terrace in Atlanta, Georgia, is a nonprofit intermediate care facility built 18 years ago that has a 90-bed Alzheimer's disease program comprising two 45-bed units (Exhibit 23-4). Budd Terrace's Alzheimer's disease treatment program occupies two floors of a seven-story facility. This program is designed for those Alzheimer's disease patients who require continuous care but who are also able to function physically.

The facility's construction was financed through funds from the U.S. Department of Housing and Urban Development. Each floor has a central corridor with

---

Exhibit 23-4 Budd Terrace, Wesley Woods Center, Atlanta, Georgia

Configuration: 90 beds in two 45-bed units of a large intermediate care facility

Rates: Private room—$65 per day, semiprivate room—$59 per day

Staffing patterns: for each 45-bed unit, average 2.3 hours per day per patient

Day shift: 0.5 registered nurse, 0.5 social worker, 1 licensed practical nurse, 4 nurse assistants

Evening shift: 1 licensed practical nurse, 3 nurse assistants

Night shift: 1 licensed practical nurse, 2 nurse assistants

Activities programming: 6–7 hours per day, 7 days per week

Points of note: private-pay patients only; only residents who are ambulatory, continent, and walk with a steady gait are accepted; all require a structured environment; outplacement assistance provided as necessary; program has a full-time director

Marketing approach: Linkages with local agencies and referrals with the center; Wesley Woods offers a continuum of geriatric care including independent living apartments, an intermediate care facility, a skilled nursing facility, and a geriatric hospital

its own dining room and large and small activities rooms. Residents are free to walk the center's expansive grounds but can be monitored because they must pass the nursing stations, located in front of the elevators, to leave the facility. Budd Terrace offers a psychosocial Alzheimer's disease treatment program, with greater staff involvement and higher activity levels than the other intermediate care floors in the facility. Activities are planned for residents six to seven hours each day.

This facility's rates, which do not include medical supplies, are the lowest of the four, with per diem rates of $65 for a private room and $59 for a semiprivate room. These lower rates reflect the lower capital costs of the facility and a lower care staffing level—approximately 2.3 hours per resident per day. Even at these rates, though, Budd Terrace only accepts private-pay patients. A limited amount of philanthropic support is available through the center's annual fund-raising drive.

CONCLUSION

Each of the case study sites highlighted above has a unique approach to the care and treatment of its residents. Each is successful in addressing the needs of the particular targeted segment of the Alzheimer's population it is designed to serve. Among these successes there are many more common themes than differences. Included are specialized programming to meet the individual needs of the residents, higher staffing levels, nonconfrontational techniques, reliance on private payment of facility fees, facility designs that provide maximum freedom of movement within a confined area, and marketing of the program through community resources.

The Report on the Advisory Panel on Alzheimer's Disease of the U.S. Department of Health and Human Services finds that "specialized programming leads to better behavioral outcomes and better quality of life for all involved."[8] Caregivers at each of the case study sites agree. This specialized programming, while taking various forms, always involves additional staffing, sometimes with very specific skill levels. This, in turn, translates into increased operating costs for treatment of the Alzheimer's disease victim. This increased cost is reflected in the higher rates charged by Alzheimer's disease treatment units and their reliance on private-pay patients for the majority of their revenues.

Specialized facility design, layout, and furnishing can make the environment in which Alzheimer's disease victims live more conducive to achieving their maximum potential and maintaining their quality of life. Interestingly, these considerations do not appear to be significant drivers of cost but rather simply require different design elements than those of traditional acute and long-term care facilities. Providers stress that Alzheimer's disease treatment facilities must be designed and implemented with imagination and with an attempt to simplify and clarify the environment rather than challenge the residents.

As our population ages, the challenge of caring for a growing number of Alzheimer's disease victims will increase substantially. While certainly not the only issue related to aging and long-term care that must be addressed, the same demographic trends that are likely to assist many acute care institutions in terms of increasing occupancy levels may swamp the long-term care system. Without a major clinical breakthrough in the treatment or prevention of Alzheimer's disease, the financial implications of the 14 million Americans projected to have Alzheimer's disease by the year 2040, many of whom will require treatment, are staggering. Current strategies of relying on private-pay patients may still be appropriate, but clearly other means of payment will be required if providers are to continue to operate financially viable Alzheimer's disease treatment units.

NOTES

1. D. Gelman et al., The Brain Killer, *Newsweek* 114, no. 25 (1989):54–56; B. Bowers, Slow Death: Life with Alzheimer's Is Often the Hardest on Families of the Sick, *Wall Street Journal,* May 2, 1990, A1.

2. U.S. Senate Special Committee on Aging, *Developments in Aging: 1989,* Rept. 101-249, vol. 1, 101st Congress, 2d sess., 1989 (Washington, D.C.: U.S. Government Printing Office, 1990).

3. U.S. Department of Health and Human Services, *Report of the Advisory Panel on Alzheimer's Disease, 1988–1989,* Pub. No. (ADM) 89-1644 (Washington, D.C.: U.S. Government Printing Office, 1989).

4. Who Can Afford a Nursing Home, *Consumer Reports* 53, no. 5 (1988):200–202.

5. National Association of Insurance Commissioners, Long-Term Care Insurance Model Regulation, in *Model Laws, Regulations, and Guidelines* (Kansas City, Mo.: National Association of Insurance Commissioners Publications, 1989).

6. U.S. Department of Health and Human Services, *Report on the Advisory Panel on Alzheimer's Disease, 1988–1989,* 25.

7. Ibid., 23.

8. Ibid.

Chapter 24

Financing Retirement Communities: The Changing Picture

Judith L. Horowitz and Margo P. Kelly

There are two types of retirement communities, those that provide health care services (either directly or indirectly) and those that do not. A continuing care retirement community (CCRC) offers housing and health care services to residents for their lifetime. The range of health care services available and the method of financing those services varies significantly among CCRC organizations. The health care services may include long-term nursing care or be limited to emergency or short-term nursing care and may be provided through an entrance fee, a rental fee, or on a fee-for-service basis. The housing units may be of a rental, condominium, cooperative, or entrance-fee type.

The American Association of Homes for the Aging distinguishes three types of CCRCs. Type A offers "all-inclusive" contracts, including fully paid nursing care for as long as necessary. Type B communities offer most of the same amenities as Type A but limit the number of days of nursing home care provided at no cost. Type C communities generally operate on a fee-for-service basis. Type A facilities generally have the highest fees, Type C the lowest.[1]

The retirement community concept is not new; the first retirement communities were developed in the 1920s. Early retirement centers were generally sponsored by religious or fraternal organizations. In the late 1940s, the concept of retirement community living became an established option for older Americans as middle-class Americans developed the requisite financial resources to take advantage of the independence and security offered by retirement communities. While retirement communities built before the 1970s generally operated under a fee-for-service contract, those built in the 1970s and 1980s used predominantly all-inclusive contracts, with all services offered to all residents paying the same charges regardless of services actually received.

Source: Reprinted from *Topics in Health Care Financing,* Vol. 17, No. 4, pp. 49–61, Aspen Publishers, Inc., © 1991.

Initially, retirement communities were nonprofit organizations. However, as older Americans became recognized as an affluent market segment, real estate developers and hotel chains such as Marriott and Hyatt entered the retirement community market and began to develop for-profit retirement communities.

Many CCRCs developed during the 1970s and 1980s have encountered financial difficulties as the entrance fees and monthly maintenance fees proved inadequate to provide for residents' health care needs and the inflationary pressures encountered. By 1988, 24 states had developed regulations for CCRCs in an attempt to prevent financial difficulties in new developments.[2]

In response to the financial difficulties of the all-inclusive CCRC model and the diversified needs of the elderly population, more CCRCs are charging for services on a fee-for-service basis. Communities are moving from the concept of continuing care to that of a continuum of care.[3] In some cases, residents do not have the protection afforded by a contract or lease; neither are they guaranteed a place in a nursing center should they need it. Instead, they are promised a priority place on the waiting list.

Additionally, the concept of a nonrefundable entrance fee is being replaced by partially or fully refundable entrance fees, and there are now rental developments and condominium developments. In the 1990s, a continued move may be seen away from the nonrefundable entrance fee concept, with an increase in the array of services and types of communities available.

MAJOR FINANCING VEHICLES

Financing Capital Development

Retirement community development may be financed by a wide variety of vehicles, the most common of which are tax-exempt bonds, taxable bonds, and commercial loans. (Loans through the U.S. Department of Housing and Urban Development for retirement communities, while technically available, are very limited and are therefore not discussed in this chapter.) Traditionally, tax-exempt bonds have been the favored financing alternative. However, the Internal Revenue Code of 1986 and the 1988 Tax Act imposed many restrictions on the use of tax-exempt bonds to finance projects such as retirement communities.

The pressures associated with the federal budget deficit will result in continued legislative initiatives to reduce or eliminate tax-exempt debt, and we anticipate that a growing proportion of future developments will be financed by taxable vehicles. If a development does not qualify as a 501(c)(3) corporation, taxable bonds or other commercial vehicles may be used. Taxable bonds usually have higher interest rates and shorter maturities than the tax-exempt issues.

Commercial financing is increasingly available as conventional lenders become more educated about retirement communities. Projects financed through commercial loans are most often rental projects because the lenders are more comfortable with this approach and view the projects as being similar to traditional real estate developments. Conventional lenders are generally less comfortable with endowment-type projects. Commercial loans usually entail lower upfront financing costs but have higher interest rates than bond financing. Additionally, commercial financing may require larger equity contributions, letters of credit, or personal guarantees.

With continued legislative pressure to reduce or eliminate tax-exempt debt and the entry of real estate developers, hotel chains, and other proprietary entities into the retirement community market, it is anticipated that an increasing number of retirement communities will be financed commercially.

Financing Operations

In the 1970s and 1980s, many CCRCs required a nonrefundable entrance fee and monthly maintenance fees. The entrance fee was designed to guarantee the resident health care for life. Many of the CCRCs developed during this time experienced financial difficulties as the actuarial basis and inflationary assumptions used to project health care expenses resulted in significant underestimates of actual costs. Additionally, many potential residents resist paying a nonrefundable entrance fee. In the future, services will probably continue to be unbundled and provided on a fee-for-service basis. Furthermore, the number of CCRCs structured as rental or condominium projects will increase, with monthly rental or maintenance fees structured to cover the cost of services provided. Long-term health insurance may be offered to residents of retirement communities on a discounted basis or as an option for residents or may be included as part of the costs used to set monthly rental rates or maintenance fees. Such insurance is designed to minimize the owner and operator's risk and cost of providing health care services to CCRC residents.

TAX-EXEMPT BOND FINANCING

Of the available financing options, tax-exempt bonds generally offer the lowest interest rate, longest amortization period, and smallest equity contribution. As a result, tax-exempt bonds have been the most favored vehicle used to finance retirement communities. The federal deficit, however, has spurred legislation aimed at reducing or eliminating tax-exempt debt. The requirements imposed by the 1986 Internal Revenue Code and the Technical Miscellaneous Revenue Act of

1988, as well as proposed legislation such as the Donnelly Bill, have significantly limited the number of retirement communities that qualify for tax-exempt bond financings. If a project is able to qualify, however, tax-exempt bonds remain an attractive financing vehicle.

Definition of Qualified Bond

The provisions of the Internal Revenue Code of 1986 as amended classify bonds issued to finance projects used by Section 501(c)(3) organizations as private activity bonds. Qualified 501(c)(3) bonds are nontaxable. The code defines a "qualified 501(c)(3) bond" as any private activity bond if two conditions are met:

1. All the property that is financed is owned by a Section 501(c)(3) organization or a governmental unit.
2. Ninety-five percent of the bond proceeds are used for the exempt purpose of the Section 501(c)(3) organization.

Qualified Nonhospital Bonds

Of the two types of private activity qualified 501(c)(3) bonds, those used to finance CCRCs are "qualified nonhospital bonds." Two revenue rulings describe the criteria that must be met for a retirement community to qualify for tax-exempt bond financing: Rev. Rul. 79-18, 1979-C.B. 19X and Rev. Rul. 72-124, 1972-1C.B. 145. Under these revenue rulings, elderly housing must address three primary needs of elderly persons: housing, health care, and financial security.

Housing must be designed to meet some of the physical, emotional, recreational, social, religious, and other needs of elderly persons. For example, a facility might provide ramps and elevators to aid those with physical limitations. Health care must be provided by the organization or through arrangements with other facilities.

The financial security criterion is satisfied if:

- the organization is committed to maintaining (to the extent economically feasible) any person who becomes unable to pay regular charges
- housing is within the financial means of a significant segment of the community's elderly persons
- services are provided at the "lowest feasible cost"

Qualified Management Contracts

To qualify for tax-exempt financing, in addition to addressing the primary needs of elderly persons, any retirement community that is managed by an organization other than a Section 501(c)(3) organization must have a "qualified management contract." A management contract is qualified if:

- the contract term does not exceed five years (including renewal options)
- the Section 501(c)(3) organization may terminate the contract without cause or penalty at the end of three years
- management fees are not based on a share of net profits
- at least 50 percent of the management fee is on a fixed-fee basis

Use of Proceeds and Costs of Issuance

The Internal Revenue Code requires that 95 percent of the tax-exempt bond proceeds be used for the exempt purpose of the Section 501(c)(3) organization. Five percent of the proceeds may be used for nonqualifying costs, including issuance costs such as attorney's fees and underwriter's discounts. However, issuance costs paid for with the bond proceeds may not exceed 2 percent of the aggregate face amount of the bonds.

$150-Million User Cap

Each Section 501(c)(3) organization issuing qualified nonhospital bonds may use tax-exempt bonds only to finance projects totaling $150 million or less. The $150-million user cap separately aggregates projects financed before and after August 16, 1986. As long as the debt is outstanding, the debt is included in calculating the issuer's user cap, even if the retirement community is no longer owned by the issuer.

Additionally, lessees and nonqualifying managers and other defined groups are subject to the $150-million user cap. This restriction is designed to prevent related parties from circumventing the user cap.

Information Reporting and Public Approval Requirements

In addition to complying with the criteria and restrictions outlined above, issuers of tax-exempt debt must obtain authority to issue from appropriate elected officials and comply with information-reporting requirements. If the information reporting is not completed within the stated period, the tax-exempt status of the issue is at risk.

Provisions of the 1988 Tax Act

The Technical and Miscellaneous Revenue Act of 1988 (1988 Tax Act) amended the Internal Revenue Code so that acquisitions of existing retirement communities could not be financed with qualified Section 501(c)(3) bonds unless the community was substantially renovated or the acquisition was of a "qualified residential rental project." To be a "qualified residential rental project," at least 20 percent of the rental units must be occupied by tenants with incomes that are 50 percent or less of the area median gross income, or 40 percent of the rental units must be occupied by tenants with incomes that are 60 percent or less of the area median gross income.

The issuer must decide before bond issuance which of the above two requirements to apply and must apply the requirement during the qualified project period, which begins when 10 percent of the units are occupied and ends on the latest of these dates:

- the date 15 years after 50 percent of units are occupied
- the first day on which no tax-exempt bonds issued for the project are still outstanding
- the date on which assistance provided to the project code Section 8 of the United States Housing Act of 1937, as amended, terminates

Refunding Restrictions

The code permits advance refunding of qualified Section 501(c)(3) bonds. Refunding is considered advance refunding if the prior bonds are not redeemed within 90 days after refunding bonds are issued. However, advance refunding is subject to numerous restrictions.

Current refunding of qualified bonds is not subject to limitations of the code. However, the following provisions apply to current refunding:

- public approval
- 2 percent restriction on issuance costs

- arbitrage rules
- information reporting
- change in ownership

TAXABLE FINANCING

Taxable Bonds

Taxable bond financing has been and will continue to be a popular vehicle for financing retirement communities. Taxable bonds are available for more projects than tax-exempt bonds because of the myriad restrictions on tax-exempt bonds. However, maturities of taxable issues are generally shorter and interest rates are usually higher than for tax-exempt issues. Additionally, the upfront financing fees are more expensive than those for commercial loans.

Commercial Mortgage Financing

As retirement communities become an established industry, more banks and insurance companies are willing to provide traditional mortgage financing for retirement communities. These lenders favor rental-type projects, which they view and evaluate similarly to other real estate developments. Interestingly, foreign banks may be more receptive to financing retirement centers than domestic banks. Foreign banks find the retirement center investment opportunity appealing for several reasons:

- The U.S. dollar is devalued.
- Foreign banks are not subject to U.S. banking regulations and are not limited as to the states or counties in which they lend money.
- U.S. real estate investments are viewed as relatively safe investments.

An added advantage for the borrower is that the loan underwriting provisions of foreign banks are sometimes not as rigorous as those of domestic banks.

CREDIT ENHANCEMENTS

To enhance the marketability of bonds (taxable or tax-exempt) and lower the stated interest rate, credit enhancements may be obtained. Credit enhancements include bank letters of credit and personal, federal, or insurance company guarantees.

When bonds or mortgages are secured by some form of credit enhancement, the purchaser looks to the financial strength of the credit guarantor in assessing the financial risk rather than to the strength of the borrower or the feasibility of the project.

Letters of credit may be obtained from domestic or foreign banks. As in the case of mortgage lending, foreign banks are more interested in providing letters of credit for retirement center developments than are U.S. institutions. Additionally, foreign banks may be more willing to provide letters of credit on projects that domestic banks view as somewhat risky.

Credit enhancement fees are structured in a variety of ways. Banks will generally charge one to one and one-half points annually. Some insurance companies do not charge annual fees but charge substantial upfront fees and increase the mortgage amount to cover the fees. Federal Housing Authority (FHA) mortgage insurance may also be used and may have lower upfront fees and annual fees. However, the FHA places many requirements on services that may or must be provided, and obtaining FHA commitments may be a time-consuming process.

FUNDING ONGOING OPERATIONS

Residents of CCRCs pay either a one-time entrance fee and monthly maintenance fees or monthly rental fees. Contract terms may vary, and entrance fees may be nonrefundable, partially refundable, refundable on a declining basis over time, or fully refundable. Monthly maintenance fees may be all-inclusive or just cover basic housing needs, with access to health care services or other amenities provided on a fee-for-service basis. In the past, an entrance fee was analogous to the purchase price for a unit and was based on capital costs. Maintenance fees were based on the operating costs of the facility.

Set-up Research

Regardless of the precise contract structure, four tasks must be undertaken prior to the establishment of entrance and maintenance fees:

1. market assessment
2. calculation of expected fill-up and turnover
3. projection of health care utilization
4. projection of operating expenses and cash flow

Market Assessment

The market assessment should include a review of the age, gender, and economic demographics in the proposed service area and an analysis of the competitive market. In 1988, the average entrance fee for two-bedroom units nationally was $86,815, $68,823, and $56,011 for Type A, B, and C communities, respectively. Monthly fees for units averaged $1,149, $980, and $729 respectively.[4] The typical resident of a CCRC is an unmarried female over 75 years of age. While such national statistics may be helpful as guidelines in setting fees, research on the local market is critical to ensure that the project is priced competitively. In addition, the experience of other area providers in penetrating the market and achieving target occupancy and turnover rates should provide the potential developer with important information. The market assessment must also determine whether a sufficient pool of potential residents with adequate financial resources exists in the service area.

Calculation of Fill-up and Turnover

Based on the market analysis, primarily the age, gender, and economic distribution of the population and the profile of existing competitors, a fill-up term is calculated. The fill-up term is an estimate of the number of units to be occupied each month until the facility is at capacity. The initial census profile reflects the number (single versus double occupancy), age, and gender of residents.

The census profile is then modified to reflect mortality, morbidity, and withdrawal assumptions. These actuarial assumptions are key elements in the financial projections for a CCRC. Mortality assumptions provide an estimate of the length of time a resident will live after entering the CCRC, morbidity assumptions are used to project the future demand for health care services, and withdrawal assumptions are used to estimate the number of residents who will leave the CCRC for other reasons. Together, these assumptions are used to project unit turnover. The frequency of unit turnover, an estimate of the time to reoccupy a vacated unit, and a profile of replacement residents are all used in the development of a resident profile.

Health Care Utilization

If health care services are to be provided to residents as part of their entrance or monthly maintenance fees, it is important to project the volume and type of utilization expected so that fees can be set to cover costs. Projections of health care utilization incorporate the initial census profile, the profile of replacement residents, and the actuarial assumptions about mortality and morbidity.

Projection of Operating Expenses and Cash Flow

Operating expenses are those associated with the day-to-day functioning of the facility and typically include the salaries and supply costs of administration, plant operation and maintenance, food service, housekeeping, laundry, and health care services.

Establishing Entrance and Maintenance Fees

Entrance and maintenance fees must reflect the actual capital and operating costs of the facility. If entrance fees are to be set to cover capital costs (e.g., depreciation and principal), a present-value model of expected cash flow should be used. Such a model must incorporate assumptions about inflation rates as well as unit turnover and reoccupancy.[5]

Refundable Entrance Fee Approach

As discussed earlier, the industry trend is away from nonrefundable entrance fees to fully or partially refundable entrance fees. The analysis is essentially the same for establishing the fees for a refundable or nonrefundable entrance fee project; the only difference is the calculation of the increase in the endowment fee necessary to fund the refunds. The additional entrance fee requirement is invested, and this fee, together with interest earnings, is used to refund entrance fees as required. The additional entrance fee required to offer refunds or partial refunds is calculated relying on the projected mortality and withdrawal statistics for the initial and replacement residents as well as assumptions relative to the rate of interest earnings.

If a nonrefundable entrance fee was set at $84,000, the fee for a 50 percent refundable unit should be $106,703, assuming the average resident remains in the CCRC for 8 years and an 8 percent rate of return is generated by reserves. The calculations are as follows:

Entrance fee required	$ 84,000
Amount to be refunded (percent)	0.50
Refund guaranteed	$ 42,000
Present value factor (8 years at 8 percent)	÷ 1.85
Additional entrance fee required	22,703
Entrance fee with 50 percent refund	$106,703

Nonentrance Fee Approach

To estimate the maintenance fees required for a rental-type development, the analysis is essentially the same as that performed in the nonrefundable entrance fee model. The only difference is that all costs, including capital, must be financed through monthly fees. A present-value analysis is still required so that maintenance fees are set high enough to fund a reserve for financing future cost increases caused by increased health care utilization; thus, maintenance fees can be increased only to keep pace with inflation. If maintenance fees are set on an annual basis to cover only projected costs for that year, the resident would be forced to pay maintenance fees that increase much more rapidly than inflation as the resident's age and health care utilization increases. The resultant fee increases would not be tolerated by residents and would result in significant turnover of units.

The following case study illustrates the financial performance of a Type B retirement community.

Case Study

King's Bridge Retirement Center, Inc., is a 206-unit retirement community located in the Atlanta metropolitan area. Efficiency, one-bedroom, and two-bedroom residential units are available. The facility began operation in September 1985. The inability of the retirement center to meet certain covenants and payment requirements of its original loan agreement and the resultant decision of the original trustee to accelerate the maturity of the bonds necessitated the refinancing of the bonds. In 1987, bonds were issued by the Residential Care Facilities for the Elderly Authority of DeKalb County, Georgia. The information presented in this case study is from the official statement for the 1987 bond issue.[6]

Of the 206 residential units, 155 require entrance fees and monthly maintenance fees, whereas 51 are available for rental. Entrance fees may be nonrefundable or refundable based on the preference of the tenant. In 1987, refundable entrance fees were 25 to 52 percent greater than nonrefundable fees for the same unit, as shown below. Entrance fees were projected to increase 4 percent per year.

Unit Type	Nonrefundable Endowment	Refundable Endowment
Efficiency	$25,500	$38,800
Two-bedroom	$75,900	$94,700

King's Bridge is a Type B community, with health care benefits limited to 30 days per year at a skilled nursing facility of the resident's choice. Other services available at King's Bridge include a main dining area, lounges and kitchenettes, coin-operated laundries, a house laundry, a clinic with a four-bed infirmary, an activities room, a workshop, a beauty shop, and other recreational activities.

As of December 31, 1986, 15 months after the facility began operation, 109 units (53 percent of the total units) were occupied, only 10 of which were rental units. The projected utilization for the entrance-fee and rental units is presented in Table 24-1. As indicated, King's Bridge was expected to reach 96 percent occupancy of both the entrance-fee and rental units by 1989, four years after it began operation.

Table 24-1 Forecast Utilization

Utilization Type	1987[*]	1988[*]	1989–1991[*]
Apartments—Entrance-fee units			
Average number of units available	155	155	155
Number of units occupied at year end	127	149	149
Average number of units occupied	113	142	149
Average percentage occupancy	73%	91%	96%
Apartments—Rental units			
Average number of units available	51	51	51
Number of units occupied at year end	34	49	49
Average number of units occupied	20	46	49
Average percentage occupancy	40%	91%	96%

[*]All figures are as of September 30 unless otherwise indicated.

Source: Residential Care Facilities for the Elderly Authority of DeKalb County (Georgia). Official statement issued on January 28, 1987, in conjunction with issuance of $14.5 million in Series 1987 Bonds.

Monthly maintenance fees for 1987 are provided below for single-occupancy efficiency and two-bedroom units.

Unit Type	Monthly Maintenance Fee for Entrance-Fee Units	Monthly Maintenance Fee for Rental Units
Efficiency	$398	$775
Two-bedroom	$795	$1,785

As shown, monthly maintenance fees are significantly higher for the rental units. Maintenance fees were projected to increase 6 percent annually for entrance fee units and 4 percent for rental apartments.

Even with the projected increase in utilization and escalation in monthly fees, King's Bridge was still forecast to show an operating loss through 1991, three years after it reached 96 percent occupancy. Table 24-2 provides the forecast revenue and expense statements.

Table 24-2 Forecast Statements of Revenues and Expenses (in thousands)

Item	Year Ending September 30				
	1987	*1988*	*1989*	*1990*	*1991*
Operating revenues					
Monthly maintenance fees	$1,271	$2,025	$2,240	$2,368	$2,492
Other operating revenues	74	108	118	123	128
Entrance fees earned	155	369	377	388	402
Total operating revenues	$1,500	$2,502	$2,744	$2,897	$3,022
Operating expenses					
Administrative and maintenance salaries	185	192	200	208	216
Insurance	68	70	73	76	79
Marketing expenses	92	92	28	31	34
Dietary expenses	441	529	581	605	629
Housekeeping expenses	148	160	169	176	183
Utilities	166	215	234	247	260
Management fees	60	60	60	60	60
Health care expenses	125	131	138	145	152
Other operating expenses	113	118	123	127	133
Total operating expenses	$1,398	$1,567	$1,606	$1,675	$1,746
Excess of revenues over expenses before fixed charges, nonoperating revenues, and extraordinary item	$ 102	$ 935	$1,138	$1,204	$1,276
Fixed charges					
Interest expenses (Series 1987 bonds)	1,390	1,269	1,269	1,269	1,269
Interest expenses (other)	113	96	88	80	73
Letter of credit fees	66	65	47	47	47
Depreciation	424	424	424	424	424
Amortization, financing costs (Series 1987 bonds)	25	25	25	25	25
Total fixed charges	$2,018	$1,879	$1,853	$1,845	$1,838
Excess of expenses over revenues before nonoperating revenues and extraordinary item	($1,916)	($ 944)	($ 715)	($ 641)	($ 562)
Nonoperating revenues	155	190	239	247	244
Excess of expenses over revenues before extraordinary item	($1,761)	($ 754)	($ 476)	($ 394)	($ 318)
Extraordinary item (early extinguishment of long-term debt)	(1,439)	0	0	0	0
Excess of expenses over revenues	($3,200)	($ 754)	($ 476)	($ 394)	($ 318)

Source: Residential Care Facilities for the Elderly Authority of DeKalb County (Georgia). Official statement issued on January 28, 1987, in conjunction with issuance of $14.5 million in Series 1987 Bonds.

As is typical with many nonprofit retirement communities, King's Bridge is not projected to generate an excess of revenues over expenses until the project is occupied and debt is paid down. However, King's Bridge was projected to generate cash flow adequate to cover debt service requirements (Table 24-3).

SHOULD HOSPITALS INVEST IN CCRCs?

In response to declining profit margins and a mature inpatient market, many hospitals are seeking to diversify into nonacute care services. Is the CCRC market an option hospitals should consider? Based on the 1988 and 1989 annual surveys of diversification activities conducted by *Hospitals,* hospitals have not been particularly successful in the retirement community market. In 1988, only 36.3 percent of those hospitals investing in retirement communities made money.[7] In 1989, the proportion of hospitals reporting profits on retirement communities decreased to 25.7 percent.[8]

Additionally, as demonstrated above, retirement communities themselves do not generally generate positive net income until units are fully occupied and debt service is reduced.

Table 24-3 Ratio of Forecast Cash Available to Estimated Annual Debt Service on the Series 1987 Bonds (in thousands)

Item	Year Ending September 30				
	1987	1988	1989	1990	1991
Funds available for debt service on Series 1987 bonds	$2,385	$2,534	$1,228	$1,417	$1,531
Unrestricted cash, beginning of year	8	100	100	100	100
Entrance fee fund	0	957	1,985	1,732	1,674
Bond fund, beginning of year	0	317	317	317	317
Forecast cash available for debt service	$2,393	$3,908	$3,630	$3,566	$3,622
Estimated annual debt service (Series 1987 Bonds)					
Interest	$1,390	$1,269	$1,269	$1,269	$1,269
Other					
Developer's fee	260	140	140	140	140
Letter of credit fees	66	65	47	47	47
Total annual debt service requirement	$1,706	$1,474	$1,456	$1,456	$1,456
Ratio of forecast available to total annual debt service requirement	1.40×	2.65×	2.49×	2.45×	2.49×

Source: Residential Care Facilities for the Elderly Authority of DeKalb County (Georgia). Official statement issued on January 28, 1987, in conjunction with issuance of $14.5 million in Series 1987 Bonds.

Retirement community investments appeal to hospitals as hospital management believes that ownership in a retirement community may increase acute care market share and diversify revenue sources by increasing primary care and home health care revenues. These benefits are usually overestimated. Additionally, most hospitals lack the management expertise to be successful in the CCRC market. Hospitals may obtain increased revenues and image enhancement by joint-venturing CCRC projects with experienced professionals, entering into contracts to provide health care services to retirement community residents, or developing health maintenance organization or preferred provider organization agreements with retirement communities rather than developing a hospital-sponsored CCRC.

CONCLUSION

CCRCs will continue as an attractive life-style alternative for elderly Americans. To meet the needs of the aging population, new CCRCs will be developed. Estimates of future demand for CCRCs vary, but all projections indicate the significant demand for additional CCRCs will increase into the 21st century. The range of services available within the CCRC and the different types of CCRCs available will increase, providing residents the ability to select services and life styles best suited to their needs. More large units, in terms of square feet of living space, and fewer efficiency-type units will be developed. More projects will be financed by taxable vehicles, and fewer nonrefundable entrance-fee models will be developed.

NOTES

1. Communities for the Elderly, *Consumer Reports* 55, no. 2 (1990):123–131.

2. M.D. Kelly, State Regulation of Continuing Care Retirement Communities, paper presented at the Continuing Care Retirement Community Seminar, Captiva, Florida, June 1988.

3. Communities for the Elderly.

4. D. Dannenfeldt, Easy on the Glitz, but Long on Success, *Modern Healthcare's Eldercare Business* (1990):20–22.

5. J. Horowitz and J.B. Ryan, Structuring the Life-Care Contract To Minimize Financial Risk, *Topics in Health Care Financing* 10, no. 3 (1984):66–76.

6. Residential Care Facilities for the Elderly, Authority of Dekalb County (Georgia), Official Statement for Residential Care Facilities Refunding Revenue Bonds (King's Bridge Retirement Center, Inc., Project), Series 1987, issued January 28, 1987.

7. F.G. Sabatino, The Diversification Success Story Continues: Survey, *Hospitals* 63, no. 1 (1989):26–32.

8. F.G. Sabatino, Survey Managed Care Led 89 Diversification Improvements, *Hospitals* 63, no. 1 (1990):56–59.

Chapter 25

Food Service Management in Long-Term Care

Stephen Lawrence

Quality. Satisfaction. Cost. Compliance. These are a few of the pertinent challenges food service administrators often find testing their competence. In the fast-paced and unpredictable profession of food service management, industry leaders are increasingly expected to provide quality programs; ensure customer, staff, and resident satisfaction; maintain affordable costs; and ensure regulatory compliance.

In theory, the expectations seem simple. They are reasonable and well defined, controllable and concise. In reality, the factors that separate winners from losers, good programs from bad programs, are forever changing.

Successful food service administrators need to be well versed in many areas. Because health care changes and residents' individual prognoses differ, food service administrators continually need to evaluate menus and feeding systems, staffing and work patterns, equipment and dining areas, costs and reimbursements in order to satisfy facility objectives and ensure a good quality of life for residents.

THE ROLE OF FOOD SERVICE IN LONG-TERM CARE

Socialization

For many of us, mealtime provides an opportunity to gather with family and friends. It is the time of the day to catch up on news, to seek respite, to interact with others, to socialize.

At a stage in life when losses are common, residents need frequent stimulation and support to ensure a healthy self-esteem and wholesome frame of mind. As they have, during much of their lives, experienced dining as a social activity, residents often welcome the chance to eat with others. Meals present residents the same opportunities afforded to the noninfirm. By allowing peers to congregate, meals can become focused, celebratory events rather than periods of loneliness.

330

Many authorities believe malnutrition, widespread among the elderly, is largely attributable to loneliness.[1] Residents need friends and companions, and without them there is often a loss of appetite. Even though residents function at different levels, often passive socialization is as effective as active socialization in providing residents with support and companionship.

It is important not to lose sight of the fact that residents were independent before they became residents and had their own individual food likes and beliefs. Many have cooked at one time or another. Probably many, especially homemakers, feel they are culinary experts.

To capitalize on what many residents feel comfortable doing, food service and activities departments can work together to establish food-related activities. This can enhance individual self-worth by respecting the residents' culinary heritage and habits while creating additional arenas of socialization.

Sample activities include the following:

- Cooking or baking groups. Small groups of residents are assisted by a staff member. Foods may be served to other residents or sold to benefit the resident council fund.
- Social hours. Residents assist in planning special or regular gatherings. They may cut vegetables, make dips, or pour beverages.
- Basket making. Groups of residents prepare and arrange fruit baskets that are placed at nursing units for visitors, families, and residents.
- Food committee. Staff work with a resident group to maintain open lines of communication with the food service department. Food service stays attuned to menu likes and dislikes, and residents feel a part of the process.
- Seasonal, ethnic, or holiday dinners. Residents and staff work together to plan special dinners for residents.

Leaving home and losing independence and self-sufficiency present great challenges for the long-term care resident. It is a time of adjustment unlike any other time in life. Many residents become bitter, depressed, and antagonistic. Many adjust, however, and realize that by working with nursing home staff they can achieve an enjoyable, participatory normalcy to living. As Susan D. Dickes so accurately described, "Meals are often the last bastion of control, choice, and enjoyment for the residents of a long term care facility."[2]

Nutrition

Good nutrition and healthy eating patterns take on added importance in long-term care. As a result of the use of DRGs (diagnosis-related groups) and the provision of improved community health care services, residents enter long-term care more acutely ill than in times past. Generally, residents' nutritional needs are greater as a consequence. Common diseases prevalent among the elderly include heart disease, bone disease, cancer, diverticulosis, brain disease, gum disease, and diabetes.[3] Because of the natural degenerative problems that can affect individual nutritional status, the food service department must establish a positive interface with all disciplines to satisfy residents' nutritional requirements. Common degenerative problems, in addition to chronic diseases include these:[4]

- confusion as a result of change in environment
- psychological problems, including depression
- poor dexterity
- loss of coordination
- deterioration of eyesight or hearing
- socialization void
- constipation or incontinence

Assessing the Resident

An effective, comprehensive care plan starts with the nutritional assessment. This is historically done by the dietitian but is often performed by a diet technician. Frequently, dietitians formulate a personalized nutritional care plan utilizing a systems approach. This approach encompasses four parts: assessment, planning, implementation, and evaluation. The assessment includes gathering diet history information, performing a physical examination and laboratory tests, and taking anthropometric measures such as height and weight. The data gathered in the assessment are used in determining the plan. The plan lays out which measures will be utilized in fulfilling the goals outlined in the care plan. The third part of a systems approach is the implementation of the plan and the monitoring and documenting of the resident's response to the plan. Finally, the results of the implemented plan are measured and evaluated.

As a resident's eating pattern changes, for psychosocial, medical, or environmental reasons, so too should the resident's nutritional care plan. The systems approach enables dietitians to intervene quickly and to make responsive changes accordingly.

How Rigid a Diet?

There are differing philosophies as to how rigid a nursing home diet should be. Some believe that strict adherence to a prescribed diet will prevent further health deterioration and deter additional complications. Many disagree, however, believing that someone who is incapacitated and has little hope of regaining independence deserves the right to consume the kinds of foods he or she prefers.

The clinical and production components of a food service department need to work together to agree on a more liberalized interpretation of the geriatric diet. This may mean using less salt and less fat, minimizing purchasing of preprocessed foods (possibly high in sodium), using fresh vegetables and fruits, and allowing for the consumption of generous amounts of fiber and ample amounts of fluids. The residents' personal physicians should be consulted regarding the facility's menu preparation policies. Dietitians may want to obtain written releases from physicians to afford them the latitude to occasionally provide residents with menu items not normally congruent with the therapeutic diet plan. As the facility will not want to cause medical complications by serving the wrong kind of food, a physician's clearance is preferred.

The food service department has to balance clinical requisites against residents' individual food preferences. Changes in medical conditions and nutritional needs require the clinical team to monitor nutritional status and develop necessary interventions. However, interventions should not be rigidly implemented without regard for each resident's lifelong eating behaviors and preferences.

Dining Accommodations

To encourage residents' participation in meals, careful consideration must be given to decor of the dining areas. The dining areas should be well lit, well ventilated, clean, and well organized. Background music can create a soothing feeling, but too much noise can be distracting. Small groups at each table are more intimate, but if residents don't get along or distress one another, then meals will not be pleasant. If a resident has a lack of mobility or poor motor skills, then an alternative table height, adaptive feeding devices, and the use of a lapboard should be considered. Residents will have different needs in the dining room. Some may need coaching, some may need partial assistance, and others may need total assistance. Some residents may only need staff to open cereal, milk, or juice cartons.

Mealtimes should be respected. It is important that residents do not feel rushed while eating, and self-feeding should always be encouraged. Maintenance or housekeeping crews should put off cleaning or performing maintenance work until meals are over. Facilities may also want to avoid the passing of medications at meals.

Cyclical Menus

No matter how talented the culinary team, if the menu items selected do not reflect the personal preferences and ethnic diversity of its customer base, its efforts will be misdirected. Residents should be involved in the evaluation of menu items, and, since it is difficult to satisfy everyone all of the time, items selected should possess a broad appeal.

The food service department will want to gauge resident acceptance and consumption of meals. This can be done formally or informally, by observation in the dining room, plate waste logs, or formal audits of food quality and acceptance based on staff and resident surveys. Whatever the process, there are other key factors to consider when developing a menu: staffing patterns and production feasibility, equipment capability and space, feeding systems, therapeutic and nutritional necessities, regulatory requirements, and budgetary constraints.

Further, the food service department must consider the differing clienteles it is preparing for when writing menus. For example, if the department is responsible for feeding employees or servicing a Meals on Wheels program in addition to feeding residents, then the menu has to represent the consensus of all the different groups. Ideally, the department will have the staffing resources to serve different menus to the various feeding groups it prepares for. Also, the facility should decide whether the menu will be selective, partially selective, or nonselective. Again, how much can be offered to the residents depends on the priority given to selection and the staffing and budgetary resources the department has.

It is important to understand that there is much more to long-term care food and nutrition services than the grinding and pureeing of foods. Food service responsibilities in long-term care are much broader than in other forms of volume feeding. The food service department must work with the other disciplines involved in resident care in creating a family feeling within the facility. This might mean a midafternoon meal upon the return of a resident from the doctor, a special cake for Sunday evening to celebrate a son's visit, the procuring of nontraditional foods, or a half-hour of a staff member's time to just sit and listen. Successful food service departments do what they have to do to ensure acceptance and to understand that the opportunity available to them to make a difference in someone's life goes beyond hot food and hearty soups.

MANAGEMENT AND ORGANIZATION

Leadership Sets the Tone

As I thought about management and how I would explain my interpretation of it, I referred to Webster's dictionary for help. The initial definition of *management* is the "process of managing." Definitions of *manage* include "to direct or control the use of," "to exert control over," and "to make submissive."[5]

Summary of Contents

First Encyclopedic coverage of Long-Term Care — Your private consultant on hand at all times!

Increasing responsibilities. Limited resources. Residents arriving older and sicker, more infirm than ever. With increasing expectations and demands from

LONG-TERM CARE ADMINISTRATION HANDBOOK

Seth B. Goldsmith

AN ASPEN PUBLICATION

with those issues.

From how to reduce the problems - and costs! -- from TQM through negotiating your own contract ... from planning a new Alzheimer's Disease case unit through forecasting a future need for ADL caregivers ... from reducing bureaucracy in your facility through choosing between bank loans, tax-exempt bonds, real estate investment trusts, and FHA insured loans -- you'll have the knowledge and tools you need to proceed efficiently and successfully.

You'll learn how to ...

- staff specialized programs
- manage resources better through individualized nursing care plans for

- avoid deceptive durable medical equipment vendors
- implement a new adult day care center
- dovetail your leadership role with that of medical directors

You'll get the broad-based back-ground information, the detailed how-tos, and sample materials you need -- all geared to your perspective, your problems, and your objectives.

Steering you knowledgeably, reliably through the long-term care landscape of pitfalls and opportunities.

There's never been a resource so

...y members, the community, and regulatory agencies.

Long-term care administrators face problems and pressures unique in the health care industry -- and now you have the resource that tackles those challenges head-on. An encyclopedic handbook that covers a wide range of long-term care administration issues directly and in depth.

Right at hand -- your own consultation with more than 40 leading long-term care professionals.

The LONG-TERM CARE ADMINISTRATION HANDBOOK is an extraordinary collection of specialized, advanced expertise presented by long-term care administrators, consultants, academics, planners, attorneys, ...hitects, and nurses.

Chapter by chapter, the handbook explores the many, specific issues you face ... and presents practical, ready-to-apply answers and materials for dealing

each resident
- structure a mental health program elderly residents can accept
- select and cultivate members of your board
- structure an employee contract to avoid problems later on
- manage charges of sexual harassment
- protect facility assets through corporate reorganization
- develop a marketing plan for existing services or a new program
- use computers for resident care management
- improve your revenue and accounts receivable cycle
- manage a capital project fund development program from needs assessment through goal
- develop a new menu for residents that better meets their needs ... and yours
- do accurate construction budget estimating
- reduce legal risks
- contract management operations to independent agencies

exclusively devoted to your work, so completely dedicated to benefitting you.

With the **LONG-TERM CARE ADMINISTRATION HANDBOOK** within easy reach, you'll save time researching a new effort or a new solution. You'll avoid the loss of time to solutions that don't work ... the loss of dollars to mistakes you never had to make.

More importantly, you'll be able to strengthen your performance and that of your entire facility -- at every level -- with innovations, model programs, and procedures you otherwise might never have considered at all!

Certainly, management in the long-term care industry demands skills in controlling and directing processes and people. However, a certain amount of free-thinking, individual assertiveness, and responsible risk taking is also crucial. Accordingly, effective decision making and organizational success should be attributed not just to competent management but also to inspired leadership.

Leadership is difficult to define and arduous to teach. It is the art of transforming the common into the uncommon, of creating instead of conforming, of questioning before accepting.

As Drucker writes in *The Practice of Management,* "There is no substitute for leadership. But management cannot create leaders. It can only create the conditions under which potential leadership qualities become effective; or it can stifle potential leadership."[6]

What is the tie-in to food service management? There will be many difficult tasks that food service administrators will be expected to accomplish in the years to come: providing quality programs at reduced costs, creating and overseeing revenue-generating ventures, implementing employee retention and recruitment programs, responding to environmental issues and trash management, remaining abreast of food advances and product availability, remaining mindful of changes in the resident population and responding to growing needs, and keeping attuned to regulatory requirements. With industry changes encouraging creativity and fresh thinking, with resident outcomes overshadowing antiquated policy manuals, the opportunity exists for food service leadership to help frame the fiscal, social, and moral boundaries within which the profession functions.

Establishment of Objectives

Before a food service department can function efficaciously as a cohesive unit within an organization, the facility must first establish the objectives it intends food service to meet. The specificity of the objectives is critical for achieving desired results. The objectives may be outlined by the governing board, corporate planners, facility administrators, or the food service director. The objectives may delineate who the facility will feed, where the feeding and serving will occur, the levels of dining or service to be offered, and the budgetary parameters within which the department needs to work.

It is by means of the objectives that the senior management and the food service administrator can identify the needs and formulate the structure of the food service department.

Planning and Organization

The planning process of the department involves the interpretation of facility and department objectives and the formulating of strategies as to how best to achieve them. The process will be continuous, and the monitoring of systems, products, staffing patterns, and feeding options will be never ending. For example, a department objective might be "to serve high-quality, freshly prepared foods consistently." Within this general objective, more specific measures should be listed, such as "only fresh produce will be used" or "standardized recipes will be developed" or "choice-grade meats will be purchased." Specific objectives should be monitored and systems changed as the need arises.

One task that was mentioned earlier was the writing of the menu. Writing the menu is arguably the most important function within the department, especially at the outset, because it is the menu that determines equipment needs, staffing requirements, feeding systems, and food and sundry specifications. Facilities that do not put menu planning at the beginning of food service planning risk equipment duplication, service inefficiency, and cost overruns. The type of meal delivery system and accompanying menu should be established before kitchens, service elevators, dining rooms, storage areas, sculleries, and so on, are constructed and equipment procured. For example, if a facility utilizes a centralized tray-line form of feeding and dining areas are not close to the main kitchen, then additional personnel might be required to deliver food carts. Had the dining areas been placed near the kitchen or had service elevators been installed near the kitchen and dining areas, the food cart delivery function probably could have been assigned to already scheduled personnel.

Once the planning phase is completed, the organizational chart and the positions required for meeting established needs are created. Time studies may be used to help design daily work routines. These routines and the standards for performance evaluation must be objective and be based on actual requirements, not on personal ability or lack of ability. Drafted simultaneously are the job descriptions, which should list the position's basic purpose, general accountabilities and requirements, and location in the organizational chart (i.e., the lines of authority must be indicated).

Alternatives in Organizational Structure

A facility has options in the structural organization of its food service department. The size and scope of services often determine whether a facility chooses to hire an administrative dietitian or a food service director to lead the department. Both can bring valuable experiences to the facility. Departments are traditionally separated into two components, production and clinical nutrition, and management has to ensure a workable interface between the two to ensure effective delivery of services.

Food Production

Frequently the purchasing responsibility will be assumed by the food service director or supervisor. This individual will establish specific product specifications, inventory par levels, and purchasing protocols. Purchasing and inventory responsibilities should remain separate from production responsibilities. This will allow production staff to concentrate on preparing quality products and allow the person in charge of purchasing to focus on procuring quality and cost-effective supplies. It can also serve as a checks-and-balances means of inventory control.

The larger the facility and the greater the number of meals to be prepared, the greater the need for production supervision. Some facilities are able to use the cooks for supervising, but larger facilities require production supervisors or chefs to coordinate and supervise meal preparation. The production coordinator will be responsible for production schedules, recipe development and training, therapeutic and master menu adherence, cost control, and sanitation. Depending on the size of the facility, the coordinator may or may not actually cook for meal service.

The third component under the food production umbrella is service (tray assembly and delivery). Some facilities may decide to place all resident care services, including tray assembly, under clinical nutrition supervision. This may happen in large homes of 300 or more residents. More often than not, the food service supervisor will work with diet technicians in assembling trays and monitoring the process. Effective supervision during tray assembly ensures portion control, meal assembly accuracy, attractiveness and quality of trays, and proper serving temperatures. The actual serving of meals or trays is often performed by nursing staff. Nursing personnel know the residents well and understand all of the individual needs and idiosyncrasies that residents can have.

Sanitation is important in any food service operation, and in the highly regulated health care field it takes on added importance. Sanitation involves many areas within food service, including food and supply storage, food preparation, food handling and service, food holding and transportation, personal hygiene, environmental sanitation, and warewashing. State and local sanitation codes need to be obtained and procedures written in congruence with them. Management needs to provide in-service education for staff and to monitor sanitation consistently.

I could write several pages on sanitation, but since this is not a food service textbook, I will spare the reader. However, I would like to offer a perspective on sanitation that is often lost sight of.

Patrons of food establishments are sensitive to the sanitation conditions and practices. Whether the establishment be a restaurant, cafeteria, or nursing home kitchen, the patrons will notice when a cook is smoking in the kitchen, when a cook's uniform is soiled, when a food server's hair is long and uncontrolled, and when a kitchen is just plain filthy. The patrons are not going to say anything to the management, because they know if management was on top of the situation, conditions would be different. But they will communicate their misgivings to friends.

In a long-term care facility, if staff do not feel comfortable eating meals because of sanitary conditions, those feelings will be transferred to the residents.

Food service personnel need to understand the impact good sanitation practices can have in ensuring customer or resident satisfaction.

Clinical Nutrition

The clinical team will be headed by a dietitian. This person may or may not be registered, and whether he or she is part-time or full-time depends on state regulations and the size of the facility. Hopefully, the facility will select someone who shares the same nutritional ideology and who will complement the food service's delivery of services.

Dietitian

The primary responsibility of the dietitian is the nutritional care of the residents. This responsibility requires the assessment, planning, application, and monitoring of each resident's nutritional status and constant communication with other resident care disciplines. The dietitian is also a manager and will be responsible for formulating and directing the nutritional team to ensure that resident and facility nutritional objectives are met.

Nutritional Support Staff

The composition of the nutrition team will vary depending on the size and nature of the facility. Some facilities need the technical experience of a diet technician, who can assist the dietitian with assessments, care planning, counseling, and monitoring. In some cases, the diet technician will assume supervisory responsibilities within the clinical team.

Nutrition assistants or diet clerks often assume responsibility for patient feeding. They function as the day-to-day link between the clinical team and the production team. Their responsibilities may include menu selection and tallying, record keeping, quality control, and checking of the tray line. It will be the nutrition assistant's responsibility to ensure that the meals ordered are the meals that are served.

MAKING IT ALL WORK

The Director

I remember vividly a situation years ago when I first became involved in management. I was on the road and had to telephone my supervisor for advice. After advising me as to how best to handle the situation, he said to me, "So you want to be a manager, son, well let's see how you can manage now."

The director of food service will be confronted with many situations, and his or her span of accountability will be far-reaching. The director will need expertise in food production, nutrition, purchasing, budgeting, staff management, cost control, quality assurance, customer service, equipment maintenance, facility design, and catering.

The director must have effective communication skills and be able to work well with other department heads, since food service needs extend well outside the kitchen walls. The director must depend on housekeeping, maintenance, nursing, and materials management to ensure efficient operations. The director oversees the facility's lone production line and must make certain meals are produced and served on time. The director will have to instill in the management team a philosophy of pitching in and helping line staff to ensure that quality meals are served consistently.

These responsibilities make the director's job difficult. When uncontrollable and unscheduled circumstances arise, such as absences, product shortages, equipment malfunctions, spontaneous function requests, health department inspections, and fire drills, the director has to drop everything and utilize all of his or her resources to ensure resident meal service. Whereas other departments can cancel or reschedule work duties, food service rarely has that option, and it is the director's leadership and decision-making abilities that guarantee meal service is efficient and uninterrupted.

Staffing around Needs

Finally, effective food service departments are staffed around established needs and well-defined systems. It is crucial that a facility evaluate every dimension of food delivery from a systems point of view before creating an organizational chart or master work schedule. What does this mean? It means that after needs are established—such as how many staff are required to work the tray line, how many staff are required for scullery, or how many meals can be prepared by a cook—a time and work analysis is performed and daily work schedules are established. Daily work schedules are written for created positions and include specific time frames within which specific tasks are to be completed. It is through this approach that departments can prepare budgetary estimates while realistically accounting for specific work duties.

A facility can spare itself the likeliness of inefficiency and confusion by establishing positions around needs and not around individuals. It is through individual strengths and weaknesses that systems become vulnerable and inconsistency prevalent. If a function has been designed around an individual, what happens when that person is not available or leaves the organization? Does someone new come in and establish his or her own way of operating? What happens to the other departments, employees, and disciplines that interface with that position?

A facility needs to ensure constancy of systems regardless of who staffs a particular position. Smooth delivery of resident meal services depends on each food service employee working together consistently.

FINANCIAL MANAGEMENT

The financial control of any operation is one of the most important functions of management. This is especially true of food service. The food service director must develop prudent strategies to ensure consistent delivery of meal services within established budgetary parameters.

As was mentioned earlier, clearly defined objectives need to be established before financial planning can proceed. Such objectives are the basis for developing systems, creating staffing patterns, writing menus, costing meals, and formulating policies. In addition, records should be maintained and reports generated to provide the director with the information needed to investigate costs and control them.

The Operating Budget

The annual operating budget functions as the financial plan for the food service department. As changes occur in facility objectives and department needs, budgets may need to be altered. By separating the annual budget into 12 monthly periods, months can be planned differently and changes can be made more readily. Budget preparers should utilize historical data and inflationary projections in preparing budgets. Additionally, any change in operations that may affect cost projections, such as staffing patterns or supply consumption, should be factored in.

Information necessary in developing a comprehensive operating budget is listed below:[7]

• forecast of number of patient days and average food cost per patient day

- forecast of number of nonresident meals such as staff meals, special functions, stipend meals, and so on
- total salary, wage, and benefit expenses
- total expense for resident and nonresident meal service
- total costs for supplies such as disposables, serviceware replacement, cleaning agents
- continuing education

The formation of an operating budget is crucial to the overall success of the food service department. After budgets are planned, managers must continue staff education programs to ensure adherence to established policies and written procedures.

Budget Control

Effective department planning centers around the menu. When thinking about controlling costs and maintaining budgetary allowances, the menu is an important place to start. Departments should have in place effective measures to coordinate production, such as standardized recipe cards, meat and poultry pull sheets, production sheets with accurate meal counts, and established portion sizes. Accordingly, employees will need appropriate equipment to satisfy production expectations, such as scales, portion control scoops, ladles, and quart dippers. Overproduction is a common source of waste in a kitchen. Food production employees need to be mindful of costs and be motivated to control them. Employees also need to be trained to utilize foods and leftovers efficiently while ensuring quality and controlling product costs.

The storage of foods and sundries is also a significant factor in effective budget control. Supplies need to be stored in a proper environment, and correct refrigerator and freezer temperatures, proper lighting, and moisture prevention controls need to be in place.

Efficient receiving practices are another important factor in controlling costs. Receiving personnel should be oriented to food service products and be aware of product specifications and quality. Receiving personnel should have copies of product purchase orders in advance of delivery so that discrepancies may be handled at the time of delivery. Ideally, receiving should be separated from individual departments, including the food service department. Separating purchasing and receiving functions can serve as an effective checks-and-balances method.

Employee scheduling is also an integral part of budget control. Wage and salary lines often constitute the largest portion of operating expenses for a food service department. Using care in creating work routines, as well as cross-training staff and hiring of part-timers, can help prevent overtime.

Purchasing

Ideally, facilities have separate purchasing or materials management departments to procure needed supplies. Many long-term care facilities are not large enough for a separate department, and purchasing is handled by the food service director. It is important for a facility to understand the importance of purchasing and the time required to stay current with trends and changes in product availability and pricing. This is especially true of foods, including fish, produce, meat, and poultry. Again, to allow for checks and balances, it may be preferable to have ordering performed by a food service person but have actual purchasing handled by a purchasing department. Some of the different types of procurement systems commonly used are listed below.

Centralized. A separate department buys supplies and issues them to individual departments. Receiving may also be centralized or be handled by department. Vendors will meet with the purchasing department to receive orders but may meet with individual department heads to showcase new products.

Bid. There are two types of bidding systems, formal and informal (or contractual and noncontractual). In a formal bidding contract, vendors are given invitations to bid that contain specific product specifications, delivery agreements, quantities, payment terms, and so on. Prices may be guaranteed, but this is not always feasible. Formal bidding is common among large facilities. In informal bidding, common among smaller facilities, bids do not reflect quantities and may be given over the telephone.

Group Purchasing. It is possible for several institutions to consolidate their purchasing activities, generating volume for selected vendors and providing pricing benefits for the members. Members may pay a small fee to cover administrative expenses. The disadvantage is that the facilities may have to reach consensus on available product lines and specifications.

One-Stop Shopping. In one-stop shopping, a facility purchases all products from one supplier. The advantage is that less time is spent retrieving bids and processing quotations. The disadvantage is that the facility has no alternative source of products should the primary supplier not have the products available. Also, there is no built-in price protection mechanism, as there is when suppliers are bidding against one another.

Prime Vendor. In this scenario, a facility guarantees that 60 percent of its business will go to a prime vendor. This is common among purchasing groups. The prime vendor will bid, and the bids are calculated on the 60 percent estimated sales volume. The facility provides the vendor with purchasing volume information in advance.[8]

Purchasing Ethics

There are several questions regarding purchasing management must consider. First, are purchasing contracts awarded solely on the basis of compliance with established criteria such as product specifications, price, quality, service, delivery, and payment terms? A facility can become vulnerable when bids are not awarded using established criteria alone. It risks losing its purchasing edge when sales are awarded to vendors because of friendships, alliances, or corporate pressure.

Second, are vendor prices confidential? Salespeople lose their incentive to offer facilities the best price available to garner business when they are aware of the pricing they have to beat. For example, if vendor A has bid $12.00 for tomatoes and vendor B is aware of it, vendor B may bid $11.95 and win the contract. If vendor B had not known of the competitor's bid, maybe he or she would have bid $11.25. In addition, management loses the respect of vendors when it fails to maintain confidentiality. Salespeople will want to peruse food storage areas to discover the source of products purchased, but letting them in to do this is, in my opinion, a bad policy. In my dealings with salespeople in competitive situations, I am frank as to whom else I purchase from. This is acceptable and in fact helps maintain open, trustworthy, and objective relationships.

Third, should facility managers accept any personal gratuities such as tickets to sporting events, product rebates, bottles of liquor, and so on? Accepting such gifts obviously puts managers in a compromising situation. What if vendor A gives a manager a bottle of wine for Christmas and vendor B comes in and gives the same manager four tickets to a professional basketball game? That would be a situation I would not want to put myself in. I always like to retain the prerogative to deal or not deal with any vendor at any time based on the nonsubjective factors I mentioned earlier.

Finally, how a facility deals with questions of ethics depends on its entire management philosophy. How it conducts business with vendors is a reflection on the facility as a whole and on the authorized buyer. Does the facility exhibit character, show good moral judgment, and live up to standards of business etiquette? Whatever the facility chooses to do, hopefully it will gain an understanding of the leverage it has as a purchasing power and will never lose it.

INTERDEPARTMENTAL RELATIONSHIPS

Directing a food service department goes well beyond hiring staff, writing menus, and developing policies. It is not possible, in managing a food service department, to completely control all of the situations and decisions that affect a department. Management often is unable to control the external circumstances it may be forced to deal with. It can, however, remain cognizant of the department's original purpose, mission, and operating philosophy and not deviate from them. Managers must be content with controlling the controllable, or in this case managing the departments for which they are accountable. Managers must attempt to work within or change the parameters of the external factors (e.g., other departments) to satisfy their own departmental needs. This is easier said than done. For a start, department heads must educate their colleagues, in addition to their own employees, as to their goals, directions, intentions, and needs. Colleagues will respond more positively and offer their own departments' assistance to food service, if they feel they have been a part of the decision-making process.

Whether it is a matter of the housekeeping department setting up tables for a special function, stripping dining room floors, or washing the kitchen ceiling, the efficiency and effectiveness of the food service department often depend on the amount of support or lack of support the department receives from other departments.

CONCLUSION

It is not always possible to predict the future of an industry. Health care analysts, however, all agree that the long-term care industry will continue to grow for years to come. This grants food service leaders the opportunity to create new ways of feeding, new ways of providing compassion and care, and new ways of leading.

Finally, it might be useful to consider a theory of leadership that may help define what will be expected of food service managers in the future: the theory of cartwheels. This theory professes that managers must do what they have to do, buy what they have to buy, serve what they have to serve, change what they have to change, and lead where they have to lead to ensure that satisfying residents' food-related requests is the standard, not the exception. In short, it means they must do cartwheels.

NOTES

1. E.N. Whitney et al., *Understanding Normal and Clinical Nutrition* (St. Paul: West Publishing, 1987), 567.

2. S.D. Dickes, "Mutiny or Bounty?" *Contemporary Long-Term Care,* September 1989, 100.

3. E.N. Whitney et al., *Understanding Normal and Clinical Nutrition,* 555.

4. Ibid., 571.

5. *Webster's Dictionary II* (Boston: Houghton Mifflin, 1984), 433.

6. P.F. Drucker, *The Practice of Management* (New York: Harper & Row, 1986), 158.

7. R.P. Puckett and B.B. Miller, *Food Service Manual for Health Care Institutions* (Chicago: American Hospital Publishing, 1988), 84.

8. Ibid., 234–235.

Chapter 26

Developing an Effective Social Work Department

Harvey M. Shankman

The social worker is the first long-term care facility staff member that most families come into contact with. That initial encounter creates a perception about the professionalism, warmth, and effectiveness of the facility.

In a nursing facility, social workers are acutely visible at times of crisis, which include preadmission planning, postadmission adjustments, the resident's physical and cognitive decline, and the resident's death. The social worker's professional skills and empathy impact not only the resident's quality of life but also the family's and ultimately the community's perception of that long-term care facility.

Most social workers handle intake, admissions, transfers, discharges, counseling, financial planning, health care clarification, staff in-service, problem mediation, and documentation. A responsive, professional social service department is crucial to a well-run facility. The facility's first step in providing high-quality, efficient social services is to ensure staff have proper credentials.

PROFESSIONAL SOCIAL WORKER CREDENTIALS

In social work, the master's degree (MSW) is considered the best indication of a professional level of training and competence. Quality-oriented facilities prefer to fill their social work positions with MSWs because of their extensive training in human behavior, interviewing, psychopathology, aging, and case work and group work skills. Social workers with bachelor degrees are also qualified, although their classroom and field training curriculum is less extensive. Besides the academic degree, other relevant credentials and regulations include the following:

- *Licensing.* Most states license social workers, and a nursing facility must comply with the standards mandated by its state government.

- *Certification.* The National Association of Social Workers (NASW) confers the credential of Member of the Academy of Certified Social Workers (ACSW) on MSWs who have had two years of supervised postgraduate experience and have passed a national examination.
- *Joint Commission Standards.* The Long Term Care Division of the Joint Commission on Accreditation of Healthcare Organizations states social service personnel must be "currently licensed, registered, or certified in accordance with federal, state, and local requirements." The Joint Commission standards reflect high expectations, emphasizing the social worker's duties in the areas of counseling, advocacy, provision of access to community resources, and development of resident and family councils.
- *HCFA.* In contrast, the Federal Health Care Financing Administration has set extremely low requirements. HCFA mandates skilled nursing facilities with more than 120 beds to employ one qualified, full-time social worker. This regulation, as of April, 1992, identifies a social worker as an individual who has a bachelor's degree in social work or in a human services field and has one year of supervised experience in a health care setting. (In the author's opinion, a more realistic requirement would be one MSW for every 50 to 60 beds.)

Assuming that a nursing facility has qualified social work staff, this paper will move on to identify program elements of an effective Social Service Department.

INTAKE

Most referrals to nursing facilities are made by an adult daughter, who is usually overwhelmed and feeling guilty. This woman, typically in her late fifties, is probably a member of the "sandwich generation." She faces the stress of meeting not only the overwhelming needs of her medically fragile parent but also the emotional and financial needs of her own children, who may be in college, buying a house, or about to have a child. She and her husband are facing their own health problems due to aging and their own financial needs as retirement rapidly approaches.

Prior to contacting the long-term care facility, the daughter has had to contend with her parent's medical crisis, which frequently included hospitalization. Unfortunately, medical jargon used by care providers, such as *myocardial infarction, dementia, transient ischemic attacks, incontinence, prosthesis, cerebral vascular accident, DRGs,* and so on, is often never fully explained. The adult child only knows for sure that Mom (or Dad) will be discharged in several days and that it is her responsibility to find a nursing home. The physician and nursing staff rarely discuss with the family tangible issues such as Medicare, Medicaid, or nursing facility costs, and emotional issues are usually avoided like the plague.

THE INITIAL FAMILY INTERVIEW

Families today are much more knowledgable about what to look for and what questions to ask when seeking a nursing facility. They have often received materials on how to select a nursing home from hospital social workers, local offices on aging, the area long-term care ombudsman's program, and so on. Also, many adult children have participated in support groups run by organizations such as the Alzheimer's Association, where information about what to look for in a long-term care facility is readily shared.

The following is a list of suggestions regarding the first interview:

- When possible, the applicant, all adult children, and significant others should be present during the first interview. This will prevent misinformation, repetition, and confusion.
- It is clinically informative to interview the applicant and the family both jointly and separately.
- Even when obvious, the social worker should ask the family members why they are there and give them a chance to tell their story.
- Accurate medical and social histories are essential. The social worker should ensure that the family members understand the applicant's diagnoses and prognoses.
- Authorizations for the release of medical information should be obtained.
- Alternatives to nursing home placement should be explored, and the family members should always be asked what they have already tried.
- The facility's cost of care should be reviewed as well as the applicant's eligibility for Medicare and Medicaid.
- The applicant and family should tour the facility.
- If the facility cannot accommodate immediate placement, the social worker should assist the family in working out a short-term solution.
- The social worker should help the family to develop a consensus on advanced medical directives (e.g., a living will or durable power of attorney).
- A financial plan, taking into account the applicant's savings, assets, eligibility for Medicare and Medicaid, and prepaid burial expenses, should be discussed.
- A family plan of action should be developed, with one family member being given the responsibility for follow up.

In view of all the above information to be obtained and the plethora of feeling erupting from the applicant and family, it should not be surprising that more than one interview may be necessary. It is also not unusual for the adult children to come in alone for the first interview, since many are overwhelmed and need help in order to tell their parent that nursing home placement is necessary. Other times the parent is demented and unable to actively participate in decision making.

Although the first family interview is stressful and may require crisis intervention techniques, it also represents an opportunity for the adult children and the applicant to see the nursing facility as capable of playing a positive, helpful role. In spite of often unyielding pressure from the administration to "keep the beds filled at all times," the social worker must never function as a rental agent. Instead, by permitting the family members the time to tell their story, by taking a complete social history, by explaining medical terminology and its significance, by offering financial information, and by explaining what life is like in a long-term care facility, the social worker can establish a significant helping relationship. The social worker will have had the opportunity to counsel, educate, and provide direction and information to a family in crisis. If done well, a bonding process will often occur, permitting the family to feel a sense of trust and security in the social worker and the nursing facility he or she represents. The resulting bond will prove invaluable in follow-up interviews and at times of significant change following admission. Since many high-quality nursing homes have waiting lists, this bond will also be a decisive factor in the family's decision at a later time if during the interim their parent was placed at another facility.

WAITING LISTS

When a waiting list exists, it is essential that the social worker maintain monthly contact with the family. One family member should be designated as the liaison. It is helpful to request that the family liaison be the one to initiate the monthly contact with the social worker to guarantee it takes place. Families are often worried that their parent will be forgotten without regular contact, and the contact permits the social worker to maintain the bond with the family.

If the waiting period is six months or longer, health information may have to be updated prior to admission. It is always helpful for the social worker to keep additional signed medical release forms in the applicant's chart, since updated medical and hospital records will be necessary. When a long waiting period occurs, the social worker may want to consider referral to an adult day-care center if appropriate. Should an interim nursing facility become necessary, it is very meaningful to the applicant and family if the social worker visits. Making a visit will also give insight into the applicant's and the family's adjustment to an institutionalized setting.

When the applicant reaches the top of the waiting list, it is beneficial to arrange a lunch visit. This permits the soon-to-be-admitted resident an additional opportunity to become familiarized with staff, a potential roommate, facility routines, and the layout of the building. It also provides the social worker with an additional opportunity to validate the applicant's physical, social, and emotional needs.

THE PREADMISSION CONFERENCE

The preadmission conference is an opportunity for the applicant, family, and nursing facility staff to prepare for the admission, which should occur very soon after. The following should be accomplished during the preadmission conference:

- an introduction to the staff, unit, room, and if appropriate, the roommate (this helps lessen the anxiety of the soon-to-be resident and the family)
- the gathering of updated medical information, including a current list of medications
- an explanation of what medical and ancillary services will be offered to the resident during the first month
- a reminder of what clothing, personal items, furniture, and so on, are appropriate to bring at the time of admission
- a reminder of what financial arrangements must be finalized at the time of admission

A successful preadmission conference will give the family and the soon-to-be resident a sense of control over the imminent admission. It also may provide an opportunity to complete administrative paper work so that the social worker can spend more time with the new resident on the day of admission. Lastly, it is an ideal time to set up a postadmission family conference, which should occur a month after the admission.

RELOCATION ADJUSTMENT

It will take a new resident up to six months to become adjusted to the nursing facility. Even if the resident was previously in another nursing home, each facility has its own environment, staff, daily routines, and activities. The term *admission fog* aptly describes the anxiety, confusion, and disruption that impacts new residents. In most cases, the fog lifts within three to six months, and the resident achieves his or her optimal level of functioning.

The role the family plays can assist or hinder the new resident's adjustment. If the family is conflicted and tenuous, the adjustment will be much harder for the resident. If the family is nurturing yet firm that the placement is the only alternative, the adjustment period will often be easier and shorter. If the family is about to go out of town, it is prudent to delay the admission until the family returns. In situations where the resident is having an adjustment problem, the social worker should promptly involve the family in searching for a solution.

Frequent visits by the family at the time of admission help to reduce the relocation effect and should be encouraged. Ideally the family will visit 15–20 minutes per day for the first two weeks. These visits will reduce the resident's and family's anxiety and will also allow the staff to establish a relationship with the family. Following the first two weeks, the family should be encouraged to develop a visitation pattern that is less intense and that fits with the lifelong relationships and dynamics of the family.

INDIVIDUAL COUNSELING

Social workers labor at building trusting relationships with their clients and then use those relationships to help the clients do as much of their own problem solving as possible. If the social worker assigned to the new resident must be replaced by another after admission, an orderly transfer should take place over a 30-day period. The resident must be introduced and given an opportunity to develop a trusting relationship with the new social worker.

The social worker should regularly visit each resident, even during periods when a resident's condition remains stable. Regular family contact is also beneficial, and family members should be encouraged to call or stop by the social worker's office whenever they have a question.

SOCIAL SERVICE DEPARTMENT HOURS

An effective social service department will provide for some flexibility in its hours of operation. Since many family members work during the day, it is helpful to offer one evening per week or time during the weekend for social work appointments. To avoid hardship, the social workers can rotate to cover the added hours. More often than not, however, one social worker will actually enjoy having one day a week with a 1:00 PM to 9:30 PM schedule. This one late workday will provide the social worker with many unanticipated benefits, such as improved relationships with the second shift, a less pressured time to meet with families and residents, and quiet time to catch up with paper work. It is also very helpful for the social worker to schedule open office hours during which residents and families are invited to drop by to visit. This informal arrangement can help the social worker maintain a strong relationship with residents and families with whom he or she would not ordinarily schedule an appointment. Not surprisingly, for this arrangement to be effective, the social worker's open office hours must be well publicized.

Some social service departments sponsor an annual or biannual open house to allow families to meet with staff and learn about new programming or changes at the facility. Maintaining strong resident and family relationships proves advantageous to social workers, especially when the inevitable crises of long-term care occur.

The social worker will have many opportunities to offer one-on-one counseling to the resident, particularly when a family crisis occurs or when the resident feels isolated or depressed, is upset about a roommate, is experiencing a physical or mental change, or must move to a different living unit.

The insight into the resident and family gained by the social worker through interviews and counseling is invaluable to the interdisciplinary team in providing high-quality care and in formulating a comprehensive resident plan of care.

USE OF GROUPS

Social workers are trained in group work while in graduate school and should utilize their skills on an ongoing basis. Depending on the interests and needs of the residents, groups may focus on relocation adjustment, reminiscence, education, therapeutic issues, or some common task. In spite of the fact that many residents blossom in groups and that groups are easy to set up in nursing homes, this modality is underutilized in most facilities.

Many facilities have a group designed for new residents. This group lessens the anxiety of new residents by permitting them to express their feelings about their physical and cognitive losses as well as their feelings about placement. This type of group also aids the participants in developing relationships with each other, clarifying where things are located in the building, and encouraging involvement in activities and programs.

FAMILY ADJUSTMENT GROUPS

Today's nursing home resident is older, more frail, and less likely to play an active role in decision making. Professionals report that 60–70 percent of all nursing home admissions have a diagnosis of dementia, have five or more medical diagnoses, and are taking five or more medications. The increase in acuity level makes it even more necessary for the social worker to work closely with the family. Support groups for adult children of cognitively impaired residents should be considered as a possible supplement and, in some cases, even an appropriate alternative to individual counseling.

Even in the case of a cognitively impaired resident, that individual's ability to adjust to nursing home placement is linked to the family's adjustment. If the family remains anxious, projects feelings of neglect onto the staff, or is overly involved in care issues, an optimal adjustment will never occur. In some instances, a family will not respond to individual counseling but will benefit greatly from a group experience. Family groups can be assembled to address the issues of orientation, admission, physical and cognitive decline, education, ongoing support, and so on. A family council is a good example of a task-oriented group that often becomes an excellent booster of the facility.

Guilt is the most common feeling displayed by families, and to some degree it may be inevitable. Adult children often feel guilty that their parent cannot be cared for at home. Spiritually, the children may wonder how they can "Honor thy Mother and Father" by placing them in an institution. Also, children with high personal expectations may feel very upset that they are abandoning the parent. Although individual counseling helps many children, group support from peers may be necessary for others.

One population often overlooked consists of well spouses. Spouses living in the community have a very stressful role. They are married and yet have partners too physically or cognitively impaired to function in a mutual relationship. The well spouse is often shunned by married friends who do not know what to say and therefore avoid contact. The well spouse is expected to be nurturing to the institutionalized mate and to visit regularly, even though the ill spouse may not know who the well spouse is. The well spouse may be afraid to go out socially or express upset to the children, may become overly involved in the ill spouse's care, or may exhibit depressed behavior. Many well spouses are good candidates for a group, and every facility should consider a spouse group.

DOCUMENTATION

Increasingly, all disciplines are spending significant amounts of the workday meeting documentation requirements. Social services is no exception, and ensuring high-quality documentation is essential. The social worker must compile various intake materials, preadmission histories, admission summaries, monthly notes, quarterly notes, plans of care, and multiple forms of correspondence with families, health providers, and social service agencies. Specialized documentation may often be necessary to meet various state Medicaid requirements. The following suggestions can make some of this documentation burden more manageable:

- Whenever possible, social service documentation should be typed. This not only gives the notes, summary, or history high visibility but also makes the information more likely to be read by other members of the interdisciplinary team. In small facilities lacking a social service secretary, a word processor for the social worker is often a solid investment.
- Social service staff should be encouraged to attend seminars and workshops on writing plans of care, minimum data sets, and other specialized documentation. Too often these workshops are only offered to nursing and medical records personnel, and key elements of proper documentation are never fully shared with social services.
- The social service department should make a documentation audit part of its regular quality assurance program. By doing so, problem areas can be immediately identified and rectified rather than coming to light during a state licensure and certification survey.

PROFESSIONAL INVOLVEMENT

An effective social service department challenges itself to reach beyond the walls of the long-term care facility. Social workers should be involved in local, state, and national gerontological and professional organizations. They should serve as field instructors for social work students from nearby universities. They should be encouraged to volunteer as speakers on aging and to participate in aging support groups. These outside activities invariably generate innovative ideas, such as intergenerational activities, oral histories programs, and resident newsletters.

By actively participating in the field of gerontology, social workers not only increase their knowledge and sharpen their professional skills but also promote a positive image for their long-term care facility. As the acuity level of nursing facility residents rises and the sophistication and expectations of families expand, the social worker's role must evolve in new ways in order to help maintain the vitality of the facility's programs and services. Having an effective social service department is crucial if the facility is to meet the major challenges of providing high-quality care during the last decade of this century.

BIBLIOGRAPHY

Abrahamson, J. 1983. Social services in long-term care. In *Creative Long-Term Care Administration,* ed. K.G. Gordon and R. Stryker. Springfield, Ill.: Charles C Thomas.

Brody, E.M. 1977. *Long-Term Care of Older People: A Practical Guide.* New York: Human Sciences Press.

Burger, S., et al. 1986. *A Guide to Management and Supervision in Nursing Homes.* Springfield, Ill.: Charles C Thomas.

Joint Commission on Accreditation of Healthcare Organizations. 1989. *Joint Commission 1990 Long Term Care Standards Manual.* Chicago: Joint Commission on Accreditation of Healthcare Organizations.

Silverstone, B., and Hyman, H.K. 1982. *You and Your Aging Parent.* New York: Pantheon Books.

Chapter 27

More Than Passing Time: Activities Programs in New York City Nursing Homes

United Hospital Fund of New York

This report is the product of the United Hospital Fund's Nursing Homes–Long Term Care Committee, which, for the last three decades, has worked to improve the quality of life in New York City nursing homes. Founded in 1962, the Committee visits nursing homes throughout the city, creating a public presence in institutions that all too often exist on the periphery of community interest. The volunteer members of the Committee observe interactions between staff and residents, evaluate the physical environment, and take note of the types of therapy and activities programs available. The Committee also publishes reports, which provide qualitative and quantitative information about individual facilities. The reports, updated frequently, have proven valuable for individuals who must choose a nursing home either for themselves or for a relative, as well as for community and hospital social services staff involved in the nursing home placement process.

Over the years, the focus of the Committee's work has changed, reflecting changes in the nursing homes themselves. As regulatory oversight has improved and the number of overt deficiencies has declined, and as the population of nursing homes has grown older and frailer, the Committee's mission has shifted from identifying gross abuses to improving the quality of life for all residents. Most recently, the Committee has focused on activities programs, an increasingly important factor in determining quality of life, but one which is not always accorded the attention and resources it deserves.

In an effort to identify the elements of successful activities programs, as well as the problems that too often limit their scope and effectiveness, the Nursing Homes–Long Term Care Committee prepared this report. It follows a year of intensive efforts, during which Committee members developed and administered a survey, visited nursing homes to follow up on survey results, and met with

Source: Copyright United Hospital Fund of New York, 1992. This report was written by Ellie King, with the assistance of Deborah E. Halper, Irving Brickman, Judy Levin, and Phyllis Brooks.

activities directors, academic experts, administrators, and government officials to discuss their findings.

The report would not have been possible without the efforts of a great number of people, first and foremost, the volunteers on the Nursing Homes–Long Term Care Committee, who have devoted untold hours to the Committee and to this project. Ellie King, former chairperson of the Committee and author of the report, deserves special recognition; her knowledge of and commitment to the subject inform the pages that follow. The report was enriched by the insights of Irving Brickman, long-time Committee member, and Judy Levin, staff associate, who did substantial work on the report. I would also like to acknowledge, gratefully, the contributions of the members of the advisory committee, who were instrumental in helping to establish a direction for the project, and the activities directors and staff who participated in the survey and follow-up discussions. Finally, the report owes a great deal to the efforts of Deborah E. Halper, Director of the Fund's Division of Education and Community Services, who has provided invaluable support and guidance to the Committee for the past five years. This project serves admirably as a benchmark for the Committee's mission and activities in the years ahead.

Bruce C. Vladeck
President
United Hospital Fund of New York

INTRODUCTION

Out of the experience of the two world wars came a recognition of the need for some form of recreation in medical settings, initially for the wounded, subsequently for disabled and hospitalized veterans, then for the mentally ill and disabled, and finally for everyone requiring long-term care. By the end of the 1960s, activities programs were well established as one of the services routinely provided in nursing homes, but there was no real consensus on their underlying principles or status within the institution. Recreation was, and still is, seen as a means of fulfilling a variety of functions, from simple entertainment and diversion to significant therapeutic intervention as part of an overall care or rehabilitation program.

This report, the product of the United Hospital Fund's Nursing Homes–Long Term Care Committee, is based on visits to nursing homes, meetings with staff, and a survey of directors of activities programs. In addition to describing the range of programs offered, the report discusses how programs are designed and evaluated, identifies problems in developing and providing services, profiles model programs, and makes recommendations for future policy and programmatic directions. Before the Committee's findings are described, however, a brief review of pertinent changes in the nursing home population and code over the past 20 years is in order.

Older and Frailer Residents

As the number of elderly people increases rapidly, it is the oldest, frailest, and sickest among them who are placed in nursing homes. This trend is reinforced by several factors in addition to the aging of the population. The number and variety of community-based programs for the elderly (e.g., adult day care, long-term home health care) have grown, enabling many elderly people who formerly would have been institutionalized to remain at home. In addition, reimbursement changes in both hospitals and nursing homes have encouraged nursing homes to admit the frailest patients. Since 1986, hospitals in New York State have been paid under a prospective case payment system, which creates incentives to reduce the length of hospitalization. Thus, patients are discharged earlier, often while still in need of services either in nursing homes or at home. At the same time, under the resource utilization groups (RUGs) payment system, nursing homes are paid most for those patients who use the most resources and are thus encouraged to admit patients who need the greatest amount of care.

As a result of these changes, the profile of the nursing home population today is quite different than it was 10 years ago. Approximately 45 percent of all nursing home residents are now over the age of 85, usually with multiple physical, psychological, or chronic problems; many are wheelchair-bound. As steadily increasing numbers of them require substantial care, the nursing home has come to more closely resemble a health care facility than a residential center.

Regulatory Issues

New York State regulations mandate that nursing homes provide activities to promote residents' sense of "usefulness and self-esteem" and encourage voluntary, individual choice among the activities offered. Recent revisions of the state's nursing home code, which took effect on October 1, 1990, brought the state in compliance with the federal Omnibus Budget Reconciliation Act (OBRA) of 1987, which emphasized the importance of increasing individual residents' rights as a means of improving overall quality of care and life. Among the legislation's provisions was the directive that the use of restraints be significantly reduced. When implemented, this requirement will have tremendous implications for activities programs because previously restrained residents will now need additional supervision and care, as well as a range of safe and stimulating activities. It is worth noting that the legislation targets those residents currently least able to participate in programs of any kind. The OBRA-driven code revisions also mandate activities that meet the special needs of those with hearing, visual, and mental impairments, as well as activities that respond to residents' "interests, education and experience."

If the revisions in the nursing home code significantly expanded the charge of activities programs, they did little to resolve the underlying dispute about the role and status of recreation in nursing homes. Indeed, the code continues to take a rather casual view of the demands of such programs. For example, in language virtually unchanged from earlier versions, the code lists three broad options for qualification for the position of activities director, despite the greatly increased need for personnel who are specially trained to devise programs appropriate for residents with complex physical and psychological disabilities and to recognize even minimal response to stimulation.

THE STATE OF THE ACTIVITIES ART

The Nursing Homes–Long Term Care Committee's yearlong study of activities programs revealed serious and systemic problems, but at the same time a variety of encouraging and effective solutions. It was clear that the questions the Committee raised in its survey (Appendix 27-A) were considered important; many were already being addressed by those in the field. Response to the survey was positive, with 83 surveys of 157 returned (53 percent) (Table 27-1).

The most fundamental problem—activities programs' lack of a clear-cut identity—emerged in the response to the survey's first question, "What is the department called. . .and what is its goal?" Just under half the respondents (49 percent) use the federal and state term *activities*, while 31 percent use the term *therapeutic recreation* or *recreation therapy.* Another 13 percent simply use the term *recreation.* Finally, one nursing home, in an echo of an earlier era, calls its program *leisure time activities.* The variety of titles suggests that there is no real consensus about the role activities programs play in nursing homes.

Table 27-1 Response to Survey

	Total Facilities	Surveys Received	Percentage
Voluntary	61	40	66
Proprietary	91	39	43
Municipal	5	4	80
Total	157	83	53

Statements of program goals or mission are less varied; virtually all appear to be either paraphrases of or direct quotations from the New York State code, which reads:

> to meet. . . the interests and the physical, mental and psycho-social well-being of each resident. . . to promote and maintain the resident's sense of usefulness to self and others, [to] make his or her life more meaningful, [and to] stimulate and support the desire to use his or her physical and mental capabilities to the fullest extent.

To determine how effectively program objectives are implemented and to identify obstacles, the Committee made special visits to nursing homes and undertook an analysis of the basic elements of activities programs and of the institutional and administrative environment in which they take place. To be effective, Committee members concluded, an activities program must carefully assess residents' needs, design and implement programs to meet these needs, take steps to ensure participation, and systematically evaluate program outcomes.

Assessment: The Essential First Step

The resident's physical, mental, and social skills and needs must be carefully and accurately assessed in order to develop a good match with the activities program. Under New York State regulations, a comprehensive clinical and psychosocial assessment must be carried out within 14 working days of admission; interviews with the new resident are to be given primary consideration in any subsequent decisions. It is not surprising, therefore, that almost all facilities (92 percent) reported that interviews with the residents themselves are the most important factor in determining their abilities and interests.

Since most residents are sick, confused, disoriented, or hard of hearing, however, it takes considerable skill, sensitivity, and tenacity to obtain information that will be useful in developing the activities plan. A frequent problem, given staff shortages, is the lack of time in which to elicit a response. The assessor must have strong interviewing skills in order to overcome these obstacles.

Next in importance, according to almost 60 percent of the respondents, are the staff's interdisciplinary conferences at which preadmission information and the minimum data sets (MDS+), New York's resident assessment instrument, are discussed. For activities directors who have limited training or experience with regressed or frail residents, the MDS+ can serve as a useful tool in establishing the resident's physical and cognitive abilities. However, a link must then be made between this essentially clinical information and the resident's past interests and experiences in order to formulate a comprehensive care plan. The MDS+ cannot substitute either for the skill needed to integrate the resident's physical, emotional, and other needs in developing an activities program or for the sensitivity and intuition of a nursing home's staff.

Interviews with family members ranked third in importance, perhaps not surprisingly in a country where adult children frequently live far from their aged parents. Relatives are not always a reliable source of information, however; some may have forgotten small but significant details. Others, for a variety of reasons, may have selective memory or even misinformation (e.g., Did Mother really love to cook or did she cook only because she had to? Was Dad really an avid sports fan or was he just trying to be "one of the boys"?). Finally, family members may themselves be preoccupied and worried, still trying to cope with their decision to place their parent in a nursing home. Nevertheless, given the increasing numbers of disoriented and sick residents, family interviews remain an important, if not primary, factor in developing an activities plan, and several activities directors indicated their belief that greater efforts should be made to locate and work with family members.

Evaluation: Measuring the Immeasurable

Like program development, evaluation is often constrained by the nature of the current nursing home population. Resident interviews were identified by 89 percent of the facilities as the most important factor in evaluating a program's success. A close second was resident council feedback; staff feedback was a distant third (Figure 27-1). Again, given today's nursing home population, interviews with residents may not elicit an adequate response. Resident councils, typically—and necessarily—composed of the most mobile and alert among the population, are always vocal in suggesting activities, but may not be adequately representative of the wishes or needs of the majority. They can help to obtain feedback, however. Several facilities evaluate their programs with the assistance of residents' representatives who attend programs for the more regressed population and report back on the response, if any.

In practice, however, it is generally the staff who determine through daily observation what types of stimulation elicit a positive reaction from which residents. Ideally, everyone on staff from housekeepers to nurses should be sensitive to what constitutes a response, which may be as little as the blink of an eye, but interviews indicate that it is usually the activities staff and sometimes the aides and orderlies who make these judgments.

Attendance lists are usually required for group programs, but they may be inadequate for purposes of evaluation, since they may not reflect either resident interest or degree of participation, except if attendance is exceptionally low. And even

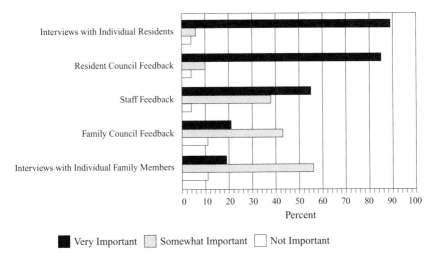

Figure 27-1 How programs are evaluated. *Source:* Based on responses to a survey conducted by the Nursing Homes–Long Term Care Committee of the United Hospital Fund.

low attendance may be misleading; it may indicate a lack of awareness of the activities schedule as much as a lack of interest.

Ensuring Participation

Even the best-designed and most appealing activities may fail to attract residents if efforts are not made to ensure participation. Calendars are the traditional way of informing residents and staff of scheduled activities, but their usefulness is limited. Some calendars are too small and difficult for residents to see and read, but even when the monthly schedules posted in the hallways are legible, colorful, and imaginative, residents and staff do not necessarily use or remember to look at them.

The survey found that most facilities rely on staff reminders (77 percent) and individual calendars (73 percent) to inform residents of the activities schedule. A combination of the two probably works best, but these methods have their drawbacks. Individual calendars, even when marked to indicate an individual's preferred programs, may be forgotten or misplaced. Some activities directors enlist the nursing staff, particularly the aides, to remind residents about specific programs, with mixed results. Some aides are very helpful and know and care if a resident participates in activities; others may say that reminders are not their responsibility and that they don't have the time to constantly check the schedule. It helps when the activities director and staff notify each unit's nursing staff which activities offered that day will be most appropriate for which residents.

However, time constraints and lack of personnel in many facilities may make this procedure difficult to do on a regular basis.

Most often, reminders are made over the public address system, again, with mixed results. For example, observers report that announcements may be made too late to allow residents to be taken to another floor, or even to the unit day room. In addition, experts emphasize that some residents need reminders every few minutes, and particularly disoriented or forgetful residents may need an escort just to get to the right place. These efforts take time, almost always the activity staff's time, stretching their usually small numbers to the limit. Add to the problem the fact that most facilities (88 percent) rely on activities staff to transport residents to and from activities, and it becomes clear that simple logistics can cut into the duration, frequency, and above all the quality of the programs. Clearly, the traditional methods of encouraging participation need to be re-examined in light of the current resident population; what worked years ago may no longer be effective.

PROGRAM PROFILES

Designing appropriate programs for today's nursing home population is complex and challenging. In the past, residents were generally able to participate more fully, and activities such as current events discussions could be arranged for large groups in a common area. Today's nursing home residents are sicker, require more care, and vary considerably with regard to ability and level of need. Those who are most mobile, many of them Alzheimer's patients, are frequently disoriented and unable to concentrate; those who are mentally alert are frequently too frail to participate in traditional large group programs. Cognitive and physical impairments must be dealt with realistically, but not used as an excuse for failing to provide appropriate activities. Conversely, the resident who chooses *not* to participate in a group activity must be given that option; staff must determine whether this decision is symptomatic of withdrawal or depression or merely the manifestation of a natural desire to be left alone for a while. Activities staff must also strike a balance between group and independent activities and offer unstructured options, including the opportunity to sit on the sidelines and watch.

The most important factor in developing programs is residents' interests, according to 95 percent of the respondents, followed by the residents' ethnic and religious background (64 percent) (see Figure 27-2). The types of patients and their level of functioning (case mix) were considered very important by about 54 percent of the respondents; others relied on suggestions by family members. Although the educational background of the residents ranked last, a substantial number of the respondents considered it somewhat important in developing programs.

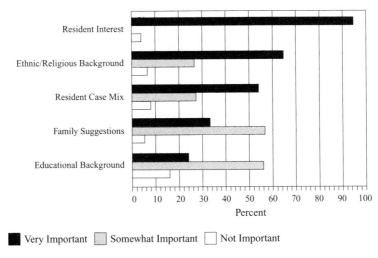

Figure 27-2 Factors considered in developing programs. *Source:* Based on responses to a survey conducted by the Nursing Homes–Long Term Care Committee of the United Hospital Fund.

Despite even the best efforts to meet needs and tastes on an individual basis, however, the reality seems to be that, at least at first, the resident must be fit into existing programs. Most facilities have monthly or semimonthly special events for residents, often built around food and entertainment. There are usually monthly birthday parties; other facilitywide programs include observances of national and religious holidays, in-house talent shows, and performances by professional entertainers. The entire staff is necessarily involved in these programs, with the activities director acting as the primary coordinator. For the most mobile and alert residents, traditional programs ranging from bingo and crafts to trips to baseball games and concerts are both popular and appropriate, although observations during visits suggest that the number of residents participating in these programs has been steadily declining. These residents are also likely to enjoy independent activities like painting or reading.

Programs for more impaired residents fall into three overlapping categories: those for residents with dementia who are cognitively impaired but physically mobile; those for mentally alert residents who are unable to leave their units but able to participate in group day room programs; and finally, those for residents who are very ill and require individual attention.

Programming for Residents with Dementia

Programming for cognitively impaired residents is a particular challenge for the activities director. These residents have by definition medical or functional problems that inhibit participation in regular programs. Compounding the challenge, there are differing degrees of dementia, and its manifestations tend to be unpredictable, varying in kind and intensity from day to day and even from minute to minute. Other problems in designing and running programs for residents with dementia include short attention spans, difficulty understanding, varying levels of impairment, and mistrust of the staff facilitators.

To further complicate planning, there is the issue of whether it is better to work with dementia residents separately or to integrate them with other residents. Keeping dementia patients together may make it easier to deal with wandering residents and minimize disruptions for those without dementia. On the other hand, there are some advantages to placing dementia residents in small groups with other residents for sensory programs, music, reminiscence, and physical activity. Not only does "mainstreaming" promote the functioning of residents with dementia, but it may ease the burden on staff, since many activities are appropriate for other residents as well and may be provided jointly.

For patients, individual attention usually elicits positive responses, but because it is very staff-intensive, it is difficult for facilities to provide full-scale, full-time individual programs. Nevertheless, all but three facilities that answered the survey identified some form of special individualized program for residents with dementia. Typically, these programs are offered for only a short time a few days a week. But even when programs are offered daily, there is still a tremendous amount of time when residents have no activity or therapy.

A particular problem in dementia programming is striking a balance between avoiding frustration, for example, from not being able to find the right word, and infantilization. Simple, familiar tasks like stuffing envelopes, folding napkins, and chopping vegetables are often used to integrate a resident into larger projects. Working with specially manufactured large-piece jigsaw puzzles with adult themes is particularly popular and may be useful for exercising stiffened fingers as well. Several activities directors emphasized that what may strike visitors as infantilization, such as the use of children's toys and games, is usually not resented, but rather welcomed by the residents for whom they are intended.

Walking, either indoors or outdoors, is a simple solution to the problems created by the short attention spans, excess energy, and tendency to wander that so often characterize the dementia or Alzheimer's patient. Setting aside safe, interior space is often impractical, however, as is providing regular and appropriate escorts for outside excursions. Only three facilities listed walking as a separate activity.

Clearly, a wide range and variety of programs are necessary. The challenge in designing programs—whether for residents with dementia or for more alert residents—is finding imaginative ways to incorporate activities programs in the daily care routine.

In the Day Room

For those patients who are mentally alert but unable or unwilling to leave their unit, activities are most often provided in the day room. The survey results indicate that these activities routinely include many of the same components as dementia programs, such as reality orientation and reminiscence, but generally incorporate more music and exercise. Rhythm bands and singing are almost universal, as are bingo, word games, and adaptive sports. Shuffleboard and games that can be played with a volleyball or beach ball are also common and relatively easy to arrange, even in a medium-sized day room.

Analysis of day room activities suggests that resident participation is greatest when the program is geared to a fairly wide range of functioning levels simultaneously. For example, the response to music may vary from enthusiastic singing to very tentative tapping of a finger or foot. Other activities may require more encouragement from staff on the sidelines, during a ball game, for instance. In the absence of any sign of interest on the part of an individual resident, some quiet conversation in a corner may be in order.

For the Very Disabled

Programs for bedbound residents must, of necessity, rely heavily on one-on-one attention. The techniques most commonly used are similar to those used for dementia residents and, in the case of sensory, music, and reminiscence programs, may sometimes overlap.

In most cases, however, for these residents whose mental faculties remain sound despite severe physical debilitation, the survey indicates a reliance on visits by volunteers when they are available or by "adopted" grandchildren from neighborhood schools. Individual sessions, whether with staff or volunteers, tend to be less frequent than group programs for these patients, usually weekly, and sometimes disappear completely, particularly during school vacations. Even in homes with large staffs and many volunteers, it is hard to offer individual programming on a regular and frequent basis; if programs are offered even four times a week for one-half hour—a somewhat ambitious schedule—there is still considerable time without active stimulation or interaction.

STAFFING: THE HEART OF THE MATTER

Although there are obvious similarities among certain types of activities, there is enormous variety in the ways programs are designed and implemented. Their effectiveness reflects the equally varied sizes, backgrounds, training, sensitivity, and creativity of the activities staff, particularly the activities director.

There is no state requirement regarding the number of activities personnel a nursing home must employ. As one would expect, the larger facilities have larger activities staffs. However, Committee members observed that staff size may not be the most important factor in determining the quality of a program. Homes with small staffs, if efficiently deployed and supplemented by the facility's other resources, may offer an interesting and effective program. Many respondents listed ten or more staff names on the activities roster, often enlisted part-time from other departments. When other staff or volunteers help with logistics and refreshments, for example, the activities staff are free to spend more time on the content of the program itself. Some activities directors enlist the nursing and housekeeping staff who see the residents every day to encourage attendance at activities or to work with a specific resident needing individual attention. In rare instances, nursing aides and other staff help with an activity, usually reality orientation but sometimes activities like singing or sewing.

This type of interdisciplinary approach can be significantly enhanced by facilitywide in-service training in the various elements of activities programs, from recognizing a positive response to the specific skills and techniques needed to elicit one. Unfortunately, such opportunities are usually infrequent, usually occurring only once a year. These opportunities should be made the most of; nursing and social services staff should definitely be included, and an effort should be made to include other staff and volunteers as well. Providing more in-service training is one way to enhance and improve activities programs where resources are limited.

The Question of Credentials

With few exceptions, the quality of the activities program depends on the expertise and talent of the activities director and his or her staff. Instinct and common sense are crucial but difficult to identify or define and impossible to measure. With training and experience, however, these important qualities can be effectively utilized and enhanced.

The survey showed that, for the most part, the largest facilities not only have the largest staffs but also the largest number with some formal training and certification. Just under one-third of the respondents listed activities personnel with master's degrees, most of them in therapeutic recreation, but many in music, art, social work, or psychology. Many of those holding master's degrees in therapeutic recreation have undergraduate degrees in music or art.

The academic requirements for a degree in therapeutic recreation at either the undergraduate or the graduate level generally include classes in psychology, sociology, and physiological science; specialized courses in the philosophy of leisure and recreation; training in program planning and hands-on "facilitation techniques"; as well as an internship of one semester or more. Colleges within New York City offering this type of curriculum include New York University, Lehman College, and Kingsborough Community College.

Many activities staff in nursing homes in New York City who lack formal training enroll in a 64-hour course for activities leaders offered by the Zeman Center of the Jewish Home and Hospital. Offered over the span of nine weeks, the class typically enrolls 10 to 15 students at a time.

It is always difficult to generalize about the benefit and value of formal training. Observations and meetings suggest that training is useful and important in gaining certain skills and insight, but those without it may be able to compensate by being creative and adaptable. A minimally educated nursing assistant under some circumstances may be more helpful with disoriented residents than a graduate psychologist. But a good training program will help develop skills and knowledge. The challenge for the administrator is to recognize good instinct and talent during the recruitment process and to encourage and support as much innovation as possible. The administrator should also emphasize and promote in-service training as a way to build the skills of the activities staff.

Volunteers

The same evaluation must be made with regard to potential volunteers, whether family members, students, members of community groups, or well-intentioned neighbors. A volunteer with special talent in the arts, for example, may offer badly needed assistance with entertainment and large group programs, but special sensitivity training and supervision may be required if the volunteer is to work with more regressed residents. In many homes, volunteers are most often asked to help with transportation and the more traditional activities like crafts.

Some facilities, especially smaller proprietary facilities, have voiced reluctance to recruit volunteers; their typically small activities staffs do not have the time to screen and supervise them properly. In addition, many, if not most, volunteers are themselves elderly, and some need extra care and attention. Proprietary facilities have a particularly difficult time recruiting volunteers, who typically prefer to donate their time at nonprofit facilities, which they perceive—rightly or wrongly—as more deserving of their services.

PROBLEMS AND PITFALLS

From the perspective of the activities directors, there are several problems to be overcome in developing appropriate and effective programs. Some are obvious and have already been alluded to; others are more subtle. Both kinds are difficult to surmount.

When asked to identify the three biggest problems they face in providing activities to residents, over 70 percent of the activities directors listed staffing (Figure 27-3). Personal interviews revealed that the problem is only partially the result of financial constraints; indeed, few directors (less than 25 percent) indicated budget, either for staff or for supplies, as a major problem. Rather, there are simply too few adequately trained people in the field. Throughout the New York metropolitan area, health care institutions vie for a small pool of specialized activities personnel; nursing homes compete not only with more spacious, luxurious suburban facilities, but also with nursing homes in other neighborhoods of the city, where the physical plant or working conditions may be more attractive. There is also competition with other types of institutions such as senior centers.

Compounding the staffing problem is the inevitable burden of paper work; on visits, some directors reported that they spend an average of 25 percent of their time preparing the notes and reports mandated by regulations. Although there is no substitute for the staff's own evaluations of the residents' participation in activities, computer-based information systems and extra clerical assistance might help reduce the workload associated with some of the more routine paper work.

Second in importance only to staffing is the question of transportation, specifically, the time and effort it takes to transport residents to programs. Almost 57 percent of the respondents considered it among the top three problems they face. Personal interviews evoked expressions of frustration. Although there is usually no lack of assistance for off-site excursions, the daily routine of pushing a wheelchair or escorting a resident to the auditorium or day room usually falls to the activities staff and any available volunteers (Figure 27-4).

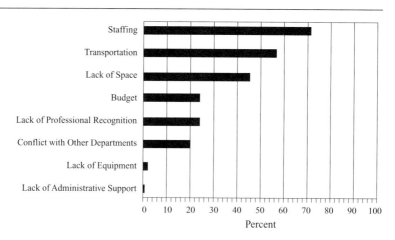

Figure 27-3 The biggest problems in providing activities to residents. *Source:* Based on responses to a survey conducted by the Nursing Homes–Long Term Care Committee of the United Hospital Fund.

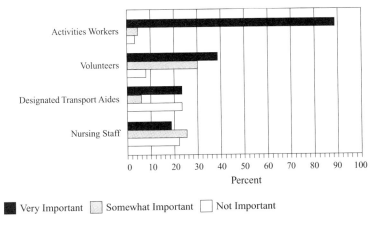

Figure 27-4 How residents are transported to programs. *Source:* Based on responses to a survey conducted by the Nursing Homes–Long Term Care Committee of the United Hospital Fund.

The "battle of the elevators" is an integral part of the transportation problem. Because of physical plant limitations, comparatively few facilities have enough elevators to prevent seemingly interminable waits. In addition, some equipment, like the new and more comfortable reclining geri-chair, is large and occupies even more space in already overcrowded elevators. The result is late and lower attendance at off-unit programs and the frequent relegation of many residents to day room television. Some facilities are moving activities to sites that are more accessible to the residents whenever feasible given other space constraints.

The problem that ranks third, according to survey respondents, is lack of space for both programs and supplies. Again, this is a particular problem in older buildings, where one large room, usually the main dining room, serves as auditorium, game room, and arts and crafts studio. Supplies are crammed into a closet or onto shelves in the activities director's office. The situation on the units in older facilities is still less satisfactory. When these nursing homes were built, more of the population were ambulatory, and there was little or no need for day room activities; lounges on each floor, built to hold a few visitors at a time, are frequently small and dimly lit. Renovated and more recently constructed facilities usually include larger and brighter day rooms, but still there is generally insufficient space for more than one group activity at a time, little or no space to accommodate several one-on-one sessions simultaneously, and virtually no place for residents to walk off excess energy.

Further exacerbating the space problem, those residents who do not enjoy the formal activity being offered and prefer to watch others tend to congregate in the crowded corridors near the nursing station or in equally cramped lobby areas. Residents like to observe activity, but the patio areas and terraces that were designed for quiet sitting and watching often face away from the main entrance or street and therefore provide little visual stimulation.

Budget—for salaries and supplies—and lack of professional recognition are not coincidentally ranked equally as problems by respondents, almost one-quarter of whom listed both as significant difficulties. To the extent possible, the administration that places a high value on the activities program and its importance to the well-being of the residents will try to allocate more funds for salaries. Approval of funds for supplies and other resources is also indicative of recognition but is considered less crucial to the effectiveness of a program. The simplest supplies can be adapted to a variety of uses, given a degree of creativity and ingenuity. Simple supplies may, in fact, be even more effective for more regressed residents than more elaborate equipment because they are familiar and more likely to be accepted.

Lack of professional recognition by other departments within the facility is a problem that is more difficult to overcome. An all-too-common opinion is that activities have no therapeutic value and exist to keep residents occupied when there is nothing more important for them to do. This perception, although less prevalent in recent years, is still manifest in scheduling conflicts with other departments for both time and space. Although personal and medical needs should and always do take precedence and formal activities are therefore never scheduled until after the morning care routine, it is important to minimize scheduling conflicts with doctors' visits, clinic appointments, and therapy sessions.

WHAT WORKS: SOME THINGS OLD, SOME THINGS NEW

The Committee found during its visits to nursing homes and from its survey that chronic problems of time, space, and staffing—as well as newer problems related to the changing nursing home population—can be reduced through a combination of ingenuity, flexibility, and, perhaps most important, administrative support. Over and over again, Committee members observed staff introducing new ideas and making imaginative use of limited resources. Some of the most promising of these innovations are described below.

Activities for Patients Who Cannot Leave the Unit

Given the increasing number of frail residents, programs must be designed for those who are no longer able to go to another part of the home for an activity. Sometimes, this simply means modifying traditional programs. For example, bingo is hardly a new idea, but several facilities have adapted the game to the needs of frailer residents by assisting them individually, even at the bedside. The game is then not only enjoyable but a form of cognitive stimulation. Other facilities make use of a strolling musician, usually a guitarist, to bring music programs to the unit; a popular, and increasingly affordable, variation is a portable keyboard which enables one person to "play" a variety of instruments at the same time.

Ideally, the program will make available adaptive materials. In one program, Committee members observed a specially constructed braided ball, which residents can hold and manipulate more easily. Appropriate puzzles, games, and audiocassettes should be available both during regularly scheduled activities programs and when they are not scheduled. One program is able to bring many programs to residents by means of a closed circuit television system.

The use of small groups for activities programs emerged from the survey, discussions with the advisory committee, and the Committee's on-site visits as a particularly effective technique. Although such programs are staff-intensive and often require staff who have specific training and skills in small group work, they are extremely effective in engaging residents' interest and meeting their needs at the appropriate level. Even if a resident does not actively participate in a small group, he or she may enjoy sitting on the periphery. Committee members have even observed one or two former wanderers and disruptive residents sitting quietly on the outside of a group.

Programs for Residents with Dementia

A number of facilities make use of "activity aprons" with snaps, zippers, and other sensory material for residents with Alzheimer's, who need to release energy by moving their hands. The aprons are available commercially, but some homes have made them in house as well.

Sometimes, changing the time of day at which an activity takes place can make a big difference. In one facility, physical exercise has been adapted to meet the needs of residents with dementia, who are often agitated at night. A late afternoon or evening exercise program appears to decrease this "sundown syndrome."

Reaching a Diverse Patient Population

A growing challenge for activities directors is to develop programs that are suitable for residents across a range of functioning levels. One nursing home holds its monthly birthday parties on different floors rather than in the main dining room; the highest functioning residents attend and suggest the songs, dance, and play tambourines to add the necessary festive tone to the proceedings.

Similarly, the traditional current events program can be adapted to reach a wide range of functioning levels. In one home, the highest functioning residents read selected portions of the newspapers aloud and then, with the help of the activities leader, discuss the stories with the mid-level residents. The lower functioning residents are shown the photographs in the paper to stimulate discussions about the past.

Tying in Activities to Residents' Past Experiences

Activities are usually most successful when the programs are based on familiar events and experiences, helping residents to maintain continuity with the past. Examples range from a weekly "happy hour," at which wine, beer, and cheese are served under close supervision, to ethnic or religious activities to gardening—if only in a potted plant on a small patio.

Reminiscence groups are common, along with creative variations. In several instances, humor is used as a therapeutic tool, as residents recollect old jokes, listen to old radio programs, and watch old movies. In another case, the traditional sing-along is transformed into a discussion group, drawing in residents who normally do not verbalize but who can remember the lyrics to old songs. In one home, links to the past are explored during the current events program; residents discuss what taxes or food prices used to be, for example, or what used to be considered bad taste.

Similarly, reality orientation is most effective when related to familiar experiences. Focusing on residents' educational and religious background can be an effective way to engage residents. In one case, in a facility with many Jewish residents, the group leader discusses the day's religious rituals. In another nursing home, activities staff bring in spring flowers and autumn leaves to remind residents of the change of seasons and even arrange for residents to feel rain or snow, which provides not only continuity with past experiences but sensory stimulation.

Intergenerational programs, which recall the experience of being a parent or grandparent, seem to be meaningful for many residents. Many nursing homes have programs with local schools, which provide young volunteers. One facility maintains a child day-care center, supported by grants. Residents are able to interact with, cuddle, or simply watch the children, while the facility is able to provide a valuable service for staff and the community. Pet therapy also provides an opportunity for emotional expression and reinforces feelings of being cared for and loved. Programs that allow residents to "adopt" a cat or dog are particularly effective and popular.

Some Innovative Staffing Solutions

One facility supplements its very small full-time staff with part-time college students. This allows the director to assign activities personnel to every floor every day. Although chronic staff turnover is a problem, observers felt the trade-off in terms of staff morale and enthusiasm was worth it.

In an effort to free activities staff from time-consuming chores, another facility has hired a recreation aide who is responsible for transporting residents and distributing supplies and refreshments on one or two specially assigned floors. The same aide is also available to help with floor programs when needed.

A Little Peace and Quiet

Most residents benefit from a quiet physical environment; even well-oriented residents can be overwhelmed by the cacophony of loud public address announcements and the blaring of radio and television sets, compounded periodically by the activity leader's microphone. For a resident with dementia, the noise can lead to fright, agitation, and perhaps even violent behavior. Resident participation in programs appears to be greatest when the public address system is restricted to emergency use and when the television in the activity room is turned off during the program.

Integrating Activities into an Overall Care Plan

The comprehensive approach to care, which integrates all aspects of a resident's routine and medical needs and involves all departments, was universally recommended by the experts consulted. During the course of many on-site interviews, it became evident that nursing staff are often as eager for help with behavioral problems as activities staff are for help with their programs and that mutual planning can be beneficial. This will become even more the case with the new regulations regarding restraints. When restraints are released, activities must provide stimulation to occupy those likely to fall and to keep agitated and restless residents from wandering. In effect, nursing care and activities need to become increasingly integrated. Daily grooming may become an activity; singing a few old songs may become part of nursing care. Activities should be viewed as a tool that can be incorporated into different aspects of professional care.

The comprehensive approach has achieved remarkable therapeutic results in a model program called the personalized care model (PCM). In the PCM, a nurse's assistant has complete responsibility for a cluster of 8 to 10 residents during the day, including many of their activities. One facility (the Jewish Home and Hospital for Aged, Bronx, New York) has had some success with this model, but it can be difficult to implement. Strong administrative and nursing support is needed in order to re-evaluate and redefine work roles.

To fill the gaps in which no formal activity is scheduled, one nursing home has trained the aide assigned to the day room to lead at least two short programs a day, whether in reality orientation, exercise, or simple question-and-answer games. The same aide is also responsible for normal day room nursing duties such as toileting and feeding. Not only has this enabled the nursing home to add on-unit programs at times when there would not normally be activities staff to lead them, but it has also proven to be an effective form of staff recognition for the aides, who are given the opportunity to play a larger role in planning resident routines.

At other nursing homes, activities are merged with the rest of the daily routine. For instance, a resident who undergoes physical therapy in the morning may receive follow-up in an afternoon exercise program. One facility transforms occupational and physical therapy into socialization activities in themselves; the residents spend several hours with others in the therapy rooms watching, talking, and listening to piped in music when they are not taking treatment themselves. In the relatively cramped confines of the building, this type of scheduling solves space, time, and transportation problems simultaneously.

Sometimes, continuity may be achieved by making an effort *not* to segment the day into different tasks. At one facility, Committee members saw a nurse quietly hook up nutrition containers for tube feeders without disrupting a well-attended music therapy session in the day room.

ESSENTIAL ISSUES: POLICY AND PROGRAMMATIC RECOMMENDATIONS

Activities programs play a critical role in improving the quality of life for nursing home residents. Activities must be designed not just to fill empty blocks of time but to meet the needs and interests of individual residents as effectively as possible. If the institutional structure poses constraints, it also creates significant opportunities for improving the quality of life for residents at similar functioning levels. What follows is a series of suggested next steps to address some of the issues raised in this report.

Recognize activities programs as a key element both in determining and in assuring quality of life. For too long, uncertainty about the proper role and potential contributions of activities programs has limited their scope and impact. As the nursing home population continues to age and increases in frailty, activities programs will play an increasingly important role, both in assuring quality of life and in contributing to residents' basic safety. Their value must be recognized by both those within the facility—the administrators, nursing staff, and other employees—and those without—family members, regulators, and the general public.

Identify ways to provide additional training and support to activities directors and activities staff. A standardized certification process for activities personnel through a formal academic curriculum is a highly desirable goal and can be achieved through the National Council for Therapeutic Recreation Certification (NCTRC). (Special grandfathering provisions that stipulate additional training could be arranged for staff already in place.) More immediately, hands-on experience and access to information on new developments are essential. Nursing homes should explore ways to share training opportunities; they should also develop vehicles (e.g., newsletters) to encourage staff at different facilities to share ideas and expertise.

Improve in-service training, both for activities staff and for other staff, like nursing aides, who may help provide activities. In order to ensure that the best use is made of all available resources, regular and frequent in-service training on activities techniques should be provided. This training would improve the programs already scheduled, extend programs by using staff other than the activities staff, and generally aid in the provision of care.

Foster increased cooperation and coordination among departments. The entire staff should be made aware of how carefully thought out activities can benefit the residents and in some cases modify inappropriate behavior. Activities staff must be acknowledged as an integral part of the caregiving team, and the activities program must become part of other daily routines (e.g., dressing, washing up), with all staff members stimulating and working with the resident as much as possible at all times. In addition, the staff should encourage and facilitate resident participation in appropriate group activities; this will necessarily involve close coordination and accommodation of the residents' scheduled appointments with other departments.

Develop better methods to evaluate the success of activities programs. As discussed earlier, resident feedback on programming is difficult to obtain, and evaluation depends largely on monitoring of responses by staff and, when possible, family members. Given the limitations on time and resources, staff must be trained in interviewing skills to help them quickly and accurately assess residents' needs and interests. Staff should also be better trained to recognize and measure responses. Development of accurate measurement techniques and evaluation methods is also needed to better determine program effectiveness and value.

Develop and support creative solutions to the transportation problem. Many solutions have been tried, from employing special transportation aides to scheduling *all* programs on the units to avoid the problem completely. To begin with, facilities should explore the possibility of locating programs in different areas of the home and of using smaller groups.

Intensify training and recruitment of volunteers. Carefully screened and trained volunteers invariably enhance the range and quality of activities programs, but the effectiveness of recruitment techniques varies widely, particularly among proprietary facilities. The activities director should work closely with the administrator in identifying potential volunteers among family members, neighbors, members of local organizations, and employees of local businesses. As with the staff itself, the sensitivity and talent of the prospective volunteers, not their number, are the most important factors. Regular and formal public recognition of volunteers' efforts should be routine. Finally, exchanges of information rather than competition among facilities might greatly enhance the volunteer recruitment efforts.

Encourage a comprehensive rethinking of activities by long-term care professionals in all disciplines, academics, public officials, and representatives of private organizations. Activities programs must be re-examined in the much larger context of the important role they play in determining the quality of life for an increasingly elderly, sick, and frail resident population. The re-evaluation process should include an analysis of the types of programs being offered; their range, size, and location; the success with which they are meeting current needs; and ways to adapt them to better meet needs. Issues that deserve special attention include the physical environment in which the activities take place, the extent to which the environment is conducive to participation, and the value of small groups in dealing with residents with dementia and other severe impairments.

ACKNOWLEDGMENTS

The Nursing Homes–Long Term Care Committee gratefully acknowledges the contributions of the Recreation Advisory Committee, whose members include Nancy Curry, Director of Recreation, Fairview Nursing Home, Forest Hills, N.Y.; Linda Dianto, Recreation Director, Coler Memorial Hospital and Home, New York, N.Y.; Fidelma Dolan, Assistant Administrator, Terence Cardinal Cooke Health Care Center, New York, N.Y.; Marian Finkelstein, Director of Therapeutic Recreation, Beth Abraham Hospital, Bronx, N.Y.; Charles Fisch, Public Health Social Work Consultant, Office of Health Systems Management, New York State Department of Health, New York, N.Y.; Fred Greenblatt, Director of Therapeutic Recreation, The Jewish Home and Hospital for Aged, Bronx, N.Y.; Claudette Lefebre, Department Chair of Recreation and Leisure, Physical Education and Sports, New York University, New York, N.Y.; Jane Rosenthal, Administrator, Menorah Nursing Home, Brooklyn, N.Y.; Patrick Russell, Administrator, Park Nursing Home, Rockaway Park, N.Y.; Deborah Schindler, Director of Therapeutic Recreation, Chapin Home for the Aged, Jamaica, N.Y.; Stuart Waldman,

Director of Activities, Menorah Nursing Home, Brooklyn, N.Y.; and John Zeiss, Associate Director, Coler Memorial Hospital and Home, New York, N.Y. The Committee also wishes to thank staff at the following nursing homes, which it visited in order to study activities projects: Aishel Avraham Residential Health Facility, Brooklyn, N.Y.; Coler Memorial Hospital and Home, New York, N.Y.; Dry Harbor Nursing Home, Queens, N.Y.; Frances Schervier Home and Hospital, Bronx, N.Y.; Greenpark Care Center, Brooklyn, N.Y.; and Meadow Park Nursing Home, Queens, N.Y.

ABOUT THE NURSING HOMES–LONG TERM CARE COMMITTEE

Since 1962, the volunteers of the United Hospital Fund's Nursing Homes–Long Term Care Committee have worked to improve the quality of nursing home care in New York City. In addition to this special report, the Committee prepares reports on individual facilities that contain extensive factual information. The Committee also publishes a guide, *Facilities for the Aging: How to Choose a Nursing Home*. All of these publications are made available to hospitals and agencies making nursing home referrals, as well as to interested individuals.

ABOUT THE UNITED HOSPITAL FUND

The United Hospital Fund is a nonprofit organization that for over a century has been a source of philanthropic aid and leadership for the New York City health care community. All of the Fund's activities and programs reflect a basic commitment to the survival of voluntarism and voluntary institutions and to the provision of the highest quality of care.

Through its Division of Voluntary Initiatives, the Fund provides aid to voluntary groups in developing programs that will improve patient care and community health education, guide citizen action on legislative issues affecting health care, and assist in monitoring conditions affecting patient care in municipal hospitals and area nursing homes.

Survey of
Nursing Home Activity Programs

Date
_____

Name of facility
_____   Director (name)
                                   _____

Number of residents
_____   Name and title of person completing
                                   form, if different

Please complete this survey, which will be the basis for a report on the current state of activity programs. Return to the United Hospital Fund by April 19, 1991.

1. What is the Department called (e.g., activities, therapeutic recreation), and what is its goal?

Please answer the following questions by circling the response that best fits your facility. 1 = very important, 2 = somewhat important, and 3 = not important. Please provide any additional information under the "other" category.

2. How do you initially assess residents to plan activities for them?
   a. 1 2 3   interdisciplinary meetings
   b. 1 2 3   resident interviews
   c. 1 2 3   family interviews
   d. _____   other (please specify)

3. What factors do you consider in developing programs?
   a. 1 2 3   ethnic/religious background
   b. 1 2 3   resident interest
   c. 1 2 3   family suggestions
   d. 1 2 3   educational background
   e. 1 2 3   case mix of residents
   f. _____   other (please specify)

4. Do you evaluate the success of your programs? _____ yes _____ no

   If yes, how?
   a. 1 2 3   individual resident interviews
   b. 1 2 3   resident council feedback
   c. 1 2 3   individual family member interviews
   d. 1 2 3   family council feedback
   e. 1 2 3   staff feedback
   f. _____   other (please specify)

5. How do you ensure residents are aware of the activities schedule?
   a. 1 2 3   using staff reminders
   b. 1 2 3   individualized calendars
   c. 1 2 3   attendance list
   d. _____   other (please specify)

6. Is the Resident Council involved in the development of activity schedules?
   _____ yes _____ no

   If yes, how?
   a. 1 2 3   suggests activities at council meetings
   b. 1 2 3   volunteers to help the more regressed residents
   c. 1 2 3   helps raise funds for special events
   d. _____   other (please specify)

7. Who transports residents to programs?
   a. 1 2 3   activities workers
   b. 1 2 3   nursing staff
   c. 1 2 3   designated transport aides
   d. 1 2 3   volunteers
   e. _____   other (please specify)

8. Do you have any programs geared specifically to residents with dementia?
   _____ yes _____ no

   If yes, please list
      Program   *Frequency*
   a. _____   _____
   b. _____   _____
   c. _____   _____

9. Please describe any innovative program(s) that you have developed in the past year and indicate (use back of page if needed) how often they are offered to residents.

10. Please attach your most recent activity program calendar. Feel free to attach any recent annual or monthly report that conveys the type and number of activities.

11. Please list types and frequency of in-service training received by activity program staff.
    a. _____
    b. _____
    c. _____

12. Are other departments, such as nursing and social work, included in activity in-service training? _____ yes _____ no

    If yes, please list departments
    a. _____
    b. _____
    c. _____

13. Do other departments such as occupational therapy, physical therapy, social services, and nursing work with you to help implement and plan activities?
    _____ yes _____ no

    If yes, please describe the process

14. Are nursing aides involved in planning and implementing programs (e.g., facilitating day room programs)? _____ yes _____ no

If yes, please indicate how important nursing aides are in each role below:
1 = very important, 2 = somewhat important, and 3 = not important

a. 1 2 3 transportation
b. 1 2 3 leading activities
c. 1 2 3 helping with one-on-one stimulation
d. 1 2 3 suggesting activities
e. _____ other (please specify)

15. Are volunteers involved in activities? _____ yes _____ no

If yes, please indicate how important volunteers are to these activities below:
a. 1 2 3 escorting to activities
b. 1 2 3 helping with large group activities
c. 1 2 3 one-on-one sessions
d. 1 2 3 facilitating specific activities
e. 1 2 3 planning programs with community groups (e.g., churches, schools)
f. _____ other (please specify)

16. Please check the 3 biggest problems that you see in providing activities to residents.
a. _____ budget
b. _____ staffing
c. _____ conflicts with other departments
d. _____ lack of space
e. _____ lack of equipment
f. _____ transportation
g. _____ support of administration
h. _____ lack of recognition as profession
i. _____ other (please specify)

17. What type of information, resources, or educational programs would you find helpful in enhancing your activity program?

18. Indicate the name, educational background, and experience of your activity program staff in the chart below:

Name	Type of Certification	Last Educ. Degree	Length of Service in Field	Employment Classification (staff or consultant)	Special Expertise (e.g., music, dance)	Memberships in Professional Organization(s)

19. We would like to identify what activities are available for residents at different levels of functioning and how well residents at various levels are served by activity programs. We have chosen to look at the four places where activities generally occur—in the resident's room, in the unit or day room, off the unit in an activity or dining room, or outside the facility. We want to understand what activities (e.g., music) are available at each location. For instance, as shown below, for frailer bed- or room-bound residents, there might be three programs available, twice a week, which reach 5 to 10 residents during the session.

SAMPLE

Location of Activity	Program Type	Frequency	Approximate Number of Residents Participating
Bed- or room-bound	1. Music	2/wk	10
	2. Sensory awareness	1/wk	15
	3. Pet therapy	2/yr.	5

We have identified the most typical types of activities as follows: music, reminiscence, storytelling, crafts, discussion, sensory awareness, pet therapy, movement, trips. Please choose from this list and feel free to add to it or use your own terminology.

Location of Activity	*Program Type*	*Frequency*	*Approximate Number of Residents Participating*
a. Bed- or room-bound (residents confined to bed or room)	1. _____ 2. _____ 3. _____ 4. _____	_____ _____ _____ _____	_____ _____ _____ _____
b. On unit (residents not able to leave floor)	1. _____ 2. _____ 3. _____ 4. _____	_____ _____ _____ _____	_____ _____ _____ _____
c. Off unit (program in activity or dining room)	1. _____ 2. _____ 3. _____ 4. _____	_____ _____ _____ _____	_____ _____ _____ _____
d. Independent activity (residents who are able to go outside)	1. _____ 2. _____ 3. _____ 4. _____	_____ _____ _____ _____	_____ _____ _____ _____
e. Other (please list)	1. _____ 2. _____ 3. _____ 4. _____	_____ _____ _____ _____	_____ _____ _____ _____

Source: Courtesy of United Hospital Fund of New York.

Chapter 28

Chaplaincy Services in Long-Term Care

Herbert H. Friedman and Rabbi Zev Schostak

The chaplain is a most vital member of the multidisciplinary resident care team. He interfaces with major department heads on matters of critical importance to the well being of the residents.[*] The chaplain may also work closely with administration in matters of religious policy and procedures as well as chair or participate on its ethics committee. Most importantly, the chaplain serves residents in his primary capacity, which is to provide or coordinate religious services and pastoral counseling.

The scope of the chaplain's role is determined by the size and structure of the facility in which he serves. In smaller facilities, the chaplain may serve in a more limited capacity, on a part-time or consultant basis. At the very least, he would be expected to lead or coordinate religious services and programming for his faith; he may also be responsible for arranging religious services for other faiths through his contacts with community clergy. Beyond this most basic responsibility, the chaplain is often expected to provide pastoral counseling to the residents and their families; the extent of this service, however, varies from facility to facility. These primary chaplaincy roles—conducting and coordinating religious services and providing counseling—are recognized as standard in long-term care.

The Joint Commission on Accreditation of Healthcare Organizations declares that "patients/residents desiring spiritual services have their spiritual needs met" by "religious services . . . within the facility . . . outside the facility (if patients/residents are capable of attending) and/or patients/residents have contact and/or private consultation with members of the clergy."[1] In larger facilities, where the chaplain serves full time or nearly full time, he may also be expected to perform any or all of the following tasks: (1) conducting regular rounds and charting his visits on the residents' records, (2) serving on multidisciplinary resident care

---

[*]Many chaplains appointed to long-term care facilities today are women (e.g., Catholic Sisters, Conservative or Reform Jewish clergy). However, for the sake of stylistic expediency, this chapter employs male pronouns when necessary.

teams and interdisciplinary committees, (3) visiting residents in hospitals, (4) participating on ethics committees, and (5) conducting resident or staff programs.

To appreciate the unique position of the chaplain in long-term health care, it is important to distinguish between religiously sponsored facilities, whose primary mission is to meet the needs of a particular religious group, and other facilities. In a facility sponsored by or operating under the aegis of a religious group, the chaplain's role is pivotal. He is charged with creating a religious ambiance reflecting his faith's traditions by providing a full complement of spiritual services, holiday programming, and outreach to community resources (e.g., local clergy, lay ministers, and church or synagogue clubs or auxiliaries). In a religiously sponsored facility, the chaplain would likely assume an activist role on questions of religious policy or ethics by advocating positions consonant with those of his faith. He would be viewed by other department heads as a coequal and in some facilities would indeed be granted full departmental status. In a nondenominational facility, however, his role is usually more limited. He would serve primarily as a coordinator or provider of religious services, not necessarily as a catalyst for new programming or policy making. If he is the sole member of the clergy on staff, he would, of course, make every effort to provide equal access for residents of different faiths to their respective religious services; indeed, this is true in a religiously sponsored facility as well. In a nondenominational facility, the chaplain or outside clergy may serve on the institution's ethics committee or consult with administration on religious matters; nevertheless, he would rarely assert his personal moral and religious beliefs on policy matters out of respect for other theological doctrines and sensitivity to secular ethicists (though he would, of course, represent the views of his faith tradition).

PASTORAL ROLES AND RELATIONSHIPS WITHIN THE ORGANIZATION

The chaplain's position within a particular organizational structure, including the lines of accountability, is chiefly determined by the administration's or institutional perception of his role. If he is perceived to be primarily a spiritual counselor for residents, their families, and staff, then he might be positioned and budgeted as either part of the department of social services or recreation or as part of the administration (in facilities where he does not have his own department). Consequently, he would report to the appropriate director or administrator. Indeed, in a recent study of the pastoral functions most valued by both nonprofit and for-profit hospital administrators, counseling patients and their families was rated significantly higher than religious functions.[2] Additionally, the accreditation process for chaplaincy certification, CPE (clinical pastoral education), includes supervised clinical work similar to that of social workers and psychologists.

In a religiously sponsored facility, however, where religious concerns and ambiance are primary, pastoral services may be accorded full departmental status. In fact, it may be argued that in any health care setting, the chaplain plays a most critical role beyond patient or resident care: He serves the spiritual and emotional needs of staff through personal counseling, educational publications, and workshops. "Since the chaplain ministers not only to patients and their relatives, but also to the entire hospital community, he should report to the person who also views the hospital in that same broad perspective: the chief executive officer or administrator."[3]

In summary, the administration's perception of the chaplain's major role and job description will determine whether he operates under the aegis of another department or is accorded full departmental status. "The level at which the hospital chaplain reports is a combination of factors, but is mainly a function of the internal organizational structure of a specific institution."[4]

STRUCTURE OF PASTORAL SERVICES

In a facility representing a particular religious denomination, chaplaincy staffing will reflect that denomination. The head chaplain and his colleagues will generally be ordained as ministers or rabbis by that denomination; they may be career health care chaplains or may have served previously in local parishes, synagogues, or religious schools of that faith. In these facilities, the staff chaplain serves in two major roles: He provides religious services to residents of his own faith and counsels residents of all faiths. In order to meet the religious needs of residents of other denominations, he must establish contacts with other clergy and coordinate their services with the facility. This is particularly important because many outside clergy serve voluntarily at various community health care facilities on a part-time basis and their availability is limited even as the demands on their time increase. Hence, it is most critical that the institutional chaplain maintain a cordial relationship with clergy of other faiths, accommodating their schedules and needs, so that they will continue to serve the facility regularly on a pro bono or nominal stipend basis.

In a nondenominational facility, the head chaplain may be appointed from the religious denomination most representative of the resident population. He, too, is expected to coordinate religious services with other local clergy. Unlike large nondenominational hospitals, however, where clergy representing the Protestant, Catholic, and Jewish denominations serve in pastoral care departments on a full-time basis, nondenominational long-term care facilities are not generally budgeted for this arrangement. Rather, the facility chaplain engages the services of other clergy on a part-time paid or voluntary basis.

The size of the long-term facility will generally dictate the size of the pastoral care staff. "For an acute care hospital, the American Hospital Association suggests one chaplain for every 50 patients. This ratio will vary with the acuity of the patients served. Thus, for long-term institutions the ratio may expand to one chaplain for every 350 patients."[5]

INTERFACING WITHIN THE ORGANIZATION

The chaplain's organizational role vis-à-vis other departments in the facility is most significant. He regularly interfaces with several major department heads and their staffs, and his role within the organization may be better understood by describing his relationships with them. The chaplain's role is especially critical in view of the fact that, in many ways, he also serves as a facilitator on behalf of the residents. Often residents turn to him with their problems and grievances—as a court of last resort. He may thus become a sort of personal ombudsman to resolve their problems, wherever possible, through the appropriate departments. His integrity and credibility assure residents that their needs and concerns will not be dismissed when, in their mind, everything else has failed. Moreover, the chaplain's close relationships with major department heads and administration, as well as his professional training as a counselor, often make him an ideal candidate for mediating or moderating interdepartmental differences. He can be, and often is, the spiritual glue that bonds closer relationships between departments as well as between the residents. Finally, his considerable contacts with the surrounding community and his intense involvement with the key players within the facility enable him to serve as a respected communicator of the institution's philosophy and programs as well as a catalyst for or coordinator of innovative projects reflecting community needs and interests.

Following is described the chaplain's role with other departments in order of the frequency of his contacts with those departments.

Social Services

In a study of the perceptions of the chaplain's role by the three major groups— patients and families, staff, and the chaplains themselves—several important conclusions emerged:

> The three groups saw the chaplain's main role as giving comfort . . . The positive nature of comments from patients' relatives and

staff show the importance of the chaplain's role: (from patients and rel-atives) "Cared about us in time of needing someone". . . "Someone the family could talk and discuss with". . . "no words of mine can express the words of comfort the chaplain gave to myself and my late wife in our time of need."

And from the staff: "Often, it is necessary to provide emotional sup-port for the staff in a crisis situation, pending death of a young person". . . "The chaplain was of substantial benefit in dealing with the family."

Chaplains and medical and nursing staff saw the chaplain as most effective in the role of communicator, while patients and relatives rated the chaplain as communicator slightly below the role of helping with practical details. . . And patients and relatives gave the chaplain the highest effectiveness rating overall."[6]

This research underscores the fact that the chaplain's primary role is that of counselor to residents and their families. He helps allay their fears and anxieties upon admission and provides emotional support thereafter when they are lonely, depressed, or suffering from chronic illness or debilitating disease. The chaplain may counsel residents and families about medical ethical treatment decisions and, finally, offers both hope and comfort when a resident is dying. Though much of what the chaplain does has been labelled as social work, one should never con-fuse the role of the chaplain with that of the social worker. The chaplain operates on a different level, infusing spiritual values and religious experience when coun-seling residents and their families and praying with them. It is the chaplain who helps residents to recognize their own spiritual resources when facing a crisis or their own mortality. It is the chaplain who comforts them when they feel lonely, abandoned, and worthless by validating their self-worth as human beings created in the image of God. Finally, it is the chaplain who inspires residents with the beliefs of his faith tradition, enabling them to make the most of their remaining days on earth and evoking the ultimate hope of immortality of the spirit.

As part of his daily routine, the chaplain works closely with the department of social services. He is informed of all new admissions and is in touch with unit social workers to ascertain information fundamental to his work with residents and their families. The chaplain may also review new residents' charts before meeting with them.

In the initial interview, he will probe many vital areas. Is the new resident lucid? Can he or she both comprehend others and communicate with them? If so, how has the resident adjusted to admission? Is the resident generally hostile, withdrawn, depressed, or optimistic? What about the resident's religious affilia-tions and degree of spiritual commitment, if any? (Some chaplains administer standardized spiritual inventories such as the spiritual profile assessment to make this determination.)[7]

Are the family members actively involved with the resident or are they essentially passive? Do they express guilt, anger, or resentment about the resident's condition? About their own? In general, what in the family's history and its interpersonal dynamics has given rise to the current state of the relationships? Do the family members require pastoral counseling to enable them to deal with the guilt feelings of placing their loved one in a long-term care facility? Do they want their family clergyperson contacted? Do they need guidance about the ethical concerns involved in advance directives or the issues of life support systems?

Medicine and Nursing

Although both the department of medicine and the department of nursing are worthy of separate mention, the long-term care chaplain may not be able to prioritize their relative importance vis-à-vis *his* role in the facility. To the chaplain, medicine and nursing are essentially two sides of the same coin: delivery of appropriate health care to the residents. Medicine is charged with the diagnosis of the resident's conditions and the prescription of appropriate treatments, medications, and therapies, while nursing's role is the delivery of these and other vital services to the residents. Organizationally, in terms of day-to-day management of resident care, nursing is certainly the most critical of all disciplines. Indeed, the designation of long-term care facilities as skilled nursing facilities or as nursing homes reflects the predominant position of nursing services. Overwhelmingly, the greatest number of employees in long-term care are nurses and nursing aides, a fact that should not be lost on anyone assessing the organizational power structure of any long-term care facility. As a result, the chaplain's relationship with each of the departments is most critical. He must possess a general understanding of the resident's medical conditions and what *realistic* treatment options are available to the resident or his or her proxy. At the same time, the chaplain must maintain an ongoing relationship with the nursing staff, who, more than anyone else, constantly administer to the resident's needs and are abreast of the latest developments of his or her condition.

The chaplain must be familiar with the physiology of aging and how it impacts on the residents. He must understand that their feelings of frustration and upset about chronic pain and loss of function and control are often legitimate. Indeed, there are many physiological losses that are a part of the aging process: "The blood flow decreases. Hearing of high-pitched sound diminishes. We lose up to 50 percent of our sensitivity to taste and smell. Resistance to infection decreases and people become more susceptible to disease. There is a loss of tissue and vascular elasticity, and there are structural changes in the size of the brain."[8]

These physiological losses are compounded by the multiple medical conditions and complications that are the usual lot of the long-term care resident. Strokes, Parkinson's, Alzheimer's and other advanced stages of dementia, for example, often impair the ability of the resident to communicate with others. The chaplain must be both sensitive and patient as he uses other modalities to communicate (e.g., touch and hearing or eye and body language when the resident is deaf or hard of hearing). He must also bolster the spirits of family members and friends, who often become increasingly frustrated with their loved one's deteriorating condition and occasionally direct their misplaced anger against staff. Indeed, the chaplain may become an important resource for crisis intervention, serving as a buffer between the resident and family and the facility.

Finally, it is important that the chaplain have a working knowledge of what medications and therapies may be beneficial and, above all, what a realistic prognosis might be. For example, certain potent pain-killing drugs may depress respiration; other milder pain relief medications may aggravate a urinary tract infection. Thus, the chaplain, working in concert with the physician, can help the resident and his or her family understand the limitations imposed by the multiple complications and accept realistic treatment alternatives. In fact, some have even suggested that this is one of the ways chaplains can play a role in reducing medical costs. Pastoral care services "can be beneficial in reducing the need for drugs, medical interventions, or extended care. When a patient's prognosis indicates that death is imminent and hospice care is a viable alternative or that further treatment is of no benefit, spiritual counseling is of utmost importance in helping patients and their families to make treatment decisions."[9]

With all of this intense work with the residents and their families, the chaplain must also serve the spiritual and emotional needs of the medical and nursing staff (as well as other resident care staff, e.g., social workers, therapeutic recreation personnel, and occupational therapists), who encounter disability, physical and mental deterioration, chronic pain, and death and dying on a daily basis. He must be available to them for private consultation and personal counseling. The chaplain must also be the spiritual catalyst in developing workshops and seminars to address these most critical staff needs. In this way, the chaplain can make a most valuable contribution to reducing emotional burnout and possibly decreasing staff turnover.[10]

Therapeutic Recreation

In many facilities, religious services and the holiday and educational programming conducted or coordinated by the clergy are scheduled through the department of therapeutic recreation. It is vital that the chaplain appreciate the unique contributions of recreation therapy in providing residents with wholesome and meaningful group experiences (and, in the cases of bedridden residents, one-on-one experiences). Indeed, the chaplaincy's programming is often presented as part of therapeutic recreation. When a holiday comes, the chaplain may provide background information through talks, video presentations, religious school entertainment, and printed materials. He may present weekly Bible classes or conduct discussion groups on issues of interest to the residents. The chaplain, if properly trained, may even lead group therapy and meditation sessions. It should be noted, however, that those residents who attend therapeutic recreation programs are generally more lucid than those who do not attend. In addition, many alert residents cannot always attend these programs due to scheduling conflicts with rehabilitation therapy, various medical services, or personal matters. Consequently, the chaplain must reach out to residents on the units—in dining rooms, in lounge areas, and at the bedside—to provide pastoral services to the residents who cannot attend scheduled group programs. In fact, some facilities equipped with closed-circuit television offer live presentation of all therapeutic recreation and pastoral programming.

Dietary

Chaplains occasionally receive resident complaints about the only major area where residents exercise some degree of control—menus and food. Quite often, residents' complaints about the taste of the food are unfounded, because people, as they age, usually lose about 50 percent of their sense of taste. Indeed, when residents regularly reject the main and alternate menu selections, frequently they are sending a quite different message to the powers that be: They are unhappy with something else that is happening in their lives, and they want action. The chaplain must be sensitive to their concerns—both real and imagined—so that he can properly address them. What is most important is that the chaplain attempt to counsel them with reality-based therapy. Residents must come to accept their situation and learn to live, as best as possible, with the physical limitations imposed by their age and medical conditions.

In a Jewish facility providing kosher food services, the chaplain or rabbi is often charged with the responsibility of supervising these services through the dietary department. This would demand that the chaplain be both knowledgeable about the applicable Jewish laws and about current developments in the field of kosher food certification. In addition, the chaplain may be required to direct and supervise the dietary staff's adherence to kosher standards and procedures.

Finance and Budgeting

Although the chaplain might not have a direct relationship with the finance department, the chaplaincy is, of course, subject to the budgeting process. Accordingly, the director of pastoral services will be expected to prepare a budget that realistically projects his department's needs. Among the major budget items in the pastoral department are these: staff salaries and benefits (including clergy and secretarial), religious items (e.g., sacramental supplies and prayer books), office equipment and supplies, books, periodicals, and professional dues. It should be noted, however, that the department of pastoral care is particularly cost-effective, since many community clergy and religious laypersons serve in a voluntary capacity. "Because of the use of non-salaried workers in the department, the pastoral care department is very effective for the services provided."[11]

Public Relations

The chaplain, by virtue of his extensive contacts with local clergy, churches, synagogues, and religious institutions, can be a most effective spokesperson on behalf of the facility. He may be invited to represent the institution at public functions and charitable events. He may be asked to deliver invocations, sermons, and speeches and to serve on philanthropic boards and committees. The chaplain, acting on behalf of the department of volunteers, may address interested community groups in order to recruit new volunteers; indeed, some chaplains have established parachaplaincy programs in their facilities consisting of specially trained volunteers who assist in ministering to the spiritual needs of the residents. Some chaplains also reach out to the community by creating special public service programs within their facility in conjunction with other departments, such as group sessions for residents' families who have difficulty coping with the placement of their loved ones in a long-term care facility or with the emotional and spiritual conflicts that attend aging and chronic disease. The chaplain may also be the catalyst for multigenerational religious programs featuring presentations by choral and dramatic groups of local religious schools. He and other area clergy may conduct discussion groups and workshops focusing on a wide range of bioethical issues and chaplaincy concerns. Finally, the chaplain, who holds the unique position of ministering to the spiritual needs of the residents and providing pastoral counseling to them and their families, can create the best possible public relations image—reaching out to the sick and elderly in their time of need and touching their lives with meaning and purpose.

CONCLUSION

Because the elderly continue to be the fastest growing segment of the population, new facilities will be established and existing ones will expand to meet the increased demand. With the ever-increasing advances in medical technology, more of our frail and acutely ill elderly can be kept alive through sophisticated life support systems. There is also an increasing emphasis by the regulatory agencies and society as well on the "quality of life." This means that the chaplaincy in the 21st century will face bold challenges. The chaplain will be significantly more than the traditional provider of religious services. He will be the pastoral counselor to residents, families, and staff. He will become the professional in-house ethicist who will work closely with the resident care disciplines in establishing protocol and policy for medical ethical decision making. He will play an active, if not pivotal, role on the facility's ethics committee. Finally, he will serve as a spiritual resource for guidance and strength to residents, families, and staff as they face life-and-death medical decisions. At these most critical times, his expertise in ethics, his moral leadership of the resident care staff, and, above all, his compassion and concern as a chaplain will set the spiritual tone of the long-term care facility of the future.

NOTES

1. Joint Commission on Accreditation of Healthcare Organizations, *Long Term Care Standards Manual* (Chicago: Joint Commission on Accreditation of Healthcare Organizations, 1990), 78.

2. M.Y. Manns, The Valuation of Pastoral Care by Hospital Administrators: A Survey of Selected For-profit and Non-profit Institutions, *Journal of Health Care Chaplaincy* 3, no. 1 (1990):5–22. Listed among the three most valued pastoral functions were these: "Show kindness and concern to a patient" (no. 1), "help a patient to face death with calmness and dignity" (no. 2 for for-profit administrators), "listen to a patient talk about God" (no. 2 for nonprofit administrators), and "provide support to a patient's family (no. 3). Three of the five least valued functions are the same for administrators of for-profit and nonprofit institutions: "Talk with a patient about religious beliefs," "refer a patient to a member of the clergy," and "read scripture to a patient" (pp. 12–15).

3. D.N. Peel, The Chaplain's Place on the Healing Team, *Dimensions in Health Service* 57 (1980):40.

4. D. Saylor, Pastoral Care: The Chaplain's Perspective, *Journal of Nursing Administration* 20 (1990):16.

5. Ibid., 15.

6. C.D. McKechnie, The Role of a Chaplain in Crisis, *Hospital Administration in Canada* 19 (1977):22. See also G.W. Barger et al., The Institutional Chaplain: Constructing a Role Definition, *The Journal of Pastoral Care* 38, no. 3 (1984):176–185.

7. E. McSherry and W.A. Nelson, The DRG Era: A Major Opportunity for Increased Pastoral Care Impact or a Crisis for Survival? *The Journal of Pastoral Care* 41, no. 3 (1987):201–211.

8. T. Weiner et al., *Old People Are a Burden but Not My Parents* (Englewood Cliffs, N.J.: Prentice-Hall, 1983), 26.

9. C.H. Homer and M.A.T. Hamilton, Pastoral Care, Social Services: Role in Reducing Medical Costs, *Hospital Progress* (June 1984):62.

10. R.S. Crum, The Chaplain as Staff Development Agent, *Care Giver* 2, no. 4 (1985):39–42.

11. D. Saylor, Pastoral Care: The Chaplain's Perspective, *Journal of Nursing Administration* 20, no. 2 (1990):17.

Chapter 29

Adult Day Care

Richard S. Lamden, Concetta M. Tynan, and Jan Warnke

As advanced health care improves and increases the longevity of older persons, so do the options for care. In the forefront of the rapidly growing home and community-based services is adult day care (also referred to as adult day health or adult day health care). This often underutilized service provides a unique setting for persons who require some assistance with tasks of daily living but do not need 24-hour care. Through the provision of a structured day program in a safe, supervised setting, functionally impaired elderly and disabled adults are able to remain in the community, and caregiving families can maintain their employment. The provider notion of prevention is the mainstay of adult day care. Through early involvement in a program, a client can maintain some independence while gaining a renewed sense of self-worth. The large costs, both financial and human, when nursing home placement is premature and inappropriate force society to seek and utilize new alternatives.

Inherent in the continuum of care philosophy is the premise that services provided must meet the individuals' needs and be offered in the least restrictive environment. It is incumbent upon service providers to be aware of options available so that clients can be directed and referred to the service that can best meet their needs.

THE HISTORY OF ADULT DAY CARE

Adult day care, in the form of day hospitalization, originated in Europe and was implemented most successfully in Great Britain under the pioneering direction of Lionel Cosin. Responsible for the first developments in the United States in the 1960s, Cosin developed a therapeutic day program at Cherry Hospital in Goldsboro, North Carolina, that was intended to prepare patients for discharge by teaching and promoting independent living skills. Early expansion of centers was due, in part, to the efforts of a grass roots movement that pushed for recognition and funding. However, development of new centers was inhibited as a result of the general lack of expertise regarding the concept and implementation of adult day care.

The advent of Title XIX and XX reimbursement during the 1960s allowed low-income elderly to begin accessing the services in small numbers. The competition for limited funding with other essential services, particularly nursing homes, caused slow growth and center closures. In spite of difficult beginnings, centers expanded from a mere 15 in 1973 to over 2,100 currently. A major force shaping the future and destiny of adult day-care services was the development of national standards in 1984 by the National Institute of Adult Day Care (NIAD). This organization, a constituent unit of the National Council on the Aging (NCOA), has from its inception strived not only to increase the visibility of adult day care but also to set forth guidelines for practitioners as an impetus toward professionalism.

DEFINING THE CONCEPT

Adult day care fills the gap between loosely structured senior centers and full-time residential care. It is important to differentiate adult day care from the other two types of services. Both senior centers and adult day care offer meals, recreation, and socialization. The latter, however, has as its main framework an individual plan of care, and it serves more impaired clients. The primary distinctions between adult day care and nursing homes are the amount of time individuals use the services and the acuity level. Adult day care, as the name implies, provides care during daytime hours. The client returns to his or her residence at the end of the day.

Having been developed as a fragmented service defined according to treatment emphasis (e.g., medical, psychiatric, or social), adult day care emerged with a lack of direction and multiple types of programs. Although programs were flexible and responsive to the specific needs of clients and locales, the diverse models of care created confusion. As the representative body of the providers, NIAD established generic guidelines and standards intended to be used as a tool by practitioners for defining, planning, and implementing quality care:

> Adult day care is a community-based group program designed to meet the needs of adults with functional impairments through an individual plan of care. It is a structured, comprehensive program that provides a variety of health, social and related support services in a protective setting during any part of a day but less than 24-hour care.
>
> Individuals who participate in adult day care attend on a planned basis during specific hours. Adult day care assists its participants to

remain in the community, enabling families and other caregivers to continue caring at home for a family member with an impairment.[1]

Recognizing the program diversity necessary to adapt to the changing needs of the population served, the generic position is emerging as the dominant model. Regardless of definitions, the center and staff must be able to respond fully to the needs of the clients.

PLANNING AND DEVELOPING THE SERVICE

Adult day care serves a broad range of people. It can provide structure and mental stimulation for a person with Alzheimer's. It can provide socialization, nutrition, and health monitoring for someone who is frail and isolated. Or it can offer rehabilitation and respite for a young stroke victim and the working spouse.

Though characteristics vary, clients tend to fall into two general categories: (1) adults with emotional, mental, or physical impairments who require structured care in order to maintain independent functioning, and (2) adults with disabilities who require restorative and rehabilitative services in order to attain maximum independent functioning. It is necessary for the adult day-care center to define the target population it intends to serve so that programs and staff can meet the clients' needs.

Prior to developing an adult day-care center, it is prudent to thoroughly analyze the reasons for wanting to establish it. Existing organizations need to examine their mission statement and goals to ascertain the need for and compatibility of this service. New organizations need to carefully assess the appropriateness of developing a day-care facility. Since adult day care is not typically a high revenue producer, the rationale may be to create a continuum of care so that clients can be retained in the system. Independent centers may focus more on community needs.

Planning and developing an adult day-care center begins with a feasibility study. This is not as difficult as it sounds. One needs to locate individuals who represent the community in the area of services for the aging and set up a meeting to discuss the development of a facility. An initial brainstorming session could evolve into the creation of a formal planning committee.

The planning committee should undertake a needs and feasibility assessment to answer such questions as these:

- Is there a need? Is there a gap in the continuum of care? Is there a target group needing this service?
- What funding sources are available for maintaining the program? Are they private or public?

- Is there community support for such a program?
- What is the best location? Is it accessible to those who will be attending? If the program will be housed in an existing building, how much renovation is necessary to meet regulations?
- Is the program accessible by public transportation? Is it going to provide transportation for clients?
- Will the staff necessary for the program be hard to find?
- What, if any, is the competition?

After these questions are addressed, the committee might then turn its attention to the paperwork and filings necessary to become a legal entity, including

- the preparation of a pro forma budget, including startup costs
- the identification of job categories and the development of job descriptions and personnel policies
- the creation of a plan for publicity and marketing
- the development of admission policies
- the establishment of a certification or licensing process and the development of operating policies

In planning for the development of a physical structure to house adult day care, several steps should be taken. Licensing and regulation play a vital role in the implementation process.

In many states, the department of health services (or its counterpart agency) usually is the agency responsible for the adoption, administration, and enforcement of regulations. It is the purpose of the department to supplement the efforts of conscientious providers by establishing and enforcing minimum standards of operation, including standards for facilities, equipment, and personnel.

Organizations contemplating the establishment of an adult day-care program should complete and submit an application requesting licensure to the department of health services, usually on a form prescribed by the department. Generally licenses are issued annually.

Any change of ownership, administration, or location of a licensed adult day-care program will require a new application for licensure.

Upon receipt of the application for licensure, it is customary for the licensing agency to schedule an appointment to inspect and investigate the space, the planned program activities, and the standards of care being proposed by the facility.

A well-designed facility is vital in providing and supporting adult day-care activities. In fact, the environment plays a significant role in improving the clients' social interaction and functional capacity. Of prime consideration in planning a facility is safety and security. The clients should be able to move through the center with ease.

The facility should be warm, inviting, and homelike and should allow for the performance of activities of daily living, promote social contact, and stimulate the visual, tactile, auditory, and olfactory senses.

The site should have sufficient space to accommodate the number of clients being served. It is common practice for state licensure to require a certain number of square feet per client, excluding offices, reception area, restrooms, and hallways.

The site should have adequate access for handicapped vans, which may be used to drop off clients. It should be within easy reach of public transportation and not be located on a very busy road, making ingress into the area difficult. There should be spaces identified for handicapped parking and a ramp for easy access to the building without the need to climb stairs.

The site should also have a covered area for exterior recreation where clients can enjoy gardening and other activities. The area should have outdoor furniture and benches for seating. The reception area should make visitors and clients feel welcome and be attractively decorated with soft colors. The reception area serves as a central center where clients are checked in. A phone should be placed in this area for clients to use if they need to make a call. A closet nearby for outer garments and rainwear is a nice convenience.

Since some clients may be wheelchair-bound, there should be wheelchair-turning space of at least 5' × 5' in entrance doors and restrooms, door opening widths of at least 32", thresholds level with the floor, lever-type controls on faucets and doors, grab bars at all toilets, angled mirrors at sinks, and at least 29" clearance under sinks and 27" clearance under tables.

Adjustable blinds to protect elderly persons' eyes from the glare of sunlight should also be considered, as should the use of parabolic filters in fluorescent lighting. Chairs should be vinyl laminated with high backs and round arms, and there should be a clear kick space below the front edge of the seat. Tables should be round and laminated. All furniture edges and corners should be rounded because of the possibility of falls.

An adult day-care center includes a kitchen for the preparation of meals and snacks. The kitchen may be designed for therapeutic use (e.g., helping impaired adults to relearn cooking skills).

Because the elderly need fluid frequently, a water fountain (handicap accessible) should also be provided. And, of course, a fire extinguisher should be readily available (usually in the kitchen area).

The equipment needed for day care includes most equipment that would be customary for a reception area, offices, a nurse's office, restrooms, a kitchen, a conference room, and classrooms. In purchasing equipment, it is necessary to keep in mind the new ADA rules as they relate to the handicapped.

Equipment for activities might include beach balls, adaptive sports equipment, quilting supplies, puzzles, frames, books, ceramic supplies, games, bingo prizes, seasonal decorations, paints, theatrical props, a movie projector, a television, a VCR, a stereo, a radio, a computer, a sewing machine, a kiln, and a large clock.

Minimum staffing is in most cases determined by state licensure. Because of financial constraints, the team consists of professionals (social worker, registered nurses, etc.) and nonprofessionals working together, including a director, a secretary (depending on size of the center), an activity coordinator, an activity assistant, and in some cases a certified nursing assistant. There should usually be two staff members for the first ten clients. With larger clienteles, the ratio of staff to clients should be 1:8. The number of positions will vary depending on the size and scope of the program.

At the time of the licensure inspection, it would be beneficial to have a personnel record for each employee. The record should include a verification of an annual tuberculosis skin test, an annual chest x-ray, or a physician's statement noting no symptomatic evidence of current pulmonary tuberculosis disease and current documentation of certification for CPR and first-aid training. A food handler certificate should be included for staff who are responsible for serving and supervising meals or snacks if the local health department requires it.

The facility should have adequate insurance, including the minimum property and casualty coverage applicable in the state as well as appropriate liability coverage.

Once the inspection has taken place and the license has been obtained, it must be conspicuously posted in the center. This license is not transferrable from facility to facility. Although the rule may vary slightly from state to state, a separate license is required for each location when more than one facility is operated by the same person or agency.

If a center is to achieve success, it must be attentive to the uniqueness of each new applicant entering the program. Like other needs-driven services (e.g., hospital care, nursing homes), adult day care is approached reluctantly by most consumers. Decisions for admission are generally executed by a family member, caregiver, or casemanager, and this often results in resistance. Integrating a new client requires forethought and sensitivity if maximum acceptance and adjustment are to be achieved.

During the initial inquiry, it is necessary to evaluate the appropriateness, needs, and interests of the potential client. A brief screening by the social worker can determine the functioning level of the applicant and type of intervention needed. A visit to the center is crucial for the applicant and family or caregiver so that the program can be explained and demonstrated. A home visit by a staff member can provide further insight into the applicant's need for service and can begin to establish a trusting relationship. A medical release, completed by the primary physician, indicating absence of tuberculosis should be obtained prior to or upon admission. Enrollment is completed when financial and transportation arrangements are finalized and admission documents and contracts are discussed, signed, and distributed.

Matching a staff person and a well-adjusted client with the new client for a minimum of one week can often ensure a positive transition. It is recommended that an interdisciplinary assessment (e.g., by activities, nursing, and social work staff) be completed within the first week so that a care plan can be developed. The assessment should include a health profile, a social history, a review of support systems, ADL (activities of daily living) skills, mental and emotional status, strengths, needs, activity interests, and community and financial resources. An initial discharge plan is developed that determines alternative services should the client leave the program. The plan incorporates input from each team member and provides the framework for all intervention. The selection of problems to be dealt with, goals, and approaches by each discipline allows for coordination of services and guides all staff activity. When possible, clients and families need to be involved so that full understanding and cooperation can be achieved.

IMPLEMENTING THE PROGRAM COMPONENTS

Having established how the center will serve the client, program implementation begins with a dual focus—on the goals and objectives of the program and on those of the client. With the core essential services in place (i.e., health monitoring, nutrition, personal care, social work, and therapeutic activities), the staff can concentrate on how to assist the client in complying with the plan of care in order to increase or maintain his or her functioning level.

Emphasis on wellness and health maintenance is the mainstay of the program. Although enrollment requires a physician's release and a tuberculosis test, many clients neglect routine medical care, thus hastening physical decline. Health supervision by the center's registered nurse, even only a few times per week, can help a client to maintain his or her capacity for self-care and community residence. The initial nursing assessment, which identifies the client's diagnosis, medical history, medications, diet, mobility, orientation, and bowel and bladder control, establishes the client's health status so that the nurse can observe and react to changes of condition. Monitoring of blood pressure, pulse, and weight is performed monthly. In compliance with physician's orders, medications, treatments, and supplemental feedings can be administered. Supportive nursing for colostomy or ileostomy maintenance, nail and foot care, gastrostomy tube feeding, bowel and bladder training, maintenance therapy, health monitoring, and so on, can also be made available. Acting as a liaison, the nurse communicates concerns to the primary physician and family or caregiver. If indicated, referrals are made to rehabilitation therapists and other health services in the community.

Health education is provided on an individual and group basis. The center's nurse is primarily responsible for any emergency care needed.

As a major component of health care for the elderly and disabled, good nutritional diets and habits are a necessity often neglected. The provision of a well-balanced meal or snack, even if just once a day, can ensure at the least a minimum level of nutrition. Prescribed therapeutic diets and supplements should be included in the center's menu. Clients needing feeding assistance or special adaptive equipment should be accommodated. A registered dietitian, either on staff or acting as a consultant, can provide the expertise necessary to properly monitor clients' diets. All staff, particularly direct care staff, should be present during snacks and meals to assist with and oversee food consumption. Cultural and ethnic preferences as well as seasonal and religious food celebrations need to be observed, if possible. For clients unable to prepare food at home, arrangements should be made for the provision of home-delivered meals.

Assistance with and training in activities of daily living (e.g., ambulating, bathing, dressing, grooming, and toileting) are essential if the functional capacity of clients is to be maintained or improved. Physical decline can often be delayed when independent functioning is encouraged. A functional status report completed by the registered nurse prior to admission and reviewed at care conferences is instrumental in determining the abilities and disabilities of the client. Direct care staff must be knowledgeable about safe body mechanics as they relate to transfer and ambulation. Heavy-care clients (e.g., those who need two-person transfers or who are bowel incontinent or total feeders) require special consideration.

Decline or loss of mental or physical functioning affects all aspects of a person's life, including family relationships. Increased dependence, functional losses, and role changes may cause stress and anxiety. The social worker is instrumental in helping the client and family to acknowledge and accept the need for services and to make a smooth transition into the program. Through individual and group counseling, feelings and issues can be discussed and resolved. Since many clients come to adult day care with numerous problems, referrals often need to be made to other community resources.

Diminished participation in social, recreational, and community activities promotes decline in personal growth and the ability to enjoy life. The goal of an activity program is to keep clients interested, involved, and active while at the center. Though providing fun and enjoyment is one objective, the underlying purpose is to stimulate and motivate individuals so they can reach their highest functional potential. All activities should be designed for persons with different goals and levels of ability. Selection of specific crafts, groups, games, field trips, entertainment, and so on, should be based on the individuals' needs and abilities. Staff expertise, environmental limitations, and budgetary constraints also must be considered.

Hamill and Oliver point out that "the purpose of therapeutic in contrast to diversional activities is to stimulate changes in the participants' ability from dysfunctional to functional."[2] Therefore, individualization of activities is vital. Initially and at each care conference the following objectives are focused on:

- identifying the client's current abilities
- preventing further deterioration
- improving function to the highest possible level

Appropriate activities are then identified and planned.

Transportation is an essential part of any adult day-care program. Without it, the program could not exist. In 1986, Von Behren conducted a study that uncovered a variety of transportation solutions.[3] In 56 percent of the centers, staff provided transportation, 32 percent of the centers contracted for transportation, while 10 percent relied on public transportation.

In those communities where special-needs transportation systems exist, it may be possible to engage the appropriate organizations in developing a transportation program. Some programs function more successfully by purchasing vehicles and developing their own transportation system. Many programs utilize a combination of transportation options. No method of transportation the adult day-care center chooses is without its problems, but the program that provides its own transportation tends to exercise more control over its operation.

The dynamic growth of adult day-care facilities over the past 20 years provides a clear indication that adult day care will be a vital part of the long-term care continuum. Although many models exist, this chapter has focused on the overall concept. The model used as the basis of the chapter is a large adult day-care program that serves approximately 80 people per day and is located on the same campus as a 161-bed nursing care facility. The adult day-care program has been in operation since 1967.

NOTES

1. National Council on the Aging, *National Institute on Adult Day Care, Standards and Guidelines for Adult Day Care,* 2d ed. (Washington, D.C.: National Council on the Aging, 1990), iv.

2. C.M. Hamill and R.C. Oliver, *Therapeutic Activities for the Handicapped Elderly* (Rockville, Md: Aspen Systems, 1980).

3. R. Von Behren, *Adult Day Care in America: Summary of a National Survey* (Washington, D.C.: National Council on the Aging, 1986), 19.

Chapter 30

Durable and Home Medical Equipment

Fredlee J. Shore

During the last 20 years, the health care delivery system has grown significantly in both size and sophistication. Where once consumers confronted only single practitioners, they must now interface with large group practices administered by professional office managers and comptrollers; where once many hospitals and nursing facilities were operated as nonprofit entities for the benefit of all in need, there is now a substantial for-profit sector and continuing major corporate restructuring of nonprofits in order for them to compete effectively in the common marketplace; and where once a hospital was a hospital, the Visiting Nurse Association was a home health agency, and a durable medical equipment company provided equipment and services, it is now increasingly difficult to distinguish market share as the various organizations begin to diversify into one or more areas. In short, the delivery of quality health care has evolved into big business, and accompanying this evolution has come a significant rise in government interference through legislated regulation.

As a consequence of the ever-increasing federal and state regulation, the various components that make up the total health care delivery system must learn to cooperate with each other so that the system can provide quality care for the patient in the most efficient and cost-effective manner for the provider and the payer. In order to accomplish this, no single provider of health care services or supplies can continue to operate in a vacuum. For the system to work efficiently, each provider must be educated about what services are available, who provides the various services, where each service can be found, how the services and commodities are reimbursed, and what criteria and documentation are required for reimbursement in the various venues. While managed care and reimbursement methodology may significantly narrow the choice of individual organizations in selecting business partners, no one sector will have the ability to provide all health care services. Regardless of who controls the purse strings and who directs traffic, both the care recipients and the care providers will benefit from an educated, harmonious interface.

The business organizations that provide equipment and supplies to home care patients have commonly been referred to as durable medical equipment (DME) companies. However, with the advent of new technologies and expanded markets, new nomenclature was required to update the industry image. Home medical equipment (HME) has now come to include not only durable equipment such as basic walking aids and wheelchairs but also customized seating and positioning, oxygen and other respiratory therapies, home infusion therapy and total parenteral nutrition, wound care, urologicals, and ostomy supplies.

While much of the new technology has allowed postacute care and much chronic care to be performed in the home environment, the regulatory push to use DRGs has produced a patient who is sicker at discharge and whose needs cannot always be met at home. This fact, combined with the availability of either government or private reimbursement for necessary services, has produced a long-term care patient who is on average both older and sicker than in any previous period of time. Add life-prolonging advanced technology and the reductions in reimbursements that have hit health care providers across the board and it is easy to see why the need for cooperation among a variety of supplier groups has increased.

HME providers have historically formed mutually beneficial relationships with acute care facilities, physicians, and long-term care organizations. Although there are some pitfalls in these relationships, and although federal regulations provide opportunities for close scrutiny of certain ventures, it is certainly more cost-effective to combine available resources to better serve the patient. This chapter will examine the various HME services needed in a long-term care facility and how they can be most effectively provided and reimbursed. For the purposes of this discussion, the following services and products will be included: home infusion therapy and parenteral and enteral nutrition, wound and decubitus care, urologicals and ostomy supplies, incontinent products, oxygen therapy, DME, and orthotics and prosthetics.

SERVICES AND PRODUCTS

Since the population of long-term care facilities has altered substantially over the last 20 years, it follows that the needs of this population have also altered. Because of this and the availability of more technologies and techniques to enhance quality of care, questions now arise as to who should receive what equipment and services and how the system should pay for the care provided. The wealthy sector of the long-term care elderly population either opt to pay privately for home care or only qualify as private-pay residents in long-term care facilities. In addition, the recent availability of long-term care insurance through commercial carriers has added new options for those with sufficient disposable income for the relatively expensive premiums. Those able to remain at home are afforded certain reimbursement benefits by government payers not available in skilled nursing facilities (SNFs). The issues facing SNFs and intermediate care facilities (ICFs) are related to government regulations affecting Medicare Parts A and B and Title XIX (Medicaid) payments, where applicable.

Durable Medical Equipment

DME comprises walking aids, wheelchairs and seating systems, beds, patient lifts, and various other pieces of equipment that, by definition, are medically necessary or therapeutic in nature, can withstand repeated use, and are employed in the patient's home. If a patient resides at home and the diagnosis indicates the medical necessity of a specific piece of equipment, Medicare Part B will pay 80 percent of the allowable charges. If the patient is also a Title XIX recipient, this program will pick up the copay or, in some cases, the full charge of a denied item, depending on the individual state guidelines. However, an ICF or SNF does not qualify as "home," and consequently reimbursement for DME is not covered under Part B of the Medicare program. Similarly, the cost of DME is not reimbursed separately under Title XIX programs but is included as part of the per diem rate assigned by each program to each facility.

Given these restrictions, what options are available to long-term care facilities and how can cross-industry cooperation facilitate these options? Although Medicare B excludes DME from its coverage umbrella in long-term care facilities, orthotics and prosthetics continue to be covered. In addition, the Medicare Part A intermediary can be billed directly by the facility for equipment required by Medicare patients in a Medicare-approved SNF. Lastly, if the nursing home resident qualifies for Title XIX, certain customized equipment is reimbursable in an individual consideration or prior authorization mode. Consider the following situations.

Many nursing home residents enter facilities with their own wheelchairs. Frequently, a change in condition can create seating problems that aggravate an existing diagnosis and appear to make a specific wheelchair obsolete for the user. Along with a physical and occupational therapy evaluation, a rehabilitation dealer can either fabricate a total seating system or create one from prefabricated modular parts. The seating system and the labor costs are reimbursable under the Medicare Part B orthotics coverage and can be billed directly to the Part B carrier by the rehabilitation provider. If the patient is also eligible for Title XIX, the copay will be reimbursed through that program.

If a patient is either a straight Medicaid recipient or has only Medicare Part A coverage and Medicaid, reimbursement for custom equipment is available under

Title XIX, provided that the recipient is not in a Medicare SNF bed. The variable in cases of custom equipment (e.g., a manual or power wheelchair) is a question of definition. Currently, the HME industry regards as custom any specialized wheelchair regardless of whether the adaptations were done in house or during the manufacture of the item. A custom wheelchair would limit use of the equipment to one person due to specifications determined by that patient's special requirements and measurements. If HCFA develops its own definition of custom, the scope of reimbursable items will be narrowed.

If a facility has a Medicare SNF patient who requires a piece of equipment, the facility, under Part A, can purchase the equipment, bill it directly to the Part A intermediary, and submit the cost on its cost report. Depending on the cost of the purchased item, it could be amortized as capital equipment over a period of time. All other DME for patient use is the responsibility of each facility, as is the maintenance of all facility-owned equipment. Although many equipment manufacturers have long-term care and hospital divisions and sell directly to nursing facilities and hospitals, contracted relationships with local distributors are frequently as cost-effective as direct purchase. In terms of good will and service requirements, a facility might be wise to promote purchases from competitive distributors in order to ensure prompt response to requests for service on equipment and delivery of general supplies.

The last item of concern for administrators regarding DME is repairs and general maintenance. Repairs on patient-owned equipment are reimbursable under both Medicare Part B and Title XIX. It is vital that purchase statistics be kept on each piece of patient-owned equipment in order to ensure payment. Information such as date of purchase, make and model number, and previous repairs should be available to the technician. The claims can be submitted directly to the Part B carrier by the HME company. For facility-owned equipment, a service agreement with a local vendor is worth considering, especially if the facility has purchased equipment from the vendor. This type of scheduled maintenance would contain costs, keep equipment in maximal condition, and guarantee prompt service even on unscheduled repairs. A sample maintenance agreement used by Agawam Medical Equipment, Inc., is presented in Appendix 30-A.

Oxygen Therapy

Along with DME, oxygen therapy presents a reimbursement problem for long-term care patients. Due to the large expenditures on oxygen and oxygen-related therapies, heavy regulation has resulted in reimbursement cuts and severe justification requirements.[1] Couple this with the ever-present specter of increased liability and the result is a new focus on managing the oxygen patient. Although

Medicare B does not reimburse for oxygen therapy in a SNF or ICF, Medicare Part A and most Title XIX programs that cover these services follow the Medicare guidelines determined by HCFA for home oxygen patients. These guidelines include limitations on specific diagnoses, proper physician completion of the oxygen certificate of medical necessity form 484, and selection of the most appropriate and least costly oxygen delivery system.

Given the limitations set by government regulations, what are the options available to a long-term care facility and its oxygen patients? Consideration should be given to reimbursement potential, documentation requirements, and patient mix.

If the facility is located in a part of the country where the vast majority of patients receive their oxygen by means of a concentrator, and in addition the facility has a patient mix consisting mainly of bed-confined, continuous use residents, a contractual agreement between the facility and a local vendor is the easiest and probably the least costly arrangement for both parties. The vendor agrees to supply concentrators with compressed gas emergency backup units for a fixed price per unit per month. For Title XIX patients, the expense is covered under variable costs. The remaining patients are billed privately. The facility's medical records for each patient serve as documentation of medical necessity.

If the patient and modality mix are more diversified, a vendor of choice should be selected to service individual oxygen patients. While each patient has the right to choose a supplier, developing a relationship with one or two vendors reduces documentation errors and ensures prompt service. It is essential that the facility be cooperative and timely in supplying completed paper work in order to avoid payment delays for the vendors. In most cases where Medicare Part B and Title XIX are the payers, a Medicare denial must be obtained before Title XIX can be billed. Cooperation between the facility's medical personnel and the vendor will allow for appropriate documentation for the modality selected and prevent the need for multiple submissions of the same claim. This approach is the least costly to the facility both in time and expense.

For a facility with Medicare SNF beds, the second option can be used for those residents qualifying under Title XIX, or the facility can bill Part A under ancillary charges on its cost report. This is a relatively new approach, and the facility is responsible for all recordkeeping. In addition, payment is slow. However, if the facility can contract locally for a good price per pound of liquid oxygen, the reimbursement will cover the cost of equipment rental and oxygen. Because only the oxygen is covered, the contracted rate must be low enough to cover the equipment (tank) rental.

While other creative arrangements may exist, it has been my observation that the first two options have proven track records with regard to long-term success and cost-effectiveness. The last option requires careful record keeping, which may prove expensive in total staff time.

Infusion and Nutrition Therapy

In addition to the increased need for DME and oxygen therapy, two of the fastest growing HME services are home infusion therapy and parenteral and enteral nutrition (PEN) therapy. The development of highly sophisticated infusion and enteral pumps has enabled these therapies to be safely administered at home with minimal use of skilled nursing services. In terms of cost, both therapies can be maintained at home at less cost to third-party payers than the equivalent treatment in an acute care facility. Unfortunately, government reimbursement for these therapies is tightly regulated and slowly disbursed, and the rates make collection crucial to survival.[2] It is worth noting that home infusion therapy is covered under the DME benefit in Medicare B. This coverage imposes certain restrictions, among them that a permanent pump must be used, that the certificate of medical need must be entirely completed by the physician, and that the patient must reside at home, not in an institution. The private sector of third-party payers has set a trend toward case management and utilization review organizations, whose primary focus is cost-containment and appropriateness of therapy. Coverage in an institutional setting would vary from company to company. However, it seems likely that payment for home infusion therapy would have to be privately guaranteed for long-term care patients.[3]

Fortunately, reimbursement for PEN therapy is available from government payers in both ICF and SNF situations, provided the beneficiary meets all other coverage requirements. Since compliance with these requirements is essential to prompt payment, a review of Medicare PEN guidelines is appropriate to ensure complete understanding of the documentation and billing process. Unlike infusion therapy, which is covered under the DME provision of Medicare, PEN therapy is covered under the prosthetic device benefit provision. This requires that the patient have an internal body organ that is permanently dysfunctional or inoperative. The test of permanence can be met if the impairment is considered to be long term (90 consecutive days from the initial onset of treatment). Medicare Part B will also cover related nutrients and supplies if treatment criteria are met.

Total parenteral nutrition (TPN) is covered under Medicare Part B if severe pathology to the alimentary or gastrointestinal tract results in severe nutritional deficiencies although oral intake is adequate. An example of an acceptable diagnosis for TPN would be a massive small bowel resection or intestinal obstruction due to carcinoma. TPN is administered by means of a parenteral pump. Once the criteria have been established, coverage is approved on an individual basis by the carrier and must be reviewed every three months. Each claim must be accompanied by a doctor's prescription and substantial medical documentation, including proof of the prosthetic device's benefit and specification of the amounts and types of nutrients required by the patient.

As in TPN, the documentation for enteral nutritional therapy requires three month renewals, proof of benefit, and specification of amounts and types of nutrients. However, enteral therapy is administered either through a nasogastric, jejunostomy, or gastrostomy tube by means of gravity. The use of an enteral pump is allowed only if it can be documented that gravity administration is medically inappropriate due to some physiologic reaction such as aspiration. Enteral nutritional therapy is considered medically necessary if the patient's gastrointestinal tract is functioning but the structures necessary to permit food to reach the digestive tract are nonfunctioning. Certain neuromuscular diseases that interfere with ingestion and reconstructive surgery due to head and neck cancer are among the acceptable diagnoses for this therapy.[4]

It should be noted here that, whereas parenteral and enteral nutritional therapies are covered, nutritional supplements are not reimbursed under the Medicare benefit because they do not meet the prosthetic device benefit criterion. Once a patient is determined to meet the eligibility requirements for PEN therapy, reimbursement does not discriminate based on whether the patient is at home or in an ICF or SNF. However, the complexity of the documentation and reimbursement procedure may influence how an SNF chooses to provide and bill these therapies. The following explanation of terms used in the ensuing discussion are necessary to avoid confusion. PEN items refer to all equipment and nutritional substances necessary for this therapy. The provision of PEN items by an SNF occurs when these items are purchased by the SNF for provision to the patient. The following reimbursement options are available in a SNF for PEN therapy.

Part A Reimbursement. If the beneficiary is a Medicare SNF patient and the nursing home provides PEN items, then coverage is available under Medicare Part A. The cost of the items for PEN therapy appears on the SNF's cost report. PEN therapy under Part A is billed to the intermediary under the following classifications: Enteral nutrients are considered food and are a part of routine costs; parenteral nutrients are classified as IV drugs and are billed as ancillary products. No Part B coverage is available when the SNF provides PEN to Part A beneficiaries. On the other hand, if PEN is supplied by an outside vendor to a resident, the items may be billed under the Part B prosthetic provision for Part A beneficiaries as long as the coverage requirements are met.

Non-Part A Reimbursement. If a beneficiary is not a Part A patient, PEN is covered under the Part B prosthetic benefit regardless of who furnishes the PEN items.[5] For those patients eligible for Title XIX, the copay is covered under that program. If only Title XIX coverage is available, most programs require prior authorization before the service can be provided. As indicated at the beginning of this section, PEN claims represent a discipline and documentation mode different from that for HME claims. Consideration should be given to the degree of difficulty in filing claims and receiving payment through the SNF and the time saved by arranging for PEN services to be provided and billed through a local vendor. No matter what option is chosen, an understanding of the coverage criteria and reimbursement methodology is essential.

Wound Care, Decubitus Care, Urological, Ostomy, and Incontinence Supplies

The last area where there is a great deal of cross-industry involvement is in the provision of wound care and decubitus care products and urological, ostomy, and incontinence supplies. While many of these items are reimbursable under the Medicare Part B provision, some are not, and the facility must decide how best to provide necessary supplies. According to Lisa Thomas-Payne, president of Medical Reimbursement Systems in Highlands Ranch, Colorado, "there is a rapidly growing number of nursing home patients who are bed- or chair-confined, chronically ill and who quickly incur skin breakdown. The nursing home looks for ways to obtain wound care supplies for their patients that won't cost the nursing home."[6] She suggests that the Medicare B supplier is the obvious choice because the program has a mechanism to reimburse the provider. In this manner, the nursing home effectively cares for its residents with no monetary outlay and no delay in payment. However, it is incumbent upon the facility to work in conjunction with the provider in supplying the appropriate documentation for Medicare reimbursement. In the case of wound care and decubitus care products, the following information must appear on the certificate of medical need: the primary problem causing the bed- or chair-confinement, the stage of the decubitus, the location and number of wounds, and the surgical procedure (or debridement).

If the facility has the mechanism to bill Part B, it may do so, and reimbursement will be according to the carrier allowables. A nonprofit facility might want to consider creating a for-profit billing service to avail itself of the profits that may occur from billing the Part B carrier for wound care and for other disposables as well. If the facility prefers using an outside Medicare Part B vendor, the location of the provider should be considered when making the choice. Because of the significant growth in this market, the possibility of fraud and abuse by providers is very real. For example, some suppliers operate outside the jurisdiction where the service is supplied but submit claims within their own jurisdiction. Although this issue may be resolved shortly through new legislation, the facility should not be linked with an ethically questionable provider.

The mechanism for the reimbursement of urological and ostomy supplies is the same as for wound care items. The documentation is slightly less cumbersome and demanding, requiring a diagnosis of permanent incontinence for urologicals and the date of resection surgery for ostomy claims. These claims are reimbursed under the prosthetic benefit provision of Medicare Part B, and the diagnoses must indicate that the items being used are replacing permanently nonfunctioning internal organs. While some large for-profit chains have developed a very sophisticated inventory tracking system that allows them to negotiate lucrative contracts with distributors and to closely monitor patient usage for Part B billing, most facilities benefit from long-term care providers who also do Part B billing.[7] An indication of the trend toward this type of arrangement is the dynamic growth in this segment of 10–12 percent in 1990 versus an industry average of 6 percent.[8]

CONCLUSION

Regardless of the facility's size or its legal status as a for-profit or nonprofit entity, the long-term care industry and the HME industry are becoming more involved as partners in the delivery of care to the elderly and handicapped. In this chapter, the necessity of providing quality care at the least costly rate has been discussed. The legal and ethical reputation of both the facility and the associated suppliers has also been presented as an issue worthy of serious consideration. So, what should you look for in an HME Medicare Part B provider? I would suggest that the lowest price is not always the best measure of a reliable company. You want to be certain that the company has a professional image, that its primary care base includes the services it is providing to your residents, and that it is able to provide the services when needed. Although sometimes bigger is better, when high-tech services such as oxygen therapy and PEN are involved, the smaller company that specializes in these services is often exactly what you want. Research its reputation in the provider community, investigate its longevity, and be sure that it has a proven track record, because ultimately the responsibility for quality patient care is yours.

NOTES

1. J. Lucas, Oxygen Decisions, *Continuing Care* 10, no. 10 (1991):12.

2. L. Thomas-Payne, Paying the Provider, *Infusion Therapy Focus: A Supplement to Homecare* 13, no. 3 (1991):6.

3. Ibid., 8–9.

4. Blue Cross and Blue Shield of South Carolina, *Parenteral and Enteral Nutritional Therapy: Provider Manual,* April, 1987, pp 15, 23–24.

5. Part B Carrier–South Carolina, *Medicare Advisory,* October 1991.

6. L. Thomas-Payne, Healing Wound Care Reimbursement, *Pressure Ulcer Prevention: A Supplement to Homecare* 13, no. 6 (1991):86–87.

7. J. Bowe, More Bang for the Buck, *Contemporary Long Term Care* 14, no. 11 (1991):48–50. Manor Health Care Corporation decreased its cost by 2.4 percent between June 1990 and June 1991 by using distributor contracts for high-volume purchases. A bar code system also tracked supplies by patient usage and insurance-billing capabilities.

8. LTC Dealers' Growth Tops Industry Norms, *Medical Products Sales* 22, no. 11 (1991):21.

Appendix 30-A

Sample Service Agreement and Proposal

Wheelchair Service Agreement

<u>Company name</u> or its duly authorized agent (hereinafter collectively referred to

as _____) agrees to perform certain maintenance and/or

service work on _____ located at _____ for

_____ (hereinafter referred to as Purchaser).

The purchaser, having read the Wheelchair Service Proposal and understand-

ing that the Proposal terms are incorporated by reference, desires the following:

_____

_____

I, _____, have read and understand the terms of this Service

Agreement and the Service Proposal which is incorporated into this agreement.

<u>Company name</u> and I have executed this Agreement this _____ day of

_____, 19____.

_____   _____
             Purchaser   Company

Source: Courtesy of Agawam Medical Equipment, Inc., Agawam, Mass.

Wheelchair Service Proposal

I. TERM OF AGREEMENT: This Agreement shall become effective on the date it is accepted by Purchaser and shall remain in effect for the period of one (1) year.

II. STATEMENT OF WORK TO BE PERFORMED:

A. INITIAL INSPECTION: Company shall complete an initial inspection and maintenance service of all _____ owned by the Purchaser that are to be included in this inspection. Make, model, and serial number for each wheelchair or other equipment will be recorded at this initial inspection. A detailed written estimate for each wheelchair or other equipment needing repair will be provided. Company will repair only those wheelchairs or other specified equipment authorized by the Purchaser.

B. MAINTENANCE SERVICE WILL INCLUDE THE FOLLOWING ON AN "AS NEEDED" BASIS:

1. Adjustment of brakes and bearings
2. Lubrication of slide tubes
3. Replacement of spokes, rubber tips, hand grips, and brake tips
4. Tightening and replacement of all nuts, bolts, and other hardware, as needed
5. Professional cleaning of all bright metal parts
6. Cleaning of upholstery and application of upholstery protectant
7. Mechanical inspection

III. SCHEDULED MAINTENANCE, CLEANING, AND INSPECTION SERVICES:

A. EVERY 12 MONTHS: Includes only the initial maintenance services listed in Section I of this contract and will be priced on the per hour basis listed in Section VII of this contract.

B. EVERY 6 MONTHS: Includes the initial inspection and maintenance services listed in Section I and one scheduled maintenance service during the one-year term of this contract. Price for the six-month schedule is listed in Section VII of this contract.

C. EVERY 3 MONTHS: Includes the initial inspection and maintenance services listed in Section I and three (3) scheduled maintenance services during the one-year term of this contract. Price for the three-month schedule is listed in Section VII of this contract.

At the time of the scheduled service, Company will inspect the _____ for any needed repairs. Company will provide a detailed estimate for each wheelchair or other equipment containing a description of the work to be performed, cost of the parts, and estimated labor required to complete repairs. Company will repair only the wheelchairs and other equipment approved by the Purchaser.

IV. UNSCHEDULED REPAIRS: Repair work identified by the Purchaser at any time will be performed by Company. Company will provide a detailed estimate in writing reflecting a description of the work to be completed, the cost of the parts, and estimated labor required to repair. Company will repair only those wheelchairs and other equipment approved by the Purchaser.

V. INSPECTION AND ACCEPTANCE: Upon completion of repairs and re-delivery of all wheelchairs or other equipment to the Purchaser, the Purchaser's authorized representative will inspect the equipment and the parties will agree that all repair work previously identified and approved has been completed.

VI. MISCELLANEOUS:

   D. NOTICES: All notices required or permitted under this agreement shall be in writing.

   E. ENTIRE AGREEMENT: This agreement constitutes the entire agreement among the parties. It supersedes any prior arrangement or understanding among them, and it may not be modified or amended in any manner other than in writing signed by both parties.

   F. GOVERNING LAW: This agreement and the rights of the parties shall be governed by the laws of the State of _____.

VII. PRICING:

   A. A labor rate of $35.00 per hour for manual wheelchairs and other non-electric equipment and $45.00 per hour for power wheelchairs and other power equipment will be applied on a pro-rata basis for each repair, with a minimum charge of $20.00 per manual wheelchair or non-power equipment and $30.00 per power wheelchair or other power equipment. There is no delivery or pick-up charge.

   B. INSPECTION, CLEANING, AND MAINTENANCE SCHEDULE:

      1. EVERY 12 MONTHS
         a. Manual equipment $50.00
         b. Power equipment $65.00

2. EVERY 6 MONTHS
   a. Manual equipment $30.00
   b. Power equipment $40.00
3. EVERY 3 MONTHS
   a. Manual equipment $20.00
   b. Power equipment $30.00

Note: Minimum service would be 10 wheelchairs and/or other pieces of equipment.

VIII. WARRANTY: Company warrants all repair work for 90 days from the date of completion. If repairs must be re-worked as a result of Company's failure to complete repair correctly, there will be no charge for the re-work.

    The Purchaser has been informed and agrees that Company is not a manufacturer of the required parts used in servicing the equipment and is not responsible for the design or adequacy of the same or for any manufacturing defects. The Purchaser agrees to accept whatever warranties on parts which are offered by the manufacturer in lieu of any warranty by Company.

    Company has not prescribed the equipment and makes no representations or warranties of any kind, including with regard to merchantability of the fitness of the equipment for any particular purpose of the Purchaser, its employees, or its patients.

IX. PAYMENT: Payment will be due within thirty (30) days from the date of service.

Chapter 31

Durable Medical Equipment: Looking beyond the Sales Pitch

Denise Finn-Rizzo

Durable medical equipment (DME) can be viewed as a basic component in the provision of long-term care services. It is a tool of the trade, an instrument of implementation, and as such it presents a great challenge for the long-term care administrator. Although there have been attempts to describe and define this category of products, there is no strictness to the term *durable* and no clear definition of *medically necessary.* Medicare classified DME as items that are usable over and over again by patients, primarily serve a medical purpose, are not useful to individuals who are not sick or injured, and are appropriate for use in the home.[1] This definition is inconsistent with actual practice. Examples of DME include oxygen equipment, wheelchairs and other walking aids, and wound care, urological, and ostomy supplies. Can wound care supplies be used over and over again by patients? Is a foam cushion fitted for a 50-kilogram, wheelchair-bound quadriplegic useful to a 90-kilogram patient with end-stage cardiac failure? These and many other questions arise as the long-term care administrator tries to meet the residents' DME needs.

The major objective of this chapter is to provide long-term care administrators with a solid working knowledge of the DME business. It attempts to raise consciousness levels among administrators and equip them with the armor necessary to protect not only the institution they represent but, more importantly, the residents under their charge. The issues to be discussed include the following: How can a long-term care administrator protect the institution and its residents from the dealings of disreputable DME suppliers? What are some strategies in the management of facility-owned DME items? What are some alternative mechanisms for providing and paying for equipment that is not reimbursable? How can a long-term care administrator play a role in developing public policy regarding the definition of DME and establishing mechanisms for payment?

THE UNCERTAINTY OF REIMBURSEMENT

Reimbursement for DME items has been unpredictable. Denials have been common. What has been "allowed" is what has been approved based on previous claims that have historically been paid.[2] The key factors that have surfaced in the elusive search for reimbursement are primary payer source and current residence of patient or level of bed. All decisions as to whether to obtain necessary and helpful items for patients become complicated by these factors.

Furthermore, the provision of DME items seems to be payment-driven rather than needs-driven. According to a recent article in *U.S. News and World Report,* there is evidence that DME items are supplied to individuals who have no use for them.[3] There is evidence that some Medicare patients are barred from admission to skilled nursing facilities (SNFs) because the conditions of coverage are "so vague, so variable, and so arbitrarily applied" that the institutions refuse to take the risk of no reimbursement.[4] Perhaps long-term care patients likewise do not receive the devices they truly need unless there is some mechanism of payment or reimbursement. It is probable that all too often a piece of equipment is not supplied to an individual because of the perception that reimbursement will not be forthcoming. How many times has a social worker, nurse, or physical therapist assumed that "insurance won't pay" and therefore did not even discuss the topic with the resident or the family?

The uncertainty of reimbursement, coupled with the nature of long-term care and its customers, makes for a foggy picture. Provider-to-customer relationships may be multitiered and include the resident, the family, the facility, the supplier, the physician, and perhaps contracted therapy services. To make matters even more complex, elderly individuals are susceptible to Alzheimer's disease and other cognitive impairments. Given all this, making a decision to purchase or even discuss use of an item for a patient is obviously a monumental task.

There is perhaps no other form of health care that must balance the players and components so frequently and in so many ways as long-term care. While acute care can and must maintain an aggressive attitude in order to accomplish its goal of patient discharge, ambulatory care must sit back and let the patient take the reins and drive his or her own course. Long-term care vacillates between the two—it often has to be both aggressive and laid-back. A long-term care facility has a responsibility to see to it that its residents' needs are met. Yet it must allow the residents freedom of choice and flexibility, since the facility is essentially the residents' home. The ties that bind the efforts in long-term care are the longevity of contact and the provision of residency services. All actions and activities within this setting must revolve around the fact that the resident is a consumer— a consumer of services, a consumer of goods, and a consumer of equipment.

As its name implies, long-term care exists within a larger continuum, the continuum of time. Long-term care decisions, therefore, are unlike other medical decisions. The decision makers sometimes can afford the luxury of time, which is not possible in other medical care settings. Problems in long-term care often do not spring up overnight. They evolve more slowly and often can be predicted. Time may be available for thought, exploring other options and alternatives, and weighing the implications of different decisions. In pursuing reimbursement for some common DME services, the mechanisms of payment and the implications of each path taken can be explored. The get-it-done-yesterday attitude predominant in other health care settings may not apply. Time can be used as a factor to take the long-term care administrator out of the hard-sell environment.

Long-term care has as one of its primary but unwritten responsibilities the conservation of resources. Residents may be housed at a particular facility for two weeks or 12 years. In other words, long-term care is unpredictable. There is the potential for the luxury of time, but this potential carries with it a responsibility to more critically analyze decisions.

As health care providers, long-term care facilities have the responsibility to equip themselves properly. This is entailed by their responsibility to meet the needs of all residents they accept. They must decide, however, whether to provide all that is needed by a resident under their comprehensive service package or place the burden of payment for DME necessities back on the resident and his or her reimbursement options. Common practice has encouraged looking at who is paying for the bed when considering a DME purchase. If the primary objective is to get the resident what is needed or would be helpful, then the secondary objective becomes to maximize use of available reimbursement mechanisms. It must be remembered that the long-term care facility has a responsibility to provide what would be useful to the resident or at least assist the resident in its purchase.

The challenge before the long-term care administrator thus becomes how to provide for the needs of the residents given the realities of unpredictable reimbursement for DME items, lack of knowledge on the part of health care providers as to the mechanisms and amount of payment for DME items, limited financial resources on the part of the residents, and multiple party involvement in the customer-supplier relationship.

UNDERSTANDING THE DME WORLD

Provision of required equipment cannot be accomplished without some sort of relationship between the long-term care facility and the DME source. However, long-term care administrators must be wary of relationships with DME suppliers and approach them with caution. In order to be a player in the DME reimbursement game, the long-term care administrator must understand the DME world from a broader perspective. Recent debate has occurred over allegations of fraud and abuse on the part of DME suppliers, particularly with regard to the Medicare reimbursement system. The nursing home industry has been involved in some questionable dealings, although the most publicized cases concern hospital-based joint venture referral practices and telemarketing scams that have defrauded Medicare beneficiaries living in their own homes.

To successfully pull off a telephone solicitation sale, the DME supplier contacts the beneficiary directly, obtains the beneficiary's Medicare number, the name of the primary physician, and some indication of the medical problems. The supplier then forwards a completed certificate of medical necessity to the physician for his or her signature. The physician signs and returns it to the DME supplier, thinking that perhaps the patient is truly in need of the listed items or the family is requesting the items.[5] If the physician fails to return a signed certificate in a timely fashion, the supplier may harass him or her into signing.[6] Once the completed certificate is in the DME supplier's hands, the supplier can deliver the items to the patient, perhaps claiming that "your doctor ordered them." Items may be added to the list after the physician has signed. Given the sales pitch over the phone and upon delivery, the beneficiary has difficulty refusing or returning the goods. Medicare is billed and the items sit in the closet unused.

Other examples of deceit initiated by DME suppliers include the practice of maintaining "on file" signatures that can be used to submit new claims on behalf of Medicare beneficiaries. DME suppliers have also been known to obtain more than one provider number and to submit duplicate billings for the same service under different numbers, thus receiving multiple payment for the same service.

The types of fraud and abuse that should be of most concern to long-term care administrators include carrier shopping and unbundling. Carrier shopping is a phenomenon that has its roots in the days prior to the Omnibus Budget Reconciliation Act of 1987 (OBRA '87), when the process of pricing DME was left to the individual carrier. With the initiation of OBRA '87, established fee schedules were mandated. As a result, one fee schedule for each Medicare carrier area was calculated, but it was done using "historical reasonable charges." In effect, this locked into place numerous variations in reimbursement levels for DME among the carriers.[7] To practice carrier shopping, the DME supplier tries to learn as much as possible about a particular carrier's reimbursement levels and coverage policies. The objective is to maximize reimbursement for its products. Armed with the knowledge of which carrier will pay the most, how many units of each DME category are allowed before reimbursement is cut back or disallowed, and who applies the least amount of policy-related red tape, the supplier is ready for action.[8] Submissions are directed toward best return. Mechanisms are set in place that allow the DME nomads to utilize multiple business localities and submit billings in the areas with the highest reimbursement rates.[9] Although this practice has been minimized by OBRA '90 through the establishment of national DME limits, the phase-in time of three years allows such pricing inequities to continue until late 1993.

Unbundling in relationship to DME is a process by which claims for equipment are inflated greatly beyond actual cost by separate billings for each component of the total item. In some instances, one carrier may be billed for the total item whereas another carrier may be billed for separate components of the item.[10] Ostomy equipment is often subject to the practice of unbundling. A pouch containing a bag, skin barrier, and adhesive may cost a DME supplier approximately four dollars. The reimbursement rate can be more than doubled if the supplier files an individual claim for each component.[11] Overinflated charges result in an inappropriate profit margin. Nursing homes must be wary of the DME supplier who proposes to take over uncollected accounts receivable, specifically equipment and supply claims. Once reassigned, the supplier can reimburse the long-term care facility at the face value of the invoice and then send the unbundled claims to Medicare to reap additional reimbursement.

DME suppliers also sometimes engage in questionable practices in the provision of oxygen and related supplies to patients. With the implementation of prospective reimbursement for oxygen, a single monthly payment modulated by flow rate replaced retrospective reimbursement. The incentive was created for DME providers to reduce their costs for oxygen therapy as a way of maintaining or increasing profitability. This creates a major conflict, as the cheapest form of oxygen delivery is often not the best for the patient.[12] Suppliers became unwilling to assume any additional costs for more versatile equipment, such as the transtracheal catheter. Patients have been routinely told, "Medicare does not pay for your oxygen catheter anymore."[13] Physicians were even sold the same bill of goods. An Alabama-based study examining oxygen reviews revealed that in most cases the prescribing physician did not know what type of oxygen delivery system the patient was using.[14] Misleading information abounds. Physicians and patients are being incorrectly told by certain suppliers that Medicare will no longer pay for ambulatory liquid systems and that if subscribers who use oxygen want portable systems, the combination of a concentrator and a high-pressure gas cylinder in a stroller would be reimbursed.[15] Such systems may be appropriate for individuals who are bedridden but are not appropriate for any individual who intends to travel outside the home. With regard to nursing homes, concentrators potentially leave residents tied to their rooms and discourage trips away from the facility and even walking about the facility.

A long-term care facility must also be cautious in using DME providers who operate on an unassigned claims basis. A participating supplier is one who chooses to participate, one who voluntarily agrees to accept assignment for all covered services furnished to Medicare beneficiaries. Also implied is an agreement to accept Medicare's approved amount as payment in full for services furnished during the year of participation. To accept assignment means to request direct payment from the Medicare program and to agree to accept the Medicare-approved charge as payment in full for the service. The approved charge comprises the Medicare B payment and the applicable deductible and coinsurance.[16]

A DME supplier may advertise using the phrase "Medicare accepted," yet may operate on an unassigned claims or nonparticipating basis. The practice of asking Medicare recipients to pay at the time of sale while making promises that reimbursement will be sent directly to the recipient at the "Medicare allowable" rate ensures the vendor of cash in hand yet often surprises the recipient when payment received falls significantly short of outlay. Some DME providers will not take assignment on claims that are less than a certain dollar value (e.g., $100). This practice means the Medicare recipient has to produce the money up front. The DME provider, by law, must bill Medicare for such items, but any denials for payment are then the responsibility of the recipient. Most Medicare recipients do not have the resources or the energy to deal with a carrier denial or know how to initiate the claims review or resubmission process.

CONTRACTING: PROTECTING THE LTC FACILITY

How can a long-term care administrator protect the facility and its residents from the dealings of disreputable DME suppliers? One obvious method is to develop a contractual relationship. The roles and responsibilities of both parties, the nursing home and the DME supplier, must be clearly defined. It is preferable from the nursing home's point of view for the contract to be prepared by the nursing home administrator and then submitted to the contractor. The contract should be clear and include a description of services, an indication of the duration of the agreement, a list of qualifications, a statement of acceptable charges as well as those anticipated to be used, a delineation of billing and payment mechanisms, and the date and signatures of both parties. Instituting an initial six-month (trial) contract before signing for a longer period allows the long-term care facility a chance to re-evaluate the contract conditions at an early date.[17] The facility should be looking for a supplier that has the ability to deliver good-quality supplies and equipment on time and at a reasonable cost. Of course, the ability to deliver under emergency circumstances, ideally seven days a week, 24 hours a day, is also certainly attractive.

A statement from the facility describing what it considers professional behavior and what it considers the responsibility of the supplier is mandatory. Some clause prohibiting the reassignment or subsale of the contract to other providers might serve to protect the long-term care facility and minimize costs. It is not out of bounds to include a clause that allows management the right to review the accounts payable file.[18] The facility would be wise to state that the vendor must abide by state, federal, and local regulations.[19] The incorporation of an industry standard code of ethics, such as that specified by the National Association of

Medical Equipment Suppliers, could have protective value. Although it would seem to be a basic assumption, a policy requiring ethical business practices is a necessity. This policy, however, does not totally relieve the facility of all responsibility. Any action taken by a vendor can be attributed to the purchasing organization. DME suppliers do not constitute an allied health discipline but merely sell or rent products to support treatment modalities.[20] It is therefore important that a supplier be sought with professional connections—for example, connections with a respiratory therapist, a physical therapist, or a nurse (either on staff or available through contract). A close look at the supplier's internal operations may assist the nursing home administrator in making the decision whether to establish a relationship. Are there written policies and procedures that protect the rights of the customer? An insistence that the supplier be a participant in both Medicare and Medicaid programs and be willing to bill other third parties and commercial carriers should be stated. A vendor that will take the responsibility to bill Medigap carriers may be more attractive. The contract should also specify the process by which the DME vendor handles denials.

Another method to determine whether a vendor is reputable is to investigate its reputation within the local health care community. Tactics include contacting the better business bureau, the local chamber of commerce or business association, hospitals, home health agencies, and other nursing homes to confirm levels of satisfaction with the particular supplier. Asking the DME supplier for references and actually contacting those references is one way to avoid ultimate dissatisfaction. If dealing with a national company, contacting professional organizations such as the Health Industry Distributors Association, the Health Industry Manufacturer's Association, the Joint Commission for Accreditation on Home Care, the American College of Health Care Administrators, and the American Health Care Association may prove beneficial.

The old adage to shop around and try before you buy should not be forgotten. The administrator should also not think that one and only one contract can exist. It may be beneficial to explore group purchasing options. A supplier may only carry one or two brands that the facility's staff do not consider optimal. The use of multiple suppliers may enhance the variety of items the long-term care administrator can make available to the residents and may also serve the purpose of lowering costs.

CARING FOR FACILITY-OWNED EQUIPMENT

In the case of facility-owned DME, such as mobility aids, the long-term care administrator has the option of purchasing through a local distributor or directly from an equipment manufacturer. Utilization of the local distributor may provide the advantage of prompt response to requests for service and delivery of supplies as well as a mechanism for providing scheduled maintenance and controlling costs. If the long-term care facility has no means of providing for the upkeep of such equipment as walkers and wheelchairs, a local supplier who is able to offer a service contract may seem a reasonable alternative. However, a thorough exploration of other options should be conducted before agreements are made. Individuals with expertise in equipment repair may already be employed by the long-term care facility. The occupational therapist, the physical therapist, the maintenance worker, or even the electrician may be qualified and willing to serve as a repair person.

Other resources within the community could also be investigated as possible providers of repair services. Perhaps repairs could be contracted out to the regional vocational or technical high school or community college. Local medical institutions such as hospitals, HMOs, outpatient clinics, and other long-term care facilities might be willing to share technical and repair personnel or subcontract repair services. Through utilizing this approach, the long-term care facility may secondarily establish or strengthen provider-to-provider relationships that may prove profitable in the long run (e.g., by increasing interinstitutional referrals).

BILLING FOR DME

The importance of maintaining a cooperative relationship between vendor and facility cannot be understated. In many circumstances, successful reimbursement will depend upon proper documentation and timely submission of claims. There is a significant degree of difficulty in filing claims, enough to make billing through a local vendor often more cost-effective than maintaining the necessary support systems for direct facility reimbursement. A vendor directly billing for DME must have access to the customer—the resident. The facility must weigh whether it wants to expose the residents to this third party. In instances where vendors are given direct access, the long-term care facility is wise to ensure that residents have access to information about other DME supplier options, thus guaranteeing freedom of choice.

Vendors given direct access must be comfortable with and enjoy the elderly. If they are not given direct access, some mechanism for assessing satisfaction with services and payment arrangements must be devised. Vendors given the authority to bill carriers directly for all services provided may follow denials with one and only one resubmission before bills are sent either directly to the resident or to the long-term care facility. Although having an agreement in which the vendor bills for DME items may seem attractive to the long-term care facility, caution must be maintained.

By purchasing supplies from the DME provider and billing for them itself, the nursing home can protect its residents from the possibility of DME rip-offs. Quality of care must be the balancing counterweight to efficiency.[21] Although costly in operations maintenance, this method ensures that the long-term care facility remains in control. The long-term care facility can also make certain that an all-out effort is made to collect reimbursement. By internally maintaining billing proceedings for DME supplies, claims denied yet medically necessary can be aggressively pursued until a satisfactory resolution is obtained. Since DME reimbursement has been allocated based on historical practice, there is room for play within the system. Denials for equipment that is medically necessary can and should be appealed and payment aggressively sought. When denials are received, the carrier should be asked to provide details in writing of what is unacceptable, why it is unacceptable, and what supporting documents are necessary.[22] Any demonstrable cost savings should be explained. If the long-term care facility takes the position that the equipment will provide what is truly necessary for the individual resident, the chance of success in reimbursement can only be increased. Although time consuming and energy-intensive, taking a case-by-case approach and remaining persistent may begin to change reimbursement practices and patterns and result in the optimal provision of necessary equipment.

The importance of protecting against the consequences of dealing with disreputable DME suppliers cannot be understated. Although billing through a local vendor may often seem more cost-effective than maintaining the necessary support systems for direct facility reimbursement, the cost to the facility can be overwhelming. But in order to internally run an efficient accounts receivable department with some expertise in DME billing, mechanisms must be set in place to track costs and dates and otherwise provide the proper documentation.

Most long-term care facilities already have existing policies and documentation procedures that complement the DME billing process. For those that do, the task is to extract the necessary information, set up regular reviews, and implement procedures that make DME billing a matter of routine. Facilities fortunate enough to have computerized networks can abstract billing information more readily. For the manually oriented facility, an expanded charge ticket system in which the requisition for an item paralleled the certificate of medical necessity form would serve as the primary data collection tool. Review of DME utilization could be included in social service rounds now in place for determining levels of care and reviewing cases. Sticker systems attached to the front of patient charts serve as reminders for data collection. Precalculated dates for recertification could be flagged and information gathered prior to those dates. Cooperation between physicians, therapists, and the departments of nursing, utilization review, social services, and accounts receivable is necessary if the long-term care facility is to have a direct hand in the reimbursement process.

KEEPING ABREAST OF CHANGES: A KEY TO SUCCESSFUL REIMBURSEMENT

The education of providers is a key element in the provision of DME to consumers. Since there are so many who interface with residents in a long-term care facility, the process of keeping staff up to date with current trends and reimbursement requirements is a formidable one. Nonetheless, this knowledge base does not belong strictly within the walls of the billing department but must be diffused throughout the system in order to optimize compliance and reap the benefits of maximum reimbursement. Informing physicians, social service personnel, nursing department personnel, and physical and occupational therapists is a vital part of the process.

There are mechanisms within Medicare Parts A and B and Title XIX that serve to update the provider routinely as to what is billable and what are the requirements for successful reimbursement. Newsletters are issued by carriers on a regular basis, and these usually include a section on DME that advises providers of upcoming changes in requirements for reimbursement or changes in codes. Excerpts from these newsletters can be included in the long-term care facility's newsletter, posted on staff break room bulletin boards, or even included as a payroll stuffer. Screening for dates of DME use and review can be done as a routine part of social service rounds. Grand rounds can focus on reimbursement of DME. Supplier contracts can and should include a clause assigning staff education responsibilities to the supplier. Quick on-unit presentations must be done each time a new piece of equipment is introduced. DME suppliers can be invited on a quarterly basis to present new technologies and equipment that may be of benefit to the resident. The presentations should mention who the devices would be useful for, their cost, the sources of payment, and any necessary requirements for documentation or review of product use.

The establishment of a billing department position for an expert in DME claims is worth considering. Such an individual could directly access carriers through their telephone claims assistance departments and thus be able to find out why specific claims are not being processed or are being denied. Action can then be directed at rectifying the problem and resolving payment. The provider relations department can help guide the long-term care facility through the process of claims submission for new services. It can also provide information about new services and how to bill for them. Seminars sponsored by provider services departments are often worthwhile to attend.

A basic understanding of the claims review process can decrease the number of denials. Like most large insurers, Medicare relies on an automated review system. Computers are programmed to screen claims with certain procedure codes. If the claim does not meet the screening parameters, the computer suspends the claim, which is then manually reviewed. The initial review is done by a reviewer trained by carrier personnel and generally lacking in medical education or clinical expertise. If a claims reviewer is uncertain about whether to pay or deny the claim, a nurse or physician employed by the carrier may be consulted. It is likely that a claim denied on initial review has no further medical review. Seat lift chars and transcutaneous electrical nerve stimulators are examples of DME items that HCFA requires carriers to screen.[23]

The billing department and the departments in direct contact with the residents and families must be closely linked. Encouraging the billing department to access the physician directly in order to promote proper documentation of the rationale for equipment and proper completion of claim forms may minimize denials. More important, education must be aimed at those who spend the bulk of their time with the residents, namely, the aides. Aides will often be able to best identify resident needs. Many residents are without the benefit of therapy services, yet the provision of an adaptive piece of equipment may make the difference in maintaining independence in ADL tasks. Nurses in particular must expand their thinking to include reimbursement mechanisms by direct exposure to Medicare and Medicaid information. Educating the staff about the complexities of health policy and regulation must be viewed as essential. The facility, by incorporating some basic concepts into its orientation program, can encourage new employees to expect this type of education and make them less intimidated by the facility's philosophy regarding DME.

Staff can no longer afford to be forced into tight and specific roles that preclude knowledge of DME. It is time to destroy interprofessional boundaries often mistakenly interpreted as barriers.[24] Those who have the responsibility of caring for a nursing home resident must care for the whole person. Heightening awareness of DME on the part of all its staff members is one of the ways the nursing home can truly meet the needs of its residents.

BEYOND REIMBURSEMENT

What approach can the long-term care administrator take when a requested item is not reimbursable and the resident's financial situation does not allow the luxury of out-of-pocket purchase? In such instances, contingency plans must be in place to provide the resident with what is needed in order to ensure comfort or maximize function. Leasing options should be explored, particularly in cases where the item would be useful to the individual for only a short time or the individual is unsure of its benefit. In facilities with computer systems, a facilitywide equipment database can be established to track items owned by the institution and provide information about their current location and use.

The time has come for the concept of recycling to be applied to the DME field. *Durable* implies the ability to utilize a piece of equipment over and over again.

Used equipment can be purchased from private sources. Reimbursement can be pursued through a subscriber-initiated claim form.[25] Aggressive marketing will assist long-term care administrators in acquiring equipment already used by others. When residents are discharged or expire, active solicitation of items belonging but no longer of use to them must take place. Families can be approached and requests made for donations. If the relationship has been satisfactory, in most instances families will be more than willing to donate articles that can be of use to others. Mention can also be made of the need for medical supplies and equipment in quarterly or annual newsletters. Nonprofit facilities have the advantage of being able to offer tax deductible status for donations. All facilities have a responsibility to their residents to ensure that all donated equipment is in good operating order. Documentation of this should be on file.

Community resources must also be utilized. Many local home care agencies and town-run senior centers have established loan closets for pieces of equipment such as walkers, wheelchairs, and the like. The development of good community relations with such organizations places a long-term care facility in a position to approach them with the suggestion that they provide "bridge loans" of equipment. Such loans may serve to supply residents with necessary pieces of equipment on a temporary basis while they are awaiting determination of reimbursement possibilities or recovering from a temporary problem. A long-term care facility is a community member that serves community residents and often boosts the local economy through the provision of jobs and services. As a result, the concept of taking care of itself and its own must be left behind. The long-term care facility is a community player with community output and input. Asking for assistance from the community is not a sign of weakness but rather a realization that the facility is a part of the community.

Community organizations often rally around a specific cause. Local libraries may provide an area directory of resources. Societies such as the Multiple Sclerosis Society, the American Cancer Society, the Red Cross, the Muscular Dystrophy Association, the Lion's Club, the local Jaycees, or the St. Vincent De Paul Society might respond to the requests of an individual resident in need of an item because of a diagnosis-related disability. United Way funds may provide special program monies that are allocated for medically indigent adults and often can be used for necessary equipment.[26] Spreading the word among the staff members, particularly those who belong to a church or civic club, can result in assistance to the patient. Even families or volunteers may know of organizations or individuals who would be willing to adopt a resident.[27]

Local community groups are often happy to serve as sponsors for individual patients who may not be able to afford DME items that would truly increase comfort levels or assist in the maintenance of independence. Some groups may tend to focus on a certain diagnosis. Access to appropriate groups can be achieved by obtaining chamber of commerce listings. Making telephone contact with such groups on a routine basis can be an assigned task of the marketing or public relations department. The facility may have to take no for an answer the first time around, but repeated soft-sell efforts sometimes prove fruitful. The might of a case-specific scenario gives the potential sponsor some way of identifying with a particular individual. When all else fails and needed equipment is purchased out of pocket by the resident, he or she should be advised to save slips and other purchase documents for the purpose of justifying possible medical expense tax deductions.

THE ROLE OF THE FACILITY IN SHAPING DME POLICY

In the provision of DME services to the long-term care resident, the choice of supplier is taken out of the hands of the resident and the family. The nursing facility is placed in a position of making the most appropriate choice for the resident and the family. The DME supplier becomes the agent of the long-term care facility. Their reputations become intertwined, and therefore the importance of choosing a reputable vendor cannot be underestimated.

However, the long-term care facility's responsibility goes beyond dealing exclusively with reputable vendors and extends into the realm of patient advocacy. The facility must inform insurance carriers of any knowledge of wrongdoing on the part of DME suppliers. Long-term care dollars must be safeguarded, which can be done only by communicating with carrier utilization review departments and the inspector general's office.

Long-term care facilities must step out into the community to educate potential users and the general public about DME. They also must support DME-related research. For example, one important question is whether nursing home personnel consciously or unconsciously consider a resident's financial status when deciding whether to provide or even discuss DME. The answers to this and other pertinent questions need to be discovered.

Gaps exist in the availability of items that help residents maintain as independent a life style as possible. Long-term care facilities bear the responsibility to assist with the definition of DME and create mechanisms for reimbursement. Only through documenting the need for DME services and items and demonstrating their usefulness can progress be made in the area of reimbursement. The push for legislation must balance flexibility (so that individuals can receive the assistance they need) and rigidity (so that DME suppliers are deterred from abusing the system). Further research is certainly needed to uncover the actual benefits of DME use. Finally, nursing home reimbursement must encourage the efficient and equitable allocation of resources, particularly resources that are limited now and perhaps will be more limited in the future.

NOTES

1. U.S. Department of Health and Human Services, Health Care Financing Administration, *The Medicare 1991 Handbook* (Washington, D.C.: U.S. Department of Health and Human Services, Health Care Financing Administration, 1991), 91.

2. S. Thomas, Assisting and Adapting the Home Environment, in *Home Nursing Care for the Elderly,* ed. M. Hogstel (Bowie, Md.: Brady Communications Company, 1985), 126.

3. G. Witkin et al., Health Care Fraud, *U.S. News and World Report,* February 24, 1992, 34–43.

4. R. Cogen, Medicare Coverage in the Skilled Nursing Facility, *Journal of Long Term Care Administration* 17, no. 3 (1989):18.

5. Witkin, Health Care Fraud, 37.

6. *Medicare Fraud and Abuse by Durable Medical Equipment Suppliers,* hearing before the Subcommittee on Oversight of the Committee on Ways and Means, House of Representatives, 102nd Congress, 2d sess. (Washington, D.C.: U.S. Government Printing Office, 1992), 91.

7. Ibid., 62.

8. Ibid., 92.

9. Ibid., 92.

10. Ibid., 62.

11. Ibid.

12. W. O'Donohue, Home Oxygen Therapy: Why, When and How To Write a Proper Prescription, *Postgraduate Medicine* 87, no. 2 (1990):59–61.

13. W. O'Donohue, New Problems in Home Oxygen Therapy, *American Review of Respiratory Diseases* 140 (1989):1813.

14. O'Donohue, Home Oxygen Therapy: Why, When and How To Write a Proper Prescription.

15. Ibid.

16. *The Medicare Participating Physician and Supplier Program,* Blue Cross and Blue Shield of Massachusetts, November 1991, 1.

17. S. Burger et al., *A Guide to Management and Supervision in Nursing Homes* (Springfield, Ill.: Charles C Thomas, 1986), 118.

18. Ibid., 118.

19. Ibid., 149.

20. *Medicare Fraud and Abuse,* 111.

21. S. Burger et al., *A Guide to Management and Supervision in Nursing Homes,* 116.

22. Ibid., 146.

23. E. Hirschfeld, Medically Unnecessary Denials: Where the Standards Come from and How Physicians Can Participate, *JAMA* 262 (1989):3193.

24. M. Mittelman, Rehabilitation Issues from an Insurer's Viewpoint: Past, Present and Future, *Archives of Physical Medical Rehabilitation* 61 (1980):589.

25. U.S. Department of Health and Human Services, *The Medicare 1991 Handbook, 25.*

26. J. Marvan-Hyman, Improvising and Adapting to the Home Setting in Delivering Care: Skills Needed, in *Home Health Care Nursing,* ed. S. Stuart-Siddall (Gaithersburg, Md.: Aspen Publishers, 1986), 195.

27. K. Stoltz, Community Organizations: A Source of Assistance, *Nursing Homes and Senior Citizen Care* 39 (1990):27.

Chapter 32

Strategic Planning in
Long-Term Care

Mark E. Toso

INTRODUCTION

Within the health care community, the elderly population has been viewed as a market segment that requires special attention because of its large impact on resource requirements and because of the aging of American society. In 1950, 16.9 percent of the American population was over 55 years old. In 1980, 20.9 percent of the population was over 55 years old. Table 32-1 indicates that the trend toward an older population will increase dramatically from the year 2000 to 2050. In the year 2000, 22.0 percent of the population will be over 55, and in the year 2020, 30.9 percent of the population will be over 55 years old.[1] The graying of the American population is one of the most significant demographic changes of the 20th and 21st centuries.[2] Despite the difficulties facing health care organizations today, the planning process must begin to deal with the health care needs of members of this market segment, the so-called baby boomers, as they begin to march past age 65 in the year 2010.

Table 32-2 indicates that the payment amounts for Medicare and Medicaid have grown at an average annual rate of 9.7 percent, from $88 billion in 1983 to $153.1 billion in 1989. Nursing home expenditures have grown from $2.1 billion in 1965 to $43.1 billion in 1988. Medicare normally represents 35–45 percent of a hospital's revenues, and Medicaid represents in excess of 40 percent of a nursing home's revenues. The percentage of Medicare and Medicaid reimbursement by type of service is shown in Table 32-3. Medicare outpatient service payments grew at a compound growth rate of 21.8 percent from 1966 to 1984, and Medicaid outpatient service payments grew at a compound growth rate of 17.2 percent from 1973 to 1985. Medicare home health service payments grew at a compound growth rate of 22.8 percent from 1969 to 1984, and Medicaid home health service payments grew at a compound growth rate of 37.1 percent from 1973 to 1985.[3] These rates of increase cannot be sustained for an elderly population that is growing and a tax base to fund these expenditures that is shrinking.

Table 32-1 Actual and Projected Growth of the Elderly Population, 1900–2050

Year	Total Population*	55–64		65 and over		85 and over	
		Popu-lation*	Per-centage	Popu-lation*	Per-centage	Popu-lation*	Per-centage
1900	76,303	4,009	5.3	3,084	4.0	123	0.2
1950	150,697	13,295	8.8	12,270	8.1	577	0.4
1980	226,505	21,700	9.6	25,544	11.3	2,240	1.0
1990	249,731	29,090	8.4	31,799	12.7	3,461	1.4
2000	267,990	23,779	8.9	35,036	13.1	5,136	1.9
2010	283,141	34,828	12.3	39,269	13.9	6,818	2.4
2020	296,339	40,243	13.6	51,386	17.3	7,337	2.5
2030	304,339	33,965	11.2	64,345	21.1	8,801	2.9
2040	307,952	34,664	11.3	66,643	21.6	12,946	4.2
2050	308,856	37,276	12.1	67,081	21.7	16,063	5.2

*Population is given in thousands.

Source: U.S. Senate Special Committee on Aging in Conjunction with the American Association of Retired Persons, *Aging America: Trends and Predictions,* 1984.

Table 32-2 Medicare and Medicaid Reimbursements, 1983–1989 (in billions)

Year	Total Payments	Medicare Payments	Medicaid Payments
1983	$88.0	$55.6	$32.4
1984	94.8	60.9	33.9
1985	107.1	69.6	37.5
1986	115.1	74.2	40.9
1987	125.2	77.7	47.5
1988	138.0	87.1	50.9
1989	153.1	98.4	54.7
Percent Growth Per Year	9.70%	10.00%	9.10%

Source: Health Care Financing Administration, *Health Care Financing, Program Statistics, Medicare and Medicaid Data Book, 1988,* U.S. D.H.H.S. Pub. No. 03270, 1988.

Table 32-3 Medicare and Medicaid Reimbursement by Type of Service

Service	Medicare (1984)	Medicaid (1985)
Hospital Inpatient	65.0%	28.4%
Physician	25.0	6.3
Outpatient	6.3	4.8
Home Health/Other	2.9	17.0
Nursing Home	.8	43.5

Source: Health Care Financing Administration, *Health Care Financing, Program Statistics, Medicare and Medicaid Data Book, 1988,* U.S. D.H.H.S. Pub. No. 03270, 1988.

Strategic planning has as one of its goals the allocation of scarce resources among competing objectives. In the 1980s, the planning processes undertaken emphasized improving market share. However, given the historically low operating margins of health care organizations and the desire on the part of the federal government, the state governments, and employers to hold down the rate of increase in health care expenditures, the 1990s' planning processes will place more of an emphasis on the financial viability of strategic plans. "Financially driven strategic planning is based upon the assumption that the results of the planning efforts should improve the organization's financial position."[4]

THE NURSING HOME INDUSTRY

The ability of the nursing home industry to adequately provide services to the elderly population in the future is not clear. Nursing homes today rely on Medicaid for 50–60 percent of their total revenues, according to Fitch Investor Services, Inc.[5] Fitch is one of three rating agencies that evaluate the creditworthiness of health care organizations, and it is the only rating agency that maintains a set of standards to evaluate the ability of nursing homes, continuing care retirement communities, and other housing options for the elderly to acquire debt in the capital markets. Given the growth in the elderly population, it is reasonable to assume that the demand for nursing homes and housing for the elderly will require significant capital investment, since most nursing homes are operating near capacity, as shown in Table 32-4.

The primary factors determining whether a health care organization will have the ability to obtain debt in the capital markets are the payer mix, the management, and the service area competition.[6] Although the demographic trends indicate that the demand for nursing homes and elderly housing should be strong, the

Table 32-4 Number of Nursing Homes, Beds, and Residents, 1967–1986

	1967	1976	1986
Nursing Homes	14,488	16,426	17,122
Beds (in thousands)	765	1,318	1,568
Residents (in thousands)	696	1,215	1,437
Occupancy Rates	91.0%	92.2%	91.6%
Beds per 1,000 (+65)	40.7	57.5	53.8

Source. Health Care Investment Analysts, Inc. and Arthur Anderson, *The Guide to the Nursing Home Industry,* 1990.

Table 32-5 Nursing Home Expenditures as a Percentage of National Health Care Expenditures

	Expenditures (in billions)		Nursing Home/ National Health Care
	Nursing Home	National Health Care	
1960	$0.5	$23.7	2.11%
1965	2.1	35.8	5.87
1970	4.7	65.1	7.22
1975	10.1	116.8	8.65
1980	20.6	219.4	9.39
1985	35.2	425.0	8.28
1988	43.1	539.9	7.98

Source: Health Care Investment Analysts, Inc. and Arthur Anderson, *The Guide to the Nursing Home Industry,* 1990.

present reliance on Medicaid for financing long-term care is at best an inadequate solution. The financial stress placed upon state governments to fund Medicaid has resulted in significant cutbacks in Medicaid funding in most states. This is clearly demonstrated in Table 32-5, which shows that nursing home expenditures as a percentage of total health expenditures have declined since 1980. This decline was due, in part, to the passage of the Omnibus Budget Reconciliation Act of 1987 (OBRA '87), which eliminated the distinction between skilled nursing facility (SNF) beds and intermediate care facility (ICF) beds and ultimately required higher staffing ratios in nursing homes. Another significant reason for the slower growth in nursing home expenditures was the funding of home health services by Medicare and Medicaid and other payers. Home health will continue to grow in the 1990s, but it is expected that the significant increase in the over 75 population will reverse the decline in the relative size of nursing home expenditures shown in Table 32-5. Economic forecasters have projected that national health expenditures as a percentage of gross national product will continue to grow from 12 percent in 1990 to 13 percent in 1994.[7] As the population ages, a larger percentage of the health care expenditures will be spent for long-term care services.

Support for health care services for the elderly varies significantly by state. Table 32-6 indicates the number of beds per 1,000 persons over 65 and the net revenue per resident day in 1988. It shows that each state supports the funding of nursing home beds and the availability of nursing home beds based upon the political climate within each state. The midwestern states appear to have more beds available for persons over 65 than the rest of the country. The payment rates per resident day appear to mirror the cost of living within the geographic area. The most striking statistic is that 50 percent of the elderly are located within ten states (California, Florida, Illinois, Massachusetts, Michigan, New Jersey, New York, Ohio, Pennsylvania, and Texas).

Table 32-7 summarizes some national performance indicators for nursing homes. According to these data, the average nursing home has 100 beds, a Medicaid mix of 61.86 percent, a loss from operations of $1.08 per day, and a debt to asset ratio of 57.00 percent. In order to be successful in the nursing home industry in the 1990s and beyond, it will be necessary to develop a plan that is responsive to the critical issues in the specific environment (e.g., demographics, reimbursement, payer mix, and competition) so as to accomplish the organization's mission. Without financial viability, an organization's goals and objectives cannot be achieved, and it is clear that financing for long-term care will be particularly vulnerable when the baby boomers near retirement age.

STRATEGIC PLANNING PROCESS

Strategic planning is the process of allocating the financial and human resources of an organization to meet its goals and objectives. The planning process evaluates the products and services of the organization, the markets the organization serves, the structure and financial capability of the organization, and the mission statement and then makes an assessment of the alternative strategic choices available to the organization. Based upon an assessment of these factors and others, the health care organization develops regarding its markets, products, and services strategies that allocate its resources in the most effective manner.

Table 32-6 Nursing Home Statistics by State, 1988

State	Net Revenue per Resident Day	Beds per 1,000 Persons Aged 65 and over	Population over 65 (1980) (in thousands)	Rank (1980)
Alabama	$41.19	42.9	440	10
Alaska	na	40.0	12	51
Arizona	na	36.5	307	28
Arkansas	na	58.0	312	27
California	57.62	38.4	2,214	1
Colorado	55.30	60.0	247	33
Connecticut	74.45	65.8	365	26
Delaware	62.40	53.5	59	48
Florida	63.24	27.5	1,688	3
Georgia	39.18	58.2	517	16
Hawaii	88.69	16.8	76	45
Idaho	53.95	45.8	94	41
Illinois	42.66	86.9	1,262	6
Indiana	54.87	86.4	585	13
Iowa	38.13	84.4	388	24
Kansas	38.27	87.1	306	29
Kentucky	42.96	62.3	410	21
Louisiana	34.98	70.7	404	22
Maine	62.89	53.9	141	36
Maryland	60.94	52.8	396	23
Massachusetts	70.72	63.5	727	10
Michigan	50.49	44.7	912	8
Minnesota	53.82	84.7	480	18
Mississippi	38.60	53.9	289	31
Missouri	51.50	68.8	648	11
Montana	50.27	61.6	85	43
Nebraska	na	77.2	206	35

Table 32-6 (continued)

State	Net Revenue per Resident Day	Beds per 1,000 Persons Aged 65 and over	Population over 65 (1980) (in thousands)	Rank (1980)
Nevada	60.45	26.5	66	47
New Hampshire	71.32	62.6	103	40
New Jersey	75.12	42.7	860	9
New Mexico	61.17	45.7	116	38
New York	82.68	41.7	2,161	2
North Carolina	52.06	32.9	603	12
North Dakota	54.70	74.2	80	44
Ohio	53.50	67.3	1,169	7
Oklahoma	54.59	72.7	376	25
Oregon	54.32	38.0	303	30
Pennsylvania	65.04	48.3	1,531	4
Rhode Island	55.37	63.9	127	37
South Carolina	44.11	33.1	287	32
South Dakota	na	80.9	91	42
Tennessee	40.06	53.4	518	15
Texas	38.68	61.6	1,371	5
Utah	54.01	47.9	109	39
Vermont	63.77	57.8	58	49
Virginia	57.07	39.3	505	17
Washington	58.82	54.0	432	20
West Virginia	55.41	36.0	238	34
Wisconsin	53.20	86.7	564	14
Wyoming	51.76	60.8	37	50
United States	51.27	53.6		

Source: U.S. Senate Special Committee on Aging in Conjunction with the American Association of Retired Persons, *Aging America, Trends and Projections,* 1984, and Health Care Investment Analysts, Inc. and Arthur Anderson, *The Guide to the Nursing Home Industry,* 1990.

Table 32-7 Nursing Home Industry National Averages, 1988

Indicator	Median Value
Beds	99
Occupancy Rate	95.61%
Medicaid Percentage	61.86%
Net Revenue per Resident Day	$51.27
Expense per Resident Day	$52.35
FTEs per Average Daily Census	0.74
Total Profit Margin	1.20%
Current Ratio	1.42
Average Age of Plant (years)	7.45
Debt Service Coverage Ratio	1.21
Long-Term Debt:Total Assets (%)	57.00%

Source: Health Care Investment Analysts, Inc. and Arthur Anderson, *The Guide to the Nursing Home Industry,* 1990.

Figure 32-1 provides a schematic of the planning process that health care organizations have typically followed. In order to serve the long-term care or elderly market most successfully, it is critical to know the elderly market.

Environmental Assessment

Internal Profile

The internal profile evaluates the past utilization and financial performance of the organization. It indicates the kind of patients the organization has historically served, where the patients have historically lived, and what referral patterns exist. Based upon this information, the historical service area is defined. The internal profile also outlines the organization's human resources (i.e., managers, nurses, physicians, and other health care professionals). The human resource profile might include a description of the perceptions that employees, community members, and clinicians have of the organization based upon interviews with key individuals within the organization and from the community. Perceptions can have as much influence on an organization as facts.

One of the most critical components of the internal profile is a description of the financial capacity of the health care organization, including a list of its SWOTs (strengths, weaknesses, opportunities, and threats). This capability

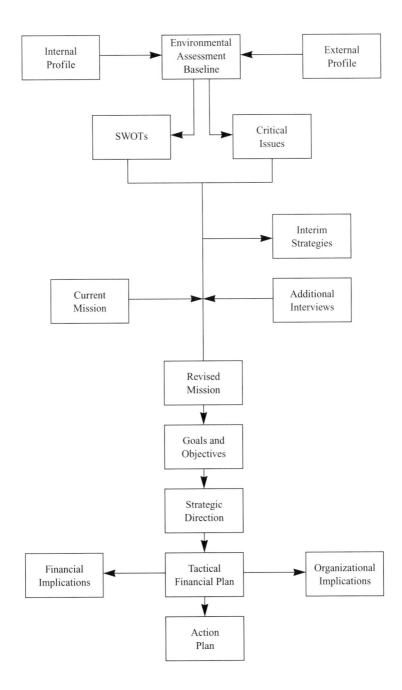

Figure 32-1 Overview of the Planning Process

defines the limits within which decision making should occur. After evaluating the internal data and preparing the internal profile, management should be able to define the strengths and weaknesses of the organization based upon its present position. See Exhibit 32-1 for a list of the most important data to include in the internal profile of a long-term care facility.

External Profile

The external profile of the elderly market should focus on the items listed in Exhibit 32-2. After evaluating the external factors affecting the health care organization's environment, the planning group should be able to make an assessment of the opportunities and threats that the health care or long-term care organization currently faces.

Exhibit 32-1 Internal Profile Data of Special Relevance for Long-Term Care Facilities

1. Patient Profile
   • Demographics
   • Patient origin
2. Elderly utilization by service
3. Elderly utilization by physician
4. Elderly utilization by DRG
5. Discharge planning experience
   • Administratively necessary days and experience
   • Policies and procedures experience
   • Placement success or failure
   • Service gaps

Exhibit 32-2 External Profile Data of Special Relevance for Long-Term Care Facilities

1. Service area demographics
   • Population by type, by age, by area; historical and projected; age groups 55–64, 65–74, 75–84, 85+
   • Sex
   • Marital status
   • Home ownership
   • Income
   • Employment
   • Race and ethnic characteristics
   • Third-party payer mix changes
2. Sociographics
   • Living situations
   • Support systems
3. Health status

continues

Exhibit 32-2 (continued)

4. Competitor profile
   - Types of competitors
     — Other hospitals (elderly utilization, elderly programs)
     — Long-term care facilities
     — Home health agencies
     — Ambulatory care facilities
     — Physicians
   - Utilization by service
   - Market share by service and by area
   - Charge structure of competitors
   - Known future plans for expansion or contraction
   - Existing referral patterns for competitors
5. Nuances of the elderly market
   - Elderly culture
   - History of programs for the elderly
   - Factors of importance to the elderly
     — Family and friends
     — Social activities
     — Financial concerns
     — Independent living
   - Preferred characteristics of particular programs
6. Evaluation of unmet health needs
   - Current
   - Projected
7. Health care human resources availability
   - Nurses
   - Technicians
   - Managers
   - Physicians
8. Regulatory changes
   - Certificate of need laws
   - Reimbursement changes
     — Medicaid
     — Medicare
     — Long-term care insurance
     — Home health
     — Managed care programs
     — Other payers
   - Third-party payer mix changes
9. Technology changes
10. Political environment
    - State government's future plans
    - Federal government's future plans
    - Insurance companies' future plans
    - Managed care companies' future plans
    - Organization support within political structure
    - Licensing requirements

The Elderly Market

The elderly market is heterogeneous and has many levels of segmentation. It includes the following dualities: independent living versus assisted living; living alone versus family or group living; fully functional versus functionally limited; good health versus chronic medical problems; full faculties versus mental impairment; affluent versus economically disadvantaged; and employed versus retired.

People in this multisegmented market are seeking a wide range of services, and therefore many opportunities exist for long-term care providers. Among the desired services are daily living support services provided in the home, social services for the independent healthy, care for chronic conditions in an outpatient setting, complete care in a residential setting, intensive inpatient care for the acutely ill, and caring support for the dying.

Services currently provided to the elderly are often not designed for the elderly. In order to provide appropriate services, health care organizations serving the elderly must be sensitive to the characteristics, needs, and preferences of those being served. Accessibility problems, including transportation, scheduling, and spatial configuration problems, should be addressed. Many services needed by the elderly are currently not provided, primarily because of lack of funding or because of the high cost of providing the service.

Additionally, the provision of services to the elderly usually occurs in the absence of coordinated care planning and management. This is unfortunate, since many providers may be involved, such as a hospital, physician, nursing home, home health agency, or day-care program. In addition, appropriate providers of acceptable quality may not be available, and reimbursement is not consistent across providers (and is even nonexistent for many). The lack of coordinated care planning and management leads to suboptimal care for some elderly patients and a discharge crisis for many hospitals. Physicians can play a key role in the successful provision of services to elderly patients, a role based upon the faith elderly patients have in their physicians.

The range of services required by the elderly is associated with a range of sources of payment: Medicare, Medicaid, supplemental (Medigap) insurance, long-term care insurance, and private payment. In order to maintain financial viability, health care organizations serving the elderly must be knowledgeable about reimbursement, have the ability to market to the private-pay market segment, and manage efficiently within narrow constraints. The provision of services to the elderly is strongly influenced by regulation. As the baby boomers age, this voting block, along with organizations like the American Association of Retired Persons (AARP), will impact regulation that affects funding for services to the elderly population.

What services and products can health care organizations provide to the elderly market? Table 32-8 presents a matrix consisting of care sites versus elderly patient care status and identifies some of the services that have been offered. Table 32-9 presents a matrix showing the typical payers for the services listed in Table 32-8. Providing services to the elderly community requires that the reimbursement for cost-efficient services be improved. Recently, long-term care insurance added home health care as a benefit, which allows the elderly to plan financially for care in the home. Health care planning for the elderly must anticipate the changing reimbursement and insurance climate in order to be in a position to provide the services that will be necessary.

Critical Issues and Planning Assumptions

If there are immediate threats to the health care or long-term care organization providing services to the elderly, interim strategies should be developed. In the absence of immediate problems, the focus should be on the future. Using an analysis of the strengths, weaknesses, opportunities, and threats, the organization should identify the critical issues confronting the organization and develop the planning assumptions that will be used to develop alternative strategies. The planning assumptions also define the criteria for the analysis of alternative strategies (Exhibit 32-3).

The Organization's Mission, Goals, and Objectives

A mission statement defines the purpose of the organization. A mission statement can be very simple and short or it can be very specific. For example, it might include a lengthy description of the organization's goals, functions, and services, the community it serves, and its relationship to other providers. In order for the mission statement to have any significance, it must be understandable to the employees of the organization and the market it serves. The mission statement should provide the foundation for future growth consistent with the values and beliefs of the people who run the organization. Two sample mission statements follow:

> The organization will provide a full range of primary and secondary health services to the service area population, along with selected tertiary programs.

> The organization will provide a continuum of services to the senior residents of the area, coordinating services as needed to ensure optimal care. This continuum may include acute care, long-term care, and supportive home and community services.

Table 32-8 The Elderly Market Service Matrix

Care Site	Care Status					
	Independent Good Health	Chronic Condition	Acute Illness	Rehabilitation Recovery Assistance	Permanent Living Assistance	Terminal Illness
Specialized Facility				Rehabilitation hospital	Alzheimer's psychiatric hospital	Hospice
Residential	CCRC Retirement community	CCRC Congregate living Assisted living		Skilled nursing facility	Sk lled nursing facility Rest home Respite	Skilled nursing facility
Inpatient Facility	Membership programs	Membership programs	Diagnosis Treatment	Transition unit	Swing beds	End-stage care
Outpatient Facility	Routine maintenance Education	Diagnosis and treatment of disease Information	Follow-up	Outpatient rehabilitation		
Community	Social activities Health screening	Social activities Day care Monitoring			Family counseling	Family counseling
Home	Services Transportation	ADL assistance Home health Durable medical equipment				

Table 32-9 The Elderly Market Payment Matrix

Care Site	Care Status					
	Independent Good Health	Chronic Condition	Acute Illness	Rehabilitation Recovery Assistance	Permanent Living Assistance	Terminal Illness
Specialized Facility				Medicare Medicaid Commercial insurance	Medicaid Private pay Grants	Medicare Private pay
Residential	Private pay	Private pay		Medicare Medicaid LTC insurance Commercial insurance	Private pay Medicaid LTC insurance Commercial insurance	
Inpatient Facility	Private pay	Private pay	Medicare Medicaid Commercial insurance Private pay	Private pay	Medicare	
Outpatient Facility	Medicare Commercial insurance Private pay	Medicare Commercial insurance Private pay	Medicare Commercial insurance Private pay	Medicare Medicaid		
Community	Private pay	Private pay Medicaid			Private pay	Private pay
Home	Private pay	Medicare Private pay LTC insurance	Medicare Private pay		Medicare Private pay	

Note: The payment sources are continually changing; however, the above payers have historically been the primary payers.

Exhibit 32-3 Criteria for the Analysis of Strategies

- Consistency with mission and values
- Fulfillment of goals and objectives
- Market demand or unmet need
- Impact on market reputation
- Impact on market share
- Impact on competition
- Barriers to entry
- Partnership potential
- Impact on health care professionals
  — Physicians
  — Nurses
  — Technicians
- Need for new health care professionals
  — Physicians
  — Nurses
  — Technicians
- Fit within product portfolio
- Resources required (capital, human, other)
- Management expertise
- Capacity issues
- Financial impact
  — Reimbursement changes
  — Insurance changes
  — Profitability potential
  — Cash flow requirements
  — Financing requirements
- Control
- Degree of risk
- Responsibility and timing

The strategic planning process will generally not change the purpose of the organization. The goals and objectives set by the organization to accomplish the mission will change as the environment changes. This can easily be seen in today's increasingly competitive health care environment. As the environment changes, it will become necessary to determine whether the organization can accomplish its original mission. For example, many health care organizations were established to provide a full range of health care services. Because of the greater competition, some can no longer provide the full range of services and remain financially viable.

A detailed set of goals are established that determine what must be done in order to accomplish the mission of the organization. The objectives of the organization include measures of performance that allow management to determine whether the goals have been achieved. The goals and objectives follow from the mission and further define the direction of the organization. Three sample objectives follow:

To capture ___ percent of the long-term care market as defined by skilled nursing beds.

To serve at least ___ percent of the elderly acute care market.

To reduce the annual number of administratively necessary days by ___ percent.

Strategic Direction and Action Plans

The long-term care organization must evaluate the alternative strategies using the criteria for analysis established previously. The selection of a set of strategies to follow will be based upon both subjective and objective criteria. If individual strategies meet the requirements for the criteria for analysis but the sum of several strategies is not within the ability of the organization, then the organization must develop a method to rank the strategies and ration the organization's capital and human resources in the most efficient way possible.

The strategic planning process must identify short-term, intermediate-term, and long-term strategies. For those strategies that can be implemented immediately, action plans (or business plans) need to be prepared. Appendix 32-A contains an outline of elements that might be included in an action plan.

STRATEGIC IMPERATIVES IN LONG-TERM CARE

At the beginning of this chapter, it was noted that the elderly population will require more health care services because of two factors: the increase in the absolute numbers of the elderly population, and the increase in longevity of the elderly population. Additionally, the federal government, the state governments, employers, HMOs, and other payers will pressure the health care system to control the rate of increase in health care expenditures. These trends are in conflict with each other and will bankrupt the system if reasonable alternatives are not developed.[8]

The role of strategic planning in a health care or long-term care organization is to deal with the realities of the present and anticipate which changes will occur in the future. However, without changes in the financing system for health care services for the elderly, reasonable access cannot be ensured by health care or long-term care organizations as they exist today. The financial vulnerability of the long-term care industry will require planners to focus on the financial viability of the services being offered if the organizations are to accomplish their mission.

NOTES

1. U.S. Senate Special Committee on Aging and the American Association of Retired Persons, *Aging America, Trends and Projections* (Washington, D.C.: Government Printing Office, 1984).

2. Ibid.

3. U.S. Department of Health and Human Services, Health Care Financing Administration, *Health Care Financing, Program Statistics, Medicare and Medicaid Data Book, 1988,* HCFA pub. no. 03270 (Baltimore: HCFA, 1988), 7,10–11.

4. M.C. Jennings, What Is Financially Driven Strategic Planning? *Topics in Health Care Financing* (Gaithersburg, Md.: Aspen Publishers, 1988), 1–8.

5. Fitch Investor Services, *Not-for-Profit Nursing Home Rating Guidelines* (New York: Fitch Investors Services, 1991).

6. Ibid.

7. Bernstein Research, *The Future of Healthcare Delivery in America* (New York: Sanford C. Bernstein and Co., April 1990).

8. J. Tedesco, *Financing Quality Care for the Elderly* (Chicago: The Hospital Research and Educational Trust, 1985), 20–21.

Long-Term Care Action Plan Elements

I. Definition of strategy

    A. What type of service will be provided by the organization?

    B. What needs will be met by the service?

    C. Who will operate the business? What provider?

    D. What services or products will be offered?

        1. To which segments?

        2. When?

        3. Where?

        4. At what price?

    E. Are there any special constraints or limitations?

    F. What results are expected?

    G. What guidelines exist to monitor performance?

II. Primary market research

    A. Techniques

        1. Surveys

        2. Focus groups

        3. Interviews

    B. Populations

        1. Physicians

        2. Consumers

        3. Patients

        4. Referral sources

        5. Discharge placements

III.   Secondary data sources

    A. Census data

    B. Home health agencies

    C. Senior centers

    D. State agencies

    E. Trade associations

    F. Churches and synagogues

IV.   Internal data sources (health care system or long-term care provider)

    A. Patient origin

    B. Age profile (segmented by sex, area, 5-year increments)

    C. Payers

    D. Physicians serving the elderly

    E. Referral sources

    F. Admissions/days/ALOS

    G. Outpatient Visits

    H. DRGs

V.   Market analysis or plan

    A. Product or service definition

       1. Place description

    B. Target market segments

       1. Description

       2. Size

       3. Future trends

    C. Competitor profile

       1. Current and anticipated

       2. Performance and image

       3. Future plans

       4. Potential threats

    D. Regulatory climate

       1. Favorable or unfavorable

       2. Future changes

    E. Price determination

F. Promotional plan
   1. Media selection
      a. Print
      b. TV
      c. Radio
   2. Direct mail
      a. Timing
      b. Target audiences
      c. Budget

Development of Demand Projections

VI. Organizational structure
   A. Long-term care facility (system)
   B. Hospital cost center
   C. Separate corporation, hospital owned and operated
   D. Joint venture
      1. Physicians
      2. Another hospital
      3. Developer
      4. Long-term care provider
      5. Other
   E. Management contract
      1. By hospital
      2. For hospital
   F. Lease arrangement
VII. Legal and regulatory requirements
   A. Contractual arrangements
      1. Partners
      2. Management firms
      3. Vendors
   B. Licensing requirements
   C. Certificate of need

VIII. Resource requirements

    A. Personnel

        1. Development

        2. Operations (clinical, management, and marketing)

    B. Facility

        1. Space

        2. Construction

        3. Utilities

    C. Equipment

    D. Supplies

    E. Marketing

        1. Upfront

        2. Ongoing

    F. Outside professional services

        1. Legal

        2. Accounting

        3. Architectural

IX. Projected financial performance

    A. Costs

        1. Project costs

        2. Operating expenses

    B. Revenues

        1. Demand projections

        2. Reimbursement assumptions

        3. Private-pay assumptions

    C. Financing needs

        1. Project financing

        2. Working capital

    D. Financing sources

        1. Mortgage

        2. Bond issue

        3. Sponsor equity

        4. Grants

   5. Philanthropy

X. Incremental financial forecasts (five years)

   A. Income statements

   B. Cash flow statements

   C. Balance sheets

   Assessment of Financial Feasibility of Action Plan

Chapter 33

Architecture for Long-Term Care Facilities

Ronald L. Skaggs and H. Ralph Hawkins

INTRODUCTION

Long-term care facilities design emerged as a result of changes in reimbursement mechanisms. The advent of Medicare and Medicaid in 1967 focused attention on the extended care setting as a means of reducing the cost of hospitalization and delivering more cost-effective care. This new emphasis reduced the then-current utilization of hospitals through shortening the length of stay. As the average American grew older and the benefits of extended care became available, many facilities were designed and built in the form of "nursing homes." However, the relevant government programs proved to be costly, and resources for funding began to dwindle. Eventually, reimbursement was reduced, which greatly impacted the fledgling long-term care industry.

Currently, the industry is facing new challenges. Hospitals, which were once a source of referrals, are getting into the market of providing long-term care as part of the continuum of care. This tactic has been relatively simple to implement, since hospitals could convert underutilized nursing units into long-term care, skilled, or intermediate nursing beds. In addition, other organizations, such as home health agencies, provided extended care to patients at home so that they would not have to be institutionalized at all. Day-care programs also allowed the elderly to be under supervision during the day, when family members were working, but at home in the evening and overnight, when family members were at home. All of these programs were aimed at keeping costs to a minimum while providing appropriate long-term care.

Long-term care may take place in a variety of facilities. The setting may be a hospital or a free-standing center. The facilities may provide individually or jointly a range of services, including skilled nursing, intermediate care, assisted living, and specialized services (e.g., services for those who are ventilator-dependent or have Alzheimer's). Other programs may augment these services, such as day care, respite, or independent living programs.

Initiating the design and construction of a long-term care project involves a variety of tasks. However, if the development is handled using experienced professionals, it can result in a well-designed, aesthetically pleasing, and functional facility. The following section is a brief overview of the development process and the main design considerations.

THE ARCHITECT'S ROLE

Architects are responsible for the design of buildings that accommodate the space requirements for the organizations' operational goals. When designing for a long-term care facility, an architect seeks to balance the functional requirements against the aesthetics (building appearance), cost (budget constraints), technology (how the building will be put together), and time (schedule for design and construction). The architect works with the long-term care facility administrator and others involved in the planning process to establish project requirements, design the appropriate facility to meet these requirements, and assist in administering the construction activities as they relate to the design documents.

Services provided by the architect can include feasibility consultation, facility development (master) planning, functional and space programming, site evaluation, basic architectural and engineering services, interior and graphic design services, facility management services, and other services that may be deemed appropriate. Various owner-architect contracts are available from the American Institute of Architects. The most common contract form is the AIA B-141, which outlines basic architectural and engineering services, along with methods of payment, and provides for the inclusion of additional services.[1] The planning and design process often is carried out by a multidisciplined team of planning consultants, architects, engineers, equipment planners, interior designers, graphic designers, landscape architects, and other specialists.

Feasibility Consulting Services

These services are often required at the beginning of a project to assess current market conditions, projected needs, and financial capacity. The resulting database provides the mechanism to determine the advisability of beginning a new long-term care facility project. Feasibility services are often provided by a health planning consultant, although many architectural firms offer such services. Also, individual institutions may have in-house planners capable of accomplishing required feasibility tasks.

Facility Development (Master) Planning Services

A facility development plan establishes a framework for existing building and site use that can accommodate future facility and program needs. Such a plan is based on current institutional considerations, including project goals, present site features, building size and capacity, and existing programs. After the investigation of current status, the information gathered is reviewed and evaluated for program compliance, functional performance, and establishment of space needs for immediate, intermediate, and long-range development. Subsequently, a final facility plan can be devised that identifies facility development strategies, proposed site development, future locations of departmental activities, and proposed growth options.

Functional and Space Programming Services

The functional and space program serves as the basis for the design of a long-term care facility. It describes how the building is to work and includes documentation describing appropriate relationships between various departments within the facility. Individual department operational considerations are outlined, and room-by-room space specifications are provided. Establishment of the functional and space program occurs after extensive data collection and reviews with operational entities. The program sizes each department and its component spaces based on operating concepts, staffing requirements, equipment needs, and patient accommodations.

Basic Architectural and Engineering Services

Typically, the basic architectural and engineering design process as defined in the AIA B-141 consists of five phases of activity, each subsequent phase characterized by more specificity and a greater level of detail. The first phase is the schematic design phase, in which the architect prepares preliminary sketches, models, drawings of room-by-room plans, preliminary specifications, and an early statement of probable construction cost for owner review and approval.

After approval of schematic design, the design development phase is initiated. In this phase, the size and character of the long-term care facility are described in greater detail. This includes indicating major materials, room finishes, and mechanical, electrical, and structural systems. Typically, a more detailed estimate of probable construction cost is presented, along with the design development documents, for owner review and approval prior to moving into the next phase.

During the construction documents phase, the architects and engineers prepare the detailed working drawings and specifications that the contractor will use to build the project after establishing final construction prices. These drawings and specifications will ultimately be made a part of the construction contract established between the owner and contractor.

The bidding or negotiation phase can vary substantially from one project to another. In certain cases, a contractor may become involved in the project prior to the completion of contract documents with the intent of arriving at a negotiated maximum construction price prior to the completion of plans. In other cases, a list of qualified contractors may bid completed plans and specifications. In either case, great care is required in evaluating the competence of the contractors under consideration as well as the mechanical, electrical, and plumbing subcontractors.

After the contractor is selected and a contract for construction is established, the construction phase begins. There should be a preconstruction conference between the owner, architect, and contractor prior to actual construction, which is the longest phase of the development process. The architect serves as the owner's agent, making periodic visits to the construction site to observe construction progress. Back in the office, the architect and engineers review shop drawings, process contractor pay requests, change orders, and perform other administrative functions in support of the construction activity.

Additional Services

Interior and graphic design services are often offered as an option in addition to basic services. such services typically include space and furniture planning; selection of such building interior items as draperies, bed spreads, carpets, indoor plants, and special lighting; and color coordination of furniture and furnishings with the building materials and finishes. Graphic design typically includes the development of exterior signage, interior signage, and wall graphics.

Facility management services are of relatively recent development. They are in part an offspring of computer-aided design and drafting. Capital investment in facilities is an ever-increasing management burden. Following initial construction and occupancy of a building, computer-aided facilities management provides the resources to coordinate the ongoing necessary modifications of the internal configuration of the facility and the associated furnishings, equipment, and mechanical and electrical systems. Computer-aided facilities management provides the ability to rapidly produce the necessary drawings and related documents for ease of alteration while simultaneously maintaining a continuous record of the current state of the facility and its associated systems, furnishings, and equipment.

The best time during the development process to bring the architect on board is as early as possible, preferably at the feasibility study stage or during site selection. The organization may wish to institute an architect selection process. Architect selection should begin with the establishment of a select list of qualified architectural firms. Each firm on the list should be invited to submit its qualifications based on an established set of criteria. A sample application is included in *Selection of Architects for Health Facility Projects*, which is published by the American Hospital Association.[2]

After the receipt of the qualifications of the firms and the evaluation of their appropriateness for the proposed project, a smaller number of firms, possibly three to five, should be invited to be interviewed. In addition to interviewing each firm, the organization may wish to contact previous references as well as visit similar projects designed by each firm. Interviews can take place at the owner's place of business or at the architect's office. Visiting each firm's office can be an effective means of understanding the firm's internal operations.

TYPES OF LONG-TERM CARE FACILITIES

Long-term care facilities come in a wide variety of types. There are, in addition to facilities for the elderly, facilities for physical rehabilitation, psychiatric care, mental retardation, and head trauma. Detailed discussions on architecture for rehabilitation and psychiatric facilities are available in the *Encyclopedia of Architecture*.[3] Regarding facilities for the elderly, there is a full spectrum of facility types that differ primarily in terms of level of dependence. At the lower end of the spectrum are elderly housing units and senior centers.

Elderly Housing

Elderly housing comprises numerous housing types, ranging from single-family residences to multiunit apartments. Facilities also range from single-level to high-rise buildings and often include a variety of shared support functions, including social centers, meal service, housekeeping, and related services. The common denominator is that they contain dwelling units, which vary to meet different housing and life-style needs. Typically, an elderly housing complex has a mix of efficiency, one-bedroom, and two-bedroom accommodations.

Senior Centers

Senior centers provide day-care and community interaction services to the elderly in a nonresidential setting. Such centers can be free-standing, part of a church or school, or the focus of a continuing care retirement community. Most senior centers consist of a large group meeting lounge and activity rooms supported by meal service capabilities, administrative and counseling services, and outdoor recreation space.

In the middle of the long-term care facility spectrum are residential care facilities typically referred to as independent living and assisted living centers. The major difference between such facilities is the level of dependence or assistance required by facility residents.

Independent Living Centers

Independent living facilities are intended to support a variety of levels of independence. Facilities at one end of the continuum are similar to elderly housing or leisure retirement communities in that health care is not available. The other end of the continuum consists of housing where the average resident can maintain an independent life style while also having access to on-site health care services and often assisted living or nursing services.

Assisted Living Centers

Assisted living facilities offer personal services that support various daily activities including bathing, dressing, taking medications, and dining. Such facilities would typically include health care and often nursing services on site. The primary feature of an assisted living facility is that the residents are unable to function independently and require some level of personal services on a daily basis.

At the higher end of the long-term care facility spectrum are nursing-related facilities, including intermediate care, skilled nursing, and specialized care facilities. Such facilities are often free-standing, although there is a growing trend toward combining such facilities with independent and assisted living centers as a way of providing a full continuum of care.

Intermediate Care Facilities

Intermediate care facilities are designed to provide minimal nursing services to residents requiring limited medical care. Residents are often able to get around but require continuous supervision in regard to medication or activities of daily living and often require periodic physical, occupational, or recreational therapy. Nursing units in intermediate care facilities commonly contain semiprivate rooms and are supported by a central meal service as well as housekeeping and various therapeutic support functions.

Skilled Nursing Facilities

Residents of skilled nursing facilities are typically bedridden and often have multiple health problems requiring continuous nursing care and supervision.

Many residents are incontinent or have debilitating illnesses affecting their ability to function on their own. Skilled nursing facilities commonly consist of nursing units that contain 40–60 beds each and have a mixture of private and semiprivate rooms.

Special Care Facilities

Special care facilities provide special services for individuals with distinct medical needs. Alzheimer's facilities, which are increasing in number, have physical design characteristics that address the special needs of residents with Alzheimer's disease. Such facilities require special provisions for security because of the tendency of these residents to wander. Careful attention to lighting, color, and signage can assist in orienting facility residents while appropriate assignment of space and views to the outside or other areas can help staff maintain awareness. Other types of special care facilities include facilities for individuals who are ventilator-dependent, are comatose, or have suffered head trauma. Such facilities often include selected acute care-related diagnostic and treatment functions in order to satisfy resident treatment needs and state licensing requirements.

CODES AND STANDARDS

Long-term care facility design, depending on types of services provided, may be subject to a wide range of codes and standards as well as licensing requirements. When acquiring, renovating, or designing a new facility, it is prudent for an architect and engineer to perform an evaluation of all applicable design requirements. These requirements vary significantly from state to state. Even within a single state, application and interpretation may vary among the various local, state, and federal regulatory agencies. This multiplicity of review can be time consuming and ultimately costly to a long-term care facility operator seeking to respond to pressing facility needs. In the case of conflicting codes and standards, the most restrictive regulation usually applies.

The purpose of codes and standards is to assure the public that long-term care facilities are safe and that their design contains the functional components necessary to provide the appropriate services.

The codes that apply to long-term care facilities generally will include a model building code, such as the Uniform Building Code or Standard Building Code. In addition, model building codes may be amended by the government prior to being promulgated. These codes are generally used in conjunction with a compatible mechanical, electrical, plumbing, and fire code. Many times, these local codes are interpreted differently by the chief building official and the local fire department officials. Another code frequently used is the National Fire Protection Association 101–Life Safety Code.

All of these codes are intended to provide for the safety of occupants and ensure proper construction techniques. There are many sections addressing structural integrity, mechanical systems, and electrical systems, but the major concerns are occupant safety and protection of the structural elements from fire.

Standards for long-term care facilities are typically used to guide the provision of proper space and equipment. The most widely used manual of standards is *Guidelines for Construction and Equipment of Hospital and Medical Facilities.*[4] This document is published by the American Institute of Architects with assistance from the U.S. Department of Health and Human Services. It contains general standards as well as specific chapters on skilled nursing, rehabilitation, and outpatient facilities. However, many states develop individual standards through their departments of health.

The purpose of using standards is to give consumers, providers, and third-party payers a certain level of assurance that the facility is able to provide the services that are offered. The standards also assist architects and consultants in the development of space programs and in functional planning.

In addition to having to meet codes and standards, many long-term care facilities pursue accreditation or membership in associations that also have certain design requirements. Typically, these organizations refer to the codes and standards already discussed, but it is not uncommon for specific design issues to be addressed. One of the most commonly sought accreditations is from the Joint Commission on Accreditation of Healthcare Organizations. In the required Joint Commission reviews, members of the accreditation team may also interpret codes and standards differently than the other reviewing agencies. As a result, it is necessary to evaluate the potential impact of these accreditation facility reviews.

Because of the number and variety of codes and standards, there is a substantial amount of redundancy, especially in the area of life safety systems. However, it is the responsibility of the providers and architects to provide a safe facility design, which means having to comply with the codes. It is important to note that fire safety reports show health care facilities have proven to have excellent safety records.

Another emerging issue in long-term care design concerns new services that do not fit standard definitions. For example, subspecialty facilities like head trauma, behavioral, or Alzheimer's units may not fall into existing codes and standards categories. Standard definitions are not always applicable, and the regulatory agencies are not always flexible in their interpretations. Flexibility would allow creative approaches to providing long-term care services, but it may impact licensing requirements and therefore also reimbursement.

Reimbursement, many times, is based on specific licenses the facility holds. Third-party payers, public and private, are adamant that facilities offer standardly defined services. This creates an impediment to emerging types of facilities. However, many insurers are beginning to give recognition to creative and cost-effective forms of care.

Long-term care facilities, as well as almost every type of building, have experienced the impact of the Americans with Disabilities Act of 1990 (ADA). The ADA is designed to eliminate discrimination based on disability. It covers employment practices and calls for the elimination of architectural as well as communication and transportation barriers in public and commercial facilities. It applies to almost all types of buildings, including buildings slated for construction and those already existing. New buildings completed and ready for first occupancy after January 26, 1993, must be designed and constructed to be "readily accessible" to individuals with disabilities. A facility is also subject to the new construction requirements if a completed application for a building permit or permit extension is filed after January 26, 1993. A new building that does not meet these criteria may be considered to be an "existing facility," in which case it will be required to remove barriers in public accommodations where such removal is "readily achievable." The term "readily achievable" means "easily accomplishable and able to be carried out without much difficulty or expense."

The ADA is not enforced by state or local governing agencies, and therefore construction documents are not necessarily reviewed by these agencies (or any federal agency) for compliance with the ADA. Consequently, compliance may not be determined until proven in court. In the absence of any authoritative and binding clarification of any standards in question, it is recommended that the standards should be construed liberally (in favor of the disabled).

Even though long-term care facilities are beset with a number of codes, standards, and agency reviews, the trend is toward consistency and acceptable alternative methods and designs that demonstrate equivalent performance and quality. Coordination among federal, state, and local agencies reviews is becoming more usual as well. A thorough review of codes and standards early in the acquisition, renovation, or construction of a long-term care facility is not only appropriate but required.

SITE CONSIDERATIONS AND SELECTION

Before beginning the development of a new long-term care facility, careful attention should be given to site appropriateness, whether the organization owns an existing site or is acquiring a new site. If site acquisition is required, purchasing a site based on low cost alone can result in major problems, even to the point that the property can be developed only at extreme cost (or not at all). The following issues should be carefully considered before settling on the final site.

Location

The facility's location can have a major effect on the organization's ability to serve residents and to attract and retain qualified physicians and employees. Road accessibility and proximity to other related facilities can improve the image of the facility and its chances of success. When evaluating a location, consideration should be given to the distance between the site and related health facilities and other types of facilities, such as shops, churches, restaurants, financial institutions, recreational facilities, and the availability of public transportation.

Zoning

Checking zoning regulations is extremely important, primarily to ensure that the type of facility planned will be authorized to be constructed by the reviewing authorities. If the zoning is not appropriate, the question should be raised as to whether rezoning is possible and, if so, how long the rezoning procedure would take. Various site restrictions such as setbacks, height restrictions, and easements should be carefully evaluated. In addition, zoning regulations regarding the adjacent land should be ascertained. The site assessment should also include the types of future development permitted in the surrounding area. Obviously, adjacent and surrounding land compatibility is important to ensure the facility will have suitable neighbors.

Property Size and Usability

A mistake often made in land acquisition is the selection of too small of a site or a site configuration that is difficult to build on. In addition to space for the building itself, there must be sufficient space for access roads and parking, appropriate landscaping, and possible expansion. Available utilities should be ascertained, as should the need for any preconstruction site modifications. Factors affecting usability include drainage, subsurface conditions (e.g., the water table), topography, and existing vegetation. If part of the site is on a flood plain, it should be determined how much of the site is usable outside of the flood plain.

Intermediate care and skilled nursing facilities of 100–120 beds typically require approximately 5 acres of developable land, while the addition of housing facilities, dependent on the number of living units, can push developable land requirements into the 20-acre range. Sufficient acreage should be included for outdoor activities for residents.

Site Amenities

Although subjective, the attractiveness of a potential site is a consideration. If objectionable noise or odors or other negative factors such as heavy traffic exist, alternative sites should be evaluated. Positive factors include attractive views, interesting topography, and available trees or vegetation.

PUBLIC AND ADMINISTRATIVE SERVICES

A long-term care facility typically has an area for receiving the public and an area to house the administration of the facility. The nature of the public area will depend on the services provided and size of the facility. Public reception begins at the front door and lobby. The front door usually opens into a vestibule that provides an air trap between the exterior and the lobby. The lobby should be designed so it is sufficiently large to receive visitors and residents but also provides a control point for those entering the facility. The lobby should have access to public toilets, a drinking fountain, and a public telephone. Other possible amenities may include a newsstand and even a small convenience store or gift shop to provide essentials to residents. The reception area should be directly adjacent to the lobby and be readily accessible to those entering the facility. It may consist of a desk or counter in the lobby or an enclosed room with a window opening into the lobby. The reception function is sometimes combined with the switchboard function. If the switchboard function is at this location, it is prudent to provide a communications closet to house telephone equipment.

Administrative functions, depending on the level of care provided, include administrative office and business office functions. The administrative area usually includes space for the administrator, the chief financial officer, possibly an assistant administrator, and often a director of nursing. It also usually includes space for secretarial support as well as a coffee bar, a coat closet, a conference room, a copy room, a supply closet, and sometimes a private toilet. The business area may provide space for a number of employees involved in accounts receivable and payable and in insurance. Many facilities provide private rooms or cubicles for resident registration or account review. The business area also may include a copy room, a supply room, an auditor's office or conference room, and rooms for other support activities. Smaller facilities may combine many of these operations, both in terms of space and staffing.

Areas often accessible to the public as well as residents include dining facilities and recreation and group activity rooms. Use of these areas by family members, friends, and even other members of the community can be encouraged to good effect. For example, many long-term care facilities provide special discounts for the elderly in their dining facilities so that elderly persons living independently may be exposed to the facilities they may ultimately require. Encouraging public use of recreation and group activity rooms is also an excellent way of exposing outsiders to activities within the facility, including education courses, arts and crafts activities, games, and social events.

Guidelines for Construction and Equipment of Hospital and Medical Facilities requires that the combined area for dining and recreation in a skilled nursing facility should be based on a total of at least 30 square feet per bed or be at least 225 square feet total. The factor may be reduced to 25 square feet per bed if the facility has 100 beds or more. At least 14 square feet of this number is to be provided for dining. Additionally a minimum of 50 square feet of storage for equipment and supplies is to be provided at or near the recreational area. Sheltered workshops may also be available for residents and outpatients.

DIAGNOSTIC AND TREATMENT SERVICES

Long-term care services do not traditionally focus on diagnosis or treatment— beyond what is required to maintain maximum levels of health and independence. Individuals are typically diagnosed and treated in an acute care setting, but they may require ongoing treatment and maintenance after transferring to a long-term care facility. This treatment and maintenance function usually only requires minimal area.

Exam Room

Generally a multipurpose exam and treatment room of 100–120 square feet is sufficient for typical medical interventions, such as routine examinations or minor treatment. The room should be flexible so it can be used for a wide range of services, including routine physical examinations and gynecological, proctological, ophthalmological, and even dental examinations. Minor treatment may also occur, so adequate lighting is essential. A lavatory for handwashing should be provided within the room. A work counter, storage cabinets, and a writing surface are also essential. A nearby toilet is sometimes desirable, not only for resident use but also for specimen collection. This exam room may be located in a central area or in a resident care unit.

Physical and Occupational Therapy

If rehabilitation therapy is part of the program for long-term care, physical and occupational therapy services should be provided. Physical and occupational therapy space requirements vary according to program and equipment. Generally, the therapy departments are combined in one location unless more extensive rehabilitation services are provided. Space requirements for providing minimal physical and occupational therapy services include an administrative and clerical area, patient reception area, supplies storage, personal effects storage, clean and soiled utility rooms, a janitor's closet, access to the conference room for in-service training, and convenient access to toilets, including a toilet for handicapped persons. If outpatient services are provided, other requirements include convenient access from parking areas, covered entrances for patient drop-offs during inclement weather, and dressing rooms and shower facilities. *Guidelines for Construction and Equipment of Hospital and Medical Facilities* is a good resource for more detailed planning.

Pharmacy

Each facility must plan for the procurement, delivery, and proper distribution of pharmaceutical products. Although a pharmacy does not have to be on site, 24-hour access must be provided.

RESIDENT CARE SERVICES

Long-term care services are provided in a variety of areas within a facility. This section primarily addresses resident rooms and nursing units and discusses general design considerations. It also contains several sample floor plans that indicate new directions in resident room and nursing unit design.

Resident Rooms

The resident room in a long-term care facility is generally where the resident interacts with nursing and medical staff and his or her family or friends. Much of the resident's daily routine occurs there. Although many facilities have multibed rooms to encourage social interaction, there is a growing trend toward private rooms or at least more privacy in multibed rooms. Configurations of multibed rooms are changing to give more privacy to each resident than is provided by a cubicle curtain (see Figure 33-1).

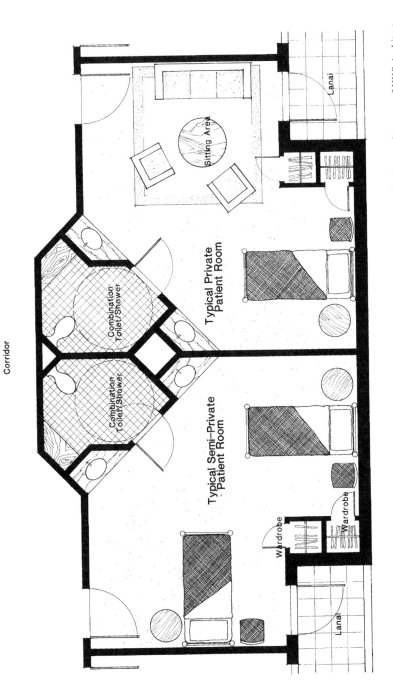

Figure 33-1 Typical patient room at G.N. Wilcox Memorial Medical Center Skilled Nursing Facility, Lihue, Hawaii. *Source:* Courtesy of HKS Architects, Dallas, Texas.

More room space is needed in a long-term care facility than in an acute care setting because of the greater length of stay. Many newer designs provide an area for sitting and a desk for writing. Wardrobe requirements also exceed those for acute care facilities, and wheelchairs must be accommodated. Resident rooms must meet minimum standards. Most codes require a minimum of 120 square feet for a private room and 100 square feet per bed for multibed rooms. These space requirements are exclusive of toilets, closets, wardrobes, alcoves, and vestibules. Multibed rooms cannot contain more than four beds, and only one bed can intervene between another bed and the window. All resident rooms must have an operable window of sufficient size for natural light and ventilation. The window may be keyed if the key is kept at the nurse's station. A sink for handwashing is not required if one is provided in the nearest toilet, but it is advisable to have a sink in multibed rooms. This allows residents to wash even if the toilet is occupied.

Toilet and Bathing Facilities

The toilet and bathing facilities in a long-term care setting often differ from acute care types of facilities. For example, it may be decided that bathing facilities should not be readily accessible to residents except when assisted by an attendant. This is an especially good policy for older residents or residents who have been brain damaged and whose equilibrium is in question. One solution is to centralize bathing facilities and provide showers and peninsular bathtubs that are equipped with hoists or devices to ensure safety. In skilled nursing facilities, a minimum of one bathtub or shower must be provided per 12 beds. In addition, residents must have access to one bathtub per nursing unit and to a handicapped shower in the centralized facilities. Bathing areas must also have associated areas for drying and dressing as well as space for attendants and wheelchairs. However, for reasons of convenience and flexibility, the long-term care facility may choose to provide bathing facilities in each room. Regardless of location, access to a nurse call in the bathing areas is important because of the possibility of falls.

The current trend is toward showers instead of tubs. Statistically fewer accidents occur in showers, probably because of the relative ease of walking directly into the washing area. One related issue is the height of the rim around the shower basin. Many propose no rim, only a sloping floor to the floor drain. The advantage of this design is that there is no tripping hazard and it is relatively easy to roll a resident into the area using a shower chair. The disadvantage is that water sometimes spreads onto the floor area. This problem can be remedied in two ways. First, a small sill of one-half inch or less could provide a small barrier to the water without being an obstacle for the resident. Second, a flush drain could be installed as the barrier between the shower and remaining area. It is important to note that this approach is more costly than installing a conventional shower basin.

Conventional shower basins are still popular and are used in most facilities. The rim of conventional basins is not a major obstacle for ambulatory residents but does act as a barrier for shower chairs. There are also seamless acrylic stalls with integral grab bars and a seat that are designed for health care use. However, any properly designed shower in a long-term care facility should have grab bars at the periphery. Also, a showerhead fixed to a flexible hose is to be preferred over a fixed head, since it allows attendants to bathe residents more thoroughly.

A handicapped-accessible toilet should be provided on each unit, and this toilet can serve as a resident training toilet. If centralized bathing facilities are provided, residents must have access to a toilet that does not require them to pass through a public area. This toilet can also serve as a training toilet.

The resident room toilet should also contain a water closet, handwashing lavatory, mirror, paper towel dispenser, and shelf for personal hygiene items. The water closet should preferably be placed at handicapped height. This sitting height is more easily attained by elderly and infirm residents. It is also advisable to have grab bars on each side of the toilet to ease access. These bars may be the swing-away type. A nurse call should be within easy reach of the toilet in case of a resident fall. Sometimes the nurse call is placed between the toilet and the shower so as to serve both areas. The handwashing lavatory must be at an appropriate height to serve sitting and standing residents. The handwashing fixture's valves should be provided with wing blades for easy operation. The mirror is best located above the lavatory, but it should have a tilting mechanism for residents in a wheelchair. The shelf for the storage of personal hygiene items should be within easy reach of the lavatory. Toilets and bathing facilities must be appropriate for the specific type of care provided. In addition, provisions for handicapped residents must meet applicable codes and standards.

The Resident Care Unit

The resident care unit comprises individual resident rooms and the support area. The support area at a minimum includes the nurses station, a staff toilet, access to the staff lounge, a medication room, a nourishment station, clean and soiled utility rooms, a peninsular tub, access to the exam room, an activity room, a janitor's closet, wheelchair and stretcher storage, storage for personal belongings, and general storage. The size of the resident care unit can vary according to the services. For example, a 60-bed unit may be appropriate for skilled nursing care (see Figure 33-2), whereas a smaller unit would be adequate for Alzheimer's care (see Figure 33-3). *Guidelines for Construction and Equipment of Hospital and Medical Facilities* recommends that at least 5 percent of the total beds be in

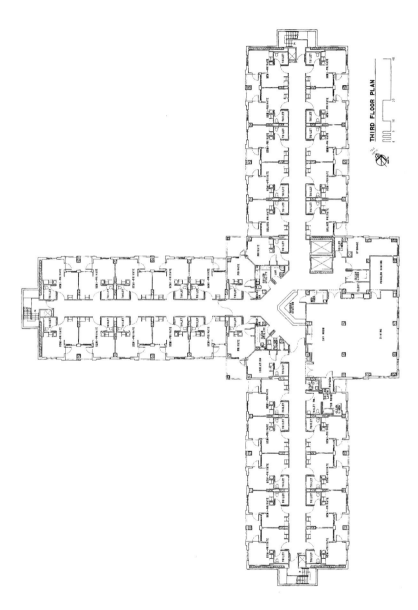

Figure 33-2 Skilled nursing facility plan. *Source:* Courtesy of HKS Architects, Dallas, Texas.

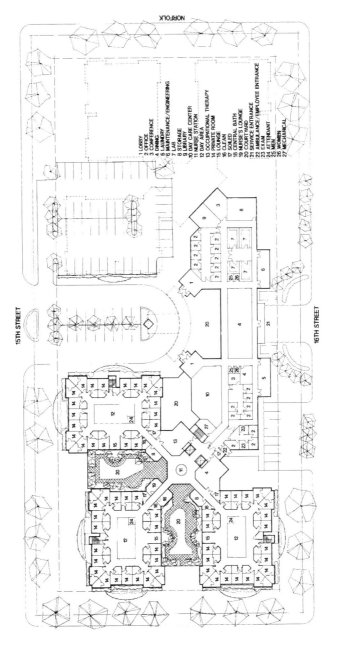

1 LOBBY
2 OFFICE
3 CONFERENCE
4 DINING
5 LAUNDRY
6 MAINTENANCE/ENGINEERING
7 LAB
8 STORAGE
9 LIBRARY
10 DAY CARE CENTER
11 NURSE STATION
12 DAY AREA
13 OCCUPATIONAL THERAPY
14 PRIVATE ROOM
15 LOUNGE
16 CLEAN
17 SOILED
18 CENTRAL BATH
19 NURSE'S LOUNGE
20 COURTYARD
21 SERVICE ENTRANCE
22 AMBULANCE/EMPLOYEE ENTRANCE
23 EXAM
24 ATTENDANT
25 MEN
26 WOMEN
27 MECHANICAL

NORFOLK

15TH STREET

16TH STREET

Figure 33-3 Alzheimer's care facility plan. *Source:* Courtesy of HKS Architects, Dallas, Texas.

private rooms that have toilet and bathing facilities. Many of the support functions may support more than one resident care unit if conveniently located.

The nurses station should be centrally located. Ideally, it should permit viewing of all resident corridors if not the door openings into each room. The activity room should preferably be located near the nurses station for observation purposes. Also, it is common for residents to congregate around the nurses station, so if the activity room is nearby, it may reduce corridor congestion. The nurses station location should allow observation of those entering and exiting the unit. The nurses station should include areas for medical charting, administrative duties, and storage of supplies, and it should be near handwashing facilities.

Several support functions must be convenient to both the nurses station and the exam rooms. The medication preparation area should be within, or at least within sight of, the nurses station. The nourishment station may be outside of the nurses station, but it must be conveniently located. The nurses working on the unit should also have easy access to a staff toilet and lounge. Clean supplies and linen may be kept in a single clean utility room. The soiled utility room should contain a work area, a storage place for soiled linen, a waste receptacle, and a clinical service sink. Wheelchairs and stretchers should be stored in alcoves or equipment storage rooms and not in corridors.

The activity room is a popular gathering place within a long-term care facility. Some of the amenities that are desirable include natural light, views, and flexibility of layout. Since many residents may be somewhat restricted physically, the exposure to natural light and views provides an orientation to time of day and season. Access to outdoor courtyards can also be beneficial to residents, since it reduces the closed-in feeling many residents experience during their long lengths of stay. The layout may include both quiet and noisy activity areas. The areas may need a physical or acoustical separation to mitigate conflict of activities. The quiet area could be used for reading, watching television, or listening to music. The noisy area could be used for games or other social activities. Long-term care facilities are often able to attract volunteer groups that provide various kinds of entertainment, such as choir groups. It is suggested that this be considered when planning the area.

Design Considerations

Long-term care facilities must be designed specifically with residents in mind. Many of the residents suffer with mobility, hearing, seeing, and equilibrium problems. Consequently, many design issues need to be resolved. For example, it is important that corridors be equipped with handrails on both sides and have minimal protrusions so as to reduce bumping and tripping. Sharp edges, slippery floor finishes, and tripping hazards are unacceptable. Walls should be protected from wheelchair hubs and footpads to prevent unsightly damage. Changes in floor levels and communicating stairs should be avoided. Floor patterns must be as unconfusing as possible to those with eyesight problems, who may interpret darker colors as steps or level changes. Contrasting colors at the wall base assist those with seeing problems in identifying the change of planes. Contrasting colors for door frames can help in the identification of openings. Doorways should be adequate for passage by patients in wheelchairs, walkers, canes, and other orthotic or prosthetic devices. Graphics should be easily readable and easy to find. Design features that aid orientation and wayfinding are generally desirable.

BUILDING SUPPORT SERVICES

A long-term care facility needs certain support functions to provide for proper delivery of care. These functions have their own space requirements, including food preparation and distribution areas, general storage, a housekeeping area, and employee facilities.

Dietary

The dietary services area includes a receiving area, refrigerated and dry food storage, a preparation area, a serving and dining area, a clean up and washing area, a staff toilet, and a waste removal area. Distribution of food, either through a servery or tray carts, should be planned carefully.

Meals can be served in a central dining area, in the activity area of a nursing unit, or in the resident's room. They can also be delivered to nursing units using thermal trays or hot and cold carts. Dietary services are an important component of long-term care from both a clinical and an enjoyment perspective.

General Storage

General storage consists of a receiving dock, breakdown area, work area for the purchasing clerk, and general storage area. Supplies are delivered by a variety of trucks, including 18-wheelers, semi-tractors, bobtails, and vans, so it is important that the dock facilities be flexible. The breakdown area is usually adjacent to the dock and is used to unpack larger containers. A trash dumpster is usually nearby for discarding waste. The purchasing clerk typically has a view of the dock area, the general storage area, and the dispatchment of items from the stores. The general storage area includes open shelves accessible by corridor rows. Secured storage may be required for more expensive items to prevent pilfering.

Housekeeping Area

The housekeeping area is a storage area for cleaning supplies and some cleaning equipment, such as floor buffers and vacuum cleaners. The housekeeping area is augmented by janitor's closets located conveniently throughout the facility.

Employee Facilities

Employee facilities within long-term care facilities vary significantly depending on number of employees. In many cases, the facilities consist only of a lounge and toilets. However, larger facilities will also contain locker and shower areas. This area should be designed according to program need.

Engineering Services

Engineering services are responsible for operating and maintaining heating, ventilation, and air conditioning systems. General maintenance is usually also one of the responsibilities. Grounds maintenance may be contracted out or provided on site by engineering services.

MECHANICAL, ELECTRICAL, LIGHTING, AND PLUMBING DESIGN CONSIDERATIONS*

General Considerations

Support systems, such as the mechanical, electrical, lighting, and plumbing systems, are often overlooked in relation to the overall architecture of a long-term health care facility until they cease to function properly. In most cases, the users are the elderly, and this simple fact is neglected by many support system designers. The physical problems of the elderly, such as decreased vision, decreased hearing, and arthritis, should affect the selection of engineering systems. Yet the

*This section is contributed by Rick Rome, P.E., CCRD Partners, Dallas, Texas.

high standards and intricate design details used for hospital facilities are usually not required for long-term facilities.

Another support systems design issue sometimes overlooked concerns building codes and state standards. Several states do not have separate standards for long-term facilities. In many other states, these standards are simply modified hospital standards. In all cases, these standards prescribe what is minimally acceptable in the design of the systems. However, many designers use these standards as if they reflected the best options available. Combine this with the fact that many of the standards are based on young to middle-aged users rather than senior citizens and it is no wonder that many inferior systems are designed and installed.

Mechanical Systems

The mechanical systems comprise the heating, ventilating, and air conditioning systems and the various subsystems that support them. The majority of the basic design concepts for these systems are established by the American Society of Heating, Refrigeration and Air Conditioning Engineers, the local building codes, and state standards.

- The design temperature for the heating season should be 75°F to compensate for the increased sensitivity of older people to colder temperatures.
- Insulated and tinted glass should be used in the rooms to limit the temperature gradient at the glass and to reduce the glare experienced in the room.
- Unlike state standards for hospitals, many state standards for long-term care facilities do not specify the filtration efficiency that the supply air to the rooms should have. Eighty percent final filters should be considered for the supply air, which matches most state requirements for patient rooms.
- Many states do not specify the number of air changes of outside air that should be introduced into each room. It is recommended that a minimum of two changes of outside air with six changes of supply air per hour be provided. This should adequately ventilate the space and prevent stale air.
- Exhaust air change rates of two to four per hour should be provided to reduce the institutional odors that are often experienced.
- Heat lamps in the bathrooms provide the elderly with additional comfort after bathing.
- Air supply diffusers should be designed for low terminal velocities in the range of 25 feet per minute, thus reducing the feeling of drafts within the space.
- Thermostats with larger numbers should be utilized for ease of viewing by residents.

Electrical Systems

Electrical power and special systems in long-term care facilities are very tightly controlled by NFPA 70 (National Electric Code), with little room for variation. Additional considerations are discussed below.

- Electrical outlets should be located 24 inches above the finished floor for easier accessibility.
- Two TV outlets should be provided in each room, one 12 inches below the ceiling for a wall bracket location and the other 24 inches above the floor for mounting a TV on a stand.
- Emergency nurse call switches should be provided in two locations—one at the bed and one in the bathroom. Integration of lighting, television, and intercom controls into the call station at the bed is recommended.
- When establishing the fire alarm system for the facility, consideration should be given to the reduced hearing capacity of the elderly. Solutions include decreasing the space between speakers, providing higher wattage speakers, and locating smoke alarms in the resident's rooms.

Lighting Systems

When considering lighting for the living areas in a long-term care facility, care should be devoted to providing lighting that renders colors truly and gives character to the room. In addition, proper placement of light fixtures, either in the ceiling or on the wall, can provide an appropriate stimulus for the residents.

- Because of the illumination needs of the elderly, maximum illumination levels of 50 foot-candles should be provided in the living and bed areas, and 25–30 foot-candles in the corridors.
- Proper emergency lighting in the rooms and corridors can assist in preventing any confusion. Corridors should be designed for an emergency lighting level of 3–5 foot-candles instead of the more common 1 foot-candle level.
- Glare caused by a strong light source or windows at the end of a hallway can confuse an elderly person and obscure the definition of the space. This problem can be minimized by utilizing diffused light sources.
- Aging eyesight impacts the ability to perceive depth and discriminate details. The eye also has a difficult time adjusting to lighting changes. To aid with these problems, sudden changes in lighting level should be avoided. Moving from a dim corridor into a bright room can cause temporary blindness and

possibly even cause a trip or fall. Provision of lighted vestibules between a bright room and dimmer corridors can minimize such problems.

• Light fixtures that provide true color rendition are preferable, particularly in resident bathrooms.

• The use of illuminated light switches is recommended because of the limited night vision of many of the elderly.

Plumbing Systems

Plumbing systems are tightly controlled by the local building codes, the state health codes, and the National Fire Protection Association.

• Wrist blade faucet trim is recommended on all patient lavatories.

• Installation of a fixed or fold-down seat in the tub or shower should be considered. A detachable spray head is recommended for bathing.

• A slip-resistant finish on the floor of the tub or shower should be provided, with integral grab bars on the walls.

• The domestic hot water temperature should not be higher than 110°F, nor lower than 100°F.

CONSTRUCTION OPTIONS

There are a variety of construction approaches available in delivering the completed long-term care facility. The most common has been the conventional design-bid-construct approach. This approach follows a sequential pattern: First the architect and engineers prepare design documents; next general contractors submit bids; then a construction contract is awarded, typically to the lowest bona fide bid submitted; and finally the construction phase begins. The primary advantage of this approach is that the organization receives a firm cost before construction begins, although there is no assurance that bids will be within the established budget.

An alternative approach is to establish a design-construct team that includes the contractor. The contractor is thus involved during the design phase and has the ability to provide a negotiated construction contract with a guaranteed maximum price after the full project scope is established. In this approach, construction management techniques are often utilized. Construction management is the process of including construction expertise in the formative stages of a project in order to provide construction concept and cost-control input. The construction manager is responsible for cost estimates and budget control, design review for constructability, construction scheduling, prepurchasing of critical materials and equipment, and direction of all construction activities. When appropriate, the design-construct team approach affords the opportunity to start construction before all design documents are complete.

A third alternative is the design-build approach, where a single-source "turn-key" organization or a consortium consisting of an architect and a contractor is hired to develop a building design and to provide a fixed price. Since plans are typically in a preliminary form when the fixed price is established, a greater level of risk is placed on the builder, and there is the possibility that the quality of the construction may be reduced as unknown costs appear.

Variations or combinations of these methods are possible, depending on specific contract requirements. The advantages and disadvantages of available approaches must be weighed in light of the facility's needs before a plan of action tailored to the specific requirements can be initiated.

COST ESTIMATING

Throughout the design of a long-term care facility, estimates of probable construction and development costs should be reviewed in order to control the cost of the completed project. Costs per square foot are often quoted, but the variety of components included may differ. As a result, comparison of costs per square foot of various projects can be misleading.

It is recommended that cost control be approached by formulating a total project budget containing not only construction costs but all other developmental investments made by the long-term care facility. A common format for budgeting includes the following.

- *Building cost.* Typically the cost for the structure and all internal space and systems. This cost typically includes expenditures for all construction within five feet of the building exterior.
- *Site development cost.* Commonly includes cost of all construction work outside of the five-foot building line. This construction consists of non-building development such as extensions of existing utility services, new utility services, site lighting, grading, walks, drives, parking lots, and landscaping.
- *Fixed equipment cost.* Includes cost of all items that are installed before completion of the building and that are a part of the construction contract, such as lockers, food service equipment, laundry equipment, and any medical equipment fixed to the building.

- *Construction cost.* The sum of the building cost, site development cost, and fixed equipment cost, with appropriate provision for inflation and estimating contingencies.
- *Land cost.* All costs of land, including purchase price and cost of site preparation, not included in the construction cost.
- *Movable equipment cost.* Includes the cost of depreciable equipment that typically has five years of life or more and is not normally purchased through construction contracts. Movable equipment comprises large items of furniture and equipment that have a reasonably fixed location in the building but are capable of being moved.
- *Professional fees.* Fees for services provided by various professionals involved in the project development, including architectural and engineering services.
- *Owner's contingency.* Funds set aside to provide a buffer to absorb normal growth in schematic design and design development, variations in bidding, unforeseeable construction conditions, and change orders.
- *Administrative cost.* Includes costs for such items as soil tests, site survey, legal fees, printing costs and related expenses that the owner must pay in connection with building construction.
- *Financing cost.* Cost of interim financing that may be required for land acquisition and construction. Estimates of this cost should be established.
- *Total project cost.* The sum of all development costs listed above.

Not only is it necessary to prepare a detailed budget initially and have all members of the design team and the owner in full agreement on it, but it is also necessary to update the estimate often to incorporate current selections of building elements and systems and to confirm current prices in the marketplace.

EMERGING DESIGN CONSIDERATIONS

Long-term care facilities are facing unprecedented change. Demographically, our population is growing older and will be requiring more long-term care than ever before. Concurrently, hospital reimbursement is encouraging shorter and shorter lengths of stay—thereby encouraging transfer to long-term care facilities. As hospitals become super acute tertiary facilities, long-term care facilities will become more like hospitals of the past. In fact, many new hospitals that have moved to new quarters are converting their old buildings into various types of long-term care facilities. Many of these facilities are offering new services, including care for individuals with Alzheimer's disease, head injuries, and cancer.

In general, the acuity of the long-term care residents' conditions is increasing. Many facilities are also providing a hybrid of various services to accommodate residents' needs. As reimbursement allows long-term care facilities to provide a setting for extended care, these facilities over time will play a larger role in the delivery of health care services.

The design of long-term care facilities provides a unique challenge, since the care needs of residents must be balanced against their ongoing desire for the highest level of independence possible. Facilities can and should provide an attractive homelike ambience rather than the more common institutional atmosphere. In addition, careful attention must be given to making provisions for the full continuum of long-term care in order to support the variation in level of independence.

The architect should be involved in new facility development early on in order to assist in addressing the myriad issues that arise throughout the planning of a project. Siting the buildings; sizing the complex; establishing the appropriate layout; choosing building materials, finishes, and mechanical and electrical systems; and establishing reasonable construction cost expectations are all part of developing long-term care facilities that will effectively serve their residents.

As the population in the United States continues to mature, the long-term care facility will continue to emerge as a major type of health care building. The expanded need for new and updated facilities will provide the opportunity to develop facility designs that recognize and support resident dignity and contribute to the improvement of care.

NOTES

1. *AIA Document B-141—Owner/Architect Agreement* (Washington, D.C.: American Institute of Architects, 1987 edition).

2. American Hospital Association, *Selection of Architects for Health Facility Projects* (Chicago: American Hospital Association, 1975).

3. J.A. Wilkes, *Encyclopedia of Architecture* (New York: Wiley, 1988).

4. American Institute of Architects, *Guidelines for Construction and Equipment of Hospital and Medical Facilities,* 1987 ed. (Washington, D.C.: American Institute of Architects Press, 1987).

Chapter 34

Innovation in Long-Term Care Facility Design

David M. Dunkelman

THE NEED FOR INNOVATION

There are four driving forces for innovation in the development of new facilities for older people.

Demographics

In the year 1900, average life expectancy was 47.3 years. Today, average life expectancy for 40-year-old white females is 92 years. After 3,000 years of recorded history—and within the span of only several generations—we have almost doubled life expectancy. The numbers are astounding. In 1940, there were 300,000 Americans over the age of 85. In 2040, when those 40-year-old women turn 90, there will be 16 million over the age of 85.

For the past ten years, approximately 25 percent of Americans over age 85 have been in nursing home care. Simply because of the limits of human and financial resources, such a high percentage will no longer be possible.

The problems related to the design of buildings are exacerbated by the fact that the nursing home population has "aged in." Today's residents are much older and more frail and need a very different program and environment than the typical home resident just ten years ago.

Labor

Another issue is the labor shortage that is now surfacing. It is the byproduct of a confluence of demographic trends: fewer young people; a monumental failure of the education system, which is producing a less skilled, less employable young work force; and upwardly mobile women in the work force, depleting the candidates willing to remain in low-level, dead-end professions. Some believe we have just begun to experience the effects of this labor shortage. It will be an ongoing reality in all health care, particularly in nursing homes. Many tasks will have to be reassessed and redistributed. New products and new ideas will have to replace the dependence on a huge pool of low-paid aides engaged in dead-end, unfulfilling chores. Facilities will need to be designed in ways that contribute to more efficient, appropriate care provision.

Government

The government sees the looming deluge of frail older people. Its goal is to remove itself from what it considers an impossible financial burden and an unattractive ideological one. It recognizes that the current structure and system of services must be basically reconfigured.

The government has three available tactics: to raise the threshold levels at which an older person can access government funds for services, to shorten the time for which services are available, and to reduce reimbursement rates for services delivered. All of these tactics can have a dramatic impact on programs and buildings.

New Expectations

Higher expectations and stricter regulations, which are a product of the maturation of the nursing home field, are forcing nursing homes to deliver quality of care and life more efficiently and in ways not mandated during earlier stages of the industry's development. Consistent with the law of unintended consequences, these regulations and higher expectations are quickening the rate of burnout for those who cannot adapt. They are also forcing nursing home care to develop into a new specialty. Project and architectural decisions and choices must anticipate and react to those stricter regulations and higher expectations. Design innovations are a logical response.

THE ROLE OF THE MANAGER

The administrator plays a variety of roles in the design process. In essence, the administrator's task is to translate resources, whether human or financial, into affection. And unlike many other health care settings, which have more precise, limited goals, long-term care has the mission of providing quality *time* for residents. With that as background, let us turn our attention to what actually happens in a new project development.

An interesting idea is suggested in a passage from a Kurt Vonnegut novel, in which there is a lawyer who explains that between the time a person dies and his or her will is probated, the presumptive heirs have not yet developed an emotional attachment to the legacy. During that period, the property of the estate has no owner (which, of course, provides an opportunity for the lawyer scoundrel in the novel). In a way, this is like a nonprofit home: It belongs to no one person but to different people at different times depending on the history, the personalities, and the issues confronting the organization.

The nature of a building project exaggerates this phenomenon. By definition, a project entails a major shift in relationships, goals, and agendas. There are new players (consultants) and novel risks and opportunities. But the administrator provides the continuity by setting the format and filling the gaps. He or she does it by painting pictures, by creating context. As translator and mediator between residents, staff, families, the board, and consultants, the administrator shapes themes—and therein lies his or her power.

DIFFICULTIES IN DEVELOPING INNOVATIVE PROJECTS

Many involved with innovation in nursing home design have been surprised at the difficulties they have had to face. The purpose of this section is to explore the reasons for these difficulties and to suggest how to overcome them. Nursing home design is complex because four major components must be aligned and synchronized. Each of these four components involves its own set of relationships and each has its own set of obstacles. The four components are

1. the government[*]
2. the facility or sponsoring organization
3. the gerontological experts
4. the inherent nature of innovation

Government

History of the Government's Role

The government is a major partner and leader of nursing home care as we know it today. This differs from many other industries that evolved entrepreneurially

---

[*]Even in the states with no certificate of need process, there are other regulatory and review conditions that make government a major player in any new project.

and only later were regulated by government. In long-term care, it can be argued that the government itself is often the initiator of change. An analogy may help flesh out this idea.

The government of the state of Israel was, in a sense, in existence before its inhabitants arrived. Obviously, there were already some Jews in "Palestine," but for many citizens the government was the initiator and advocate of their freedom and citizenship and the primary socializer and employer in their new lives. Consequently, the relationship between Israelis and the state of Israel even today is very different from the relationship to government of their counterparts in America, where, for the most part, people immigrated specifically because of the absence of government.

The nursing home industry mirrors the Israeli experience, at least more closely than other American industries. The passage of Title XIX (Medicaid) of the Social Security Act in 1965 was the mechanism that shaped the form of the modern nursing home movement. Because the average nursing home resident has always been relatively old (today, approximately 86), and because there is an inescapable correlation between old age and indigence for so many, currently only government has the resources to provide the base of care. For these same reasons, government will continue to be the dominant force and shaper of long-term care in the future, and, again similar to the Israeli analogue, providers expect this.

Changes in Government Expectations

But government's expectations have changed. The industry has grown quickly, and because of the gerontological revolution and more sophisticated interventions, government is now demanding three things from nursing homes:

1. quality of care (medical issues)
2. quality of life (psychosocial issues)
3. fiscal responsibility (delivering the above at a reasonable cost)

An example of increasing expectations has occurred in New York State. Historical social concern and activism, combined with intensive analysis, have led to groundbreaking interlocking sets of regulations.

In the 1970s, New York State developed a system of Sentinel Health Events (SHEs), which were statistically based measures of quality of care. The Long Term Care Survey is a second-generation instrument, a more sophisticated way to measure and raise quality of care standards. The New York Quality Assurance System is a tool to measure and raise quality of life standards, and Resource Utilization Groups constitute a sophisticated method of measuring the staff time (cost) of delivering care. Even if all these new standards had not been promulgated, the cost of care would have risen because labor is more expensive and specialized and nursing home residents are more frail.

Nursing homes are being forced to try to meet these new expectations with insufficient resources (labor and money) and using buildings built to support programs and populations entirely different. The explosion in program variety and sophistication, the new expectations, and the very progressiveness of New York State, reflected in its higher new standards, are forcing homes to build or adapt physical environments which will allow the reconciliation of these goals and resources.

Just as geriatrics has evolved into a specialty, gerontologic nursing, gerontological therapies, and food delivery and social work in long-term care facilities have grown in complexity and uniqueness and become fields of specialty. Their maturation also demands that architectural forms and interior features be developed that support these new fields.

Government's Changed Expectations and Conservatism

There is a difficulty with government's involvement with the evolution of new architectural models. Because government is the traditional initiator and prime mover of the nursing home industry, it has developed sets of regulations that encourage or discourage a vast array of provider behaviors. Historically, government regulations often relate to features, objects, and items that are measurable because these are easy for the government's agents to evaluate and observe for compliance. A sponsor or designer may meet a code but not satisfy a need. Regulations, except for a few, do not deal with possibilities for facilitating behavior but are rather driven by other issues (e.g., protection).

The increase in regulation is a prime example of the post–World War II growth of administrative law, and it makes a broad, integrated overview almost impossible. An analogue is the tax code, which has become a vehicle for social policy and therefore is fraught with diverse, sometimes contradictory, goals and policies. In both cases, there is a tangle that can cause new ideas and initiatives to be lost, as is discussed by Robert Murphy in *The Body Silent*. Murphy blames

> the proliferation of an increasingly intrusive and impenetrable bureaucracy, which in our modern age has enveloped business and education as well as government. Bureaucracy renders the work of authority opaque, remote, and incomprehensible. It imposes a structure and an order that is impersonal and inimical. And it defies reduction to the far simpler notions about society that most people carry around in their heads. To make matters worse, bureaucracies are devised as rational, systematized organizations, but in operation they often are as capricious, arbitrary, and irresponsible as Wonderland's Red Queen.[1]

It is not necessarily simple-mindedness, stupidity, or lack of progressiveness that inhibits innovation. Other factors include the potential enormousness of the implications of operationalizing the behavior desires, making any change, as well as the inability to find decision makers and concise regulations to battle. The initiator of change must forge a consensus in a land where both formal power and informal power are veiled.

The Facility

A number of factors have made innovation difficult within the facility as well.

The Chief Executive Officer

Because the reimbursement mechanism has become so complex and because adequate response is so critical for a facility's survival, more CEOs come from fiscal, not gerontological, backgrounds. Therefore, they are less sensitive to certain issues and less able to reach beyond the existing framework. Many of these MBAs are not schooled in techniques of social change and become victims of, rather than activists in, gerontological or long-term care policy. Or, worse, some rally behind a single issue and fail to get at the larger issues that influence people, not just systems.

The Board

With the increased specialization in the field, with the change from homes for the aged to modern health care facilities, volunteer boards often have been relegated to financial overseers. Planning and change require time, which volunteer board members often are not willing to give or do not have. Board members may be experts in their own field, company, or industry or in community work but can still be naive about aging and design. People often appear to have an intuitive understanding of both aging and design, but a little knowledge is usually not enough. Good design for older people is *not* intuitive. Board members or a lay subgroup must study and become involved in order to act. It is too much for one person or one CEO. It is not unusual for projects to suffer severely without board support and commitment. In fact, for-profit or large hospital-sponsored systems may emerge as instigators of change in the future, since these organizations utilize special planners and lobbyists to shepherd their projects through the bureaucracy.

Inadequate Administrative Programs

From the new gerontological perspective, there are insufficient numbers of administrators trained as transfer agents. Too many administrative degree programs are in traditional public health, hospital, or generic "health care" disciplines, which suffer from insufficient grounding in conceptual gerontological issues. Often gerontologists are social work trained but not necessarily schooled in the full set of management, government, and health care issues. Programs could be comprehensive but they are now rather limited.

Organizational Characteristics of Nursing Homes

Some traditional organizational characteristics of nursing homes militate against innovation. Hage and Aiken have found that the following organizational characteristics are related to high levels of innovation:[2]

- a high degree of complexity in the professional training of organizational members
- a substantial decentralization of power
- a low level of formalization
- a relative lack of emphasis on volume (as opposed to quality or production)
- a relative lack of emphasis on efficiency in the provision of services
- a high degree of job satisfaction among staff

An analysis of the basic profile of many nursing homes, in light of these characteristics, may suggest they do not provide an environment conducive to innovation.

First, until recently there have been relatively few professional staff in nursing homes. The majority of the labor force is paid minimum wage.

Second, power is generally highly centralized, since relatively few staff members have the management skills and access to information to make decisions. There is often one administrator or nurse with predominant responsibility and control, in large part because of the dependent characteristics of many of the residents. In few other organizational environments can the personality of one individual be so dominant.

Third, nursing homes are generally extremely formalized because of the vast variety of detailed regulations and activity schedules with which the relatively undereducated staff must comply. Only with precise rules, schedules, and routines can the administrator ensure continuity of care. But this same formalization militates against innovation and gets between the caregiver and direct responsiveness to the older person.

Fourth, there are enormous government and financial restraints that emphasize volume (as opposed to quality) and efficiency, both of which are negatively correlated with innovation. With increased government cutbacks in an already resource-poor environment, the focus must be on efficiency in order to take care of the basics. There is little remaining energy, money, or staff time for experimentation related to innovation.

Fifth, the nursing home environment currently does not engender much job satisfaction. The work is hard and repetitious, the pay is low, and there are few opportunities for advancement. The "customer" is seldom grateful and too often ungracious. The combination results in low job satisfaction and high turnover, which are also negatively correlated with innovation.

Gerontological Experts

The third set of actors are the gerontological experts (e.g., architects and consultants) who play such an integral role in project development. There are a number of factors that limit their effectiveness in fostering innovation.

Lack of Experts and Limited Basis for Expertise

The relatively new body of knowledge regarding the effects of environmental modifications on programs, resident behaviors, and finances is often inaccessible. As a consequence, there are an insufficient number of trained transfer agents and specialists. Because of this, facility project development involves improvisation and blind groping. For even well-intentioned novices there is no outline, no text, no form to follow, no standards by which to winnow out the charlatans and the inexperienced consultants. Many consultants earn money by doing things by the book, and they do not question the underlying concepts. They deliver prepackaged and standardized formulae and engage in back room politics. Boards may be reluctant to hire a consultant who is unable to guarantee a cost, for it is difficult to estimate the unknowns and the time needed for change.

Breakdown in Information Transfer

There is an insufficient flow of information among providers, regulators, and research centers (i.e., there are too few models and examples and too little applied research). Too much information must be obtained orally and too little is presented in easy-to-read formats. There have been few nursing homes built recently, often because of government policy. And those built are generally stripped-down cookie-cutter molds (the overwhelming concerns being approval and construction costs). These facilities test few questions of interest and provide little data upon which others can build. They are monuments to past theories, perhaps decked out with a few trendy colors but often more stripped down than the facilities they replace.

Low Status of Long-Term Care

There is an anti-institutional bias that pervades the entire process. Despite the fact that there are three nursing home beds for every two hospital beds nationally, ageist attitudes and anachronistic ideas encourage the view that nursing homes snatch away, not encourage, independence. This closed-loop cycle becomes a self-fulfilling prophecy that slows down the influence of progressive ideas. Attitudinal roadblocks abound: "Older people can't learn continence." "What do you mean wandering has value?" "That won't work for these people."

No Mechanism for Instituting Changes

The complexity of the new architectural design ideas often prevents the resulting designs from fitting the format of the reviewing agency. The designs are not easily processed, take a longer amount of time to review, and are therefore disruptive to the equilibrium of the system. Thus new ideas have a hard time taking hold.

The Inherent Nature of Innovation

The previous three sections have indicated the myriad problems that prevent innovation in nursing homes. One arrangement that may facilitate innovation is a constructive alliance among these three parties: state policy makers, gerontological experts, and the long-term care facility. Such an alliance would demand ongoing dialogue, realistic understanding of the other parties' constraints, a shared vision regarding certain critical elements, and a continuity of relationship over an extended period of time.

With the current state of the art, it takes an extraordinary confluence of vision among policy makers, experts, and facilities to achieve innovation in nursing homes. Furthermore, not only do the human actors facilitate or inhibit innovation, but innovation itself may exaggerate or mitigate the difficulties experienced by a group of people working together. Finally, what makes an innovation more or less attractive will affect the likelihood of its utilization. Zaltman, Duncan, and Holbeck studied the characteristics of innovation,[3] and a few of these characteristics are discussed below.

Economic and Social Costs

Costs can be either economic or social. Economic costs include the initial costs of adopting an innovation and the continuing costs of keeping it in operation. Social costs involve changes in status within the organization as individuals and groups gain or lose power because of the new developments. Either type of cost is likely to be viewed as exorbitant by opponents and minimized by proponents of a proposed change.

Nursing home innovation may be inherently more difficult than most kinds, because the nursing home administrator, the board, and government, each with very different perceptions, must approve the economic and social costs. For example, it may be possible to invest more capital into the project initially in order to lower operational costs over the life of the building. But the relationship between physical structure and operations—how staff and residents may function more efficiently—has been addressed rarely, even by government. There are currently few definitive empirical studies available to board and government policy makers. In addition, the very structure of the government reviewing agency may increase the difficulties. The number and range of issues facing an agency may mean that those reviewing the certificate of need are entirely separate from those dealing with operations. Thus, the certificate-of-need reviewer may treat as irrelevant even empirically supported operational savings resulting from innovative design.

Social costs are also often neglected by government agencies dealing with nursing home innovation. The agencies generally have developed administrative precedents, sometimes committed to writing, that are really previous resolutions regarding the complex web of issues already confronted. Each precedent or policy is the result of a balancing of issues and players. Few refer to the social costs of having to retrain the elderly, for example, or fostering dependency.

Substantial innovation threatens the sometimes fragile equilibrium of an agency. By reformatting an issue or presenting an old issue in a new light, a series of previous resolutions may be subject to revision, resulting in the arousal of the government community to a level unanticipated by the innovating home's administrator and board.

Compounding these internal reviewing agency problems are background societal issues. Government administrative bodies are often, by default, forced to grapple with and decide issues not addressed by the legislative and judicial branches. Given our litigious society and the possible large financial impact of decisions, government agencies obviously have reason to assume a conservative, defensive posture. As a result, a request that fits within the existing framework of precedents is more likely to be addressed and approved.

Communicability and Complexity

The communicability and complexity of an innovation are also correlated with utilization. Clarity regarding the potential results of an innovation is associated with likelihood of adoption. More complex innovations are less likely to be adopted.

Unfortunately, innovation in nursing home design is often complex and abstract. There are several reasons for this. First, long-term care is multidisciplinary and must deal with an enormous range of open-ended medical and psychosocial issues. Research and clinical experience are finding that the various aspects of aging are intricately interrelated. Nutrition, exercise, support systems, state of mind, brain function, mobility, appropriate housing, and physical capacity are not isolated variables, nor can they be effectively addressed in isolation. Because of this, nonintegrated programs that address only limited aspects of an elderly person's life tend to fragment the individual and are often inadequate.

Additionally, the issue of nursing home design innovation is abstract and laden with paradox. To explain, person-environment fit theory describes and analyzes how a person and his or her environment interact. Older frail people tend to become increasingly more dependent on their environment for mobility, eating, toileting, cueing memory, and stimulating thought. In a nursing home, the person and environment become so closely intertwined that they define one another. That is, the more appropriately designed and supportive the environment, the more fully functional and independent the older person becomes.

The issues that radiate from this notion are often incalculable. If innovative designs are used in the construction of a new facility for a known nursing home population, the very fact of placing the residents in a better designed, more supportive environment redefines their abilities. This is one reason for the proliferation of multilevel arrangements. Innovation can be centrifugal, moving older people "outward" toward less restrictive, less expensive, more dignified, and more appropriate settings.

Therefore, a nursing home designer is not designing for an existing population but for an anticipated population—really for a population that will be transformed by its use of the new environment. And building a variety of innovative service options compounds the ambiguity and difficulties. It is necessary to anticipate not only the impact of a given program on future, perhaps very different cohorts but also the effects of any given program on other programs. The swirl of different service options and the recategorization of changing populations makes the results of innovation exciting and challenging but also complex and therefore lacking in the clarity associated with likelihood of adoption.

Complexity in design is also caused by the separate but interlocking resident spaces required in a nursing home. There are at least four basic kinds of areas that can be distinguished based upon privacy: the private areas (bedroom and bathroom), the semiprivate areas (the unit or floor), the public areas (dining room and lobby), and the area between these and the adjacent population. Each has its own attendant issues, assumptions, and value judgments, and each is a building block for the next area.

The difficulty is one of balance. Each area demands detailed analysis of many separate variables, many of which are gerontological unknowns. The characteristics and costs of each space may compete with those of the other spaces, which is why many projects have brilliant isolated innovations but fall short overall. They do not function as hoped for because of unanticipated, countervailing forces caused by other segments of the design.

Yet residents respond on a conscious and unconscious level to *all* the alternatives and assumptions presented in the total environment. The design must anticipate how residents will function in the total environment and blend the various programmatic or design features into an integrated whole that will provide an accessible range of options to future residents and will allow each of the carefully designed elements to function as planned.

An analogy may help explain the difficulties in creating the linkages and proper proportions among the different components. Imagine the task of using a freehand technique to blow up four small, intricate drawings to billboard size while retaining the proper balance.

In sum, the multidisciplinary nature of long-term care itself, the dynamic way in which design and residents interact, and the various space components of the building all make innovative design abstract and complex and militate against adoption.

Return on Investment

It is obvious that innovations will be selected that yield high returns on investment. The situation is more complex when an innovation emanates from the non-business sector, such as innovation in a nonprofit nursing home. For example, there are a number of ways to define return on investment in a nursing home, such as actual repayment of capital, operational savings, and enhanced quality of life. Each of the major groups tend to weigh these variables from different perspectives. But for nursing home innovation to be attractive, it must pass the difficult test of good return on investment from *each* of the groups.

Unfortunately, the results of innovation are not easily quantified. A nursing home is not like a hospital, which is generally short-term and deals with specific conditions that can be cured and measured. The clarity of these results, in contrast to the relative unclarity of nursing home results, may be related to the greater success hospitals have had in receiving approvals for their innovations.

Compatibility

The more compatible the innovation is with the existing system, the more likely it is to be adopted. This, of course, implies that organizations are likely to be conservative in their innovations, since what is compatible is unlikely to be radical. Whereas nursing home innovations may have an evolutionary, step-by-step genesis gerontologically and may be a logical extension of changes in government policy, it is very possible that the innovations are perceived as outside the framework of the existing government system. Consistent with the law of unanticipated consequences, the full future implications of existing government policy may not yet have been foreseen by governmental policy makers themselves. The design innovations may thus be perceived as incompatible with the existing system and thus less readily adopted.

Status Quo Ante

In the case of an innovation, there is always the question of whether the innovation is reversible. Can there be a return to the previous state of the organization? Related to this is the question of whether the innovation or technological policy is divisible. Can a little bit at a time be tried or does a total package have to be adopted? Many nursing home innovations that necessitate a certificate of need are capital-related. They deal with physical structure, which has a long life, and therefore they are not easily reversible. Ironically, designing flexibility into the building structure in order to facilitate modification later may increase the initial costs and thus render the innovations even less financially and politically feasible.

Gatekeepers

Probability of adoption is also affected by whether an innovation must pass through several steps of approval or only one or two. The greater the number of gatekeepers, the more likely that the innovation will be turned down. Because nursing home innovations develop as responses to hands-on care of residents, new ideas must flow up through the organization and then to the board, special consultants, bankers, and government. The long succession of gatekeepers may effectively kill, block, or inhibit many innovations that might otherwise survive a less prolonged gauntlet of review.

Implications

In light of the myriad obstacles to innovation—the organizational conservatism, the regulatory mine fields, the paradoxes, ironies, and difficulties of innovation itself—it seems logical to ask why any innovation occurs at all. Thankfully, the answer is simple. Innovation in nursing home design occurs because it must. It grows from the commitment and faith of individuals. The demographic revolution and our more sophisticated expectations require that we find new ways to deliver more services while expending fewer resources.

As for the question of how it occurs, individuals are stepping forward throughout the system, innovators who are capable of enormous bursts of energy and possess reserves of perseverance, to support innovation through extended periods of modification and frustration. Policy makers at the head of government agencies are encouraging internal entrepreneurs. Nursing home boards are looking for executives who can act as change agents and are themselves more prepared to take risks. Gerontological experts are moving beyond the rarefied environment of academe and are networking and learning to apply their insights to the outside world. And these efforts are increasingly supported by the general public, which no longer views aging issues solely as elderly issues. Despite the artificial arguments about generational conflict, the current power generation, the baby boomers, are recognizing that these issues relate directly to their own parents and their own future lives.

What are the implications of this turbulent world of innovation? What is the state of innovation? What is the environment in which these people will function? What is the texture and tenor of their world? It is difficult to arrive at any absolute rules, but certain perspectives and overviews may be possible. Many innovative nursing home design projects have common elements, at least superficially. But even if it was possible to tease apart the sundry variables, it would be difficult to determine the comparative weight of each. The range of variables makes each project sui generis. Consequently, anecdotal, ideographic, or formula-based summaries are often less than helpful. As shown by the previous discussion, a more open-ended, fluid construct will more appropriately map the complex state of innovative design in nursing homes.

Reflections

Because design innovation must emanate from the nursing home itself, it is the nursing home culture that is critical. The development of an organization seems to unfold in successive stages. At each stage, the organization deals with the issues it is prepared to address. This idea can be visualized using a wave analogy. As the waves approach shore, each successive wave is relatively independent, yet it bears a relationship to and has some interaction with neighboring waves. Most importantly, they generally move in the same direction, but with different speeds and magnitudes. Analogously, different nursing home organizations deal with novelty and change in different ways. Each home is in fact innovating, but the speed and strength of the innovation is a function of its expectations and perceptions of older people—who they are, what they can be.

This construct helps explain why homes within geographic proximity to each other may be innovating and stretching equally but achieve very different results, perhaps even reflecting the thinking of different eras. This is not to suggest that innovation can be plotted on a line. On the contrary, because the foundation of nursing home services is hands-on care, innovative ideas bubble up from myriad directions. New technologies may restructure certain traditional problems, but nursing home innovation is not primarily technologically driven and therefore not predictable. Rather, nursing home innovation is more a matter of piecing together fragmented ideas, experiments, and partial solutions into an integrated functioning whole.

Finally, there is no one marketplace for the ideas. There are isolated pockets of intense innovative activity and new themes and directions, but there are also gaps and anachronisms. As in the Renaissance, innovations reach different citadels through serendipitous contact and through word of mouth. Much of the cross-pollination is accomplished by wandering minstrels and balladeers. Ideas are reinterpreted, misinterpreted, lost and rediscovered, and adapted into different forms and settings.

The maturation of the alliances among government agencies, gerontological experts, and nursing homes will create a climate for innovation and a framework within which approaches and solutions will be organized, formalized, and disseminated. The strength of these alliances will move us through this intermittent prehistorical phase and toward the realization of new, responsive, and mature models and forms of nursing home design.

THE ORDER AND PROCESS OF PROJECT DEVELOPMENT

Maslow's hierarchy of needs suggests that there is a rank order to an individual's needs. Specifically, Maslow suggests that lower-level needs must be satisfied before the individual will act to satisfy higher-level needs.

Interestingly, there is a similar dynamic involved in the development of innovative nursing home design. Although it is an intergroup, not an individual, dynamic, innovative design process requires a predetermined sequence of separate formal and informal approvals, and it is necessary to secure the lower-level approvals before the process can move on to higher-level approvals. In a sense, the needs of each group must be met in order to secure approval from that group and in order to move to the next higher level. Approvals must typically be obtained from the following groups and individuals in the following order: the administrator, the board of directors, the architect or consultant, the state government, banks, staff, families, and residents.

The Administrator

The suggested order of approvals generally starts with the administrator. As the paid professional, the administrator must bring a sense of the "state of the art" to the organization. Even if the administrator is not the initiator, it is his or her responsibility to be the theme setter, the person who shapes priorities. The process of innovative design may fail even with the administrator's support, but without that support it will not even begin.

The Board of Directors

The board is the policy-setting group for the organization. If peopled and positioned properly, it can act as ambassador to the general community and arouse the community's support for major organizational efforts. To accomplish innovative design, the board must understand the need for and must be willing to take risks. The motivations of individual board members may differ. Their objectives may include better resident care, long-term reduction of operational costs, or any number of egocentric goals. It is not critical that the board members share similar motivation, only that they concur that it is worthwhile for the organization to risk community and organization assets on innovative design. If they do not make a conscious decision to embark on such an adventure, the innovative process will probably not begin. If it does begin, the process will be scuttled later as the problems inherent in innovation design arise.

The Architect

The concurrence between the administrator and the board on the need to develop innovative design results in the selection of an architect. Beyond the often bizarre and unpredictable selection process, there exists a basic paradox. Architects may be quite articulate, innovative, and thoughtful, but they generally have little understanding of the culture and dynamics of a nursing home. The selected architect must therefore be educated by the administrator before translating his or her innovative concepts into drawings. Once this process begins, the architect, a relative newcomer to program and process, becomes the driver of the innovation. He or she shapes and creates the "visible product." The architect's design may frustrate the intent of the administrator and board, but from this point it is an architect-driven process, and the architect generally prevails. The art is in jump-starting an intimate collaboration that allows shared shaping of the design. When, as frequently is the case, this kind of partnership does not occur, the hope for innovative design dies.

The State Government

The administrator and the board, with architect drawing in hand, must then approach the state for approvals—for a certificate of need (if this is required) and for affirmation that the specific innovative design satisfies written and unwritten state codes. In most states, the process of review is sufficiently complex, with overlapping policy issues intermittently arising and submerging, that one person in the bureaucracy or one issue can defeat the overall design. The lines of authority and responsibility in the bureaucracy are often so opaque, so hidden from the nursing home organization, that the actual reason or set of reasons for disallowance may never become apparent. What will be presented and articulated to the organization is the most defensible reason for disallowance, one based on the strongest possible precedent.

For the bureaucracy to approve the innovation, it must feel comfortable about the applicant organization, its motivation, its skill and adeptness at developing the actual innovation, and its trustworthiness and skill at orchestrating consensus within the bureaucracy itself. There also must be a desire in the bureaucracy for improvement. When these understandings and confidences merge, people within the bureaucracy are enabled to form a coalition to change the status quo and to make the effort to redirect the prior set of precedents. This despite the fact that it puts them at risk for failure as well as establishes new precedents that can open up other unanticipated avenues of approach.

Banks

If the state gives initial approval, the organization then must look to the financial community to back the project. The financial community generally is sufficiently sophisticated to recognize that the nursing home industry is sui generis. It looks at the project using real estate and cash flow criteria, analyzes underlying organizational and community strengths, and carefully scrutinizes the approval of the state, which to a large degree will determine the timetable for construction and operations (and who will ultimately finance operations over the long haul). Recognizing the complexity of such a venture, the banks will insist upon written and verbal assurances from each and all of the previous players—the board, the administrator, and the state—before they will commit to participation.

The Staff

After proper alignment of the administrator, board, state government, and financial institutions, the issues are presented to the staff. The staff may have been engaged early in the initial excitement of designing a building and been encouraged, through their participation, to make it their own. Even if that does not happen and the administration (with the paid consultants) designs the building, it is the staff that ultimately takes control of the building once it is built and interprets that building to the community. Because people in the community, in this instance primarily families of potential residents, have the least knowledge about the internal workings of a nursing home, it is the lower-level employees' interpretation that will shape their views of the nursing home's innovative design. Therefore, the administrator may be well advised to include the staff in the design process early, if only for internal and indirect marketing reasons.

Families

Because the actual residents are generally frail and poor self-advocates, the community views their families as the true users of the home. It is the families who will interpret the experience of being a resident (consciously or subconsciously flavored by their experience of being a family member), and their interpretation is what will most strongly shape the outside community's view of the new facility. There is generally little prior family involvement in the innovation process, for family members are primarily focused on the personal experience, the suffering of their parent. However, after completion of the building, the design will be scrutinized in-depth by families, who will make their determinations basically upon their perceptions of the care that is being provided.

Residents

Residents are the last to be involved with the innovation process. Whereas all previous participants make decisions in the name of the residents, the residents themselves generally have little input into the design process. Typically, a resident's view will be shaped by the feeling and reactions of the staff and the family. The latter will transmit a sense of excitement and satisfaction with the new upscale facility or will foster feelings of disappointment and embitterment toward the squandered opportunity and the lack of concern for resident welfare in the facility design. Disappointment is easily engendered, since residents with chronic debilitating disease often view yesterday as better than today and two weeks ago as better than yesterday. The past tends to be seen through a golden haze, however unpleasant it was at the time, for today's pain and sorrows are much more vibrant than those experienced previously.

CONCLUSION

The model described in this chapter suggests that there is a logical order in the orchestration and accomplishment of innovation. Yet once achieved, the interpretation of the innovation as successful or unsuccessful begins at the top and goes downward. This means that an organizational effort that leaves out the involvement of the real users of the facility—residents, families, and staff—until late in the process risks failure, even if the effort has achieved a dramatic and positive physical design. For it is the perceptions and interpretations of those users that will ultimately determine whether the financiers, the state government, the board, the community, and the administrator evaluate the venture as a folly or as a successful innovation that allows the residents to achieve an enhanced sense of dignity and well-being.

NOTES

1. R.F. Murphy, *The Body Silent* (New York: Henry Holt and Company, 1987), 43–44.
2. J. Hage and M. Aiken, *Social Change in Complex Organizations* (New York: Random House, 1970).
3. G. Zaltman et al., *Innovations and Organizations* (New York: Wiley Interscience, 1973).

Chapter 35

Assisted Living: Supporting Frail Elders in Alternative Residential Environments

Anne Harrington

Assisted living is a "hot" concept in long-term care and aging. It's also the subject of considerable controversy. Some believe that it is an entirely new option for elders and represents the wave of the future in supportive residential living. Others think that it is merely a new phrase for housing and services that have been available for years. Without waiting for consensus, many state policy makers are working on plans to implement assisted living programs as they scramble to find alternatives to "budget buster" Medicaid accounts. This chapter sorts through some of the key issues and examines the significance of this new alternative for the nursing home industry.

WHAT IS ASSISTED LIVING? A MASSACHUSETTS CASE STUDY

Confusing Terminology

"Assisted living" is a phrase used by many (including the American Association of Homes for the Aging [AAHA]) to designate a wide variety of residence-with-supportive-services alternatives for older people. Places that offer assisted living services may be known as rest homes, board and care homes, group foster homes, continuing care retirement communities, elder housing, or congregate housing, to name just a few of the designations. Because they provide more than housing, assisted living settings can serve elders who are quite frail.

Note: The term "rest home" has been widely accepted and used for years. Some providers, however, feel that this language is outdated and somewhat misleading. These homes are no longer primarily a place of respite for people who may be discharged from a hospital prior to their return home. Although the term has been retained throughout this chapter because of its likely familiarity to readers, "assisted living facility" or "residential care facility" is more appropriate.

Source: Reprinted from *Continuum,* January/February, April, and June 1992, Association of Massachusetts Homes for the Aging, with permission of Anne Harrington, Ph.D. © 1992.

500

As defined by Robert Newcomer and Leslie Grant, this type of living (which they generically label "residential care") "refers to the provision by a non-relative of food, shelter, and some degree of protective oversight and/or personal care that is generally nonmedical in nature."[1]

By protective oversight and personal care, the authors mean supervising residents' medications, helping them with one or more of their functional needs such as bathing or grooming, cleaning residents' rooms, doing their laundry, and assisting with arranging transportation or other support services.

Not all would agree that assisted living should be so broadly defined, however. Advocates of a narrower definition often have specific characteristics in mind such as the arrangement of the physical space or the degree of personal choice and control that they feel is unique to assisted living.

While there is no universal agreement about its fundamental characteristics, perhaps more importantly, confusion about assisted living is due to ambiguity about the type and intensity of client needs, the quality of care, and the actual services provided in the different settings.

Using the broad definition of assisted living as applied to a traditional array of residential options for older people, for instance, are all rest homes or all board and care facilities or all continuing care retirement communities the same? Are they consistently different from each other in predictable ways—ways that consumers can readily understand? Looking at rest homes in particular, do all rest homes serve clients with similar physical and mental needs? Do they offer a menu of services that is the same from one setting to another? Do they cost the same? The answer to all of these questions is an emphatic no.

Rest Homes as Assisted Living

Massachusetts rest homes are as different from each other as the older residents who live in them. Some of them are very "upscale"; others cater to a moderate or a low-income clientele or a mixed population. Some of the buildings are small and homelike. Others are large and more impersonal. In some, the majority of the residents are the deinstitutionalized mentally ill. In others, the homes reflect the genteel tradition of a bygone era.

At the core of rest homes and other assisted living communities, however, is a mission to serve older people who are, by and large, physically healthy.

Jane Bellegarde, administrator of Merrimack River Valley House in Lowell, Massachusetts, talks about the historic mission of rest homes. In the past, the typical old age home served people who were mostly independent and able to take care of themselves but who needed general supervision, monitoring of medications, and some form of assistance with functional needs. Many seeking admission may also have been unable to continue to do housekeeping, meal preparation, and maintenance chores associated with living alone. At the time of admission, they were expected to be mentally alert, with only very mild confusion, if any, and able to walk and move around unassisted. As they got older, if some of the residents became more confused or developed a medical problem, they were moved to a nursing home. Others were able to live out their days in the home.

Although there have been many changes since then, today's rest homes and other forms of assisted living continue to see themselves as an important part of the continuum of elder care. As in the past, they believe that they offer a homelike residential experience for a largely independent population at a lower cost than a nursing home. By and large, most tend not to provide medical services, unless on a special basis or unless the home has nursing beds (and trained nursing staff).

Beyond this core of similarity, however, assisted living providers offer highly differentiated services in different kinds of settings to different populations at costs that can range from $30 a day to more than three times that amount, excluding extra supportive services (continuing care retirement communities excepted).

What Do State Regulations Say?

If the existence of state regulations is any measure, Massachusetts rest homes (or level IV resident care facilities, as they are called) *are* different from other types of assisted living. Unlike congregate housing and all the other residential alternatives, licensed level IV homes must conform to a significant amount of regulation and to preset reimbursement ceilings.

Let's start with the state's idea of what a rest home is. In Massachusetts, it is a facility that provides "a supervised supportive and protective living environment and support services incident to old age for residents having difficulty in caring for themselves and who do not require level II or III nursing care or other medically related services on a routine basis."[2] In other words, it's not a nursing home. It's a home that provides supportive services to people who do not have regular medical needs.

What about the staffing? What does the state require? One "responsible person" must be on the premises at all times. Not a nurse or a nurse aide. A responsible person. This is defined as a mature high school graduate 21 years or older who speaks English and the primary language spoken by residents. For homes with less than 20 beds, responsible persons should be available during the waking hours in a ratio of 1 person to 10 residents. For larger homes, a minimum of one responsible person should be available 24 hours a day for each unit (up to 60 beds).

What about medications? Who handles that? Can medications be self-administered? Perhaps. The regulations also allow for administration of certain medications by a person who has successfully completed one approved training course on dispensing medications. One course. Otherwise, a free-standing level IV home must have a licensed consultant nurse for 4 hours a month per unit, a consultant dietitian to review special diets every 3 months, and a cook "as needed." The nurse must review medications every 6 months and provide services to residents in the case of a "minor illness of a temporary nature." Also, social services should be provided as needed, along with 20 hours of activities "suited to the needs of residents."[3]

Although Massachusetts requirements for level IV homes cover many things, from the physical plant and equipment and supplies to how often the bed linen should be changed, rest homes are not much different from other types of assisted living environments when it comes to who is supposed to live and work there. What is offered is supposed to be based on the needs of residents who are more independent than frail. *(Note:* Community Support Facilities are a special type of licensed level IV home in Massachusetts. More than 50 percent of their residents have some mental illness diagnosis, and for that reason these facilities have many more regulations and staffing requirements than conventional level IV homes.)

Changing Needs—Increasing Frailty

Since July 1991, Massachusetts Medicaid officials have implemented a policy of making it more difficult for older people with "light care needs" to get into a nursing home. Rest homes are getting more referrals from people who have multiple needs. They are also seeing more dementia and emotional problems.

Rosalyn Piro, administrator of the Caldwell Home in Fitchburg, Massachusetts, is seeing people "with lots of dementia needs" as well as people who are incontinent. (Incontinence is a big issue for these facilities because of the demands for more staff, more laundry, more supplies, and hotter water. Traditionally, level IV facilities do not admit people who are incontinent.) In response to a hypothetical situation, she says that she might be willing to take in someone with mild dementia needs. She has a nurse consultant six hours a week and is able to provide "lots of personal care." In evaluating a person with dementia, she assesses her other residents' needs and considers how much supervision the applicant requires.

For Bellegarde in Lowell, Massachusetts, the new realities of who is seeking admission to her home cause her to "worry about the expectation level for level IVs." Applicants are more frail, sometimes confused or emotionally troubled, and some have "transfer assist" needs (i.e., they need help moving from one place to another). But in addition to more physical and cognitive needs, many requesting admission are in their 90s! Since the resident average age is already 88 years, she expects new residents will be pushing that average higher—and will require more services as well.

Valerie Emerton, administrator of the German Home in Lawrence, Massachusetts, sees the same change—people seeking admission who are in wheelchairs, others with oxygen or insulin requirements, and people who are incontinent.

Who Pays?

Funding sources have a lot to do with what kind of assisted living a person qualifies for and the services available in that setting. In HUD-financed elder housing, many residents receive monthly rent subsidies from the federal government. Until recently, however, federal assistance has not paid for supportive services, with the notable exception of HUD's Congregate Housing Services Program. (HUD has now acknowledged this need through a commitment to fund service coordinators, but matching demand to limited funds has been a vexing problem.) In Massachusetts-subsidized congregate housing, limited state home care dollars have restricted services to residents with the highest levels of frailty.

Unlike most other types of assisted living, rest homes offer a program of supportive services for *all* residents. Supplemental Security Income (SSI) and Emergency Aid to the Elderly, Disabled, and Children are two of the more common forms of public assistance that can help to defray expenses. If a person qualifies for SSI, for example, he or she must have income below approximately $720 a month and no more than $2,000 in assets. The state will supplement the difference between this income and the rate that the state allows the home to charge. Selling a home as part of "spending down" to qualify for SSI is common.

Massachusetts sets a cap on the rates that a licensed level IV home can charge its publicly subsidized residents. Unfortunately for level IV homes, the Massachusetts Rate Setting Commission uses a payment formula that reimburses facilities for costs based on what happened two years earlier. Consequently, if a home incurs increased costs, as many did in 1991 in response to tougher Medicaid nursing home eligibility requirements and frailer applicants to rest homes, these are not reflected in the state's allowable rates until two years later. There is no mechanism for appeal. Because the state maintains no historical data on resident health status, it has no information on which to base a rate adjustment due to changed needs.

State Policies for Community-Based Residential Programs

The Massachusetts example demonstrates that in many respects there is little to distinguish a rest home from a congregate home (defined as providing private or shared quarters along with some shared common space such as dining and socializing areas) or from a board and care home (an unlicensed boarding house with services). The major difference is the presence or absence of state regulation and licensure. (In licensed level IV homes, significant regulations apply as compared with other types of assisted living. Available penalties for breaking the rules include being cited by the state Department of Public Health, fines, delicensure or decertification, and, in very egregious circumstances, criminal prosecution.) The major similarity across these settings is the people whom they serve. Although there have been some changes in recent months, it is the same population of elders who are looking to get their needs met wherever they live! It is really habit and history that is causing rest homes to be viewed as down-sized nursing homes.

As Massachusetts implements two new programs—a group adult foster care program and a managed care program in publicly funded housing—important public policy questions emerge. What's going to happen in the rush to create new community-based alternatives to nursing homes? When personal care services are reimbursed through Medicaid's adult group foster care program, will more regulations be added to elderly housing to make *them* safer and more protective environments? Will they too become more medicalized and therefore more government controlled? Or will they be allowed to grow and diversify as elder housing and congregate housing and board and care homes have traditionally been allowed to do? And what about the state's policy for rest homes? What group of older people should they serve and what reimbursement is appropriate, given the level of need of their residents? Is it time for a more flexible state approach that incorporates rest homes as one type of assisted living?

WHAT'S BEHIND THE NEW BUZZWORDS: "HOSPITALITY MODEL," "CATERED LIVING," AND "RESIDENTIAL ALTERNATIVES"?

Imagine that you are a provider of services to older people and that you are in charge of a residence with supportive services. Most of your residents are in their eighties. Some are very independent. They may take public transportation, do volunteer work either in your facility or elsewhere, or drive their own cars. Many, though, are quite frail. They require some type of assistance—perhaps a reminder to take medications or assistance with meals, housekeeping, transportation, bathing, or getting dressed.

In this hypothetical scenario, is it possible to say with certainty what type of residential setting is being described? Is it a rest home? A board and care home? Congregate housing? Senior housing? A continuing care retirement community?

Without more information, it could be any of these settings. Knowledge of the needs of the residents and the services offered are typically not enough to determine which form of assisted living is being provided.

An identical floor plan could belong to a congregate housing site, a level IV facility (a rest home), or a board and care home. In these settings, each resident may have his or her own private room and shared common areas such as a dining room or a place to socialize with friends. Staffing patterns could also be similar—aides, kitchen staff, housekeeping staff, transportation staff. Nursing might be available on staff or as needed (through contracts with local home health agencies).

What if we add another piece of information? Our residence serves primarily private-pay clients. Does this help us to narrow it down? Not necessarily. All forms of assisted living may be offered on a private-pay basis. If, on the other hand, our residence serves a low or moderate income group, we have ruled out most continuing care retirement communities, which tend to serve a more affluent population.

If, after thorough investigation, we discover that this residence is regulated and licensed by the state and the facility is in Massachusetts, we are ready to solve the mystery. We have identified a rest home. Had we been told that it was an unregulated facility, we would still be in the dark. The possibilities would still include senior housing, congregate housing, board and care homes, and the non–health care areas of continuing care retirement communities.

The point is that there are many different types of assisted living settings offering services for independent, frail, and sometimes even very frail older people. Labels alone offer little help in identifying what goes on in them.

Just How New Is Assisted Living?

Housing with supportive services provided by a nonrelative (our definition of assisted living) has a long history, as we saw in the Massachusetts example. Terms like *senior housing, congregate housing,* and *rest home* were used to differentiate one form of supportive residential living from another. The fact that the physical layout and the needs of clients living in congregate housing were often very similar to those for rest homes and unlicensed homes was ignored. The variation from one rest home to another or from one congregate housing site to another was also ignored.

It was the differences between these environments that counted. After all, rest homes were state-regulated and licensed. They evolved from a more medicalized model of health care. Weren't they just a step down from nursing homes? What about much of the senior housing funded by the federal government in the 1960s? Weren't these residents really more independent? And weren't people living in congregate housing somewhere between independent living and "custodial" care—but closer to independence?

Beyond the different labels, funding sources, and government regulations or lack thereof, there was also an important reality for residents. They knew that if they developed more needs, they would have to move somewhere else. Where they went would depend on the level of assistance they required and the amount of money they had. Perhaps it would be to congregate housing or a rest home or a nursing home. But maintaining independence (or faking it) was as real as the fear of having to move someday.

To today's older consumer, the newer assisted living communities may seem entirely different. They frequently offer self-contained apartments. There may be more "amenities." Supportive services may be purchased separately or included in the monthly fees. Prices may be "upscale" and there may be an entrance fee in addition to the monthly fees. For residents, there's another crucial difference: It is okay to need assistance.

However, all assisted living environments, old or new, share a common philosophy that focuses on the independence of the resident and the residence itself as a person's home.

Shifting Priorities: Medical Model Is Out, Hospitality In

Government policy makers caught on. They knew all along that people living independently had a variety of unmet needs. However, it took a fiscal crisis of enormous proportions to begin a massive shift in outlook and funding priorities at the federal and state levels.

We are seeing evidence of that shift today. The new priorities are to create and fund nonmedicalized residential alternatives for independent and frail elders. To limit the use of nursing homes through changed Medicaid eligibility criteria and make them more like subacute hospitals. To keep the middle class from "spending down" to Medicaid and to recoup expended funds from their estate if they require publicly financed assistance. And to create "managed care" programs for older adults that hopefully prevent or postpone institutionalization. Driving it all is the government's fiscal motivation to save public dollars, limit spending, and restrict Medicaid access.

The medicalization of elder care is presumed to be the cause of budget buster state Medicaid programs. Consequently, the medical or hospital model has lost favor in the eyes of government policy makers, who now speak of its limited usefulness for the majority of older people. Studies are widely quoted that document older people's desire to live in their own homes. Nursing homes, solidly rooted in the medical model, are "out," appropriate only as a last resort. Protective, supervised environments are passé.

What's "in" is the hotel model. Maintaining independence through supportive services offered in a residential, homelike setting. Developing a contractual relationship between the individual who pays the rent or fee for housing and services and the provider.

The model has important implication for staff, who, like the hotel concierge, make arrangements for residents basically responsible for their own "evenings out." Implicitly and explicitly, the resident is the ultimate decision maker, responsible for requesting and using services and programs.

Licensure and Regulation

Assisted living requires a new set of ideas about state licensure and regulation. The medical model uses the acuity of the individual as its benchmark. Government reimbursement follows need, primarily defined in terms of health care. In Massachusetts nursing homes, the places of greatest need for chronic care, the case mix Medicaid reimbursement system uses a scoring system to identify residents as somewhere between "light" and "heavy" care and bases its reimbursement to facilities on these scores, with more money paid for heavier care residents.

Assisted living challenges all that. If a resident becomes very frail and wishes to remain at home, he or she may not have to go to a nursing home. Theoretically, that resident can live in an assisted living setting as long as he or she wishes to remain there, can pay for services, and is permitted to by the assisted living contract. A move may be unnecessary. Given the level of need that can be met in assisted living, acuity may not be the defining difference between regulated and unregulated environments. It all depends on what state regulations permit.

Consultant David Roush argues that a critical factor in future state decisions about whether a community is regulated or not should be the kind of relationship that gets structured between providers and older people. In assisted living environments, the relationship often works out as follows: "I (the consumer) am the decision maker. This is my home. I choose the services. I want you (the provider) to remind me to take my medications or help me to get dressed in the morning. I am still in charge of my life." Perhaps in these situations, there may not have to be regulation or licensure.

On the other hand, if a provider must exercise direct responsibility for care and services, similar to what happens in a hospital or a nursing home, where there is a significant degree of protective oversight and supervision, then perhaps that environment *should* be regulated and licensed.

In a situation like Massachusetts, however, where the state is still working out its position on assisted living, providers can be caught in a quandary about liability issues, licensure, and regulation. Fear of liability and state regulation drives many, often at the advice of counsel, to make distinctions between acts that require licensed health care workers (and that may, therefore, trigger facility licensure and regulation) and acts that do not.

One area where this plays out is the distinction between reminding residents to take their medications and actually dispensing medications. Medication reminders arguably can be done by anyone regardless of setting or staff qualifications, since the final decision to take the medication belongs to the resident. On the other hand, dispensing medications, unless performed by an outside vendor like a certified home health agency, may require facility regulation and licensure.

It is common to find assisted living providers instructing their nonmedical staff to set out trays with medications in individual compartments and to offer medication reminders. Many have also developed arrangements with home health agencies for nurses to make visits as needed. This avoids potential liability problems and regulatory oversight by the state, they hope.

Providers interested in avoiding regulation may also use great caution from the outset in deciding the number and type of services they will offer, whether services will be offered on site or off, and whether they will be performed by their own staff.

Government officials may have little experience with this type of supportive living. Should it be subject to regulation? If so, how much? What type? By whom? If not, what are the risks? Assisted living opens up whole new areas for federal and state decision making about where to draw the line between consumer protection and individual risk. It also raises questions about what services and programs should be funded, and for whom.

The consensus that seems to be emerging in Massachusetts and elsewhere is that the medical model of assistance is too expensive and may not be appropriate for assisted living.

Who Is Really Served in Assisted Living?

Who really needs assisted living? Why do older people make the change to assisted living in the first place? Although precise statistics are nonexistent and figures depend on how one defines "assisted living," Victor Regnier, author of *Best Practices in Assisted Living,* estimates that about 40 percent of the people coming into assisted living have some degree of confusion (probably mild) and 40 percent have trouble with incontinence.[4] There is undoubtedly some overlap in these numbers due to older people who have difficulty in both areas. In the experience of Bill Carney, an assisted living consultant who manages the John Bertram House in Salem, Massachusetts, his state's numbers are lower than the national figures. He believes that approximately 33 percent have some confusion and 33 percent have urinary incontinence. "If you eliminated [people with] incontinence and confusion," states Carney, "you'd eliminate most of the clients seeking supportive environments."

In states still debating their views on alternative environments, many assisted living providers who serve a cognitively impaired group of residents may feel that they are not free to make independent decisions about what is in the residents' best interest. The issue of medication administration is a case in point. For example, asks Carney, what happens if a resident with manic-depressive tendencies chooses not to take his or her medication? What if that resident becomes agitated and disturbs other residents? What is the responsibility of the provider in this situation? Is a hands-off policy appropriate?

Sorting Out the Questions

Assisted living raises many unresolved questions. The following list is an attempt to identify some of the critical ones:

- What's the right model for assisted living? Considering some of the people being served in assisted living environments, is "hospitality" the best model for people who may have cognitive problems or who take psychotropic medications?
- Who is at risk? What is the risk? What is the role of the provider in minimizing risk (e.g., the overnight supervision of very frail elders at risk of nursing home placement)? What is the role of the state in setting up safeguards?
- Should there be regulation? If yes, should it be based on a health model, a consumer protection model, or some hybrid?
- What amount of state regulation is desirable and what entity should do the regulating?
- Are there aspects of the current regulatory and certifying system that work well? What are they? Where are they?
- What are the parts of the system that do not work well and create obstacles to providing supportive services?
- What about licensure and certification? Should places be licensed or the people who work in them? Should licensure or certification be limited to health caregivers or should it be broad enough to include personal care assistants?
- Should there be a special category of residential care facilities that serve primarily older people with cognitive impairments who may also have other needs (e.g., incontinence)?

- If regulations establish only basic consumer protection safeguards to protect against fraud, abuse, and negligence, should the state also encourage the voluntary adoption by providers of a higher set of assisted living standards?

- What are fair admissions criteria? Can providers legally refuse admission to those who may upset the mix of healthy and infirm?

- What kind of services can appropriately be provided in assisted living settings?

- Can or should the state expect cost savings from these assisted living alternatives?

- Is nursing home placement prevented or postponed?

- If older people are being diverted into community-based settings by Medicaid policy makers, what system of checks and balances can be set up to ensure appropriate placement and care?

- What about private-pay elders? Do new state programs serve their needs? Are costs for supportive services going to be driven up for people not eligible for publicly funded programs?

- What happens to those who "spend down" in assisted living? Where do they go? How do they access services and housing? What is the provider's responsibility? What is the state's responsibility?

These and many other questions need to be publicly discussed and debated. The recognition that the current long-term care system cannot continue presents a unique opportunity for states, providers, and consumers.

STATES ARE SCRAMBLING TO FIND ALTERNATIVES TO NURSING HOMES

In states all across the country, massive experimentation is taking place. It involves the redirection of millions of dollars from nursing homes to community-based residential programs, affects thousands of older people, and promises to fundamentally reshape the way retirement housing is provided in the future. Consumers, state regulators, and the whole spectrum of elder service and housing providers are all being affected.

The driving forces behind the state-by-state experiments include consumer desire to "age in place" in home and community-based settings, state and federal governments' desperation over budget buster Medicaid programs, and a recognition that cost-effective innovation is the only way to avoid fiscal and programmatic collapse in the near future. Reliance on increasingly restrictive Medicaid benefits or other old ways of doing business just will not suffice.

This experimentation has a name. It is called assisted living. As we have seen, there is little agreement about how to define it, design it, or fund it. Whether and how to regulate it or license it. Whether to develop one basic statewide model or take a more laissez-faire approach. Whether to target it to the poor, the rich, or everyone in between. Whether it is the great new wave of the future or just another passing fad.

Regardless of the lack of consensus, this form of residential living appears to be taking hold and consumers are fueling a growing demand. In Oregon, developers cannot build assisted living communities fast enough; waiting lists in existing communities are commonplace.

What accounts for the excitement? After all, we have had various sorts of housing with supportive services in the past, such as congregate housing and rest homes. HUD has also acknowledged the need for adding services and service coordinators to public housing.

Narrowly defined, however, assisted living is new. Depending on who you talk to, it may refer to a specific kind of physical environment—a private apartment, private bath, kitchenette, and a locking door on the outside of each unit, for example. But the physical setup is meant to be just a reflection of a much broader philosophy that emphasizes privacy, expanded care choices, respect for individuality, personal decision making and control, and maximum independence—all within a homelike environment. Given the needs of residents who typically require assistance with such things as bathing, dressing, and medications and who may also be confused or incontinent, this option can meet the needs of frail older people and do it in a "consumer friendly" way.

Given a lack of policy, leadership, and funding for assisted living at the federal level, states have become de facto labs for experimental programs and new regulations. Sometimes, a state starts an assisted living program after a provider develops the initial concept and makes it work in the private sector; then the state agrees to step in and fund it for a Medicaid population. That is what happened in Oregon. In other states, it may take an out-of-control budget to get policy makers seriously interested in figuring out how to create and fund community-based alternatives for frail elders.

Regardless of how states get into it, however, two things are certain. Every state in the nation is taking a long, hard look at assisted living and assessing its viability. And secondly, with programs being created and implemented on a state-by-state basis, it is clear that each state regulating assisted living will probably do it differently.

Oregon

Oregon has a highly successful track record in providing residential alternatives like assisted living and adult foster care. Medicaid nursing home utilization by people over age 65 has shown a steady decline since 1982. According to Dick Ladd, administrator of the Senior and Disabled Services Division, nursing home costs account for a significantly smaller percentage of Oregon's total long-term care budget than in other states—about 65 percent in Oregon vs. more than 90 percent in most other states.[5]

Assisted living is defined in the regulations as "an apartment complex that provides nursing home level non-medical support in a way that allows for increments of service to be added to or taken away from a client's total care package as that client's condition changes." The assisted living unit shall consist of "single occupancy units [220 square feet] with lockable doors, private bathrooms, and kitchenettes." These are the "key structural ingredients," according to Rosalie Kane et al., *Meshing Services with Housing: Lessons from Adult Foster Care and Assisted Living in Oregon.*[6]

Although assisted living is defined very specifically in terms of the physical environment, the rules about providing services are more ambiguous. They do not stipulate a basic core of services or required staffing levels. Instead, providers must have the ability to meet the needs of residents at all times.

According to Keren Brown Wilson, developer of the first private assisted living project in the state and one of the contributors to Oregon's assisted living regulations, 24-hour 'care capability' for "providing or coordinating routine nursing care such as medication management, injections, nail and skin care, dressing changes, health monitoring, non-skilled catheter care, and other nursing tasks" and other types of required capabilities put a lot of responsibility on providers.[7] They must be proactive on the resident's behalf—identifying needs and preferences and making sure that needs are met. This applies even to ancillary services. In her words, "It is the responsibility of the provider to act as a case manager [for each resident."]*

Generally, to meet nursing needs, assisted living providers either contract directly with a nurse or hire a nurse on staff. This nurse is responsible either for providing direct care or supervising unlicensed staff whom he or she authorizes to perform certain tasks (e.g., medication administration). There is very little use of third-party providers, Wilson explains. It's simply too expensive to contract with an outside home health agency, for instance, whose own overhead would get factored into the final bill.

Residents are typically in their mid-eighties and require assistance with multiple activities of daily living. Many have need of incontinence care, Alzheimer's assistance, or some type of routine nursing care such as dressing changes, medications, or injections. Eighty-four percent are "mobility impaired." Some require behavioral intervention and supervision. The majority need 24-hour "custodial" supervision.

Note: Keren Brown Wilson interviewed by telephone 5/20/92.

At the higher end of impairment, one 87-year-old resident has had two strokes, a fractured hip, is unstable when walking unassisted, is confused, and has an indwelling catheter and a colostomy. This resident is being served appropriately in assisted living, despite these multiple needs.

The success of Oregon's program can be measured in several ways. One is the declining utilization of nursing homes. Another is its cost-effectiveness. Assisted living costs, on average, about 80 percent of the Medicaid nursing home rate for level III residents (according to Kane's report). In addition, assisted living seems to provide an empowering milieu for residents so they tend to do more for themselves and may even improve, especially when they move into assisted living from another more restrictive setting. Improved behavioral outcomes were reported by Kane et al. in their study. Finally, there have been no problems with liability so far. Despite some controversy about the Nurse Delegation Act, no provider has been sued.

Of the many factors that have contributed to Oregon's success in designing and implementing a workable program, a few stand out, including these[8]:

- A consolidated bureaucratic apparatus for gaining access to all elder services, both at the state and local level. Consumers and providers deal with only one entity at each level; state officials are able to make tough budgetary decisions about programs because all of the aging programs are administered by one agency.

- A comprehensive philosophy and clear vision about what assisted living is. This includes a vocabulary defining new roles, responsibilities, and relationships in this environment (e.g., "managed risk," "shared responsibility," and "bounded choice").

- A flexible, nonprescriptive regulatory approach.

- A law that permits nurses to delegate responsibility for certain routine tasks to less skilled staff acting under their supervision (known as the Nurse Delegation Act).

- A commitment by regulators, providers, and residents to work things out as problems or differences of opinion arise.

- A single assessment process that prescreens everyone interested in nursing home placement, including privately paying clients.

- A five-tiered reimbursement system that compensates providers based on the intensity of resident need.

- Care plans that are developed and agreed to by staff, residents, and families.

- A needs-driven, personalized approach to care for residents who are or may become quite frail. Services are "unbundled" and made available only when needed.

- An outcome-based system (i.e., the state evaluates providers based on resident outcomes, not on the temperature of the water or the date on the fire extinguisher).

Oregon now has 785 assisted living apartments in 18 licensed facilities and hopes to add 1,000 more units by the end of 1992, according to a preliminary report of the National Academy for State Health Policy.[9] Of the existing licensed facilities, there is an average of about 50 units per site. When these sites reach capacity, about 24 percent of the residents will be receiving Medicaid assistance.

It's important to point out that nursing homes continue to play an important role in Oregon. Although a wide range of physical and cognitive frailty and aging in place is accommodated in assisted living, residents who become totally and permanently bedfast and are unable to ask for assistance are not considered suitable for this environment. (However, an exception is possible if a facility can demonstrate that it can safely meet the needs of such a resident.)

Washington

The state of Washington is developing a new assisted living program that is similar in many ways to Oregon's. The program, sponsored by the Department of Social and Health Services, is intended "to test a variety of service models within assisted living standards proposed by the Department." According to Charles Reed,[*] Assistant Secretary, the state hopes to have contracted for 180 units of assisted living by late August 1992. (Forty-five are currently in operation and have been for a year.)

The statewide demonstration involves a low-income population who would otherwise qualify for intermediate nursing care (ICF or level III care). A flat rate of $45 a day has been set. This is higher than the $20 a day rate for state-funded congregate care but only 58 percent of the ICF-level nursing home rate. Medicaid waivers and Title XIX personal care monies are being used to fund the program.

All units must be private, 220–square foot, handicapped-accessible apartments with private bathrooms, refrigerators, and "cooking capacity" (i.e., a hot plate or microwave). Congregate meals are required, along with access to common areas. Services include personal care, behavior management, incontinence care, and specified nursing services, such as medication administration and injections. Facilities have the option of providing additional services such as therapies, sterile dressing changes, and catheter and ostomy care.

---

[*]*Note:* Charles Reed interviewed by telephone 5/18/92.

Because Washington has no nurse delegation act, implementation of the staffing aspect of the program differs from the Oregon model. Nurses are required to be on staff and available for unscheduled resident needs 24 hours a day. (In Oregon, there is no required staffing pattern and unlicensed staff can perform many care tasks.)

The state expects to contract with existing licensed boarding homes rather than build new assisted living facilities. Of the state's 12,000 licensed board and care beds, 3,000 are state-funded congregate. Assisted living is seen as an important alternative that fills in the gap between congregate and nursing home care. And with the state projecting that it will be at nursing home bed capacity by the year 2005 (its bed limit is 45 per 1,000 residents), the assisted living demonstration will provide valuable information about alternative residential living for frail elders.

Florida

Florida has a new law that allows providers to care for more impaired residents than in its regular adult congregate housing program. The regulations, now finalized, apply to a new licensure category called extended congregate care (ECC). ECC homes have to be dually licensed both as adult congregate living facilities and as extended congregate care facilities. Oregon's Keren Brown Wilson consulted with Florida state officials in the development of the program.[*]

Although the law is in place, reaching agreement on the regulations was more difficult. The state was temporarily mired in controversy with its for-profit nursing home association about the scope of proposed regulations, which would allow assisted living providers to care for some of the same type of residents as nursing homes. State officials worked out a compromise and implementation is underway.

Initial admission rules are similar for all congregate facilities. To get in, a resident must have a statement from a physician or nurse practitioner indicating that he or she does not require 24-hour nursing care, can have needs met in a nonmedical, non-nursing facility, has no apparent sign of infectious disease, is capable of self-administration of medications with assistance or supervision, and is capable of "self-preservation in an emergency"—with staff assistance. In addition, the medical report must stipulate whether the individual is independent in daily functional needs or requires supervision or one-on-one assistance.

What the state will permit as residents "age in place" in assisted living is defined in the new rules and is unique to ECC facilities. ECC residents can be bedridden for up to 14 consecutive days and can be totally dependent in up to

---

[*]Note: This section describes the Florida regulations, as of September 1992.

three activities of daily living—dressing, grooming, toileting, bathing, and eating. (An exception is made for quadriplegics, paraplegics, and people with muscular dystrophy or multiple sclerosis or other neuromuscular disease as long as they can communicate their needs and do not require facility assistance with complex medical problems.)

Residents become ineligible for aging in place in extended congregate care when one of the following needs or situations arises: a condition that requires 24-hour nursing supervision, more than 14 consecutive days of being bedridden, four or more functional impairments, cognitive impairment to the point where the resident cannot make simple decisions, treatment for level 3 or 4 pressure ulcers (sores), needs beyond transfer assistance, danger posed to self or others, or a medically unstable condition in a person with special health problems for whom no therapy regimen has been established.

To emphasize the importance of giving residents choices, Florida requires that providers must offer a minimum set of choices such as remaining in the same room, participating in activities sponsored by the facility, being part of the service planning, and taking part in local community activities.

Besides setting up criteria for admissions, discharge, and personal decision making, Florida's regulations highlight another important difference in its assisted living program—its adaptation to congregate housing and life style. Shared quarters and shared living space differentiate its assisted living program from those in many other states, particularly Oregon. In Florida, semiprivate rooms and apartments are permitted, along with private rooms and apartments. In shared quarters, there can be up to two residents to a room (four in other congregate facilities). The amount of square footage is also significant. It is okay to have a very small private room or even small shared quarters! In private quarters, for example, the minimum is 80 square feet of usable floor space per room. Bathrooms can be shared by as many as four residents. And because it is a congregate facility, the amount of shared living and socializing space is stipulated.

Meals may illustrate another part of the difference, although it remains to be seen how the new rules for extended congregate care get played out. Residents living in all congregate settings "shall be encouraged or assisted to eat at tables in dining areas." Given the congregate nature of extended care facilities, there is an implied expectation that meals will continue to be served in a group setting. How does this fit in with the requirement in the proposed rules that extended care facilities must give residents choices, especially about participation in activities of the community? What if some choose to eat alone in their own rooms or apartments? Which one will be encouraged—eating with others or making a personal decision?

As in all congregate facilities, unlicensed staff will be allowed to get medications, do reminders, open the bottle or container, and steady any part of the resident's body. "Self-administration" of medications means that the final act of putting medication in the mouth is done by the resident. What is defined as "administration of medication" to a resident is limited to licensed professionals.

Extended congregate care regulations contain many other requirements for licensure, including the types of staff needed, training, resident service plans, record keeping, allowable services, and the development of facility-specific mechanisms to encourage residents to make personal choices and decisions and facility-specific policies and procedures to allow residents to age in place.

New York

The New York model is least like the others described in this chapter. According to a new law effective in January 1992, assisted living is defined in terms of the providers who offer it and the types of residents who need it. It is not defined in terms of a private room or apartment or a prescribed amount of square footage. Assisted living is a hybrid that combines supportive housing with home care services. The aim is to provide housing and needed services "in the least restrictive environment possible" to people who are medically eligible for nursing home placement. Assisted living is expected to offer a more intensive level of services than is available through "adult homes" (comparable to residential care facilities) or "enriched housing" (similar to congregate housing).

Under the current proposal, the Assisted Living Program (ALP) must be doubly licensed—as an adult home or enriched housing program *and* as a home care or certified home health agency or as a long-term home health care program. In addition, projects must be located in areas of unmet need. To pay for services, the provider will get either a private rate payment or a capitated payment (50 percent of the resident's RUGS classification for nursing home care) for Medicaid-eligible residents. (Covered services include nursing, personal care, home health aides, therapies, medical supplies and equipment, personal emergency response, and adult day health.) Funding for the housing portion will be based on SSI or private payments.

Residents who are in need of continual nursing or medical care, are chronically bedfast or chairfast, or are cognitively or physically impaired to a point that compromises safety are ineligible for assisted living under the proposed regulations.

Two state agencies and various divisions expect to regulate the program. The Department of Social Services (DSS) will have general oversight. However, each of the component parts will be separately regulated. The Department of Health will regulate the home care agency. The DSS's Division of Medical Assistance will be responsible for personal care. And the DSS's Division of Adult Services will review and regulate the housing.

New York hopes to eventually have 4,200 assisted living units, which are expected to save an estimated $61.8 million in averted nursing home costs, according to the National Academy for State Health Policy report.[10]

SUMMARY

Assisted living is a form of residential living that is highly variable from one state to another. In Oregon, it is called "assisted living," in Florida "extended congregate care," in Rhode Island "sheltered care," in Pennsylvania "personal care," and in Colorado "alternative care." It not only has different names, it can actually look physically different, offer different services, and be staffed differently. It can be suitable for frail people who would otherwise be in a nursing home and may need "regular nursing care" (Oregon) or it can exclude people because they cannot walk or move about without staff assistance (current regulations in New Hampshire). It can be part of a major state initiative intended to divert people from nursing homes through expanded community-based alternatives and restricted nursing home access (Massachusetts proposal) or be just another type of residential living available to older people (Colorado). It can involve new construction (Oregon) or existing housing (Washington).

By its very nature, then, assisted living can take many different forms and serve widely different needs. Each state has tailored its assisted living policies to its own spectrum of available services, its own financing constraints, and the nature of the state itself. A program for a state that has fewer than three million residents many of whom live in rural areas (Oregon) may not work in a densely populated area that forces greater economies of scale (New York).

Perhaps the greatest strength of assisted living is its adaptability to a wide range of needs of people as they age and its strong emphasis on individuality and consumer choice. Perhaps it matters less whether resident rooms are private or shared and whether the unit is an apartment with its own kitchen and bathroom. As long as consumers get to decide, they will "vote" their preference. A critical role for states is to figure out where to draw the line between encouraging flexibility, independence, and reasonable risk and providing adequate resident safeguards.

NOTES

1. R. Newcomer and L. Grant, Residential Care Facilities: Understanding Their Role and Improving Their Effectiveness, in *Aging in Place: Supporting the Frail Elderly in Residential Environments,* ed. D. Tilson, (Glenview, Ill.: Scott, Foresman & Co., 1990).

2. Department of Public Health, *105 CMR 150.000–159.000: Long-Term Care Facilities* (Commonwealth of Massachusetts, 1990), 597.

3. Ibid.

4. V. Regnier et al., *Best Practices in Assisted Living: Innovations in Design, Management, and Financing* (Los Angeles, Calif.: University of Southern California, 1991).

5. M. Southwick, Reforming the Long-Term Care System, Oregon-Style, in *Continuum: A Report on Aging and Long-Term Care in Massachusetts,* vol. 2, no. 4, ed. A. Harrington (Boston, Mass.: Association of Massachusetts Homes for the Aging, 1991).

6. R. Kane et al., *Meshing Services with Housing: Lessons from Adult Foster Care and Assisted Living in Oregon* (Minneapolis, Minn.: University of Minnesota, 1990), 113.

7. K.B. Wilson, Assisted Living: A Model of Supportive Housing, in *Advances in Long-Term Care* (New York: Springer Publishing, in press), 1–2.

8. Ibid. Also, K.B. Wilson, Assisted Living: The Merger of Housing and Long-Term Care Services, in *Long-Term Care Advances: Topics in Research, Training, Service, and Policy.* Vol. 1. (Durham, N.C.: Duke University Center for the Study of Aging, 1990).

9. R.C. Ladd et al., *Building Assisted Living into Public Long-Term Care Policy: A Discussion Paper* (National Academy for State Health Policy, 1992).

10. Ibid.

Chapter 36

Risk Management for Nursing Homes: A Primer

George A. Balko III

When a plaintiff's lawyer works to build a malpractice case against a provider of health care services, he or she seeks to go beyond the mere demonstration that an injury was inflicted upon his or her client. Malpractice requires more than just showing there was a mistake that caused injury. It also requires showing that the accepted standard of care was not maintained. This often includes showing what the health care provider does and does not do to ensure the delivery of the highest quality of care to the patient. The lawyer will often try to show that the provider ought to have avoided the error that caused the injury or, at the very least, ought to have been able to discover the error shortly after it was made and taken steps to treat the injury.

In other words, to maximize the potential recovery the lawyer will try to develop a picture that includes what went on before, during, and after the infliction of the injury on his client. The more damning the circumstances the lawyer can portray, the more effective and successful will be his or her case.

The purpose of this chapter is to indicate what an administrator of a long-term care facility can do to ensure that, when a lawyer begins an investigation of the circumstances surrounding an injurious event, the lawyer will see a picture that is not conducive to pointing fingers at the health care providers. To the greatest extent possible, the administrator wants to limit the lawyer's case to the single event causing the injury. This requires work to be done long before any event occurs to bring a lawyer snooping. The administrator must devise and implement a plan that ensures the provision of careful, well-monitored, and high-quality health care services.

What is the best strategy for achieving this? Communication, communication, communication!

THE IMPORTANCE OF RECORDKEEPING

Not enough can be said about the need to keep a comprehensive and careful medical chart for each resident. A clear, comprehensive, understandable, chronological narrative of a resident's condition and all the care that has been delivered to that resident tells a compelling story of what care was necessary and when and why. Such a record pre-empts any suggestion that anything happened other than exactly what appears in the record.

Of course, there are legal and ethical issues concerning the obligation of keeping accurate charts and entries on the delivery of care. Those issues are beyond the scope of this chapter. Here we will address why precise, legible, consistent records are important tools in depriving a plaintiff's attorney of ammunition in a malpractice action.

In investigating a claim for malpractice, the attorney always makes a review of the relevant medical records one of the initial parts of his or her analysis. The purpose of this is not only to learn the history of the client's care and medical condition but also to look "between the lines" of the records to see how competently that care has been delivered and recorded by the people responsible for the care.

It is said that history is not what has happened but rather what has been recorded as having happened. This is nowhere more true than in medical records. If the records are incomplete, spotty, illegible, or incomprehensible, a lawyer will be able to challenge any assertion by the health care provider that a certain event took place. Moreover, the lawyer will be able to point to the gaps in the legible record as indications of carelessness and may even try to impute that carelessness to the overall delivery of health care at the institution. Few things can seem more damning to a jury than a convincing argument to the effect that even the health care providers do not know exactly what happened during the period of time at issue.

It is vital that the administrator establish a standardized set of rules for the creation and maintenance of data in a medical chart. The requirements for the types of data kept will necessarily vary somewhat depending on the nature of the institution and the type of care being provided to the residents. However, certain basic rules ought to be included in any set of rules for keeping charts.

The records must be legible. This is not so that the lawyer reviewing the chart does not have to confront the notorious problem of trying to read photocopies of scrawled writing. Rather, it is so that a subsequent provider of some particular service can easily and quickly read and review the recent history on the resident's condition and care. It too often occurs that some act was taken because the provider misread what had been done before either for or with the resident. This compounds one negligent act with another and sets the stage for the suggestion to the jury that the institution is rife with carelessness.

One hears the comment, "Well, if I can read my writing in the record, that is good enough." It is not. Only the most vain of care providers would ever think that no one else will have need to read his or her notes or know what he or she did with or for a resident. An experienced personal injury lawyer, a paralegal, or a retained medical expert will be reviewing those records. If they have trouble reading and deciphering notations written by the provider, they will undoubtedly try to suggest, if not prove, that no provider could have read the handwriting, even the writer. Most people have experienced situations where they could not read something they wrote in a hurried scrawl some time before. It is not too hard to at least suggest that a provider's writing was partly indecipherable even to the provider. Illegible writing is not much better than no writing at all.

The records must be orderly. There must be a clear organizational scheme in place for how charts are ordered. New additions to the records must go where they are supposed to go, they must be added in a timely manner, and they must be put in their proper place immediately after creation. This may sound obvious, but it does happen that additions to a medical chart are not placed in their proper location as soon as they are created but are added at a later time. Sometimes a page gets lost, sometimes it gets put in the wrong place. Eventually it may be found and put in the right place. If some emergency occurs before that record is returned to its proper place, however, potentially important information will be missing that could affect a health care provider's evaluation of what to do in an emergency. Such a situation is indefensible and can be damning in a trial.

The records must be complete. This should go without saying, but attorneys often have the experience of hearing a nurse, for instance, say that some tasks or activities are not precisely reported in the records. The nurse then explains that they are not recorded because "they are always done the same way," or "they are the particular variations on the standard protocols that we follow in our wing." This leads to the suggestion that the people in charge of the institution are not actually in control. Worse, a lawyer can argue from this that the administration does not even really know exactly what is going on in the "front lines" of resident care.

Another problem with incomplete records is that they make it difficult to prove that something did not happen. Residents of long-term care facilities often "recall" certain things as having happened that either did not occur or that occurred at some other time. A resident might relate such a "memory" to family members or a lawyer. If the alleged event does not seem consistent with proper treatment, it might attract attention. The additional fact that the alleged event is not reflected in the record leads to suspicion and feeds a lawyer's interest in pursuing the matter further—just because he or she does not know exactly what further investigation might uncover. A complete record gives the lawyer this answer up front and takes away some of the motivation to dig further.

Finally, corrections to the record should be made but should be inserted in the chart at the points when the corrections are made. For example, if it is determined that there is an error in the past records, the correction should not be squeezed in at what would have been the correct location had the entry been timely. Rather, the correction should be entered, full size and without embarrassment, at the end of the chart at the time the correction is being made. The correct entry should of course make reference to the time and date where it ought to have been made. Also, there ought to be, at the proper time and date, a brief reference directing the reader to the later note. However, it is not acceptable to try to cram in the entire correct entry into the record at the place it originally should have been located.

There are several reasons for later placement. First, it shows that the institution acknowledges that mistakes in recordkeeping sometimes occur. That is a fact that will gain the institution substantial sympathy if it is admitted and will engender much distrust and doubt if it is denied. Second, it avoids the risk of a later-added note being incompletely written because there is not enough space on the original page to fit in everything that ought to be said. Third, it avoids disputes over when the later-added note was actually written. Putting the note at the end of the chart as it currently exists tells exactly when it was written. This helps personnel later remember exactly what information was available to them at any particular time as they made decisions about what treatment to provide. Perhaps more important, it helps avoid suggestions that the record for any particular time has been subsequently doctored.

A clean, crisp medical chart virtually denies the plaintiff's lawyer the opportunity to suggest indifferent or careless treatment of his or her client. It also mitigates any suggestion by the lawyer—even without solid proof—that "other things" were going on in the institution that contributed to or compounded the injury. And, to some minds, it shows that the institution cares about each and every resident to the extent that it wants to be sure to have the best possible running record of the resident's treatment and condition history, not only for posterity but also for any emergency situation, when the review of the chart will have to be fast and furious and under time constraints.

COMMUNICATION WITH STAFF

All of the formal requirements for recordkeeping and other protocols will not be enough if the administration does not communicate on a regular basis with the staff. Communication with the staff should include extensive discussions on recordkeeping. These discussions should not be restricted to explaining what to do or how to do it. They should also include repeated explanations as to why detailed, clear, accurate recordkeeping is important.

The staff should be made aware of the goals and philosophy of the institution. They must understand that attention to detail at every level and in every activity helps produce and maintain high levels of quality in the delivery of services and good morale, both among the staff and among the resident population. They must also understand that good morale supports a good reputation and breeds success—success in which every staff member can share, both emotionally and financially.

Good morale will serve the institution well if and when a possible lawsuit is being investigated or pursued. It minimizes the risk of discontented employees who could provide ammunition for the lawyer's guns. Contented employees, especially those who feel they have a personal stake in the reputation and success of their workplace, are much less likely to give testimony that is critical of the procedures followed at that workplace. They are also more likely to attend to little details. Those details can seem like a burden to do, but they are vital. Their omission may provide the plaintiff's lawyer with the opportunity to point at myriad examples of "lack of attention to detail," which could raise doubts about the quality of every service provided.

The administration must communicate the importance of good recordkeeping. It is not enough merely to state in the abstract that records are important and should be meticulously kept. The administration must demonstrate care and concern in concrete ways. It should routinely pull charts randomly and review them using all the criteria discussed above. The staff should be informed that particular records are being reviewed. If the reviewers find the records well done, they should tell the appropriate staff members. If the records are somehow deficient, the reviewers should cite the specific deficiencies and offer suggestions for improvement.

When a high-level administrator does this kind of reviewing, it sends a strong message to front-line personnel that quality counts in the institution. The same effect cannot be obtained if only immediate supervisors review charts. If the staff knows the administration cares and is looking at their work, they will strive to improve their work product. This serves to improve the quality of service delivered to the residents. It helps reduce the likelihood of error. It builds an environment that will give a lawyer the least opportunity to find problems that could enhance his or her attempts to portray the institution as careless and prone to error.

COMMUNICATION WITH RESIDENTS AND FAMILIES

It is frequently commented upon in legal circles that lack of communication with patients, or even perceived lack of communication, is one of the most significant factors contributing to the bringing of malpractice lawsuits. A long-term care resident who feels that he or she was not adequately consulted or kept informed is much more likely to want to prosecute a lawsuit than one who feels warmly toward his or her health care provider.

Certainly communication alone is not going to fend off a lawsuit if there has been a major injury due to malpractice. Often, however, the harm is less than catastrophic, and the resident might not initially be sure he or she wants to pursue legal action. A feeling of "not being cared about properly" (as distinguished from not being cared for properly) may well be, for the resident, the deciding factor in whether to go ahead with legal action.

In most medical situations, but perhaps especially in the extended care situations, communication with the family of the patient is as critical as communication with the patient him- or herself. Family members often are the ones who decide whether legal action will follow an incident where some injury occurs. How they feel about the institution will influence the decision they ultimately reach.

It is vital, therefore, to cultivate a good relationship and good feelings with the families of residents. This requires work before as well as after any accident occurs.

Administrators should show personal interest in and awareness of each resident. Of course, to what extent this can be accomplished depends greatly on the dynamics and the size of the institution. It is not necessary for an administrator to meet with or talk to family members every time they come to the institution. Encourage staff personnel who have frequent direct contact with the resident to take aside a family member and to give an update on how the resident has been since the family's last visit. The administrator who can do this personally, even once or twice a year, can demonstrate a personalized commitment by the institution to the care of the resident. A perception by the family of that commitment may well determine whether a family comes to believe an injury was caused by an honest mistake (and is therefore forgivable) or was caused by unpardonable malpractice.

If an injury-causing accident has already happened, the administration should still communicate with the family and the resident. It is advisable not to try to hide anything that will likely be uncovered in an investigation. At the same time, it is advisable to be careful of what is said. The best strategy is to stick to statements of fact and to promises that the institution will do whatever can be done to rectify the situation.

If the administration acts as if there is something to hide, the resident or family will sense that. So will their lawyer. If the administration acts as if there is nothing to hide, it can dull the suspicions that will encourage a lawyer or his or her client to move toward litigation.

No one—not a jury, not an insurance adjuster, not an experienced personal injury lawyer—expects that all health care services can always be delivered without error. Mistakes happen. Everyone realizes that. People are willing to make allowances and to forgive mistakes made in good faith. It is the compounding events and circumstances that often generate a disposition to pursue litigation.

The more culpable a lawyer thinks he or she can make an institution or a health care provider look, the more likely the lawyer is to think a lawsuit will probably be successful. The lawyer will convey this opinion to the client, and it will be all the harder to settle a valid claim or to fend off a dubious one without a lawsuit. The less forthcoming the institution is, the more suspicious the resident or family will be—and the more likely they will be to consider litigation to "get to the bottom" of the situation.

If the institution has already set the tone by convincing the resident or family that it does its best to keep them informed and to treat them as partners in the health care program, the institution's after-incident efforts will be all the more fruitful.

CONCLUSION

It is impossible to avoid all litigation. If there has been an injury caused by negligence, a basis exists for a claim for damages. If the injured party and the wrongdoer (or the wrongdoer's insurer) cannot agree on fair compensation, the typical result is a trial. The more serious the injury, the larger the claim and the more likely that litigation will ensue.

Similarly, where there exists a strong difference of opinion as to whether an injury has been committed by the wrongful act of a health care provider, litigation is the ultimate means of deciding the issue. Some lawyers prefer to put their clients' claims into suit early rather than trying to resolve the claims without resort to litigation. There is little that can be done to fend off lawsuits in those situations.

However, there are ways to avoid litigation. The best strategy is to ensure that care and attention to detail become part of the routine way things are done. If that can be done, the lawyer of any potential plaintiff will be denied the kind of materiel that can turn a simple case into a complex and more damaging one. In essence, the institution engages in a form of damage control in advance. The result, hopefully, will be the avoidance of litigation, its cost, and the attendant bad publicity.

Chapter 37

Planning Long-Term Care Services: A Guide for Acute Care Hospitals

Cathy Sullivan Clark and Susanna E. Krentz

New service development in hospitals in recent years has focused to a great extent on nonacute care programs. The development of such programs has helped to stem the flow of business away from the hospitals as their acute care volumes have dwindled. Among the services frequently developed is the entire array of long-term care services. These services are particularly attractive given an aging average national population.

Under the Medicare prospective payment system for inpatient care, hospitals face strong economic incentives for the early discharge of elderly patients. Yet, given the complexity of elderly patients' illnesses and the fact that many older persons do not have adequate support at home, it is often difficult to discharge these patients directly from an acute care setting to home. Arranging for support services may be equally difficult, due to an insufficient supply or a complete lack of the needed services.

By developing long-term care services, hospitals can guarantee that appropriate after-care services are available, better meeting patient needs while at the same time freeing up acute care resources for more appropriate uses and controlling patient care costs.

THE CONTINUUM OF LONG-TERM CARE SERVICES

While many acute care hospitals may be interested in developing long-term care services, individual hospitals are likely to vary significantly in terms of the specific long-term care services they ultimately develop. Long-term care refers to a continuum of services, ranging from intermittent ambulatory services to institutionally based services offered on a 24-hour basis:

Source: Reprinted from *Topics in Health Care Financing,* Vol. 17, No. 4, pp. 73–82, Aspen Publishers, Inc., © 1991.

- ambulatory and home care services
  - — home health care, durable medical equipment
  - — homemaker and chore services
  - — adult day care
  - — meals programs, personal emergency response systems
- Linkages and assessment services
  - — assessment services, case management
  - — follow-up and evaluation
- Institutional and housing services
  - — nursing home care (custodial, intermediate, skilled)
  - — independent and assisted living
  - — respite care
  - — inpatient hospice

The choice of a specific service will depend on the particular strengths and resources of a hospital and the unique market conditions facing it.

Persons with long-term illnesses are likely to move along the long-term care continuum over time, requiring different types of care during various stages of their diseases. Individual long-term care services may be provided on a stand-alone basis by a hospital or may be combined to facilitate continuity of care.

PLANNING LONG-TERM CARE SERVICES: STEPS IN THE PROCESS

This chapter provides a framework for planning long-term care services. The steps in the planning process are briefly described. A case study example follows that provides important lessons regarding how and how not to plan for long-term care services.

Regardless of the type of long-term care services being considered for development, the steps in planning are the same. They include development of a market assessment and development of a feasibility assessment. Each of these is described in more detail in the sections that follow.

Development of a Market Assessment

A market assessment for any new long-term care service typically includes four components:

1. delineation of service area
2. demographic and socioeconomic profile
3. competitor profile
4. regulatory review

The market assessment is undertaken with the goal of answering this question: Does a need exist for an additional program of this kind in our market? To answer this question, the potential market size for the new service must be determined, based on the delineation of a service area and the completion of a demographic and socioeconomic profile. This is followed by the development of a competitor profile and a regulatory review, both of which help in assessing the case with which a new participant can enter the market for a particular service.

The service area should represent the geographic region from which the majority of the program patients are expected to be drawn. The hospital's service area for acute care can be used as the starting point for defining the service area for a new program. However, the service area for the new service will not necessarily be identical to the hospital's existing service area, nor will the service areas for all long-term care services be the same.

Once a service area has been defined for a new program, a demographic and socioeconomic profile should be completed. This provides valuable information for the estimation of the potential market size for the service. The demographic and socioeconomic profile might include

- current and projected population by age and gender
- distribution of target population by living arrangement (e.g., living alone, living with spouse)
- median household income of target population
- distribution of households within target population by household income
- functional abilities (e.g., bathing, dressing, getting outside) of target population

A full range of demographic information is typically available from both demographic and market research firms. Information regarding functional limitations (at a national level) can be obtained from the National Center for Health Statistics and combined with service area demographic data to develop area-specific estimates of functional abilities.

The data gathered as part of the demographic and socioeconomic profile are critical inputs for the determination of market size for a proposed new program. Statistics regarding population size, living arrangements, and functional abilities are useful in projecting the number of individuals who could potentially benefit from the new service. Household income statistics are useful in estimating the degree to which the target population can afford to pay for poorly covered or non-covered services. Because long-term care insurance is not readily available, many long-term care services will need to be supported entirely by direct payments from patients.

The next component of the market assessment is the competitor profile. Through the competitor profile, the hospital can gain an understanding regarding capacity of existing services and, subsequently, can develop reasonable estimates of utilization for a proposed new program. The competitor profile can also provide insight regarding what features are likely to be most attractive to patients and can assist in evaluating the relative desirability of competing in a given market.

At a minimum, a competitor profile should include all similar programs within the defined service area. Programs located near but not within the service area should also be profiled if they draw significantly from the potential service area. A typical competitor profile might include the following for each program:

- location
- ownership
- number of years in operation
- program capacity
- program volume
- patient mix (age, place of residence, payer mix)
- range of services offered
- fee schedule
- financial performance
- reputation or current satisfaction level of users

To a great extent, the actual content of the competitor profile depends on what data are available. However, even in the absence of public information, a comprehensive competitor profile can be gleaned from personal interviews with medical staff and other individuals (both inside and outside the hospital) familiar with the local long-term care market. Community service directories published by local social service agencies often provide an excellent foundation for the development of a competitor profile.

The final step in the development of a market assessment is the identification of regulatory barriers to entry. The most common of these are certificate-of-need (CON) regulations and licensure requirements. CON regulations, which still exist in many states, typically apply to inpatient services (especially nursing home services) as well as to all classes of services requiring capital expenditures in excess of a predetermined amount. Depending on the service under consideration, licensure requirements may affect such aspects of the program as facility design, quality assurance, and staffing. When regulatory barriers exist, the likelihood, timing, and associated cost of obtaining regulatory approval for the proposed program must be included in the market assessment. An otherwise attractive program for which regulatory approval is not likely to be easily or inexpensively obtained might be abandoned in favor of an alternative service to which stringent or costly regulatory requirements do not apply.

Development of a Feasibility Assessment

The purpose of the market assessment is to determine whether a need exists for a particular program or service; the goal of the internal feasibility assessment is to determine whether a particular organization should respond to the market opportunity. The feasibility assessment includes two major components, projections of utilization and projections of most likely financial impact.

Based on the total potential market size for a proposed program or service, projections of utilization for the planned program can be developed. Because the goal of many hospital-sponsored long-term care services is to guarantee appropriate and adequate after-care services for acute care patients, existing hospital records can provide valuable information regarding the likely utilization of new long-term care services. Personal interviews with likely referral services can also provide an excellent foundation for the development of reasonable and achievable utilization projections. These might include interviews with such diverse individuals as representatives of the local council on aging, physicians, representatives of caregiver support groups, local clergy, and employees of the human resource departments of local businesses. For services whose supply is regulated, such as nursing home services, input from government planning or approval agencies can also prove useful.

The feasibility assessment for any potential new program or service would be incomplete without a projection of the program's most likely financial impact. This requires both the projection of revenues and the estimation of development and operating expenses. To accurately estimate the incremental financial impact of a proposed new service, only incremental costs should be considered. Fixed costs, such as overhead, that might be reallocated among services as a result of a new program but will not change in total should be ignored. In general, financial projections should be developed for a three- to five-year period for all potential new programs to accurately account for startup costs, increasing third-party contractual allowances, and the learning curve. The projections of revenues and expenses for a potential service are combined to develop a pro forma income statement. The results of the pro forma statement can then be used to calculate key financial ratios for the program, including operating margin, return on investment, and debt service coverage.

Projections of the most likely financial impact of a proposed long-term care service represent only the first step of the financial assessment. An equally important step involves the development of sensitivity analyses. Through sensitivity analysis, key assumptions to the financial forecast can be varied individually to assess the impact on overall financial performance of failure to achieve each assumption. As such, the results of sensitivity analysis can aid in evaluating the level of risk associated with developing individual long-term care services.

CASE STUDY: COMMUNITY HOSPITAL

In its recently completed strategic plan, Community Hospital identified the development of long-term care services as a top priority. For several reasons, key members of the hospital's board of trustees were particularly interested in both nursing home services and congregate housing, to be provided at the hospital's existing facility. For the last several years, the hospital had very successfully operated 20 of its licensed beds as swing beds. Recent increases in demand for acute care services, however, coupled with reimbursement incentives to reduce length of stay, led the board to consider the development of a dedicated nursing home. At the same time, members of the hospital's finance department were concerned about the operating efficiency of certain support areas at the hospital, such as dietary services, and were looking for ways to maximize the use of existing capacity. They suggested congregate housing, both as a strategy for achieving the strategic plan objective regarding long-term care and as a means for improving productivity. A management task force was convened and charged with responsibility for investigating the market feasibility of developing either nursing home services or congregate housing or both. Based on the results of the market studies, the board hoped to determine whether the hospital should proceed with the development of financial forecasts for the potential new services.

The task force first determined service areas for the potential new programs. Because the nursing home was intended primarily to provide care to patients referred from the hospital, its service area was defined as the hospital's primary service area based on current patient origin data. This included five zip code areas south of the hospital. The communities immediately north of the hospital, which were not included in the service area, were generally acknowledged to be adequately served by nursing homes already located in these northern communities.

The potential service area for congregate housing was defined on the basis of distance rather than hospital use patterns. This was consistent with the experience of existing congregate living facilities, which had found that the majority of individuals interested in congregate living were not willing to relocate. The potential service area for congregate housing at Community Hospital was defined as the entire region within a ten-mile radius of the hospital. This service area included part of the service area for the nursing home as well as portions of communities to the north of the hospital not included in the nursing home service area.

Having defined the potential service areas for the two programs, the task force continued with the development of service area demographic and socioeconomic profiles. The results of these analyses are summarized in Table 37-1. While the results of the market profiles confirmed many of the hypotheses management had regarding the potential service areas, the task force was surprised to learn that over 50 percent of the elderly households in both service areas had annual incomes of less than $15,000. This was potentially worrisome, knowing that a congregate housing facility would need to be supported entirely by payments from residents themselves, as third-party coverage would not be available.

Armed with the results of the demographic and socioeconomic profiles, the task force set out to complete perhaps the most important pieces of the market assessments: projections of need and likely utilization. Exhibits 37-1 and 37-2 provide estimates of need for additional nursing home services and congregate housing in their respective service areas. Ability to pay was a key determinant of the size of the total market for congregate housing. In this case, the potential market was defined to include all households with a head of household 70 years of age or older (the population most likely to use congregate housing) and with an annual income between $20,000 and $30,000. The targeted income range was determined based on the estimated monthly rental fee for the proposed congregate housing. Use of both a minimum income level and an income ceiling to narrow the target population guaranteed a relatively homogeneous resident population for the proposed facility, a condition that existing sponsors of congregate housing had found to be essential.

Members of the task force were pleased to find that some need existed locally for both nursing home services and congregate housing, although they conceded

Table 37-1 Results of Demographic and Socioeconomic Profile

Criterion	Nursing Home Service Area	Congregate Housing Service Area
Population and Households		
1990 Population, 65+ Years	5,460	9,843
Forecast Change in 65+ Population, 1990–1995	15.1%	20.2%
1990 Households, with Head of Household 70+ Years	2,087	3,829
Distribution of Elderly Households by Household Income, 1990		
<$15,000	61.8%	54.7%
$15,000–$19,999	11.3%	12.7%
$20,000–$24,999	8.1%	9.5%
$25,000–$29,999	5.0%	5.8%
$30,000–$34,999	3.4%	3.6%
$35,000–$49,999	6.4%	6.9%
$50,000+	4.0%	6.8%

Exhibit 37-1 Estimated Nursing Home Beds Needed in 1990

Service area population, 65+ years	5,460
Beds needed per 1,000 population	36.9
Total beds needed for service area residents	201
Less existing beds in service area	130
Net beds needed for service area residents	71
Plus beds needed for patients from outside service area	18[*]
Total net beds needed	89

[*]Assumes 20 percent of beds will be filled by individuals from outside the primary service area.

Exhibit 37-2 Estimated Need for Congregate Housing in 1990

Service area households with head of household 70+ years	3,829
Percent of households with annual income of $20,000–$30,000	15.3%
Total potential market, number of households	585
Estimated penetration rate	5.0%[*]
Estimated need, number of units	29
Existing service area capacity—number of units	19
Net need, number of units	10

[*]Industry standard.

that the net need for additional congregate housing was probably insufficient to warrant investment in this area. A special session of the Community Hospital's board of trustees was called to review the results of the market feasibility analyses developed by the management task force. Based on these analyses, the board authorized the development of financial forecasts for a 60-bed nursing home but decided not to pursue the development of congregate housing services. The decision not to develop congregate housing was based only partly on the findings of the market assessment. Members of the board also recognized that success in congregate housing would require expertise in real estate development and management, an expertise that did not exist among the hospital's management team.

The hospital's financial staff began the work of developing financial projections for a proposed nursing home facility. Based on the results of its competitor profile, they assumed the following regarding utilization at the new facility:

- an overall occupancy rate of 96 percent
- allocation of 85 percent of beds for intermediate care, with the remaining 15 percent for skilled nursing care
- a resident mix of 68 percent Medicaid-covered and 32 percent self-pay

While the task of developing financial projections was certainly not new to the finance department, members of the department soon learned that they knew relatively little about nursing home operations and could not easily make assumptions regarding the financial performance of a nursing home facility based on their own hospital experience. To avoid major errors in assumptions, the task force interviewed representatives of both existing similar programs and major third-party payers. The purpose of the interviews was twofold: to test the reasonableness of assumptions regarding revenues and expenses, and to identify likely future changes in either payments or costs.

As a result of its interviews, the task force avoided many common mistakes in developing financial forecasts for long-term care services. The task force found, for example, that assumptions regarding revenue were too optimistic, both underestimating the potential bad debt attributable to private-pay patients and overestimating reimbursement from third parties, particularly in the later years of the forecasts. Based on the interviews, the task force also greatly modified its initial projections of salaries and benefits expenses. In particular, the original staffing assumptions for the new facility, while reasonable for acute care services, were found to be much too generous given both the level of care needed by nursing home residents and the level of reimbursement available for such services. In retrospect, all members of the task force recognized how important their interviews with outside sources had been in developing reasonable financial forecasts. On several occasions, they reflected on how far wrong they could have been in their projections had they not relied on experts for guidance. In fact, the exercise of developing projections served as an important lesson for the group regarding the relative risk of the proposed project for the hospital.

The task force did use the hospital's prior experience as a basis for developing expense estimates for the proposed project. Because the new nursing home was planned to use certain ancillary services at the hospital, such as medical records, dietary services, and laundry and linen, forecasts of expenses for these areas were based on existing departmental cost data. The costs of program development, including preplanning costs, site preparation, construction, and equipment, were based on quotes from potential contractors and vendors. Depreciation expense was calculated based on industry-standard estimated useful lives of all depreciable assets. Assumptions regarding the terms of debt, planned to be used to partially finance the project, were made consistent with the terms of existing debt held by the hospital.

Table 37-2 summarizes the calculations used to forecast net revenue for the nursing home for the first full year of operation. The forecast for year 1 staffing and salary expenses for the proposed nursing home are provided in Table 37-3. Table 37-4 provides a summary of the assumptions used to project nonsalary expenses for year 1.

The projected revenues and expenses for the proposed nursing home, provided in Table 37-5, were presented to the board along with a recommendation that the hospital pursue the development of a 60-bed facility. While the initial planning

Table 37-2 Net Revenue Forecasts for Year 1

Level of Care	Payer	Average Daily Census	Forecast per Diem Revenue	Forecast Daily Revenue
Intermediate	Medicaid	33.3	$50.38	$1,677.65
	Private pay	15.6	$73.60	1,148.16
Skilled	Medicaid	5.9	$90.00	531.00
	Private pay	2.8	$90.00	252.00
Total		57.6		$3,608.81
Number of days per year				365
Total annual net revenue				$1,317,216

Table 37-3 Forecast Staffing and Salary Expenses for Year 1

Position	Full-Time Equivalents (FTEs)	Salary Expense per FTE	Total Salary Expenses
Administrator	1.0	$45,000	$ 45,000
Medical consultant	0.3	$60,000	18,000
Registered nurse	5.0	$26,500	132,500
Nurse's aide	13.5	$13,000	175,500
Activity therapist	1.0	$22,000	22,000
Dietitian	1.0	$40,000	40,000
Dietary aide	4.0	$13,000	52,000
Housekeeper	1.0	$11,500	11,500
Maintenance worker	0.5	$18,500	9,250
Total salary expenses			$505,750
Fringe benefits as percent of salary expense			x 20.0
Fringe benefit expenses			$101,150
Total salary and benefit expenses			$606,900

process had taken six months and a substantial amount of staff time to complete, members of the board of trustees agreed that the time and effort were well spent. The board voted to allocate the necessary capital resources to the proposed nursing home project, confident that the risks associated with development were reasonable in light of the expected future benefits.

CONCLUSION

Although the case study presented in this article focuses on only two long-term care services, the range of services that might be developed by an acute care hos-

Table 37-4 Nonsalary Expense Assumptions for Year 1

Category	Assumption
Patient Care Supplies	$2.43 per patient-day
Ancillary Services	$1.79 per patient-day
Maintenance	$1.23 per gross square foot
Laundry and Linen	$2.53 per patient-day
Housekeeping	$0.56 per gross square foot
Dietary	$8.73 per patient-day
Utilities	$3.89 per gross square foot
Insurance	$500 per bed
Administration	$7,000 fixed expense
Bad Debt	13.4% of private-pay revenues

Table 37-5 Pro Forma Income Statement for Year 1

Category	Projection
Net Revenue	$1,317,216
Operating Expenses	
Salaries and Benefits	$ 606,900
Patient Care Supplies	51,088
Ancillary Services	37,633
Maintenance	18,450
Laundry and Linen	53,191
Housekeeping	8,400
Dietary	183,540
Utilities	58,350
Insurance	30,000
Administration	7,000
Bad Debt	68,538
Depreciation	80,226
Interest	65,475
Total Operating Expenses	$1,268,791
Excess of Revenue over Expenses	$ 48,425

pital is broad. While individual hospitals may be interested in developing any number of these at one time, a lack of resources internally may dictate that they must choose among the desired programs. The steps described in this chapter provide a framework for making such choices, as they constitute a common set of evaluation questions that can be used regardless of the service being considered. For most hospitals, the initiative for the development of long-term care services will result from the strategic planning process. However, practical decisions regarding how best to enter the long-term care market must result from a more analytical framework, such as the one described here.

Chapter 38

Contract Facility Management in Long-Term Care

Susan S. Bailis and Alan D. Solomont

In the increasingly complex and competitive U.S. health care environment, providers of all kinds agree on the need for better facility management practices. The question is whether to develop management expertise internally or to purchase it from outside sources. Hospitals have been grappling with this question since the 1970s, and now long-term care facilities are facing it as well. This chapter explores contract management in long-term care. Although both hospitals and nursing homes may contract for services on a departmental basis—particularly in the areas of housekeeping and dietary services—the discussion below focuses on full-service contract management, an arrangement in which day-to-day administrative responsibilities for a facility are assumed by a separate management organization, which reports to the facility's owner or board of directors and may hire key personnel. Under contract management, the owner sets policy for the managed facility and continues to have legal responsibility.[1]

BACKGROUND

Like so much else in contemporary health care, contract management in long-term care is a relatively recent phenomenon. Changes in demographics, medical care, and public policy have all contributed to the new long-term care landscape. Simply stated, more people are living longer, and these older people increasingly experience chronic illness and disability requiring long-term care.[2] At the same time, all aspects of health care delivery—clinical, administrative, regulatory, financial—have become more complex. With only scarce resources available for long-term care, all providers face the intractable reality of these conditions. Some independent providers have continued to operate nursing homes by developing skills internally in an attempt to adapt to new conditions, while others have sold their facilities to multifacility organizations known as nursing home chains. For others, contract management has been the solution to today's increasingly challenging environment.

Prior to the enactment of Medicare and Medicaid in 1965, long-term care was an individual matter.[3] Most elderly people were cared for at home by their families. Those who had access to extended care outside their families' homes found it in "rest homes" or "homes for the aged." These facilities tended to be nonprofit homes run by religious or charitable organizations as part of their missions. There were also some public facilities, often for military veterans, and some proprietary, owner-operated homes. With the introduction of the Medicare and Medicaid programs providing public payment for the care of the elderly, many proprietary rest homes were converted into nursing homes. The proprietary sector grew as the availability of public payment attracted small business people to the nursing home industry. Many new nursing homes were "Mom and Pop" operations— where "Mom" was a nurse and "Pop" served as the business manager.

At the same time that the nursing home landscape was becoming populated with proprietary facilities, the concept of contract management was developing in hospitals. Prior to the enactment of Medicare and Medicaid, most hospitals were voluntary nonprofits, public institutions, or owned by a group of physicians. In response to these new programs, however, investor-owned hospitals grew rapidly. In the recession of the 1970s, these investor-owned hospitals sought new markets for their administrative skills, a market that they found in contract management.[4]

Concurrently, hospitals began to see contract management as a solution for a variety of reasons. As an organizational structure, it offered relative ease of implementation. To a large proportion of mission-directed, nonprofit and public hospitals, it guaranteed continued autonomy and board control. A study conducted in the mid-1980s revealed the distinguishing characteristics of hospitals entering into contract management arrangements. While the study found that hospitals of all ownership types were equally likely to enter into contract management agreements, there were other identifying variables. Small rural hospitals were drawn to full-service contract management, especially in the Southeast, Great Plains, and West. More recently, large urban hospitals have looked to contract management as a way to respond to a difficult market. Although contract management may have been especially appealing to small rural hospitals from the beginning, the traditionally more stable contingent of large urban hospitals has been buffeted by increasing competition and changes in reimbursement. While this shakeout occurred, there was a tremendous growth in hospitals under contract management—the number of contract-managed hospitals grew at a 20–35 percent annual rate from the mid-1970s to the early 1980s.[5]

Nursing homes were also changing in the 1970s and 1980s. Spurred on by the demand for long-term care services resulting from changes in demographics and medical care and by the availability of reimbursement, the nursing home business has grown into a $53.1 billion industry with more than 1.6 million beds.[6] To continue to expand in the more complicated health care environment, the developing nursing home industry found itself in need of both capital and management expertise. National chains sprang up to meet both the capital and management needs, providing economies of scale by purchasing many small providers. Examples include Beverly Enterprises and The Hillhaven Corporation, the two largest nursing home ownership chains in the industry. These and other chains supplied both capital and management together with the benefits of economies of scale. In the economic downturn at the beginning of the 1990s, however, purchases of nursing homes slowed, making contract management an attractive option to owners who might once have sold to a chain.[7]

For nonprofit and government-owned nursing homes, contract management has historically provided an alternative to ownership by a national chain. Contract management separates management and capital, an arrangement suited to these types of nursing homes, which have different capital needs than the proprietary sector while sharing the need for better management. Although the nonprofits control a much smaller share of the nursing home industry than proprietary nursing homes, they make up a significant sector, increasingly buttressed by the strong entry hospitals themselves have made into long-term care.

Hospitals were drawn to long-term care for a variety of reasons—the widespread shortage of nursing home beds in the mid-1980s, reimbursement requirements leading to earlier discharge of patients, and competitive pressures to diversify their services into a full continuum of care. Hospitals first purchased existing nursing homes, later began to build them, and most recently moved to the conversion of acute care beds into skilled nursing beds. Currently in Massachusetts, 20 hospitals (14 percent of the total number in the state) own or have other formal affiliations with long-term care facilities. Nationwide, the 1990 AHA Survey indicates that 238 responding hospitals reported ownership of a total of 112 long-term care units.[8]

The entry of hospitals into long-term care presents the greatest opportunity for contract management in the nursing home industry. The reason is twofold: with nearly two decades of experience to draw on, the hospital industry is familiar with contract management, and, increasingly, hospitals are aware that long-term care is a separate part of the health care business that requires specialized expertise.[9] In the long-term care environment, reimbursement is quite different and localized, regulation is more detailed, average length of stay is greater, margins are smaller, resources are in much shorter supply, and skilled nursing is the basis of the clinical program. In fact, hospital contract managers are reluctant to branch out into long-term care because of these factors.

CONTRACT MANAGEMENT OPERATIONS

When a nursing home decides to enter into a contract management agreement, the key issues between owner and manager center on striking an equitable balance between responsibility and control. Any contractual agreement between these two parties must address duties, authority, and risk as well as specifying the duration of the agreement, circumstances for its termination, and the manager's compensation. There is no one formula for all situations. The manager's authority tends to be greater if the facility is in distress, if the owner lacks long-term care experience, or if the facility is a passive investment.[10]

The most important lesson for the management company is that the fundamental charge is not only managing the facility but simultaneously managing the relationship with the owner. To be successful, the manager must understand the goals of ownership, which may in some ways compete with typical business goals. The manager needs to approach each situation individually, recognizing differences among owners. Although all owners are looking for expert financial management, the nonprofit sector in particular is seeking management congruent with mission; for the manager, the ability to express the values of the owner, combined with management skill, becomes critically important.

Duties

The management agreement sets forth the manager's duties in order to provide for all essential services and to minimize the potential for later disputes between owner and manager. Under a contract management arrangement, the management company reports to the nursing home's owner and board. Although operating under the directives of the owner and the board, the manager must have clear responsibility for day-to-day management. The management agreement may include a provision that the manager follow the policies and provisions of the owner but that the manager exercise reasonable judgment where no specific policies are set forth.

Authority

Critical issues of authority include budgeting, reporting, contracting with third parties, spending, and personnel.

Budgeting. The budgeting process helps the owner and manager define common financial goals. The management agreement needs to establish budgeting authority; typically, management prepares the budget for the owner's review.

Reporting. Financial and operational information needs to be reported on a timely and accurate basis, and management should be sure that its reports serve the owner's needs and work with the owner's established systems. Reporting promotes good internal controls and helps identify potential areas for improvement.

Third-Party Contracting. The agreement should set forth the manager's authority for third-party contracting. Both the manager and owner must recognize that they have existing relationships with attorneys, accountants, insurers, and ancillary providers; the management company itself may offer ancillary services. Selection of third-party vendors and professionals should be made to best serve the facility.

Spending. Which name—the manager's, the owner's, or the facility's—is on the bank account, and which party controls access? The agreement must also establish acceptable spending limits and provisions for emergency expenditures.

Personnel. Oversight of key personnel may be dealt with in a variety of ways according to individual conditions. In general, the most effective contract management results when the manager hires, supervises, and compensates the administrator. This personnel authority many extend to other key personnel, such as the controller or director of nursing. The management agreement should contain a provision regarding retention of the administrator in the case of termination of management services.

Risk

Insurance provisions address the question of which party is responsible for which risks. Legally, the owner is the licensee and therefore the provider; the manager is working on the owner's behalf. In fact, the manager also has exposure to risk. It is the province of the manager to see that appropriate insurance is obtained and maintained, paid for by the owner. The policies should cover the manager as an additional insured, and the management agreement should specify that the owner and insurer notify the manager prior to the cancellation of any insurance coverage.

Business Issues: Term and Compensation Provisions

No set standard exists for the length of management terms. The term needs to be long enough for progress to be made and measured—three- and five-year tenures are common. The agreement should spell out termination provisions for each party. Compensation may also be handled in a variety of ways, depending on attitudes of risk and reward on the part of both the manager and the owner. Arrangements may include a percentage of revenue, a flat fee, or a fee with an incentive provision. The federal tax code does contain restrictions on incentive compensation for a for-profit manager of a nonprofit nursing home. Because Medicaid and Medicare play such an important role in nursing home administration, it should be noted that contract management is affected by these programs. Medicaid reimbursement regulations vary from state to state.

THE REAL WORLD OF CONTRACT MANAGEMENT

In examining trends and issues in contract management, it is possible to forget that they are derived from circumstances and decisions ultimately involving individual elderly and disabled people. To explore what contract management can mean in the actual practice of delivering long-term care, it is necessary to examine some actual cases.

Each of the cases sketched here is part of the experience of The A/D/S Group, a Massachusetts long-term care company that has grown out of a family-owned set of proprietary nursing homes. The experience of the family-owned nursing homes over the past 30 years helped build specialized nursing home management skills as the industry itself matured. In 1985, The A/D/S Group began to offer those skills to other providers and has managed more than 20 facilities. Due to the company's geographic focus, all of the cases that follow are drawn from Massachusetts, but the lessons they illustrate are more broadly applicable.

An Inner-City Nursing Home: Ethnic Issues and Labor Strife

In response to a clear need for services in the minority community in the 1920s, African-Americans opened a home for the elderly in a predominantly minority area of Boston. Owned by a nonprofit organization, this home served its community steadily until the 1970s, when expansion, regulatory problems, and labor strife combined to create nearly two decades of severe trouble.

In 1970, the board approved the demolition of the original building to make way for a new 240-bed facility. By the middle of the decade, the nursing home was facing financial and managerial problems, and the quality of care was significantly diminished. At the same time, the home faced its first union organizing drive, among its service workers. By 1979, conditions had deteriorated so far that the home lost its Medicaid certification and was placed in the protection of a court-appointed receiver who lacked health care experience but had the trust of the African-American community. To manage the facility, the receiver designated a major Boston teaching hospital with sound geriatric services but no nursing home management experience. The nursing home board, anxious to protect the facility's identification with the minority community, placed restrictions on the hospital's management authority.

Throughout the 1980s, the nursing home remained in receivership and experienced multiple problems, including Medicaid decertification, two more union organizing drives, and a bitter strike. The three-week strike, which took place in

1987, debilitated the weak home. Morale plunged and antipathy burgeoned as the service workers ended up settling for the original management offer and returned to work for administrators who had struggled to keep the home open with no reward for their efforts. Further, the resident census was diminished beyond recovery during the strike, as admissions were frozen and the most frail patients were relocated.

By late 1989, the Massachusetts Department of Public Health was visiting on almost a daily basis, the prospect of decertification again loomed, and the facility was hemorrhaging financially, losing more than $1 million for the year. In a desperate effort to keep the nursing home open, the receiver decided to bring in a specialist in nursing home management. Aggressively implementing new systems and redeploying personnel, The A/D/S Group was able to address the quality of care issues and stop the financial loss. In 1992, the nursing home emerged from the receivership it had entered 12 years earlier. Although labor issues persist—including a ten-day strike in 1992—a labor-management committee is now in place and both sides are working to achieve stability in labor relations while operating without financial losses. Contract management has played a significant role in stabilizing a facility whose ongoing mission is servicing elderly residents of the minority community.

A Hospital Seeks Vertical Integration through Acquisition

In the late 1960s, a new proprietary nursing home opened its doors in an affluent Boston suburb. For a time, it flourished. By the mid-1980s, however, the nursing home was facing stiff competition, a nursing shortage, and a tight market for service workers; the family ownership decided to sell. They found a ready buyer in a hospital eager to expand into the long-term care field. The hospital, located in a largely working class neighborhood of Boston that abuts the suburban community, wanted to expand its market to a new, more upscale area. The hospital was confident in its decision, because three years earlier it had made a successful initial foray into the long-term care field by purchasing a stable nursing home in its own traditional market area.

The hospital's confidence proved to be ill-founded. In its desire to expand, it acquired a nursing home that had begun to deteriorate and needed significant investment to correct deferred maintenance needs, frayed staff relationships, and patient care problems. The hospital would find operating a troubled nursing home a very different proposition from running a successful, stable facility. Moreover, the hospital, in its enthusiasm to attain vertical integration, had miscalculated fundamental issues in strategic planning and marketing. Its clinical staff and patients were strongly focused on Boston neighborhoods, not the new suburb; the hospital's physicians had never seen the suburban home as a preferred location home for their patients, and the hospital's ownership did not change their attitude. The more serious miscalculation, however, was the hospital's belief that it could penetrate a competitive acute care market through nursing home ownership. The revenue stream flows from hospital to nursing home, and in any case the nursing home had firmly established admitting relationships with other institutions. The hospital had also anticipated that the nursing home could maintain its traditional high private census, but the problems it was experiencing in management, maintenance, and labor made such a scenario impossible.

The nursing home became more and more troubled, encountering serious regulatory and quality of care difficulties. In 1987, a new administration at the hospital called on specialists to manage the nursing home. The strategy The A/D/S Group pursued depended on strong administration and a new heavy-care population with higher reimbursements related to the higher level of acuity. Together with this new patient population, A/D/S brought in a new management team to address regulatory problems. The situation turned around sufficiently for the hospital to sell the nursing home in 1992. The hospital is now concentrating its efforts in its primary market area in Boston, where it continues to operate its earlier acquisition, also under contract management.

A Hospital Builds a New Nursing Home: Planning from the Ground Up

For nearly a century, a community hospital served the health care needs of a town west of Boston. By the mid-1980s, the hospital, like so many others, was looking for a way to provide a multilevel system of care to its market area. A strategic planning study in 1986 identified elderly services as a need in the community, and the hospital explored developing both congregate housing and a long-term care facility, the latter a particular priority because of the critical shortage of nursing home beds in Massachusetts at the time. Abutter opposition soon quashed the congregate housing plans, but the community was enthusiastic about the nursing home.

The hospital decided to build a new nursing home immediately adjacent to the hospital on its wooded campus. The proximity of acute care services would prove to be a strong marketing benefit for the new facility. Although the hospital wanted to build, it did not wish to assume the entire risk of such an enterprise, and it went shopping for a joint venture partner both to share the risk and to manage the construction process. Understanding from the outset that nursing homes are a separate business and require specialized services that the hospital could not provide internally, the hospital stipulated that its joint venture partner have specific long-term care experience.

The A/D/S Group entered the project in a consulting role while the hospital sought a joint venture partner and initiated discussions with two potential partners. When both potential alliances fell through, the hospital analyzed the situation again and, determining that it could accomplish the project without an equity partner, engaged A/D/S as both the developer and eventual manager of the facility. This decision was crucial to the project's success, for knowing how the building will function once built is as important as knowing the development process. Having the manager involved as developer also helped ensure that the project would come in on budget—particularly important in this project because the hospital's board wanted to develop the nursing home essentially without the hospital's credit backing.

When the actual development process began, The A/D/S Group worked with the hospital and an oversight committee to assemble a development team, including an architect, an interior designer, and a construction company. The developer also advised the hospital on financing the $8 million project. This development was the first tax-exempt, stand-alone, hospital-sponsored nursing home project in Massachusetts. The developer advised, structured, and facilitated the financing, identifying both the issuer and underwriter.

In this case, the involvement of an outside company was critical to success. Although much of the hospital's energy was devoted to a merger with a nearby community hospital in the final months of construction, the nursing home opened on time and under budget in the spring of 1992. The project is a success because the hospital set overall direction and delegated implementation to the team of long-term care experts it had assembled to handle development.

CONCLUSION

Contract management is becoming increasingly significant in long-term care; its role is likely to grow as long as the factors that support it continue. These include the increased sophistication and cost of health care technology, the complexity and variability of reimbursement arrangements, the aging of the population, and the transfer of older and sicker patients to nursing homes. Also, hospitals are entering the long-term care field in greater numbers. Both control of costs and quality of care are necessary. All of these factors call for specialists in long-term care to manage nursing homes.

If contract management is here to stay, what are the conditions under which it can provide the greatest benefit? The most important factor is trust between owner and manager, fostered by the manager's sensitivity to each owner's individual situation and concerns. The owner must recognize that a specialist is needed. With direction from the owner and board, the manager needs sufficient authority to manage productively. Involving the manager as early as possible solves existing problems sooner and prevents potential problems from developing. This may be an ideal scenario for contract management, but the elderly and disabled deserve no less.

ACKNOWLEDGMENTS

The authors wish to thank the following people for contributing their insights to the preparation of this chapter: Jane Barry, Stephen Fraser, David Gottlieb, Richard Killigrew, Joanne Mukerjee, Karen Nemeth, Sarah Porter, Alan Rosenfeld, and Jonathan Truslow. Susan Geib provided research and editorial assistance. Staff at the American Health Care Association, American Hospital Association, Massachusetts Hospital Association, and National Health Lawyers Association were particularly helpful in locating information.

NOTES

1. J.M. Lowe, Contract Management of Health Care Facilities: Structural Models, *Health Care Management Review* 6, no. 4 (1981):18.

2. For an overview, see C.J. Evashwick and L.G. Branch, Clients of the Continuum of Care, in *Managing the Continuum of Care,* ed. C.J. Evashwick and L.J. Weiss (Gaithersburg, Md.: Aspen Publishers, 1987), 45–56.

3. For an overview, see C.L. Estes and P.R. Lee, Social, Political, and Economic Background of Long Term Care Policy, in *Long Term Care of the Elderly: Public Policy Issues,* ed. C. Harrington et al. (Beverly Hills, Calif.: Sage Publications, 1985), 17–39.

4. T.G. Rundall and W.K. Lambert, The Private Management of Public Hospitals, *Health Services Research* 19 (1984):527.

5. Lowe, Contract Management, 18–19; J.A. Alexander and B.L. Lewis, Hospital Contract Management: A Descriptive Model, *Health Services Research* 19 (1984):465–469; J. Newald, What's Ahead for the Full-Service Contract Management Industry? *Hospitals,* May 20, 1987, 70–76; J.R.C. Wheeler and H.S. Zuckerman, Hospital Management Contracts: Institutional and Community Perspectives, *Health Services Research* 19 (1984):499.

6. K.R. Levit et al., National Health Expenditures, 1990, *Health Care Financing Review* 13, no. 1 (1991):36. There were 1,690,481 certified beds in 1991, according to the Health Care Financing Administration and the U.S. Bureau of the Census (information courtesy of the American Health Care Association).

7. J. Bowe, There's No Substitute for Experience, *Contemporary Long-Term Care,* October 1990, 32, 94.

8. Massachusetts information courtesy of the Massachusetts Hospital Association; *AHA Hospital Statistics,* 1991–1992 edition (Chicago: American Hospital Association, 1991), 232.

9. Bowe, There's No Substitute, 34; J. Burns, Long-Term Care Chains Show Slight Growth, *Modern Healthcare,* May 18, 1992, 82.

10. This discussion of contract management operations is informed throughout by Glenn P. Hendrix and Keith E. Linch, Long Term Care Facility Management Agreements (Paper presented at the National Health Lawyers Association Long Term Care and the Law Conference, Las Vegas, February 12–14, 1992).

Index

National Institute of Adult Day Care, 396
Needs of residents
  emotional, 20-21
  individual, 19-21
  spiritual, 384
Negotiations, in budgetary process, 267-268
New York, 518-519
Non-profit organizations
  corporate reorganization of, 160-165, 166-180
  debt-financing in, 269
  social role of, 277, 278
  tax issues, 254
  types of, 160, 163-165, 172-173
Nurse's aides, 76-77
Nursing department
  in adult day care, 401
  chaplaincy services and, 389-390
  continuing education for, 69-70
  design of, 472
  director of education, 73-74
  establishing philosophy for, 59-60
  gerontological specialists in, 78-80
  head nurse, 74
  infection control, role in, 68
  nurse's aide in, 76-77
  policies/procedures for, 63-65
  practice guidelines for, 65-66
  in quality assurance process, 62-63
  in risk management, 63
  role in long-term care, 56-59
  selecting practice model for, 60-61
  staff development in, 67, 69
  staff nurse in, 74-75
  standards of care in, 61-63
  supervisor, 72-73
  turnover in, 68-69
  ward clerks, 77-78
Nursing director
  assistant, 72
  medical director and, 36
  qualifications for, 56-57, 71-72
  role of, 57, 59
  staffing responsibilities, 68
Nursing Home Reform Act of 1988, 17
Nursing homes
  current state of, 433-435
  demographics of, 33-34
  development of, in U. S., 16-17
  as facility title, 192
  national associations for, 16-17
Nutrition
  in adult day care program, 401

as component in food service, 331-332
dietitian's role in, 338
home medical equipment for, 409-411
needs assessment, 332

O

OBRA. *See* Omnibus Budget Reconciliation Act of 1987
Omnibus Budget Reconciliation Act of 1987
  on activities planning, 357-358
  assessment in, 214
  compatible standards of care for, 217-218
  on computerized information management, 41
  durable medical equipment reimbursement and, 420
  information management in, 213-214
  patient rights in, 53
  role of medical director in, 33, 35, 39, 43, 46
ORBITS bar coding system, 264
Oregon, 512-515
Oxygen therapy equipment, 407-408, 421

P

Pareto chart, 233
Patient Accounts Volunteer Experience, 184
Patient Self-Determination Act, 85-86
Payroll management, 265
Peer counseling, in mental health program, 104
Performance evaluations, of CEO, 158
Personalized care model, 373
Pharmacology
  in assessing mental health, 100
  psychopharmacology, 15
Pharmacy, designing space for, 466
Philanthropy, 254-255. *See also* Fund raising
  acknowledging donations, 288
  donor motives for, 282
  role of, 277, 278
  sources of, 281, 287-288
Physician(s)
  bylaws for, 44-45
  in designing diet, 333
  factors in consumer appraisal of, 192
  recognition of mental health problems by, 98
  role of, in nursing homes, 34-35
  staffing arrangements for, 44
Plumbing systems, 477
Pneumonia, 13
Political issues in caregiving, 10-11